enVisionmath 2.0

SCOTT FORESMAN · ADDISON WESLEY

Volume 2 Topics 8–16

Authors

Randall I. Charles
Professor Emeritus
Department of Mathematics
San Jose State University
San Jose, California

Jennifer Bay-Williams
Professor of Mathematics
Education
College of Education and Human
Development
University of Louisville
Louisville, Kentucky

Robert Q. Berry, III
Associate Professor of
Mathematics Education
Department of Curriculum,
Instruction and Special Education
University of Virginia
Charlottesville, Virginia

Janet H. Caldwell
Professor of Mathematics
Rowan University
Glassboro, New Jersey

Zachary Champagne
Assistant in Research
Florida Center for Research in
Science, Technology, Engineering,
and Mathematics (FCR-STEM)
Jacksonville, Florida

Juanita Copley
Professor Emerita, College
of Education
University of Houston
Houston, Texas

Warren Crown
Professor Emeritus of Mathematics
Education
Graduate School of Education
Rutgers University
New Brunswick, New Jersey

Francis (Skip) Fennell
L. Stanley Bowlsbey Professor
of Education and Graduate and
Professional Studies
McDaniel College
Westminster, Maryland

Karen Karp
Professor of Mathematics
Education
Department of Early Childhood
and Elementary Education
University of Louisville
Louisville, Kentucky

Stuart J. Murphy
Visual Learning Specialist
Boston, Massachusetts

Jane F. Schielack
Professor of Mathematics
Associate Dean for Assessment
and Pre K-12 Education,
College of Science
Texas A&M University
College Station, Texas

Jennifer M. Suh
Associate Professor for
Mathematics Education
George Mason University
Fairfax, Virginia

Jonathan A. Wray
Mathematics Instructional
Facilitator
Howard County Public Schools
Ellicott City, Maryland

PEARSON

Glenview, Illinois   Boston, Massachusetts   Chandler, Arizona   Hoboken, New Jersey

Mathematicians

Roger Howe
Professor of Mathematics
Yale University
New Haven, Connecticut

Gary Lippman
Professor of Mathematics and
Computer Science
California State University,
East Bay
Hayward, California

ELL Consultants

Janice R. Corona
Independent Education
Consultant
Dallas, Texas

Jim Cummins
Professor
The University of Toronto
Toronto, Canada

Common Core State Standards Reviewers

Debbie Crisco
Math Coach
Beebe Public Schools
Beebe, Arkansas

Kathleen A. Cuff
Teacher
Kings Park Central School District
Kings Park, New York

Erika Doyle
Math and Science Coordinator
Richland School District
Richland, Washington

Susan Jarvis
Math and Science Curriculum
Coordinator
Ocean Springs Schools
Ocean Springs, Mississippi

Velvet M. Simington
K-12 Mathematics Director
Winston-Salem / Forsyth County
Schools
Winston-Salem, North Carolina

PEARSON

ISBN-13: 978-0-328-82745-9
ISBN-10: 0-328-82745-2

Digital Resources

You'll be using these digital resources throughout the year!

Go to PearsonRealize.com

MP
Math Practices Animations to play anytime

Learn
Visual Learning Animation Plus with animation, interaction, and math tools

Practice Buddy
Online Personalized Practice for each lesson

Assessment
Quick Check for each lesson

Games
Math Games to help you learn

ACTIVe-book
Student Edition online for showing your work

Solve
Solve & Share problems plus math tools

Glossary
Animated Glossary in English and Spanish

Tools
Math Tools to help you understand

Help
Another Look Homework Video for extra help

eText
Student Edition online

PEARSON
realize™ Everything you need for math anytime, anywhere

KEY

And remember, your eText is available at PearsonRealize.com!

Contents

TOPICS

1. Generalize Place Value Understanding

2. Fluently Add and Subtract Multi-Digit Whole Numbers

3. Use Strategies and Properties to Multiply by 1-Digit Numbers

4. Use Strategies and Properties to Multiply by 2-Digit Numbers

5. Use Strategies and Properties to Divide by 1-Digit Numbers

6. Use Operations with Whole Numbers to Solve Problems

7. Factors and Multiples

8. Extend Understanding of Fraction Equivalence and Ordering

9. Understand Addition and Subtraction of Fractions

10. Extend Multiplication Concepts to Fractions

11. Represent and Interpret Data on Line Plots

12. Understand and Compare Decimals

13. Measurement: Find Equivalence in Units of Measure

14. Algebra: Generate and Analyze Patterns

15. Geometric Measurement: Understand Concepts of Angles and Angle Measurement

16. Lines, Angles, and Shapes

This shows how fraction strips can be used to determine equivalent fractions.

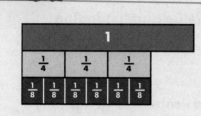

TOPIC 8 Extend Understanding of Fraction Equivalence and Ordering

Math and Science Project 407

Review What You Know 408

My Word Cards 409

8-1 **Equivalent Fractions: Area Models**......................411
4.NF.A.1, MP.1, MP.2, MP.5

8-2 **Equivalent Fractions: Number Lines**...................417
4.NF.A.1, MP.1, MP.3, MP.4, MP.5, MP.7

8-3 **Generate Equivalent Fractions: Multiplication** 423
4.NF.A.1, MP.2, MP.3, MP.4

8-4 **Generate Equivalent Fractions: Division** 429
4.NF.A.1, MP.1, MP.2, MP.3, MP.4, MP.6

8-5 **Use Benchmarks to Compare Fractions** 435
4.NF.A.2, 4.NF.A.1, MP.1, MP.2, MP.3, MP.8

8-6 **Compare Fractions**....................................441
4.NF.A.2, 4.NF.A.1, MP.2, MP.3, MP.5

8-7 **MATH PRACTICES AND PROBLEM SOLVING**
Construct Arguments................................447
MP.3, Also MP.1, MP.2, MP.5, 4.NF.A.1, 4.NF.A.2

Fluency Practice Activity 453

Vocabulary Review 454

Reteaching..455

Topic Assessment 457

Topic Performance Assessment 459

This shows how you can use fraction strips to model the addition of fractions.

| 1 |
| $\frac{1}{10}$ | $\frac{1}{10}$ | $\frac{1}{10}$ | $\frac{1}{10}$ | $\frac{1}{10}$ |

$\frac{1}{10}$ | $\frac{1}{10}$

TOPIC 9 Understand Addition and Subtraction of Fractions

Math and Science Project 461
Review What You Know 462
My Word Cards 463

9-1 **Model Addition of Fractions** 465
4.NF.B.3a, MP.1, MP.2, MP.3, MP.4, MP.5

9-2 **Decompose Fractions** 471
4.NF.B.3b, MP.2, MP.4, MP.5

9-3 **Add Fractions with Like Denominators** 477
4.NF.B.3a, 4.NF.B.3d, MP.1, MP.3, MP.4, MP.7

9-4 **Model Subtraction of Fractions** 483
4.NF.B.3a, MP.1, MP.2, MP.4, MP.5, MP.6

9-5 **Subtract Fractions with Like Denominators** 489
4.NF.B.3a, 4.NF.B.3d, MP.2, MP.3, MP.4

9-6 **Add and Subtract Fractions with Like Denominators** 495
4.NF.B.3a, MP.2, MP.4, MP.5

9-7 **Estimate Fraction Sums and Differences** 501
4.NF.B.3a, MP.1, MP.2, MP.3, MP.4, MP.8

9-8 **Model Addition and Subtraction of Mixed Numbers** 507
4.NF.B.3c, MP.2, MP.3, MP.5

9-9 **Add Mixed Numbers** 513
4.NF.B.3c, MP.1, MP.2, MP.3, MP.8

9-10 **Subtract Mixed Numbers** 519
4.NF.B.3c, MP.1, MP.2, MP.3, MP.8

9-11 **MATH PRACTICES AND PROBLEM SOLVING**
Model with Math 525
MP.4, Also MP.1, MP.2, MP.5, 4.NF.B.3d, 4.NF.B.3a

Fluency Practice Activity 531
Vocabulary Review 532
Reteaching 533
Topic Assessment 535
Topic Performance Assessment 537

You can use a number line to help multiply fractions and whole numbers.

$$\frac{0}{3} \quad \frac{1}{3} \quad \frac{2}{3} \quad \frac{3}{3} \quad \frac{4}{3} \quad \frac{5}{3} \quad \frac{6}{3}$$
$$0 \qquad\qquad\qquad 1 \qquad\qquad\qquad 2$$

$$\frac{1}{3} \times 4 = \frac{4}{3}$$

TOPIC 10 Extend Multiplication Concepts to Fractions

Math and Science Project 539
Review What You Know 540
My Word Cards 541

10-1 **Fractions as Multiples of Unit Fractions: Use Models** 543
4.NF.B.4a, MP.2, MP.4, MP.7

10-2 **Multiply a Fraction by a Whole Number: Use Models** 549
4.NF.B.4b, 4.NF.B.4a, 4.NF.B.4c, MP.2, MP.4, MP.7, MP.8

10-3 **Multiply a Fraction by a Whole Number: Use Symbols** . . . 555
4.NF.B.4b, 4.NF.B.4a, 4.NF.B.4c, MP.2, MP.4, MP.6, MP.7

10-4 **Multiply a Whole Number and a Mixed Number** 561
4.NF.B.4c, MP.1, MP.3, MP.7

10-5 **Solve Time Problems** 567
4.MD.A.2, 4.NF.B.4c, MP.1, MP.2, MP.3, MP.4, MP.5

10-6 **MATH PRACTICES AND PROBLEM SOLVING**
Model with Math 573
MP.4, Also MP.1, MP.2, MP.6, 4.NF.B.4c, 4.NF.B.3d, 4.MD.A.2

Fluency Practice Activity 579
Vocabulary Review 580
Reteaching 581
Topic Assessment 583
Topic Performance Assessment 585

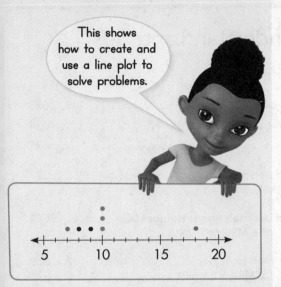

This shows how to create and use a line plot to solve problems.

TOPIC 11 Represent and Interpret Data on Line Plots

Math and Science Project 587

Review What You Know 588

My Word Cards 589

11-1 **Read Line Plots** 591
4.MD.B.4, MP.2, MP.3, MP.6, MP.7

11-2 **Make Line Plots** 597
4.MD.B.4, 4.NF.A.1, MP.2, MP.3, MP.6

11-3 **Use Line Plots to Solve Problems** 603
4.MD.B.4, 4.NF.B.3d, MP.1, MP.2, MP.5, MP.8

11-4 **MATH PRACTICES AND PROBLEM SOLVING**
Critique Reasoning 609
MP.3, Also MP.1, MP.2, MP.4, 4.MD.B.4

Fluency Practice Activity 615

Vocabulary Review 616

Reteaching 617

Topic Assessment 619

Topic Performance Assessment 621

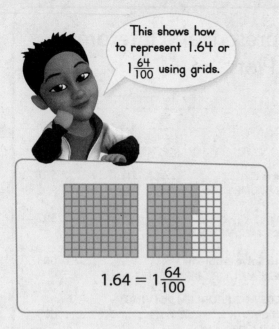

This shows how to represent 1.64 or $1\frac{64}{100}$ using grids.

$$1.64 = 1\frac{64}{100}$$

TOPIC 12 Understand and Compare Decimals

Math and Science Project 623
Review What You Know 624
My Word Cards 625

12-1 **Fractions and Decimals** 627
4.NF.C.6, MP.2, MP.3, MP.4

12-2 **Fractions and Decimals on the Number Line** 633
4.NF.C.6, MP.1, MP.2, MP.4, MP.6, MP.7

12-3 **Compare Decimals** 639
4.NF.C.7, 4.MD.A.2, MP.2, MP.3, MP.5

12-4 **Add Fractions with Denominators of 10 and 100** 645
4.NF.C.5, MP.1, MP.2, MP.3, MP.4, MP.5

12-5 **Solve Word Problems Involving Money** 651
4.MD.A.2, 4.NF.C.6, MP.1, MP.2, MP.4, MP.7, MP.8

12-6 **MATH PRACTICES AND PROBLEM SOLVING**
Look For and Use Structure 657
MP.7, Also MP.1, MP.2, MP.3, MP.4, MP.6, 4.NF.C.7, 4.MD.A.2

Fluency Practice Activity 663
Vocabulary Review 664
Reteaching 665
Topic Assessment 667
Topic Performance Assessment 669

This shows how metric units are related.

Metric Units of Length

1 m	= 1,000 mm
1 cm	= 10 mm
1 m	= 100 cm
1 km	= 1,000 m

TOPIC 13 Measurement: Find Equivalence in Units of Measure

Math and Science Project 671
Review What You Know 672
My Word Cards 673

13-1   **Equivalence with Customary Units of Length** 679
4.MD.A.1, 4.MD.A.2, 4.NF.B.3d, 4.NF.B.4c, MP.1, MP.6, MP.7, MP.8

13-2   **Equivalence with Customary Units of Capacity** 685
4.MD.A.1, 4.MD.A.2, 4.NF.B.3d, 4.NF.B.4c, MP.1, MP.2, MP.8

13-3   **Equivalence with Customary Units of Weight** 691
4.MD.A.1, 4.MD.A.2, 4.NF.B.3d, 4.NF.B.4c, MP.1, MP.2, MP.6, MP.8

13-4   **Equivalence with Metric Units of Length** 697
4.MD.A.1, 4.MD.A.2, MP.1, MP.3, MP.5, MP.6, MP.8

13-5   **Equivalence with Metric Units of Capacity and Mass** 703
4.MD.A.1, 4.MD.A.2, MP.1, MP.2, MP.6, MP.8

13-6   **Solve Perimeter and Area Problems** 709
4.MD.A.3, 4.MD.A.2, 4.NBT.B.5, 4.NF.B.4c, MP.1, MP.2, MP.3

13-7   **MATH PRACTICES AND PROBLEM SOLVING**
Precision 715
MP.6, Also MP.1, MP.2, MP.4, 4.MD.A.2, 4.MD.A.3, 4.NBT.B.5, 4.NBT.B.4

Fluency Practice Activity 721
Vocabulary Review 722
Reteaching 723
Topic Assessment 725
Topic Performance Assessment 727

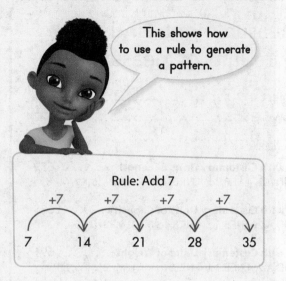

This shows how to use a rule to generate a pattern.

Rule: Add 7

+7   +7   +7   +7

7   14   21   28   35

TOPIC 14 Algebra: Generate and Analyze Patterns

Math and Science Project 729
Review What You Know 730
My Word Cards 731

14-1   **Number Sequences** 733
4.OA.C.5, MP.1, MP.2, MP.4, MP.5, MP.7, MP.8

14-2   **Patterns: Number Rules** 739
4.OA.C.5, MP.2, MP.7

14-3   **Patterns: Repeating Shapes** 745
4.OA.C.5, MP.2, MP.3, MP.6, MP.7

14-4   MATH PRACTICES AND PROBLEM SOLVING
Look for and Use Structure 751
MP.7, Also MP.1, MP.2, 4.OA.C.5

Fluency Practice Activity 757
Vocabulary Review 758
Reteaching 759
Topic Assessment 761
Topic Performance Assessment 763

This shows how to measure and draw angles.

TOPIC 15 Geometric Measurement: Understand Concepts of Angles and Angle Measurement

Math and Science Project 765
Review What You Know 766
My Word Cards 767

15-1 **Lines, Rays, and Angles**...............................771
4.MD.C.5, 4.G.A.1, MP.2, MP.4, MP.6, MP.7

15-2 **Understand Angles and Unit Angles**.................777
4.MD.C.5a, MP.1, MP.2, MP.3, MP.4

15-3 **Measure with Unit Angles** 783
4.MD.C.5a, 4.MD.C.5b, MP.1, MP.3, MP.4, MP.5, MP.8

15-4 **Measure and Draw Angles** 789
4.MD.C.6, MP.1, MP.2, MP.3, MP.5, MP.6

15-5 **Add and Subtract Angle Measures** 795
4.MD.C.7, MP.1, MP.2, MP.3, MP.4, MP.7

15-6 **MATH PRACTICES AND PROBLEM SOLVING**
Use Appropriate Tools 801
MP.5, Also MP.1, MP.2, MP.4, 4.MD.C.6, 4.MD.C.7

Fluency Practice Activity 807
Vocabulary Review 808
Reteaching..809
Topic Assessment 811
Topic Performance Assessment 813

This shows how to draw lines of symmetry in a figure.

TOPIC 16 Lines, Angles, and Shapes

Math and Science Project 815
Review What You Know 816
My Word Cards 817

16-1 **Lines** 821
4.G.A.1, MP.3, MP.4, MP.6

16-2 **Classify Triangles** 827
4.G.A.2, MP.3, MP.6, MP.8

16-3 **Classify Quadrilaterals** 833
4.G.A.2, MP.2, MP.3, MP.6, MP.7, MP.8

16-4 **Line Symmetry** 839
4.G.A.3, MP.2, MP.3, MP.5, MP.7

16-5 **Draw Shapes with Line Symmetry** 845
4.G.A.3, MP.1, MP.2, MP.3, MP.4

16-6 **MATH PRACTICES AND PROBLEM SOLVING**
Critique Reasoning 851
MP.3, Also MP.1, MP.2, MP.6, MP.7, 4.G.A.2

Fluency Practice Activity 857
Vocabulary Review 858
Reteaching 859
Topic Assessment 861
Topic Performance Assessment 863

STEP UP to Grade 5

STEP UP Lessons Opener.......................................865

1. Understand Decimal Place Value......................867

2. Compare Decimals......................................871

3. Use Models to Add and Subtract Decimals............875

4. Estimate the Product of a Decimal and
   a Whole Number..879

5. Find Common Denominators............................883

6. Add Fractions with Unlike Denominators..............887

7. Subtract Fractions with Unlike Denominators.........891

8. Multiply Fractions and Whole Numbers................895

9. Divide Whole Numbers by Unit Fractions.............899

10. Model Volume...903

These lessons help prepare you for Grade 5.

Glossary..G1

Math Practices and Problem Solving Handbook

Math practices are ways we think about and do math.

Math practices will help you solve problems.

Math Practices

 MP.1 Make sense of problems and persevere in solving them.

 MP.2 Reason abstractly and quantitatively.

MP.3 Construct viable arguments and critique the reasoning of others.

 MP.4 Model with mathematics.

MP.5 Use appropriate tools strategically.

 MP.6 Attend to precision.

 MP.7 Look for and make use of structure.

 MP.8 Look for and express regularity in repeated reasoning.

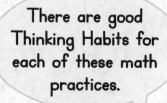

There are good Thinking Habits for each of these math practices.

Make sense of problems and persevere in solving them.

Good math thinkers make sense of problems and think of ways to solve them.

If they get stuck, they don't give up.

Here I listed what I know and what I am trying to find.

Mia buys 2 T-shirts for $7 each and a dress that costs $15. She uses a $4 coupon and pays with $40. How much change will Mia get back?

What I Know:
- Mia has $40 and a $4 coupon.
- Mia buys 2 T-shirts for $7 each.
- Mia buys a dress for $15.

What I need to find:
- The amount of change Mia gets.

Thinking Habits

Be a good thinker! These questions can help you.

- What do I need to find?
- What do I know?
- What's my plan for solving the problem?
- What else can I try if I get stuck?
- How can I check that my solution makes sense?

MP

Good math thinkers know how to think about words and numbers to solve problems.

I drew a bar diagram that shows how things in the problem are related.

Sam buys a box of 6 thank you cards that costs $12. How much does each thank you card cost?

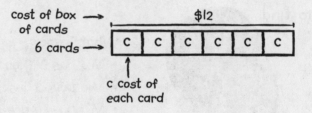

cost of box of cards ⟶

6 cards ⟶ | c | c | c | c | c | c |

$12

↑ c cost of each card

$12 ÷ 6 = c

Each card costs $2.

Thinking Habits

Be a good thinker! These questions can help you.

- What do the numbers and symbols in the problem mean?

- How are the numbers or quantities related?

- How can I represent a word problem using pictures, numbers, or equations?

MP.3 Construct viable arguments and critique the reasoning of others.

Good math thinkers use math to explain why they are right. They can talk about the math that others do, too.

I wrote a clear argument with words, numbers, and symbols.

Jackie drew a number line and placed a point at $\frac{2}{3}$. Bonnie drew a number line and placed a point at $\frac{2}{3}$ as well. Which student correctly marked the point?

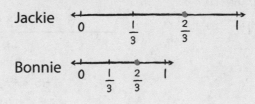

Jackie

Bonnie

$\frac{2}{3}$ is correctly marked on both number lines. The two number lines are different lengths, but both show three equal parts.

Thinking Habits

Be a good thinker! These questions can help you.

- How can I use numbers, objects, drawings, or actions to justify my argument?

- Am I using numbers and symbols correctly?

- Is my explanation clear and complete?

- What questions can I ask to understand other people's thinking?

- Are there mistakes in other people's thinking?

- Can I improve other people's thinking?

MP.4 Model with mathematics.

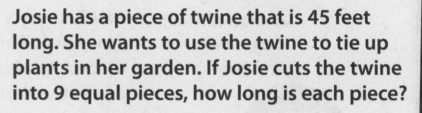

Good math thinkers choose and apply math they know to show and solve problems from everyday life.

Josie has a piece of twine that is 45 feet long. She wants to use the twine to tie up plants in her garden. If Josie cuts the twine into 9 equal pieces, how long is each piece?

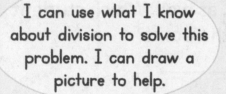

I can use what I know about division to solve this problem. I can draw a picture to help.

45 feet

t t t t t t t t t

$45 \div 9 = t$

Each piece of twine is 5 feet long.

Thinking Habits

Be a good thinker! These questions can help you.

- How can I use math I know to help solve this problem?

- How can I use pictures, objects, or an equation to represent the problem?

- How can I use numbers, words, and symbols to solve the problem?

Use appropriate tools strategically.

Good math thinkers know how to pick the right tools to solve math problems.

I decided to use counters because I could make an array to solve the problem.

Hank has $13 in his wallet. He earns $15 more for mowing a lawn. He would like to download movies that cost $7 each. How many movies can Hank download? Choose a tool to represent and solve the problem.

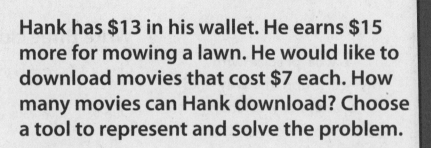

$13 + $15 = $28
$28 ÷ $7 = 4
Hank can download 4 movies.

Thinking Habits

Be a good thinker! These questions can help you.

- Which tools can I use?
- Why should I use this tool to help me solve the problem?
- Is there a different tool I could use?
- Am I using the tool appropriately?

MP.6 Attend to precision.

Good math thinkers are careful about what they write and say, so their ideas about math are clear.

I was precise with my work and the way that I wrote my solution.

Write three clues to describe a square.

Clue 1: I have 4 right angles.

Clue 2: I have four sides that are the same length.

Clue 3: I have 2 sets of sides that are parallel.

A square has 4 right angles, 4 sides with the same length, and 2 sets of parallel sides.

Thinking Habits

Be a good thinker! These questions can help you.

- Am I using numbers, units, and symbols appropriately?
- Am I using the correct definitions?
- Am I calculating accurately?
- Is my answer clear?

Math Practices and Problem Solving Handbook

MP.7 Look for and make use of structure.

Good math thinkers look for relationships in math to help solve problems.

I used what I know about basic facts to solve the problem.

Use <, >, or = to compare the expressions without calculating.

$3 \times 6 \bigcirc 3 \times 9$

$3 \times 6 < 3 \times 9$ because $6 < 9$.

Thinking Habits

Be a good thinker! These questions can help you.

- What patterns can I see and describe?

- How can I use the patterns to solve the problem?

- Can I see expressions and objects in different ways?

MP.8 Look for and express regularity in repeated reasoning.

Good math thinkers look for things that repeat, and they make generalizations.

I used reasoning to generalize about calculations.

Cathy has arranged some shells in two different ways. One array has 2 rows with 6 shells in each row. The other array has 6 rows with 2 shells in each row. Do both arrays have the same number of shells? Explain.

Yes, both arrays have the same number of counters. The arrays are the same except that the number of shells in the rows and columns are reversed.

Thinking Habits

Be a good thinker! These questions can help you.

- Are any calculations repeated?
- Can I generalize from examples?
- What shortcuts do I notice?

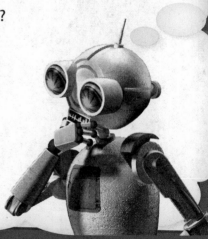

Problem Solving Guide

Math practices can help you solve problems.

Make Sense of the Problem

Reason Abstractly and Quantitatively

- What do I need to find?
- What given information can I use?
- How are the quantities related?

Think About Similar Problems

- Have I solved problems like this before?

Persevere in Solving the Problem

Model with Math

- How can I use the math I know?
- How can I represent the problem?
- Is there a pattern or structure I can use?

Use Appropriate Tools Strategically

- What math tools could I use?
- How can I use those tools strategically?

Check the Answer

Make Sense of the Answer

- Is my answer reasonable?

Check for Precision

- Did I check my work?
- Is my answer clear?
- Did I construct a viable argument?
- Did I generalize correctly?

Some Ways to Represent Problems

- Draw a Picture
- Make a Bar Diagram
- Make a Table or Graph
- Write an Equation

Some Math Tools

- Objects
- Grid Paper
- Rulers
- Technology
- Paper and Pencil

Math Practices and Problem Solving Handbook

Problem Solving Recording Sheet

This sheet helps you organize your work.

Name **Carlos**

Teaching Tool
1

Problem Solving Recording Sheet

Problem
Lynda wants to buy a bike that costs $80. Her father will help by paying for $20. She will earn the rest by walking dogs. She earns $6 for each dog she walks. How many dogs does Lynda need to walk in order to have enough money for the bike?

MAKE SENSE OF THE PROBLEM

Need to Find	**Given**
Number of dogs to walk	Earns $6 per walk
	Bike costs $80
	Dad's part is $20

PERSEVERE IN SOLVING THE PROBLEM

Some Ways to Represent Problems

☐ Draw a Picture
☑ Make a Bar Diagram
☐ Make a Table or Graph
☑ Write an Equation

Some Math Tools

☐ Objects
☐ Grid Paper
☐ Rulers
☐ Technology
☑ Paper and Pencil

Solution and Answer

$80
| $20 | d dollars |

Dad's money   Lynda's money

$20 + d = 80$

Lynda must earn $60.

Money earned → $60
Dogs walked → $6 d

$60 \div \$6 = 10$

Lynda must walk 10 dogs.

CHECK THE ANSWER

I used operations that undo each other to check my work.

$10 \times \$6 = \$60$ $\$60 + \$20 = \$80$

My answer is reasonable.

T1

Bar Diagrams

You can draw a **bar diagram** to show how the quantities in a problem are related. Then you can write an equation to solve the problem.

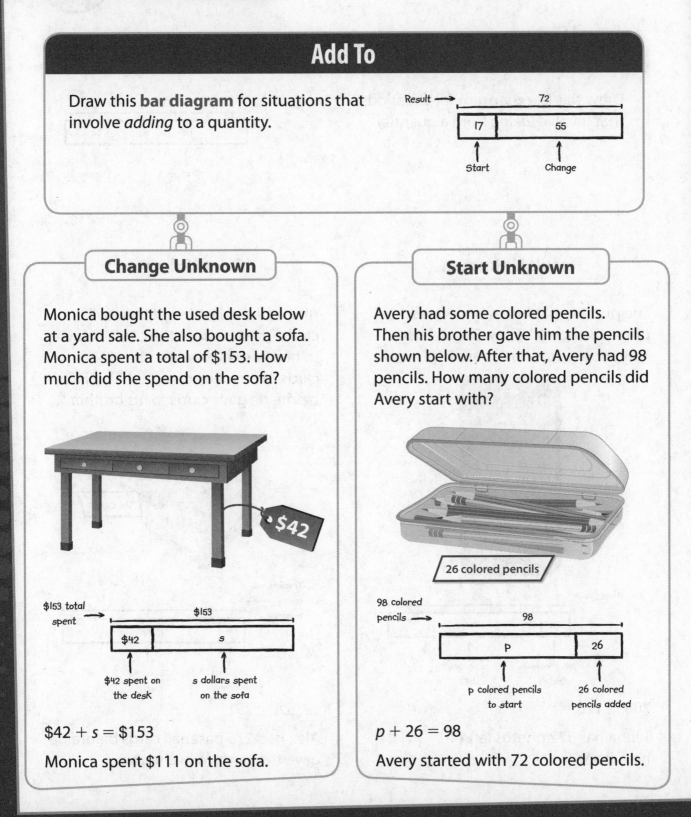

Add To

Draw this **bar diagram** for situations that involve *adding* to a quantity.

Result → 72

17 | 55

Start   Change

Change Unknown

Monica bought the used desk below at a yard sale. She also bought a sofa. Monica spent a total of $153. How much did she spend on the sofa?

• $42

$153 total spent → $153

$42 | s

$42 spent on the desk   s dollars spent on the sofa

$42 + s = $153

Monica spent $111 on the sofa.

Start Unknown

Avery had some colored pencils. Then his brother gave him the pencils shown below. After that, Avery had 98 pencils. How many colored pencils did Avery start with?

26 colored pencils

98 colored pencils → 98

p | 26

p colored pencils to start   26 colored pencils added

p + 26 = 98

Avery started with 72 colored pencils.

Bar Diagrams

You can use bar diagrams to make sense of addition and subtraction problems.

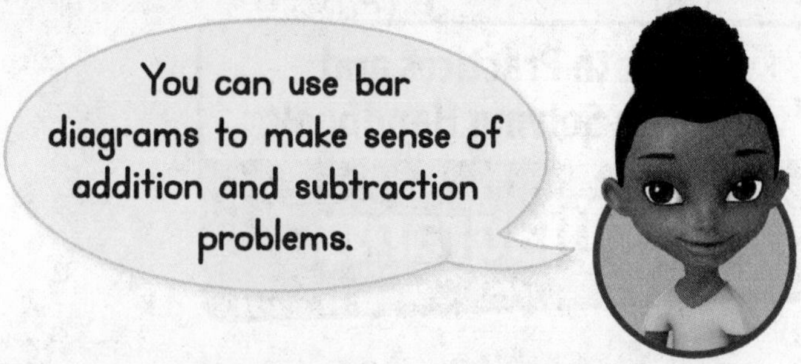

Take From

Draw this **bar diagram** for situations that involve *taking* from a quantity.

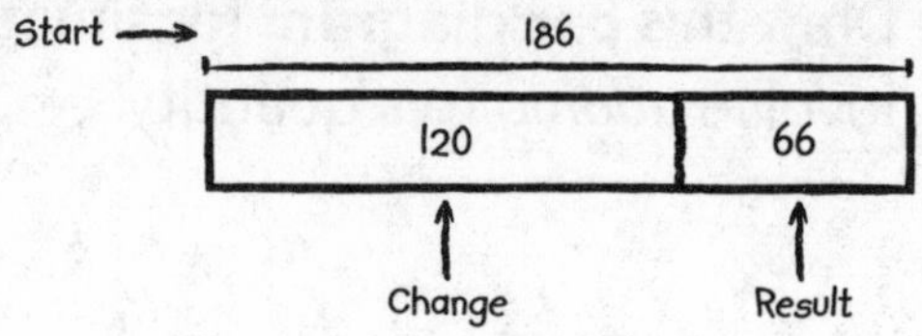

Start ⟶ 186

| 120 | 66 |

↑ Change   ↑ Result

Result Unknown

The number of photos on Jenna's phone is shown below. She deleted 128 photos. How many are left?

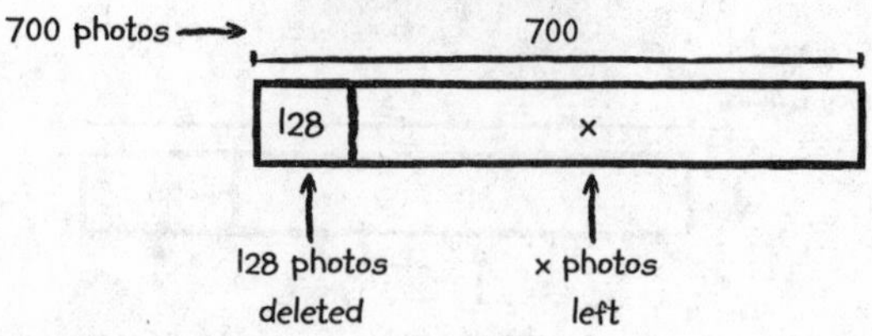

700 photos

700 photos ⟶ 700

| 128 | x |

↑ 128 photos deleted   ↑ x photos left

$700 - 128 = x$

Jenna has 572 photos left on her phone.

Start Unknown

Alex had a collection of baseball cards. Then he gave the cards below to his brother. Now Alex has 251 cards. How many cards did Alex have before he gave cards to his brother?

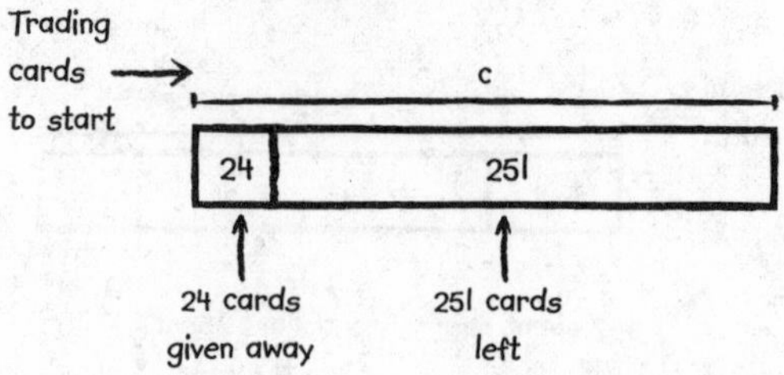

24 cards

Trading cards to start ⟶ c

| 24 | 251 |

↑ 24 cards given away   ↑ 251 cards left

$c - 24 = 251$

Alex had 275 baseball cards before he gave the cards to his brother.

The **bar diagrams** on this page can help you make sense of more addition and subtraction situations.

Put Together/Take Apart

Draw this **bar diagram** for situations that involve *putting together* or *taking apart* quantities.

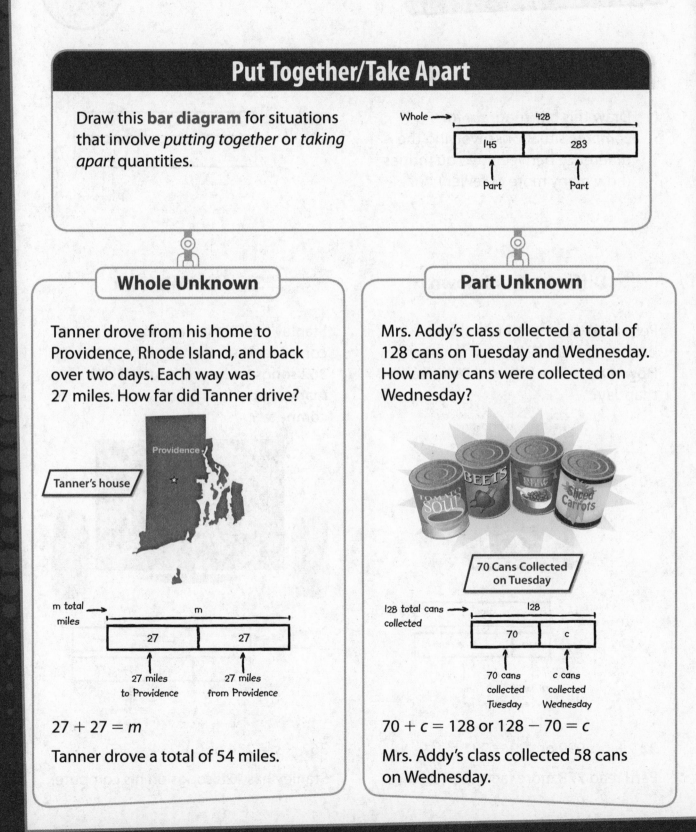

Whole ⟶

428	
145	283

Part   Part

Whole Unknown

Tanner drove from his home to Providence, Rhode Island, and back over two days. Each way was 27 miles. How far did Tanner drive?

Providence
Tanner's house

m total miles ⟶

m	
27	27

27 miles to Providence   27 miles from Providence

$27 + 27 = m$

Tanner drove a total of 54 miles.

Part Unknown

Mrs. Addy's class collected a total of 128 cans on Tuesday and Wednesday. How many cans were collected on Wednesday?

BEETS   BEEF STEW   Sliced Carrots   TOMATO SOUP

70 Cans Collected on Tuesday

128 total cans collected ⟶

128	
70	c

70 cans collected Tuesday   c cans collected Wednesday

$70 + c = 128$ or $128 - 70 = c$

Mrs. Addy's class collected 58 cans on Wednesday.

Bar Diagrams

Pictures help you understand a problem.

Compare: Addition and Subtraction

Draw this **bar diagram** for *compare* situations involving the difference between two quantities (how many more or fewer.)

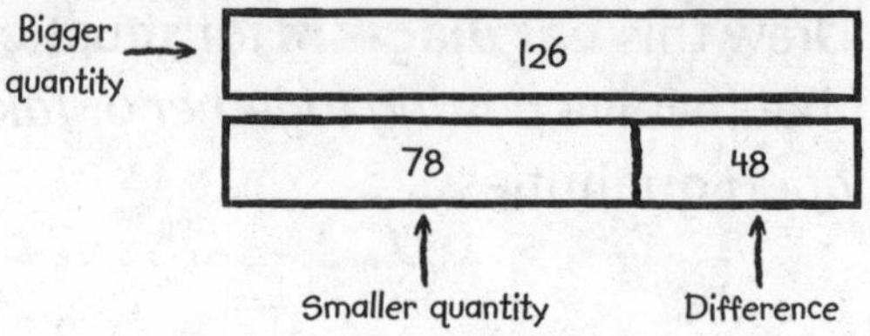

Bigger quantity → | 126 |

| 78 | 48 |

↑ Smaller quantity ↑ Difference

Difference Unknown

Perri read the entire book shown below. Jay read 221 facts in the book. How many more facts did Perri read than Jay?

999 FACTS ABOUT REPTILES

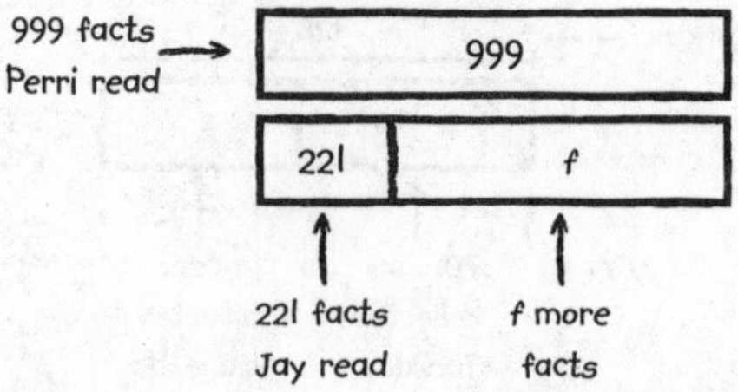

999 facts Perri read → | 999 |

| 221 | f |

↑ 221 facts Jay read ↑ f more facts

$221 + f = 999$ or $999 - 221 = f$

Perri read 778 more facts than Jay.

Smaller Unknown

Stanley has 234 fewer songs on his computer than Joanne. Joanne has 362 songs on her computer. How many songs does Stanley have on his computer?

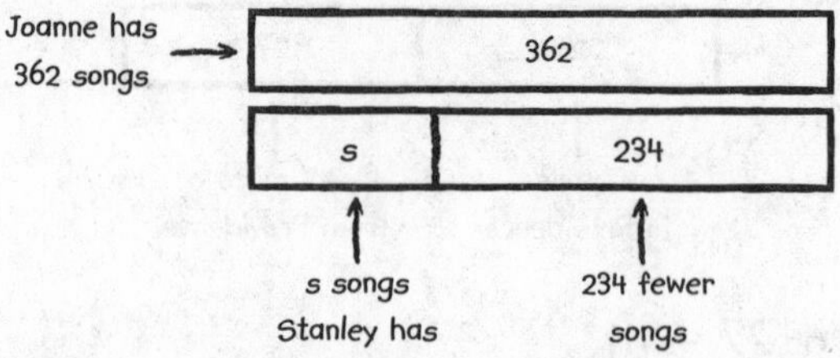

Joanne has 362 songs → | 362 |

| s | 234 |

↑ s songs Stanley has ↑ 234 fewer songs

$362 - s = 234$ or $s + 234 = 362$

Stanley has 128 songs on his computer.

The **bar diagrams** on this page can help you solve problems involving multiplication and division.

Equal Groups: Multiplication and Division

Draw this **bar diagram** for situations that involve *equal groups*.

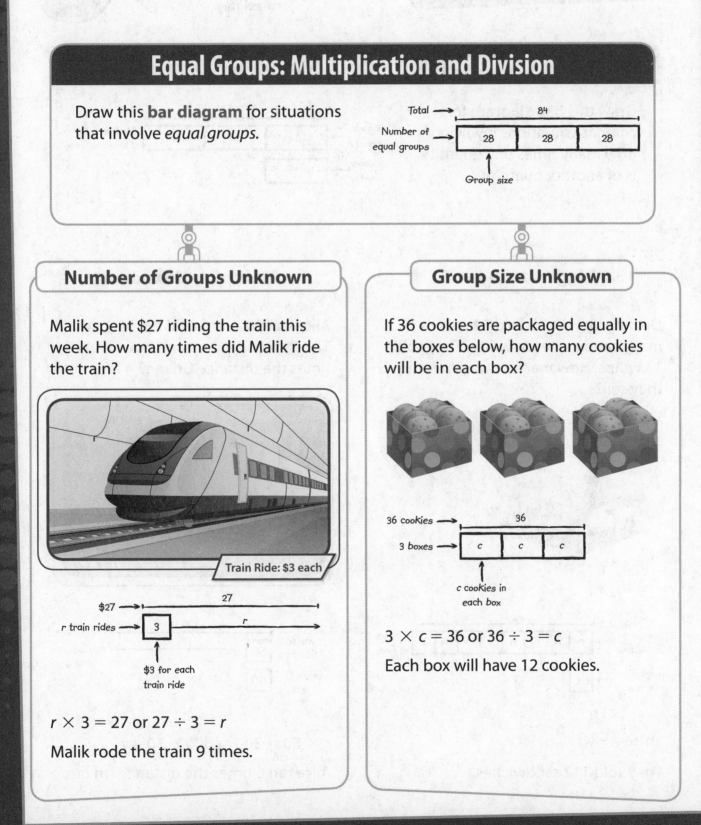

Total → 84

Number of equal groups → 28 28 28

Group size

Number of Groups Unknown

Malik spent $27 riding the train this week. How many times did Malik ride the train?

Train Ride: $3 each

$27 → 27

r train rides → 3   r

$3 for each train ride

$r \times 3 = 27$ or $27 \div 3 = r$

Malik rode the train 9 times.

Group Size Unknown

If 36 cookies are packaged equally in the boxes below, how many cookies will be in each box?

36 cookies → 36

3 boxes → c c c

c cookies in each box

$3 \times c = 36$ or $36 \div 3 = c$

Each box will have 12 cookies.

Bar Diagrams

Bar diagrams can be used to show how quantities that are being compared are related.

Compare: Multiplication and Division

Draw this **bar diagram** for *compare* situations involving how many times one quantity is of another quantity.

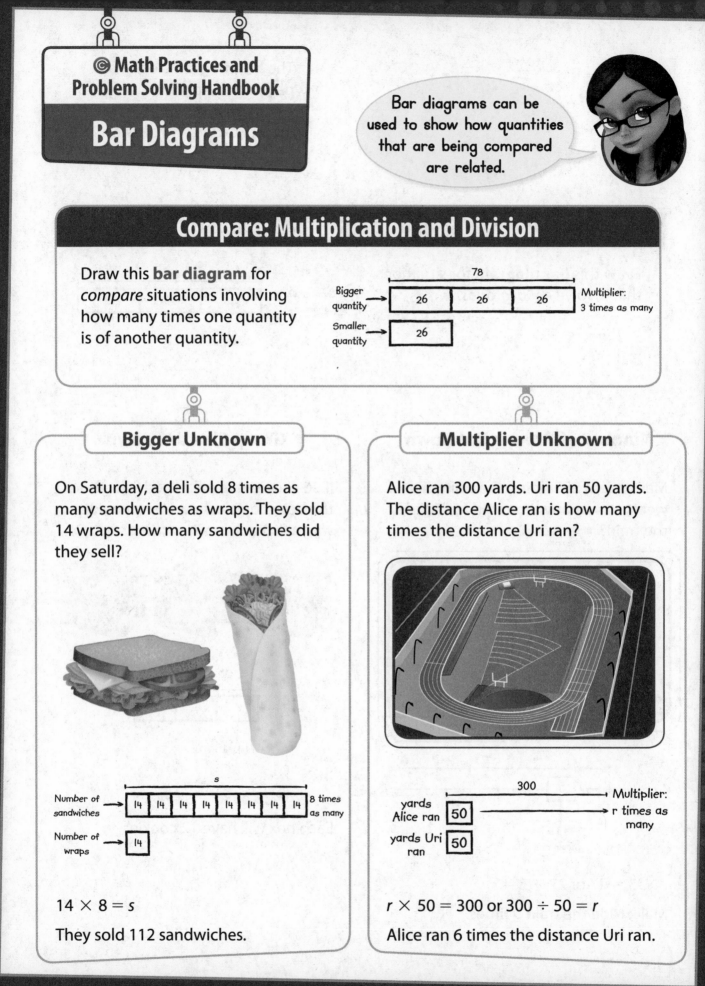

78

Bigger quantity → | 26 | 26 | 26 |

Smaller quantity → | 26 |

Multiplier: 3 times as many

Bigger Unknown

On Saturday, a deli sold 8 times as many sandwiches as wraps. They sold 14 wraps. How many sandwiches did they sell?

s

Number of sandwiches → | 14 | 14 | 14 | 14 | 14 | 14 | 14 | 14 | 8 times as many

Number of wraps → | 14 |

$14 \times 8 = s$

They sold 112 sandwiches.

Multiplier Unknown

Alice ran 300 yards. Uri ran 50 yards. The distance Alice ran is how many times the distance Uri ran?

300

yards Alice ran | 50 |

yards Uri ran | 50 |

Multiplier: r times as many

$r \times 50 = 300$ or $300 \div 50 = r$

Alice ran 6 times the distance Uri ran.

Extend Understanding of Fraction Equivalence and Ordering

Essential Questions: What are some ways to name the same part of a whole? How can you compare fractions with unlike denominators?

Some animals use their senses differently from humans. The entire body of a catfish is covered with taste-sensitive cells.

They use their sense of taste to locate food that is far away in the water.

Lots of animals have special ways of receiving information. Here is a project about senses.

Math and Science Project: Senses

Do Research Use the Internet or other resources to find information about how animals use special senses, such as echolocation, electricity, or magnetism. Include information about where the animal lives and how the special sense is used.

Journal: Write a Report Include what you found. Also in your report:

- Some spiders rely on sight to receive information about food. Spiders can have as many as 8 eyes. Draw a picture of a spider with many eyes, using some shaded circles as eyes and some empty circles as eyes.

- Write a fraction that names shaded spider eyes to total spider eyes. Write three equivalent fractions.

Name _____

Review What You Know

A-Z Vocabulary

Choose the best term from the box.
Write it on the blank.

- denominator
- numerator
- fraction
- unit fraction

1. A symbol, such as $\frac{2}{3}$ or $\frac{1}{2}$, used to name part of a whole, part of a set, or a location on a number line is called a _____.

2. The number above the fraction bar in a fraction is called the _____.

3. A fraction with a numerator of 1 is called a _____.

Unit Fractions

Write a fraction for each statement.

4. 2 copies of $\frac{1}{6}$ is _____.

5. 3 copies of $\frac{1}{3}$ is _____.

6. 4 copies of $\frac{1}{5}$ is _____.

7. 2 copies of $\frac{1}{10}$ is _____.

8. 7 copies of $\frac{1}{12}$ is _____.

9. 3 copies of $\frac{1}{8}$ is _____.

Fraction Concepts

Write the fraction shown by each figure.

10.

11.

12.

13.

14.

15.

Parts of Wholes

16. © MP.3 **Construct Arguments** Is $\frac{1}{4}$ of the figure below green? Explain.

17. This picture shows a square. Shade in $\frac{3}{4}$ of the square.

My Word Cards

Use the examples for each word on the front of the card to help complete the definitions on the back.

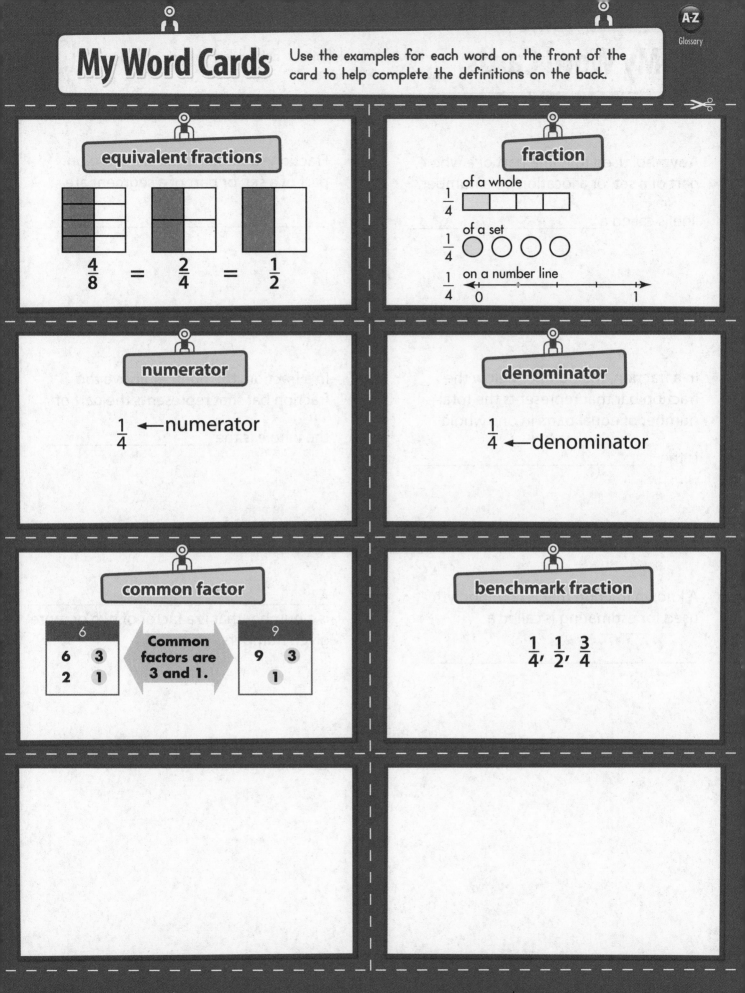

equivalent fractions

$$\frac{4}{8} = \frac{2}{4} = \frac{1}{2}$$

fraction

of a whole
$\frac{1}{4}$

of a set
$\frac{1}{4}$

on a number line
$\frac{1}{4}$ 0   1

numerator

$\frac{1}{4}$ ←numerator

denominator

$\frac{1}{4}$ ←denominator

common factor

6
6 3
2 1

Common factors are 3 and 1.

9
9 3
1

benchmark fraction

$$\frac{1}{4}, \ \frac{1}{2}, \ \frac{3}{4}$$

My Word Cards

Complete each definition. Extend learning by writing your own definitions.

A symbol used to name part of a whole, part of a set, or a location on a number line is called a _____.

Fractions that name the same region, part of a set, or part of a segment are _____.

In a fraction, the number below the fraction bar that represents the total number of equal parts in one whole is the _____.

In a fraction, the number above the fraction bar that represents the part of the whole is the _____.

A known fraction that is commonly used for estimating is called a _____.

A _____ is a number that is a factor of two or more given numbers.

Name _____

Solve & Share

Lena has yellow tile on $\frac{1}{4}$ of her kitchen floor. Write another fraction equivalent to $\frac{1}{4}$. **Solve this problem any way you choose.**

I can ...
recognize and generate equivalent fractions.

© **Content Standard** 4.NF.A.1
Mathematical Practices MP.1, MP.2, MP.5

Choose appropriate tools strategically. You can use area models or fraction strips to solve this problem.

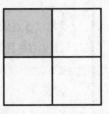

Look Back! © **MP.2 Reasoning** How do you know your fraction is equivalent to $\frac{1}{4}$?

Essential Question What Are Some Ways to Name the Same Part of a Whole?

A

James ate part of the pizza shown in the picture at the right. He said $\frac{5}{6}$ of the pizza is left. Cardell said $\frac{10}{12}$ of the pizza is left. Who is correct?

Equivalent fractions name the same part of the same whole.

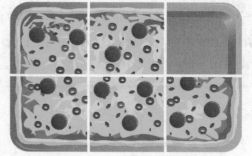

fraction $\begin{cases} \frac{5}{6} \end{cases}$ ← numerator
← denominator

B One Way

Use an area model. Draw a rectangle and divide it into sixths. Shade $\frac{5}{6}$. Then divide the rectangle into twelfths.

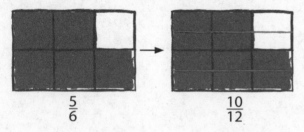

$\frac{5}{6}$ → $\frac{10}{12}$

The number and size of parts differ, but the shaded part of each rectangle is the same. $\frac{5}{6}$ and $\frac{10}{12}$ are equivalent fractions.

C Another Way

Use a different area model. Draw a circle and divide it into sixths. Shade $\frac{5}{6}$. Then divide the circle into twelfths.

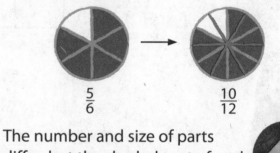

$\frac{5}{6}$ → $\frac{10}{12}$

The number and size of parts differ, but the shaded part of each circle is the same. $\frac{5}{6}$ and $\frac{10}{12}$ are equivalent fractions.

Both James and Cardell are correct because $\frac{5}{6} = \frac{10}{12}$.

Convince Me! © **MP.2 Reasoning** Mia ate $\frac{1}{4}$ of a pizza. Matt ate $\frac{2}{8}$ of another pizza. Did Mia and Matt eat the same amount of pizza? Explain.

Name _____

☆ Guided Practice *

Do You Understand?

1. © **MP.2 Reasoning** Use the area model to explain why $\frac{3}{4}$ and $\frac{9}{12}$ are equivalent.

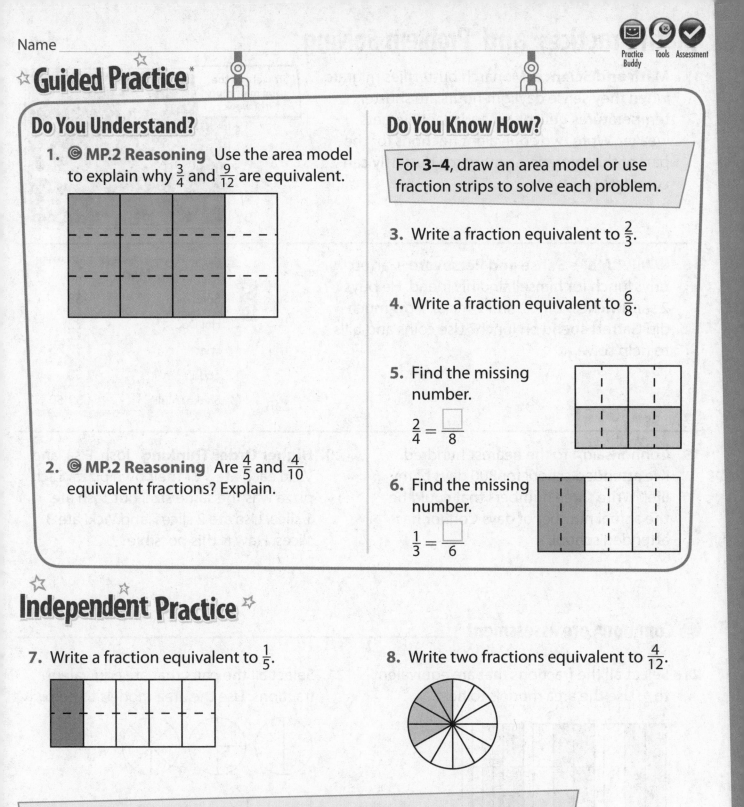

2. © **MP.2 Reasoning** Are $\frac{4}{5}$ and $\frac{4}{10}$ equivalent fractions? Explain.

Do You Know How?

For **3–4**, draw an area model or use fraction strips to solve each problem.

3. Write a fraction equivalent to $\frac{2}{3}$.

4. Write a fraction equivalent to $\frac{6}{8}$.

5. Find the missing number.

$$\frac{2}{4} = \frac{\square}{8}$$

6. Find the missing number.

$$\frac{1}{3} = \frac{\square}{6}$$

Independent Practice ☆

7. Write a fraction equivalent to $\frac{1}{5}$.

8. Write two fractions equivalent to $\frac{4}{12}$.

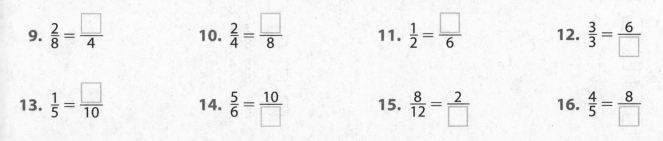

For **9–16**, draw an area model or use fraction strips to solve each problem.

9. $\frac{2}{8} = \frac{\square}{4}$

10. $\frac{2}{4} = \frac{\square}{8}$

11. $\frac{1}{2} = \frac{\square}{6}$

12. $\frac{3}{3} = \frac{6}{\square}$

13. $\frac{1}{5} = \frac{\square}{10}$

14. $\frac{5}{6} = \frac{10}{\square}$

15. $\frac{8}{12} = \frac{2}{\square}$

16. $\frac{4}{5} = \frac{8}{\square}$

Math Practices and Problem Solving

17. **Math and Science** Monarch butterflies migrate when they sense daylight hours are shorter, temperatures get colder, and plant life gets weaker. Write two equivalent fractions for the part of the migration a monarch butterfly can complete in 1 week.

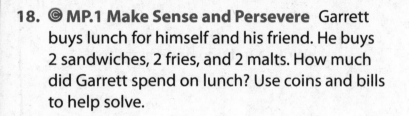

Travel $\frac{1}{5}$ of the total migration in 1 week

18. © **MP.1 Make Sense and Persevere** Garrett buys lunch for himself and his friend. He buys 2 sandwiches, 2 fries, and 2 malts. How much did Garrett spend on lunch? Use coins and bills to help solve.

DATA	Menu	
	Sandwich	$8
	Hot Dog	$2
	Fries	$2.75
	Soda	$2
	Shake/Malt	$3.50

19. Connor said, "To the nearest hundred, I've attended school for 800 days of my life!" Write three numbers that could be the actual number of days Connor has attended school.

20. **Higher Order Thinking** Josh, Lisa, and Vicki each ate $\frac{1}{4}$ of their own pizza. Each pizza was the same size, but Josh ate 1 slice, Lisa ate 2 slices, and Vicki ate 3 slices. How is this possible?

© **Common Core Assessment**

21. Select all the fractions that are equivalent to $\frac{2}{3}$. Use the area models to help.

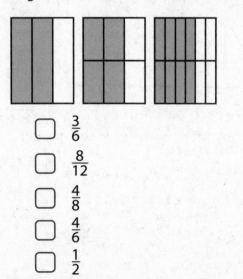

☐ $\frac{3}{6}$

☐ $\frac{8}{12}$

☐ $\frac{4}{8}$

☐ $\frac{4}{6}$

☐ $\frac{1}{2}$

22. Select all the pairs that are equivalent fractions. Use the area models to help.

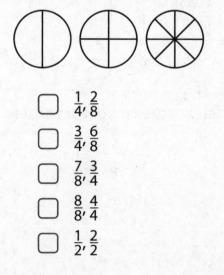

☐ $\frac{1}{4}, \frac{2}{8}$

☐ $\frac{3}{4}, \frac{6}{8}$

☐ $\frac{7}{8}, \frac{3}{4}$

☐ $\frac{8}{8}, \frac{4}{4}$

☐ $\frac{1}{2}, \frac{2}{2}$

© Pearson Education, Inc. 4

Help Practice Tools Games
       Buddy

Another Look!

Use an area model to find two fractions equivalent to $\frac{1}{2}$.

Many fractions are equivalent to $\frac{1}{2}$.

The circle is divided into 2 equal parts. The shaded part represents $\frac{1}{2}$.	Divide the circle into 4 equal parts. The shaded part represents $\frac{2}{4}$.	Divide the circle into 8 equal parts. The shaded part represents $\frac{4}{8}$.

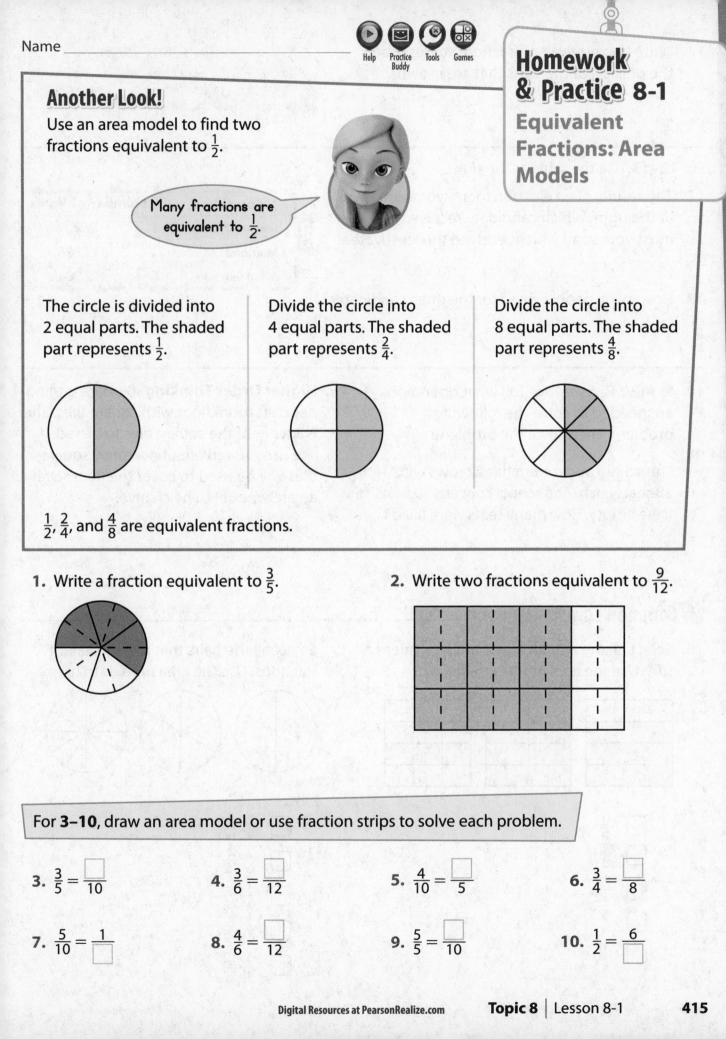

$\frac{1}{2}$, $\frac{2}{4}$, and $\frac{4}{8}$ are equivalent fractions.

1. Write a fraction equivalent to $\frac{3}{5}$.

2. Write two fractions equivalent to $\frac{9}{12}$.

For **3–10**, draw an area model or use fraction strips to solve each problem.

3. $\frac{3}{5} = \frac{\square}{10}$

4. $\frac{3}{6} = \frac{\square}{12}$

5. $\frac{4}{10} = \frac{\square}{5}$

6. $\frac{3}{4} = \frac{\square}{8}$

7. $\frac{5}{10} = \frac{1}{\square}$

8. $\frac{4}{6} = \frac{\square}{12}$

9. $\frac{5}{5} = \frac{\square}{10}$

10. $\frac{1}{2} = \frac{6}{\square}$

11. Write two equivalent fractions to describe the portion of the eggs that are brown.

For **12–13**, use the table at the right.

12. The results of an election for mayor are shown at the right. Which candidate received the most votes and which received the least votes?

DATA	Candidate	Number of Votes
	Leonard Hansen	12,409
	Margaret O'Connor	12,926
	Jillian Garcia	12,904

13. How many people voted for the three candidates?

---

14. © **MP.2 Reasoning** Tell what operations are needed to solve the following problem. Then solve the problem.

The school auditorium has 22 rows with 28 seats each. At a school concert, 19 seats were empty. How many seats were filled?

15. **Higher Order Thinking** Barbara is tiling her craft room floor with square tiles. She wants $\frac{6}{10}$ of the square tiles to be red. If she uses 18 red tiles, how many square tiles will be used to cover the floor? Draw an area model to help solve.

© **Common Core Assessment**

16. Select all the fractions that are equivalent to $\frac{3}{4}$. Use the area models to help.

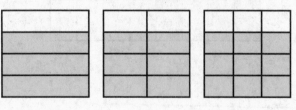

- ☐ $\frac{6}{6}$
- ☐ $\frac{2}{8}$
- ☐ $\frac{9}{12}$
- ☐ $\frac{6}{8}$
- ☐ $\frac{1}{2}$

17. Select all the pairs that are equivalent fractions. Use the area models to help.

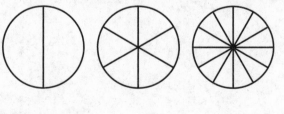

- ☐ $\frac{1}{6}, \frac{3}{12}$
- ☐ $\frac{2}{6}, \frac{4}{12}$
- ☐ $\frac{3}{6}, \frac{1}{2}$
- ☐ $\frac{1}{6}, \frac{6}{12}$
- ☐ $\frac{6}{6}, \frac{12}{12}$

Name _____

Solve & Share

Suppose you have a ruler showing fourths. Use your ruler to name a fraction that is equivalent to $\frac{2}{4}$. Tell how you know the fraction is equivalent.

I can ...
name the same amount on a number line using equivalent fractions.

Content Standard 4.NF.A.1
Mathematical Practices MP.1, MP.3, MP.4, MP.5, MP.7

You can use appropriate tools like rulers or number lines to help solve problems.

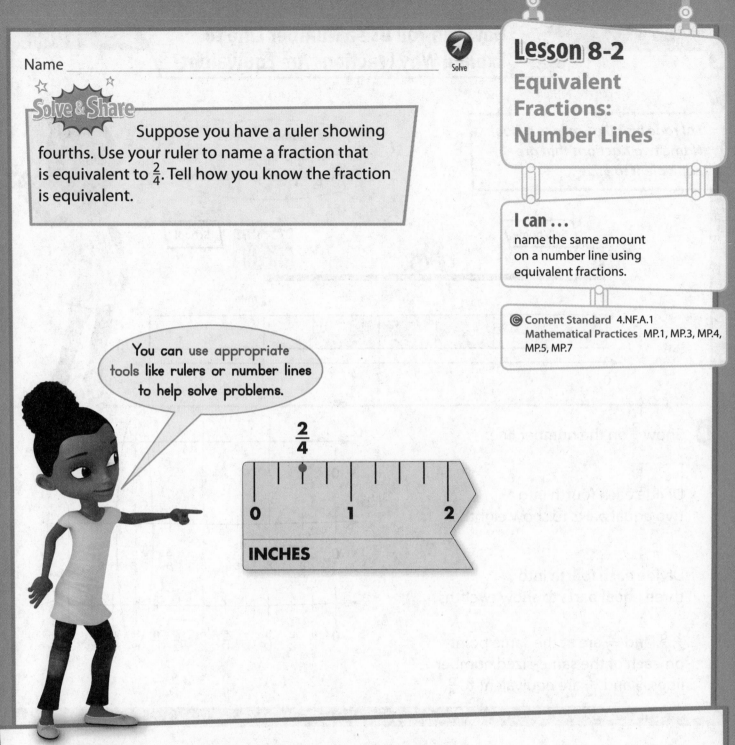

$\frac{2}{4}$

0   1   2

INCHES

Look Back! MP.4 Model with Math Do you think there is more than one fraction equivalent to $\frac{2}{4}$? Draw a picture to explain.

Essential Question: How Can You Use a Number Line to Explain Why Fractions Are Equivalent?

A

Sal rode his bike $\frac{3}{4}$ mile to school. Name two fractions that are equivalent to $\frac{3}{4}$.

A number line is another appropriate tool for finding equivalent fractions.

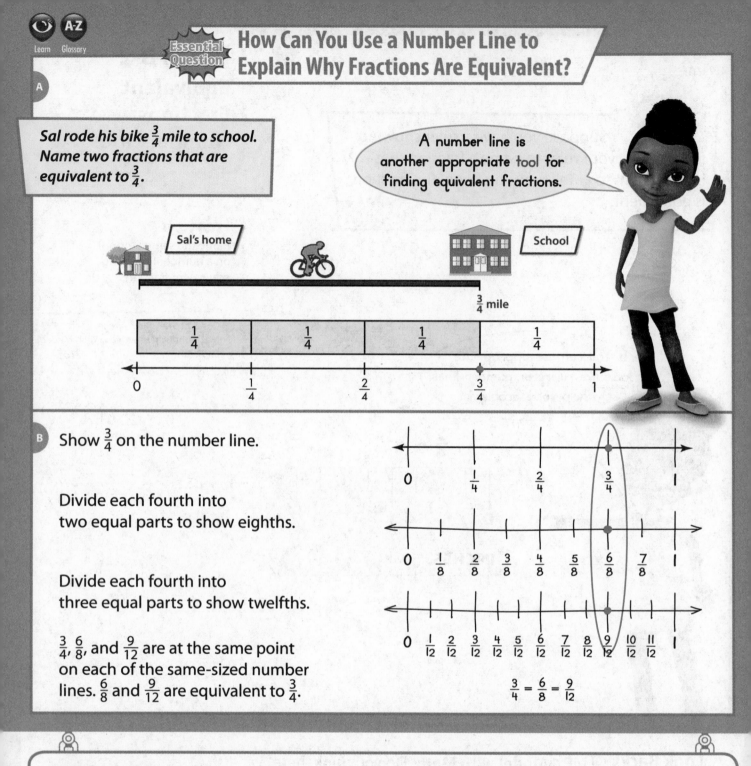

Sal's home

School

$\frac{3}{4}$ mile

| $\frac{1}{4}$ | $\frac{1}{4}$ | $\frac{1}{4}$ | $\frac{1}{4}$ |

0    $\frac{1}{4}$ $\frac{2}{4}$ $\frac{3}{4}$ 1

B Show $\frac{3}{4}$ on the number line.

Divide each fourth into two equal parts to show eighths.

Divide each fourth into three equal parts to show twelfths.

$\frac{3}{4}$, $\frac{6}{8}$, and $\frac{9}{12}$ are at the same point on each of the same-sized number lines. $\frac{6}{8}$ and $\frac{9}{12}$ are equivalent to $\frac{3}{4}$.

0    $\frac{1}{4}$ $\frac{2}{4}$ $\frac{3}{4}$

0 $\frac{1}{8}$ $\frac{2}{8}$ $\frac{3}{8}$ $\frac{4}{8}$ $\frac{5}{8}$ $\frac{6}{8}$ $\frac{7}{8}$

0 $\frac{1}{12}$ $\frac{2}{12}$ $\frac{3}{12}$ $\frac{4}{12}$ $\frac{5}{12}$ $\frac{6}{12}$ $\frac{7}{12}$ $\frac{8}{12}$ $\frac{9}{12}$ $\frac{10}{12}$ $\frac{11}{12}$

$$\frac{3}{4} = \frac{6}{8} = \frac{9}{12}$$

Convince Me! © MP.7 Use Structure The number and size of each part on two number lines are different. Can the number lines show equivalent fractions? Use the number lines above to explain.

Another Example!

You can use a number line to find equivalent fractions that are greater than or equal to 1.

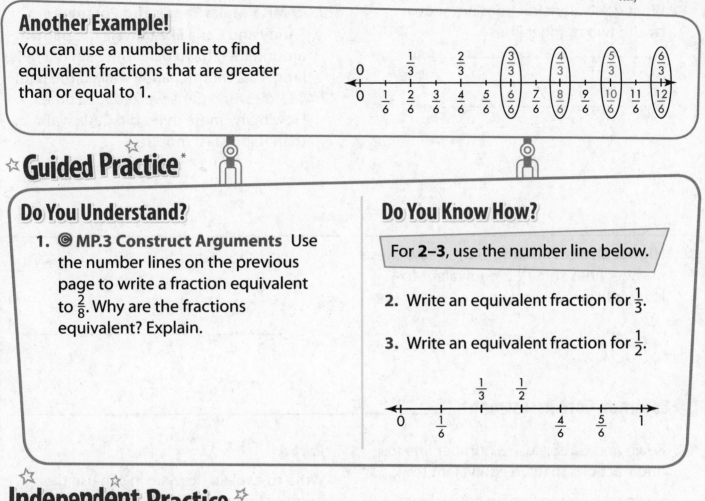

☆ Guided Practice*

Do You Understand?

1. © **MP.3 Construct Arguments** Use the number lines on the previous page to write a fraction equivalent to $\frac{2}{8}$. Why are the fractions equivalent? Explain.

Do You Know How?

For **2–3**, use the number line below.

2. Write an equivalent fraction for $\frac{1}{3}$.

3. Write an equivalent fraction for $\frac{1}{2}$.

Independent Practice ☆

For **4–5**, use the number line to find equivalent fractions. Circle the correct answer.

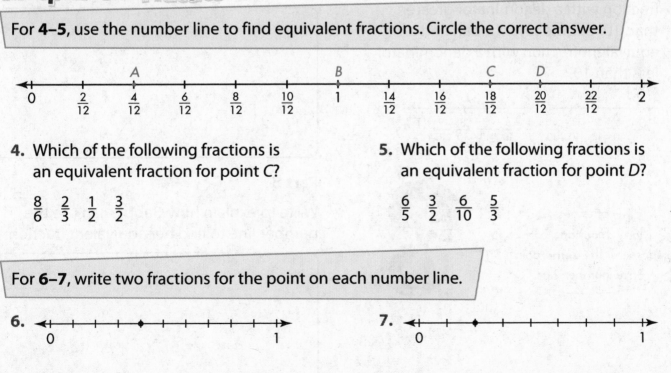

4. Which of the following fractions is an equivalent fraction for point *C*?

   $\frac{8}{6}$ $\frac{2}{3}$ $\frac{1}{2}$ $\frac{3}{2}$

5. Which of the following fractions is an equivalent fraction for point *D*?

   $\frac{6}{5}$ $\frac{3}{2}$ $\frac{6}{10}$ $\frac{5}{3}$

For **6–7**, write two fractions for the point on each number line.

6.

   0   1

7.

   0   1

Math Practices and Problem Solving

8. What equivalent fractions are shown by the two number lines?

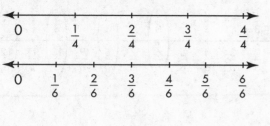

9. © **MP.1 Make Sense and Persevere**
Randy and Carla like to walk the path around their town park. The path is 2 miles long. Last month Randy walked the path 13 times, and Carla walked it 22 times. How many more miles did Carla walk than Randy last month?

10. **Higher Order Thinking** Jarred says these number lines show $\frac{3}{4}$ is equivalent to $\frac{2}{3}$. Is Jarred correct? Explain.

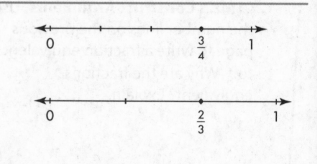

© **Common Core Assessment**

11. Kevin and Gabbie use a number line to find fractions that are equivalent to $\frac{4}{10}$.

Kevin says he can find an equivalent fraction with a denominator greater than 10. Gabbie says she can find an equivalent fraction with a denominator less than 10.

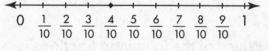

Many fractions can represent the same point on a number line.

Part A

Write to explain how Kevin can use the number line to find his equivalent fraction.

Part B

Write to explain how Gabbie can use the number line to find her equivalent fraction.

Help Practice Tools Games
      Buddy

Another Look!

You can write equivalent fractions for a point shown on a number line.

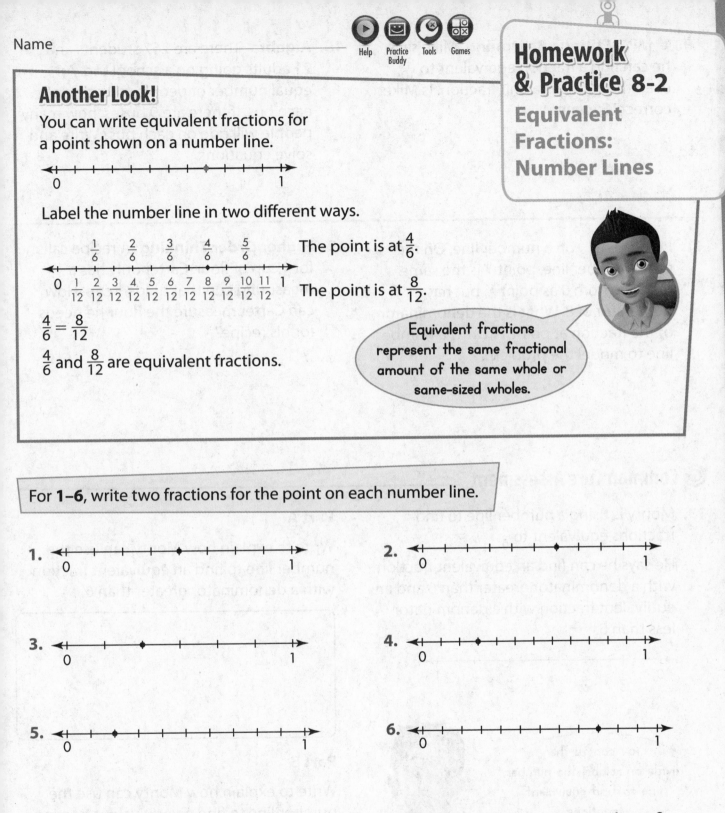

Label the number line in two different ways.

$\frac{1}{6}$ $\frac{2}{6}$ $\frac{3}{6}$ $\frac{4}{6}$ $\frac{5}{6}$

The point is at $\frac{4}{6}$.

0 $\frac{1}{12}$ $\frac{2}{12}$ $\frac{3}{12}$ $\frac{4}{12}$ $\frac{5}{12}$ $\frac{6}{12}$ $\frac{7}{12}$ $\frac{8}{12}$ $\frac{9}{12}$ $\frac{10}{12}$ $\frac{11}{12}$ 1

The point is at $\frac{8}{12}$.

$\frac{4}{6} = \frac{8}{12}$

$\frac{4}{6}$ and $\frac{8}{12}$ are equivalent fractions.

Equivalent fractions represent the same fractional amount of the same whole or same-sized wholes.

For **1–6**, write two fractions for the point on each number line.

1. 0 ———————•——————— 1

2. 0 ———————————•——— 1

3. 0 ————•——————————— 1

4. 0 ———•———————————— 1

5. 0 ——•————————————— 1

6. 0 ——————————•————— 1

7. Are $\frac{3}{8}$ and $\frac{3}{4}$ equivalent fractions? Draw a number line to decide.

8. Draw a number line to show $\frac{1}{4}$ and $\frac{2}{8}$ are equivalent.

9. **© MP.3 Critique Reasoning** Mike says he can find a fraction equivalent to $\frac{1}{10}$, even though $\frac{1}{10}$ is a unit fraction. Is Mike correct? Explain.

10. **Algebra** There are 267 students and 21 adults going on a school trip. An equal number of people will ride on each bus. If there are 9 buses, how many people will ride on each bus? Write and solve equations.

11. Point X is at $\frac{2}{3}$ on a number line. On the same number line, point Y is the same distance from 0 as point X, but has a numerator of 8. What is the denominator of the fraction at point Y? Draw a number line to model the problem.

12. **Higher Order Thinking** A recipe calls for $\frac{1}{4}$ cup of flour. Carter only has a measuring cup that holds $\frac{1}{8}$ cup. How can Carter measure the flour he needs for his recipe?

© Common Core Assessment

13. Monty is using a number line to find fractions equivalent to $\frac{4}{6}$.

He says he can find an equivalent fraction with a denominator greater than 6 and an equivalent fraction with a denominator less than 6.

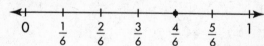

$$0 \quad \frac{1}{6} \quad \frac{2}{6} \quad \frac{3}{6} \quad \frac{4}{6} \quad \frac{5}{6} \quad 1$$

You can further divide or relabel the number line to find equivalent fractions.

Part A

Write to explain how Monty can use the number line to find an equivalent fraction with a denominator greater than 6.

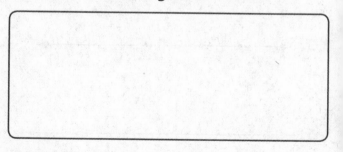

Part B

Write to explain how Monty can use the number line to find an equivalent fraction with a denominator less than 6.

Name _____

☆ ☆
Solve & Share

Wayne bought a box of muffins. Four sixths of the muffins are blueberry. Write a fraction equivalent to $\frac{4}{6}$. **Solve this problem any way you choose.**

I can ...
use multiplication to find equivalent fractions.

© Content Standard 4.NF.A.1
Mathematical Practices MP.2, MP.3, MP.4

What can you draw to model with math to help represent the problem? *Show your work in the space below!*

Look Back! © MP.2 Reasoning How are the numerator and denominator of your fraction related to the numerator and denominator of $\frac{4}{6}$?

How Can You Use Multiplication to Find Equivalent Fractions?

Essential Question

A

A librarian said $\frac{1}{2}$ of the books checked out yesterday were nonfiction. What are some fractions equivalent to $\frac{1}{2}$?

To find equivalent fractions, multiply by a fraction equal to one.

$\frac{1}{2}$ of the books checked out were nonfiction.

B Multiply by $\frac{2}{2}$.

Multiply the numerator and the denominator by 2.

$$\frac{1}{2} \times \frac{2}{2} = \frac{2}{4}$$

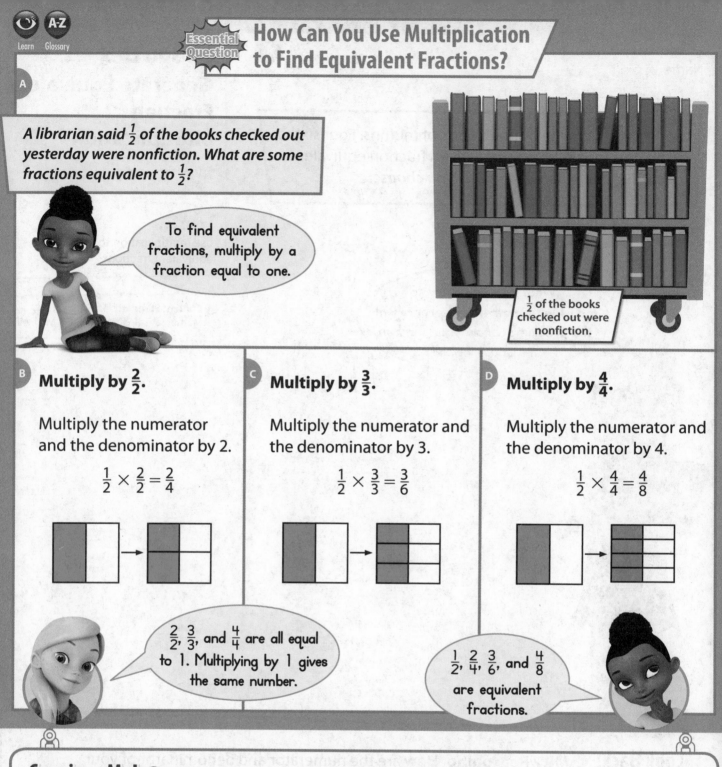

C Multiply by $\frac{3}{3}$.

Multiply the numerator and the denominator by 3.

$$\frac{1}{2} \times \frac{3}{3} = \frac{3}{6}$$

D Multiply by $\frac{4}{4}$.

Multiply the numerator and the denominator by 4.

$$\frac{1}{2} \times \frac{4}{4} = \frac{4}{8}$$

$\frac{2}{2}$, $\frac{3}{3}$, and $\frac{4}{4}$ are all equal to 1. Multiplying by 1 gives the same number.

$\frac{1}{2}$, $\frac{2}{4}$, $\frac{3}{6}$, and $\frac{4}{8}$ are equivalent fractions.

Convince Me! © **MP.3 Critique Reasoning** Kevin said, "In each of the examples above, all you are doing is multiplying by one. When you multiply by 1, the value doesn't change." Is Kevin correct? Explain.

☆Guided Practice☆

Do You Understand?

1. Use an area model and multiplication to show why $\frac{5}{6}$ and $\frac{10}{12}$ are equivalent fractions.

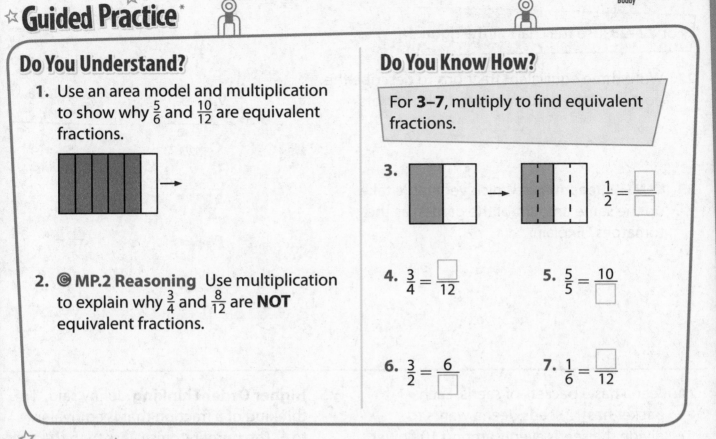

2. © MP.2 Reasoning Use multiplication to explain why $\frac{3}{4}$ and $\frac{8}{12}$ are **NOT** equivalent fractions.

Do You Know How?

For **3–7**, multiply to find equivalent fractions.

3. $\frac{1}{2} = \frac{\square}{\square}$

4. $\frac{3}{4} = \frac{\square}{12}$

5. $\frac{5}{5} = \frac{10}{\square}$

6. $\frac{3}{2} = \frac{6}{\square}$

7. $\frac{1}{6} = \frac{\square}{12}$

☆Independent Practice☆

Leveled Practice For **8–13**, multiply to find equivalent fractions.

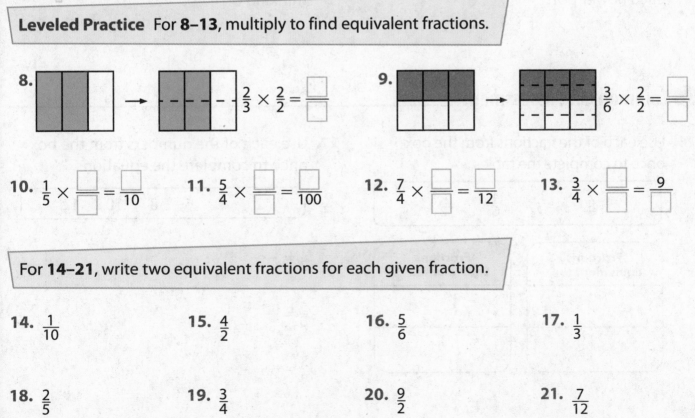

8. $\frac{2}{3} \times \frac{2}{2} = \frac{\square}{\square}$

9. $\frac{3}{6} \times \frac{2}{2} = \frac{\square}{\square}$

10. $\frac{1}{5} \times \frac{\square}{\square} = \frac{\square}{10}$

11. $\frac{5}{4} \times \frac{\square}{\square} = \frac{\square}{100}$

12. $\frac{7}{4} \times \frac{\square}{\square} = \frac{\square}{12}$

13. $\frac{3}{4} \times \frac{\square}{\square} = \frac{9}{\square}$

For **14–21**, write two equivalent fractions for each given fraction.

14. $\frac{1}{10}$

15. $\frac{4}{2}$

16. $\frac{5}{6}$

17. $\frac{1}{3}$

18. $\frac{2}{5}$

19. $\frac{3}{4}$

20. $\frac{9}{2}$

21. $\frac{7}{12}$

*For another example, see Set B on page 455.

Math Practices and Problem Solving

For **22–23**, use the chart at the right.

22. Write three equivalent fractions to describe the portion of the garden planted with carrots.

23. © **MP.2 Reasoning** Which vegetable takes up the same amount of the garden as the tomatoes? Explain.

Vegetable	Fraction of Garden Planted
Carrots	$\frac{1}{6}$
Tomatoes	$\frac{1}{4}$
Peppers	$\frac{4}{12}$
Beans	$\frac{3}{12}$

24. Jeena has 5 packets of seeds. Each packet has 12 seeds. Jeena wants to divide the seeds evenly among 10 flower pots. How many seeds can she plant in each flower pot?

25. **Higher Order Thinking** Jenny said, "I'm thinking of a fraction that is equivalent to $\frac{2}{6}$. The numerator is 8 less than the denominator." What fraction is Jenny thinking of?

© Common Core Assessment

26. Use each of the fractions from the box once to complete the tables.

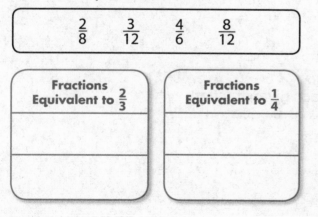

$\frac{2}{8}$ $\frac{3}{12}$ $\frac{4}{6}$ $\frac{8}{12}$

Fractions Equivalent to $\frac{2}{3}$

Fractions Equivalent to $\frac{1}{4}$

27. Use each of the numbers from the box once to complete the equations.

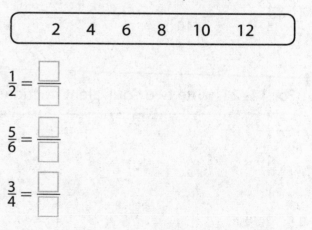

2   4   6   8   10   12

$\frac{1}{2} = \frac{\square}{\square}$

$\frac{5}{6} = \frac{\square}{\square}$

$\frac{3}{4} = \frac{\square}{\square}$

Another Look!

Find two fractions that are equivalent to $\frac{3}{4}$.

Multiply the given fraction by a fraction equal to one to find equivalent fractions.

$$\frac{3}{4} \times \frac{2}{2} = \frac{6}{8} \qquad \frac{3}{4} \times \frac{3}{3} = \frac{9}{12}$$

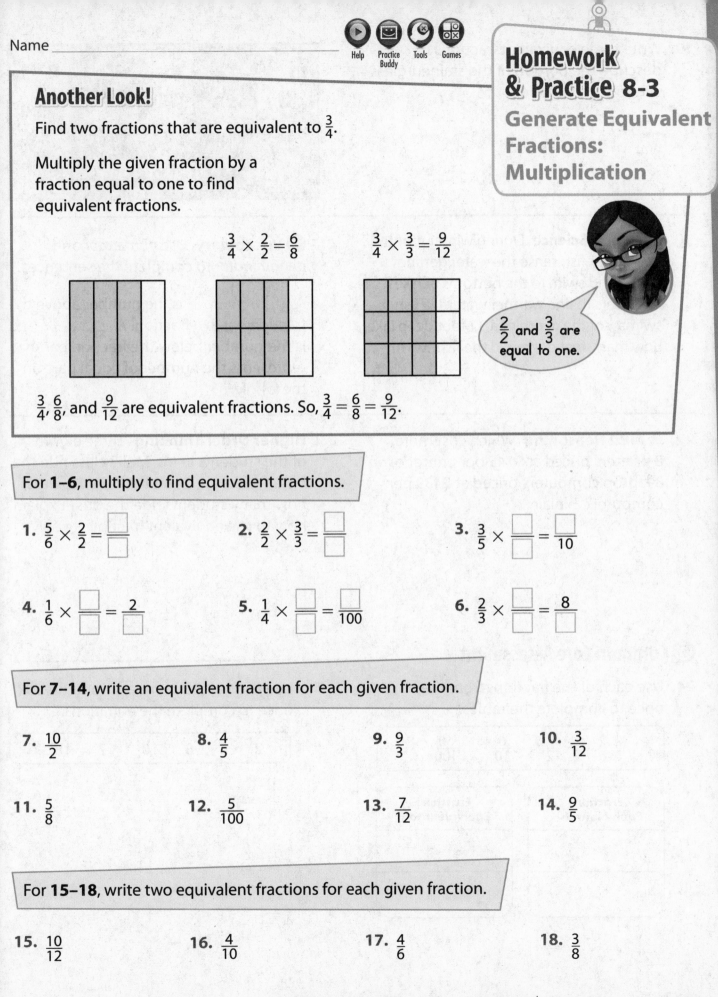

$\frac{2}{2}$ and $\frac{3}{3}$ are equal to one.

$\frac{3}{4}$, $\frac{6}{8}$, and $\frac{9}{12}$ are equivalent fractions. So, $\frac{3}{4} = \frac{6}{8} = \frac{9}{12}$.

For 1–6, multiply to find equivalent fractions.

1. $\frac{5}{6} \times \frac{2}{2} = \frac{\square}{\square}$

2. $\frac{2}{2} \times \frac{3}{3} = \frac{\square}{\square}$

3. $\frac{3}{5} \times \frac{\square}{\square} = \frac{\square}{10}$

4. $\frac{1}{6} \times \frac{\square}{\square} = \frac{2}{\square}$

5. $\frac{1}{4} \times \frac{\square}{\square} = \frac{\square}{100}$

6. $\frac{2}{3} \times \frac{\square}{\square} = \frac{8}{\square}$

For 7–14, write an equivalent fraction for each given fraction.

7. $\frac{10}{2}$

8. $\frac{4}{5}$

9. $\frac{9}{3}$

10. $\frac{3}{12}$

11. $\frac{5}{8}$

12. $\frac{5}{100}$

13. $\frac{7}{12}$

14. $\frac{9}{5}$

For 15–18, write two equivalent fractions for each given fraction.

15. $\frac{10}{12}$

16. $\frac{4}{10}$

17. $\frac{4}{6}$

18. $\frac{3}{8}$

19. Write three equivalent fractions to describe the portion of the stained-glass window that is gold.

20. Math and Science During winter months, freshwater fish sense the water getting colder and swim to the bottoms of lakes and rivers to find warmer water. If a fish swims $\frac{7}{8}$ of the depth of a 32-foot deep lake, how many feet down did the fish swim?

21. 🅰🆉 **Vocabulary** Use *numerator* and *denominator* to complete the sentences.

A _____ is the number above the fraction bar in a fraction. A _____ is the number below the fraction bar that represents the number of equal parts in the whole.

22. © **MP.2 Reasoning** Which cost more, 8 printers priced at $145 per printer or 3 laptop computers priced at $439 per computer? Explain.

23. Higher Order Thinking Three eighths of the students in Ms. Mull's class ride the bus. If there are 24 students in the class, how many students ride the bus? Explain how to use equivalent fractions to solve.

© **Common Core Assessment**

24. Use each of the fractions from the box once to complete the tables.

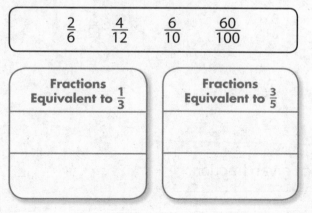

| $\frac{2}{6}$ | $\frac{4}{12}$ | $\frac{6}{10}$ | $\frac{60}{100}$ |

Fractions Equivalent to $\frac{1}{3}$	Fractions Equivalent to $\frac{3}{5}$

25. Use each of the numbers from the box once to complete the equations.

| 2 | 6 | 8 | 10 | 12 | 18 |

$$\frac{5}{6} = \frac{\square}{\square}$$

$$\frac{1}{3} = \frac{\square}{\square}$$

$$\frac{9}{4} = \frac{\square}{\square}$$

Name _____

☆ ☆
Solve & Share

Sara bought a piece of ribbon. The length of the ribbon is given in tenths. Write the length as two other equivalent fractions. *Solve this problem any way you choose.*

Solve

I can ...
use division to find equivalent fractions.

© Content Standard 4.NF.A.1
Mathematical Practices MP.1, MP.2, MP.3, MP.4, MP.6

Remember to be precise when answering the question. Use appropriate labels.

$\frac{6}{10}$ meter

Look Back! © MP.1 Make Sense and Persevere Sara wrote the following equivalent fractions: $\frac{6}{10} = \frac{3}{5}$. What two operations could Sara have used to find her equivalent fractions? Explain.

How Can You Use Division to Find Equivalent Fractions?

Essential Question

A

In early May, Fairbanks, Alaska, has daylight for $\frac{18}{24}$ of the day. What are some fractions equivalent to $\frac{18}{24}$?

Fairbanks

To find equivalent fractions, divide the numerator and the denominator by a common factor greater than 1.

A common factor is a factor two or more numbers have in common.

18 hours of daylight in May

B Two common factors of 18 and 24 are 2 and 3.

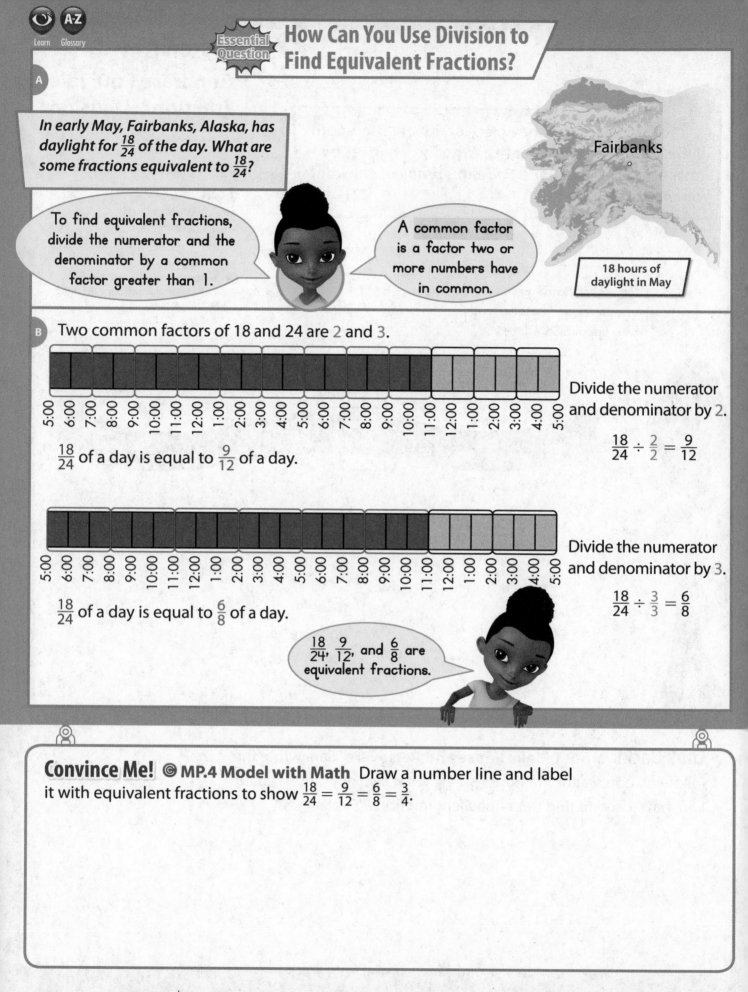

5:00 6:00 7:00 8:00 9:00 10:00 11:00 12:00 1:00 2:00 3:00 4:00 5:00 6:00 7:00 8:00 9:00 10:00 11:00 12:00 1:00 2:00 3:00 4:00 5:00

$\frac{18}{24}$ of a day is equal to $\frac{9}{12}$ of a day.

Divide the numerator and denominator by 2.

$$\frac{18}{24} \div \frac{2}{2} = \frac{9}{12}$$

5:00 6:00 7:00 8:00 9:00 10:00 11:00 12:00 1:00 2:00 3:00 4:00 5:00 6:00 7:00 8:00 9:00 10:00 11:00 12:00 1:00 2:00 3:00 4:00 5:00

$\frac{18}{24}$ of a day is equal to $\frac{6}{8}$ of a day.

Divide the numerator and denominator by 3.

$$\frac{18}{24} \div \frac{3}{3} = \frac{6}{8}$$

$\frac{18}{24}$, $\frac{9}{12}$, and $\frac{6}{8}$ are equivalent fractions.

Convince Me! © MP.4 Model with Math Draw a number line and label it with equivalent fractions to show $\frac{18}{24} = \frac{9}{12} = \frac{6}{8} = \frac{3}{4}$.

Practice Buddy   Tools   Assessment

☆ Guided Practice *

Do You Understand?

1. Use division to show $\frac{9}{12}$ and $\frac{3}{4}$ are equivalent fractions.

2. ©MP.2 Reasoning Is there a fraction with a smaller numerator and denominator that is equivalent to $\frac{4}{12}$? Explain.

Do You Know How?

For **3–8**, divide to find equivalent fractions.

3. $\frac{6}{10} = \frac{\square}{\square}$ 4. $\frac{8}{12} = \frac{\square}{\square}$

5. $\frac{8}{12} = \frac{\square}{3}$ 6. $\frac{10}{12} = \frac{5}{\square}$

7. $\frac{2}{10} = \frac{\square}{5}$ 8. $\frac{10}{100} = \frac{\square}{10}$

☆ Independent Practice ☆

Leveled Practice   For **9–16**, divide to find equivalent fractions.

9. $\frac{6}{12} \div \frac{6}{6} = \frac{\square}{\square}$

10. $\frac{70}{10} \div \frac{5}{5} = \frac{\square}{\square}$

11. $\frac{2}{6} \div \frac{2}{2} = \frac{\square}{\square}$

12. $\frac{50}{100} \div \frac{10}{10} = \frac{\square}{\square}$

13. $\frac{9}{6} \div \frac{\square}{\square} = \frac{3}{\square}$

14. $\frac{10}{4} \div \frac{\square}{\square} = \frac{\square}{2}$

15. $\frac{4}{12} \div \frac{\square}{\square} = \frac{\square}{6}$

16. $\frac{2}{8} \div \frac{\square}{\square} = \frac{\square}{4}$

For **17–24**, divide to find two equivalent fractions.

17. $\frac{20}{100}$

18. $\frac{40}{10}$

19. $\frac{16}{12}$

20. $\frac{12}{8}$

21. $\frac{24}{12}$

22. $\frac{10}{100}$

23. $\frac{90}{10}$

24. $\frac{80}{100}$

*For another example, see Set B on page 455.   **Topic 8** | Lesson 8-4   **431**

Math Practices and Problem Solving

For **25–27**, use the table at the right.

25. Complete the table at the right by writing the fraction of the day each animal sleeps and an equivalent fraction. Remember, there are 24 hours in a day.

26. Suppose the cow slept 4 more hours. What fraction of the day would the cow spend sleeping?

27. How many hours does a tiger sleep in 7 days?

Animal	Number of Hours Spent Sleeping	Fraction of the Day Spent Sleeping	Equivalent Fraction
Cat	12		
Cow	4		
Squirrel	15		
Tiger	16		

---

28. © **MP.1 Make Sense and Persevere** Ethan ate $\frac{4}{8}$ of the sandwich. Andy ate $\frac{1}{2}$ of the sandwich. The sandwiches were the same size.

   a. Whose sandwich had more equal parts?

   b. Whose sandwich had larger equal parts?

   c. Who ate more? Explain.

29. **Higher Order Thinking** If the numerator and denominator of a fraction are both odd numbers, can you write an equivalent fraction with a smaller numerator and denominator? Explain.

© **Common Core Assessment**

30. Which equation is **NOT** true?

   Ⓐ $\frac{12}{10} = \frac{6}{5}$

   Ⓑ $\frac{3}{1} = \frac{30}{10}$

   Ⓒ $\frac{6}{12} = \frac{2}{3}$

   Ⓓ $\frac{8}{6} = \frac{16}{12}$

31. There are 12 students in DeLynn's class. Eight students own pets. Which shows the fraction of the class that owns pets?

   Ⓐ $\frac{8}{12}$

   Ⓑ $\frac{1}{2}$

   Ⓒ $\frac{6}{4}$

   Ⓓ $\frac{12}{8}$

Name _____

Help Practice Tools Games
       Buddy

Homework
& Practice 8-4
Generate Equivalent
Fractions: Division

Another Look!

Use division to find two fractions equivalent to $\frac{8}{12}$.

To find an equivalent fraction, divide the numerator and denominator by any common factor other than 1.

$$\frac{8}{12} \div \frac{2}{2} = \frac{4}{6} \qquad \frac{8}{12} \div \frac{4}{4} = \frac{2}{3}$$

$\frac{8}{12}$, $\frac{4}{6}$, and $\frac{2}{3}$ are equivalent fractions.

For **1–8**, divide to find equivalent fractions.

1. $\frac{5}{10} \div \frac{5}{5} = \frac{\square}{\square}$

2. $\frac{2}{12} \div \frac{2}{2} = \frac{\square}{\square}$

3. $\frac{12}{6} \div \frac{3}{3} = \frac{\square}{\square}$

4. $\frac{40}{100} \div \frac{10}{10} = \frac{\square}{\square}$

5. $\frac{25}{100} \div \frac{\square}{\square} = \frac{\square}{4}$

6. $\frac{8}{12} \div \frac{\square}{\square} = \frac{\square}{2}$

7. $\frac{70}{100} \div \frac{\square}{\square} = \frac{7}{\square}$

8. $\frac{18}{10} \div \frac{\square}{\square} = \frac{9}{\square}$

For **9–16**, find an equivalent fraction for each given fraction.

9. $\frac{75}{100}$

10. $\frac{4}{10}$

11. $\frac{10}{12}$

12. $\frac{200}{100}$

13. $\frac{24}{100}$

14. $\frac{60}{12}$

15. $\frac{84}{100}$

16. $\frac{70}{10}$

For **17–24**, divide to find two equivalent fractions.

17. $\frac{500}{100}$

18. $\frac{4}{12}$

19. $\frac{30}{10}$

20. $\frac{60}{100}$

21. $\frac{50}{10}$

22. $\frac{6}{12}$

23. $\frac{12}{8}$

24. $\frac{18}{6}$

25. What fraction of the game spinner is red? Write two equivalent fractions.

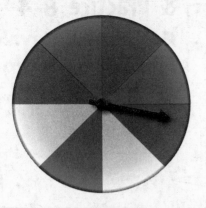

26. Solve this number riddle:
I am an odd number.
I am less than 100.
The sum of my digits is 12.
I am a multiple of 15.

What number am I?

27. It took Bob 55 minutes to clean the garage. How many seconds did it take Bob? There are 60 seconds in one minute.

28. Betty is canning 104 pears and 126 apples separately. Each jar holds 8 pears or 6 apples. How many jars does Betty need?

29. ⓒ **MP.3 Critique Reasoning** Laurie says summer is $\frac{1}{4}$ of the year. Maria says summer is $\frac{3}{12}$ of the year. Who is correct? Explain.

30. **Higher Order Thinking** Cindy is using division to write a fraction equivalent to $\frac{30}{100}$. She tried to divide the numerator and denominator by 3. She got stuck. What advice would you give her?

ⓒ **Common Core Assessment**

31. Which equation is **NOT** true?

ⓐ $\frac{10}{12} = \frac{5}{6}$

ⓑ $\frac{69}{100} = \frac{6}{10}$

ⓒ $\frac{10}{5} = \frac{200}{100}$

ⓓ $\frac{12}{4} = \frac{6}{2}$

32. There are 100 pieces of fruit in a basket. Twelve of the pieces are apples. Which shows the fraction of the fruit that are apples?

ⓐ $\frac{12}{12}$

ⓑ $\frac{12}{100}$

ⓒ $\frac{100}{12}$

ⓓ $\frac{100}{100}$

Name _____

Solve & Share

Color a part of each strip of paper below. Estimate what fraction of each strip is colored. Explain how you made your estimate. **Solve this problem any way you choose.**

I can ...
use benchmarks, area models, and number lines to compare fractions.

© Content Standards 4.NF.A.2, 4.NF.A.1
Mathematical Practices MP.1, MP.2, MP.3, MP.8

You can use reasoning. Use $\frac{1}{4}$, $\frac{1}{2}$, and $\frac{3}{4}$ to compare. Did you color more or less than $\frac{1}{2}$ of the strip? $\frac{1}{4}$ of the strip? $\frac{3}{4}$ of the strip?

Look Back! © **MP.8 Generalize** How could you tell if a fraction is greater than, less than, or equal to $\frac{1}{2}$ just by looking at the numerator and the denominator?

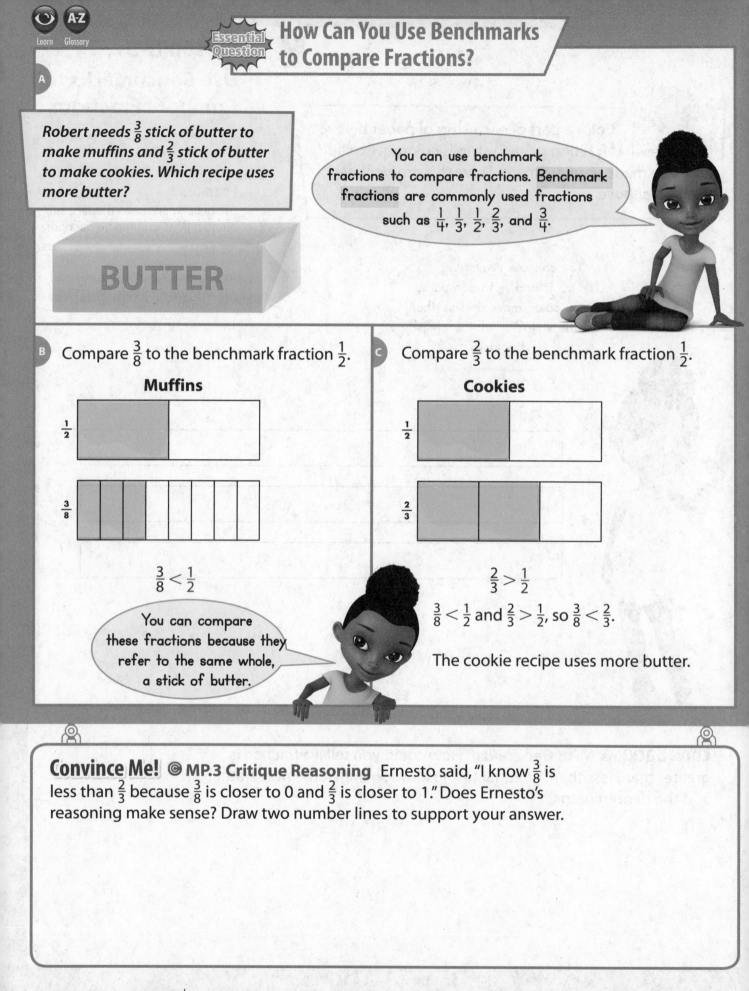

© Pearson Education, Inc. 4

Another Example!

Compare $\frac{9}{10}$ and $\frac{7}{6}$. Use 1 whole as a benchmark.

$\frac{9}{10} < 1$ and $\frac{7}{6} > 1$, so $\frac{9}{10} < \frac{7}{6}$.

☆ Guided Practice*

Do You Understand?

1. © MP.2 Reasoning Carl found $\frac{4}{8}$ is equal to $\frac{1}{2}$, and $\frac{1}{3}$ is less than $\frac{1}{2}$. How can Carl compare $\frac{4}{8}$ to $\frac{1}{3}$? Explain.

2. Write a fraction that is closer to 0 than to 1. Write another fraction that is closer to 1 than to 0. Use your fractions to complete the comparison.

$$\frac{\square}{\square} < \frac{\square}{\square}$$

Do You Know How?

For **3–4**, compare. Write $<$, $>$, or $=$.

3. $\frac{2}{6} \bigcirc \frac{4}{5}$

4. $\frac{11}{12} \bigcirc \frac{9}{8}$

5. Circle the fractions that are less than $\frac{1}{2}$.

$\frac{5}{4}$ $\frac{1}{4}$ $\frac{1}{5}$ $\frac{2}{3}$ $\frac{2}{12}$ $\frac{51}{100}$

6. Circle the fractions that are greater than 1.

$\frac{99}{100}$ $\frac{6}{5}$ $\frac{7}{8}$ $\frac{14}{8}$ $\frac{11}{10}$ $\frac{11}{12}$

Independent Practice ☆

For **7–10**, circle all the fractions that match each statement.

7. Fractions less than $\frac{1}{2}$

$\frac{3}{4}$ $\frac{1}{6}$ $\frac{6}{12}$ $\frac{4}{10}$ $\frac{5}{8}$ $\frac{5}{2}$

8. Fractions greater than $\frac{1}{2}$

$\frac{5}{8}$ $\frac{1}{4}$ $\frac{6}{3}$ $\frac{7}{10}$ $\frac{5}{12}$ $\frac{6}{12}$

9. Fractions greater than 1

$\frac{5}{4}$ $\frac{2}{3}$ $\frac{6}{6}$ $\frac{1}{10}$ $\frac{15}{12}$ $\frac{7}{8}$

10. Fractions closer to 0 than to 1

$\frac{3}{4}$ $\frac{1}{8}$ $\frac{1}{4}$ $\frac{7}{5}$ $\frac{2}{4}$ $\frac{3}{10}$

For **11–18**, compare using benchmark fractions or 1. Then write $>$, $<$, or $=$.

11. $\frac{1}{3} \bigcirc \frac{4}{6}$

12. $\frac{4}{8} \bigcirc \frac{2}{4}$

13. $\frac{7}{5} \bigcirc \frac{7}{8}$

14. $\frac{6}{12} \bigcirc \frac{4}{5}$

15. $\frac{4}{5} \bigcirc \frac{2}{5}$

16. $\frac{6}{6} \bigcirc \frac{13}{12}$

17. $\frac{8}{10} \bigcirc \frac{1}{8}$

18. $\frac{4}{4} \bigcirc \frac{10}{10}$

*For another example, see Set C on page 456.

Math Practices and Problem Solving

19. **MP.2 Reasoning** Jordan has $\frac{5}{8}$ can of green paint and $\frac{3}{6}$ can of blue paint. If the cans are the same size, does Jordan have more green paint or blue paint? Explain.

20. **Vocabulary** Write two examples of a *benchmark fraction*.

---

21. Four neighbors each have gardens that are the same size.

   a. Which neighbors planted vegetables in less than half of their gardens?

   b. Who has a larger section of vegetables in their garden, Margaret or Wayne?

Neighbor	Fraction of Garden Planted with Vegetables
James	$\frac{5}{12}$
Margaret	$\frac{5}{10}$
Claudia	$\frac{1}{6}$
Wayne	$\frac{2}{3}$

---

22. **MP.1 Make Sense and Persevere** Gavin bought 3 pizzas for a party. Each pizza had 8 slices. There were 8 other people at the party. Everyone ate the same number of slices. What is the greatest number of slices each person ate? How many slices were left over?

23. **Higher Order Thinking** How can you tell just by looking at the numerator and denominator of a fraction if it is closer to 0 or to 1? Give some examples in your explanation.

Common Core Assessment

24. Donna ate $\frac{7}{12}$ box of popcorn. Jack ate $\frac{4}{10}$ box of popcorn. The boxes of popcorn are the same size. Write to explain how to use a benchmark fraction to determine who ate more popcorn.

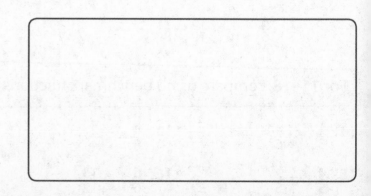

Homework & Practice 8-5

Use Benchmarks to Compare Fractions

Another Look!

Compare $\frac{6}{8}$ and $\frac{5}{12}$.

One Way

Compare the fractions to $\frac{1}{2}$.

$\frac{6}{8} > \frac{1}{2}$ $\frac{5}{12} < \frac{1}{2}$

$\frac{6}{8} > \frac{5}{12}$

Another Way

Compare the fractions to 0 and to 1.

$\frac{6}{8}$ is closer to 1 than to 0.

$\frac{5}{12}$ is closer to 0 than to 1.

$\frac{6}{8} > \frac{5}{12}$

Benchmarks can help you compare fractions.

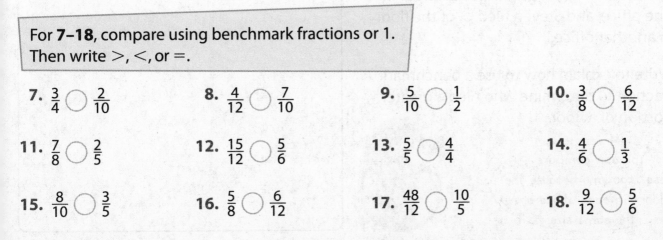

For **1–6**, write three fractions that match each statement.

1. Fractions equal to $\frac{1}{2}$

2. Fractions less than $\frac{1}{2}$

3. Fractions greater than 1

4. Fractions closer to 1 than to 0

5. Fractions closer to 0 than to 1

6. Fractions greater than $\frac{1}{2}$

For **7–18**, compare using benchmark fractions or 1. Then write $>$, $<$, or $=$.

7. $\frac{3}{4} \bigcirc \frac{2}{10}$

8. $\frac{4}{12} \bigcirc \frac{7}{10}$

9. $\frac{5}{10} \bigcirc \frac{1}{2}$

10. $\frac{3}{8} \bigcirc \frac{6}{12}$

11. $\frac{7}{8} \bigcirc \frac{2}{5}$

12. $\frac{15}{12} \bigcirc \frac{5}{6}$

13. $\frac{5}{5} \bigcirc \frac{4}{4}$

14. $\frac{4}{6} \bigcirc \frac{1}{3}$

15. $\frac{8}{10} \bigcirc \frac{3}{5}$

16. $\frac{5}{8} \bigcirc \frac{6}{12}$

17. $\frac{48}{12} \bigcirc \frac{10}{5}$

18. $\frac{9}{12} \bigcirc \frac{5}{6}$

19. Write three fractions that are greater than $\frac{1}{2}$ but less than 1.

20. © **MP.3 Critique Reasoning** Mary lives $\frac{6}{10}$ mile from school. Thad lives $\frac{9}{8}$ miles from school. Mary says Thad lives farther from school. Is she correct? Explain.

21. Mr. Phillips is mixing paint for his art class. How many 6-ounce bottles can he fill with the quantities of paint shown at the right? Explain.

Paint
64 ounces of blue
12 ounces of yellow
32 ounces of white

22. Sandra used benchmark fractions to describe some insects she collected. She said the ladybug is about $\frac{1}{4}$ inch long, and the cricket is about $\frac{2}{3}$ inch long. Which insect is longer?

23. **Higher Order Thinking** Austin said, "I know $\frac{1}{4}$ is less than $\frac{1}{2}$, so that means $\frac{3}{12}$ is less than $\frac{1}{2}$." Does Austin's reasoning make sense? Explain.

© **Common Core Assessment**

24. Kiyo and Steven are tiling the floors in an office building. Kiyo tiled $\frac{3}{6}$ of the floor in one office, and Steven tiled $\frac{5}{12}$ of the floor in another office.

Write to explain how to use a benchmark fraction to determine who tiled a greater portion of a floor.

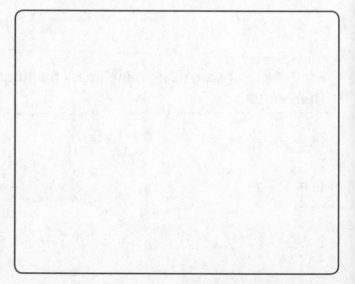

You can compare these fractions because the floors in each office are the same size.

Name _____

Solve & Share

Juan read for $\frac{5}{6}$ of an hour. Larissa read for $\frac{10}{12}$ of an hour. Who read for a longer period of time? Explain. **Solve this problem any way you choose.**

I can ...
use equivalent fractions to compare fractions.

© Content Standards 4.NF.A.2, 4.NF.A.1
Mathematical Practices MP.2, MP.3, MP.5

You can select and use appropriate tools such as drawings, number lines, or fraction strips to solve. *Show your work in the space below!*

Look Back! © MP.2 Reasoning Carlos read for $\frac{8}{10}$ of a hour. Did Carlos read for more or less time than Juan? Write your answer as a number sentence using >, <, or =.

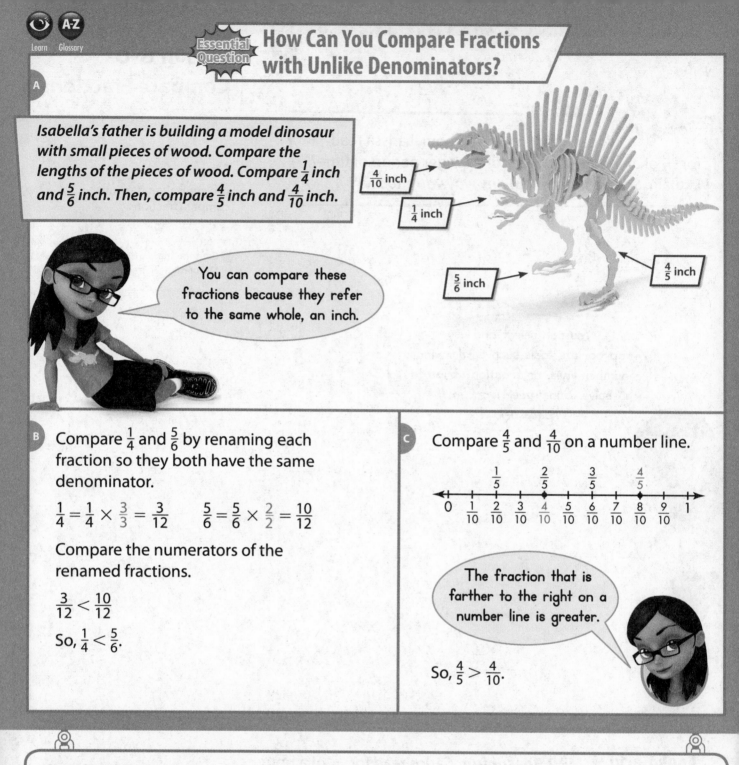

Essential Question How Can You Compare Fractions with Unlike Denominators?

A

Isabella's father is building a model dinosaur with small pieces of wood. Compare the lengths of the pieces of wood. Compare $\frac{1}{4}$ inch and $\frac{5}{6}$ inch. Then, compare $\frac{4}{5}$ inch and $\frac{4}{10}$ inch.

$\frac{4}{10}$ inch

$\frac{1}{4}$ inch

$\frac{5}{6}$ inch

$\frac{4}{5}$ inch

You can compare these fractions because they refer to the same whole, an inch.

B

Compare $\frac{1}{4}$ and $\frac{5}{6}$ by renaming each fraction so they both have the same denominator.

$$\frac{1}{4} = \frac{1}{4} \times \frac{3}{3} = \frac{3}{12} \qquad \frac{5}{6} = \frac{5}{6} \times \frac{2}{2} = \frac{10}{12}$$

Compare the numerators of the renamed fractions.

$$\frac{3}{12} < \frac{10}{12}$$

So, $\frac{1}{4} < \frac{5}{6}$.

C

Compare $\frac{4}{5}$ and $\frac{4}{10}$ on a number line.

The fraction that is farther to the right on a number line is greater.

So, $\frac{4}{5} > \frac{4}{10}$.

Convince Me! © MP.3 Critique Reasoning Kelly looked at the fractions on the right and said, "These are easy to compare. I just think about $\frac{1}{8}$ and $\frac{1}{6}$." Circle the greater fraction. Explain what Kelly was thinking.

$\frac{5}{8}$ $\qquad$ $\frac{5}{6}$

Another Example!

Compare $\frac{3}{4}$ and $\frac{6}{10}$.

Create an equivalent fraction for $\frac{3}{4}$ that has a numerator of 6.

$$\frac{3}{4} \times \frac{2}{2} = \frac{6}{8}$$

$\frac{6}{8} > \frac{6}{10}$ because 8 equal parts are each larger than one of the 10 equal parts of the same whole.

When two fractions have different denominators but the same numerators, the fraction with the greater denominator is less.

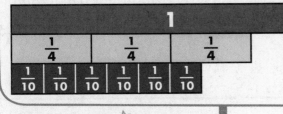

1		
$\frac{1}{4}$	$\frac{1}{4}$	$\frac{1}{4}$

$\frac{1}{10}$	$\frac{1}{10}$	$\frac{1}{10}$	$\frac{1}{10}$	$\frac{1}{10}$	$\frac{1}{10}$

☆ Guided Practice*

Do You Understand?

1. © **MP.3 Critique Reasoning** Mary says $\frac{1}{8}$ is greater than $\frac{1}{4}$ because 8 is greater than 4. Is Mary's reasoning correct? Explain.

Do You Know How?

For **2–5**, write >, <, or =. Use number lines, fraction strips, or equivalent fractions.

2. $\frac{3}{4} \bigcirc \frac{6}{8}$ 3. $\frac{1}{4} \bigcirc \frac{1}{10}$

4. $\frac{3}{5} \bigcirc \frac{5}{10}$ 5. $\frac{1}{2} \bigcirc \frac{4}{5}$

☆ Independent Practice ☆

Leveled Practice For **6–15**, find equivalent fractions to compare. Then write >, <, or =.

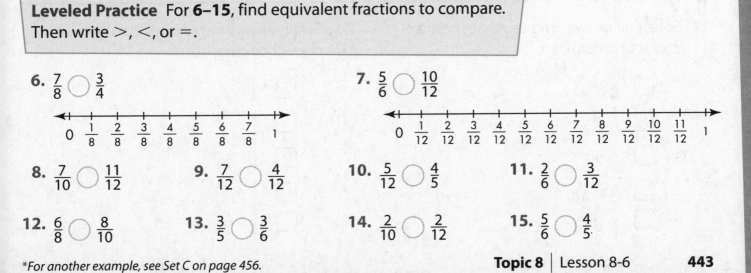

6. $\frac{7}{8} \bigcirc \frac{3}{4}$

    0 $\frac{1}{8}$ $\frac{2}{8}$ $\frac{3}{8}$ $\frac{4}{8}$ $\frac{5}{8}$ $\frac{6}{8}$ $\frac{7}{8}$ 1

7. $\frac{5}{6} \bigcirc \frac{10}{12}$

    0 $\frac{1}{12}$ $\frac{2}{12}$ $\frac{3}{12}$ $\frac{4}{12}$ $\frac{5}{12}$ $\frac{6}{12}$ $\frac{7}{12}$ $\frac{8}{12}$ $\frac{9}{12}$ $\frac{10}{12}$ $\frac{11}{12}$ 1

8. $\frac{7}{10} \bigcirc \frac{11}{12}$ 9. $\frac{7}{12} \bigcirc \frac{4}{12}$ 10. $\frac{5}{12} \bigcirc \frac{4}{5}$ 11. $\frac{2}{6} \bigcirc \frac{3}{12}$

12. $\frac{6}{8} \bigcirc \frac{8}{10}$ 13. $\frac{3}{5} \bigcirc \frac{3}{6}$ 14. $\frac{2}{10} \bigcirc \frac{2}{12}$ 15. $\frac{5}{6} \bigcirc \frac{4}{5}$

Math Practices and Problem Solving

16. Felicia drew the pictures at the right to show $\frac{3}{8}$ is greater than $\frac{3}{4}$. What was Felicia's mistake?

17. © **MP.3 Critique Reasoning** Jake said you can compare two fractions with the same denominator by only comparing the numerators. Is Jake correct? Explain.

18. Tina completed $\frac{2}{3}$ of her homework. George completed $\frac{7}{8}$ of his homework. Tina and George have the same amount of homework. Who completed a greater fraction of homework?

19. If $34 \times 2 = 68$, then what does 34×20 equal?

20. What can you conclude about $\frac{3}{5}$ and $\frac{60}{100}$ if you know $\frac{3}{5}$ is equivalent to $\frac{6}{10}$ and $\frac{6}{10}$ is equivalent to $\frac{60}{100}$?

21. Jackson played a video game for $\frac{1}{6}$ hour. Hailey played a video game for $\frac{1}{3}$ hour. Who played the video game for a greater amount of time? Explain.

22. **Higher Order Thinking** Four fourth-grade classes from an elementary school took a trip to the United States Capitol. There were 25 students in each class. At the capitol, a maximum of 40 students were allowed on a tour at one time. What was the least number of tours needed for all students to take the tour?

© Common Core Assessment

23. Select all answer choices that show a correct comparison.

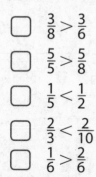

- ☐ $\frac{3}{8} > \frac{3}{6}$
- ☐ $\frac{5}{5} > \frac{5}{8}$
- ☐ $\frac{1}{5} < \frac{1}{2}$
- ☐ $\frac{2}{3} < \frac{2}{10}$
- ☐ $\frac{1}{6} > \frac{2}{6}$

24. Select all answer choices that show a correct comparison.

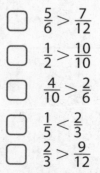

- ☐ $\frac{5}{6} > \frac{7}{12}$
- ☐ $\frac{1}{2} > \frac{10}{10}$
- ☐ $\frac{4}{10} > \frac{2}{6}$
- ☐ $\frac{1}{5} < \frac{2}{3}$
- ☐ $\frac{2}{3} > \frac{9}{12}$

Name _____

Another Look!

Compare $\frac{2}{3}$ and $\frac{1}{2}$.

One Way

Rename one or both fractions so they both have the same denominator.

Rename both $\frac{2}{3}$ and $\frac{1}{2}$.

$\frac{2}{3} = \frac{2}{3} \times \frac{2}{2} = \frac{4}{6}$

$\frac{1}{2} = \frac{1}{2} \times \frac{3}{3} = \frac{3}{6}$

$\frac{4}{6} > \frac{3}{6}$, so $\frac{2}{3} > \frac{1}{2}$.

Another Way

Rename one or both fractions so they both have the same numerator.

Leave $\frac{2}{3}$ alone. Rename $\frac{1}{2}$.

$\frac{1}{2} = \frac{1}{2} \times \frac{2}{2} = \frac{2}{4}$

$\frac{2}{3} > \frac{2}{4}$, so $\frac{2}{3} > \frac{1}{2}$.

> You can use fraction strips, number lines, or benchmark fractions to justify your comparisons.

For **1–16**, find equivalent fractions to compare. Then write $>$, $<$, or $=$. Use fraction strips or number lines.

1. $\frac{5}{6} \bigcirc \frac{2}{3}$

2. $\frac{1}{5} \bigcirc \frac{2}{8}$

3. $\frac{9}{10} \bigcirc \frac{6}{8}$

4. $\frac{3}{4} \bigcirc \frac{1}{4}$

5. $\frac{7}{8} \bigcirc \frac{5}{10}$

6. $\frac{2}{5} \bigcirc \frac{2}{6}$

7. $\frac{1}{3} \bigcirc \frac{3}{8}$

8. $\frac{2}{10} \bigcirc \frac{3}{5}$

9. $\frac{8}{10} \bigcirc \frac{3}{4}$

10. $\frac{3}{8} \bigcirc \frac{11}{12}$

11. $\frac{2}{3} \bigcirc \frac{10}{12}$

12. $\frac{7}{8} \bigcirc \frac{1}{6}$

13. $\frac{3}{8} \bigcirc \frac{7}{8}$

14. $\frac{2}{4} \bigcirc \frac{4}{8}$

15. $\frac{6}{8} \bigcirc \frac{8}{12}$

16. $\frac{1}{3} \bigcirc \frac{4}{8}$

For **17–18**, use the table at the right. The same number of students attended school each day.

17. Did more students buy lunch on Tuesday or on Wednesday?

18. Did more students buy lunch on Thursday or on Friday?

DATA	Day	Fraction of Students Buying Lunch
	Monday	$\frac{1}{2}$
	Tuesday	$\frac{2}{5}$
	Wednesday	$\frac{3}{4}$
	Thursday	$\frac{5}{8}$
	Friday	$\frac{4}{6}$

19. Number Sense Explain how you know $\frac{21}{100}$ is greater than $\frac{1}{5}$.

20. An orange was divided into 10 equal sections. Lily ate 4 sections. Manny and Emma ate the remaining sections. What fraction of the orange did Manny and Emma eat?

---

21. Which is longer, $\frac{1}{4}$ of line A or $\frac{1}{4}$ of line B? Explain.

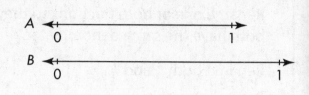

---

22. ⓒ **MP.3 Critique Reasoning** James says $\frac{5}{5}$ is greater than $\frac{9}{10}$. Is James correct? Explain.

23. Write 3 fractions with unlike denominators that are greater than the fraction shown below.

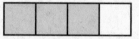

---

24. Ann works at a store in the mall and earns a wage of $8 an hour. She earns $10 an hour if she works on the weekends. Last week she worked 24 hours during the week and 16 hours on the weekend. How much did Ann earn last week?

25. Higher Order Thinking Four friends each ordered individual pizzas at a restaurant. Suzy ate $\frac{3}{8}$ of her pizza. Ethan ate $\frac{3}{5}$ of his pizza. Tenaya ate $\frac{4}{6}$ of her pizza. Sam ate $\frac{1}{3}$ of his pizza. Who ate more than half of their pizza? less than half?

ⓒ **Common Core Assessment**

26. Select all the answer choices that show a correct comparison.

- ☐ $\frac{10}{12} > \frac{5}{6}$
- ☐ $\frac{6}{8} = \frac{3}{4}$
- ☐ $\frac{1}{8} > \frac{1}{10}$
- ☐ $\frac{9}{10} < \frac{4}{5}$
- ☐ $\frac{1}{100} > \frac{1}{10}$

27. Select all the answer choices that show a correct comparison.

- ☐ $\frac{4}{12} < \frac{2}{5}$
- ☐ $\frac{6}{10} > \frac{60}{100}$
- ☐ $\frac{1}{4} < \frac{1}{10}$
- ☐ $\frac{3}{10} < \frac{1}{2}$
- ☐ $\frac{3}{5} < \frac{6}{12}$

Name _____

Solve & Share

Sherry and Karl both started their hike with a small bottle filled with water. Tia started her hike with a larger bottle that was $\frac{1}{2}$ full. At the end of the hike, Sherry and Tia's bottles were each half filled with water. Karl's bottle was $\frac{1}{3}$ filled with water. Who has the most water left? Construct a math argument to support your answer.

I can ...
construct math arguments using what I know about fractions.

© Mathematical Practices MP.3 Also MP.1, MP.2, MP.5
    Content Standards 4.NF.A.1, 4.NF.A.2

Sherry   Karl   Tia

Thinking Habits

Be a good thinker! These questions can help you.

• How can I use numbers, objects, drawings, or actions to justify my argument?

• Am I using numbers and symbols correctly?

• Is my explanation clear and complete?

Look Back! © **MP.3 Construct Arguments** If Tia's bottle was $\frac{1}{3}$ filled with water at the end of the hike, would you be able to decide who had the most water left? Construct an argument to support your answer.

Essential Question ## How Can You Construct Arguments?

A

Erin said $\frac{1}{2}$ is the same amount as $\frac{2}{4}$.

Matt said $\frac{1}{2}$ and $\frac{2}{4}$ can be different amounts.

Which student is correct?

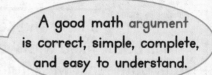

A good math argument is correct, simple, complete, and easy to understand.

What do you need to do to solve this problem?

I need to construct an argument with what I know about fraction models and ways to show $\frac{1}{2}$ and $\frac{2}{4}$.

B **How can I construct an argument?**

I can

- use numbers, objects, drawings, or models to justify my arguments.

- use a counterexample in my argument.

- give an explanation of my argument that is clear and complete.

C

Here's my thinking.

I will use drawings to show which student is correct.

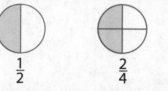

Both wholes are the same size. The $\frac{1}{2}$ and $\frac{2}{4}$ represent the same part of the whole.

These wholes are not the same size. So, $\frac{2}{4}$ of the larger circle represents more than $\frac{1}{2}$ of the smaller circle.

Both students are correct. $\frac{1}{2}$ and $\frac{2}{4}$ of the same-size whole are the same amount. $\frac{1}{2}$ and $\frac{2}{4}$ of different-size wholes are different amounts.

Convince Me! © **MP.3 Critique Reasoning** Erin also said $\frac{3}{6}$ and $\frac{5}{10}$ are **NOT** the same size because the denominators are not factors of each other. Is Erin's argument correct? Explain.

© Pearson Education, Inc. 4

Name _____

☆ Guided Practice ☆

© MP.3 Construct Arguments

Margie and Parker ordered the same-size burritos. Margie ate $\frac{4}{6}$ of her burrito. Parker ate $\frac{4}{5}$ of his burrito. Margie concluded she ate more than Parker because the fraction of the burrito she ate has a greater denominator.

1. What is Margie's argument? How does she support her argument?

2. Does Margie's conclusion make sense?

Independent Practice ☆

© MP.3 Construct Arguments

In the after-school club, Dena, Shawn, and Amanda knit scarves that are all the same size with yellow, white, and blue yarn. Dena's scarf is $\frac{3}{5}$ yellow, Shawn's scarf is $\frac{2}{5}$ yellow, and Amanda's scarf is $\frac{3}{4}$ yellow. The rest of each scarf has an equal amount of white and blue.

> When you construct an argument, you need to make sure your explanation is complete.

3. Describe how Amanda could make the argument that her scarf has the most yellow.

4. How much of Dena's scarf is blue?

5. Dena has a scarf at home that is the same length as the scarf she made in the club. The scarf at home is $\frac{6}{8}$ yellow. Dena said the scarf at home has more yellow. Is she correct?

Math Practices and Problem Solving

Snail Race

Mr. Aydin's science class had a snail race to see which snail would crawl the farthest from a starting line in two minutes. The table shows the distances the snails crawled.

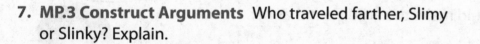

DATA	Snail	Slimy	Slinky	Curly	Pod	Stylo	Creeper
	Distance in feet	$\frac{3}{12}$	$\frac{2}{12}$	$\frac{1}{5}$	$\frac{3}{10}$	$\frac{2}{10}$	$\frac{3}{8}$

6. **MP.5 Use Appropriate Tools** Curly and Stylo traveled the same distance. Justify this conjecture using a number line or fraction strips.

7. **MP.3 Construct Arguments** Who traveled farther, Slimy or Slinky? Explain.

When I construct arguments, I give a complete explanation.

8. **MP.2 Reasoning** Who traveled farther, Creeper or Slimy? Explain.

9. **MP.1 Make Sense and Persevere** Who won the race?

Name _____

Another Look!

Gina and her brother Don made cornbread in equal-sized pans. Gina ate $\frac{1}{4}$ pan of cornbread. Don ate $\frac{3}{8}$ pan.

Tell how you can construct an argument to justify the conjecture that Don ate more cornbread.

- I can decide if the conjecture makes sense to me.

- I can use drawings and numbers to explain my reasoning.

> When you construct arguments, you use drawings and numbers to explain.

One Way

I can draw a picture of two equal-sized wholes to show that Don ate more cornbread.

$\frac{1}{4} < \frac{3}{8}$
Don ate more cornbread.

Another Way

I can use common denominators to compare $\frac{1}{4}$ and $\frac{3}{8}$. $\frac{1}{4}$ is equivalent to $\frac{2}{8}$.

Then I can compare the numerators of $\frac{2}{8}$ and $\frac{3}{8}$. Because the denominators are the same and $\frac{3}{8}$ has the greater numerator, $\frac{3}{8} > \frac{2}{8}$. Don ate more cornbread.

1. **© MP.3 Construct Arguments** A human usually has 20 baby teeth, which are replaced by 32 adult teeth. Raul lost 8 of his baby teeth. Raul said he lost $\frac{4}{10}$ of his baby teeth. Ana said Raul lost $\frac{2}{5}$ of his baby teeth. Which of these conjectures are true? Construct an argument to justify your answer.

> Remember, a good argument is correct, simple, complete, and easy to understand.

2. **© MP.3 Construct Arguments** Trip has 15 coins worth 95 cents. Four of the coins are each worth twice as much as the rest. Construct a math argument to justify the conjecture that Trip has 11 nickels and 4 dimes.

Animal Weight and Food

Molly claims when one animal weighs more than another animal, it always eats more than the other animal. She also claims that when one animal weighs less than another, it always eats less. She supports her claims with the information shown in the table.

Animal	Weight	Food Eaten
Caribou	$\frac{3}{5}$ ton	12 pounds a day
Giraffe	$\frac{7}{8}$ ton	100 pounds a day
Panda	$\frac{1}{4}$ ton	301 pounds a week
Siberian Tiger	$\frac{1}{3}$ ton	55 pounds a day

3. **MP.1 Make Sense and Persevere** Which animal eats the most? Explain.

4. **MP.2 Reasoning** Does the animal that eats the most weigh more than the other animals? Explain.

5. **MP.3 Critique Reasoning** Explain whether or not you agree with Molly's claim.

6. **MP.1 Make Sense and Persevere** Which animal eats the least? Explain.

7. **MP.2 Reasoning** Does the animal that eats the least weigh less than the other animals? Explain.

Remember, you can use words, objects, drawings, or diagrams when you construct an argument.

Name _____

Point & Tally

Find a partner. Get paper and a pencil. Each partner chooses a different color: light blue or dark blue.

Partner 1 and Partner 2 each point to a black number at the same time. Each partner subtracts the two numbers.

If the answer is on your color, you get a tally mark. Work until one partner has twelve tally marks.

I can ...
subtract multi-digit whole numbers.

© Content Standard 4.NBT.B.4

Partner 1					Partner 2
510	93	362	322	267	195
608	714	607	191	421	243
701	433	229	213	471	379
850	365	530	315	655	488
909	131	492	284	413	417
	458	120	22	506	

Tally Marks for Partner 1

Tally Marks for Partner 2

Vocabulary Review

A-Z
Glossary

Word List

- benchmark fraction
- common factor
- denominator
- equivalent fractions
- fraction
- numerator

Understand Vocabulary

Choose the best term from the box. Write it on the blank.

1. A number that names part of a whole, part of a set, or a location on a number line is a(n) _____ .

2. A commonly used fraction that helps you understand a different size or amount is called a(n) _____ .

3. The number below the fraction bar in a fraction that shows the total number of equal parts is the _____ .

4. Fractions that name the same part of a whole or the same location on a number line are called _____ .

5. The number above the fraction bar that represents part of the whole is called a(n) _____ .

For each of these terms, give an example and a non-example.

	Example	Non-example
6. Fraction	_____	_____
7. Equivalent fractions	_____	_____
8. A fraction with a common factor for its numerator and denominator	_____	_____

Use Vocabulary in Writing

9. Explain how to compare $\frac{5}{8}$ and $\frac{3}{8}$. Use at least 3 terms from the Word List in your explanation.

Set A | pages 411–422

Reteaching

Use an area model to write an equivalent fraction for $\frac{1}{2}$.

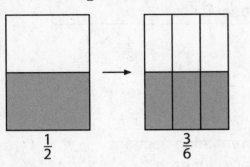

$\frac{1}{2}$ and $\frac{3}{6}$ name the same part of the whole.

$\frac{1}{2}$ and $\frac{3}{6}$ are equivalent fractions.

Use a number line to write an equivalent fraction for $\frac{1}{3}$.

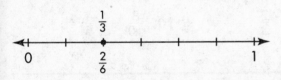

$\frac{1}{3}$ and $\frac{2}{6}$ name the same part of the whole.

$\frac{1}{3}$ and $\frac{2}{6}$ are equivalent fractions.

Remember that equivalent fractions name the same part of a whole.

Write an equivalent fraction for each fraction given.

1. $\frac{2}{8}$　　　　2. $\frac{2}{3}$

3. $\frac{1}{4}$　　　　4. $\frac{3}{5}$

Draw a number line to shown each fraction and an equivalent fraction.

5. $\frac{4}{6}$

6. $\frac{4}{10}$

Set B | pages 423–434

Find two equivalent fractions for $\frac{1}{2}$.

$\frac{1}{2} \times \frac{2}{2} = \frac{2}{4}$　　$\frac{1}{2} \times \frac{3}{3} = \frac{3}{6}$

$\frac{1}{2}, \frac{2}{4}$, and $\frac{3}{6}$ are equivalent fractions.

Find two equivalent fractions for $\frac{8}{12}$.

$\frac{8}{12} \div \frac{2}{2} = \frac{4}{6}$　　$\frac{8}{12} \div \frac{4}{4} = \frac{2}{3}$

$\frac{8}{12}, \frac{4}{6}$, and $\frac{2}{3}$ are equivalent fractions.

Remember that you can multiply or divide to find equivalent fractions.

Multiply or divide to find equivalent fractions.

1. $\frac{2}{3} = \frac{8}{\square}$　　　　2. $\frac{1}{4} = \frac{\square}{8}$

3. $\frac{1}{6} = \frac{2}{\square}$　　　　4. $\frac{3}{5} = \frac{\square}{10}$

5. $\frac{10}{12} = \frac{5}{\square}$　　　　6. $\frac{4}{10} = \frac{\square}{5}$

7. $\frac{2}{6} = \frac{1}{\square}$　　　　8. $\frac{6}{10} = \frac{\square}{5}$

Compare $\frac{5}{8}$ and $\frac{4}{10}$. Use benchmark fractions.

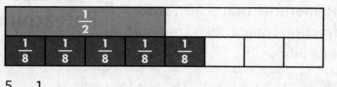

$\frac{5}{8} > \frac{1}{2}$

$\frac{4}{10} < \frac{1}{2}$

So, $\frac{5}{8} > \frac{4}{10}$.

Compare $\frac{4}{6}$ and $\frac{3}{4}$. Rename each fraction.

$\frac{4}{6} = \frac{4}{6} \times \frac{2}{2} = \frac{8}{12}$ $\frac{3}{4} = \frac{3}{4} \times \frac{3}{3} = \frac{9}{12}$

$\frac{8}{12}$ is less than $\frac{9}{12}$ so, $\frac{4}{6}$ is less than $\frac{3}{4}$.

Remember benchmark fractions are commonly used fractions such as $\frac{1}{4}$, $\frac{1}{2}$, and $\frac{3}{4}$.

Use benchmark fractions to compare. Write >, <, or = for each $\bigcirc$.

1. $\frac{5}{5} \bigcirc \frac{4}{6}$ 2. $\frac{4}{8} \bigcirc \frac{1}{2}$

3. $\frac{4}{5} \bigcirc \frac{7}{8}$ 4. $\frac{2}{3} \bigcirc \frac{4}{6}$

Compare by renaming fractions. Write >, <, or = for each $\bigcirc$.

5. $\frac{3}{4} \bigcirc \frac{5}{8}$ 6. $\frac{1}{5} \bigcirc \frac{2}{10}$

7. $\frac{2}{5} \bigcirc \frac{1}{4}$ 8. $\frac{3}{6} \bigcirc \frac{3}{4}$

9. $\frac{2}{4} \bigcirc \frac{2}{3}$ 10. $\frac{8}{10} \bigcirc \frac{4}{6}$

Think about these questions to help you **construct arguments**.

Thinking Habits

• How can I use numbers, objects, drawings, or actions to justify my argument?

• Am I using numbers and symbols correctly?

• Is my explanation clear and complete?

Remember when you construct arguments, you use drawings and numbers to explain.

Peter says $\frac{3}{4}$ of a pizza is always the same as $\frac{6}{8}$ of a pizza. Nadia says while $\frac{3}{4}$ and $\frac{6}{8}$ are equivalent fractions, $\frac{3}{4}$ and $\frac{6}{8}$ of a pizza could represent different amounts.

1. Who is correct? Explain. Use a drawing to justify your argument.

2. Use a counterexample to explain who is correct.

Name _____

1. After a bake sale, only $\frac{2}{3}$ pie remains. What fraction is equivalent to $\frac{2}{3}$?

Ⓐ $\frac{1}{3}$

Ⓑ $\frac{3}{3}$

Ⓒ $\frac{2}{6}$

Ⓓ $\frac{4}{6}$

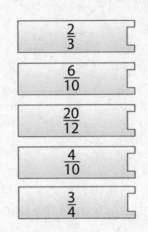

2. Leslie will use more than $\frac{1}{2}$ cup but less than 1 whole cup of flour for a recipe. What fraction of a cup might Leslie use? Explain.

3. Danielle said she read $\frac{1}{2}$ of a book. Select all the fractions that are equivalent to $\frac{1}{2}$.

☐ $\frac{3}{6}$

☐ $\frac{5}{10}$

☐ $\frac{6}{12}$

☐ $\frac{3}{5}$

☐ $\frac{6}{8}$

4. Explain how to use division to find an equivalent fraction for $\frac{9}{12}$.

5. Draw lines to match each fraction on the left to an equivalent fraction on the right.

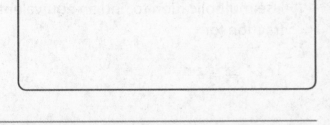

$\frac{2}{3}$		$\frac{10}{6}$
$\frac{6}{10}$		$\frac{6}{8}$
$\frac{20}{12}$		$\frac{2}{5}$
$\frac{4}{10}$		$\frac{8}{12}$
$\frac{3}{4}$		$\frac{3}{5}$

6. Compare the fractions to $\frac{1}{2}$. Write each fraction in the correct answer space.

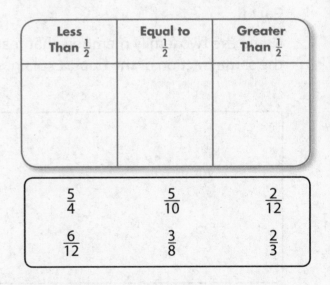

Less Than $\frac{1}{2}$	Equal to $\frac{1}{2}$	Greater Than $\frac{1}{2}$

$\frac{5}{4}$ $\frac{5}{10}$ $\frac{2}{12}$

$\frac{6}{12}$ $\frac{3}{8}$ $\frac{2}{3}$

7. For questions 7a–7d, choose Yes or No to tell if the fraction is greater than $\frac{3}{5}$.

7a. $\frac{3}{10}$ ○ Yes   ○ No

7b. $\frac{3}{8}$ ○ Yes   ○ No

7c. $\frac{5}{3}$ ○ Yes   ○ No

7d. $\frac{6}{6}$ ○ Yes   ○ No

8. The Sahas were reading a best-selling novel as a family. After the first week, they checked in with each other to see how much of the book each had read.

Fraction Read	
Mr. Saha	$\frac{2}{6}$
Mrs. Saha	$\frac{1}{3}$
Maddie	$\frac{3}{4}$
George	$\frac{2}{3}$

Part A

Who read the greatest fraction of the book?

Part B

Name the two family members that read the same fraction of the book. Explain.

9. Johnny found a fraction equivalent to the one shown by the point on the number line. Which fraction could Johnny have found?

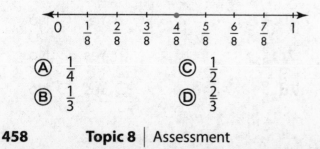

Ⓐ $\frac{1}{4}$ Ⓒ $\frac{1}{2}$

Ⓑ $\frac{1}{3}$ Ⓓ $\frac{2}{3}$

10. Bill and Gina each ate $\frac{1}{2}$ of their own pizza. Bill ate more pizza than Gina. Draw a picture and explain how that is possible.

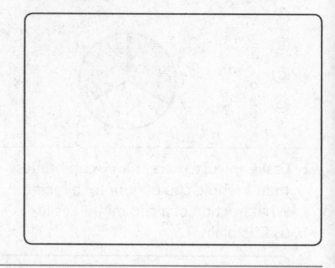

11. Use multiplication to find an equivalent fraction for $\frac{1}{3}$.

$$\frac{1}{3} \times \frac{\square}{\square} = \frac{\square}{\square}$$

12. Only one of the comparisons below is correct. Which is correct?

Ⓐ $\frac{2}{3} < \frac{1}{2}$

Ⓑ $\frac{1}{2} = \frac{3}{5}$

Ⓒ $\frac{3}{4} < \frac{4}{5}$

Ⓓ $\frac{3}{4} < \frac{2}{3}$

13. Use 1 as a benchmark to compare $\frac{6}{5}$ and $\frac{5}{6}$.

© Performance Assessment

Comparing Grasshoppers

Mrs. Rakin's class measured the lengths of some grasshoppers.
The **Grasshopper Lengths** table shows the lengths they found.

1. Mrs. Rakin asked the students to choose two grasshoppers and compare their lengths.

Part A

Henry used benchmark fractions to compare the lengths of grasshoppers A and C. Which grasshopper is longer? Explain.

Grasshopper Lengths	
Grasshopper	**Length (inch)**
A	$\frac{5}{8}$
B	$\frac{3}{2}$
C	$\frac{7}{4}$
D	$\frac{7}{8}$
E	$\frac{3}{4}$
F	$\frac{3}{8}$

Part B

Riley used a number line to compare the lengths of grasshoppers A and E. Which grasshopper is longer? Use the number line to show the comparison.

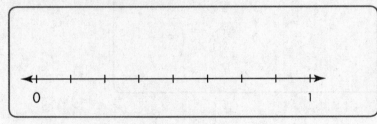

Part C

Jack compared the lengths of grasshoppers D and E. He said grasshopper D is longer. Is Jack correct? Justify the comparison using fraction strips.

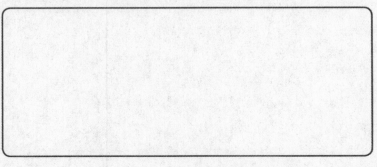

2. One group of students measured the lengths of grasshoppers in centimeters, instead of inches. The **More Grasshopper Lengths** table shows the lengths they found.

More Grasshopper Lengths	
Grasshopper	**Length (centimeter)**
G	$\frac{7}{10}$
H	$\frac{4}{5}$
I	$\frac{6}{10}$

Part A

Tommy compared the lengths of grasshoppers G and H. Which grasshopper is longer? Explain how to rename the fractions using multiplication so they have the same denominator to compare.

Part B

Venon compared the lengths of grasshoppers H and I. Which grasshopper is longer? Explain how to rename the fractions using division so they have the same denominator to compare.

Part C

Rina wants to determine if grasshopper D is longer or shorter than grasshopper G. Explain how Rina can compare the fractions.

TOPIC 9

Understand Addition and Subtraction of Fractions

Essential Questions: How do you add and subtract fractions and mixed numbers with like denominators? How can fractions be added and subtracted on a number line?

Digital Resources

Solve Learn Glossary Practice Buddy

Tools Assessment Help Games

Morse code uses a special machine to transfer information using a series of tones.

A combination of dots and dashes stands for each letter, each number, and even some whole words.

How do you write, "I love math?" using Morse code? Here is a project about fractions and information.

Math and Science Project: Fractions and Information Transfer

Do Research Morse code uses patterns to transfer information. Any word can be written using Morse code. Use the Internet or other sources to find how to write *fourth, grade,* and *school* using Morse code.

Journal: Write a Report Include what you found. Also in your report:

- Write *one* in Morse code. Write a fraction that tells what part of the code for *one* is dashes.

- Write *three* in Morse code. Write a fraction that tells what part of the code for *three* is dots.

- Write and solve an equation to find how much greater the fraction for dots is than the fraction for dashes in the word *three*.

Topic 9 461

Name _____

Review What You Know

A-Z Vocabulary

Choose the best term from the box.
Write it on the blank.

- benchmark fractions
- equivalent fractions
- denominator
- numerator

1. In $\frac{2}{3}$, 2 is the _____ of
   the fraction and 3 is the _____ of the fraction.

2. Fractions that name the same region, part of a set, or part of a segment
   are called _____ .

Equivalent Fractions

Write the missing values to show pairs of equivalent fractions.

3. $\frac{2}{3} = \frac{\square}{6}$

4. $\frac{\square}{4} = \frac{3}{12}$

5. $\frac{6}{5} = \frac{\square}{10}$

6. $\frac{1}{2} = \frac{50}{\square}$

7. $\frac{1}{5} = \frac{\square}{10}$

8. $\frac{3}{\square} = \frac{30}{100}$

Benchmark Fractions

Use the number line to find a benchmark fraction or whole number
for each given fraction.

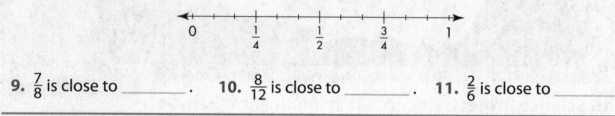

9. $\frac{7}{8}$ is close to _____ .   10. $\frac{8}{12}$ is close to _____ .   11. $\frac{2}{6}$ is close to _____ .

Problem Solving

12. Adult admission to the dog show is $16. Children's admission is $9. How much
    would it cost 3 adults and 2 children to enter the dog show?

13. Meg saved coins she found for a year. She found a total of 95 pennies, 13 nickels,
    41 dimes, and 11 quarters. She would like to evenly divide the coins into 4 piggy
    banks. How many coins will go in each piggy bank?

My Word Cards

Use the examples for each word on the front of the card to help complete the definitions on the back.

decompose

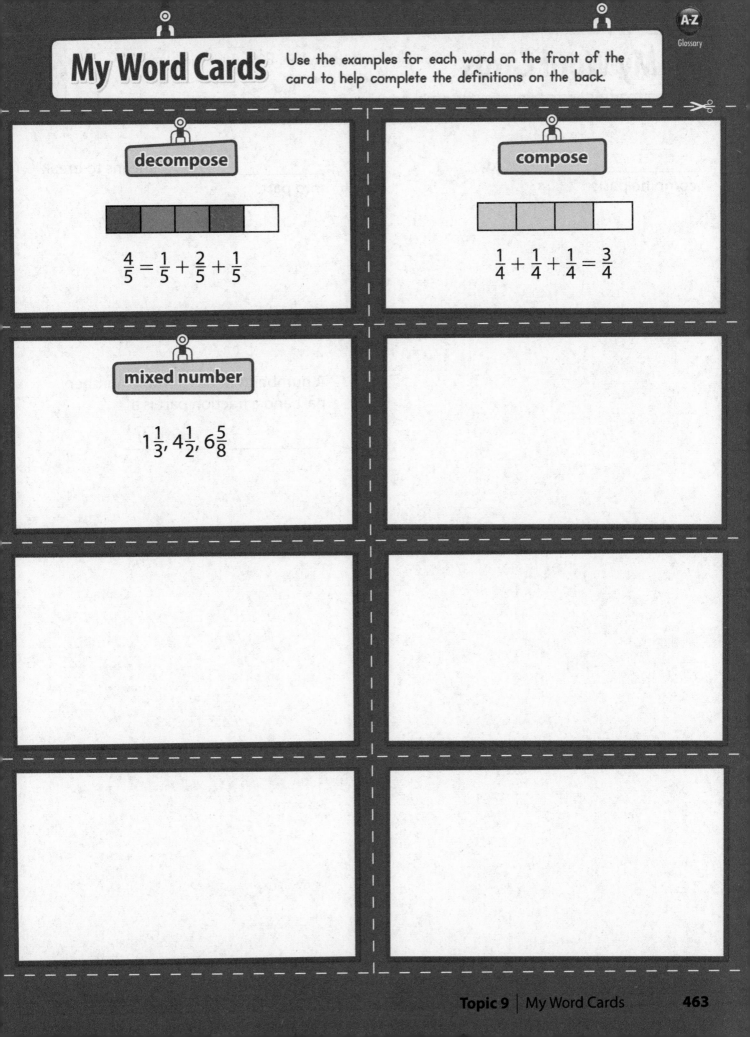

$$\frac{4}{5} = \frac{1}{5} + \frac{2}{5} + \frac{1}{5}$$

compose

$$\frac{1}{4} + \frac{1}{4} + \frac{1}{4} = \frac{3}{4}$$

mixed number

$$1\frac{1}{3}, \ 4\frac{1}{2}, \ 6\frac{5}{8}$$

My Word Cards

Complete each definition. Extend learning by writing your own definitions.

_____ means to combine parts.

_____ means to break into parts.

A number that has a whole number part and a fraction part is a

_____.

Name _____

Solve & Share

Kyle and Jillian are working on a sports banner. They painted $\frac{3}{8}$ of the banner green and $\frac{4}{8}$ purple. How much of the banner have they painted? **Solve this problem any way you choose.**

Lesson 9-1
Model Addition of Fractions

I can ...
use tools such as fraction strips or area models to add fractions.

© Content Standard 4.NF.B.3a
Mathematical Practices MP.1, MP.2, MP.3, MP.4, MP.5

You can use appropriate tools. You can use drawings, area models, or fraction strips to solve this problem. *Show your work in the space below!*

Look Back! © **MP.5 Use Appropriate Tools** Kyle says $\frac{1}{8} + \frac{1}{8} + \frac{1}{8} = \frac{3}{8}$. Jillian says $\frac{1}{8} + \frac{1}{8} + \frac{1}{8} = \frac{3}{24}$. Use fraction strips to decide who is correct.

Essential Question **How Can You Use Tools to Add Fractions?**

A

Ten canoeing teams are racing downriver. Five teams have silver canoes and two teams have brown canoes. What fraction of the canoes are either silver or brown?

You can use tools such as fraction strips to add two or more fractions.

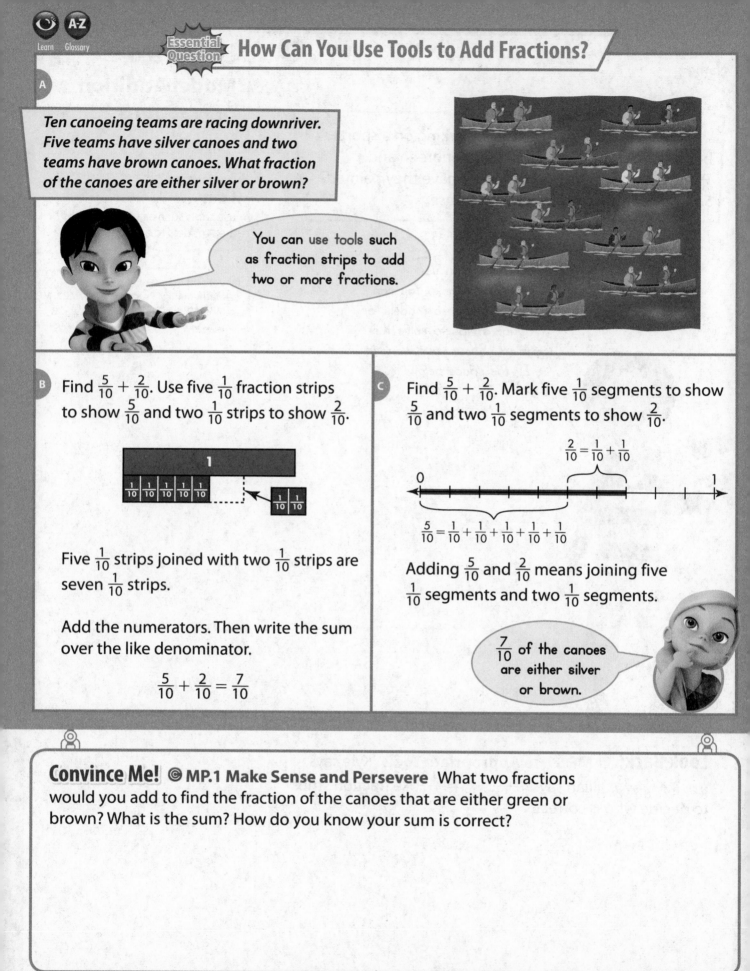

B

Find $\frac{5}{10} + \frac{2}{10}$. Use five $\frac{1}{10}$ fraction strips to show $\frac{5}{10}$ and two $\frac{1}{10}$ strips to show $\frac{2}{10}$.

Five $\frac{1}{10}$ strips joined with two $\frac{1}{10}$ strips are seven $\frac{1}{10}$ strips.

Add the numerators. Then write the sum over the like denominator.

$$\frac{5}{10} + \frac{2}{10} = \frac{7}{10}$$

C

Find $\frac{5}{10} + \frac{2}{10}$. Mark five $\frac{1}{10}$ segments to show $\frac{5}{10}$ and two $\frac{1}{10}$ segments to show $\frac{2}{10}$.

$$\frac{2}{10} = \frac{1}{10} + \frac{1}{10}$$

$$\frac{5}{10} = \frac{1}{10} + \frac{1}{10} + \frac{1}{10} + \frac{1}{10} + \frac{1}{10}$$

Adding $\frac{5}{10}$ and $\frac{2}{10}$ means joining five $\frac{1}{10}$ segments and two $\frac{1}{10}$ segments.

$\frac{7}{10}$ of the canoes are either silver or brown.

Convince Me! © **MP.1 Make Sense and Persevere** What two fractions would you add to find the fraction of the canoes that are either green or brown? What is the sum? How do you know your sum is correct?

☆ Guided Practice*

Do You Understand?

1. © MP.2 Reasoning In the problem on the previous page, why aren't the purple $\frac{1}{10}$ strips the same length as the red strip?

2. What two fractions are being added below? What is the sum?

| $\frac{1}{8}$ | $\frac{1}{8}$ | | $\frac{1}{8}$ | $\frac{1}{8}$ | $\frac{1}{8}$ |

Do You Know How?

For **3–4**, find each sum.

3. $\frac{2}{5} + \frac{1}{5}$

4. $\frac{1}{6} + \frac{1}{6}$

Independent Practice ☆

Leveled Practice For **5–16**, find each sum. Use fraction strips or other tools.

5. $\frac{3}{12} + \frac{4}{12}$

6. $\frac{4}{10} + \frac{1}{10}$

7. $\frac{2}{12} + \frac{4}{12}$

8. $\frac{1}{6} + \frac{2}{6} + \frac{3}{6}$

9. $\frac{1}{4} + \frac{2}{4}$

10. $\frac{1}{3} + \frac{1}{3}$

11. $\frac{5}{8} + \frac{1}{8}$

12. $\frac{1}{4} + \frac{3}{4}$

13. $\frac{7}{12} + \frac{2}{12}$

14. $\frac{1}{4} + \frac{1}{4}$

15. $\frac{2}{5} + \frac{2}{5}$

16. $\frac{1}{10} + \frac{2}{10} + \frac{1}{10}$

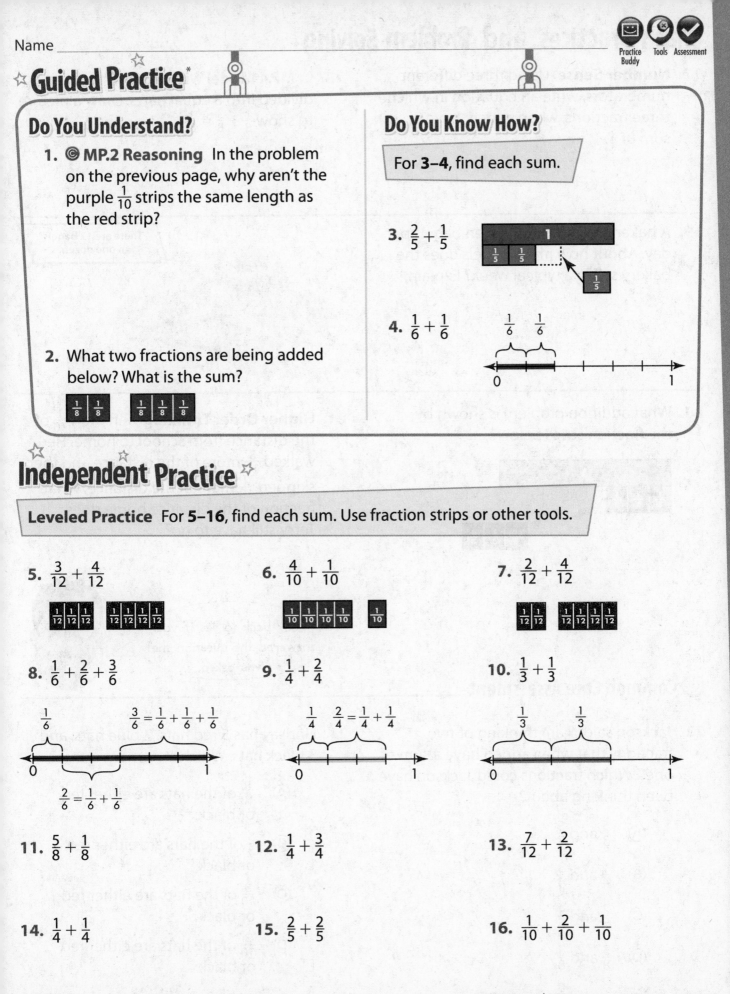

Math Practices and Problem Solving

17. Number Sense Using three different numerators, write an equation in which three fractions, when added, have a sum of 1.

18. ⓒ MP.4 Model with Math A rope is divided into 8 equal parts. Draw a picture to show $\frac{1}{8} + \frac{3}{8} = \frac{4}{8}$.

19. A bakery sells about 9 dozen bagels per day. About how many bagels does the bakery sell in a typical week? Explain.

> There are 12 bagels in one dozen.

20. What addition problem is shown by the fraction strips below?

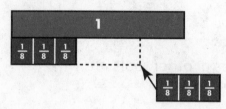

21. Higher Order Thinking Terry ran $\frac{1}{10}$ of the distance from school to home. He walked $\frac{3}{10}$ more of the distance and then skipped $\frac{2}{10}$ more of the distance. What fraction of the distance home does Terry still have to go?

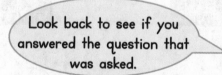

Look back to see if you answered the question that was asked.

ⓒ Common Core Assessment

22. Jackson said, "I am thinking of two fractions that when added have a sum of one." Which fractions could Jackson have been thinking about?

   Ⓐ $\frac{5}{3}$ and $\frac{5}{3}$

   Ⓑ $\frac{1}{4}$ and $\frac{3}{4}$

   Ⓒ $\frac{2}{5}$ and $\frac{4}{5}$

   Ⓓ $\frac{3}{8}$ and $\frac{4}{8}$

23. Lindsay has 5 red hats, 2 blue hats, and 3 black hats. Which statement is true?

   Ⓐ $\frac{8}{10}$ of the hats are either red or black.

   Ⓑ $\frac{5}{3}$ of the hats are either red or black.

   Ⓒ $\frac{5}{10}$ of the hats are either red or black.

   Ⓓ $\frac{3}{10}$ of the hats are either red or black.

Name _____

Homework & Practice 9-1
Model Addition of Fractions

Another Look!

Eight friends went out to lunch. Four of them had pizza. Two had hamburgers and two had soup. What fraction of the group had either pizza or soup?

You can use a circle fraction model to add fractions.

Divide a circle into eighths to represent each of the 8 people in the group.

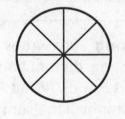

Four people had pizza. Shade 4 of the sections to represent $\frac{4}{8}$.

Two people had soup. Shade 2 more sections to represent $\frac{2}{8}$.

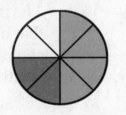

Count the number of $\frac{1}{8}$ sections. There are six $\frac{1}{8}$ sections shaded. So, $\frac{6}{8}$ of the group had either pizza or soup.

$$\frac{4}{8} + \frac{2}{8} = \frac{6}{8}$$

For **1–12**, find each sum. Use fraction strips or other tools.

1. $\frac{1}{5} + \frac{1}{5}$

2. $\frac{4}{6} + \frac{1}{6}$

3. $\frac{5}{8} + \frac{2}{8}$

4. $\frac{2}{12} + \frac{2}{12}$

5. $\frac{2}{5} + \frac{3}{5}$

6. $\frac{2}{10} + \frac{3}{10}$

7. $\frac{5}{8} + \frac{3}{8}$

8. $\frac{3}{10} + \frac{1}{10}$

9. $\frac{3}{4} + \frac{1}{4}$

10. $\frac{5}{10} + \frac{4}{10}$

11. $\frac{1}{6} + \frac{1}{6} + \frac{1}{6}$

12. $\frac{1}{12} + \frac{5}{12} + \frac{2}{12}$

13. © **MP.3 Critique Reasoning** When Jared found $\frac{1}{5} + \frac{2}{5}$, he wrote the sum $\frac{3}{10}$. Is Jared correct? Explain.

14. Number Sense Leah wrote 2 different fractions with the same denominator. Both fractions were less than 1. Can their sum equal 1? Can their sum be greater than 1? Explain.

15. Sasha has a box of antique letters. She wants to give an equal number of letters to each of her 5 friends. How many antique letters will each friend receive?

There are 130 antique letters in the box.

16. © **MP.4 Model with Math** Sandy made 8 friendship bracelets. She gave 1 bracelet to her best friend and 5 bracelets to her friends on the tennis team. Use the model to find the fraction that represents the total number of bracelets Sandy gave away.

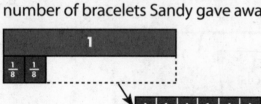

17. Higher Order Thinking Julia writes 2 fractions with the same denominator that have numerators 5 and 7. What could the denominator be if the sum is less than 1? Equal to 1? Greater than 1?

© **Common Core Assessment**

18. Billy did $\frac{1}{6}$ of his homework on Friday. He did $\frac{1}{6}$ more on Saturday. Billy still had $\frac{4}{6}$ to finish. How much of his homework did Billy do on Friday and Saturday?

Ⓐ $\frac{2}{6}$ Ⓒ $\frac{4}{6}$

Ⓑ $\frac{3}{6}$ Ⓓ $\frac{5}{6}$

19. Roberto shares a bag of almonds with 2 friends. He shares $\frac{1}{8}$ bag with Jeremy and $\frac{2}{8}$ bag with Emily. He eats $\frac{3}{8}$ of the almonds himself. What fraction of the almonds do Roberto and his friends eat?

Ⓐ $\frac{1}{12}$ Ⓒ $\frac{6}{8}$

Ⓑ $\frac{3}{8}$ Ⓓ $\frac{7}{8}$

Name _____

★ ☆ ★
Solve & Share

Karyn has $\frac{11}{8}$ pounds of chili to put into three bowls. The amount of chili in each bowl does not have to be the same. How much chili could Karyn put into each bowl? *Solve this problem any way you choose.*

How can you model the amount of chili Karyn puts in each bowl? *Show your work in the space below!*

I can ...
use fraction strips, area models, or drawings to decompose fractions.

© Content Standard 4.NF.B.3b
Mathematical Practices MP.2, MP.4, MP.5

Look Back! © **MP.5 Use Appropriate Tools** Use a drawing or fraction strips to help write equivalent fractions for the amount of chili in one of the bowls.

How Can You Represent a Fraction in a Variety of Ways?

A

Charlene wants to leave $\frac{1}{6}$ of her garden empty. What are some different ways Charlene can plant the rest of her garden?

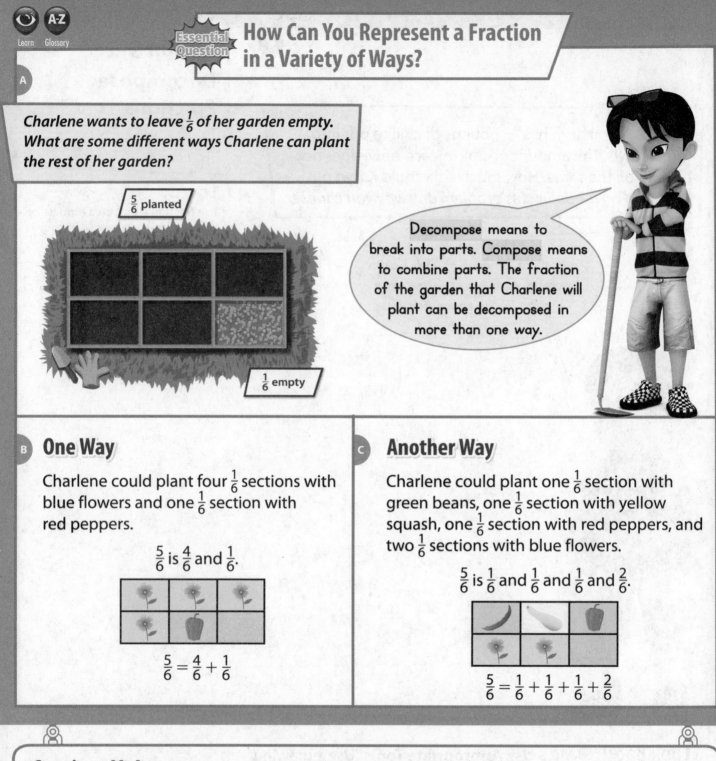

$\frac{5}{6}$ planted

$\frac{1}{6}$ empty

Decompose means to break into parts. Compose means to combine parts. The fraction of the garden that Charlene will plant can be decomposed in more than one way.

B **One Way**

Charlene could plant four $\frac{1}{6}$ sections with blue flowers and one $\frac{1}{6}$ section with red peppers.

$\frac{5}{6}$ is $\frac{4}{6}$ and $\frac{1}{6}$.

$$\frac{5}{6} = \frac{4}{6} + \frac{1}{6}$$

C **Another Way**

Charlene could plant one $\frac{1}{6}$ section with green beans, one $\frac{1}{6}$ section with yellow squash, one $\frac{1}{6}$ section with red peppers, and two $\frac{1}{6}$ sections with blue flowers.

$\frac{5}{6}$ is $\frac{1}{6}$ and $\frac{1}{6}$ and $\frac{1}{6}$ and $\frac{2}{6}$.

$$\frac{5}{6} = \frac{1}{6} + \frac{1}{6} + \frac{1}{6} + \frac{2}{6}$$

Convince Me! © **MP.5 Use Appropriate Tools** Draw pictures or use fraction strips to show why these equations are true.

$$\frac{5}{6} = \frac{3}{6} + \frac{2}{6} \qquad \frac{5}{6} = \frac{1}{6} + \frac{2}{6} + \frac{2}{6}$$

Another Example! How can you decompose $3\frac{1}{8}$?

$3\frac{1}{8}$ is 1 whole + 1 whole + 1 whole + $\frac{1}{8}$.

Each whole can also be shown as eight equal parts.

> A mixed number has a whole number part and a fraction part.

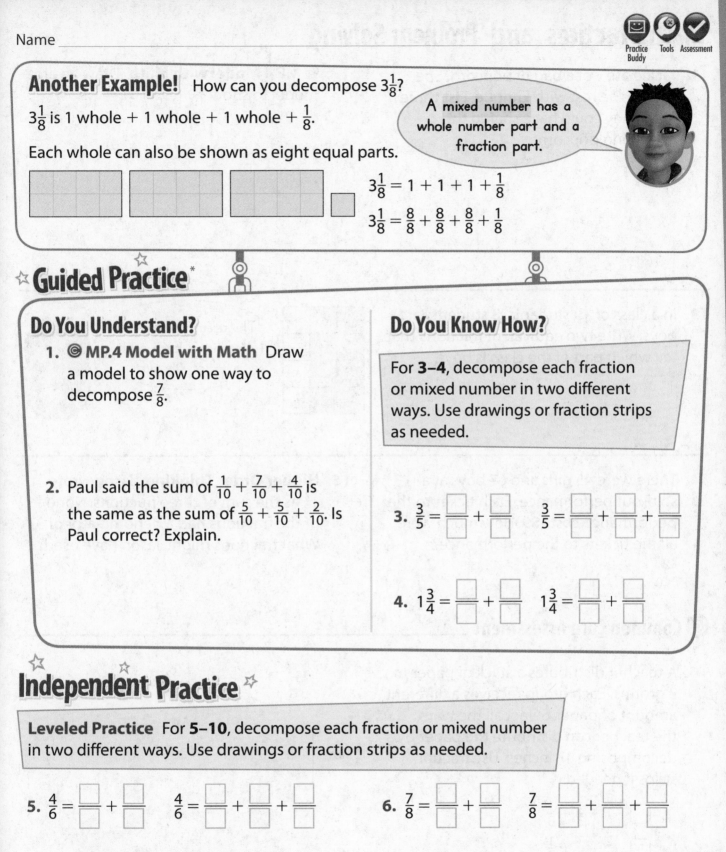

$$3\frac{1}{8} = 1 + 1 + 1 + \frac{1}{8}$$

$$3\frac{1}{8} = \frac{8}{8} + \frac{8}{8} + \frac{8}{8} + \frac{1}{8}$$

Guided Practice *

Do You Understand?

1. ⓒ **MP.4 Model with Math** Draw a model to show one way to decompose $\frac{7}{8}$.

2. Paul said the sum of $\frac{1}{10} + \frac{7}{10} + \frac{4}{10}$ is the same as the sum of $\frac{5}{10} + \frac{5}{10} + \frac{2}{10}$. Is Paul correct? Explain.

Do You Know How?

For **3–4**, decompose each fraction or mixed number in two different ways. Use drawings or fraction strips as needed.

3. $\frac{3}{5} = \frac{\square}{\square} + \frac{\square}{\square}$ $\quad$ $\frac{3}{5} = \frac{\square}{\square} + \frac{\square}{\square} + \frac{\square}{\square}$

4. $1\frac{3}{4} = \frac{\square}{\square} + \frac{\square}{\square}$ $\quad$ $1\frac{3}{4} = \frac{\square}{\square} + \frac{\square}{\square}$

Independent Practice *

Leveled Practice For **5–10**, decompose each fraction or mixed number in two different ways. Use drawings or fraction strips as needed.

5. $\frac{4}{6} = \frac{\square}{\square} + \frac{\square}{\square}$ $\quad$ $\frac{4}{6} = \frac{\square}{\square} + \frac{\square}{\square} + \frac{\square}{\square}$

6. $\frac{7}{8} = \frac{\square}{\square} + \frac{\square}{\square}$ $\quad$ $\frac{7}{8} = \frac{\square}{\square} + \frac{\square}{\square} + \frac{\square}{\square}$

7. $1\frac{3}{5} = \frac{\square}{\square} + \frac{\square}{\square}$ $\quad$ $1\frac{3}{5} = \frac{\square}{\square} + \frac{\square}{\square} + \frac{\square}{\square}$

8. $2\frac{1}{2} = \frac{\square}{\square} + \frac{\square}{\square}$ $\quad$ $2\frac{1}{2} = \frac{\square}{\square} + \frac{\square}{\square} + \frac{\square}{\square}$

9. $\frac{9}{12} = \frac{\square}{\square} + \frac{\square}{\square}$ $\quad$ $\frac{9}{12} = \frac{\square}{\square} + \frac{\square}{\square} + \frac{\square}{\square}$

10. $1\frac{1}{3} = \frac{\square}{\square} + \frac{\square}{\square}$ $\quad$ $1\frac{1}{3} = \frac{\square}{\square} + \frac{\square}{\square} + \frac{\square}{\square}$

*For another example, see Set A on page 533.

Math Practices and Problem Solving

11. Jackie ate $\frac{1}{5}$ of a bag of popcorn. She shared the rest with Enrique. List three ways they could have shared the remaining popcorn.

12. © **MP.4 Model with Math** Draw an area model to show $\frac{4}{10} + \frac{3}{10} + \frac{2}{10} = \frac{9}{10}$.

13. In a class of 12 students, 8 students are boys. Write two equivalent fractions that tell which part of the class is boys.

The area model shows 12 sections. Each section is $\frac{1}{12}$ of the class.

14. There were 45 girls and 67 boys at a sold-out performance. Each ticket to the performance costs $9. How much were all the tickets to the performance?

15. **Higher Order Thinking** Jason wrote $1\frac{1}{3}$ as the sum of three fractions. None of the fractions had a denominator of 3. What fractions might Jason have used?

© **Common Core Assessment**

16. A teacher distributes a stack of paper to 3 groups. Each group receives a different amount of paper. Select all the ways the teacher can distribute the paper by decomposing $1\frac{2}{3}$ inches. Use fraction strips if needed.

$1\frac{2}{3}$ inches

☐ $1 + \frac{1}{3} + \frac{1}{3}$

☐ $\frac{2}{3} + \frac{1}{3} + \frac{1}{3}$

☐ $\frac{2}{3} + \frac{2}{3} + \frac{1}{3}$

☐ $\frac{1}{3} + \frac{1}{3} + \frac{1}{3} + \frac{1}{3} + \frac{1}{3}$

☐ $1 + \frac{2}{3}$

Name _____

Help Practice   Tools Games
         Buddy

Homework & Practice 9-2
Decompose Fractions

Another Look!

Shannon wants to use $\frac{5}{8}$ of her garden space to plant petunias and marigolds. How can Shannon use the available space?

> There are more than two solutions to this problem.

Write $\frac{5}{8}$ as the sum of fractions in two different ways.

$$\frac{5}{8} = \frac{1}{8} + \frac{4}{8} \qquad \frac{5}{8} = \frac{2}{8} + \frac{3}{8}$$

Shannon could use $\frac{1}{8}$ of the space for petunias and $\frac{4}{8}$ for marigolds, or she could use $\frac{2}{8}$ of the space for petunias and $\frac{3}{8}$ for marigolds.

For **1–8**, decompose each fraction or mixed number in two different ways. Use drawings or fraction strips as needed.

1. $\frac{4}{8} = \frac{\square}{\square} + \frac{\square}{\square}$

   $\frac{4}{8} = \frac{\square}{\square} + \frac{\square}{\square} + \frac{\square}{\square}$

2. $\frac{7}{10} = \frac{\square}{\square} + \frac{\square}{\square}$

   $\frac{7}{10} = \frac{\square}{\square} + \frac{\square}{\square} + \frac{\square}{\square}$

3. $\frac{4}{5} =$

   $\frac{4}{5} =$

4. $\frac{3}{10} =$

   $\frac{3}{10} =$

5. $1\frac{1}{4} =$

   $1\frac{1}{4} =$

6. $2\frac{2}{3} =$

   $2\frac{2}{3} =$

> Challenge yourself! Include ways that break a fraction or mixed number into more than two parts.

7. $1\frac{3}{5} =$

   $1\frac{3}{5} =$

8. $1\frac{1}{2} =$

   $1\frac{1}{2} =$

Digital Resources at **PearsonRealize.com** **Topic 9** | Lesson 9-2 **475**

9. Yvonne ran $\frac{3}{8}$ of the race before stopping for water. She wants to stop for water one more time before finishing the race. List two ways Yvonne can do this.

$\frac{1}{8}$	$\frac{1}{8}$	$\frac{1}{8}$	$\frac{1}{8}$	$\frac{1}{8}$	$\frac{1}{8}$	$\frac{1}{8}$	$\frac{1}{8}$

10. © **MP.2 Reasoning** A teacher noticed $\frac{5}{8}$ of the students were wearing either blue shorts or white shorts. Write two different ways this could be done.

11. Connie made $1\frac{1}{3}$ pounds of trail mix for a hike. Is there a way Connie can break up the trail mix into four bags? Explain.

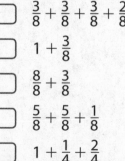

12. Jo's Donut Express earned $4,378 at a festival by selling chocolate or vanilla donuts for $2 each. If they sold 978 chocolate donuts, how many vanilla donuts did they sell?

13. **Higher Order Thinking** Mark said he can decompose $\frac{5}{6}$ into three fractions with three different numerators and the same denominator. Is this possible? Explain. Remember, you can use equivalent fractions.

© **Common Core Assessment**

14. Mrs. Evans asked the class to decompose $1\frac{3}{4}$. Which of the following are **NOT** ways to decompose $1\frac{3}{4}$? Select all that apply. Use area models if needed.

- ☐ $1 + \frac{3}{4}$
- ☐ $\frac{1}{4} + \frac{1}{4} + \frac{1}{4} + \frac{1}{4} + \frac{1}{4} + \frac{1}{4} + \frac{1}{4}$
- ☐ $\frac{4}{4} + \frac{3}{4}$
- ☐ $\frac{3}{4} + \frac{5}{4}$
- ☐ $1 + \frac{1}{2} + \frac{2}{2}$

15. Ms. Anderson showed her class how to decompose $1\frac{3}{8}$. Select all the ways Ms. Anderson could have decomposed $1\frac{3}{8}$. Use fraction strips if needed.

- ☐ $\frac{3}{8} + \frac{3}{8} + \frac{3}{8} + \frac{2}{8}$
- ☐ $1 + \frac{3}{8}$
- ☐ $\frac{8}{8} + \frac{3}{8}$
- ☐ $\frac{5}{8} + \frac{5}{8} + \frac{1}{8}$
- ☐ $1 + \frac{1}{4} + \frac{2}{4}$

Name _____

☆ Solve & Share ☆

Jonas is making nachos and tacos for a family party. He uses $\frac{2}{5}$ bag of shredded cheese for the nachos and $\frac{1}{5}$ bag for the tacos. How much of the bag of shredded cheese does Jonas use? *Solve this problem any way you choose.*

I can ...
use my understanding of addition as joining parts of the same whole to add fractions with like denominators.

© Content Standards 4.NF.B.3a, 4.NF.B.3d
Mathematical Practices MP.1, MP.3, MP.4, MP.7

You can model with math. What equation can you write to represent this problem?

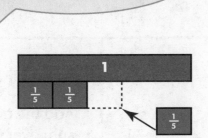

Look Back! © MP.7 Look for Relationships What do you notice about the denominators in your equation?

Essential Question # How Can You Add Fractions with Like Denominators?

A

The table shows the results of a fourth-grade Pets Club survey. What fraction of the club members chose a hamster or a dog as their favorite pet?

Add the fractions for hamsters and dogs to find the result.

Favorite Pet	
	$\frac{5}{12}$
	$\frac{4}{12}$
	$\frac{2}{12}$
	$\frac{1}{12}$

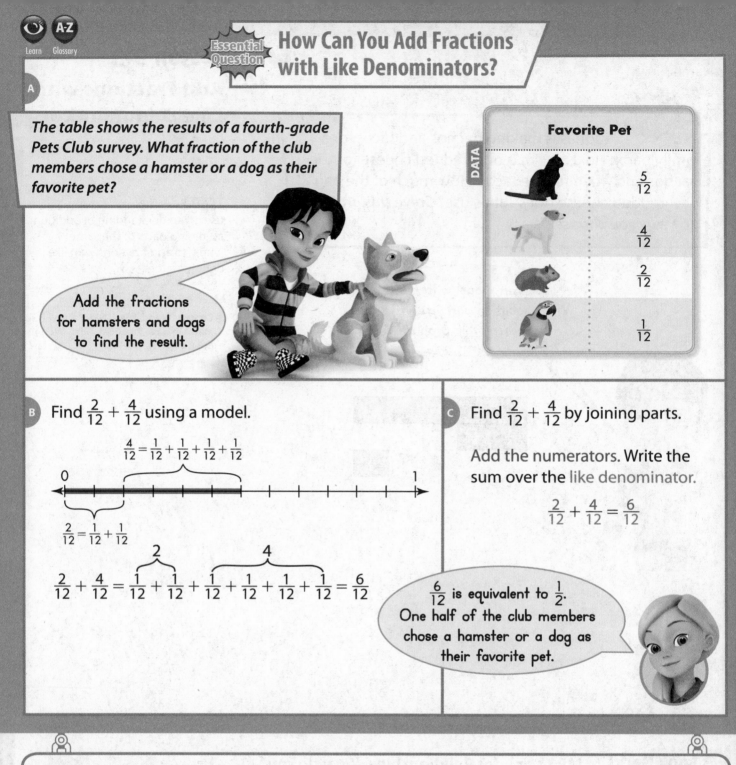

B Find $\frac{2}{12} + \frac{4}{12}$ using a model.

$$\frac{4}{12} = \frac{1}{12} + \frac{1}{12} + \frac{1}{12} + \frac{1}{12}$$

0 ——————————————— 1

$$\frac{2}{12} = \frac{1}{12} + \frac{1}{12}$$

$$\frac{2}{12} + \frac{4}{12} = \frac{1}{12} + \frac{1}{12} + \frac{1}{12} + \frac{1}{12} + \frac{1}{12} + \frac{1}{12} = \frac{6}{12}$$

C Find $\frac{2}{12} + \frac{4}{12}$ by joining parts.

Add the numerators. Write the sum over the like denominator.

$$\frac{2}{12} + \frac{4}{12} = \frac{6}{12}$$

$\frac{6}{12}$ is equivalent to $\frac{1}{2}$. One half of the club members chose a hamster or a dog as their favorite pet.

Convince Me! ⓒ **MP.3 Critique Reasoning** Frank solved the problem above and found $\frac{2}{12} + \frac{4}{12} = \frac{6}{24}$. What error did Frank make? Explain.

Practice Buddy   Tools   Assessment

Another Example!

Find $\frac{4}{5} + \frac{3}{5}$.

$$\frac{4}{5} + \frac{3}{5} = \overbrace{\frac{1}{5} + \frac{1}{5} + \frac{1}{5} + \frac{1}{5}}^{4} + \overbrace{\frac{1}{5} + \frac{1}{5} + \frac{1}{5}}^{3} = \frac{7}{5}$$

Write the fraction as a mixed number. $\frac{7}{5} = \frac{5}{5} + \frac{2}{5} = 1\frac{2}{5}$

You can write the sum as a fraction or a mixed number.

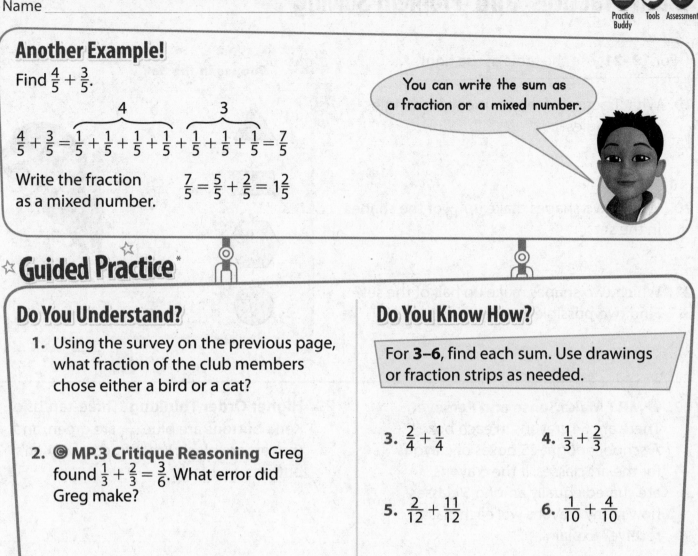

☆ Guided Practice*

Do You Understand?

1. Using the survey on the previous page, what fraction of the club members chose either a bird or a cat?

2. ⓒ **MP.3 Critique Reasoning** Greg found $\frac{1}{3} + \frac{2}{3} = \frac{3}{6}$. What error did Greg make?

Do You Know How?

For **3–6**, find each sum. Use drawings or fraction strips as needed.

3. $\frac{2}{4} + \frac{1}{4}$ 4. $\frac{1}{3} + \frac{2}{3}$

5. $\frac{2}{12} + \frac{11}{12}$ 6. $\frac{1}{10} + \frac{4}{10}$

☆ Independent Practice ☆

For **7–18**, find each sum. Use drawings or fraction strips as needed.

7. $\frac{2}{8} + \frac{1}{8}$ 8. $\frac{3}{6} + \frac{2}{6}$ 9. $\frac{1}{8} + \frac{4}{8}$

10. $\frac{3}{10} + \frac{2}{10}$ 11. $\frac{3}{10} + \frac{5}{10}$ 12. $\frac{5}{12} + \frac{4}{12}$

13. $\frac{4}{5} + \frac{3}{5} + \frac{2}{5}$ 14. $\frac{3}{10} + \frac{2}{10} + \frac{6}{10}$ 15. $\frac{2}{6} + \frac{5}{6}$

16. $\frac{3}{6} + \frac{9}{6}$ 17. $\frac{11}{10} + \frac{11}{10}$ 18. $\frac{7}{8} + \frac{1}{8}$

*For another example, see Set A on page 533.

Math Practices and Problem Solving

For **19–21**, use the table at the right.

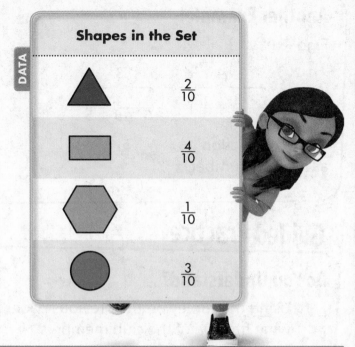

Shapes in the Set

▲	$\frac{2}{10}$
▬	$\frac{4}{10}$
⬡	$\frac{1}{10}$
●	$\frac{3}{10}$

19. What fraction of the set is either triangles or rectangles?

20. Which two shapes make up $\frac{7}{10}$ of the shapes in the set?

21. Which two shapes make up half of the set? Find two possible answers.

22. © **MP.1 Make Sense and Persevere** There are 64 crayons in each box. A school bought 25 boxes of crayons for the art classes. If the crayons are shared equally among 5 classes, how many crayons will each class receive? Explain.

23. **Higher Order Thinking** Three-tenths of Ken's buttons are blue, $\frac{4}{10}$ are green, and the rest are black. What fraction of Ken's buttons are black?

© **Common Core Assessment**

24. Draw lines connecting each fraction or mixed number on the left with the correct expression on the right.

$\frac{3}{4}$	$\frac{3}{8} + \frac{2}{8} + \frac{32}{8}$
$4\frac{5}{8}$	$\frac{2}{6} + \frac{4}{6}$
$\frac{7}{6}$	$\frac{2}{4} + \frac{1}{4}$
1	$\frac{6}{6} + \frac{1}{6}$

25. Draw lines connecting each fraction or mixed number on the left with the correct expression on the right.

$1\frac{1}{10}$	$\frac{1}{4} + \frac{2}{4} + \frac{8}{4}$
2	$\frac{1}{10} + \frac{0}{10} + \frac{10}{10}$
$\frac{6}{12}$	$\frac{3}{12} + \frac{3}{12}$
$2\frac{3}{4}$	$\frac{5}{4} + \frac{3}{4}$

Name _____

Another Look!

Find $\frac{4}{8} + \frac{2}{8}$.

When you add fractions with like denominators, add the numerators and keep the denominators the same.

$\frac{4}{8} = \frac{1}{8} + \frac{1}{8} + \frac{1}{8} + \frac{1}{8}$ $\frac{2}{8} = \frac{1}{8} + \frac{1}{8}$

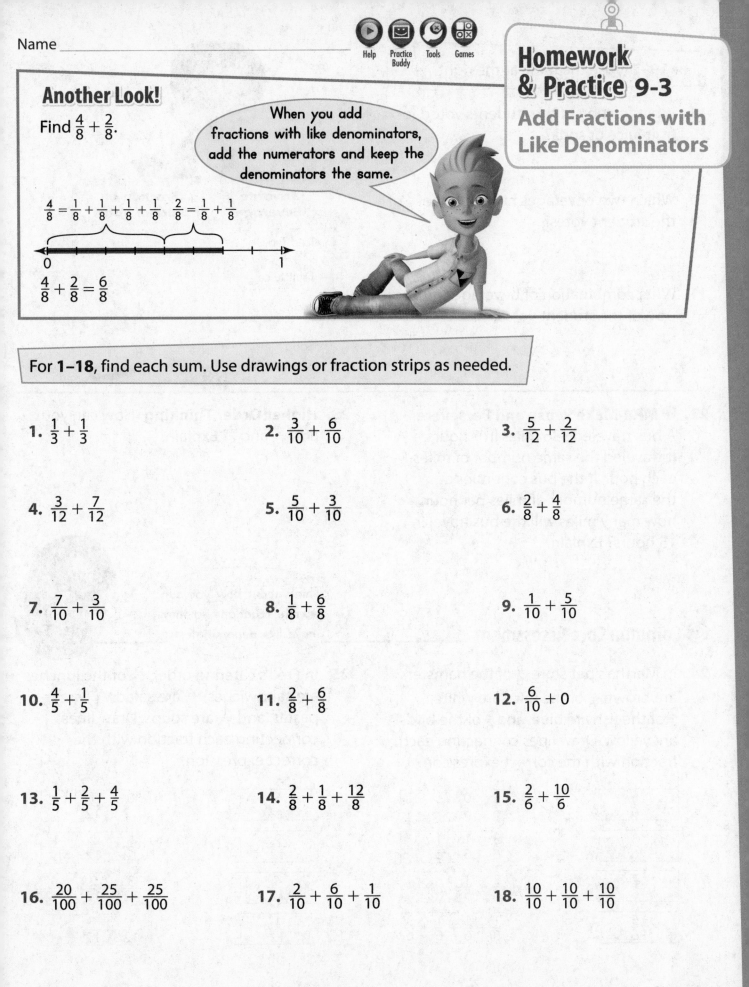

$\frac{4}{8} + \frac{2}{8} = \frac{6}{8}$

For **1–18**, find each sum. Use drawings or fraction strips as needed.

1. $\frac{1}{3} + \frac{1}{3}$

2. $\frac{3}{10} + \frac{6}{10}$

3. $\frac{5}{12} + \frac{2}{12}$

4. $\frac{3}{12} + \frac{7}{12}$

5. $\frac{5}{10} + \frac{3}{10}$

6. $\frac{2}{8} + \frac{4}{8}$

7. $\frac{7}{10} + \frac{3}{10}$

8. $\frac{1}{8} + \frac{6}{8}$

9. $\frac{1}{10} + \frac{5}{10}$

10. $\frac{4}{5} + \frac{1}{5}$

11. $\frac{2}{8} + \frac{6}{8}$

12. $\frac{6}{10} + 0$

13. $\frac{1}{5} + \frac{2}{5} + \frac{4}{5}$

14. $\frac{2}{8} + \frac{1}{8} + \frac{12}{8}$

15. $\frac{2}{6} + \frac{10}{6}$

16. $\frac{20}{100} + \frac{25}{100} + \frac{25}{100}$

17. $\frac{2}{10} + \frac{6}{10} + \frac{1}{10}$

18. $\frac{10}{10} + \frac{10}{10} + \frac{10}{10}$

19. What fraction of the students voted for fruit juice or soda?

20. Which two beverages have a sum of $\frac{5}{8}$ of the student votes?

21. What combination of beverages makes up $\frac{6}{8}$ of the student votes?

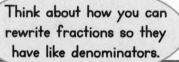

Favorite Beverage	Fraction of Student Votes
Iced Tea	$\frac{3}{8}$
Fruit Juice	$\frac{2}{8}$
Water	$\frac{1}{8}$
Soda	$\frac{2}{8}$

22. © **MP.1 Make Sense and Persevere** A bus traveled 336 miles in 7 hours. It traveled the same number of miles each hour. If the bus continues at the same number of miles per hour, how many miles will the bus travel in 15 hours? Explain.

23. **Higher Order Thinking** How can you add $\frac{3}{10}$ and $\frac{2}{5}$? Explain.

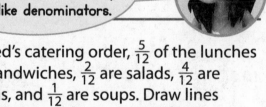

Think about how you can rewrite fractions so they have like denominators.

© **Common Core Assessment**

24. In Martha's pet store, $\frac{6}{6}$ of the hamsters are brown, $\frac{3}{6}$ of the mice are white, $\frac{2}{6}$ of the fish are blue, and $\frac{5}{6}$ of the birds are yellow. Draw lines connecting each fraction with the correct expression.

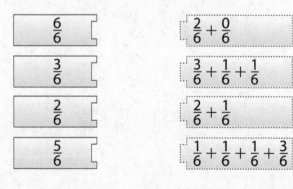

$\frac{6}{6}$	$\frac{2}{6} + \frac{0}{6}$
$\frac{3}{6}$	$\frac{3}{6} + \frac{1}{6} + \frac{1}{6}$
$\frac{2}{6}$	$\frac{2}{6} + \frac{1}{6}$
$\frac{5}{6}$	$\frac{1}{6} + \frac{1}{6} + \frac{1}{6} + \frac{3}{6}$

25. In Fred's catering order, $\frac{5}{12}$ of the lunches are sandwiches, $\frac{2}{12}$ are salads, $\frac{4}{12}$ are pastas, and $\frac{1}{12}$ are soups. Draw lines connecting each fraction with the correct expression.

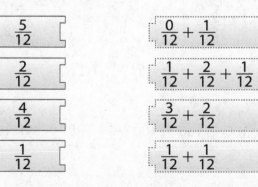

$\frac{5}{12}$	$\frac{0}{12} + \frac{1}{12}$
$\frac{2}{12}$	$\frac{1}{12} + \frac{2}{12} + \frac{1}{12}$
$\frac{4}{12}$	$\frac{3}{12} + \frac{2}{12}$
$\frac{1}{12}$	$\frac{1}{12} + \frac{1}{12}$

Name _____

Lesson 9-4
Model Subtraction of Fractions

☆ Solve & Share ☆

Mr. Yetkin uses $\frac{4}{6}$ of a sheet of plywood to board up a window. How much of the plywood is left? **Solve this problem any way you choose.**

I can ...
use tools such as fractions strips or area models to subtract fractions with like denominators.

You can select tools such as fraction strips, drawings, or area models to solve this problem. *Show your work in the space below!*

© Content Standard 4.NF.B.3a
Mathematical Practices MP.1, MP.2, MP.4, MP.5, MP.6

Look Back! © **MP.6 Be Precise** Explain why $\frac{4}{6}$ is subtracted from $\frac{6}{6}$ to find how much of the plywood is left.

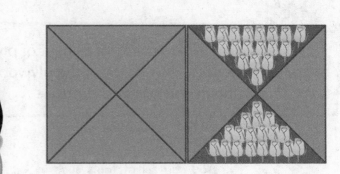
Essential Question **How Can You Use Tools to Subtract Fractions?**

A

A flower garden is divided into eighths. If $\frac{2}{8}$ of the garden is used to grow yellow roses, what fraction is left to grow other flowers?

You can use tools such as fraction strips to represent subtraction.

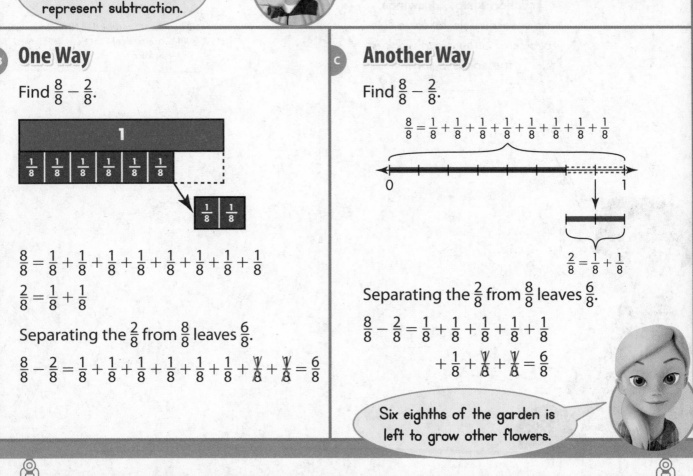

B **One Way**

Find $\frac{8}{8} - \frac{2}{8}$.

$$\frac{8}{8} = \frac{1}{8} + \frac{1}{8} + \frac{1}{8} + \frac{1}{8} + \frac{1}{8} + \frac{1}{8} + \frac{1}{8} + \frac{1}{8}$$

$$\frac{2}{8} = \frac{1}{8} + \frac{1}{8}$$

Separating the $\frac{2}{8}$ from $\frac{8}{8}$ leaves $\frac{6}{8}$.

$$\frac{8}{8} - \frac{2}{8} = \frac{1}{8} + \frac{1}{8} + \frac{1}{8} + \frac{1}{8} + \frac{1}{8} + \frac{1}{8} + \cancel{\frac{1}{8}} + \cancel{\frac{1}{8}} = \frac{6}{8}$$

C **Another Way**

Find $\frac{8}{8} - \frac{2}{8}$.

$$\frac{8}{8} = \frac{1}{8} + \frac{1}{8} + \frac{1}{8} + \frac{1}{8} + \frac{1}{8} + \frac{1}{8} + \frac{1}{8} + \frac{1}{8}$$

$$\frac{2}{8} = \frac{1}{8} + \frac{1}{8}$$

Separating the $\frac{2}{8}$ from $\frac{8}{8}$ leaves $\frac{6}{8}$.

$$\frac{8}{8} - \frac{2}{8} = \frac{1}{8} + \frac{1}{8} + \frac{1}{8} + \frac{1}{8} + \frac{1}{8}$$
$$+ \frac{1}{8} + \cancel{\frac{1}{8}} + \cancel{\frac{1}{8}} = \frac{6}{8}$$

Six eighths of the garden is left to grow other flowers.

Convince Me! © **MP.5 Use Appropriate Tools** In the problem above, suppose six sections of the garden are used for yellow roses and two other sections are used for petunias. How much more of the garden is used for yellow roses than is used for petunias? Use fraction strips or another tool to help. Write your answer as a fraction.

Name _____

Another Example!

Find $\frac{11}{8} - \frac{2}{8}$.

Use eleven $\frac{1}{8}$-fraction strips to show $\frac{11}{8}$. Take 2 strips away.

$\frac{11}{8} - \frac{2}{8} = \frac{9}{8}$

$\frac{9}{8} = \frac{8}{8} + \frac{1}{8} = 1\frac{1}{8}$

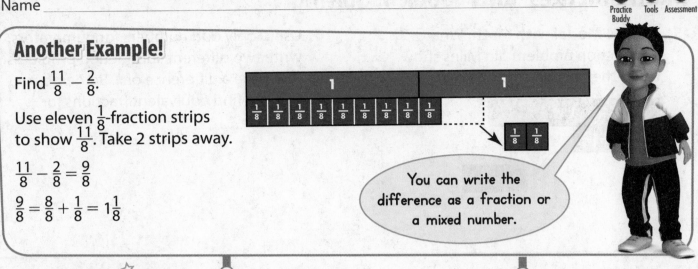

You can write the difference as a fraction or a mixed number.

⭐ Guided Practice *

Do You Understand?

1. © **MP.2 Reasoning** In the problem at the top of the previous page, suppose one other $\frac{1}{8}$ section was used to grow peonies. What fraction of the garden is now available for flowers?

Do You Know How?

For **2–5**, use fraction strips or other tools to subtract.

2. $\frac{1}{3} - \frac{1}{3}$ 3. $\frac{5}{5} - \frac{2}{5}$

4. $\frac{7}{12} - \frac{3}{12}$ 5. $\frac{7}{8} - \frac{1}{8}$

Independent Practice ⭐

Leveled Practice For **6–14**, find each difference. Use fraction strips or other tools as needed.

6. $\frac{11}{12} - \frac{5}{12}$

7. $\frac{2}{2} - \frac{1}{2}$ $\frac{2}{2} = \frac{1}{2} + \frac{1}{2}$

8. $\frac{2}{3} - \frac{1}{3}$

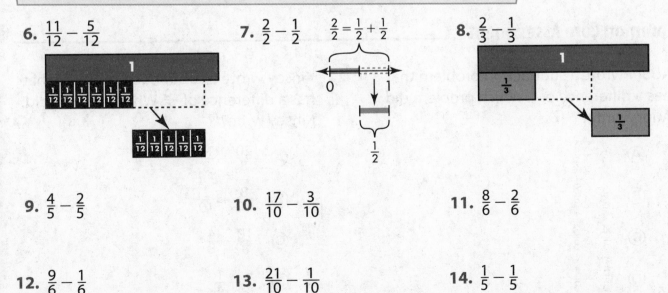

9. $\frac{4}{5} - \frac{2}{5}$ 10. $\frac{17}{10} - \frac{3}{10}$ 11. $\frac{8}{6} - \frac{2}{6}$

12. $\frac{9}{6} - \frac{1}{6}$ 13. $\frac{21}{10} - \frac{1}{10}$ 14. $\frac{1}{5} - \frac{1}{5}$

Math Practices and Problem Solving

15. ◎ **MP.4 Model with Math** What subtraction problem did Miles show using the fraction strips below?

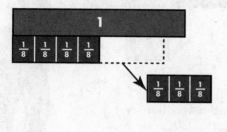

16. Using only odd numbers for numerators, write two different subtraction problems that have a difference of $\frac{1}{2}$. Remember, you can find equivalent fractions for $\frac{1}{2}$.

17. In Kayla's class, some of the students are wearing blue shirts. $\frac{6}{8}$ of the students are **NOT** wearing blue shirts. What fraction of the students are wearing blue shirts? Show your work.

18. ◎ **MP.2 Reasoning** In Exercise 17, what number represents the whole class? How do you know what fraction to use to represent this number?

19. Rick shared his bag of grapes with friends. He gave $\frac{2}{10}$ of the bag to Melissa and $\frac{4}{10}$ of the bag to Ryan. What fraction of the bag of grapes does Rick have left? Show your work.

20. **Higher Order Thinking** Teresa gave away 8 baseball cards and has 4 baseball cards left. Write a subtraction problem to show the fraction of the baseball cards Teresa has left.

◎ Common Core Assessment

21. Audry wrote a subtraction problem that has a difference of $\frac{1}{3}$. Which problem did Audry write?

Ⓐ $\frac{2}{2} - \frac{1}{2}$

Ⓑ $\frac{5}{3} - \frac{3}{3}$

Ⓒ $\frac{4}{3} - \frac{3}{3}$

Ⓓ $\frac{5}{3} - \frac{1}{3}$

22. Kinsey wrote a subtraction problem that has a difference of $\frac{10}{8}$. What problem did Kinsey write?

Ⓐ $\frac{20}{8} - \frac{10}{8}$

Ⓑ $\frac{8}{10} + \frac{2}{10}$

Ⓒ $\frac{10}{8} - \frac{4}{8}$

Ⓓ $\frac{6}{8} - \frac{1}{4}$

Name _____

Another Look!

Kimberly cut a pizza into 10 equal slices. She ate two of the slices. What fraction of the pizza is left? Remember, $\frac{10}{10}$ = 1 whole pizza.

Step 1

Divide a circle into tenths to show the pizza cut into 10 slices.

Step 2

Take away the 2 slices or $\frac{2}{10}$ of the pizza that Kimberly ate.

Step 3

Count the remaining slices and write the subtraction.

$$\frac{10}{10} - \frac{2}{10} = \frac{8}{10}$$

$\frac{8}{10}$ of the pizza is left.

For **1–12**, find each difference. Use fraction strips or other tools as needed.

1. $\frac{3}{5} - \frac{2}{5}$

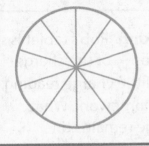

$\frac{3}{5} = \frac{1}{5} + \frac{1}{5} + \frac{1}{5}$

$\frac{2}{5} = \frac{1}{5} + \frac{1}{5}$

2. $\frac{7}{10} - \frac{3}{10}$

3. $\frac{4}{4} - \frac{2}{4}$

4. $\frac{8}{10} - \frac{5}{10}$

5. $\frac{6}{6} - \frac{3}{6}$

6. $\frac{11}{12} - \frac{7}{12}$

7. $\frac{5}{6} - \frac{2}{6}$

8. $\frac{4}{8} - \frac{2}{8}$

9. $\frac{11}{12} - \frac{8}{12}$

10. $\frac{9}{8} - \frac{2}{8}$

11. $\frac{24}{4} - \frac{18}{4}$

12. $\frac{30}{10} - \frac{20}{10}$

13. Eddie noticed that out of 10 students, one student was wearing brown shoes, and seven students were wearing black shoes. What fraction of students were **NOT** wearing brown or black shoes?

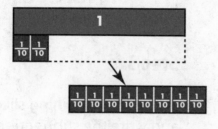

14. © **MP.1 Make Sense and Persevere**
A marathon is a race that covers about 26 miles. Cindy ran 5 miles before taking her first water break. Then she ran another 7 miles to get to her next water break. After 6 more miles, she took her last water break. About how much farther does Cindy have until she reaches the finish line?

15. **Algebra** Jeffrey has already run $\frac{3}{8}$ of the race. What fraction of the race does Jeffrey have left? Write and solve an equation.

0   1

16. **Higher Order Thinking** Rob's tablet is fully charged. He uses $\frac{1}{12}$ of the charge playing games, $\frac{5}{12}$ of the charge reading, and $\frac{3}{12}$ completing homework. What fraction of the charge remains on Rob's tablet?

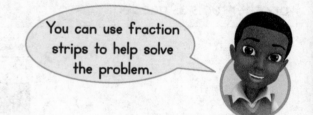

You can use fraction strips to help solve the problem.

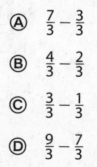

© **Common Core Assessment**

17. Roger found he had $\frac{2}{5}$ of his quarters left to use at the arcade. Which of the following subtraction problems could **NOT** be used to find the fraction of quarters Roger had left?

    Ⓐ $\frac{4}{5} - \frac{2}{5}$

    Ⓑ $\frac{3}{6} - \frac{1}{2}$

    Ⓒ $\frac{3}{5} - \frac{1}{5}$

    Ⓓ $\frac{5}{5} - \frac{3}{5}$

18. Krys has $\frac{2}{3}$ of her homework finished. Which of the following does **NOT** have a difference of $\frac{2}{3}$?

    Ⓐ $\frac{7}{3} - \frac{3}{3}$

    Ⓑ $\frac{4}{3} - \frac{2}{3}$

    Ⓒ $\frac{3}{3} - \frac{1}{3}$

    Ⓓ $\frac{9}{3} - \frac{7}{3}$

Name _____

☆ ☆
Solve & Share

Leah and Josh live the same direction from school and on the same side of Forest Road. Leah's house is $\frac{8}{10}$ mile from school. Josh's house is $\frac{5}{10}$ mile from school. How much farther does Leah have to walk home when she reaches Josh's house? **Solve this problem any way you choose.**

You can model with math. What expression can you use to represent this problem?

I can ...
use my understanding of subtraction as separating parts of the same whole to subtract fractions with like denominators.

Ⓒ Content Standards 4.NF.B.3a, 4.NF.B.3d
Mathematical Practices MP.2, MP.3, MP.4

Look Back! Ⓒ **MP.3. Critique Reasoning** Sarah wrote the expression $\frac{8}{10} - \frac{5}{10}$ to solve the problem. Jared wrote the expressions $\frac{10}{10} - \frac{8}{10}$, $\frac{10}{10} - \frac{5}{10}$, and $\frac{5}{10} - \frac{2}{10}$ to solve the problem. Who is correct? Explain.

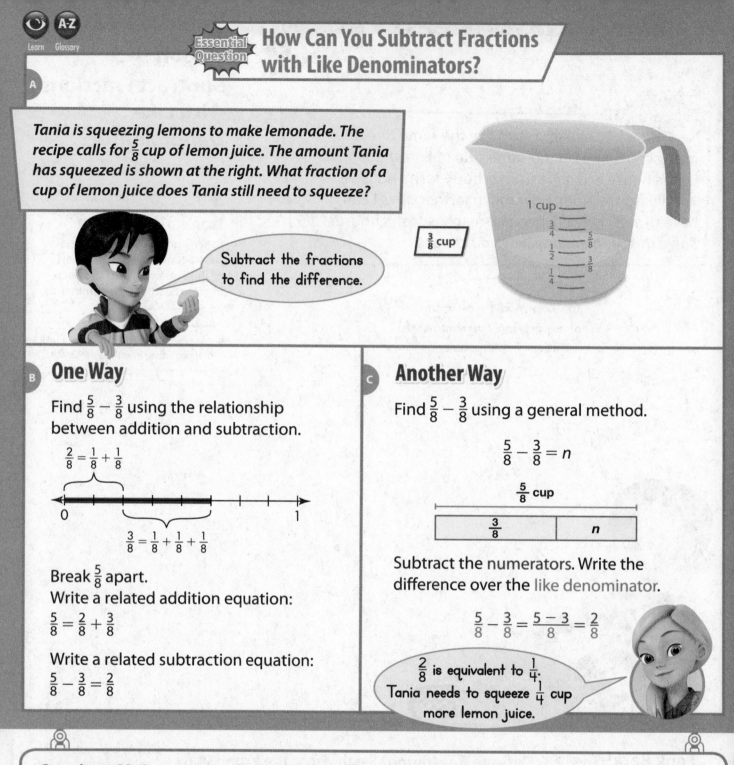

Essential Question

How Can You Subtract Fractions with Like Denominators?

A

Tania is squeezing lemons to make lemonade. The recipe calls for $\frac{5}{8}$ cup of lemon juice. The amount Tania has squeezed is shown at the right. What fraction of a cup of lemon juice does Tania still need to squeeze?

$\frac{3}{8}$ cup

1 cup
$\frac{3}{4}$
$\frac{5}{8}$
$\frac{1}{2}$
$\frac{3}{8}$
$\frac{1}{4}$

Subtract the fractions to find the difference.

B **One Way**

Find $\frac{5}{8} - \frac{3}{8}$ using the relationship between addition and subtraction.

$\frac{2}{8} = \frac{1}{8} + \frac{1}{8}$

$\frac{3}{8} = \frac{1}{8} + \frac{1}{8} + \frac{1}{8}$

0   1

Break $\frac{5}{8}$ apart.
Write a related addition equation:
$\frac{5}{8} = \frac{2}{8} + \frac{3}{8}$

Write a related subtraction equation:
$\frac{5}{8} - \frac{3}{8} = \frac{2}{8}$

C **Another Way**

Find $\frac{5}{8} - \frac{3}{8}$ using a general method.

$$\frac{5}{8} - \frac{3}{8} = n$$

$\frac{5}{8}$ cup

$\frac{3}{8}$	n

Subtract the numerators. Write the difference over the like denominator.

$$\frac{5}{8} - \frac{3}{8} = \frac{5-3}{8} = \frac{2}{8}$$

$\frac{2}{8}$ is equivalent to $\frac{1}{4}$.
Tania needs to squeeze $\frac{1}{4}$ cup more lemon juice.

Convince Me! © **MP.2 Reasoning** In the problem above, suppose Tania decided to double the amount of lemonade she wants to make. Then how much more lemon juice would Tania need to squeeze?

Name _____

☆ Guided Practice ✱

Do You Understand?

1. Ⓒ **MP.3 Critique Reasoning** Jesse has a bottle that contains $\frac{7}{10}$ liter of water. He drinks $\frac{2}{10}$ liter. Jesse says he has $\frac{1}{2}$ liter left. Is he correct? Explain.

2. Subtract $\frac{4}{10}$ from $\frac{9}{10}$. What addition sentence can you use to check your answer?

Do You Know How?

For **3–10**, subtract the fractions.

3. $\frac{2}{3} - \frac{1}{3}$

4. $\frac{3}{4} - \frac{2}{4}$

5. $\frac{5}{6} - \frac{2}{6}$

6. $\frac{9}{12} - \frac{3}{12}$

7. $\frac{9}{8} - \frac{3}{8}$

8. $\frac{17}{10} - \frac{9}{10}$

9. $\frac{4}{8} - \frac{1}{8}$

10. $\frac{1}{2} - \frac{1}{2}$

Independent Practice ☆

Leveled Practice For **11–18**, subtract the fractions.

11. $\frac{5}{6} - \frac{1}{6}$

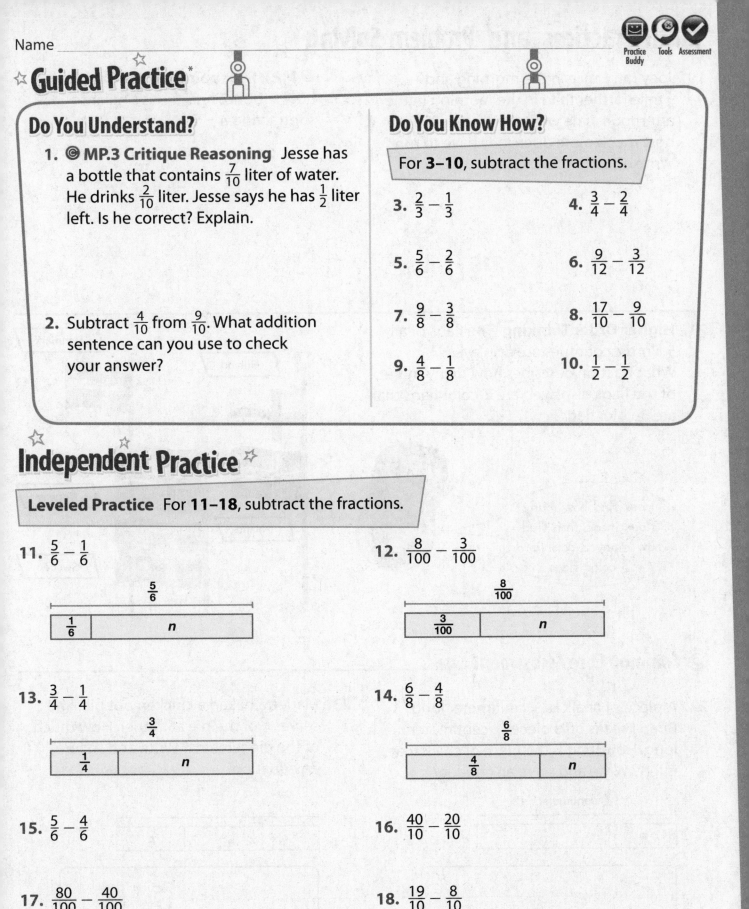

$\frac{5}{6}$	
$\frac{1}{6}$	n

12. $\frac{8}{100} - \frac{3}{100}$

$\frac{8}{100}$	
$\frac{3}{100}$	n

13. $\frac{3}{4} - \frac{1}{4}$

$\frac{3}{4}$	
$\frac{1}{4}$	n

14. $\frac{6}{8} - \frac{4}{8}$

$\frac{6}{8}$	
$\frac{4}{8}$	n

15. $\frac{5}{6} - \frac{4}{6}$

16. $\frac{40}{10} - \frac{20}{10}$

17. $\frac{80}{100} - \frac{40}{100}$

18. $\frac{19}{10} - \frac{8}{10}$

---

*For another example, see Set B on page 533.

Math Practices and Problem Solving

19. Joey ran $\frac{1}{4}$ mile in the morning and $\frac{1}{4}$ mile farther than in the morning in the afternoon. If he wants to run a full mile, how much more does Joey have to run? Write equations to explain.

20. © **MP.2 Reasoning** Write to explain how subtracting $\frac{4}{5} - \frac{3}{5}$ is similar to subtracting $4 - 3$.

21. Higher Order Thinking The flags of all 5 Nordic countries are displayed. What fraction describes how many more of the flags displayed are 2-color flags than are 3-color flags?

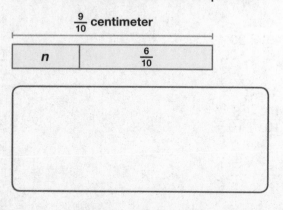

First find how many flags in all, then find how many 2-color and 3-color flags.

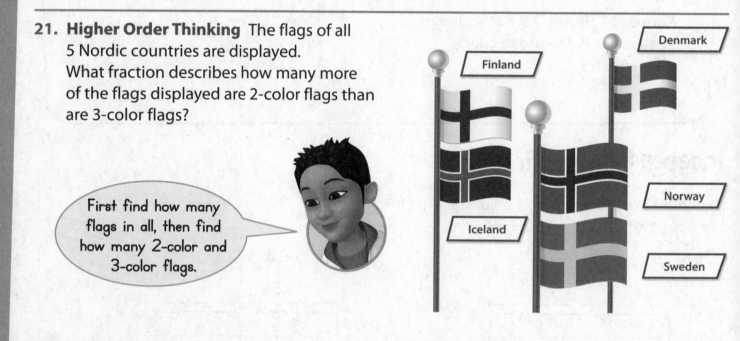

Finland
Denmark
Norway
Iceland
Sweden

© **Common Core Assessment**

22. A piece of chalk is $\frac{9}{10}$ centimeter long. Brian breaks off a piece $\frac{6}{10}$ centimeter long. How long is the piece of chalk that is left? Write and solve an equation.

$\frac{9}{10}$ centimeter

n	$\frac{6}{10}$

23. Marietta baked a chicken pot pie. She serves $\frac{2}{3}$ of the pie at dinner. How much of the pie remains? Write and solve an equation.

$\frac{3}{3}$

$\frac{2}{3}$	n

Help Practice Buddy Tools Games

Homework & Practice 9-5

Subtract Fractions with Like Denominators

Another Look!

Flora needs an additional $\frac{2}{8}$ cup flour to make her dough. The dough recipe calls for $\frac{6}{8}$ cup flour. How many cups of flour does Flora have?

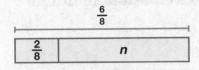

Subtract the numerators. Write the difference over the like denominator.

$\frac{6}{8} - \frac{2}{8} = \frac{4}{8}$

Flora has $\frac{4}{8}$ cup flour.

Bar diagrams can help you represent the problem.

For 1–10, subtract the fractions.

1. $\frac{6}{8} - \frac{3}{8}$

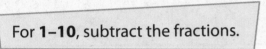

2. $\frac{4}{6} - \frac{1}{6}$

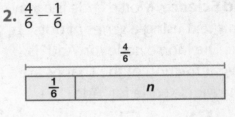

3. $\frac{4}{5} - \frac{3}{5}$

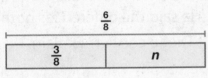

4. $\frac{3}{6} - \frac{1}{6}$

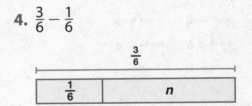

5. $\frac{97}{100} - \frac{40}{100}$

6. $\frac{5}{8} - \frac{1}{8}$

7. $\frac{10}{10} - \frac{9}{10}$

8. $\frac{17}{12} - \frac{5}{12}$

9. $\frac{33}{100} - \frac{4}{100}$

10. $\frac{50}{100} - \frac{10}{100}$

11. © **MP.4 Model with Math** An engineer was supposed to draw a line exactly $\frac{7}{10}$ centimeter long. An error was made, and he drew the line $\frac{9}{10}$ centimeter long. How much longer than needed was the line the engineer drew? Write an equation.

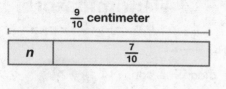

12. A mosaic wall is divided into 100 equal sections. If 30 sections are reserved for orange tiles and 40 sections are reserved for blue tiles, what fraction of the mosaic wall is left for other colors?

13. Number Sense Jonah is thinking of a 2-digit number. It is a multiple of 6 and 12. It is a factor of 108. The sum of its digits is 9. What number is Jonah thinking of?

14. In a bag of 100 balloons, 12 are red and 13 are green. What fraction of the balloons in the bag are **NOT** red or green?

15. Math and Science Morse code is a way to transmit text using a series of dots or dashes. The Morse code for "Add" is shown. What fraction of the shapes are dots in the Morse code for "Add?"

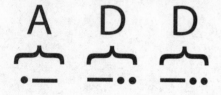

16. Higher Order Thinking Diego compared the differences for $\frac{10}{10} - \frac{1}{10}$ and $\frac{100}{100} - \frac{10}{100}$. He said the differences both equal $\frac{9}{10}$. Is Diego correct? Explain.

© **Common Core Assessment** _____

17. $\frac{5}{8}$ of Marie's marbles are red and $\frac{2}{8}$ are blue. The rest of the marbles are white. Draw a model to represent Marie's marbles. Write and solve equations to find the fraction of the marbles that are white.

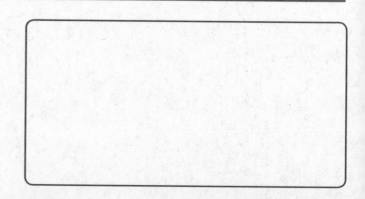

Name _____

Solve & Share

Sebastian has $\frac{6}{8}$ of the full charge left on his phone. He uses $\frac{2}{8}$ of the full charge playing a game. What fraction of the full charge does Sebastian have left? **Solve this problem any way you choose.**

I can ...
use a number line to add and subtract fractions when the fractions refer to the same whole.

© Content Standard 4.NF.B.3a
Mathematical Practices MP.2, MP.4, MP.5

You can use appropriate tools such as a number line to show this problem.

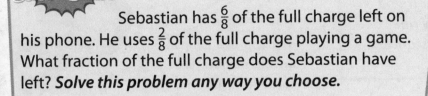

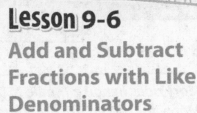

Look Back! © **MP.2 Reasoning** Write a fraction that is equivalent to the amount of a full charge that Sebastian used when playing the game.

How Do You Add and Subtract Fractions on a Number Line?

A

Mary rides her bike $\frac{2}{10}$ mile to pick up her friend Marcy for soccer practice. Together, they ride $\frac{5}{10}$ mile to the soccer field. What is the distance from Mary's house to the soccer field?

You can use jumps on the number line to add or subtract fractions.

Mary's house

Marcy's house

Soccer field

$\frac{2}{10}$ mile

$\frac{5}{10}$ mile

B

Use a number line to show $\frac{2}{10} + \frac{5}{10}$.

Draw a number line for tenths. Locate $\frac{2}{10}$ on the number line.

To add, move $\frac{5}{10}$ to the right.

$\frac{5}{10}$

0    $\frac{2}{10}$?   1

When you add, you move to the right on the number line.

C

Write the addition equation.

Add the numerators. Write the sum over the like denominator.

$$\frac{2}{10} + \frac{5}{10} = \frac{2 + 5}{10} = \frac{7}{10}$$

The distance from Mary's house to the soccer field is $\frac{7}{10}$ mile.

Convince Me! © MP.5 Use Appropriate Tools Use the number line below to find $\frac{5}{8} + \frac{2}{8}$. Can you also use the number line to find $\frac{5}{8} - \frac{2}{8}$? Explain.

0   1

Practice Buddy   Tools   Assessment

Another Example!

Find $\frac{6}{8} - \frac{4}{8}$.

Start at $\frac{6}{8}$. To subtract, move $\frac{4}{8}$ to the left. The ending point is $\frac{2}{8}$.

So, $\frac{6}{8} - \frac{4}{8} = \frac{2}{8}$.

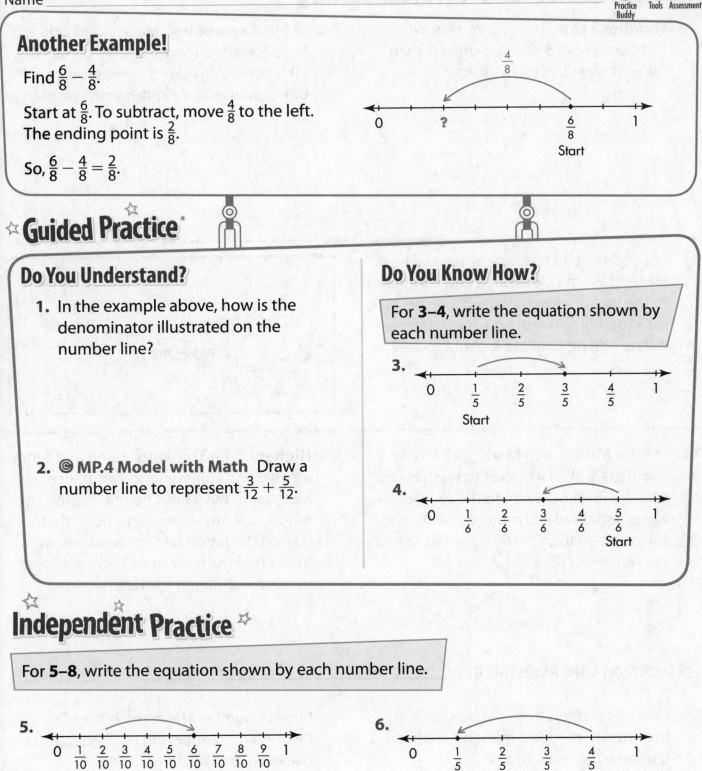

Guided Practice*

Do You Understand?

1. In the example above, how is the denominator illustrated on the number line?

2. © **MP.4 Model with Math** Draw a number line to represent $\frac{3}{12} + \frac{5}{12}$.

Do You Know How?

For **3–4**, write the equation shown by each number line.

3.

4.

Independent Practice *

For **5–8**, write the equation shown by each number line.

5.

6.

7.

8.

Math Practices and Problem Solving

9. **Number Sense** How do you know the quotient of $639 \div 6$ is greater than 100 before you actually divide?

10. **ⓒ MP.2 Reasoning** Maria saved $\frac{1}{4}$ of her allowance. Tomas saved $\frac{1}{6}$ of his allowance. Who saved a greater part of his or her allowance? Explain your reasoning.

11. Isaac started his bike ride at the trailhead. He reached the picnic area and continued to the lookout tower. If Isaac rode his bike for a total of $\frac{10}{4}$ miles, how much farther did he ride beyond the lookout tower?

Lookout Tower

Picnic Area $\frac{3}{4}$ mile

TRAILHEAD $\frac{2}{4}$ mile

12. **ⓒ MP.4 Model with Math** Ricky completely filled a bucket to wash his car. After he finished washing the car, $\frac{5}{8}$ of the water remained in the bucket. Write and solve an equation to show the fraction of the water Ricky used.

13. **Higher Order Thinking** Sarah and Jenny are running an hour long endurance race. Sarah ran $\frac{2}{6}$ hour before passing the baton to Jenny. Jenny ran $\frac{3}{6}$ hour, then passed the baton back to Sarah. What fraction of the hour does Sarah still need to run to complete the race?

ⓒ Common Core Assessment

14. Choose numbers from the box to fill in the missing numbers in each equation. Use each number once.

   a. $\dfrac{\square}{4} + \dfrac{2}{\square} = \dfrac{3}{4}$

   b. $\dfrac{8}{12} - \dfrac{\square}{12} = \dfrac{2}{\square}$

   c. $\dfrac{\square}{8} + \dfrac{2}{\square} = \dfrac{5}{8}$

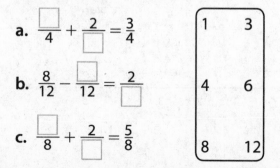

1	3
4	6
8	12

15. Choose numbers from the box to fill in the missing numbers in each equation. Use each number once.

   a. $\dfrac{3}{10} + \dfrac{\square}{10} = \dfrac{9}{\square}$

   b. $\dfrac{9}{12} - \dfrac{6}{\square} = \dfrac{\square}{12}$

   c. $\dfrac{1}{4} + \dfrac{\square}{4} = \dfrac{3}{\square}$

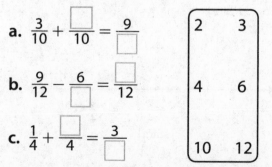

2	3
4	6
10	12

Help   Practice   Tools   Games
Buddy

Another Look!

There were 7 slices remaining of an apple pie divided into eighths. Katie and her 3 friends each ate a slice of the remaining pie. Calculate $\frac{7}{8} - \frac{4}{8}$ to find how much of the apple pie is now left.

Subtract to find how much of the pie is left.

What You Show

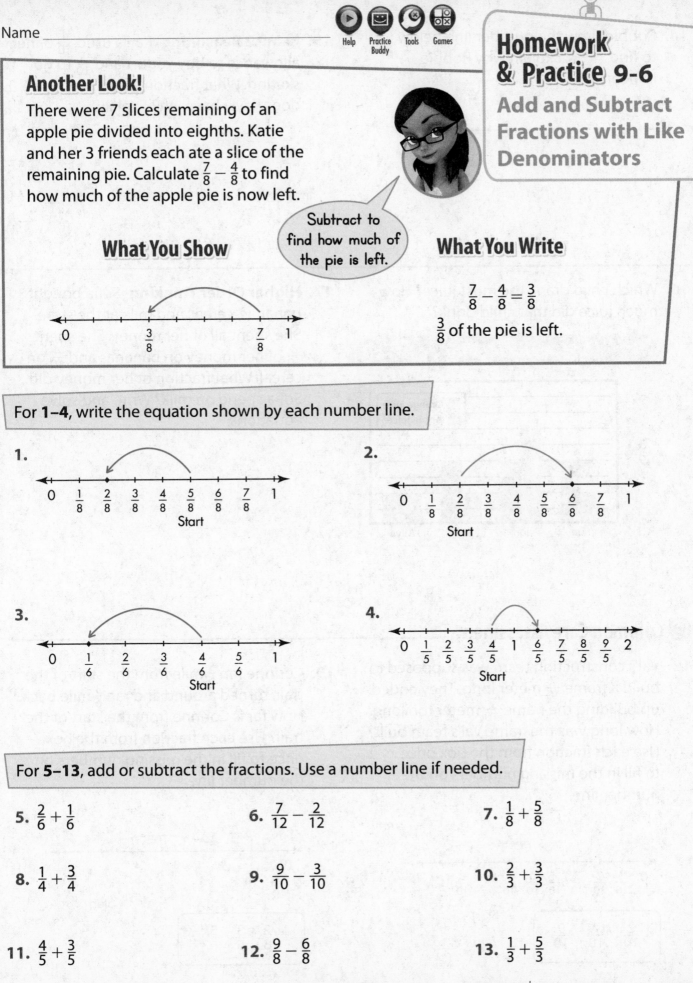

What You Write

$$\frac{7}{8} - \frac{4}{8} = \frac{3}{8}$$

$\frac{3}{8}$ of the pie is left.

For **1–4**, write the equation shown by each number line.

1.

0   $\frac{1}{8}$ $\frac{2}{8}$ $\frac{3}{8}$ $\frac{4}{8}$ $\frac{5}{8}$ $\frac{6}{8}$ $\frac{7}{8}$ 1
Start

2.

0   $\frac{1}{8}$ $\frac{2}{8}$ $\frac{3}{8}$ $\frac{4}{8}$ $\frac{5}{8}$ $\frac{6}{8}$ $\frac{7}{8}$ 1
Start

3.

0   $\frac{1}{6}$ $\frac{2}{6}$ $\frac{3}{6}$ $\frac{4}{6}$ $\frac{5}{6}$ 1
Start

4.

0   $\frac{1}{5}$ $\frac{2}{5}$ $\frac{3}{5}$ $\frac{4}{5}$ 1 $\frac{6}{5}$ $\frac{7}{5}$ $\frac{8}{5}$ $\frac{9}{5}$ 2
Start

For **5–13**, add or subtract the fractions. Use a number line if needed.

5. $\frac{2}{6} + \frac{1}{6}$

6. $\frac{7}{12} - \frac{2}{12}$

7. $\frac{1}{8} + \frac{5}{8}$

8. $\frac{1}{4} + \frac{3}{4}$

9. $\frac{9}{10} - \frac{3}{10}$

10. $\frac{2}{3} + \frac{3}{3}$

11. $\frac{4}{5} + \frac{3}{5}$

12. $\frac{9}{8} - \frac{6}{8}$

13. $\frac{1}{3} + \frac{5}{3}$

14. Robbie drew the number line below to find $\frac{4}{5} - \frac{1}{5}$. Explain why Robbie is incorrect.

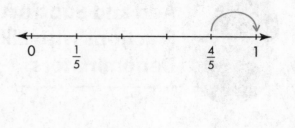

15. © **MP.2 Reasoning** Kayla used $\frac{4}{10}$ of her allowance to buy yogurt and $\frac{5}{10}$ to go skating. What fraction of her allowance does Kayla have left? Explain.

16. Which child drank the most juice? How much juice did that child drink?

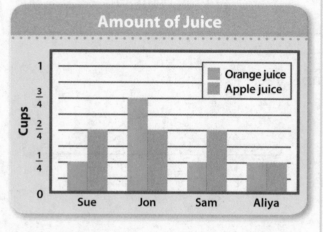

17. **Higher Order Thinking** Sofia bought bananas, cereal, and milk at the store. She spent all of her money. She spent $\frac{3}{10}$ of her money on bananas and $\frac{4}{10}$ on cereal. What fraction of her money did Sofia spend on milk? Write and solve equations.

© **Common Core Assessment** —————————

18. Val's construction team was supposed to build a frame $\frac{7}{10}$ meter long. They ended up building the frame $\frac{2}{10}$ meter too long. How long was the frame Val's team built? Use each fraction from the box once to fill in the missing numbers on the number line.

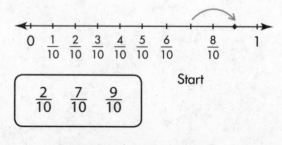

19. Corinne ran $\frac{5}{6}$ mile from the start of the trail, turned around and ran $\frac{3}{6}$ mile back. How far is Corinne from the start of the trail? Use each fraction from the box once to fill in the missing numbers on the number line.

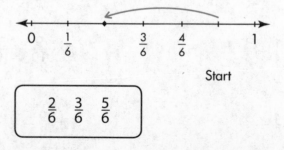

Name _____

Solve & Share

For **1–2**, use the number lines to decide if each sum is greater than or less than 1. Tell how you decided.

For **3–4**, use the number lines to decide if each difference is less than $\frac{1}{2}$ or greater than $\frac{1}{2}$. Tell how you decided.

I can ...
use number lines and benchmark fractions to estimate fraction sums and differences.

© Content Standard 4.NF.B.3a
Mathematical Practices MP.1, MP.2, MP.3, MP.4, MP.8

1. $\frac{5}{8} + \frac{8}{10}$

2. $\frac{1}{8} + \frac{1}{5} + \frac{1}{10}$

3. $\frac{7}{8} - \frac{1}{10}$

4. $\frac{9}{10} - \frac{5}{8}$

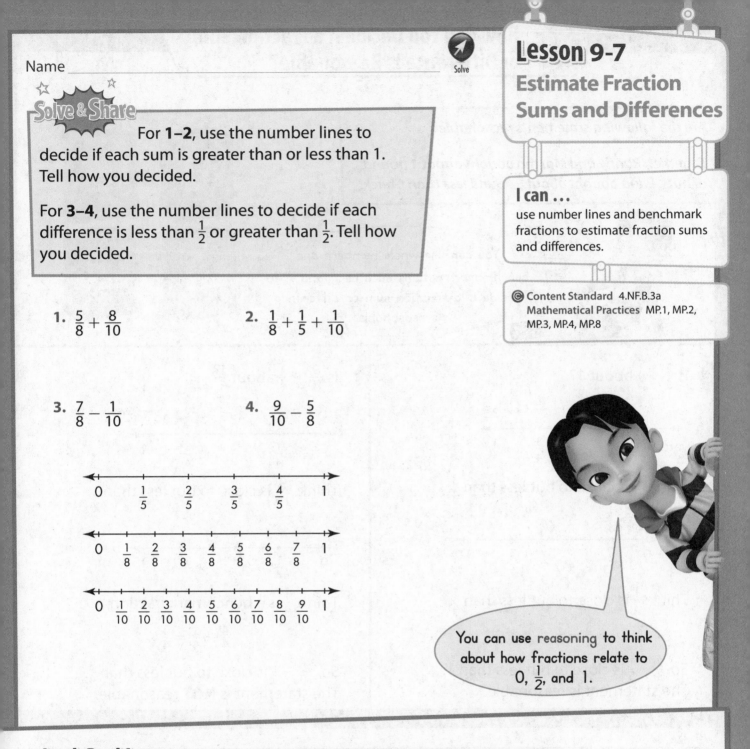

You can use reasoning to think about how fractions relate to 0, $\frac{1}{2}$, and 1.

Look Back! © **MP.8 Generalize** Which fraction in the exercises above is close to $\frac{1}{2}$? How can you use whole numbers and benchmark fractions such as $\frac{1}{2}$ to estimate fraction sums and differences?

Essential Question How Can You Decide if a Fraction Sum or Difference Is Reasonable?

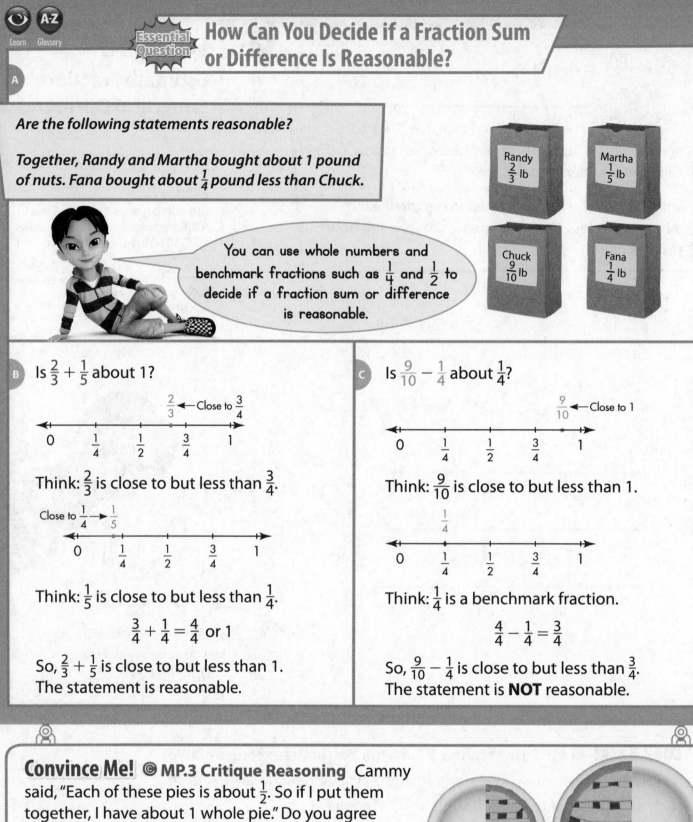

A

Are the following statements reasonable?

Together, Randy and Martha bought about 1 pound of nuts. Fana bought about $\frac{1}{4}$ pound less than Chuck.

You can use whole numbers and benchmark fractions such as $\frac{1}{4}$ and $\frac{1}{2}$ to decide if a fraction sum or difference is reasonable.

Randy $\frac{2}{3}$ lb

Martha $\frac{1}{5}$ lb

Chuck $\frac{9}{10}$ lb

Fana $\frac{1}{4}$ lb

B

Is $\frac{2}{3} + \frac{1}{5}$ about 1?

$\frac{2}{3}$ ← Close to $\frac{3}{4}$

0    $\frac{1}{4}$ $\frac{1}{2}$ $\frac{3}{4}$ 1

Think: $\frac{2}{3}$ is close to but less than $\frac{3}{4}$.

Close to $\frac{1}{4}$ → $\frac{1}{5}$

0    $\frac{1}{4}$ $\frac{1}{2}$ $\frac{3}{4}$ 1

Think: $\frac{1}{5}$ is close to but less than $\frac{1}{4}$.

$$\frac{3}{4} + \frac{1}{4} = \frac{4}{4} \text{ or } 1$$

So, $\frac{2}{3} + \frac{1}{5}$ is close to but less than 1. The statement is reasonable.

C

Is $\frac{9}{10} - \frac{1}{4}$ about $\frac{1}{4}$?

$\frac{9}{10}$ ← Close to 1

0    $\frac{1}{4}$ $\frac{1}{2}$ $\frac{3}{4}$ 1

Think: $\frac{9}{10}$ is close to but less than 1.

$\frac{1}{4}$

0    $\frac{1}{4}$ $\frac{1}{2}$ $\frac{3}{4}$ 1

Think: $\frac{1}{4}$ is a benchmark fraction.

$$\frac{4}{4} - \frac{1}{4} = \frac{3}{4}$$

So, $\frac{9}{10} - \frac{1}{4}$ is close to but less than $\frac{3}{4}$. The statement is **NOT** reasonable.

Convince Me! © MP.3 Critique Reasoning Cammy said, "Each of these pies is about $\frac{1}{2}$. So if I put them together, I have about 1 whole pie." Do you agree with this reasoning? Explain.

☆ Guided Practice *

Do You Understand?

1. © **MP.3 Construct Arguments** Use benchmark fractions to estimate $\frac{4}{10} + \frac{3}{8}$. Explain.

2. © **MP.3 Critique Reasoning** Charlie said $\frac{8}{10} - \frac{1}{5}$ is about $\frac{1}{4}$. Do you agree? Explain.

Do You Know How?

For **3–6**, use < or > to complete each equation. Use the number lines as needed.

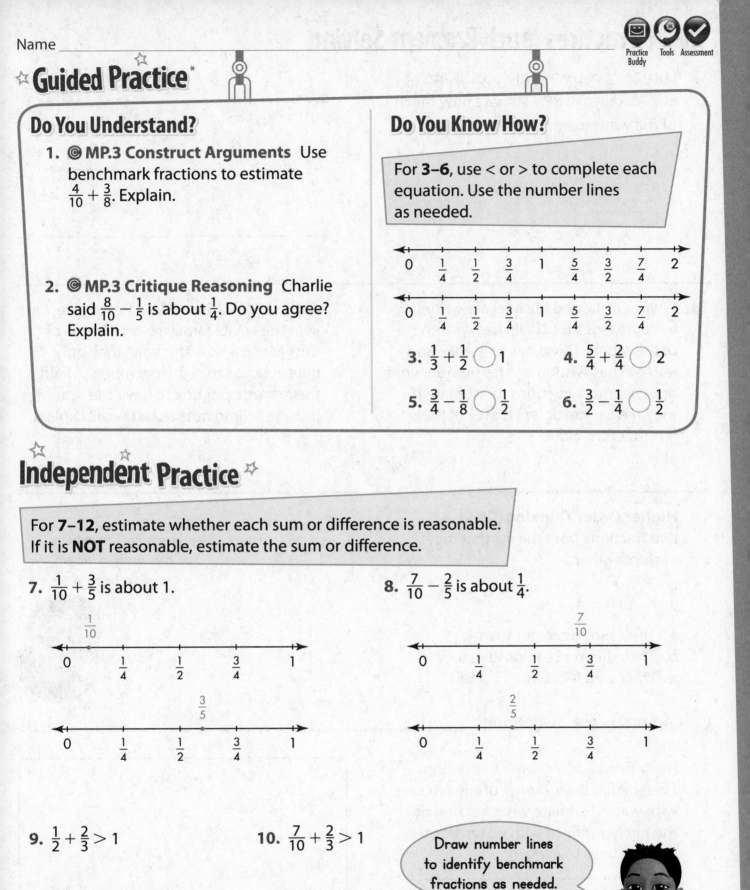

3. $\frac{1}{3} + \frac{1}{2} \bigcirc 1$

4. $\frac{5}{4} + \frac{2}{4} \bigcirc 2$

5. $\frac{3}{4} - \frac{1}{8} \bigcirc \frac{1}{2}$

6. $\frac{3}{2} - \frac{1}{4} \bigcirc \frac{1}{2}$

☆ Independent Practice ☆

For **7–12**, estimate whether each sum or difference is reasonable. If it is **NOT** reasonable, estimate the sum or difference.

7. $\frac{1}{10} + \frac{3}{5}$ is about 1.

8. $\frac{7}{10} - \frac{2}{5}$ is about $\frac{1}{4}$.

9. $\frac{1}{2} + \frac{2}{3} > 1$

10. $\frac{7}{10} + \frac{2}{3} > 1$

Draw number lines to identify benchmark fractions as needed.

11. $\frac{9}{10} - \frac{1}{8} < \frac{1}{2}$

12. $\frac{4}{5} - \frac{2}{3} < \frac{1}{2}$

Math Practices and Problem Solving

13. Lucy ate $\frac{2}{8}$ of a watermelon, Lily ate $\frac{1}{10}$, and Madelyn ate $\frac{1}{5}$. Estimate how much of the watermelon they ate. Explain.

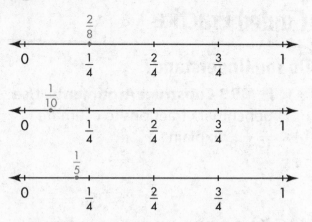

14. Gavin, Olivia, and Michael are writing a report together. Gavin has written $\frac{2}{5}$ of the report, Olivia has written $\frac{1}{8}$, and Michael has written $\frac{2}{10}$. Use number lines or benchmark fractions to estimate if they have more or less than $\frac{1}{2}$ of their report left to write.

15. **© MP.1 Make Sense and Persevere** Last year the Levitz family sold 16 boxes of nuts for $6 a box. This year, they only have 8 boxes to sell. How much should they charge per box to have the same income selling nuts as last year? Explain.

16. **Higher Order Thinking** Choose two fractions from the list that meet each condition.

$$\frac{5}{8} \qquad \frac{1}{10} \qquad \frac{3}{4} \qquad \frac{1}{5}$$

a. Their sum is greater than 1.
b. Their difference is close to 0.
c. Their sum is between $\frac{1}{2}$ and 1.

Use benchmark fractions. You can draw number lines to help.

© Common Core Assessment

17. Harry filled $\frac{1}{5}$ of a pitcher with water. Then he filled another $\frac{6}{10}$ of the pitcher with water. Estimate what fraction of the pitcher is filled with water. Use the number lines to explain.

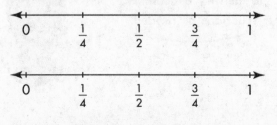

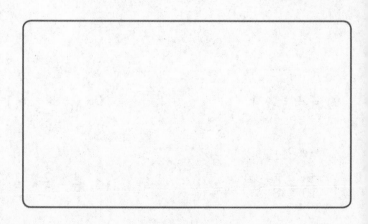

Help Practice Tools Games
Buddy

Another Look!

Jake ran $\frac{1}{10}$ of the distance to the school and walked $\frac{2}{6}$ of the distance. Estimate what fraction of the distance Jake still needs to travel to get to school.

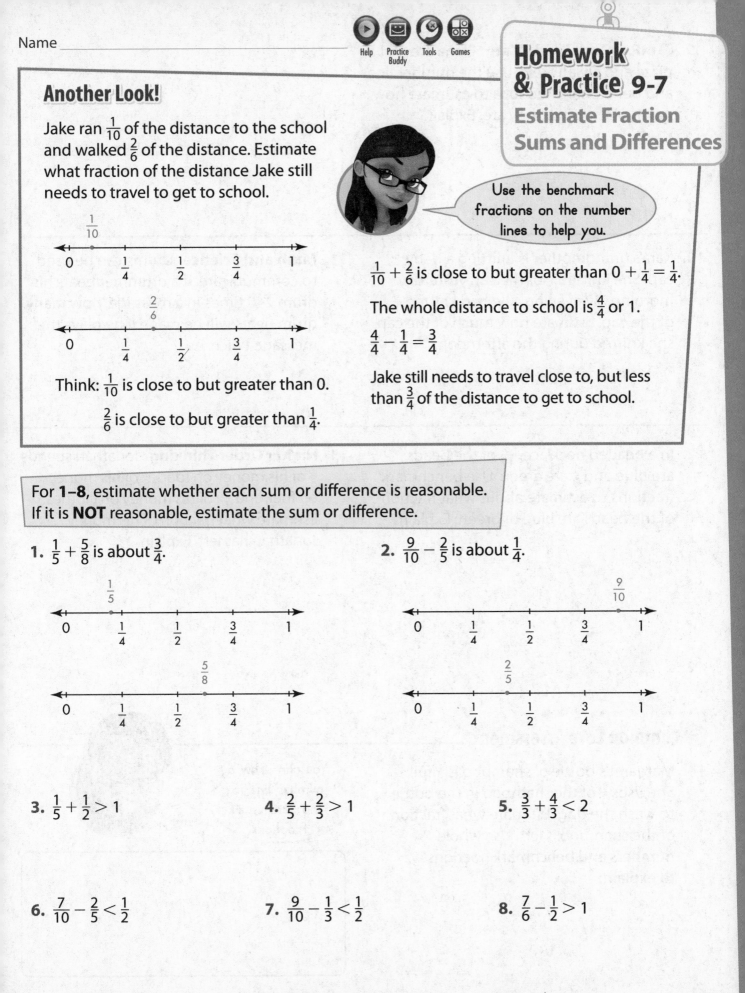

Use the benchmark fractions on the number lines to help you.

$\frac{1}{10}$

0   $\frac{1}{4}$ $\frac{1}{2}$ $\frac{3}{4}$ 1

$\frac{2}{6}$

0   $\frac{1}{4}$ $\frac{1}{2}$ $\frac{3}{4}$ 1

Think: $\frac{1}{10}$ is close to but greater than 0.

$\frac{2}{6}$ is close to but greater than $\frac{1}{4}$.

$\frac{1}{10} + \frac{2}{6}$ is close to but greater than $0 + \frac{1}{4} = \frac{1}{4}$.

The whole distance to school is $\frac{4}{4}$ or 1.

$\frac{4}{4} - \frac{1}{4} = \frac{3}{4}$

Jake still needs to travel close to, but less than $\frac{3}{4}$ of the distance to get to school.

For **1–8**, estimate whether each sum or difference is reasonable. If it is **NOT** reasonable, estimate the sum or difference.

1. $\frac{1}{5} + \frac{5}{8}$ is about $\frac{3}{4}$.

$\frac{1}{5}$

0   $\frac{1}{4}$ $\frac{1}{2}$ $\frac{3}{4}$ 1

$\frac{5}{8}$

0   $\frac{1}{4}$ $\frac{1}{2}$ $\frac{3}{4}$ 1

2. $\frac{9}{10} - \frac{2}{5}$ is about $\frac{1}{4}$.

$\frac{9}{10}$

0   $\frac{1}{4}$ $\frac{1}{2}$ $\frac{3}{4}$ 1

$\frac{2}{5}$

0   $\frac{1}{4}$ $\frac{1}{2}$ $\frac{3}{4}$ 1

3. $\frac{1}{5} + \frac{1}{2} > 1$

4. $\frac{2}{5} + \frac{2}{3} > 1$

5. $\frac{3}{3} + \frac{4}{3} < 2$

6. $\frac{7}{10} - \frac{2}{5} < \frac{1}{2}$

7. $\frac{9}{10} - \frac{1}{3} < \frac{1}{2}$

8. $\frac{7}{6} - \frac{1}{2} > 1$

9. **© MP.4 Model with Math** Elena ate $\frac{2}{8}$ of a pizza and Dylan ate $\frac{1}{5}$. Use the number lines and benchmark fractions to estimate how much of the pizza they ate. Explain.

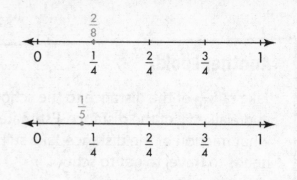

10. Kara's grandmother is knitting a baby cap. She knitted $\frac{1}{5}$ of the cap yesterday morning. By evening, she had knitted $\frac{7}{10}$ of the cap. Estimate how much of the cap she knitted during the afternoon.

11. **Math and Science** Drums can be used to communicate. If a drummer beats his drum 240 times in a message, how many drum beats will be made if he plays the message twice.

12. In a beaded necklace, $\frac{3}{12}$ of the beads are blue and $\frac{1}{3}$ are green. Use benchmark fractions to estimate about what fraction of the beads are blue or green. Explain.

13. **Higher Order Thinking** Jonathan spends $\frac{2}{8}$ of his money on food, $\frac{1}{5}$ of his money on fuel, and $\frac{2}{10}$ of his money on clothes. Estimate what fraction of his money Jonathan has left. Explain.

© Common Core Assessment

14. Margaret's bottle of shampoo is $\frac{7}{8}$ full. She uses $\frac{1}{3}$ of the shampoo in the bottle to wash the dog. Estimate what fraction of the shampoo is left. Use whole numbers and benchmark fractions to explain.

You can draw a number line to find benchmark fractions.

Name _____

Solve & Share

Tory is cutting loaves of bread into fourths. She needs to wrap $3\frac{3}{4}$ loaves to take to a luncheon and $1\frac{2}{4}$ loaves for a bake sale. How many loaves does Tory need to wrap for the luncheon and the bake sale? *Solve this problem any way you choose.*

I can ...
use models and equivalent fractions to help add and subtract mixed numbers.

© Content Standard 4.NF.B.3c
Mathematical Practices MP.2, MP.3, MP.5

You can select tools such as fraction strips or number lines to add mixed numbers.

Look Back! © **MP.2 Reasoning** How can you estimate the sum above?

Essential Question **How Can You Add or Subtract Mixed Numbers?**

A

Bill has 2 boards to use to make picture frames. What is the total length of the two boards? How much longer is one board than the other?

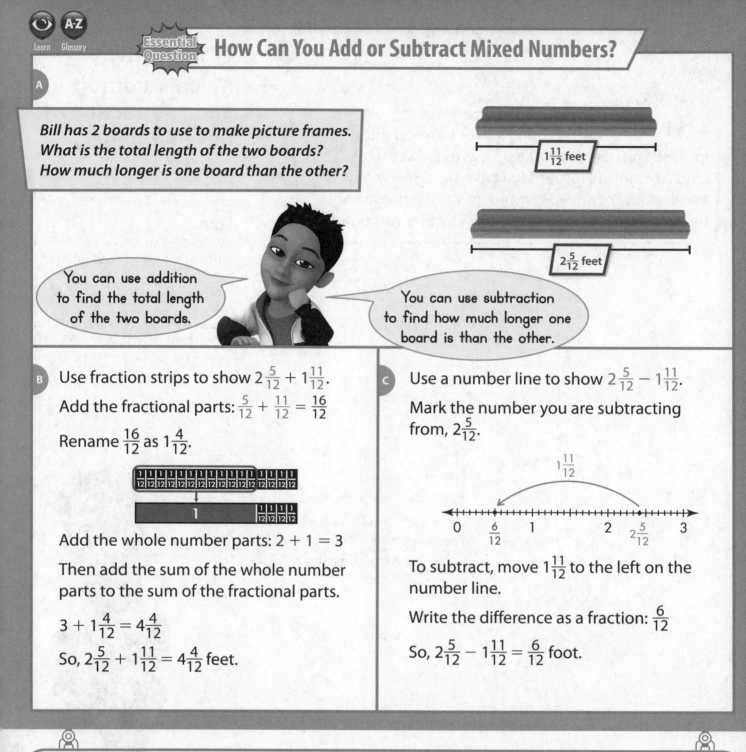

$1\frac{11}{12}$ feet

$2\frac{5}{12}$ feet

You can use addition to find the total length of the two boards.

You can use subtraction to find how much longer one board is than the other.

B   Use fraction strips to show $2\frac{5}{12} + 1\frac{11}{12}$.

Add the fractional parts: $\frac{5}{12} + \frac{11}{12} = \frac{16}{12}$

Rename $\frac{16}{12}$ as $1\frac{4}{12}$.

Add the whole number parts: $2 + 1 = 3$

Then add the sum of the whole number parts to the sum of the fractional parts.

$3 + 1\frac{4}{12} = 4\frac{4}{12}$

So, $2\frac{5}{12} + 1\frac{11}{12} = 4\frac{4}{12}$ feet.

C   Use a number line to show $2\frac{5}{12} - 1\frac{11}{12}$.

Mark the number you are subtracting from, $2\frac{5}{12}$.

$1\frac{11}{12}$

0   $\frac{6}{12}$ 1   2 $2\frac{5}{12}$ 3

To subtract, move $1\frac{11}{12}$ to the left on the number line.

Write the difference as a fraction: $\frac{6}{12}$

So, $2\frac{5}{12} - 1\frac{11}{12} = \frac{6}{12}$ foot.

Convince Me! © **MP.5 Use Appropriate Tools** Suppose Bill's boards were $2\frac{11}{12}$ feet and $1\frac{5}{12}$ feet. What would be the total length of the two boards? How much longer is one board than the other? Use fraction strips or draw number lines to show your work.

Name _____

☆Guided Practice*

Do You Understand?

1. ⓒ **MP.3 Construct Arguments** When adding mixed numbers, is it always necessary to rename the fractional sum? Explain.

Do You Know How?

For **2–5**, use fraction strips or number lines to find each sum or difference.

2. $1\frac{2}{5} + 2\frac{4}{5}$ 3. $1\frac{1}{4} + 2\frac{3}{4}$

4. $4\frac{2}{3} - 2\frac{1}{3}$ 5. $4\frac{1}{4} - 3\frac{3}{4}$

Independent Practice ☆

For **6–9**, use each model to find the sum or difference.

6. $2\frac{1}{4} - 1\frac{3}{4}$

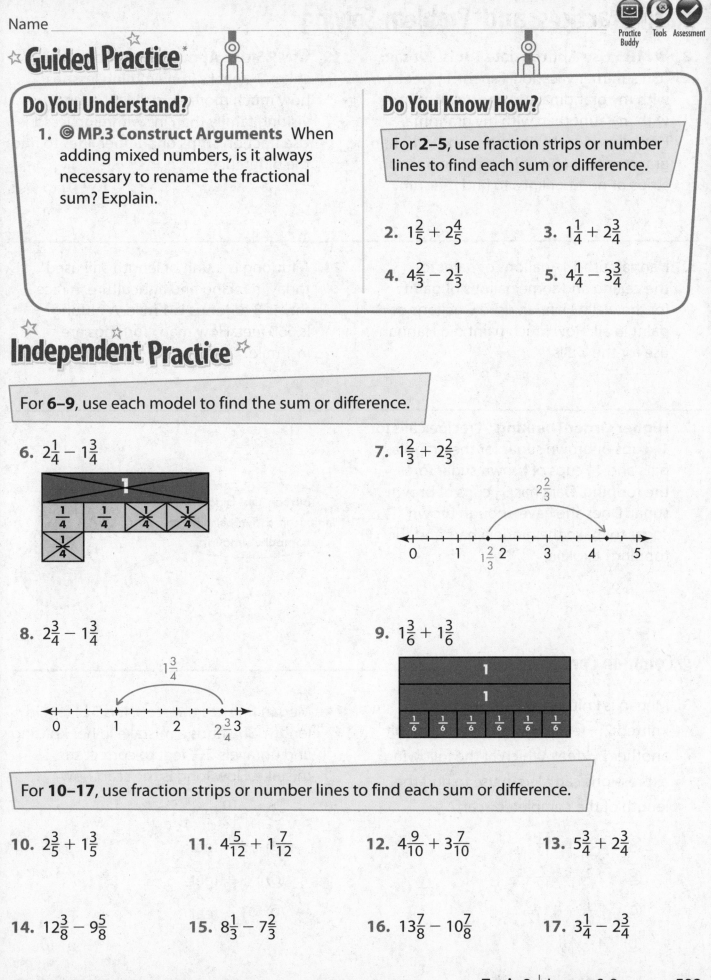

7. $1\frac{2}{3} + 2\frac{2}{3}$

8. $2\frac{3}{4} - 1\frac{3}{4}$

9. $1\frac{3}{6} + 1\frac{3}{6}$

For **10–17**, use fraction strips or number lines to find each sum or difference.

10. $2\frac{3}{5} + 1\frac{3}{5}$ 11. $4\frac{5}{12} + 1\frac{7}{12}$ 12. $4\frac{9}{10} + 3\frac{7}{10}$ 13. $5\frac{3}{4} + 2\frac{3}{4}$

14. $12\frac{3}{8} - 9\frac{5}{8}$ 15. $8\frac{1}{3} - 7\frac{2}{3}$ 16. $13\frac{7}{8} - 10\frac{7}{8}$ 17. $3\frac{1}{4} - 2\frac{3}{4}$

*For another example, see Set E on page 534.   **Topic 9** | Lesson 9-8   **509**

Math Practices and Problem Solving

18. **MP.5 Use Appropriate Tools** Kit said, "On summer vacation, I spent $1\frac{1}{2}$ weeks with my grandma and one week more with my aunt than with my grandma." How many weeks did she spend with her grandmother and her aunt? Use fraction strips or number lines to find the sum.

19. **MP.5 Use Appropriate Tools** If Kit spent $3\frac{1}{2}$ weeks in swimming lessons, how much more time did Kit spend visiting family than in swimming lessons? Use fraction strips or number lines to find the difference.

20. Hannah used $1\frac{5}{8}$ gallons of paint for the ceiling and some gallons of paint for the walls. Hannah used 6 gallons of paint in all. How much paint did Hannah use for the walls?

21. A furlong is a unit of length still used today in racing and agriculture. A race that is 8 furlongs is 1 mile. A furlong is 660 feet. How many furlongs are in 1 mile?

22. **Higher Order Thinking** A recipe calls for $1\frac{2}{3}$ cups of brown sugar for the granola bars and $1\frac{1}{3}$ cups of brown sugar for the topping. Dara has $3\frac{1}{4}$ cups of brown sugar. Does she have enough brown sugar to make the granola bars and the topping? Explain.

> You can use fraction strips or a number line to compare amounts.

Common Core Assessment

23. Megan is knitting a scarf. She has knitted $2\frac{7}{12}$ feet so far. She needs to knit another $2\frac{11}{12}$ feet. Which of the following expressions can Megan use to find the length of the completed scarf?

   Ⓐ $2\frac{7}{12} + 2\frac{11}{12}$

   Ⓑ $2\frac{5}{12} + 2\frac{7}{12}$

   Ⓒ $7\frac{1}{12} + 11\frac{1}{12}$

   Ⓓ $4 + \frac{11}{12}$

24. Megan finishes the scarf. It is $5\frac{6}{12}$ feet in length. She finds a mistake in her knitting and unravels $2\frac{4}{12}$ feet to correct the mistake. How long is the scarf now?

   Ⓐ $8\frac{10}{12}$ feet

   Ⓑ $5\frac{4}{12}$ feet

   Ⓒ $3\frac{2}{12}$ feet

   Ⓓ $1\frac{4}{12}$ feet

Help Practice Tools Games
      Buddy

Another Look!

You can use fraction strips or number lines to show the addition and subtraction of mixed numbers.

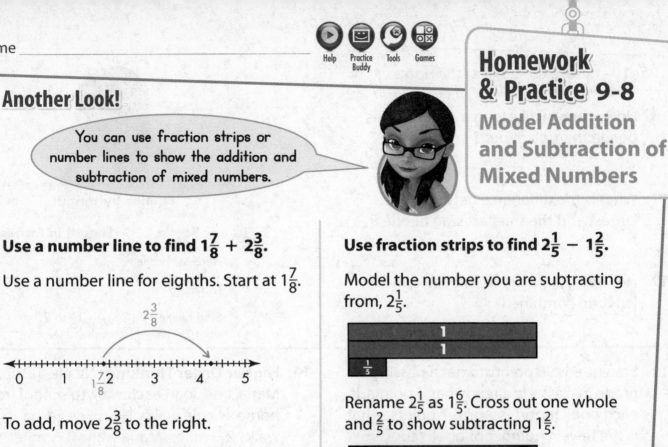

Use a number line to find $1\frac{7}{8} + 2\frac{3}{8}$.

Use a number line for eighths. Start at $1\frac{7}{8}$.

To add, move $2\frac{3}{8}$ to the right.

Write the sum as a fraction or a mixed number.

So, $1\frac{7}{8} + 2\frac{3}{8} = 4\frac{2}{8}$.

Use fraction strips to find $2\frac{1}{5} - 1\frac{2}{5}$.

Model the number you are subtracting from, $2\frac{1}{5}$.

Rename $2\frac{1}{5}$ as $1\frac{6}{5}$. Cross out one whole and $\frac{2}{5}$ to show subtracting $1\frac{2}{5}$.

Write the difference as a fraction.

So, $2\frac{1}{5} - 1\frac{2}{5} = \frac{4}{5}$.

For **1–9**, use fraction strips or number lines to find each sum or difference.

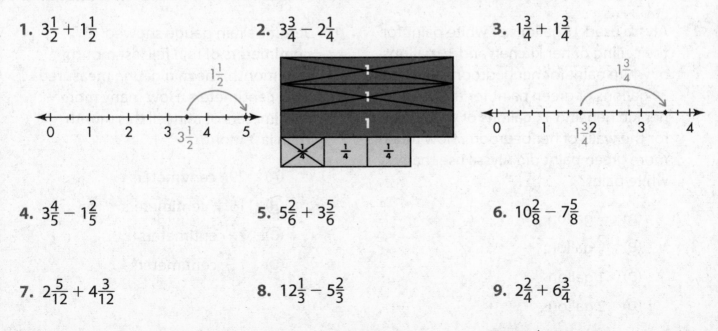

1. $3\frac{1}{2} + 1\frac{1}{2}$

2. $3\frac{3}{4} - 2\frac{1}{4}$

3. $1\frac{3}{4} + 1\frac{3}{4}$

4. $3\frac{4}{5} - 1\frac{2}{5}$

5. $5\frac{2}{6} + 3\frac{5}{6}$

6. $10\frac{2}{8} - 7\frac{5}{8}$

7. $2\frac{5}{12} + 4\frac{3}{12}$

8. $12\frac{1}{3} - 5\frac{2}{3}$

9. $2\frac{2}{4} + 6\frac{3}{4}$

For **10–12**, use the table at the right.

10. How many inches longer is a Hercules beetle than a ladybug?

11. What is the difference between the largest and the smallest stag beetles?

12. How long are a Hercules beetle and a ladybug combined?

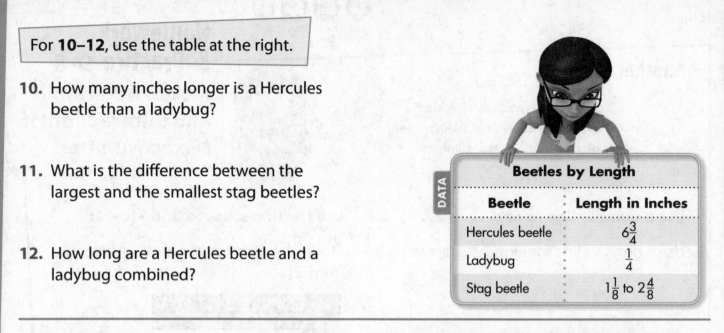

Beetles by Length	
Beetle	**Length in Inches**
Hercules beetle	$6\frac{3}{4}$
Ladybug	$\frac{1}{4}$
Stag beetle	$1\frac{1}{8}$ to $2\frac{4}{8}$

13. Stan needs 90 points to get a passing grade in class. He already has 6 points. If each book report is worth 7 points, what is the fewest number of book reports Stan can do and still pass the class?

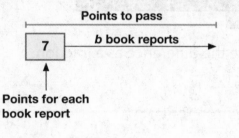

Points to pass

7 | *b* book reports →

Points for each book report

14. **Higher Order Thinking** Nicole, Tasha, Maria, and Joan each walk to school from home. Nicole walks $1\frac{11}{12}$ miles. Tasha walks $2\frac{1}{12}$ miles. Maria walks $1\frac{7}{12}$ miles. Joan walks $2\frac{2}{12}$ miles. How can you find how much farther Joan walks to school than Maria?

© **Common Core Assessment**

15. Alyssa used $1\frac{2}{3}$ gallons of white paint for the ceiling of her kitchen and $1\frac{2}{3}$ gallons of white paint for her bedroom. She used $3\frac{2}{3}$ gallons of green paint for the walls of her kitchen and $1\frac{2}{3}$ gallons of yellow paint for the walls of her bedroom. How much more green paint did Alyssa use than white paint?

Ⓐ $\frac{1}{3}$ gallon

Ⓑ $\frac{2}{3}$ gallon

Ⓒ 1 gallon

Ⓓ 2 gallons

16. Jerome's rain gauge showed $13\frac{9}{10}$ centimeters of rain fell last month. This month, the rain gauge measured $15\frac{3}{10}$ centimeters. How many more centimeters of rain fell this month than last month?

Ⓐ $29\frac{1}{5}$ centimeters

Ⓑ $15\frac{3}{10}$ centimeters

Ⓒ $2\frac{2}{5}$ centimeters

Ⓓ $1\frac{4}{10}$ centimeters

Name _____

Solve & Share

Joaquin used $1\frac{3}{6}$ cups of apple juice and $1\frac{4}{6}$ cups of orange juice in a recipe for punch. How much juice did Joaquin use? **Solve this problem any way you choose.**

I can ...
use equivalent fractions and properties of operations to add mixed numbers with like denominators.

© Content Standard 4.NF.B.3c
Mathematical Practices MP.1, MP.2, MP.3, MP.8

$1\frac{3}{6}$ cups apple juice

$1\frac{4}{6}$ cups orange juice

Generalize. You can use what you know about adding fractions to solve this problem.

Look Back! © MP.2 Reasoning Without solving the problem, use reasoning to estimate the sum. Will the sum be more or less than 3? How much more or less? Explain.

Essential Question: How Can You Add Mixed Numbers?

A

Brenda mixes sand with $2\frac{7}{8}$ cups of potting mixture to prepare soil for her plant. After mixing them together, how many cups of soil does Brenda have?

$1\frac{3}{8}$ cups sand

You can use properties of operations to add mixed numbers. When you break apart a mixed number to add, you are using the Commutative and the Associative Properties.

B Find $2\frac{7}{8} + 1\frac{3}{8}$ by breaking up mixed numbers.

$$2\frac{7}{8} + 1\frac{3}{8} = (2 + 1) + \left(\frac{7}{8} + \frac{3}{8}\right)$$

Add the fractions.	Then add whole numbers.
$2\frac{7}{8}$	$2\frac{7}{8}$
$+ 1\frac{3}{8}$	$+ 1\frac{3}{8}$
$\frac{10}{8}$	$3\frac{10}{8}$

Write the fraction as a mixed number.

$$3\frac{10}{8} = 3 + \frac{8}{8} + \frac{2}{8} = 4\frac{2}{8}$$

C Find $2\frac{7}{8} + 1\frac{3}{8}$ by adding equivalent fractions.

$$2\frac{7}{8} = 2 + \frac{7}{8} = \frac{16}{8} + \frac{7}{8} = \frac{23}{8}$$

$$1\frac{3}{8} = 1 + \frac{3}{8} = \frac{8}{8} + \frac{3}{8} = \frac{11}{8}$$

$$\frac{23}{8} + \frac{11}{8} = \frac{34}{8}$$

Write $\frac{34}{8}$ as a mixed number.

$$\frac{34}{8} = \frac{8}{8} + \frac{8}{8} + \frac{8}{8} + \frac{8}{8} + \frac{2}{8} = 4\frac{2}{8}$$

Brenda has $4\frac{2}{8}$ cups of soil.

Convince Me! © **MP.2 Reasoning** How is adding mixed numbers like adding fractions and whole numbers?

☆Guided Practice*

Do You Understand?

1. Brenda adds $1\frac{1}{8}$ cups of peat moss to her soil in the problem on the previous page. How much soil does Brenda now have? Explain.

2. Ⓒ **MP.1 Make Sense and Persevere** Use another strategy to find the sum of $4\frac{2}{8} + 1\frac{1}{8}$.

Do You Know How?

For **3–8**, find each sum.

3.
$$\begin{array}{r} 1\frac{7}{8} \\ + 1\frac{2}{8} \\ \hline \end{array}$$

4.
$$\begin{array}{r} 2\frac{4}{10} \\ + 5\frac{5}{10} \\ \hline \end{array}$$

5. $4\frac{2}{3} + 1\frac{2}{3}$

6. $6\frac{5}{12} + 4\frac{11}{12}$

7. $2\frac{1}{3} + 2\frac{1}{3}$

8. $8\frac{9}{12} + 5\frac{5}{12}$

Independent Practice ☆

Leveled Practice For **9–22**, find each sum by adding mixed numbers or by adding equivalent fractions.

9. a. Add the fractions.
   b. Add the whole numbers.
   c. Write the fraction as a mixed number.

$$\begin{array}{r} 1\frac{3}{6} \\ + 2\frac{4}{6} \\ \hline \square = \square \end{array}$$

10. a. Write the mixed numbers as fractions.
    b. Add the fractions.
    c. Write the fraction as a mixed number.

$$\begin{array}{r} 2\frac{1}{4} = \dfrac{\square}{\ } \\ + 3\frac{2}{4} = + \dfrac{\square}{\ } \\ \hline \dfrac{\square}{\ } = \square \end{array}$$

11.
$$\begin{array}{r} 2\frac{5}{6} \\ + 5\frac{4}{6} \\ \hline \end{array}$$

12.
$$\begin{array}{r} 11\frac{7}{10} \\ + 10\frac{9}{10} \\ \hline \end{array}$$

13.
$$\begin{array}{r} 9\frac{7}{8} \\ + 7\frac{5}{8} \\ \hline \end{array}$$

14.
$$\begin{array}{r} 5\frac{7}{8} \\ + 8\frac{1}{8} \\ \hline \end{array}$$

15. $4\frac{1}{10} + 6\frac{5}{10}$

16. $9\frac{7}{12} + 4\frac{9}{12}$

17. $5 + 3\frac{1}{8}$

18. $8\frac{3}{4} + 7\frac{3}{4}$

19. $2\frac{4}{5} + 7\frac{3}{5}$

20. $3\frac{2}{6} + 8\frac{5}{6}$

21. $1\frac{7}{12} + 2\frac{10}{12}$

22. $3\frac{6}{8} + 9\frac{3}{8}$

Math Practices and Problem Solving

For **23**, use the map at the right.

23. a. Find the distance from the start of the trail to the end of the trail.

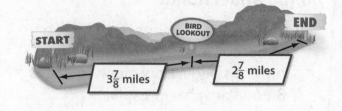

START $3\frac{7}{8}$ miles BIRD LOOKOUT $2\frac{7}{8}$ miles END

b. Linda walked from the start of the trail to the bird lookout and back. Did Linda walk more or less than if she had walked from the start of the trail to the end?

24. Joe biked $1\frac{9}{12}$ miles from home to the lake, then went some miles around the lake, and then back home. Joe biked a total of $4\frac{9}{12}$ miles. How many miles did Joe bike around the lake?

25. © **MP.2 Reasoning** The bus took $4\frac{3}{5}$ hours to get from the station to Portland and $3\frac{4}{5}$ hours to get from Portland to Seattle. How long did the bus take to get from the station to Seattle?

26. Higher Order Thinking A male Parson's chameleon can be up to $23\frac{3}{4}$ inches long. It can extend its tongue up to $35\frac{1}{4}$ inches. What are 3 possible lengths for the chameleon when its tongue is extended?

Tongue can extend up to $35\frac{1}{4}$ inches.

© Common Core Assessment

27. How long an extension cord can Julie make by attaching a $22\frac{3}{8}$ foot and a $26\frac{6}{8}$ foot cord together? Select all the possible sums.

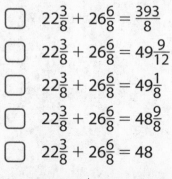

☐ $22\frac{3}{8} + 26\frac{6}{8} = \frac{393}{8}$

☐ $22\frac{3}{8} + 26\frac{6}{8} = 49\frac{9}{12}$

☐ $22\frac{3}{8} + 26\frac{6}{8} = 49\frac{1}{8}$

☐ $22\frac{3}{8} + 26\frac{6}{8} = 48\frac{9}{8}$

☐ $22\frac{3}{8} + 26\frac{6}{8} = 48$

28. Mary skips $22\frac{1}{3}$ yards down a trail, then hops another $15\frac{2}{3}$ yards. How far is Mary down the trail? Select all the possible sums.

☐ $22\frac{1}{3} + 15\frac{2}{3} = 37$

☐ $22\frac{1}{3} + 15\frac{2}{3} = 37\frac{3}{3}$

☐ $22\frac{1}{3} + 15\frac{2}{3} = 38$

☐ $22\frac{1}{3} - 15\frac{2}{3} = 6\frac{2}{3}$

☐ $22\frac{1}{3} + 15\frac{2}{3} = \frac{114}{3}$

Help Practice Buddy Tools Games

Another Look!

Randy played basketball for $2\frac{5}{6}$ hours on Saturday. He played for $1\frac{3}{6}$ hours on Sunday. How many hours did Randy play basketball on the weekend?

Add Mixed Numbers

a. Add the fractions.

b. Add the whole numbers.

c. Write the fraction as a mixed number.

$$2\frac{5}{6}$$
$$+1\frac{3}{6}$$
$$\overline{3\frac{8}{6}} = 4\frac{2}{6}$$

Randy played basketball for $4\frac{2}{6}$ hours on the weekend.

Add Fractions

a. Write the mixed numbers as fractions.

b. Add the fractions.

c. Write the fraction as a mixed number.

$$2\frac{5}{6} = \frac{17}{6}$$
$$+1\frac{3}{6} = +\frac{9}{6}$$
$$\overline{\frac{26}{6}} = 4\frac{2}{6}$$

You can add mixed numbers with like denominators using properties of operations.

For **1–12**, find each sum by adding mixed numbers or adding equivalent fractions.

1. $\begin{aligned}2\frac{10}{12}\\+3\frac{3}{12}\end{aligned}$

2. $\begin{aligned}1\frac{3}{8}\\+6\frac{6}{8}\end{aligned}$

3. $\begin{aligned}5\frac{4}{10}\\+4\frac{2}{10}\end{aligned}$

4. $\begin{aligned}10\frac{2}{6}\\+\ \ \frac{3}{6}\end{aligned}$

5. $3\frac{3}{12} + 6\frac{8}{12}$

6. $1\frac{2}{5} + 3\frac{1}{5}$

7. $2\frac{10}{12} + 3\frac{9}{12}$

8. $7\frac{2}{6} + 8\frac{5}{6}$

9. $4\frac{3}{4} + 2\frac{2}{4}$

10. $11\frac{9}{10} + 3\frac{2}{10}$

11. $5\frac{8}{12} + 3\frac{5}{12}$

12. $21\frac{11}{12} + 17\frac{5}{12}$

13. **A-Z** **Vocabulary** Use the vocabulary words *mixed number* and *fractions* to complete the sentence.

When adding mixed numbers, you first add the _____, then add the whole numbers. Finally, you write the

_____ .

14. © **MP.3 Critique Reasoning** Alan used 9 as an estimate for $3\frac{7}{10} + 5\frac{4}{10}$. He added and got $9\frac{1}{10}$ for the actual sum. Is Alan's answer reasonable?

15. Ruth needs $2\frac{1}{4}$ cups of flour for one cake recipe and $2\frac{3}{4}$ cups of flour for another cake recipe. If she makes both cakes, how much flour will Ruth need altogether?

16. A "stone" is an old unit of weight used in Ireland and England to measure potatoes. A stone is 14 pounds and 80 stones make up half of a "long ton." How many pounds is half of a long ton?

17. **Higher Order Thinking** Tirzah wants to put a fence around her garden. She has 22 yards of fence material. Does Tirzah have enough to go all the way around the garden?

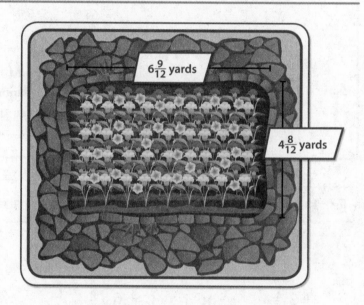

$6\frac{9}{12}$ yards

$4\frac{8}{12}$ yards

© **Common Core Assessment**

18. Pookie weighs $12\frac{7}{8}$ pounds. Rascal weighs $13\frac{3}{8}$ pounds. What is the total weight of both cats? Select all the possible sums.

☐ $26\frac{2}{8}$ pounds

☐ $26\frac{1}{4}$ pounds

☐ $\frac{210}{8}$ pounds

☐ $13\frac{3}{8}$ pounds

☐ $12\frac{7}{8}$ pounds

19. Rex weighs $30\frac{1}{4}$ pounds. Buckey weighs $50\frac{2}{4}$ pounds. What is the total weight of both dogs? Select all possible sums.

☐ $20\frac{1}{4}$ pounds

☐ 80 pounds

☐ $80\frac{3}{4}$ pounds

☐ $\frac{323}{4}$ pounds

☐ 81 pounds

Name _____

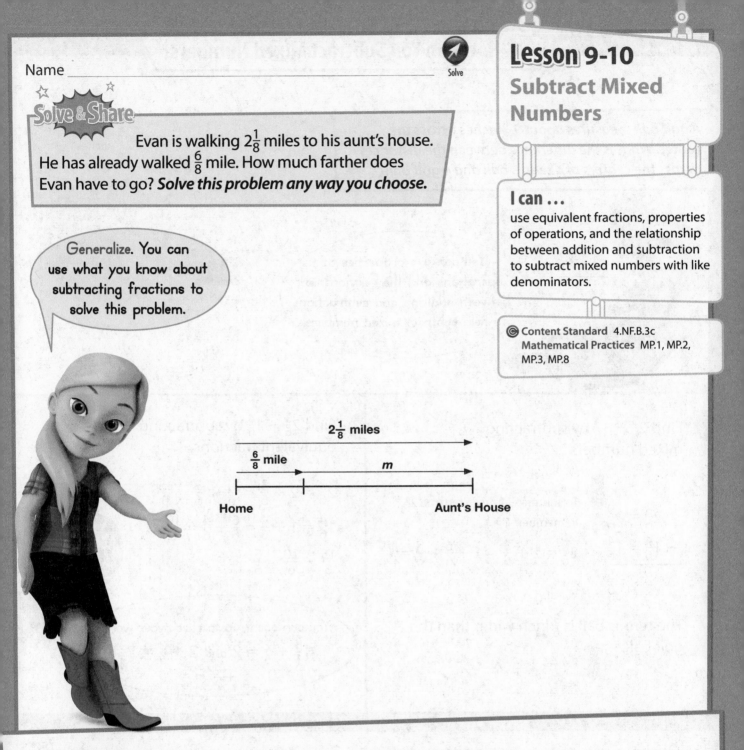

Solve & Share

Evan is walking $2\frac{1}{8}$ miles to his aunt's house. He has already walked $\frac{6}{8}$ mile. How much farther does Evan have to go? *Solve this problem any way you choose.*

Generalize. You can use what you know about subtracting fractions to solve this problem.

I can ...
use equivalent fractions, properties of operations, and the relationship between addition and subtraction to subtract mixed numbers with like denominators.

Content Standard 4.NF.B.3c
Mathematical Practices MP.1, MP.2, MP.3, MP.8

$2\frac{1}{8}$ miles

$\frac{6}{8}$ mile m

Home   Aunt's House

Look Back! MP.3 Critique Reasoning Sarah found Evan has $2\frac{7}{8}$ miles left to walk. Is Sarah's answer reasonable? Use estimation to explain.

Essential Question

How Can You Subtract Mixed Numbers?

A

A golf ball measures about $1\frac{4}{6}$ inches across the center. What is the difference between the distances across the centers of a tennis ball and a golf ball?

$2\frac{3}{6}$ inches

You can use properties of operations and the relationship between addition and subtraction to help subtract mixed numbers.

B Find $2\frac{3}{6} - 1\frac{4}{6}$ by subtracting mixed numbers.

To subtract $\frac{4}{6}$ from $\frac{3}{6}$, rename $2\frac{3}{6}$. Remember, $1 = \frac{6}{6}$.

$2\frac{3}{6} = 1\frac{9}{6}$

$\begin{array}{r} 2\frac{3}{6} = 1\frac{9}{6} \\ -\ 1\frac{4}{6} = 1\frac{4}{6} \\ \hline \frac{5}{6} \end{array}$

$2\frac{3}{6} = 2 + \frac{3}{6} = 1 + \frac{6}{6} + \frac{3}{6} = 1\frac{9}{6}$

The tennis ball is $\frac{5}{6}$ inch wider than the golf ball.

C Find $2\frac{3}{6} - 1\frac{4}{6}$ by subtracting equivalent fractions.

$2\frac{3}{6} = 2 + \frac{3}{6} = \frac{12}{6} + \frac{3}{6} = \frac{15}{6}$

$1\frac{4}{6} = 1 + \frac{4}{6} = \frac{6}{6} + \frac{4}{6} = \frac{10}{6}$

$\frac{15}{6} - \frac{10}{6} = \frac{5}{6}$

You can count up to check your work!

$1\frac{4}{6} + \frac{2}{6} = 2$ and $2 + \frac{3}{6} = 2\frac{3}{6}$

$\frac{2}{6} + \frac{3}{6} = \frac{5}{6}$

Convince Me! © MP.2 Reasoning Explain why you rename $4\frac{1}{4}$ to find $4\frac{1}{4} - \frac{3}{4}$.

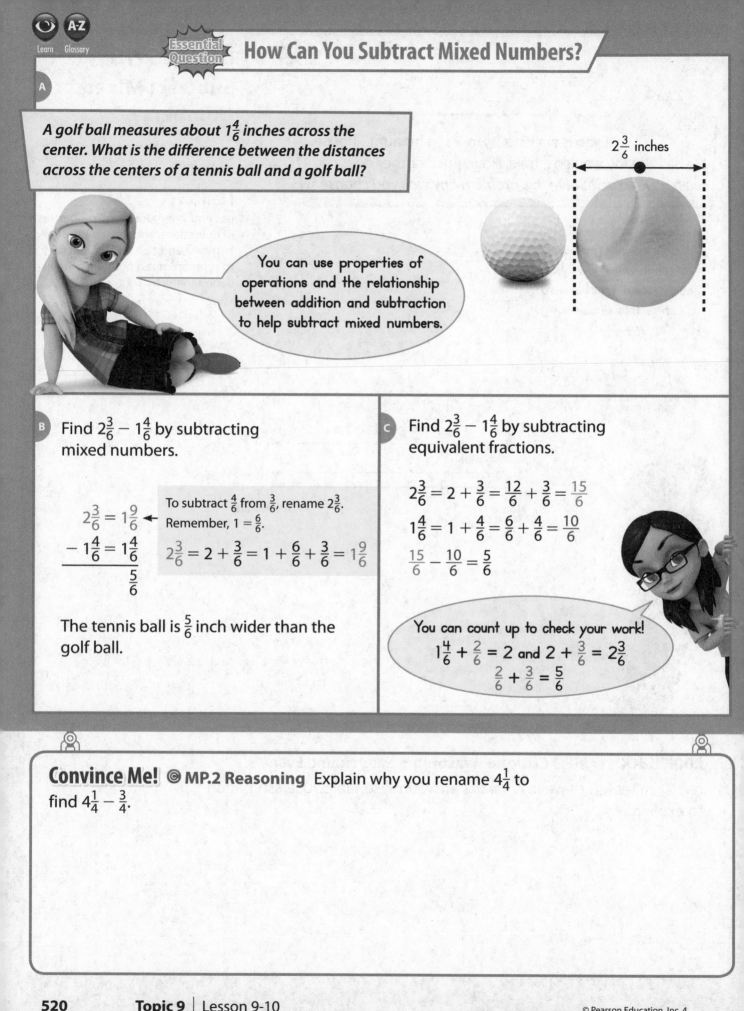

Name _____

☆ Guided Practice ☆

Do You Understand?

1. A hole at the golf course is $3\frac{3}{6}$ inches wide. How much wider is the hole than the golf ball?

2. ⓒ MP.3 Construct Arguments Why might you need to rename some whole numbers when subtracting?

Do You Know How?

For **3–8**, find each difference.

3. $\begin{array}{r} 7\frac{5}{8} \\ -\ 2\frac{4}{8} \\ \hline \end{array}$

4. $\begin{array}{r} 5 \\ -\ 2\frac{3}{4} \\ \hline \end{array}$

5. $6\frac{3}{10} - 1\frac{8}{10}$

6. $9\frac{4}{12} - 4\frac{9}{12}$

7. $4\frac{5}{6} - 2\frac{1}{6}$

8. $1\frac{9}{12} - \frac{10}{12}$

Independent Practice ☆

For **9–24**, find each difference by subtracting mixed numbers or subtracting equivalent fractions.

9. $\begin{array}{r} 8\frac{7}{8} \\ -\ 2\frac{4}{8} \\ \hline \end{array}$

10. $\begin{array}{r} 4\frac{5}{10} \\ -\ 1\frac{9}{10} \\ \hline \end{array}$

11. $\begin{array}{r} 4\frac{1}{8} \\ -\ 1\frac{4}{8} \\ \hline \end{array}$

12. $\begin{array}{r} 6 \\ -\ 2\frac{4}{5} \\ \hline \end{array}$

13. $6\frac{1}{3} - 5\frac{2}{3}$

14. $9\frac{2}{4} - 6\frac{3}{4}$

15. $8\frac{3}{8} - 3\frac{5}{8}$

16. $7 - 3\frac{1}{2}$

17. $15\frac{1}{6} - 4\frac{5}{6}$

18. $13\frac{1}{12} - 8\frac{3}{12}$

19. $6\frac{2}{5} - 2\frac{3}{5}$

20. $10\frac{5}{10} - 4\frac{7}{10}$

21. $12\frac{9}{12} - 10\frac{7}{12}$

22. $25\frac{1}{4} - 20$

23. $17 - 2\frac{1}{8}$

24. $26\frac{3}{5} - 13\frac{4}{5}$

*For another example, see Set E on page 534.

Math Practices and Problem Solving

25. The average weight of a basketball is $21\frac{1}{8}$ ounces. The average weight of a baseball is $5\frac{2}{8}$ ounces. How many more ounces does the basketball weigh?

26. What is the value of the 4 in 284,612?

27. Two of the smallest mammals on Earth are the Bumblebee Bat and the Etruscan Pygmy Shrew. How much shorter is the bat than the shrew?

Bumblebee Bat
Length $1\frac{1}{5}$ inches

28. © **MP.1 Make Sense and Persevere** The average length of an adult female hand is about $6\frac{3}{5}$ inches. About how much longer is the hand than the lengths of the bat and shrew combined?

Etruscan Pygmy Shrew
Length $1\frac{2}{5}$ inches

29. Jack made $5\frac{1}{4}$ dozen cookies for the bake sale, and his sister made $3\frac{3}{4}$ dozen cookies. How many more dozen cookies did Jack make than his sister?

30. **Higher Order Thinking** Jenna has a spool that contains $5\frac{3}{4}$ meters of ribbon. She uses $3\frac{2}{4}$ meters for a school project and $1\frac{1}{4}$ meters for a bow. How much ribbon remains on the spool?

© Common Core Assessment

31. Last week, the office used $7\frac{1}{12}$ boxes of paper. This week, they used $3\frac{5}{12}$ boxes of paper. How many more boxes did they use last week than this week? Use equivalent fractions to solve.

- Ⓐ $10\frac{1}{2}$ boxes
- Ⓑ $4\frac{2}{3}$ boxes
- Ⓒ $4\frac{1}{3}$ boxes
- Ⓓ $3\frac{8}{12}$ boxes

32. A store sold $6\frac{1}{5}$ cases of juice on Friday and $4\frac{4}{5}$ cases of juice on Saturday. How many more cases of juice did the store sell on Friday than on Saturday?

- Ⓐ 11 cases
- Ⓑ $3\frac{1}{5}$ cases
- Ⓒ $2\frac{2}{5}$ cases
- Ⓓ $1\frac{2}{5}$ cases

Help Practice Tools Games
       Buddy

Another Look!

Janet grew a pumpkin that weighs $13\frac{3}{4}$ pounds and a melon that weighs $8\frac{2}{4}$ pounds. How much heavier is the pumpkin than the melon?

Subtract Mixed Numbers

$13\frac{3}{4}$
$-\ 8\frac{2}{4}$
$\overline{\ \ 5\frac{1}{4}}$

a. Subtract the fractions. Rename whole numbers as fractions as needed.

b. Subtract the whole numbers.

Subtract Fractions

a. Write the mixed numbers as fractions.

b. Subtract the fractions.

c. Write the fraction as a mixed number.

$13\frac{3}{4} = \dfrac{55}{4}$
$-\ 8\frac{2}{4} = -\dfrac{34}{4}$
$\overline{\qquad \dfrac{21}{4} = 5\frac{1}{4}}$

The pumpkin is $5\frac{1}{4}$ pounds heavier than the melon.

You can subtract mixed numbers with like denominators using properties of operations.

For **1–16**, find each difference by subtracting mixed numbers or subtracting equivalent fractions.

1. $10\frac{3}{4}$
   $-\ 7\frac{1}{4}$

2. $7\frac{4}{6}$
   $-\ 2\frac{3}{6}$

3. 3
   $-\ 2\frac{2}{3}$

4. $17\frac{8}{12}$
   $-\ 12\frac{3}{12}$

5. $9\frac{2}{6} - 6\frac{5}{6}$

6. $4\frac{1}{5} - 2\frac{3}{5}$

7. $6\frac{3}{12} - 3\frac{4}{12}$

8. $5\frac{2}{8} - 3\frac{7}{8}$

9. $8\frac{1}{4} - 7\frac{3}{4}$

10. $2\frac{9}{10} - 2\frac{5}{10}$

11. $6\frac{5}{6} - 5\frac{4}{6}$

12. $3 - 1\frac{3}{4}$

13. $11 - 2\frac{1}{2}$

14. $42\frac{6}{10} - 10$

15. $18\frac{1}{5} - 2\frac{2}{5}$

16. $27\frac{2}{6} - 12\frac{1}{6}$

17. **A-Z Vocabulary** Use a vocabulary word to complete the sentence.

A number that has a whole number part and a fraction part is a called a(n) _____.

18. Some of the world's smallest horses include Thumbelina who stands $17\frac{1}{4}$ inches tall, Black Beauty who stands $18\frac{2}{4}$ inches tall, and Einstein who stands 14 inches tall.

   a. How much taller is Black Beauty than Thumbelina?

   b. How much taller is Thumbelina than Einstein?

19. **© MP.2 Reasoning** If Carol hangs a picture using $\frac{3}{8}$ yard of a wire that is $1\frac{1}{8}$ yards long, how much wire will Carol have left?

20. Write 6,219 in expanded form.

21. **Higher Order Thinking** Some of the largest insects in the world include the Rhinoceros Beetle, the Giant Walking Stick, and the Giant Weta Beetle. How much longer is the Giant Walking Stick than the Rhinoceros Beetle and the Giant Weta Beetle combined?

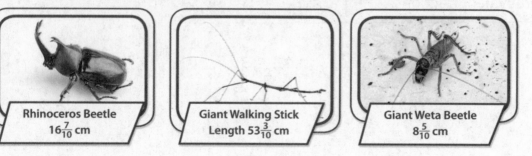

Rhinoceros Beetle
$16\frac{7}{10}$ cm

Giant Walking Stick
Length $53\frac{3}{10}$ cm

Giant Weta Beetle
$8\frac{5}{10}$ cm

© Common Core Assessment

22. Jessie needs a board $7\frac{9}{12}$ feet long. She has a board $9\frac{1}{12}$ feet long. How much of the length does Jessie need to cut from the board? Use equivalent fractions to solve.

   (A) $1\frac{1}{3}$ feet

   (B) $2\frac{8}{12}$ feet

   (C) $2\frac{2}{3}$ feet

   (D) $16\frac{10}{12}$ feet

23. Robyn ran $5\frac{3}{4}$ miles last week. She ran $4\frac{1}{4}$ miles this week. How many more miles did Robyn run last week? Use equivalent fractions to solve.

   (A) $1\frac{1}{4}$ miles

   (B) $1\frac{1}{2}$ miles

   (C) $1\frac{3}{4}$ miles

   (D) 10 miles

Name _____

Math Practices and Problem Solving

Lesson 9-11
Model with Math

Solve & Share

The table shows how long Jamie studied for a math test over 3 days. How much more time did Jamie spend studying on Tuesday and Wednesday than on Thursday?

DATA	Day of the Week	Time Jamie Studied
	Tuesday	$1\frac{3}{4}$ hours
	Wednesday	$\frac{3}{4}$ hour
	Thursday	$\frac{2}{4}$ hour

I can ...
use math I know to represent and solve problems.

Ⓒ **Mathematical Practices** MP.4 Also MP.1, MP.2, MP.5
Content Standards 4.NF.B.3d, 4.NF.B.3a

Thinking Habits

Be a good thinker!
These questions can help you.

• How can I use math I know to help solve this problem?

• How can I use pictures, objects, or an equation to represent the problem?

• How can I use numbers, words, and symbols to solve the problem?

Look Back! Ⓒ **MP.4 Model with Math** What representations can you use to help solve this problem?

Essential Question **How Can You Use Math to Model Problems?**

Brad and his father hiked the Gadsen Trail and the Rosebriar Trail on Saturday. They hiked the Eureka Trail on Sunday. How much farther did they hike on Saturday than on Sunday?

Gadsen Trail
$1\frac{9}{10}$ mile

Rosebriar Trail
$\frac{5}{10}$ mile

Eureka Trail
$\frac{6}{10}$ mile

What do you need to find?

I need to find how far Brad and his father hiked on Saturday and much farther they hiked on Saturday than on Sunday.

$2\frac{4}{10}$ miles on Saturday

$1\frac{9}{10}$	$\frac{5}{10}$

How can I model with math?

I can

- use previously learned concepts and skills.

- use bar diagrams and equations to represent and solve this problem.

- decide if my results make sense.

Here's my thinking.

Find $2\frac{4}{10} - \frac{6}{10}$.

Use a bar diagram and write an equation to solve.

$2\frac{4}{10}$ miles	

$\frac{6}{10}$	d

$2\frac{4}{10} - \frac{6}{10} = d$ $d = 1\frac{8}{10}$

Brad and his father hiked $1\frac{8}{10}$ miles farther on Saturday than on Sunday.

Convince Me! © **MP.4 Model with Math**   How do the bar diagrams help you decide if your answer makes sense?

Name _____

© **MP.4 Model with Math**

Alisa hiked a trail that was $\frac{9}{10}$ mile and Joseph hiked a trail that was $\frac{5}{10}$ mile. How much farther did Alisa hike than Joseph?

When you model with math, you use math to represent and solve a problem.

1. Draw a bar diagram to represent the problem and show the relationships among the quantities.

2. What equation can you write to represent the problem?

3. How much farther did Alisa hike than Joseph?

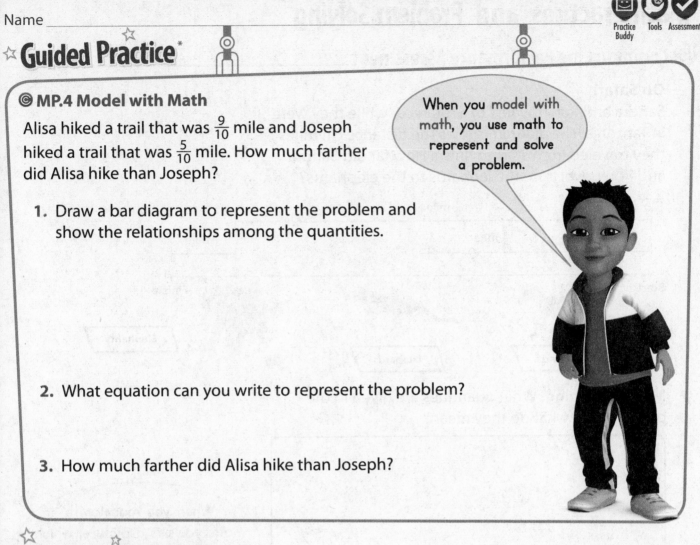

☆ **Independent Practice** ☆

© **MP.4 Model with Math**

The smallest female spider measures about $\frac{3}{5}$ millimeter in length. The smallest male spider measures about $\frac{1}{5}$ millimeter in length. How much longer is the smallest female spider than the smallest male spider? Use Exercises 4–6 to answer the question.

4. Draw a picture and write an equation to represent the problem.

5. What previously learned math can you use to solve the problem?

6. How much longer is the smallest female spider than the smallest male spider?

Math Practices and Problem Solving

© Common Core Performance Assessment

On Safari

Sandra and Ron traveled in a safari car while they were in Tanzania. The diagram shows the distances in miles they traveled from start to finish. How far did Sandra and Ron travel from the leopards to the elephants?

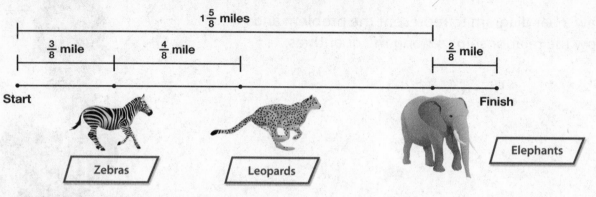

7. **MP.2 Reasoning** What quantities are given in the problem and what do they mean?

8. **MP.1 Make Sense and Persevere** What is a good plan for solving the problem?

When you model with math, you use a picture, which shows how the quantities in the problem are related.

9. **MP.4 Model with Math** Draw pictures and write and solve equations to find how far Sandra and Ron travel from the leopards to the elephants.

Help Practice Tools Games
      Buddy

Another Look!

Tina built $\frac{1}{8}$ of a model airplane on Saturday and $\frac{4}{8}$ on Sunday. She built $\frac{3}{8}$ more on Monday. How much more of the model airplane did she build on the weekend than on the weekday?

Tell how you can use math to model the problem.

• I can use previously learned concepts and skills.

• I can use bar diagrams and equations to represent and solve this problem.

• I can decide if my results make sense.

When you model with math, you use previously learned math to solve a problem.

Draw a bar diagram and write and solve equations.

$\frac{1}{8} + \frac{4}{8} = \frac{5}{8}$ on the weekend

$\frac{5}{8} - \frac{3}{8} = n$

$n = \frac{2}{8}$

$\frac{5}{8}$	
$\frac{3}{8}$	n

Tina built $\frac{2}{8}$ more of the model airplane on the weekend than on the weekday.

© **MP.4 Model with Math**

On Nick's playlist, $\frac{5}{12}$ of the songs are pop. What fraction of the songs are **NOT** pop? Use Exercises 1–3 to answer the question.

1. How can you draw a picture and write an equation to represent the problem?

2. What previously learned math can you use to solve the problem?

3. What fraction of the songs on Nick's playlist are **NOT** pop?

Ian and Rachel each made a trail mix. The amounts of ingredients they have are shown. Ian used all of the coconut, dried cranberries, and dried bananas to make his trail mix. Rachel made 2 cups of trail mix containing all of the almonds, pumpkin seeds, and granola. How much trail mix did Ian make? How much more trail mix did Rachel make than Ian?

Trail Mix Ingredients
$\frac{3}{4}$ cup almonds
$\frac{1}{4}$ cup pumpkin seeds
$\frac{2}{4}$ cup coconut
$\frac{3}{4}$ cup dried cranberries
$1\frac{2}{4}$ cup walnuts
1 cup granola
$\frac{2}{4}$ cup dried bananas

4. **MP.1 Make Sense and Persevere** What do you know, and what do you need to find?

5. **MP.5 Use Appropriate Tools** What tools could you use to help solve this problem?

6. **MP.2 Reasoning** How can you use a bar diagram to show how the quantities are related?

When you model with math, you represent the relationships in the problem.

7. **MP.1 Make Sense and Persevere** Write and solve an equation to find how much trail mix Ian made.

8. **MP.2 Reasoning** Explain how you were able to calculate how much more trail mix Rachel made than Ian.

Find a Match

Work with a partner. Point to a clue.
Read the clue.

Look below the clues to find a match. Write
the clue letter in the box next to the match.

Find a match for every clue.

I can ...
add and subtract multi-digit
whole numbers.

© **Content Standard** 4.NBT.B.4

Clues

A The sum is exactly 1,000.

B The sum is exactly 1,001.

C The difference is exactly 371.

D The difference is between 40 and 45.

E The difference is exactly 437.

F The difference is between 150 and 160.

G The sum is between 995 and 1,000.

H The sum is exactly 1,899.

409 − 252	900 − 529	909 + 990	506 + 494
580 + 417	560 − 123	601 − 560	309 + 692

A-Z
Glossary

Word List

- decompose
- denominator
- equivalent fractions
- fraction
- like denominators
- mixed number
- numerator
- whole number

Understand Vocabulary

1. Circle the label that best describes $\frac{1}{2}$.

   fraction   mixed number   whole number

2. Circle the label that best describes $1\frac{1}{3}$.

   fraction   mixed number   whole number

3. Circle the label that best describes 4.

   fraction   mixed number   whole number

4. Draw a line from each term to its example.

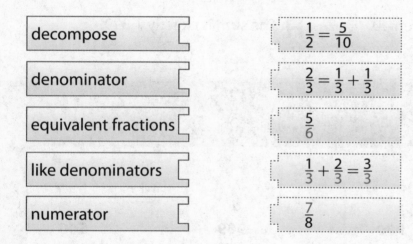

decompose	$\frac{1}{2} = \frac{5}{10}$
denominator	$\frac{2}{3} = \frac{1}{3} + \frac{1}{3}$
equivalent fractions	$\frac{5}{6}$
like denominators	$\frac{1}{3} + \frac{2}{3} = \frac{3}{3}$
numerator	$\frac{7}{8}$

Use Vocabulary in Writing

5. Find $1\frac{1}{3} + 2\frac{2}{3}$. Use at least 3 terms from the Word List to describe how to find the sum.

Set A pages 465–482

Find $\frac{5}{8} + \frac{2}{8}$.

$$\frac{5}{8} = \frac{1}{8} + \frac{1}{8} + \frac{1}{8} + \frac{1}{8} + \frac{1}{8} \qquad \frac{2}{8} = \frac{1}{8} + \frac{1}{8}$$

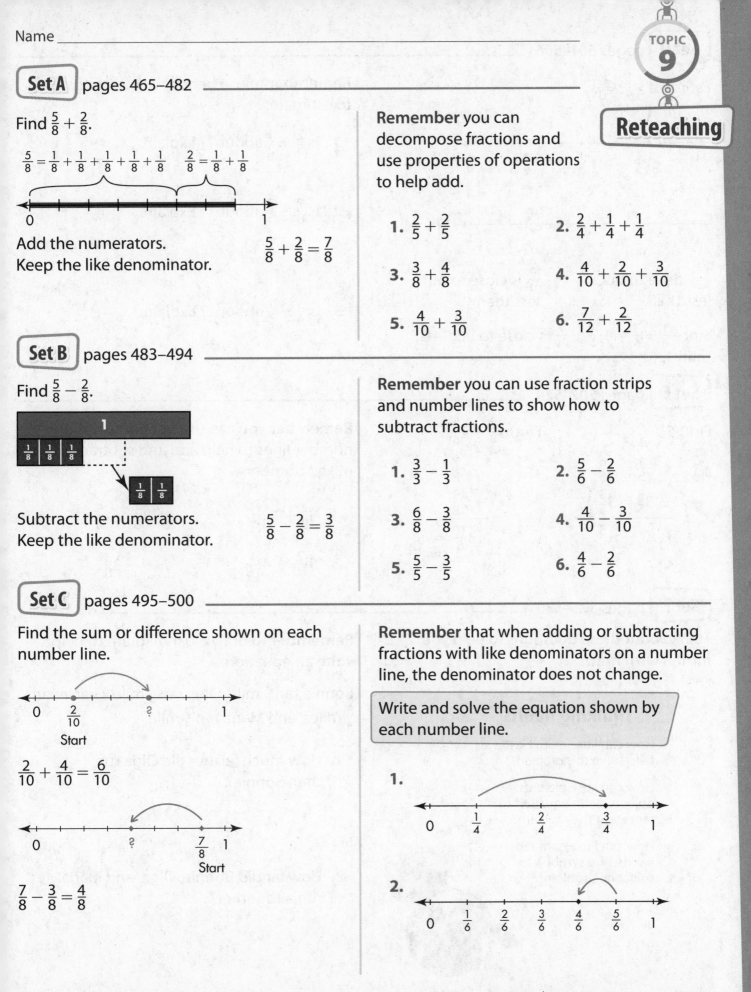

Add the numerators.
Keep the like denominator.

$$\frac{5}{8} + \frac{2}{8} = \frac{7}{8}$$

Remember you can decompose fractions and use properties of operations to help add.

1. $\frac{2}{5} + \frac{2}{5}$

2. $\frac{2}{4} + \frac{1}{4} + \frac{1}{4}$

3. $\frac{3}{8} + \frac{4}{8}$

4. $\frac{4}{10} + \frac{2}{10} + \frac{3}{10}$

5. $\frac{4}{10} + \frac{3}{10}$

6. $\frac{7}{12} + \frac{2}{12}$

Set B pages 483–494

Find $\frac{5}{8} - \frac{2}{8}$.

1

| $\frac{1}{8}$ | $\frac{1}{8}$ | $\frac{1}{8}$ |

| $\frac{1}{8}$ | $\frac{1}{8}$ |

Subtract the numerators.
Keep the like denominator.

$$\frac{5}{8} - \frac{2}{8} = \frac{3}{8}$$

Remember you can use fraction strips and number lines to show how to subtract fractions.

1. $\frac{3}{3} - \frac{1}{3}$

2. $\frac{5}{6} - \frac{2}{6}$

3. $\frac{6}{8} - \frac{3}{8}$

4. $\frac{4}{10} - \frac{3}{10}$

5. $\frac{5}{5} - \frac{3}{5}$

6. $\frac{4}{6} - \frac{2}{6}$

Set C pages 495–500

Find the sum or difference shown on each number line.

$$\frac{2}{10} + \frac{4}{10} = \frac{6}{10}$$

$$\frac{7}{8} - \frac{3}{8} = \frac{4}{8}$$

Remember that when adding or subtracting fractions with like denominators on a number line, the denominator does not change.

Write and solve the equation shown by each number line.

1.

2.

Estimate $\frac{1}{5} + \frac{7}{10}$.

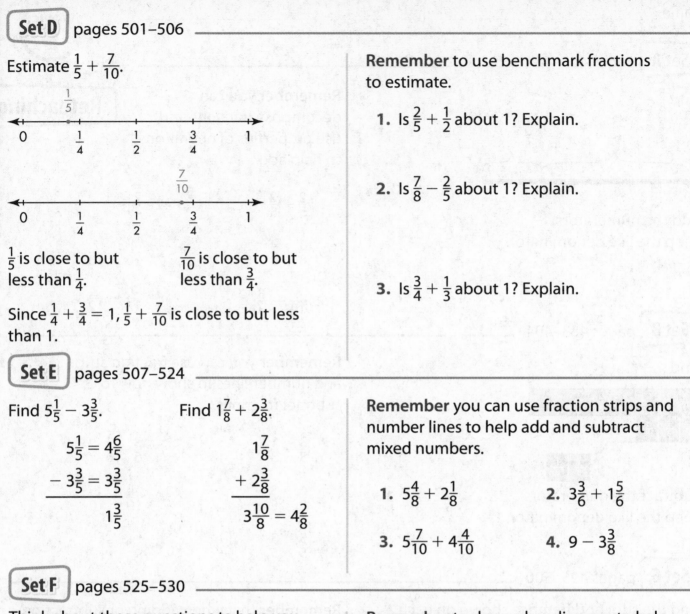

$\frac{1}{5}$ is close to but less than $\frac{1}{4}$.

$\frac{7}{10}$ is close to but less than $\frac{3}{4}$.

Since $\frac{1}{4} + \frac{3}{4} = 1$, $\frac{1}{5} + \frac{7}{10}$ is close to but less than 1.

Remember to use benchmark fractions to estimate.

1. Is $\frac{2}{5} + \frac{1}{2}$ about 1? Explain.

2. Is $\frac{7}{8} - \frac{2}{5}$ about 1? Explain.

3. Is $\frac{3}{4} + \frac{1}{3}$ about 1? Explain.

Find $5\frac{1}{5} - 3\frac{3}{5}$.

$$5\frac{1}{5} = 4\frac{6}{5}$$
$$-3\frac{3}{5} = 3\frac{3}{5}$$
$$\overline{\qquad 1\frac{3}{5}}$$

Find $1\frac{7}{8} + 2\frac{3}{8}$.

$$1\frac{7}{8}$$
$$+2\frac{3}{8}$$
$$\overline{3\frac{10}{8} = 4\frac{2}{8}}$$

Remember you can use fraction strips and number lines to help add and subtract mixed numbers.

1. $5\frac{4}{8} + 2\frac{1}{8}$

2. $3\frac{3}{6} + 1\frac{5}{6}$

3. $5\frac{7}{10} + 4\frac{4}{10}$

4. $9 - 3\frac{3}{8}$

Think about these questions to help you **model with math**.

Thinking Habits

- How can I use math I know to help solve this problem?

- How can I use pictures, objects, or an equation to represent the problem?

- How can I use numbers, words, and symbols to solve the problem?

Remember to draw a bar diagram to help write an equation.

Bonnie ran $\frac{1}{4}$ mile, Olga ran $\frac{3}{4}$ mile, Gracie ran $\frac{5}{4}$ miles, and Maria ran $\frac{2}{4}$ mile.

1. How much farther did Olga run than Bonnie?

2. How far did Bonnie, Olga, and Maria run altogether?

1. Draw lines to match each expression on the left to an equivalent expression on the right.

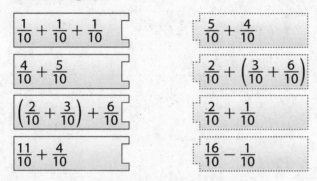

$\frac{1}{10} + \frac{1}{10} + \frac{1}{10}$

$\frac{5}{10} + \frac{4}{10}$

$\frac{4}{10} + \frac{5}{10}$

$\frac{2}{10} + \left(\frac{3}{10} + \frac{6}{10}\right)$

$\left(\frac{2}{10} + \frac{3}{10}\right) + \frac{6}{10}$

$\frac{2}{10} + \frac{1}{10}$

$\frac{11}{10} + \frac{4}{10}$

$\frac{16}{10} - \frac{1}{10}$

2. On Monday, $\frac{3}{12}$ of the students went on a field trip. What fraction of the students did **NOT** go on the field trip?

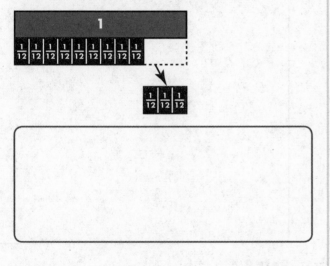

3. Riley planted flowers in some of her garden. Then, she planted vegetables in $\frac{2}{8}$ of her garden. Now, $\frac{7}{8}$ of Riley's garden is planted. What fraction of Riley's garden is planted with flowers?

Ⓐ $\frac{2}{8}$ of her garden

Ⓑ $\frac{3}{8}$ of her garden

Ⓒ $\frac{4}{8}$ of her garden

Ⓓ $\frac{5}{8}$ of her garden

4. Select all the expressions that show a way to decompose $\frac{7}{8}$.

☐ $\frac{3}{8} + \frac{4}{8}$

☐ $\frac{1}{8} + \frac{1}{8} + \frac{5}{8}$

☐ $\frac{3}{4} + \frac{4}{4}$

☐ $\frac{1}{8} + \frac{3}{8} + \frac{3}{8}$

☐ $\frac{1}{8} + \frac{2}{8} + \frac{3}{8} + \frac{1}{8}$

5. For questions 5a–5d, choose Yes or No to tell if $\frac{4}{12}$ will make each equation true.

5a. $\frac{3}{12} + \square = \frac{7}{12}$ ○ Yes ○ No

5b. $\frac{16}{12} - \square = 1$ ○ Yes ○ No

5c. $1\frac{1}{12} + \square = 5\frac{1}{12}$ ○ Yes ○ No

5d. $1\frac{5}{12} - \square = 1\frac{1}{12}$ ○ Yes ○ No

6. Use benchmark fractions to estimate sums and differences less than or greater than 1. Write each expression in the correct answer space.

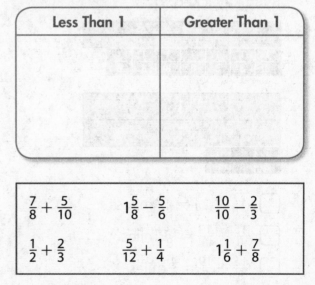

Less Than 1	Greater Than 1

$\frac{7}{8} + \frac{5}{10}$ $1\frac{5}{8} - \frac{5}{6}$ $\frac{10}{10} - \frac{2}{3}$

$\frac{1}{2} + \frac{2}{3}$ $\frac{5}{12} + \frac{1}{4}$ $1\frac{1}{6} + \frac{7}{8}$

7. Roger and Sulee each decomposed $1\frac{1}{6}$. Roger wrote $\frac{1}{6} + \frac{1}{6} + \frac{2}{6} + \frac{3}{6}$. Sulee wrote $\frac{3}{6} + \frac{4}{6}$. Who was correct? Explain.

8. It is $\frac{8}{10}$ mile from Liz's house to the market. Liz walked $\frac{6}{10}$ mile, stopped for a break, and walked the rest of the way to the market. Which equation represents Liz's walk?

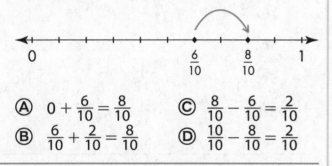

Ⓐ $0 + \frac{6}{10} = \frac{8}{10}$ Ⓒ $\frac{8}{10} - \frac{6}{10} = \frac{2}{10}$

Ⓑ $\frac{6}{10} + \frac{2}{10} = \frac{8}{10}$ Ⓓ $\frac{10}{10} - \frac{8}{10} = \frac{2}{10}$

9. Ryan kayaks $1\frac{7}{8}$ miles before lunch and $2\frac{3}{8}$ miles after lunch. Select all of the equations you would use to find how far Ryan kayacked.

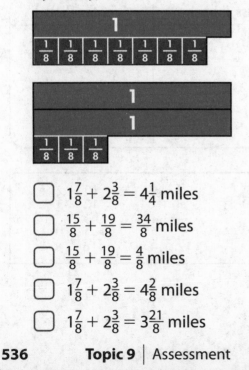

☐ $1\frac{7}{8} + 2\frac{3}{8} = 4\frac{1}{4}$ miles

☐ $\frac{15}{8} + \frac{19}{8} = \frac{34}{8}$ miles

☐ $\frac{15}{8} + \frac{19}{8} = \frac{4}{8}$ miles

☐ $1\frac{7}{8} + 2\frac{3}{8} = 4\frac{2}{8}$ miles

☐ $1\frac{7}{8} + 2\frac{3}{8} = 3\frac{21}{8}$ miles

10. The Jacobys kept track of the time they spent driving on their trip.

Driving Time	
Day	**Hours Driving**
Monday	$5\frac{3}{4}$
Tuesday	$4\frac{3}{4}$
Wednesday	$2\frac{1}{4}$
Thursday	$6\frac{3}{4}$

Part A

Find how many hours the Jacobys drove on Monday and Tuesday. Draw a bar diagram to represent the problem.

Part B

Find how many hours the Jacobys drove in all. Explain your work.

Water Race

In one of the games at the class picnic, students balanced containers filled with water on their heads. The goal was to carry the most water to the finish line. The teams are listed in the **Water Race Teams** table. The amount of water each student carried is listed in the **Water-Race Results** table.

© Performance Assessment

1. Mia will hand out the prize to the winning team.

Part A

Did Team 1 carry more or less than 2 cups of water? Tell how you estimated.

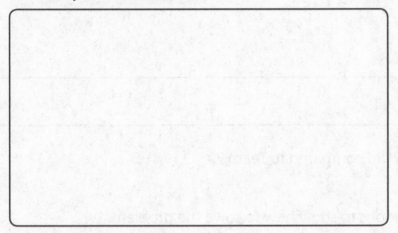

Water Race Teams	
Team	**Members**
1	Jay and Victor
2	Abbie and Shawn
3	Suki and Kira

Water Race Results	
Student	**Cups of Water**
Abbie	$\frac{5}{8}$
Jay	$\frac{6}{8}$
Kira	$\frac{5}{8}$
Shawn	$1\frac{7}{8}$
Suki	$1\frac{6}{8}$
Victor	$\frac{7}{8}$

Part B

How many cups of water did Team 2 carry? Use fraction strips to show the sum.

Part C

How many cups of water did Team 3 carry? Use the number line to show
the sum.

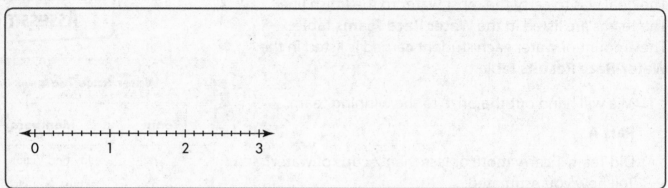

Part D

Which team carried the most water?

2. Team 1 wanted to know how they did compared to Team 2.

Part A

Draw bar diagrams and write equations to show how to solve the problem.

Part B

How much more water did Team 2 carry than Team 1? Explain how to
solve the problem using your equations from Part A. Show your work.

Extend Multiplication Concepts to Fractions

Essential Questions: How can you describe a fraction using a unit fraction? How can you multiply a whole number by a mixed number?

Digital Resources

Solve   Learn   Glossary   Practice Buddy

Tools   Assessment   Help   Games

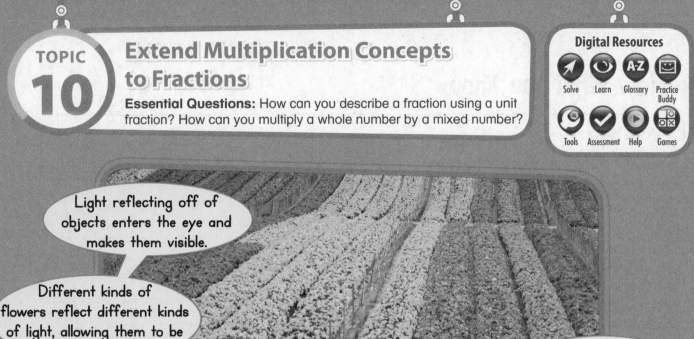

Light reflecting off of objects enters the eye and makes them visible.

Different kinds of flowers reflect different kinds of light, allowing them to be seen in color.

I could look at flowers all day! Here is a project about light and multiplication.

Math and Science Project: Light and Multiplication

Do Research Use the Internet or other sources to research the words *transparent, translucent,* and *opaque.* Write a definition for each word.

Journal: Write a Report Include what you found. Also in your report:

- List 3 examples of items that are transparent, translucent, or opaque.

- Suppose one third of each of 5 same-sized posters is covered with opaque paper. What fraction of the posters are **NOT** covered by opaque paper? Explain how to use multiplication to find what part of the posters are **NOT** covered by opaque paper.

Name _____

Review What You Know

A-Z Vocabulary

Choose the best term from the box.
Write it on the blank.

• equivalent fractions	• mixed number
• fraction	• whole number

1. A _____ has a whole number and a fraction.

2. Fractions that name the same region, part of a set, or part of a segment are called _____ .

3. A _____ has a numerator and a denominator.

Identifying Fractions

Write the fraction shown by each model.

4.

5.

6.

7.

8.

9.

Unit Fractions

Write a fraction for each statement.

10. 3 copies of $\frac{1}{6}$ is ____.

11. 9 copies of $\frac{1}{12}$ is ____.

12. 5 copies of $\frac{1}{5}$ is ____.

13. 3 copies of $\frac{1}{10}$ is ____.

14. 6 copies of $\frac{1}{8}$ is ____.

15. 7 copies of $\frac{1}{10}$ is ____.

Equivalent Fractions

16. Draw a rectangle that shows 8 equal parts. Shade more than $\frac{3}{8}$ of the rectangle but less than $\frac{5}{8}$. What fraction did you model? Use multiplication and division to write two equivalent fractions for your model.

My Word Cards

Use the examples for each word on the front of the card to help complete the definitions on the back.

unit fraction

$$\frac{1}{2}, \quad \frac{1}{3}, \quad \frac{1}{5}, \quad \frac{1}{10}, \quad \frac{1}{12}, \cdots$$

My Word Cards

Complete each definition. Extend learning by writing your own definitions.

A fraction with a numerator of 1 is a

_____.

Name _____

☆ ☆
Solve & Share

Kalil and Mara were working on their math homework. Mara wrote $\frac{4}{5}$ as $\frac{1}{5} + \frac{1}{5} + \frac{1}{5} + \frac{1}{5}$. Kalil looked at Mara's work and said, "I think you could use multiplication to rewrite your equation." Is Kalil's observation correct? Explain.

I can ...
use fraction strips or number lines to understand a fraction as a multiple of a unit fraction.

© Content Standard 4.NF.B.4a
Mathematical Practices MP.2, MP.4, MP.7

You can use reasoning to compare Mara's work and Kalil's observation.

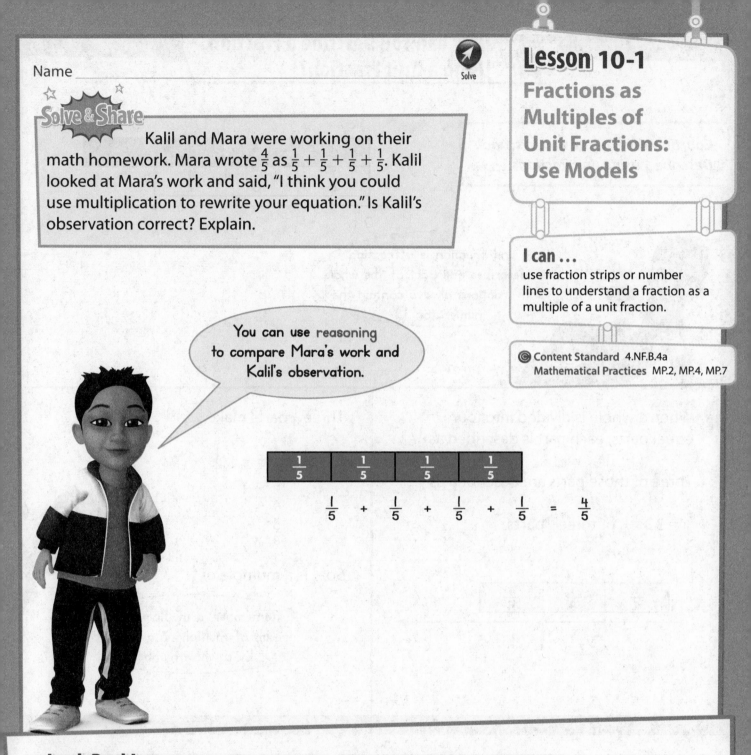

$$\frac{1}{5} \quad + \quad \frac{1}{5} \quad + \quad \frac{1}{5} \quad + \quad \frac{1}{5} \quad = \quad \frac{4}{5}$$

Look Back! © **MP.4 Model with Math** Write an equation to show the relationship between Mara's work and Kalil's observation.

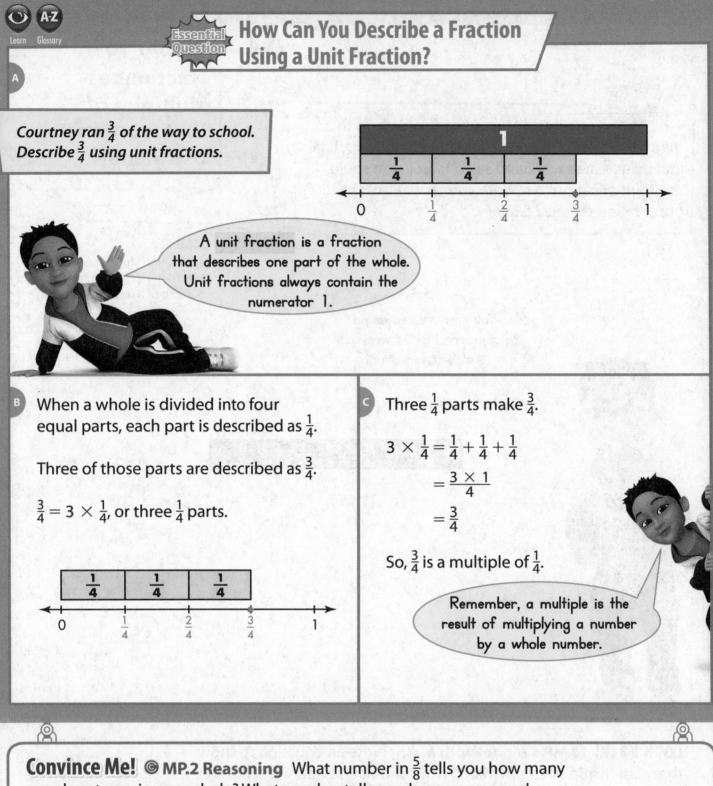

How Can You Describe a Fraction Using a Unit Fraction?

A

Courtney ran $\frac{3}{4}$ of the way to school. Describe $\frac{3}{4}$ using unit fractions.

A unit fraction is a fraction that describes one part of the whole. Unit fractions always contain the numerator 1.

B

When a whole is divided into four equal parts, each part is described as $\frac{1}{4}$.

Three of those parts are described as $\frac{3}{4}$.

$\frac{3}{4} = 3 \times \frac{1}{4}$, or three $\frac{1}{4}$ parts.

C

Three $\frac{1}{4}$ parts make $\frac{3}{4}$.

$3 \times \frac{1}{4} = \frac{1}{4} + \frac{1}{4} + \frac{1}{4}$

$= \frac{3 \times 1}{4}$

$= \frac{3}{4}$

So, $\frac{3}{4}$ is a multiple of $\frac{1}{4}$.

Remember, a multiple is the result of multiplying a number by a whole number.

Convince Me! © MP.2 Reasoning What number in $\frac{5}{8}$ tells you how many equal parts are in one whole? What number tells you how many equal parts are described? How many $\frac{1}{8}$ parts are there in $\frac{5}{8}$?

Name _____

Another Example!

Describe $\frac{5}{4}$ as a multiple of a unit fraction.

$\frac{5}{4}$ is five $\frac{1}{4}$ parts.

Some fractions are greater than 1.

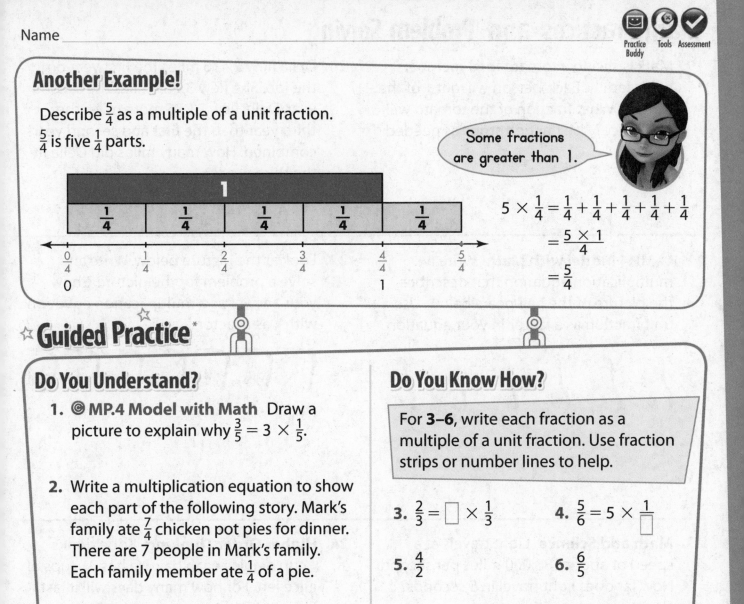

$$5 \times \frac{1}{4} = \frac{1}{4} + \frac{1}{4} + \frac{1}{4} + \frac{1}{4} + \frac{1}{4}$$
$$= \frac{5 \times 1}{4}$$
$$= \frac{5}{4}$$

☆ Guided Practice*

Do You Understand?

1. © MP.4 Model with Math Draw a picture to explain why $\frac{3}{5} = 3 \times \frac{1}{5}$.

2. Write a multiplication equation to show each part of the following story. Mark's family ate $\frac{7}{4}$ chicken pot pies for dinner. There are 7 people in Mark's family. Each family member ate $\frac{1}{4}$ of a pie.

Do You Know How?

For **3–6**, write each fraction as a multiple of a unit fraction. Use fraction strips or number lines to help.

3. $\frac{2}{3} = \square \times \frac{1}{3}$ 4. $\frac{5}{6} = 5 \times \frac{1}{\square}$

5. $\frac{4}{2}$ 6. $\frac{6}{5}$

☆ Independent Practice ☆

Leveled Practice For **7–18**, write each fraction as a multiple of a unit fraction. Use fraction strips or number lines to help.

7. $\frac{3}{4} = \square \times \frac{1}{4}$ 8. $\frac{3}{6} = 3 \times \frac{1}{\square}$ 9. $\frac{2}{5} = \square \times \frac{1}{5}$

10. $\frac{7}{10} = 7 \times \frac{\square}{10}$ 11. $\frac{8}{8} = \square \times \frac{1}{8}$ 12. $\frac{5}{12} = 5 \times \frac{1}{\square}$

13. $\frac{6}{4}$ 14. $\frac{9}{6}$ 15. $\frac{8}{5}$

16. $\frac{7}{8}$ 17. $\frac{9}{4}$ 18. $\frac{8}{6}$

*For another example, see Set A on page 581.

Math Practices and Problem Solving

19. Mark is slicing a tomato for 4 members of his family. Each person will get $\frac{1}{6}$ of the tomato. What fraction of the tomato will Mark slice? Use fraction strips as needed.

20. Delia flew 2,416 miles the first year on the job. She flew 3,719 miles the second year. Delia flew 2,076 more miles the third year than the first and second years combined. How many miles did Delia fly the third year?

21. © MP.4 **Model with Math** Write a multiplication equation that describes the picture of the half pears below. Use a unit fraction as a factor in your equation.

22. Look at the picture below. Write and solve a problem for the picture. Show your answer as a multiplication equation with $\frac{1}{2}$ as a factor.

23. **Math and Science** Light travels at a speed of about 186,000 miles per second. How far does light travel in 5 seconds? Use repeated addition to solve.

24. **Higher Order Thinking** Kobe drinks $\frac{1}{3}$ cup of juice each day. He has $2\frac{1}{3}$ cups of juice left. For how many days will it last? Show your answer as a multiplication equation with $\frac{1}{3}$ as a factor. Remember, you can write $2\frac{1}{3}$ as a fraction.

© Common Core Assessment

25. Which multiplication equation describes the fraction plotted on the number line?

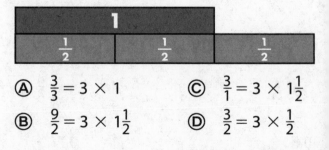

Ⓐ $6 = \frac{6}{3} \times \frac{1}{8}$ Ⓒ $\frac{1}{8} = \frac{1}{8} \times 6$

Ⓑ $\frac{6}{8} = 6 \times \frac{1}{8}$ Ⓓ $\frac{1}{8} + 6 = \frac{6}{8}$

26. Which multiplication equation describes the picture below?

Ⓐ $\frac{3}{3} = 3 \times 1$ Ⓒ $\frac{3}{1} = 3 \times 1\frac{1}{2}$

Ⓑ $\frac{9}{2} = 3 \times 1\frac{1}{2}$ Ⓓ $\frac{3}{2} = 3 \times \frac{1}{2}$

Help   Practice   Tools   Games
       Buddy

Another Look!

Use fraction strips to show $\frac{5}{8}$ as a multiple of a unit fraction.

1

$\frac{1}{8}$	$\frac{1}{8}$	$\frac{1}{8}$	$\frac{1}{8}$	$\frac{1}{8}$

0    $\frac{1}{8}$ $\frac{2}{8}$ $\frac{3}{8}$ $\frac{4}{8}$ $\frac{5}{8}$ $\frac{6}{8}$ $\frac{7}{8}$ 1

Write an equation.

$$\frac{5}{8} = \frac{1}{8} + \frac{1}{8} + \frac{1}{8} + \frac{1}{8} + \frac{1}{8}$$

$$\frac{5}{8} = 5 \times \frac{1}{8}$$

You can write any fraction as a multiple of a unit fraction.

For **1–21**, write each fraction as a multiple of a unit fraction. Use fraction strips or number lines to help.

1. $\frac{2}{4} = 2 \times \frac{\square}{4}$

2. $\frac{2}{6} = \square \times \frac{1}{6}$

3. $\frac{2}{5} = 2 \times \frac{1}{\square}$

4. $\frac{3}{3} = 3 \times \frac{1}{\square}$

5. $\frac{10}{8} = 10 \times \frac{\square}{8}$

6. $\frac{5}{2} = \square \times \frac{1}{2}$

7. $\frac{1}{6}$

8. $\frac{9}{5}$

9. $\frac{8}{3}$

10. $\frac{9}{10}$

11. $\frac{9}{12}$

12. $\frac{8}{10}$

13. $\frac{6}{3}$

14. $\frac{6}{8}$

15. $\frac{4}{12}$

16. $\frac{99}{100}$

17. $\frac{8}{12}$

18. $\frac{6}{6}$

19. $\frac{9}{8}$

20. $\frac{35}{100}$

21. $\frac{101}{100}$

22. Kevin is baking cookies. Each batch of cookies uses $\frac{1}{8}$ pound of butter. Kevin has $\frac{11}{8}$ pounds of butter. How many batches of cookies can Kevin make? Show your answer as a multiplication equation with $\frac{1}{8}$ as a factor.

23. Students are painting a mural. So far, the mural is painted $\frac{1}{4}$ blue, $\frac{2}{8}$ red, and $\frac{3}{12}$ green. Use fraction strips to determine how much of the mural has been painted. Tell the fractions you use to solve.

24. **A-Z Vocabulary** How can you tell if a fraction is a *unit fraction*?

25. **Algebra** How many $\frac{1}{6}$ parts are in $\frac{10}{6}$? Write and solve a multiplication equation with $\frac{1}{6}$ as a factor. Use p for parts.

26. **© MP.7 Look for Relationships** Mari packs the same number of oranges in each bag. How many oranges does Mari need to pack 9 bags? How can you determine the number of oranges Mari needs for 13 bags?

Number of Bags	3	5	7	9	11
Number of Oranges	9	15	21		33

27. **Higher Order Thinking** Katarina uses fraction strips to show how many thirds are in $\frac{4}{6}$. Is Katarina's model correct? Explain.

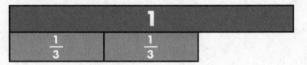

© Common Core Assessment

28. Which multiplication expression describes the fraction plotted on the number line?

$$0 \quad \frac{1}{8} \quad \frac{2}{8} \quad \frac{3}{8} \quad \frac{4}{8} \quad \frac{5}{8} \quad \frac{6}{8} \quad \frac{7}{8} \quad 1$$

- Ⓐ $\frac{5}{8} + \frac{6}{8}$
- Ⓑ $4 \times \frac{1}{8}$
- Ⓒ $\frac{1}{8} + \frac{2}{8} + \frac{3}{8} + \frac{4}{8}$
- Ⓓ $4 \times \frac{4}{8}$

29. Which multiplication expression describes the fraction strips below?

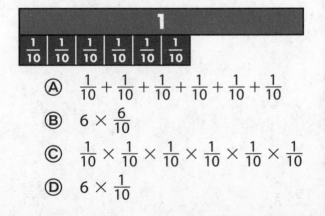

- Ⓐ $\frac{1}{10} + \frac{1}{10} + \frac{1}{10} + \frac{1}{10} + \frac{1}{10} + \frac{1}{10}$
- Ⓑ $6 \times \frac{6}{10}$
- Ⓒ $\frac{1}{10} \times \frac{1}{10} \times \frac{1}{10} \times \frac{1}{10} \times \frac{1}{10} \times \frac{1}{10}$
- Ⓓ $6 \times \frac{1}{10}$

Name _____

Solve & Share

How much tomato juice is needed for a group of 4 people if each person gets $\frac{1}{3}$ cup of juice? How much tomato juice is needed if they each get $\frac{2}{3}$ cup of juice? *Solve these problems any way you choose.*

You can use drawings or write equations to model with math. *Show your work in the space below!*

I can ...
use drawings, area models, or number lines to multiply fractions by whole numbers.

© Content Standards 4.NF.B.4b, 4.NF.B.4a, 4.NF.B.4c
Mathematical Practices MP.2, MP.4, MP.7, MP.8

Look Back! © **MP.2 Reasoning** How is multiplying $4 \times \frac{2}{3}$ cup of juice related to multiplying $8 \times \frac{1}{3}$ cup of juice?

How Can You Find the Product of a Fraction Multiplied by a Whole Number?

A

Dori lives $\frac{1}{4}$ mile from school. If she walks to and from school each day, how far does Dori walk during a school week?

Distance Walked (in miles)

	Mon	Tues	Wed	Thurs	Fri
To School	$\frac{1}{4}$	$\frac{1}{4}$	$\frac{1}{4}$	$\frac{1}{4}$	$\frac{1}{4}$
From School	$\frac{1}{4}$	$\frac{1}{4}$	$\frac{1}{4}$	$\frac{1}{4}$	$\frac{1}{4}$

You can use addition or multiplication to solve this problem.

B **One Way**

Draw a picture to show the distance Dori walks.

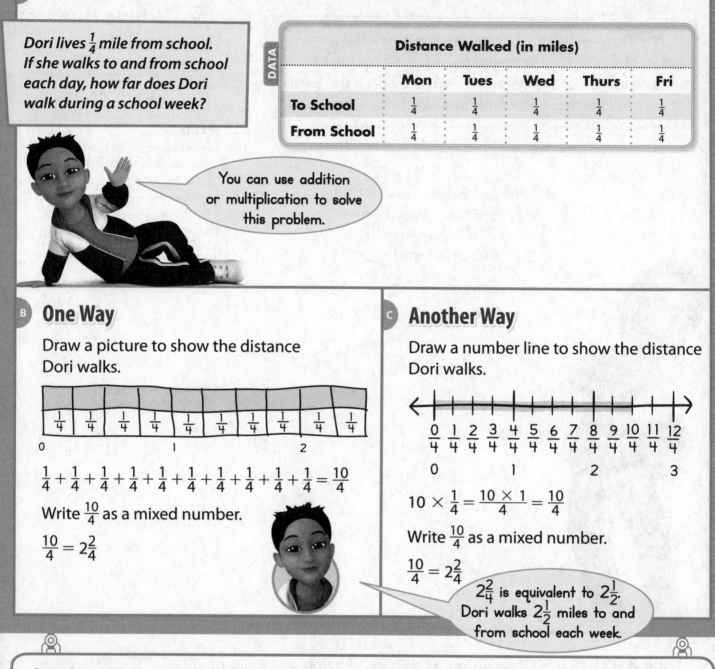

$\frac{1}{4} + \frac{1}{4} + \frac{1}{4} + \frac{1}{4} + \frac{1}{4} + \frac{1}{4} + \frac{1}{4} + \frac{1}{4} + \frac{1}{4} + \frac{1}{4} = \frac{10}{4}$

Write $\frac{10}{4}$ as a mixed number.

$\frac{10}{4} = 2\frac{2}{4}$

C **Another Way**

Draw a number line to show the distance Dori walks.

$10 \times \frac{1}{4} = \frac{10 \times 1}{4} = \frac{10}{4}$

Write $\frac{10}{4}$ as a mixed number.

$\frac{10}{4} = 2\frac{2}{4}$

$2\frac{2}{4}$ is equivalent to $2\frac{1}{2}$. Dori walks $2\frac{1}{2}$ miles to and from school each week.

Convince Me! © **MP.8 Generalize** Why can both addition and multiplication be used represent the problem above? Write an equation to explain.

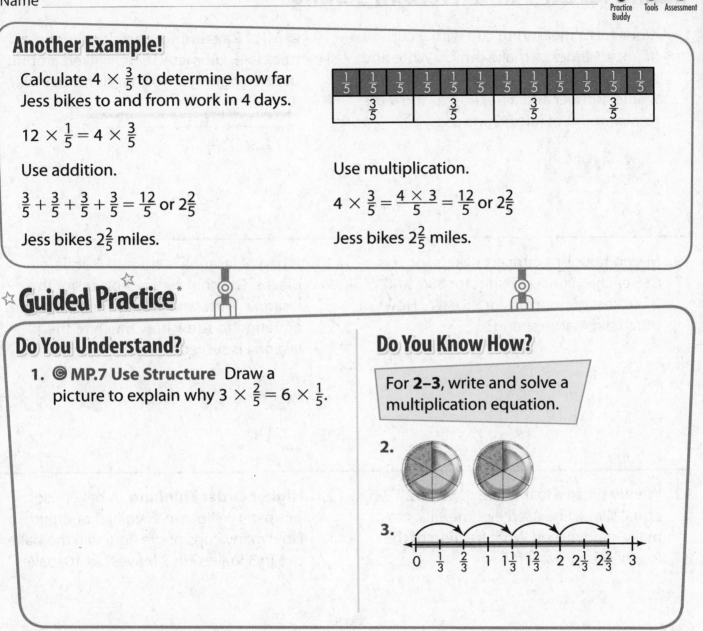

Another Example!

Calculate $4 \times \frac{3}{5}$ to determine how far Jess bikes to and from work in 4 days.

$$12 \times \frac{1}{5} = 4 \times \frac{3}{5}$$

Use addition.

$$\frac{3}{5} + \frac{3}{5} + \frac{3}{5} + \frac{3}{5} = \frac{12}{5} \text{ or } 2\frac{2}{5}$$

Jess bikes $2\frac{2}{5}$ miles.

Use multiplication.

$$4 \times \frac{3}{5} = \frac{4 \times 3}{5} = \frac{12}{5} \text{ or } 2\frac{2}{5}$$

Jess bikes $2\frac{2}{5}$ miles.

☆ Guided Practice*

Do You Understand?

1. © MP.7 Use Structure Draw a picture to explain why $3 \times \frac{2}{5} = 6 \times \frac{1}{5}$.

Do You Know How?

For **2–3**, write and solve a multiplication equation.

2.

3.

Independent Practice ☆

For **4–7**, write and solve a multiplication equation. Use drawings or number lines as needed.

4.

5.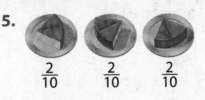

$\frac{2}{10}$ $\frac{2}{10}$ $\frac{2}{10}$

6. Calculate the distance Margo rides her bike if she rides $\frac{7}{8}$ mile each day for 8 days.

7. Calculate the distance Tom rides his bike if he rides $\frac{5}{6}$ mile each day for 5 days.

Math Practices and Problem Solving

8. Kiona fills a measuring cup with $\frac{3}{4}$ cup of juice 3 times to make punch. Write and solve a multiplication equation with a whole number and a fraction to show the total amount of juice Kiona uses.

9. © **MP.2 Reasoning** Each lap around a track is $\frac{3}{10}$ kilometer. Eliot walked around the track 4 times. How far did Eliot walk?

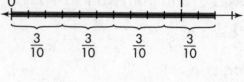

$\frac{3}{10}$ $\frac{3}{10}$ $\frac{3}{10}$ $\frac{3}{10}$

10. Margo bought 4 concert tickets for $38 each, 1 concert T-shirt for $56, and 2 buckets of popcorn for $6 each. How much did Margo spend?

11. A pan of lasagna is cut into 6 equal pieces. The chef serves 5 pieces of the lasagna. Write and solve a multiplication equation to show how much of the lasagna is served.

12. Wendy sliced a loaf of bread into 12 equal slices. She used 4 of the slices to make sandwiches. What fraction of the loaf of bread was left?

13. **Higher Order Thinking** A baker uses $\frac{2}{3}$ cup of rye flour in each loaf of bread. How many cups of rye flour will the baker use in 3 loaves? in 7 loaves? in 10 loaves?

© **Common Core Assessment**

14. Select all the expressions that represent the following story. Elaine jogged $\frac{4}{5}$ mile each day for 7 days. Use drawings or number lines as needed.

- ☐ $7 \times \frac{4}{5}$
- ☐ $\frac{4}{5} + \frac{4}{5} + \frac{4}{5} + \frac{4}{5} + \frac{4}{5} + \frac{4}{5} + \frac{4}{5}$
- ☐ $14 \times \frac{2}{5}$
- ☐ $7 \times \frac{1}{5}$
- ☐ $7 \times \frac{2}{5}$

15. Select all the expressions that represent the following story. Freddie skated $\frac{1}{2}$ mile each day for 6 days. Use drawings or number lines as needed.

- ☐ $\frac{1}{2} + \frac{1}{2} + \frac{1}{2} + \frac{1}{2} + \frac{1}{2} + \frac{1}{2}$
- ☐ $6 \times \frac{1}{2}$
- ☐ 3×2
- ☐ $6 + 2 \times \frac{1}{2}$
- ☐ 6×3

© Pearson Education, Inc. 4

Name _____

Another Look!

Georgie walked $\frac{2}{3}$ mile to and from the gym. How many miles did Georgie walk?

Find $2 \times \frac{2}{3}$.

You can use a number line to help multiply fractions and whole numbers.

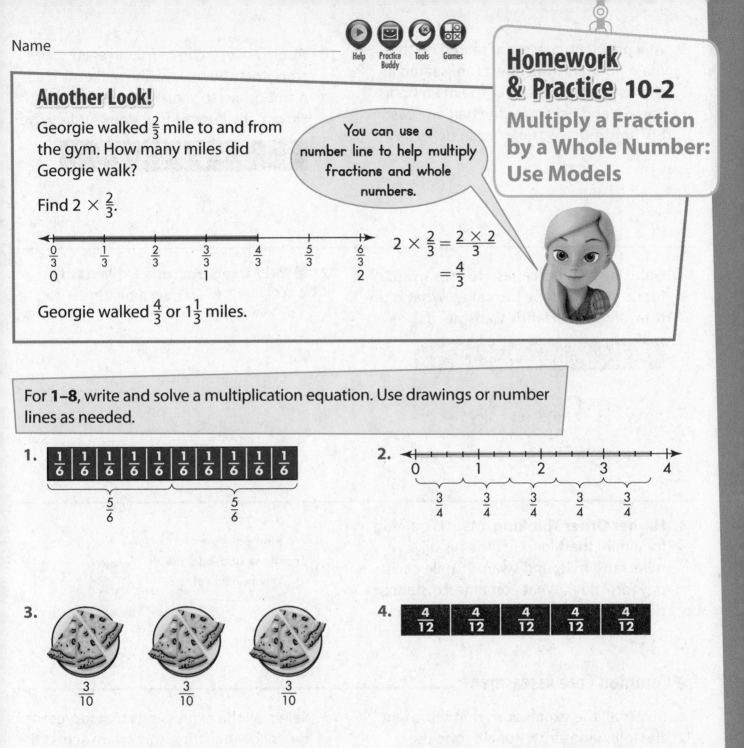

$2 \times \frac{2}{3} = \frac{2 \times 2}{3}$

$= \frac{4}{3}$

Georgie walked $\frac{4}{3}$ or $1\frac{1}{3}$ miles.

For **1–8**, write and solve a multiplication equation. Use drawings or number lines as needed.

1.

$\frac{5}{6}$ $\frac{5}{6}$

2.

$\frac{3}{4}$ $\frac{3}{4}$ $\frac{3}{4}$ $\frac{3}{4}$ $\frac{3}{4}$

3.

$\frac{3}{10}$ $\frac{3}{10}$ $\frac{3}{10}$

4.

$\frac{4}{12}$ $\frac{4}{12}$ $\frac{4}{12}$ $\frac{4}{12}$ $\frac{4}{12}$

5. Calculate the distance Penny rides her bicycle if she rides $\frac{1}{4}$ mile each day for 5 days.

6. Calculate the distance Benjamin rides his scooter if he rides $\frac{3}{5}$ mile each day for 10 days.

7. Calculate the distance Derek rows his boat if he rows $\frac{5}{6}$ mile each day for 11 days.

8. Calculate the distance Kinsey jogs if she jogs $\frac{7}{8}$ mile each day for 9 days.

9. At a play, 211 guests are seated on the main floor and 142 guests are seated in the balcony. If tickets for the main floor cost $7 and tickets for the balcony cost $5, how much was earned in ticket sales?

10. Audrey uses $\frac{5}{8}$ cup of fruit in each smoothie she makes. She makes 6 smoothies to share with her friends. How many cups of fruit does Audrey use?

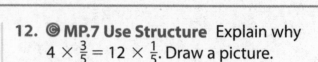

11. Gabe is making 5 capes. He uses $\frac{2}{3}$ yard of fabric for each cape he makes. What is the total amount of fabric Gabe needs?

$\frac{2}{3}$	$\frac{2}{3}$	$\frac{2}{3}$	$\frac{2}{3}$	$\frac{2}{3}$

12. © **MP.7 Use Structure** Explain why $4 \times \frac{3}{5} = 12 \times \frac{1}{5}$. Draw a picture.

13. **Higher Order Thinking** Mark is training for a mini triathlon. He rode his bike $\frac{3}{4}$ mile, ran $\frac{5}{6}$ mile, and swam $\frac{10}{12}$ mile each day for 7 days. What combined distance did Mark exercise during the week?

Find equivalent fractions and add the fractions first.

© **Common Core Assessment**

14. Select all the expressions that represent the following story. Ronald rode the rollercoaster 3 times. The rollercoaster track is $\frac{1}{4}$ mile in length. Use drawings or number lines as needed.

- ☐ $\frac{1}{4} + \frac{1}{4} + \frac{1}{4}$
- ☐ $3 \times \frac{1}{4}$
- ☐ 3×4
- ☐ $4 + 3 \times \frac{1}{4}$
- ☐ $\frac{3}{4}$

15. Select all the expressions that represent the following story. Kurt swam across the lake and back. The lake is $\frac{4}{8}$ mile across. Use drawings or number lines as needed.

- ☐ $2 \times \frac{4}{8}$
- ☐ $\frac{4}{8} + \frac{4}{8}$
- ☐ $4 \times \frac{2}{8}$
- ☐ $8 \times \frac{4}{8}$
- ☐ $2 + \frac{4}{8}$

Name _____

☆ Solve & Share ☆

A recipe for 1 gallon of fruit punch calls for $\frac{3}{4}$ cup of orange juice. How many cups of orange juice are needed to make 8 gallons of fruit punch? **Solve this problem any way you choose.**

You can use a drawing, bar diagram, area model, or equation to model with math. *Show your work in the space below!*

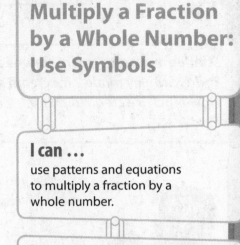

I can ...
use patterns and equations to multiply a fraction by a whole number.

ⓒ **Content Standards** 4.NF.B.4b, 4.NF.B.4a, 4.NF.B.4c
Mathematical Practices MP.2, MP.4, MP.6, MP.7

Look Back! ⓒ **MP.6 Be Precise** Look back at your solution. What units should you use to label your answer?

When Can You Use the Product of a Fraction and a Whole Number to Solve a Problem?

A

Stanley makes ice cream sundaes.
Today Stanley made 2 ice cream sundaes.
How much ice cream did Stanley use?
Find $2 \times \frac{3}{4}$.

$\frac{3}{4}$ pint of ice cream in each sundae

You can use structure when multiplying a fraction and a whole number.

B ## One Way

$2 \times \frac{3}{4} = 2 \times \left(3 \times \frac{1}{4}\right)$ $\frac{3}{4}$ is 3 copies of $\frac{1}{4}$ or $3 \times \frac{1}{4}$.

$= (2 \times 3) \times \frac{1}{4}$ Associative Property of Multiplication

$= 6 \times \frac{1}{4}$

$= \frac{6 \times 1}{4}$ Multiply the whole number and the numerator.

$= \frac{6}{4}$

$2 \times \frac{3}{4} = \frac{6}{4}$ or $1\frac{2}{4}$

C ## Another Way

$2 \times \frac{3}{4} = \frac{2 \times 3}{4}$ Multiply the whole number and the numerator.

$= \frac{6}{4}$

$2 \times \frac{3}{4} = \frac{6}{4}$ or $1\frac{2}{4}$

Stanley used $1\frac{2}{4}$ pints of ice cream to make 2 sundaes.

Convince Me! © **MP.7 Use Structure** Use properties of operations to calculate $3 \times \frac{3}{6}$. Show your work.

☆ Guided Practice ☆

Do You Understand?

1. Sarah has $\frac{1}{2}$ of a granola bar. Her friend has 5 times as many granola bars. How many granola bars does Sarah's friend have?

2. © **MP.4 Model with Math** Sue needs $\frac{5}{6}$ cup of cocoa to make one batch of chocolate pudding. She wants to make 4 batches of pudding to take to a party. Use properties of operations to help write and solve an equation to show how many cups of cocoa Sue will need for all 4 batches of pudding.

Do You Know How?

For **3–4**, multiply.

3. $8 \times \frac{1}{2}$ **4.** $13 \times \frac{3}{4}$

For **5–6**, write and solve a multiplication equation.

5. Calculate the amount of medicine taken in 10 days if the dose is $\frac{3}{4}$ fluid ounce per day.

6. Calculate the total length needed to decorate 9 boxes if each box uses $\frac{2}{3}$ yard of ribbon.

☆ Independent Practice ☆

For **7–15**, multiply.

7. $4 \times \frac{1}{3}$ **8.** $6 \times \frac{3}{8}$ **9.** $8 \times \frac{2}{5}$

10. $12 \times \frac{5}{6}$ **11.** $11 \times \frac{2}{3}$ **12.** $5 \times \frac{7}{8}$

13. $7 \times \frac{3}{4}$ **14.** $9 \times \frac{3}{5}$ **15.** $4 \times \frac{5}{8}$

For **16–17**, write and solve a multiplication equation.

16. Calculate the total distance Mary runs in one week if she runs $\frac{7}{8}$ mile each day.

17. Calculate the length of 5 pieces of ribbon laid end to end if each piece is $\frac{2}{3}$ yard long.

For another example, see Set C on page 581.

Math Practices and Problem Solving

18. A baseball team bought 8 boxes of baseballs. If the team spent a total of $1,696, what was the cost of 1 box of baseballs?

19. Oscar wants to make 4 chicken pot pies. The recipe requires $\frac{2}{3}$ pound of potatoes for each pot pie. How many pounds of potatoes will Oscar need?

20. It takes Mario $\frac{1}{4}$ hour to mow Mr. Harris's lawn. It takes him 3 times as long to mow Mrs. Carter's lawn. How long does it take Mario to mow Mrs. Carter's lawn? Write your answer as a fraction of an hour, then as minutes.

$\frac{1}{4}$ hour is 15 minutes.

21. **A-Z Vocabulary** Use *numerator*, *denominator*, and *whole number*.

When you multiply a fraction by a whole number, the _____ in the product is the same as the denominator of the fraction. The _____ in the product is the product of the _____ and the numerator of the fraction.

22. **© MP.4 Model with Math** Malik swims $\frac{9}{10}$ mile each day. How many miles will Malik swim in 8 days? Write and solve an equation.

23. **Higher Order Thinking** Sam is making 7 fruit tarts. Each tart needs $\frac{3}{4}$ cup of strawberries and $\frac{1}{4}$ cup of blueberries. What is the total amount of fruit that Sam needs for his tarts? Use properties of operations to solve.

© Common Core Assessment

24. Sean is making picture frames. Each frame uses $\frac{4}{5}$ yard of wood. What is the total length of wood Sean will need to make 12 frames? Use each of the numbers from the box once to complete and solve the equation.

$$12 \times \frac{4}{5} = \frac{\boxed{}\boxed{} \times 4}{5} = \frac{\boxed{}\boxed{}}{5} \text{ or } 9\frac{\boxed{}}{5} \text{ yards}$$

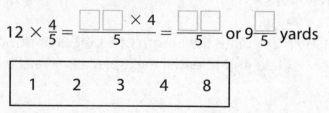

| 1 | 2 | 3 | 4 | 8 |

25. Ellen is making plant boxes. Each box uses $\frac{3}{6}$ yard of wood. What is the total length of wood Ellen will need to make 7 plant boxes? Use each of the numbers from the box once to complete and solve the equation.

$$7 \times \frac{3}{6} = \frac{\boxed{} \times 3}{6} = \frac{\boxed{}\boxed{}}{\boxed{}} \text{ or } \boxed{}\frac{3}{6} \text{ yards}$$

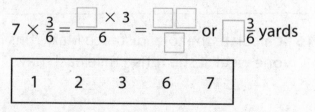

| 1 | 2 | 3 | 6 | 7 |

Name _____

Another Look!

Maria swims $\frac{3}{5}$ mile across the lake and another $\frac{3}{5}$ mile back. How far did Maria swim?

1					1

$\frac{1}{5}$	$\frac{1}{5}$	$\frac{1}{5}$	$\frac{1}{5}$	$\frac{1}{5}$	$\frac{1}{5}$

Find $2 \times \frac{3}{5}$.

$2 \times \frac{3}{5} = \frac{2 \times 3}{5} = \frac{6}{5}$ or $1\frac{1}{5}$

Maria swims $1\frac{1}{5}$ miles.

When all the groups are the same size, you can multiply to find the total.

For **1–12**, multiply.

1. $8 \times \frac{5}{12}$

2. $9 \times \frac{1}{4}$

3. $5 \times \frac{3}{5}$

4. $10 \times \frac{5}{6}$

5. $9 \times \frac{3}{10}$

6. $7 \times \frac{1}{3}$

7. $12 \times \frac{1}{5}$

8. $11 \times \frac{7}{8}$

9. $4 \times \frac{2}{3}$

10. $5 \times \frac{7}{8}$

11. $8 \times \frac{5}{6}$

12. $2 \times \frac{2}{8}$

For **13–16**, write and solve a multiplication equation.

13. Calculate the length of a scarf with 5 sections if each section is $\frac{1}{2}$ foot long.

14. Calculate the distance Kris walks in 8 days if she walks $\frac{7}{8}$ mile each day.

15. Calculate the distance Nathan rides his bike if he rides $\frac{9}{12}$ mile each day for 3 days.

16. Calculate the distance Tarryn drives if she drives $\frac{7}{8}$ mile each way to and from work, 5 days a week.

17. **© MP.2 Reasoning** Xander has 10 pieces of twine that he is using for a project. If each piece of twine is $\frac{1}{3}$ yard long, how many yards of twine does Xander have? Use properties of operations to solve.

18. The Portman's kitchen table is rectangular. The table is 4 feet wide and 8 feet long. Mrs. Portman bought a tablecloth that will cover 56 square feet. Is the tablecloth large enough to cover the table? Explain.

19. **Number Sense** Olivia is doing her math homework. For each problem, she uses $\frac{3}{4}$ sheet of paper. How many sheets of paper will Olivia need to complete 20 math problems? Use estimation to check if your answer is reasonable.

20. **Math and Science** There are 6 pure spectral colors: red, orange, yellow, green, blue, and violet. Some animals cannot see all of these colors. Bees cannot see orange or red. What fraction of the pure spectral colors can bees see?

21. Write a problem to go along with the multiplication sentence $3 \times \frac{3}{10}$. Then solve your problem.

22. **Higher Order Thinking** Lydia is making 4 loaves of rye bread and 3 loaves of wheat bread. Each loaf takes $\frac{3}{4}$ cup of sugar. How many cups of sugar will Lydia need? Explain.

© Common Core Assessment

23. Camille walks $\frac{3}{4}$ mile each day for 8 days. How far does Camille walk? Use each of the numbers from the box once to complete and solve the equation.

$$8 \times \frac{3}{4} = \frac{\boxed{} \times \boxed{}}{4} = \frac{\boxed{}\boxed{}}{4} = \boxed{} \text{ miles}$$

2	3	4	6	8

24. Corinne has cheer practice $\frac{5}{6}$ hour each day, Monday through Friday. How long does Corinne practice each week? Use each of the numbers from the box to complete and solve the equation.

$$5 \times \frac{5}{6} = \frac{5 \times 5}{6} = \frac{\boxed{}\boxed{}}{\boxed{}} = \boxed{}\frac{\boxed{}}{6}$$

1	2	4	5	6

Name _____

★ **Solve & Share** ★

Jerry is filling his sand pail and pouring the sand into a large bucket. Can the bucket hold 8 of Jerry's pails full of sand? *Solve this problem any way you choose.*

I can ...
use area models, drawings, and equations to represent and solve problems involving multiplying a whole number and a mixed number.

Ⓒ Content Standard 4.NF.B.4c
Mathematical Practices MP.1, MP.3, MP.7

Jerry's pail holds $2\frac{3}{4}$ pounds of sand.

The large bucket holds 30 pounds of sand.

You can use structure. Use what you know about multiplying whole numbers to solve this problem.

Look Back! Ⓒ **MP.1 Make Sense and Persevere** How do you know you need to multiply to solve this problem?

Learn Glossary

How Can You Multiply a Whole Number and a Mixed Number?

A

Ellie wants to make 5 blankets as gifts for her friends. It takes $2\frac{2}{3}$ yards of fabric to make each blanket. How many yards of fabric does Ellie need?

You can use appropriate tools such as bar diagrams or fraction strips to help solve the problem.

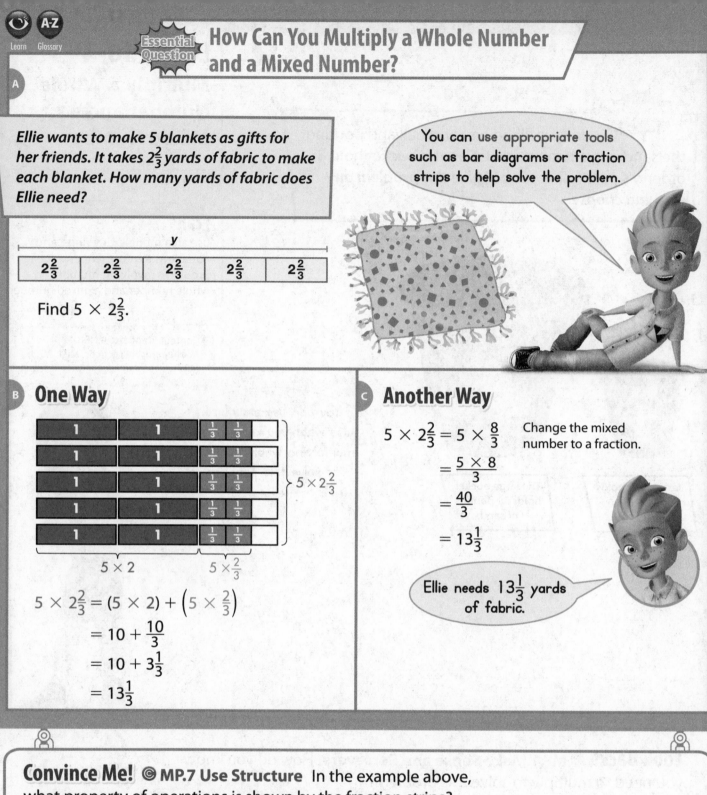

$2\frac{2}{3}$	$2\frac{2}{3}$	$2\frac{2}{3}$	$2\frac{2}{3}$	$2\frac{2}{3}$

y

Find $5 \times 2\frac{2}{3}$.

B **One Way**

1	1	$\frac{1}{3}$	$\frac{1}{3}$	
1	1	$\frac{1}{3}$	$\frac{1}{3}$	
1	1	$\frac{1}{3}$	$\frac{1}{3}$	
1	1	$\frac{1}{3}$	$\frac{1}{3}$	
1	1	$\frac{1}{3}$	$\frac{1}{3}$	

$5 \times 2\frac{2}{3}$

5×2 $5 \times \frac{2}{3}$

$5 \times 2\frac{2}{3} = (5 \times 2) + \left(5 \times \frac{2}{3}\right)$

$= 10 + \frac{10}{3}$

$= 10 + 3\frac{1}{3}$

$= 13\frac{1}{3}$

C **Another Way**

$5 \times 2\frac{2}{3} = 5 \times \frac{8}{3}$ Change the mixed number to a fraction.

$= \frac{5 \times 8}{3}$

$= \frac{40}{3}$

$= 13\frac{1}{3}$

Ellie needs $13\frac{1}{3}$ yards of fabric.

Convince Me! © **MP.7 Use Structure** In the example above, what property of operations is shown by the fraction strips? Explain how the model shows the property.

Practice Buddy   Tools   Assessment

☆ Guided Practice *

Do You Understand?

1. © **MP.7 Use Structure** In the problem on the previous page, how much fabric would Ellie need if she wanted to make 6 blankets? Explain.

2. Find $3 \times 1\frac{1}{3}$ using the two methods shown on the previous page.

Do You Know How?

For **3–4**, find each product.

3. $2 \times 2\frac{1}{4}$

n	
$2\frac{1}{4}$	$2\frac{1}{4}$

4. $2 \times 1\frac{1}{2}$

| 1 | $\frac{1}{2}$ | |
| 1 | $\frac{1}{2}$ | |

☆ Independent Practice ☆

Leveled Practice For **5–18**, find each product.

You can use fraction strips or bar diagrams to show multiplication.

5. $2 \times 3\frac{1}{2}$

n	
$3\frac{1}{2}$	$3\frac{1}{2}$

6. $2 \times 1\frac{2}{5}$

| 1 | $\frac{1}{5}$ | $\frac{1}{5}$ | | | |
| 1 | $\frac{1}{5}$ | $\frac{1}{5}$ | | | |

7. $3 \times 1\frac{5}{6}$ 8. $4 \times 2\frac{3}{8}$ 9. $8 \times 2\frac{3}{4}$ 10. $10 \times 3\frac{3}{5}$

11. $3 \times 2\frac{4}{5}$ 12. $3 \times 4\frac{7}{10}$ 13. $7 \times 4\frac{1}{2}$ 14. $9 \times 5\frac{3}{4}$

15. $11 \times 1\frac{2}{3}$ 16. $4 \times 1\frac{7}{12}$ 17. $3 \times 2\frac{1}{5}$ 18. $8 \times 9\frac{1}{2}$

Math Practices and Problem Solving

19. **©️ MP.1 Make Sense and Persevere** Joel needs 24 apples for bobbing at his party. How many pounds of apples does Joel need? Explain.

> 8 apples weigh
> $3\frac{3}{4}$ pounds

20. **©️ MP.3 Critique Reasoning** Which student, Lisa or Anthony, correctly found $3 \times 2\frac{1}{4}$? Explain.

Lisa
$$3 \times 2\frac{1}{4} = 3 \times \frac{9}{4}$$
$$= \frac{27}{4}$$
$$= \frac{24}{4} + \frac{3}{4}$$
$$= 6 + \frac{3}{4}$$
$$= 6\frac{3}{4}$$

Anthony
$$3 \times 2\frac{1}{4} = 3 \times (2 + \frac{1}{4})$$
$$= (3 \times 2) + (3 \times \frac{1}{4})$$
$$= 6 + \frac{3}{4}$$
$$= 6\frac{3}{4}$$

21. The stadium contains 8,217 blue seats and 7,236 red seats. There are 1,211 more green seats than red seats. How many seats are in the stadium?

> You can estimate to check if your solution is reasonable.

22. **Higher Order Thinking** Calculate $8 \times 7\frac{3}{4}$ with Lisa's method and then with Anthony's method above. Which method do you find easier? Explain.

©️ Common Core Assessment

23. Which expression can be used to solve the following problem? Seth has 7 cans of tuna. Each can holds $5\frac{9}{10}$ ounces of tuna. How many ounces of tuna does Seth have?

Ⓐ $(7 \times 9) + \left(7 \times \frac{5}{10}\right)$

Ⓑ $(7 \times 59) + \left(7 \times \frac{1}{10}\right)$

Ⓒ $(7 \times 5) + \left(7 \times \frac{9}{10}\right)$

Ⓓ $(7 \times 5) + \frac{9}{10}$

24. Which expression can be used to solve the following problem? Sarah has 6 copies of the same book. If each book weighs $3\frac{5}{8}$ pounds, how many pounds do all 6 books weigh?

Ⓐ $18 + 3\frac{5}{8}$

Ⓑ $18 + 3\frac{6}{8}$

Ⓒ $30 + 1\frac{7}{8}$

Ⓓ $30 + 2\frac{1}{8}$

Help Practice Buddy Tools Games

Homework & Practice 10-4

Multiply a Whole Number and a Mixed Number

Another Look!

How much flour does it take to make 3 dozen rolls if 1 dozen rolls uses $1\frac{3}{8}$ cups of flour?

Find $3 \times 1\frac{3}{8}$.

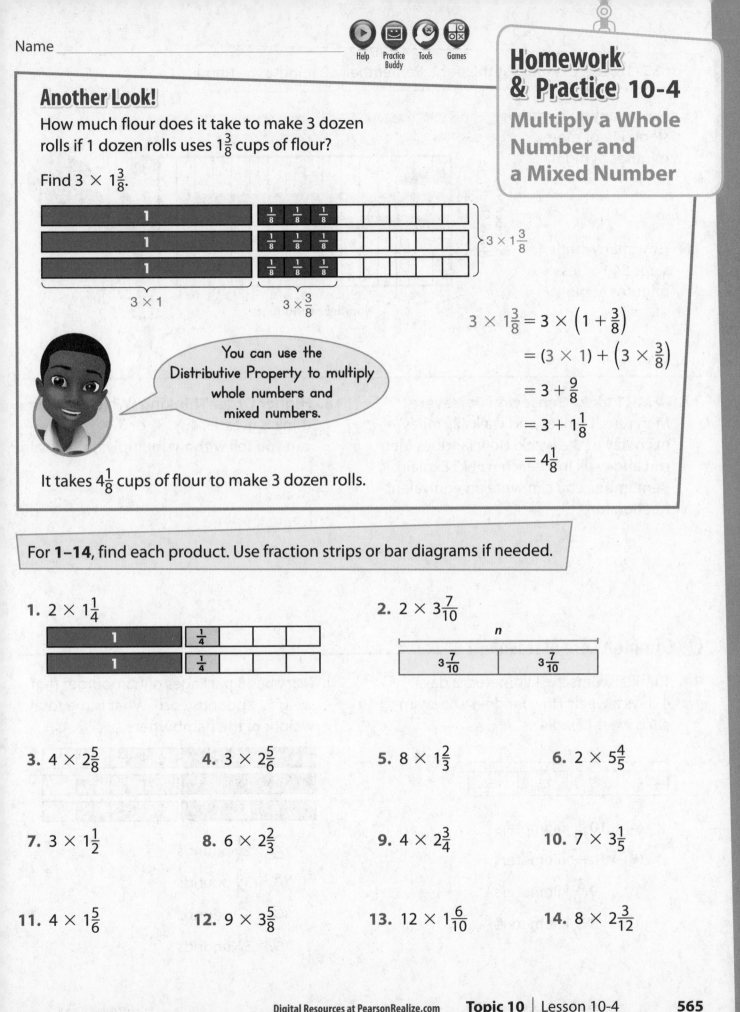

$$3 \times 1\frac{3}{8} = 3 \times \left(1 + \frac{3}{8}\right)$$
$$= (3 \times 1) + \left(3 \times \frac{3}{8}\right)$$
$$= 3 + \frac{9}{8}$$
$$= 3 + 1\frac{1}{8}$$
$$= 4\frac{1}{8}$$

You can use the Distributive Property to multiply whole numbers and mixed numbers.

It takes $4\frac{1}{8}$ cups of flour to make 3 dozen rolls.

For **1–14**, find each product. Use fraction strips or bar diagrams if needed.

1. $2 \times 1\frac{1}{4}$

2. $2 \times 3\frac{7}{10}$

3. $4 \times 2\frac{5}{8}$ 4. $3 \times 2\frac{5}{6}$ 5. $8 \times 1\frac{2}{3}$ 6. $2 \times 5\frac{4}{5}$

7. $3 \times 1\frac{1}{2}$ 8. $6 \times 2\frac{2}{3}$ 9. $4 \times 2\frac{3}{4}$ 10. $7 \times 3\frac{1}{5}$

11. $4 \times 1\frac{5}{6}$ 12. $9 \times 3\frac{5}{8}$ 13. $12 \times 1\frac{6}{10}$ 14. $8 \times 2\frac{3}{12}$

15. How many students slept 540 or more minutes at night?

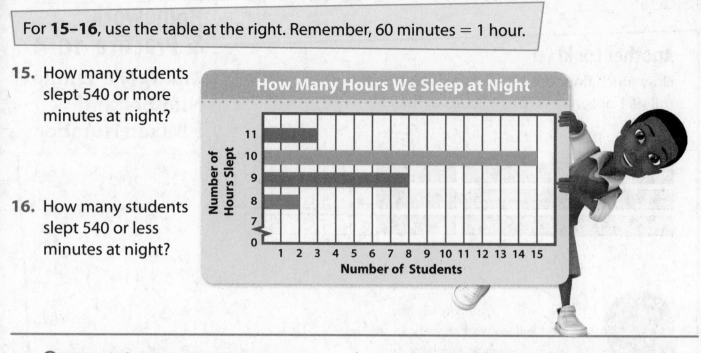

How Many Hours We Sleep at Night

16. How many students slept 540 or less minutes at night?

17. © **MP.1 Make Sense and Persevere** Meg runs $1\frac{1}{2}$ miles and walks $2\frac{1}{4}$ miles each day of the week. How far does Meg run and walk in all each week? Explain. Remember, you can write an equivalent fraction for $1\frac{1}{2}$.

18. **Higher Order Thinking** Which do you think is greater, $4 \times 3\frac{2}{5}$ or $3 \times 4\frac{2}{5}$? How can you tell without multiplying? Explain.

© **Common Core Assessment**

19. Tamika swims $2\frac{7}{10}$ kilometers a day, 4 days a week. How far does she swim each week? Find $4 \times 2\frac{7}{10}$.

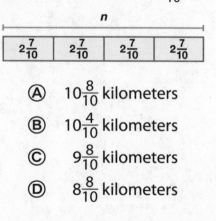

Ⓐ $10\frac{8}{10}$ kilometers

Ⓑ $10\frac{4}{10}$ kilometers

Ⓒ $9\frac{8}{10}$ kilometers

Ⓓ $8\frac{8}{10}$ kilometers

20. Mary has 3 packages of hamburger that weigh $1\frac{3}{4}$ pounds each. What is the total weight of the hamburger?

1	$\frac{1}{4}$	$\frac{1}{4}$	$\frac{1}{4}$	
1	$\frac{1}{4}$	$\frac{1}{4}$	$\frac{1}{4}$	
1	$\frac{1}{4}$	$\frac{1}{4}$	$\frac{1}{4}$	

Ⓐ $2\frac{1}{4}$ pounds

Ⓑ $3\frac{3}{4}$ pounds

Ⓒ $4\frac{1}{2}$ pounds

Ⓓ $5\frac{1}{4}$ pounds

Name _____

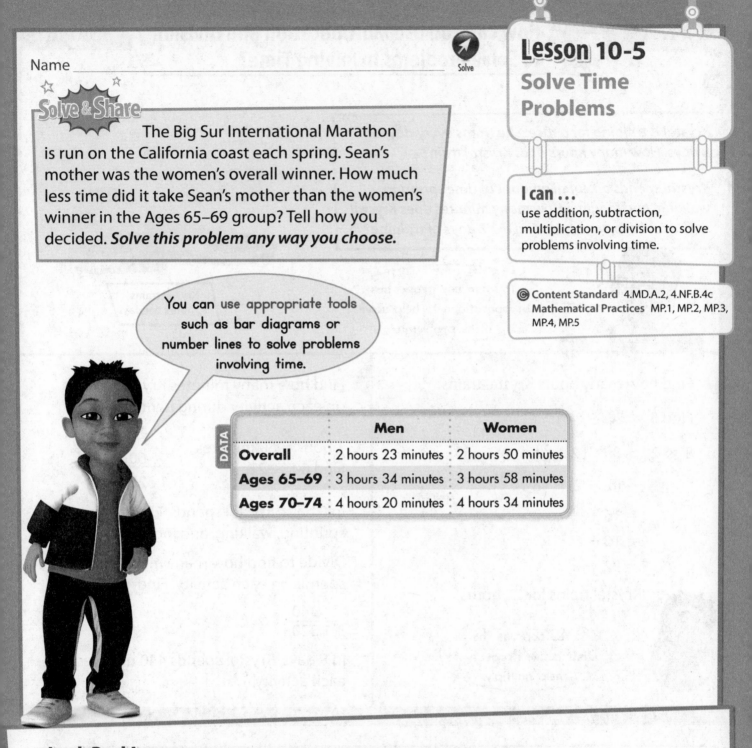

Solve & Share

The Big Sur International Marathon is run on the California coast each spring. Sean's mother was the women's overall winner. How much less time did it take Sean's mother than the women's winner in the Ages 65–69 group? Tell how you decided. **Solve this problem any way you choose.**

I can ...
use addition, subtraction, multiplication, or division to solve problems involving time.

© Content Standard 4.MD.A.2, 4.NF.B.4c
Mathematical Practices MP.1, MP.2, MP.3, MP.4, MP.5

You can use appropriate tools such as bar diagrams or number lines to solve problems involving time.

DATA	Men	Women
Overall	2 hours 23 minutes	2 hours 50 minutes
Ages 65–69	3 hours 34 minutes	3 hours 58 minutes
Ages 70–74	4 hours 20 minutes	4 hours 34 minutes

Look Back! © **MP.2 Reasoning** Was the difference in the overall men's winner and the men's winner in the Ages 70–74 group more or less than 2 hours? Explain.

Essential Question
How Can You Use Multiplication and Division to Solve Problems Involving Time?

A

Krystal is training for a race. She trains every day for 8 days. How many hours does Krystal train?

Krystal spends an equal amount of time sprinting, walking, and jogging. How many minutes does Krystal spend on each activity during her 8 days of training?

You can use properties of operations to help solve these problems.

Krystal trains $2\frac{3}{4}$ hours per day.

B Find how many hours Krystal trains.

Find $8 \times 2\frac{3}{4}$.

$$8 \times 2\frac{3}{4} = 8 \times \left(2 + \frac{3}{4}\right)$$
$$= (8 \times 2) + \left(8 \times \frac{3}{4}\right)$$
$$= 16 + \frac{24}{4}$$
$$= 16 + 6$$
$$= 22$$

Krystal trains for 22 hours.

You can use the Distributive Property to help multiply.

C Find how many minutes Krystal spends on each activity during her training.

1 hour = 60 minutes
Find 60×22.

$$\begin{array}{r} 22 \\ \times\ 60 \\ \hline 1,320 \end{array}$$

In 8 days, Krystal spends 1,320 minutes sprinting, walking, and jogging.

Divide to find how many minutes Krystal spends on each activity. Find $1,320 \div 3$.

$$\begin{array}{r} 440 \\ 3\overline{)1,320} \end{array}$$

In 8 days, Krystal spends 440 minutes on each activity.

Convince Me! © **MP.3 Critique Reasoning** Ellie said, "You can regroup the 440 minutes Krystal spent on each activity as hours." What does Ellie mean? How many hours did Krystal spend on each activity?

Name _____

Another Example!

Adding Time

Find 2 hours 32 minutes + 3 hours 40 minutes.

$$\begin{array}{r} 2 \text{ hours } 32 \text{ minutes} \\ + \ 3 \text{ hours } 40 \text{ minutes} \\ \hline 5 \text{ hours } 72 \text{ minutes} \end{array}$$

Since 72 minutes > 1 hour, regroup 60 minutes as 1 hour.

= 6 hours 12 minutes

Subtracting Time

Find 5 hours 8 minutes − 2 hours 32 minutes.

$$\begin{array}{r} \overset{4}{\cancel{5}} \text{ hours } \overset{68}{\cancel{8}} \text{ minutes} \\ - \ 2 \text{ hours } 32 \text{ minutes} \\ \hline 2 \text{ hours } 36 \text{ minutes} \end{array}$$

Since 8 minutes < 32 minutes, regroup 1 hour as 60 minutes.

☆ Guided Practice *

Do You Understand?

1. **© MP.3 Construct Arguments** How is adding and subtracting measures of time like adding and subtracting whole numbers?

Do You Know How?

For **2–3**, multiply or divide. Remember there are 60 minutes in 1 hour and 7 days in 1 week.

2. How many minutes are in $6\frac{1}{4}$ hours?

3. How many weeks are in 7,077 days?

Independent Practice ☆

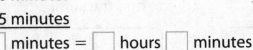
For **4–7**, add, subtract, multiply, or divide.

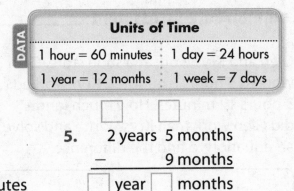

Units of Time	
1 hour = 60 minutes	1 day = 24 hours
1 year = 12 months	1 week = 7 days

4. $\begin{array}{r} 8 \text{ hours } \quad 30 \text{ minutes} \\ + \ 7 \text{ hours } \quad 35 \text{ minutes} \\ \hline \end{array}$

☐ hours ☐ minutes = ☐ hours ☐ minutes

5. ☐ ☐
$\begin{array}{r} 2 \text{ years } 5 \text{ months} \\ - \qquad\qquad 9 \text{ months} \\ \hline \end{array}$

☐ year ☐ months

6. $8 \times \frac{1}{4}$ hour $= \dfrac{\boxed{} \times 1}{\boxed{}} = \dfrac{\boxed{}}{4} = \boxed{}$ hours

7. How many weeks are in 588 days?
$588 \div 7 = \boxed{}$ weeks

*For another example, see Set E on page 582.

Topic 10 | Lesson 10-5   **569**

Math Practices and Problem Solving

For **8–9**, use the table at the right.

8. If you attend all of the activities at the reunion, how long will you spend at all of the activities?

9. There are 55 minutes between the time dinner ends and the campfire begins. What is the elapsed time from the beginning of dinner to the beginning of the campfire?

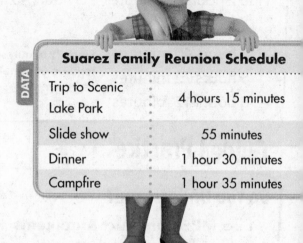

Suarez Family Reunion Schedule

Trip to Scenic Lake Park	4 hours 15 minutes
Slide show	55 minutes
Dinner	1 hour 30 minutes
Campfire	1 hour 35 minutes

10. © **MP.1 Make Sense and Persevere** The band boosters spent $4,520 on airline tickets and $1,280 on hotel costs for the 8 members of the color guard. How much was spent for each member of the color guard?

11. **Higher Order Thinking** There are 10 years in 1 decade. Dave's dog is 1 decade 2 years 10 months old. Dave is half as old as his dog. How old is Dave?

© Common Core Assessment

12. Glen and Krys work at a shoe store. Glen worked 5 hours 8 minutes. Krys worked 3 hours 12 minutes. How much longer did Glen work than Krys? Write and solve an equation to find the difference.

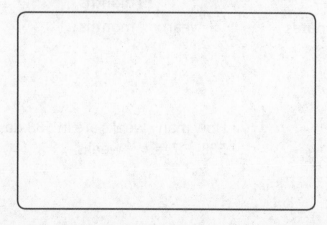

13. Henry's first flight lasts 1 hour 12 minutes. The second flight lasts 2 hours 41 minutes. How much time did Henry spend on the flights? Write and solve an equation to find the sum.

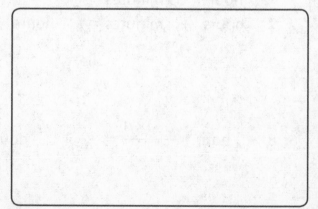

Name _____

Another Look!

You can add, subtract, multiply, or divide measures of time to solve problems.

Ann worked 5 years 7 months at her first job. She worked 3 years 3 months at her second job.

Add

How long did Ann work at her first and second job?

$$\begin{array}{r} 5 \text{ years} \quad 7 \text{ months} \\ + \; 3 \text{ years} \quad 3 \text{ months} \\ \hline 8 \text{ years } 10 \text{ months} \end{array}$$

Subtract

How much longer did Ann work at her first job than her second job?

$$\begin{array}{r} 5 \text{ years } 7 \text{ months} \\ - \; 3 \text{ years } 3 \text{ months} \\ \hline 2 \text{ years } 4 \text{ months} \end{array}$$

Ann worked 6 times longer at her fourth job than her third job. Ann worked $1\frac{1}{2}$ years at her third job.

Multiply

How long did Ann work at her fourth job?

$$6 \times 1\frac{1}{2} = (6 \times 1) + \left(6 \times \frac{1}{2}\right)$$
$$= 6 + \frac{6}{2}$$
$$= 6 + 3$$
$$= 9 \text{ years}$$

Divide

Ann was employed for 546 days at her third job. How many weeks was Ann employed? There are 7 days in one week.

$$546 \div 7 = 78 \text{ weeks}$$

For **1–9**, add, subtract, multiply, or divide.

Units of Time		
1 hour = 60 minutes	1 day = 24 hours	1 decade = 10 years
1 year = 12 months	1 week = 7 days	1 minute = 60 seconds

1.
$$\begin{array}{r} 8 \text{ hours } 12 \text{ minutes} \\ + \; 3 \text{ hours } 15 \text{ minutes} \\ \hline \end{array}$$

2.
$$\begin{array}{r} 9 \text{ weeks } 5 \text{ days} \\ - \; 1 \text{ week } 6 \text{ days} \\ \hline \end{array}$$

3.
$$\begin{array}{r} 3 \text{ hours} \quad 6 \text{ minutes } 45 \text{ seconds} \\ + \; 8 \text{ hours } 55 \text{ minutes } 20 \text{ seconds} \\ \hline \end{array}$$

4.
$$\begin{array}{r} 1 \text{ decade } 8 \text{ years} \\ - \quad\quad\quad 9 \text{ years} \\ \hline \end{array}$$

5.
$$\begin{array}{r} 12 \text{ days} \quad 6 \text{ hours} \\ + \; 8 \text{ days } 18 \text{ hours} \\ \hline \end{array}$$

6.
$$\begin{array}{r} 5 \text{ decades } 4 \text{ years } 3 \text{ months} \\ - \; 2 \text{ decades } 5 \text{ years } 6 \text{ months} \\ \hline \end{array}$$

7. How many weeks are in 42 days?

8. What is $8 \times \frac{3}{4}$ hour?

9. How many minutes are in $9\frac{1}{4}$ hours?

10. Beth works $8\frac{2}{4}$ hours, drives $1\frac{1}{4}$ hours, cooks $\frac{3}{4}$ hour, and sleeps $7\frac{2}{4}$ hours each day. How many hours of free time does Beth have each day? Remember, there are 24 hours in a day.

11. Ryan spends $10\frac{1}{2}$ hours at work each day. He has a $\frac{3}{4}$-hour lunch and receives two $\frac{1}{4}$-hour breaks. How much time does Ryan spend working? Remember, you can write an equivalent fraction for $10\frac{1}{2}$.

12. The Baltimore Marathon features a relay race. The times for each leg run by a winning team are shown in the table at the right. What is the total time it took this team to run all four legs of the marathon?

DATA

Baltimore Marathon Winner Results	
Leg of Race	Time Run
Leg 1	32 minutes 56 seconds
Leg 2	42 minutes 28 seconds
Leg 3	34 minutes 34 seconds
Leg 4	39 minutes 2 seconds

13. © **MP.4 Model with Math** What time does Mia have to leave for school if it takes 45 minutes to get to school? School starts at 7:30 A.M. Draw a number line to explain.

14. Higher Order Thinking Mr. Kent teaches 7 classes that are each 50 minutes long. He also has a 30-minute lunch break. How much time does Mr. Kent spend teaching class and at lunch?

© **Common Core Assessment**

15. If Tom brushes his teeth $\frac{1}{12}$ hour a day, how many minutes does Tom brush his teeth in 2 weeks? What units of time do you need to change to solve this problem? Write and solve equations.

16. A woman from England sneezed 978 days in a row. About how many weeks did she sneeze in a row? What units of time do you need to change to solve this problem? Write and solve an equation.

Name _____

Solve & Share

An ice cream company uses $4\frac{1}{4}$ gallons of vanilla extract and $2\frac{1}{4}$ gallons of almond extract in each vat of ice cream. How much extract is used to make 5 vats of ice cream? Use the bar diagrams to represent and solve this problem.

I can ...
use various representations to solve problems.

Ⓒ Mathematical Practices MP.4 Also, MP.1, MP.2, MP.6
Content Standards 4.NF.B.4c, 4.NF.B.3d, 4.MD.A.2

Thinking Habits
Be a good thinker!
These questions can help you.

• How can I use math I know to help solve this problem?

• How can I use pictures, objects, or an equation to represent the problem?

• How can I use numbers, words, and symbols to solve the problem?

Look Back! Ⓒ **MP.4 Model with Math** What number sentences can you write to model the problem?

How Can You Represent a Situation with a Math Model?

A

Finn gives the amount of snacks shown to the baseball team's coach every time the team wins a game. How many total pounds of snacks does Finn give the coach after the baseball team wins 3 games?

$\frac{5}{8}$ pound of red licorice

What hidden question do you need to find and solve first?

I need to find how many pounds of red licorice and peanuts Finn gives the coach when the baseball team wins a game.

$\frac{7}{8}$ pound of peanuts

Here's my thinking.

B **How can I model with math?**

I can

- use previously learned concepts and skills.

- find and answer any hidden questions.

- use bar diagrams and equations to represent and solve this problem.

C Find $\frac{5}{8} + \frac{7}{8}$ to show the total pounds of snacks.

p	
$\frac{5}{8}$	$\frac{7}{8}$

$\frac{5}{8} + \frac{7}{8} = \frac{12}{8}$ or $1\frac{4}{8}$ pounds

Find $3 \times 1\frac{4}{8}$ to show how many pounds Finn gives the coach after 3 wins.

t		
$1\frac{4}{8}$	$1\frac{4}{8}$	$1\frac{4}{8}$

$$3 \times 1\frac{4}{8} = (3 \times 1) + \left(3 \times \frac{4}{8}\right)$$
$$= 3 + 1\frac{4}{8}$$
$$= 4\frac{4}{8} \text{ pounds}$$

Finn gives the coach $4\frac{4}{8}$ pounds of snacks after the team wins 3 games.

Convince Me! © **MP.2 Reasoning** Would the answer change if $\frac{12}{8}$ pounds were used instead of $1\frac{4}{8}$ pounds to calculate the number of pounds of snacks Finn gives the coach after 3 wins? Explain.

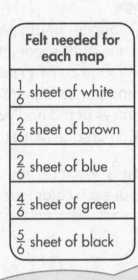

Guided Practice

© MP.4 Model with Math

Colton and his classmates are making maps of the streets where they live. How much green and black felt does his teacher need to buy so 25 students can each make a map?

Felt needed for each map
$\frac{1}{6}$ sheet of white
$\frac{2}{6}$ sheet of brown
$\frac{2}{6}$ sheet of blue
$\frac{4}{6}$ sheet of green
$\frac{5}{6}$ sheet of black

1. Draw bar diagrams and write equations to represent the problem.

2. How many green and black sheets of felt does the teacher need to buy in all? Explain.

When you model with math, you use math you know to solve a problem.

Independent Practice

© MP.4 Model with Math

Moira swims $\frac{3}{4}$ hour before school and $1\frac{3}{4}$ hours after school. For how long does she swim in 5 days? Use Exercises 3–5 to answer the question.

3. Draw bar diagrams and write equations to represent the problem.

4. What previously learned math can you use to solve the problem?

5. How long does Moira swim in 5 days? Explain.

Math Practices and Problem Solving

© **Common Core Performance Assessment** _____

Seeing Orange

Perry mixed $4\frac{2}{3}$ ounces of red paint and $3\frac{1}{3}$ ounces of yellow paint to make the right shade of orange paint. He needs 40 ounces of orange paint to paint the top of a desk and 30 ounces of another color paint to paint the rest of the desk. How many ounces of red and yellow paint should Perry use to make enough orange paint to cover the top of the desk?

6. **MP.2 Reasoning** What do you need to know to find how many ounces of each color Perry should use?

7. **MP.4 Model with Math** Draw bar diagrams and write equations to represent finding how many ounces of paint are in a batch and how many batches Perry needs to make.

When you model with math, you use a picture to show how the quantities in the problem are related.

8. **MP.6 Be Precise** How many batches does Perry need to make? Explain.

9. **MP.4 Model with Math** Draw bar diagrams. Write and solve equations to show how to find how many ounces of each color Perry should use.

Help Practice Buddy Tools Games

Another Look!

How many more cups of bananas than cups of flour are in 3 loaves of banana bread?

Tell how you can model with math to solve problems.

- I can use previously learned concepts and skills.
- I can find and answer any hidden questions.
- I can use bar diagrams and equations to represent and solve this problem.

Draw bar diagrams and write equations to solve the hidden question and the original question.

Loaf of Banana Bread

$1\frac{3}{4}$ cups of mashed bananas

$1\frac{1}{4}$ cups flour

$\frac{1}{4}$ cup applesauce

When you model with math, you can write an equation to represent the relationships in the problem.

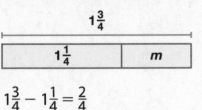

$$1\frac{3}{4} - 1\frac{1}{4} = \frac{2}{4}$$

Each loaf uses $\frac{2}{4}$ cup more of mashed bananas than flour.

$$3 \times \frac{2}{4} = \frac{6}{4} \text{ or } 1\frac{2}{4}$$

3 loaves of banana bread contain $1\frac{2}{4}$ or $1\frac{1}{2}$ cups more mashed bananas than flour.

Ⓒ MP.4 Model with Math

Aaron wraps presents in a store. In one hour, he wraps 8 games and one console. How much wrapping paper does Aaron use? Use Exercises 1–3 to answer the question.

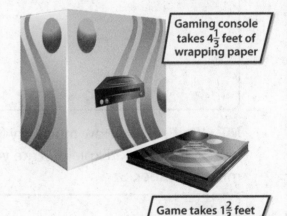

Gaming console takes $4\frac{1}{3}$ feet of wrapping paper

Game takes $1\frac{2}{3}$ feet of wrapping paper

1. Draw bar diagrams and write equations to represent the problem.

2. What previously learned math can you use to solve the problem?

3. How much wrapping paper does Aaron use? Explain.

Cat Food

Tamara feeds her cat $\frac{1}{8}$ cup canned food each day and the rest dry. She also gives her cat one treat a day. How much dry food does Tamara feed her cat in a week?

4. **MP.2 Reasoning** What quantities are given in the problem and what do the numbers describe?

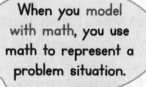

$\frac{3}{8}$ cup of food per day

5. **MP.1 Make Sense and Persevere** What do you need to find?

6. **MP.4 Model with Math** Draw bar diagrams and write equations to represent the problem and show relationships.

When you model with math, you use math to represent a problem situation.

7. **MP.6 Be Precise** How much dry food does Tamara feed her cat in a week? Explain. Write your answer as a mixed number.

8. **MP.2 Reasoning** Explain how you know what units to use for your answer.

Name _____

Point & Tally

Find a partner. Get paper and a pencil. Each partner chooses a different color: light blue or dark blue.

Partner 1 and Partner 2 each point to a black number at the same time. Each partner adds the two numbers.

If the answer is on your color, you get a tally mark. Work until one partner has twelve tally marks.

I can ...
add multi-digit whole numbers.

© **Content Standard** 4.NBT.B.4

Partner 1					Partner 2
2,814	3,043	5,776	4,565	6,015	369
3,149	6,595	3,617	6,834	3,856	194
4,097	3,343	6,496	5,502	5,537	229
5,308	3,008	3,378	4,326	4,804	468
6,127	4,291	3,183	5,677	3,521	707
	3,518	6,356	3,282	4,466	

Tally Marks for Partner 1

Tally Marks for Partner 2

A-Z
Glossary

Word List

- benchmark fraction
- denominator
- equivalent fractions
- fraction
- mixed number
- numerator
- unit fraction

Understand Vocabulary

Write T for *true* and F for *false*.

1. _____ Benchmark fractions are commonly used fractions such as $\frac{1}{4}$ and $\frac{1}{2}$.

2. _____ Equivalent fractions are fractions where the numerator and the denominator have the same value.

3. _____ The denominator of a fraction tells the number of equal parts in the whole.

4. _____ A fraction names part of a whole, part of a set, or a location on a number line.

5. _____ The numerator is the number below the fraction bar in a fraction.

Write *always*, *sometimes*, or *never*.

6. A unit fraction _____ has a numerator of 1.

7. A numerator is _____ greater than its denominator.

8. A mixed number _____ has just a fraction part.

Use Vocabulary in Writing

9. Samatha wrote $\frac{1}{2}$. Use at least 3 terms from the Word List to describe Samantha's fraction.

You can use all of the terms to describe Samantha's fraction.

Name _____

Set A | pages 543–548

Talia used $\frac{5}{8}$ yard of ribbon.

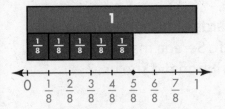

Write an equation for $\frac{5}{8}$ as a multiple of a unit fraction.

$$\frac{5}{8} = 5 \times \frac{1}{8}$$

Remember a unit fraction will always have a numerator of 1.

Write each fraction as a multiple of a unit fraction.

1. $\frac{5}{5}$ 2. $\frac{3}{8}$

3. $\frac{4}{3}$ 4. $\frac{6}{5}$

5. $\frac{15}{8}$ 6. $\frac{7}{4}$

Set B | pages 549–554

James runs $\frac{3}{5}$ mile each week. How far does James run after 2 weeks?

| $\frac{1}{5}$ | $\frac{1}{5}$ | $\frac{1}{5}$ | $\frac{1}{5}$ | $\frac{1}{5}$ | $\frac{1}{5}$ |

$\frac{3}{5}$ $\frac{3}{5}$

Use multiplication to find the product.

$2 \times \frac{3}{5} = \frac{2 \times 3}{5} = \frac{6}{5}$ or $1\frac{1}{5}$

James ran $\frac{6}{5}$ or $1\frac{1}{5}$ miles.

Remember you can record answers as fractions or mixed numbers.

Write and solve an equation.

1.
| $\frac{1}{10}$ | $\frac{1}{10}$ | $\frac{1}{10}$ | $\frac{1}{10}$ | $\frac{1}{10}$ | $\frac{1}{10}$ |

$\frac{3}{10}$ $\frac{3}{10}$

2.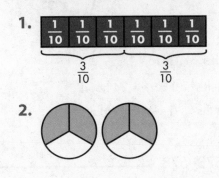

Set C | pages 555–560

Alisa has 9 puppies. Each puppy eats $\frac{2}{3}$ cup of food each day. How many cups of food does Alisa need to feed the puppies for 7 days?

Use multiplication to find how much food the puppies eat in 7 days.

$9 \times \frac{2}{3} = \frac{9 \times 2}{3} = \frac{18}{3}$ or 6 cups

$6 \times 7 = 42$ cups

Alisa needs 42 cups of food to feed the puppies for 7 days.

Remember you multiply the whole number and the numerator and write the product above the denominator of the fraction.

1. Milo makes 5 batches of muffins. In each batch he uses $\frac{2}{3}$ bag of walnuts. How many bags of walnuts does Milo use?

2. A bird feeder can hold $\frac{7}{8}$ pound of seeds. How many pounds of seeds can 12 bird feeders hold?

Find $5 \times 3\frac{1}{3}$.

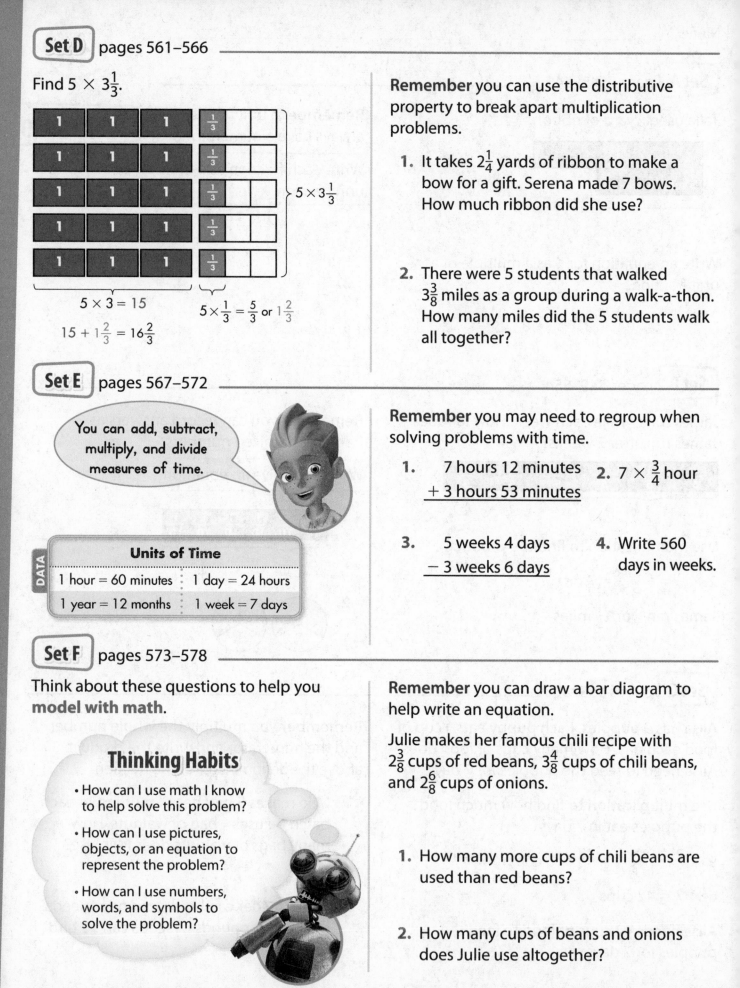

$5 \times 3 = 15$

$5 \times \frac{1}{3} = \frac{5}{3}$ or $1\frac{2}{3}$

$15 + 1\frac{2}{3} = 16\frac{2}{3}$

Remember you can use the distributive property to break apart multiplication problems.

1. It takes $2\frac{1}{4}$ yards of ribbon to make a bow for a gift. Serena made 7 bows. How much ribbon did she use?

2. There were 5 students that walked $3\frac{3}{8}$ miles as a group during a walk-a-thon. How many miles did the 5 students walk all together?

You can add, subtract, multiply, and divide measures of time.

Units of Time

DATA

1 hour = 60 minutes	1 day = 24 hours
1 year = 12 months	1 week = 7 days

Remember you may need to regroup when solving problems with time.

1.   7 hours 12 minutes
   + 3 hours 53 minutes

2. $7 \times \frac{3}{4}$ hour

3.   5 weeks 4 days
   − 3 weeks 6 days

4. Write 560 days in weeks.

Think about these questions to help you **model with math**.

Thinking Habits

• How can I use math I know to help solve this problem?

• How can I use pictures, objects, or an equation to represent the problem?

• How can I use numbers, words, and symbols to solve the problem?

Remember you can draw a bar diagram to help write an equation.

Julie makes her famous chili recipe with $2\frac{3}{8}$ cups of red beans, $3\frac{4}{8}$ cups of chili beans, and $2\frac{6}{8}$ cups of onions.

1. How many more cups of chili beans are used than red beans?

2. How many cups of beans and onions does Julie use altogether?

© **Assessment**

1. Margo practices her flute $\frac{1}{4}$ hour each day.

Units of Time
1 week = 7 days
1 hour = 60 minutes

Part A

Write and solve an equation to find how many hours Margo practices her flute in 1 week.

Part B

Use properties of operations to find how many minutes Margo practices her flute in 1 week.

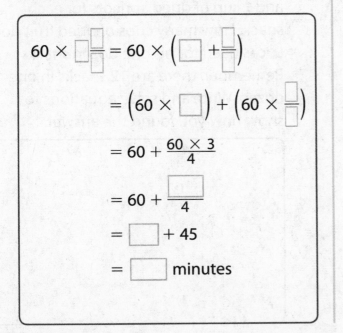

2. For questions 2a–2d, choose Yes or No to tell if $\frac{1}{2}$ will make each equation true.

2a. $6 \times \square = \frac{6}{2}$ ○ Yes ○ No

2b. $6 \times \square = 3$ ○ Yes ○ No

2c. $7 \times \square = \frac{7}{14}$ ○ Yes ○ No

2d. $7 \times \square = 3\frac{1}{2}$ ○ Yes ○ No

3. Ben played at a friend's house for 2 hours 35 minutes. Later he played at a park. He played for a total of 3 hours 52 minutes that day. How long did Ben play at the park?

Ⓐ 6 hours 27 minutes

Ⓑ 2 hours 17 minutes

Ⓒ 1 hour 17 minutes

Ⓓ 17 minutes

4. Choose numbers from the box to fill in the missing values in the multiplication equations. Use each number once.

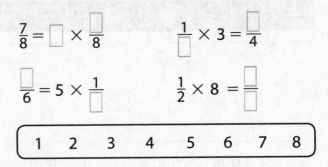

1 2 3 4 5 6 7 8

5. Chris found the product of whole numbers and mixed numbers. Draw lines to match each expression with its product.

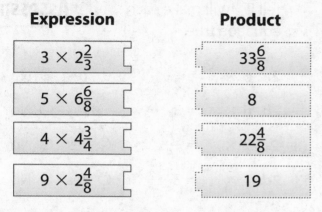

Expression	Product
$3 \times 2\frac{2}{3}$	$33\frac{6}{8}$
$5 \times 6\frac{6}{8}$	8
$4 \times 4\frac{3}{4}$	$22\frac{4}{8}$
$9 \times 2\frac{4}{8}$	19

6. Select all the expressions equal to the product of 4 and $1\frac{4}{8}$.

☐ $1\frac{4}{8} + 1\frac{4}{8} + 1\frac{4}{8} + 1\frac{4}{8}$

☐ $4 \times 1\frac{4}{8}$

☐ $4 - 1\frac{4}{8}$

☐ $4 + 1 + 4 + 8$

☐ $(4 \times 1) + \left(4 \times \frac{4}{8}\right)$

7. Complete the multiplication equation that describes what is shown by the model.

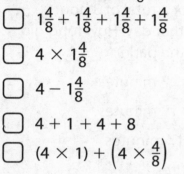

$$4 \times \frac{\square}{6} = 8 \times \frac{\square}{6}$$

8. Use a unit fraction and a whole number to write a multiplication equation equal to $\frac{7}{8}$.

9. Juan is making cookies. He makes 2 batches on Monday and 4 batches on Tuesday. He uses $\frac{3}{4}$ cup of flour in each batch. How much flour does Juan use? Explain.

10. Which multiplication expression describes the fraction shown on the number line?

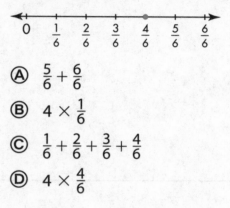

Ⓐ $\frac{5}{6} + \frac{6}{6}$

Ⓑ $4 \times \frac{1}{6}$

Ⓒ $\frac{1}{6} + \frac{2}{6} + \frac{3}{6} + \frac{4}{6}$

Ⓓ $4 \times \frac{4}{6}$

11. Lucas is making one dozen snacks for his team. He uses $\frac{1}{4}$ cup of dried cherries and $\frac{2}{4}$ cup of dried apricots for each snack. How many cups of dried fruit does Lucas need for his one dozen snacks? Remember, there are 12 snacks in one dozen. Write and solve equations to show how you found the answer.

Name _____

School Mural

Paul has permission to paint a 20-panel mural for his school. Part of the mural is shown in the **Painting a Mural** figure. Paul decides he needs help. The **Helpers** table shows how much several of his friends can paint each day and how many days a week they can paint.

Painting a Mural

Paul paints $1\frac{2}{3}$ panels a day

Helpers		
Friend	**Panels a Day**	**Days a Week**
Leeza	$\frac{3}{4}$	3
Kelsey	$\frac{7}{8}$	4
Tony	$\frac{5}{6}$	3

1. The students want to find how long it will take to paint the mural if each works on a different part of the panels a different number of days a week.

Part A

How many panels can Leeza paint in a week?
Use fraction strips to explain.

Part B

How many panels can Kelsey paint in a week?
Use equations to explain.

Part C

Paul can work 5 days a week. How many panels can Paul paint in a week?
Use multiplication equations and properties of operations to explain.

Part D

How many panels can Tony paint in a week? Draw a bar diagram.
Write and solve an equation.

2. The **Time Spent Painting Each Day** table shows
how much time each of Paul's friends helped with
the mural each day that they worked on it.

How much more time did Kelsey spend each day
than Tony and Leeza combined? Explain.

Time Spent Painting Each Day	
Friend	**Time**
Leeza	30 minutes
Kelsey	2 hours 30 minutes
Tony	1 hour 45 minutes

© Pearson Education, Inc. 4

Represent and Interpret Data on Line Plots

Essential Questions: How can you read data on a line plot? How can you make a line plot?

Digital Resources

Solve Learn Glossary Practice Buddy

Tools Assessment Help Games

Earthquakes occur when Earth's surface releases energy.

Many earthquakes occur near fault lines.

Cities, countries, and even schools have earthquake plans to keep everyone safe! Here is a project about safety and data.

Math and Science Project: Safety and Data

Do Research Use the Internet or other sources to find what causes an earthquake and how the power of an earthquake is measured. Tell how people can stay safe during earthquakes.

Journal: Write a Report Include what you found. Also in your report:

- The size, or *magnitude*, of an earthquake is measured with the Richter scale. Explain how the scale is used.

- Research the magnitudes of at least 6 earthquakes that have occurred in your lifetime. Make a table showing when they occurred and their magnitudes, and then show their magnitudes on a line plot.

Review What You Know

A-Z Vocabulary

Choose the best term from the box. Write it on the blank.

• compare	
• data	
• line plot	
• scale	

1. A _____ is a way to organize data on a number line.

2. Numbers that show the units used on a graph are called a _____.

3. _____ are pieces of information.

Comparing Fractions

Write >, <, or = in the ◯.

4. $\frac{7}{8}$ ◯ $\frac{3}{4}$

5. $\frac{1}{2}$ ◯ $\frac{5}{8}$

6. $\frac{1}{4}$ ◯ $\frac{2}{8}$

Fraction Subtraction

Find the difference.

7. $10\frac{3}{8} - 4\frac{1}{8} =$ _____

8. $5\frac{1}{4} - 3\frac{3}{4} =$ _____

9. $7\frac{4}{8} - 2\frac{4}{8} =$ _____

Interpreting Data

Use the data in the chart to answer each exercise.

10. What is the greatest snake length? What is the least snake length?

DATA	Snake Lengths (Inches)			
	$12\frac{1}{2}$	$16\frac{1}{2}$	17	24
	16	16	13	$12\frac{1}{2}$
	$18\frac{1}{2}$	$17\frac{1}{2}$	17	16

11. Which of the snake lengths are recorded more than once? Which length was recorded the most?

12. What is the difference between the greatest length and the shortest length recorded?

In this topic, you will use data to create line plots.

© Pearson Education, Inc. 4

My Word Cards

Use the examples for each word on the front of the card to help complete the definitions on the back.

line plot

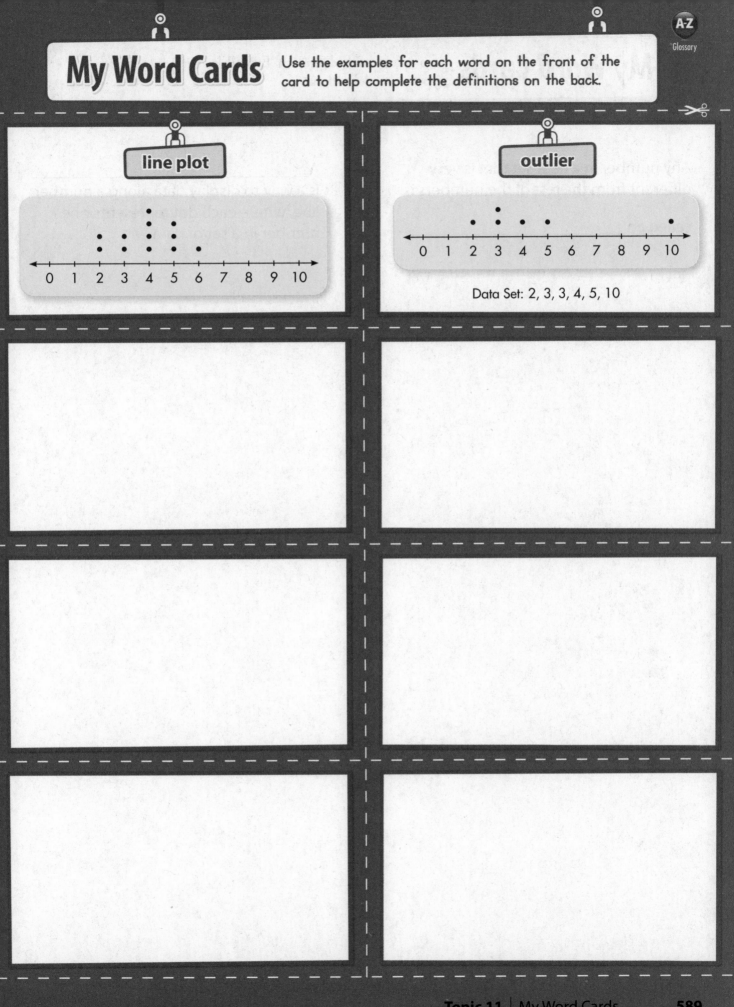

outlier

Data Set: 2, 3, 3, 4, 5, 10

My Word Cards

Complete each definition. Extend learning by writing your own definitions.

Any number in a data set that is very different from the rest of the numbers is called an _____.

A_____ is a way to display data along a number line, where each dot represents one number in a set of data.

Name _____

☆ ☆
Solve & Share

Emily went fishing. She plotted the lengths of 12 fish caught on the line plot shown below. What was the length of the longest fish caught? What was length of the shortest fish caught? *Solve this problem any way you choose.*

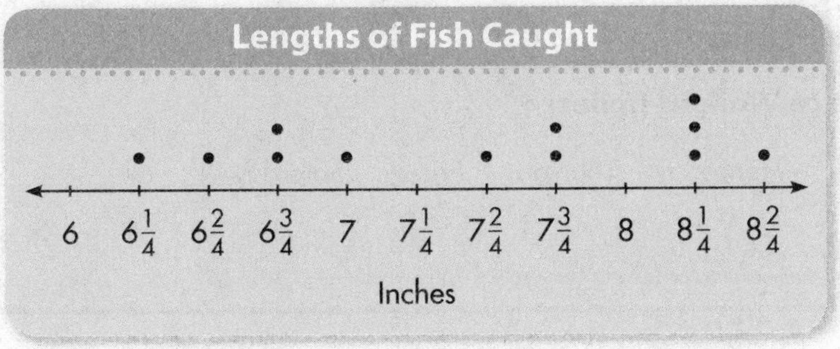

I can ...
interpret data using line plots.

© Content Standard 4.MD.B.4
Mathematical Practices MP.2, MP.3, MP.6, MP.7

Lengths of Fish Caught

| 6 | $6\frac{1}{4}$ | $6\frac{2}{4}$ | $6\frac{3}{4}$ | 7 | $7\frac{1}{4}$ | $7\frac{2}{4}$ | $7\frac{3}{4}$ | 8 | $8\frac{1}{4}$ | $8\frac{2}{4}$ |

Inches

Be precise when answering questions and use appropriate labels.

Look Back! © **MP.7 Look for Relationships** How does a line plot help you see relationships in the data?

A

A *line plot* shows data along a number line. Each dot above a point on the line represents one number in the data set. An *outlier* is any number in the data set that is very different from the rest of the numbers.

The table below shows the distance Eli walked his dog each day for seven days. How would a line plot help you identify any outliers in the data?

> Line plots make data easier to read at a glance.

DATA	Distance Walked (miles)						
	Sunday	Monday	Tuesday	Wednesday	Thursday	Friday	Saturday
	1	$\frac{1}{2}$	$1\frac{1}{2}$	1	$1\frac{1}{2}$	3	1

B Read the line plot.

Distance Walked

0   $\frac{1}{2}$ 1 $1\frac{1}{2}$ 2 $2\frac{1}{2}$ 3

Miles

The most dots are above 1 on the line plot. The most common distance is 1 mile.

The longest distance is 3 miles. The shortest distance is $\frac{1}{2}$ mile.

C Identify any outliers.

Distance Walked

0   $\frac{1}{2}$ 1 $1\frac{1}{2}$ 2 $2\frac{1}{2}$ 3

Miles

The dot above 3 is far away from the other dots on the line plot.

The distance Eli walked his dog on Friday, 3 miles, is an outlier.

Convince Me! © MP.2 Reasoning Put 4 dots on the line plot below so 3 is not an outlier. How did you decide where to place your dots?

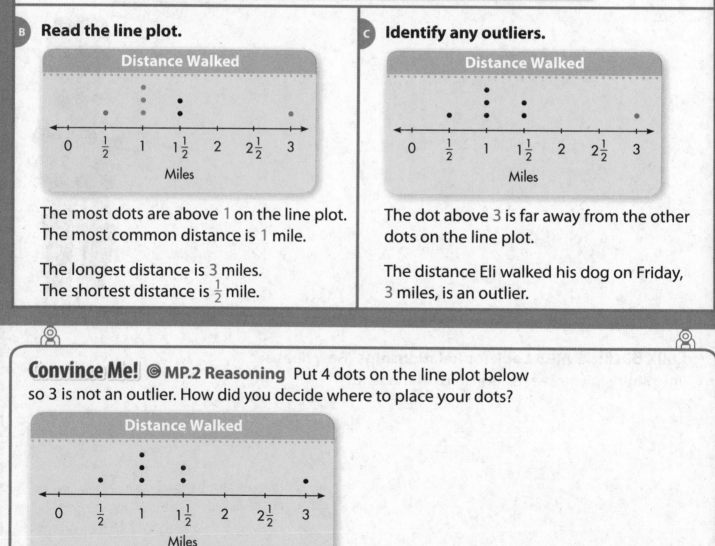

Distance Walked

0   $\frac{1}{2}$ 1 $1\frac{1}{2}$ 2 $2\frac{1}{2}$ 3

Miles

☆ Guided Practice ☆

Do You Understand?

1. © MP.3 Construct Arguments In the problem on the previous page, how do you know the distance Eli walked on Friday is an outlier by looking at the line plot?

2. If a line plot represented 10 pieces of data, how many dots would it have? Explain.

Do You Know How?

For **3–6**, use the line plot below.

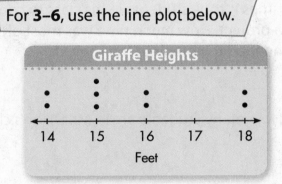

3. How many giraffes are 14 feet tall?

4. What is the most common height?

5. How tall is the tallest giraffe?

6. Is 18 feet an outlier? Explain.

☆ Independent Practice ☆

For **7–11**, use the line plot at the right.

7. How many people ran the 100-meter sprint?

8. Which time was the most common?

9. Which time is an outlier?

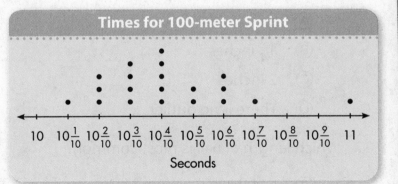

10. How many more people ran 100 meters in $10\frac{6}{10}$ seconds than in $10\frac{1}{10}$ seconds?

11. Curtis said more than half the people ran 100 meters in less than $10\frac{4}{10}$ seconds. Do you agree? Explain.

Math Practices and Problem Solving

For **12–13**, use the line plot at the right.

12. © **MP.2 Reasoning** Mr. Dixon recorded the times it took students in his class to complete a project. How much time was most often needed to complete the project?

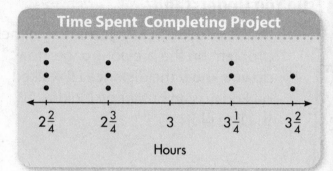

Time Spent Completing Project

$2\frac{2}{4}$　$2\frac{3}{4}$　3　$3\frac{1}{4}$　$3\frac{2}{4}$

Hours

13. How many students are in Mr. Dixon's class?

14. **Number Sense** Jorge collects sports cards. He displays his cards in an album. There are 72 pages in the album. Each page holds 9 cards. Find the number of cards in the album if half of the pages are full and the rest are empty.

15. **Higher Order Thinking** Bob listed the weights of his friends. They were 87, 98, 89, 61, and 93 pounds. Bob said there were no outliers. Is Bob correct? Explain.

© **Common Core Assessment**

For **16–17**, use the line plot at the right.

16. Which is an outlier?

　Ⓐ $\frac{3}{4}$ inch

　Ⓑ $1\frac{2}{4}$ inches

　Ⓒ 2 inches

　Ⓓ There is no outlier.

17. Which length of nail is most common?

　Ⓐ $\frac{3}{4}$ inch

　Ⓑ 1 inch

　Ⓒ $1\frac{2}{4}$ inches

　Ⓓ $2\frac{1}{4}$ inches

Each dot in this line plot represents one nail in Ed's toolbox.

Nails in Ed's Toolbox

$\frac{3}{4}$　1　$1\frac{1}{4}$　$1\frac{2}{4}$　$1\frac{3}{4}$　2　$2\frac{1}{4}$

Inches

Name _____

Another Look!

The data table shows the distances Freda ran over a period of 17 days.

A line plot shows data along a number line. Each dot represents 1 day. An outlier is a data point that is very different from the rest of the data. Which distance is the outlier?

DATA

Distance (miles)	Days
$\frac{1}{2}$	2
$1\frac{1}{2}$	4
2	5
$2\frac{1}{2}$	3
3	2
5	1

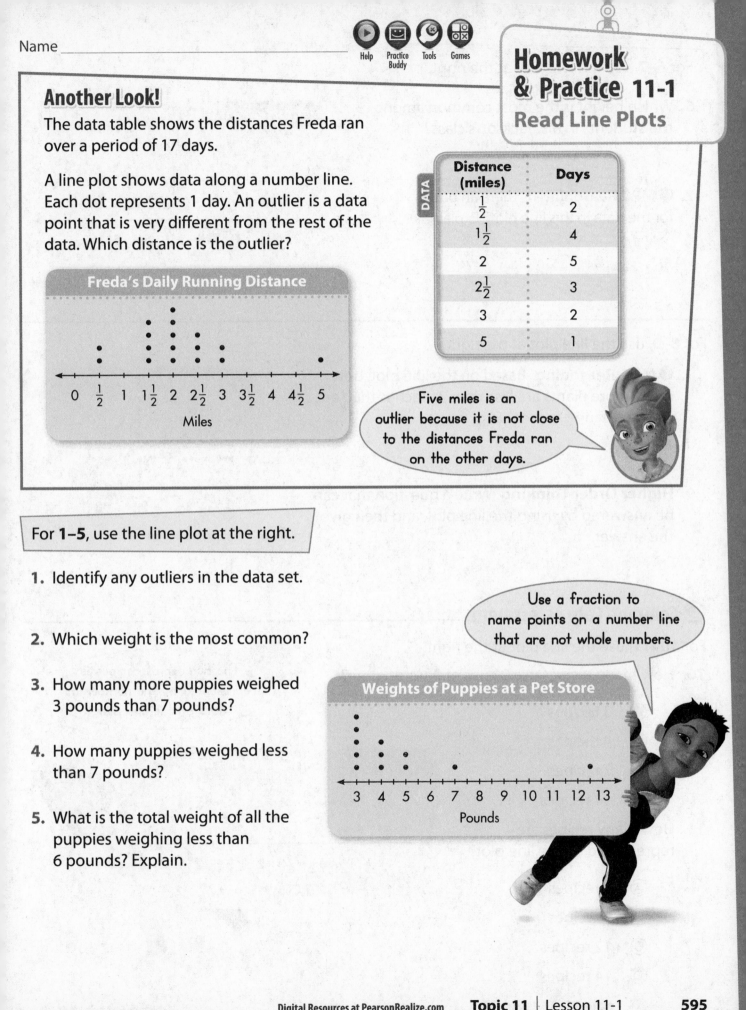

Freda's Daily Running Distance

Miles

Five miles is an outlier because it is not close to the distances Freda ran on the other days.

For **1–5**, use the line plot at the right.

1. Identify any outliers in the data set.

2. Which weight is the most common?

Use a fraction to name points on a number line that are not whole numbers.

3. How many more puppies weighed 3 pounds than 7 pounds?

4. How many puppies weighed less than 7 pounds?

5. What is the total weight of all the puppies weighing less than 6 pounds? Explain.

Weights of Puppies at a Pet Store

Pounds

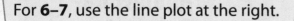

For **6–7**, use the line plot at the right.

6. Which height is the most common among the students in Ms. Jackson's class?

7. © **MP.2 Reasoning** Is there an outlier for the data in this line plot? Explain.

Heights of Students in Ms. Jackson's Class

$4 \quad 4\frac{1}{4} \quad 4\frac{2}{4} \quad 4\frac{3}{4} \quad 5 \quad 5\frac{1}{4} \quad 5\frac{2}{4} \quad 5\frac{3}{4} \quad 6$

Feet

For **8–9**, use the line plot at the right.

8. © **MP.2 Reasoning** Based on the line plot, how many more plants are less than $3\frac{2}{4}$ inches than are greater than $3\frac{2}{4}$ inches? Explain.

9. **Higher Order Thinking** Write a question that can be answered by using the line plot, and then give the answer.

Heights of Hal's Plants

$3 \quad 3\frac{1}{4} \quad 3\frac{2}{4} \quad 3\frac{3}{4} \quad 4$

Inches

© **Common Core Assessment**

For **10–11**, use the line plot at the right.

10. How many recipes use 2 cups of flour or more?

    Ⓐ 3 recipes

    Ⓑ 4 recipes

    Ⓒ 7 recipes

    Ⓓ 14 recipes

11. How many recipes are represented by the line plot?

    Ⓐ 7 recipes

    Ⓑ 9 recipes

    Ⓒ 12 recipes

    Ⓓ 14 recipes

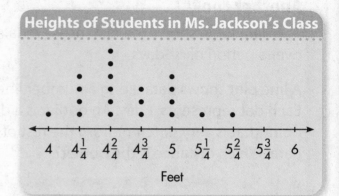

The number of recipes is represented by the number of dots on the line plot.

Flour Used in Cookie Recipes

$1 \quad 1\frac{1}{4} \quad 1\frac{2}{4} \quad 1\frac{3}{4} \quad 2 \quad 2\frac{1}{4} \quad 2\frac{2}{4} \quad 2\frac{3}{4} \quad 3$

Cups

© Pearson Education, Inc. 4

Name _____

Solve

Solve & Share

In a class of 27 students, five students have 1 pet. Three students have 2 pets. Four students have 3 pets. Two students have 4 pets. One student has 8 pets. The remaining twelve students do not have pets. Are there any outliers in this set of data? Explain. *Solve this problem any way you choose.*

I can ...
represent data using line plots.

© **Content Standards** 4.MD.B.4, 4.NF.A.1
Mathematical Practices MP.2, MP.3, MP.6

A line plot can help you be precise and organize your data. *Show your work in the space below!*

Look Back! © **MP.3 Construct Arguments** How can you use a line plot to find the data that occur most often?

Essential Question **How Can You Make Line Plots?**

A

Serena measured the lengths of her colored pencils. How can Serena make a line plot to show these lengths?

DATA

Lengths of Serena's Pencils	
Color	**Length**
Red	5 in.
Blue	$4\frac{3}{4}$ in.
Green	$4\frac{3}{4}$ in.
Purple	$4\frac{1}{8}$ in.
Orange	$4\frac{1}{2}$ in.
Yellow	$4\frac{3}{4}$ in.

You can use equivalent fractions such as $\frac{1}{2} = \frac{2}{4} = \frac{4}{8}$ to help make a line plot.

B **Making a Line Plot**

Step 1 Draw a number line and choose a scale based on the lengths of Serena's pencils. Mark halves, fourths, and eighths. The scale should show data values from the least to the greatest.

Step 2 Write a title for the line plot. Label the line plot to tell what the numbers represent.

Step 3 Draw a dot for each pencil length.

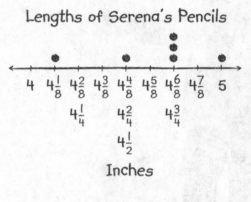

Lengths of Serena's Pencils

Inches

Convince Me! © MP.3 Construct Arguments   Complete the line plot. What is the most common shoe size? Which size is the outlier?

Shoe Sizes

4 $4\frac{1}{2}$ 5 $5\frac{1}{2}$ 6 $6\frac{1}{2}$ 7 $7\frac{1}{2}$ 8 $8\frac{1}{2}$ 9 $9\frac{1}{2}$ 10

Sizes

Shoe Sizes
$4\frac{1}{2}$, $5\frac{1}{2}$, 4, 6, 7, $5\frac{1}{2}$, 10, 6, $5\frac{1}{2}$, 6, 8, $5\frac{1}{2}$, $6\frac{1}{2}$, $5\frac{1}{2}$

Name _____

☆ Guided Practice *

Do You Understand?

1. **ⓒ MP.3 Construct Arguments** Use the table shown at the right to compare the length of Sandy's pencils with the lengths of Serena's pencils shown on the previous page. Who has more pencils that are the same length, Serena or Sandy? Which set of data was easier to compare? Why?

2. Is there an outlier for the data of Sandy's pencils? Explain.

Do You Know How?

3. Complete the line plot.

Lengths of Sandy's Pencils	
Color	**Length**
Red	$6\frac{1}{4}$ in.
Blue	$5\frac{1}{4}$ in.
Green	$6\frac{3}{4}$ in.
Purple	$5\frac{3}{4}$ in.
Orange	$6\frac{3}{4}$ in.
Yellow	$6\frac{2}{4}$ in.

Lengths of Sandy's Pencils

$$5 \quad 5\frac{1}{4} \quad 5\frac{2}{4} \quad 5\frac{3}{4} \quad 6 \quad 6\frac{1}{4} \quad 6\frac{2}{4} \quad 6\frac{3}{4} \quad 7$$

Inches

☆ Independent Practice ☆

Leveled Practice For **4–5**, use the table at the right.

4. Use the data in the table to complete the line plot.

Lengths of Rico's Bracelets

$$6 \quad 6\frac{1}{2} \quad 7 \quad 7\frac{1}{2} \quad 8 \quad 8\frac{1}{2} \quad 9$$

Inches

5. What is the length of the longest bracelet? What is the shortest length?

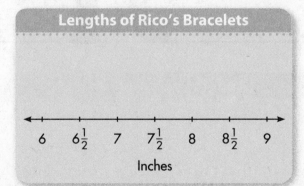

Bracelet Lengths	
8 in.	$8\frac{1}{2}$ in.
$6\frac{1}{2}$ in.	8 in.
$7\frac{1}{2}$ in.	$6\frac{1}{2}$ in.
8 in.	$7\frac{1}{2}$ in.
$6\frac{1}{2}$ in.	8 in.

*For another example, see Set B on page 617.

Topic 11 | Lesson 11-2   **599**

Math Practices and Problem Solving

6. **A-Z** **Vocabulary** Define *outlier*. Give an example using the line plot below.

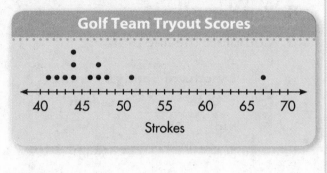

Golf Team Tryout Scores

Strokes

7. **© MP.6 Be Precise** Alyssa made a pink and white striped blanket for her bed. There are 7 pink stripes and 6 white stripes. Each stripe is 8 inches wide. How wide is Alyssa's blanket? Explain.

For **8–9**, use the table at the right.

8. Trisha's swim coach recorded her swim times each day last week. Make a line plot of Trisha's times.

9. **Higher Order Thinking** If you made a line plot of Trisha's times using 0 and 5 minutes as the boundaries, would the outlier be more or less obvious than if the boundaries of your line plot were 50 and 75 seconds? Explain.

Make sure to include a title and labels for the values on the line plot.

Day	Time
Monday	55 seconds
Tuesday	57 seconds
Wednesday	51 seconds
Thursday	72 seconds
Friday	51 seconds

© Common Core Assessment

10. Brianna is making bracelets for her friends and family members. The bracelets have the following lengths in inches:

$6, 6\frac{3}{4}, 6\frac{1}{4}, 5\frac{3}{4}, 5, 6, 6\frac{2}{4}, 6\frac{1}{4}, 6, 5\frac{3}{4}$

Use the data set to complete the line plot. Draw the dots and write the scale values.

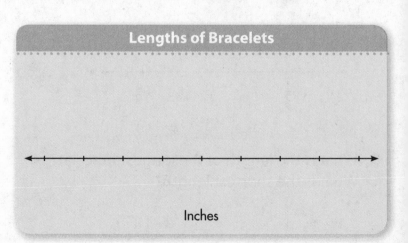

Lengths of Bracelets

Inches

Another Look!

Dorothy measured the lengths of the fingers on her left hand. She also measured the length of her thumb. Dorothy wants to make a line plot to show the measurements.

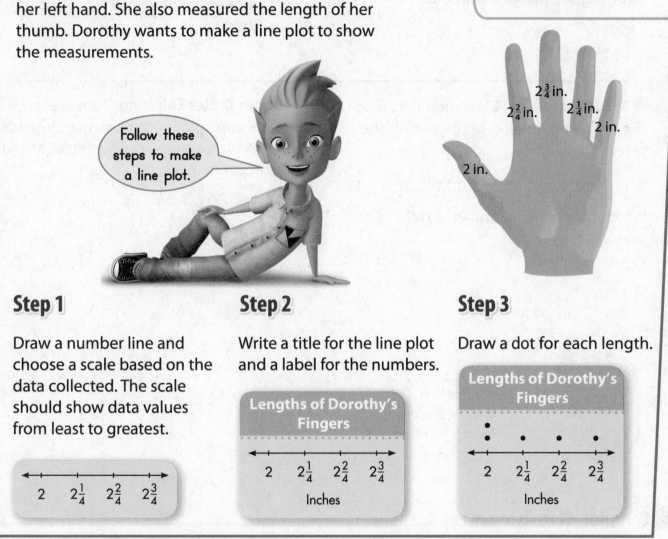

Follow these steps to make a line plot.

$2\frac{3}{4}$ in.

$2\frac{2}{4}$ in.　　$2\frac{1}{4}$ in.

2 in.

2 in.

Step 1

Draw a number line and choose a scale based on the data collected. The scale should show data values from least to greatest.

$2 \quad 2\frac{1}{4} \quad 2\frac{2}{4} \quad 2\frac{3}{4}$

Step 2

Write a title for the line plot and a label for the numbers.

Lengths of Dorothy's Fingers

$2 \quad 2\frac{1}{4} \quad 2\frac{2}{4} \quad 2\frac{3}{4}$

Inches

Step 3

Draw a dot for each length.

Lengths of Dorothy's Fingers

$2 \quad 2\frac{1}{4} \quad 2\frac{2}{4} \quad 2\frac{3}{4}$

Inches

For **1–4**, use the line plot at the right.

1. Aiden has two toy cars that measure $2\frac{1}{4}$ inches, three that measure $2\frac{3}{8}$ inches, one that measures $2\frac{7}{8}$ inches, one that measures $2\frac{1}{8}$ inches, and one that measures $2\frac{3}{4}$ inches. Use this data to complete the line plot at the right.

2. How long is Aiden's longest toy car?

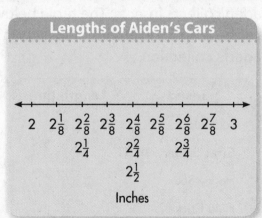

Lengths of Aiden's Cars

$2 \quad 2\frac{1}{8} \quad 2\frac{2}{8} \quad 2\frac{3}{8} \quad 2\frac{4}{8} \quad 2\frac{5}{8} \quad 2\frac{6}{8} \quad 2\frac{7}{8} \quad 3$

$2\frac{1}{4} \qquad 2\frac{2}{4} \qquad 2\frac{3}{4}$

$2\frac{1}{2}$

Inches

3. Which length appears most often on the line plot?

4. Are more cars shorter or longer than $2\frac{1}{2}$ inches?

5. A-Z Vocabulary Use a vocabulary word to complete the sentence.

An _____ fraction names the same region, part of a set, or part of a segment.

6. Math and Science Floodwalls are used to prevent damage from floods. A town built a floodwall $4\frac{4}{8}$ feet tall. Another town built a floodwall $7\frac{1}{8}$ feet tall. What is the difference between the heights of the floodwalls?

7. © MP.2 Reasoning Class members read the following number of pages over the weekend:

9, 11, 7, 10, 9, 8, 7, 13, 2, 12, 10, 9, 8, 10, 11, 12

Which number is an outlier? Explain your reasoning.

8. Higher Order Thinking Tony wants to make a line plot of the distances he rode his bike last week. He rode the following distances in miles:

$3, 4\frac{1}{2}, 6, 3, 5\frac{1}{2}, 3, 5\frac{1}{2}$

Make a line plot for the distances Tony rode.

You can draw a line plot to help you find outliers.

© Common Core Assessment

9. Caden collects insects. The table below lists the lengths in inches of insects in Caden's collection.

DATA	Insect	Length (in.)
	Ladybug	$\frac{2}{8}$
	Cross Spider	$\frac{6}{8}$
	Honey Bee	$\frac{2}{4}$
	Field Cricket	$\frac{3}{4}$
	Big Dipper Firefly	$\frac{4}{8}$
	Stag Beetle	1

Use the data set to complete the line plot. Draw the dots and write the scale values. Remember to use equivalent fractions to help write the scale values.

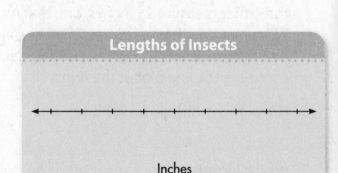

Lengths of Insects

Inches

© Pearson Education, Inc. 4

Name _____

Solve & Share

Ms. Earl's class measured the lengths of 10 caterpillars in the school garden. The caterpillars had the following lengths in inches:

$$\frac{3}{4}, 1\frac{1}{4}, 1\frac{3}{4}, 1\frac{1}{2}, 1, 1, \frac{3}{4}, 1\frac{1}{4}, 1\frac{3}{4}, 1\frac{1}{2}$$

Plot the lengths on the line plot. Write and solve an equation to find the difference in length between the longest and shortest caterpillars.

I can ...
use line plots to solve problems involving fractions.

© Content Standards 4.MD.B.4, 4.NF.B.3d
Mathematical Practices MP.1, MP.2, MP.5, MP.8

You can use tools such as a number line to display data and solve problems.

Look Back! © **MP.8 Generalize** How can a line plot be used to find the difference between the greatest and least values?

How Can You Use Line Plots to Solve Problems Involving Fractions?

A

Alma and Ben are filling water balloons. The line plots show the weights of their water balloons. Who filled more water balloons? How many more? How much heavier was Alma's heaviest water balloon than Ben's heaviest water balloon?

You can find the information you need by reading the line plots.

Weights of Alma's Water Balloons

$1 \quad 1\frac{1}{8} \quad 1\frac{2}{8} \quad 1\frac{3}{8} \quad 1\frac{4}{8} \quad 1\frac{5}{8} \quad 1\frac{6}{8} \quad 1\frac{7}{8} \quad 2 \quad 2\frac{1}{8} \quad 2\frac{2}{8}$

Pounds

Weights of Ben's Water Balloons

$1 \quad 1\frac{1}{8} \quad 1\frac{2}{8} \quad 1\frac{3}{8} \quad 1\frac{4}{8} \quad 1\frac{5}{8} \quad 1\frac{6}{8} \quad 1\frac{7}{8} \quad 2 \quad 2\frac{1}{8} \quad 2\frac{2}{8}$

Pounds

B

Who filled more water balloons? How many more?

Each dot in the line plots represents 1 water balloon.

Alma filled 20 water balloons. Ben filled 15 water balloons.

$20 - 15 = 5$

Alma filled 5 more water balloons than Ben.

C

How much heavier was Alma's heaviest water balloon than Ben's heaviest water balloon?

The dot farthest to the right in each line plot represents the heaviest water balloon.

Alma's heaviest water balloon was $2\frac{2}{8}$ pounds. Ben's heaviest water balloon was $2\frac{1}{8}$ pounds.

Subtract. $2\frac{2}{8} - 2\frac{1}{8} = \frac{1}{8}$

Alma's heaviest water balloon was $\frac{1}{8}$ pound heavier than Ben's heaviest water balloon.

Convince Me! © **MP.1 Make Sense and Persevere** How much heavier was Alma's heaviest water balloon than her lightest water balloon? How much heavier was Ben's heaviest water balloon than his lightest water balloon? Write and solve equations.

Another Example!

Rowan's class measured the snowfall for 5 days. The line plot shows the heights of snowfall they recorded. How many inches of snow were recorded? What amount of snowfall occurred most often?

Find the total number of inches of snowfall recorded.

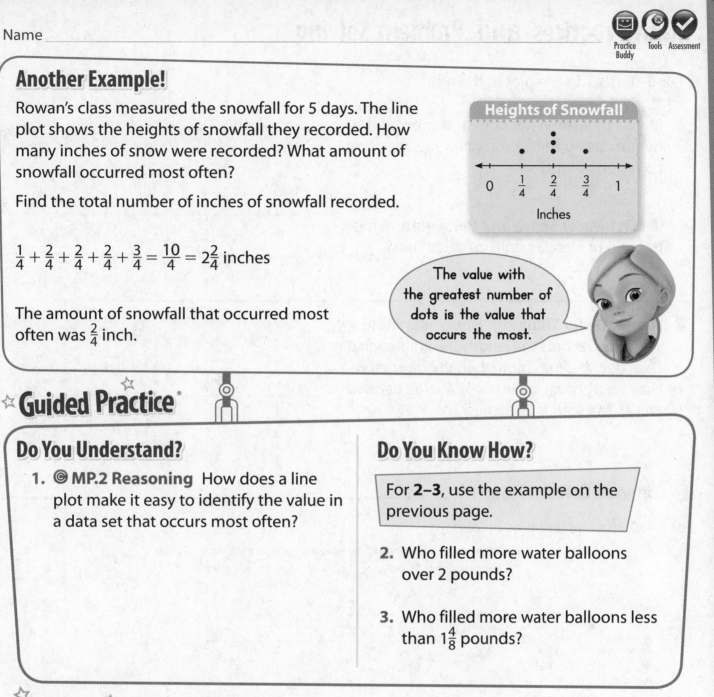

Heights of Snowfall

Inches

$$\frac{1}{4} + \frac{2}{4} + \frac{2}{4} + \frac{2}{4} + \frac{3}{4} = \frac{10}{4} = 2\frac{2}{4} \text{ inches}$$

The amount of snowfall that occurred most often was $\frac{2}{4}$ inch.

The value with the greatest number of dots is the value that occurs the most.

⭐ Guided Practice*

Do You Understand?

1. © **MP.2 Reasoning** How does a line plot make it easy to identify the value in a data set that occurs most often?

Do You Know How?

For **2–3**, use the example on the previous page.

2. Who filled more water balloons over 2 pounds?

3. Who filled more water balloons less than $1\frac{4}{8}$ pounds?

Independent Practice ⭐

For **4–5**, use the line plot at the right.

4. What is the difference in height between the tallest and shortest patients?

5. Oscar says 5 feet is the most common height Dr. Chen measured. Do you agree? Explain.

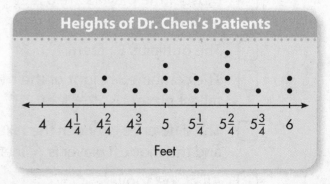

Heights of Dr. Chen's Patients

$$4 \quad 4\frac{1}{4} \quad 4\frac{2}{4} \quad 4\frac{3}{4} \quad 5 \quad 5\frac{1}{4} \quad 5\frac{2}{4} \quad 5\frac{3}{4} \quad 6$$

Feet

Math Practices and Problem Solving

For **6–7**, use the line plot at the right.

6. Marcia measured her dolls and showed the heights using a line plot. What was the most common height?

7. © **MP.1 Make Sense and Persevere** What fraction of Marcia's dolls are $6\frac{1}{2}$ inches?

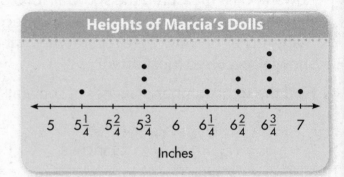

Heights of Marcia's Dolls

Inches

8. **Higher Order Thinking** Marlee is knitting a scarf. She records the length she knits each day. Each day she knits more than the day before. How many more inches does Marlee need to knit so the scarf is 30 inches?

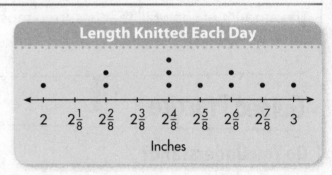

Length Knitted Each Day

Inches

© Common Core Assessment

For **9–10**, use the line plot below.

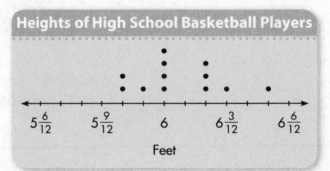

Heights of High School Basketball Players

Feet

9. Which of the following statements are true? Select all that apply.

☐ Most of the players are 6 feet or taller.

☐ The outlier is $5\frac{1}{2}$ feet.

☐ The combined height of the two tallest players is $12\frac{8}{12}$ feet.

☐ The difference between the tallest and the shortest player is $\frac{7}{12}$ feet.

☐ All of the above

10. Which of the following fractions describe the portion of the basketball players that are 6 feet tall? Use equivalent fractions. Select all that apply.

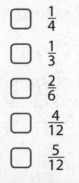

☐ $\frac{1}{4}$

☐ $\frac{1}{3}$

☐ $\frac{2}{6}$

☐ $\frac{4}{12}$

☐ $\frac{5}{12}$

Another Look!

Belle made a bracelet using beads of different sizes. The line plot shows how many beads of each size Belle used. Which length of bead did Belle use most often? How many beads did Belle use to make her bracelet?

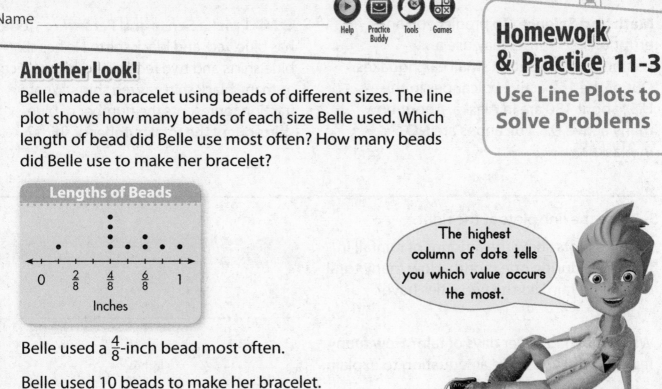

Lengths of Beads

0   $\frac{2}{8}$ $\frac{4}{8}$ $\frac{6}{8}$ 1

Inches

Belle used a $\frac{4}{8}$-inch bead most often.

Belle used 10 beads to make her bracelet.

The highest column of dots tells you which value occurs the most.

For **1–2**, use the data set below.

DATA

Length of Time to Say the Alphabet (in seconds)
5, 4, $4\frac{1}{2}$, 6, 5, $6\frac{1}{2}$, $5\frac{1}{2}$, 7, $5\frac{1}{2}$, $7\frac{1}{2}$, 6, $4\frac{1}{2}$, $4\frac{1}{2}$, $4\frac{1}{2}$, 4, 6, $4\frac{1}{2}$, $5\frac{1}{2}$, 5, $6\frac{1}{2}$

1. The table lists the length of time in seconds it takes for each student in Ms. Sousa's class to say the alphabet. Make a line plot of the data.

2. Meghan says the difference between the least amount of time it takes a student to say the alphabet and the greatest amount of time is $4\frac{1}{2}$ seconds. Do you agree? Explain.

3. Math and Science To predict volcanic eruptions, scientists may use a seismograph to detect small earthquakes. Out of the 169 active volcanoes in the U.S., about 130 are in Alaska. About how many active U.S. volcanoes are **NOT** in Alaska?

4. © **MP.1 Make Sense and Persevere** Teddy has blue, red, and black shirts. He has six blue shirts and two red shirts. He has twice as many black shirts as red shirts. What fraction represents the number of blue shirts out of the total number of shirts?

For **5–7**, use the line plots at the right.

5. The line plots show the amount of rainfall in two cities during one month. How many total days of no rain did the two cities have?

6. Which city had fewer days of rain? How many fewer? Write and solve an equation to explain.

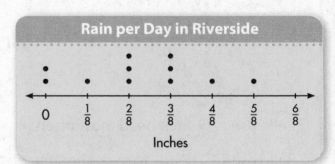

7. Higher Order Thinking Which city had the greatest amount of total rainfall? Explain.

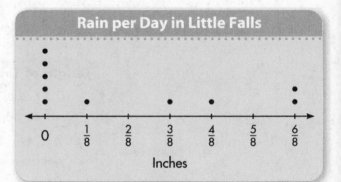

© **Common Core Assessment**

8. How many pounds of oranges do the data in the line plot represent? Use equivalent fraction to select all that apply.

- ☐ $37\frac{4}{8}$ pounds
- ☐ $37\frac{7}{2}$ pounds
- ☐ $37\frac{28}{8}$ pounds
- ☐ $40\frac{1}{2}$ pounds
- ☐ $40\frac{4}{8}$ pounds

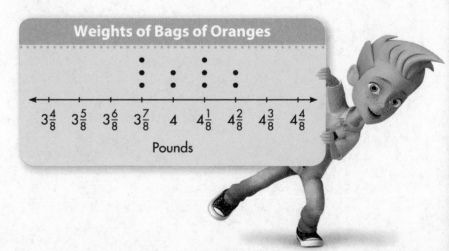

Name _____

★ ☆ ★
Solve & Share

A class made a line plot showing the amount of snowfall for 10 days. Nathan analyzed the line plot and said, "The difference between the greatest amount of snowfall recorded and the least amount of snowfall recorded is 3 because the first measurement has one dot and the last measurement has 4 dots." How do you respond to Nathan's reasoning?

Math Practices and Problem Solving

Lesson 11-4
Critique Reasoning

I can ...
use what I know about line plots to critique the reasoning of others.

ⓒ **Mathematical Practices** MP.3 Also MP.1, MP.2, MP.4
Content Standard 4.MD.B.4

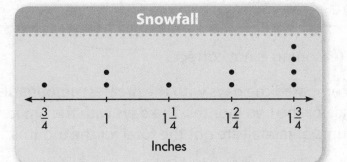

Snowfall

$\frac{3}{4}$ 1 $1\frac{1}{4}$ $1\frac{2}{4}$ $1\frac{3}{4}$

Inches

Thinking Habits

Be a good thinker!
These questions can help you.

• What questions can I ask to understand other people's thinking?

• Are there mistakes in other people's thinking?

• Can I improve other people's thinking?

Look Back! ⓒ **MP.3 Critique Reasoning** What question can you ask about the line plot above to find if Nathan's reasoning is correct?

How Can You Critique the Reasoning of Others?

A

The line plots show the amount of rainfall for two months.

Val said, "The total rainfall for February was greater than the total rainfall for January because $\frac{7}{8} + \frac{7}{8}$ equals $\frac{14}{8}$, and the highest rainfall in January was $\frac{5}{8}$."

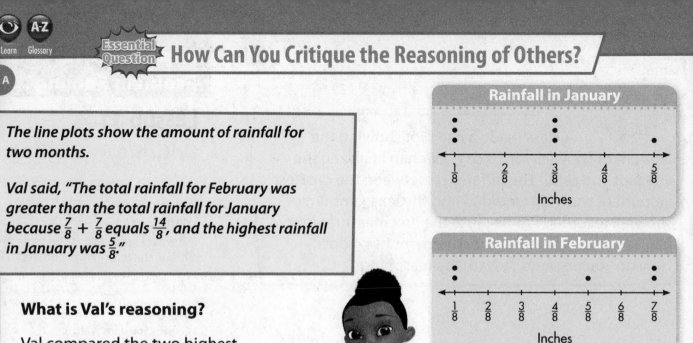

What is Val's reasoning?

Val compared the two highest amounts of rainfall for each month.

Here's my thinking.

B

How can I critique the reasoning of others?

I can

- ask questions for clarification.

- decide if the strategy used makes sense.

- look for flaws in estimates or calculations.

C

Val's reasoning is not correct.

She compared the days with the greatest amount of rainfall for the two months. The days with the greatest amounts of rainfall are not the total for the months.

Val should have added the amounts for each month. Then she could compare the amounts.

January: $\frac{1}{8} + \frac{1}{8} + \frac{1}{8} + \frac{3}{8} + \frac{3}{8} + \frac{3}{8} + \frac{5}{8} = \frac{17}{8}$ inches

February: $\frac{1}{8} + \frac{1}{8} + \frac{5}{8} + \frac{7}{8} + \frac{7}{8} = \frac{21}{8}$ inches

During February, there was $\frac{21}{8} - \frac{17}{8} = \frac{4}{8}$ inch more rain than January.

Convince Me! © **MP.3 Critique Reasoning** Bev thought January had more rainfall because it rained on 7 days and February only had rain on 5 days. How do you respond to Bev's reasoning?

Name _____

☆ Guided Practice*

ⓒ MP.3 Critique Reasoning

At a dog show, a judge wrote down the heights of 12 dogs. Cole made a line plot of the heights, shown to the right. He concluded, "The height with the most dots is $1\frac{1}{4}$ feet, so that is the greatest height of the dogs at the dog show."

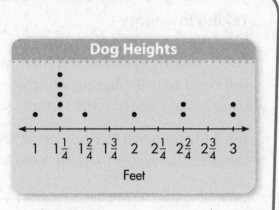

Dog Heights

Feet

1. What is Cole's conclusion? How did he reach this conclusion?

2. Is Cole's conclusion correct? Explain.

When you critique reasoning, make sure you identify flaws in reasoning.

Independent Practice ☆

ⓒ MP.3 Critique Reasoning

Natasha keeps a log of absences in her fourth-grade class. She creates the line plot shown. Each dot represents the number of absences in one week. Natasha says the total number of absences is 16 because there are 16 dots on the number line.

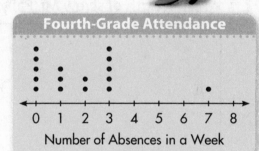

Fourth-Grade Attendance

Number of Absences in a Week

3. What is Natasha's argument? How does she support it?

4. Does Natasha's reasoning make sense? Explain.

5. Natasha also says there is an outlier in her data. Is she correct? Explain.

Math Practices and Problem Solving

© Common Core Performance Assessment

Taking Inventory

Mr. Pally is building a desk using screws of different lengths. The instructions show how many screws of each length he will need to use. Mr. Pally concludes he will use more of the shortest screws than the longest screws.

6. **MP.4 Model with Math** Draw a line plot to show the screw lengths Mr. Pally will use to build the desk.

Screw Lengths (inches)			
$\frac{3}{8}$	1	$\frac{6}{8}$	$\frac{3}{8}$
$\frac{7}{8}$	$1\frac{4}{8}$	$\frac{7}{8}$	$\frac{3}{8}$
$1\frac{4}{8}$	$\frac{6}{8}$	$\frac{3}{8}$	1
$\frac{3}{8}$	$\frac{3}{8}$	$\frac{7}{8}$	$1\frac{4}{8}$

7. **MP.2 Reasoning** How can you use the line plot to find which length of screw Mr. Pally will need the most?

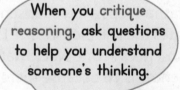

When you critique reasoning, ask questions to help you understand someone's thinking.

8. **MP.3 Critique Reasoning** Is Mr. Pally's conclusion reasonable? How did you decide? If not, what can you do to improve his reasoning?

Help Practice Tools Games
Buddy

Another Look!

Ryan's dog just had a litter of 8 puppies. He measured the length of each of the puppies. The line plot below shows their lengths in inches. Ryan says the longest puppy in the litter is $7\frac{4}{8}$ inches because $7\frac{4}{8}$ has the most dots above it.

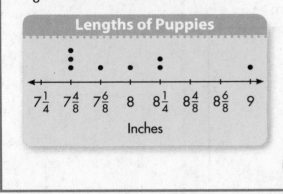

Lengths of Puppies

$7\frac{1}{4}$ $7\frac{4}{8}$ $7\frac{6}{8}$ 8 $8\frac{1}{4}$ $8\frac{4}{8}$ $8\frac{6}{8}$ 9

Inches

Tell how you can critique Ryan's reasoning.

Ryan's reasoning does not make sense. The most dots shows the most common length of puppy. To find the longest puppy, Ryan should find the dot farthest to the right on the line plot.

The longest puppy in the litter is 9 inches.

When you critique reasoning, you explain why someone's reasoning is correct or incorrect.

© **MP.3 Critique Reasoning**

Sandy made this line plot to show how many hours she read on each of 10 days. She said the difference between the greatest time and the least time she read in one day was $1\frac{3}{4}$ hours.

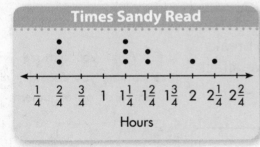

Times Sandy Read

$\frac{1}{4}$ $\frac{2}{4}$ $\frac{3}{4}$ 1 $1\frac{1}{4}$ $1\frac{2}{4}$ $1\frac{3}{4}$ 2 $2\frac{1}{4}$ $2\frac{2}{4}$

Hours

1. Tell how you can critique Sandy's reasoning.

2. Critique Sandy's reasoning.

© **MP.3 Critique Reasoning**

Liana has a collection of book series in her library. The line plot below shows how many books are in each series Liana owns. She says she has a total of 24 books.

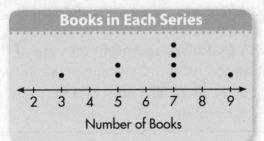

Books in Each Series

2 3 4 5 6 7 8 9

Number of Books

3. Tell how you can critique Liana's reasoning.

4. Critique Liana's reasoning.

Trivia Contest

Wallace runs a monthly trivia contest. The table shows the number of people on each trivia team. Each contestant pays a $3 entry fee to enter the contest. Wallace finds the number of contestants in the contest and concludes he will earn $171.

Team	People on Each Team
A	3
B	3
C	3
D	4
E	4
F	4
G	4
H	5
I	6
J	6
K	7
L	8

5. **MP.2 Reasoning** Draw a line plot to show the number of people on each team. Explain why a line plot can make it easier to find the most common number of people on a team.

6. **MP.1 Make Sense and Persevere** If the largest team breaks into 4 teams with 2 people on each team, how will that affect the line plot? Will it affect the amount of money Wallace earns? Explain.

When you critique reasoning, you consider all parts of an argument.

7. **MP.3 Critique Reasoning** Explain if Wallace's conclusion is reasonable. How did you decide? If not, what can you do to improve his reasoning?

Fluency Practice Activity

Find a Match

Work with a partner. Point to a clue.

Read the clue.

Look below the clues to find a match. Write the clue letter in the box next to the match.

Find a match for every clue.

I can ...
add and subtract multi-digit whole numbers.

© Content Standard 4.NBT.B.4

Clues

A The sum is between 3,510 and 3,520.

E The sum is exactly 3,584.

B The difference is exactly 3,515.

F The difference is between 3,590 and 3,600.

C The sum is between 3,560 and 3,570.

G The sum is exactly 3,987.

D The difference is between 3,530 and 3,540.

H The difference is between 1,000 and 2,000.

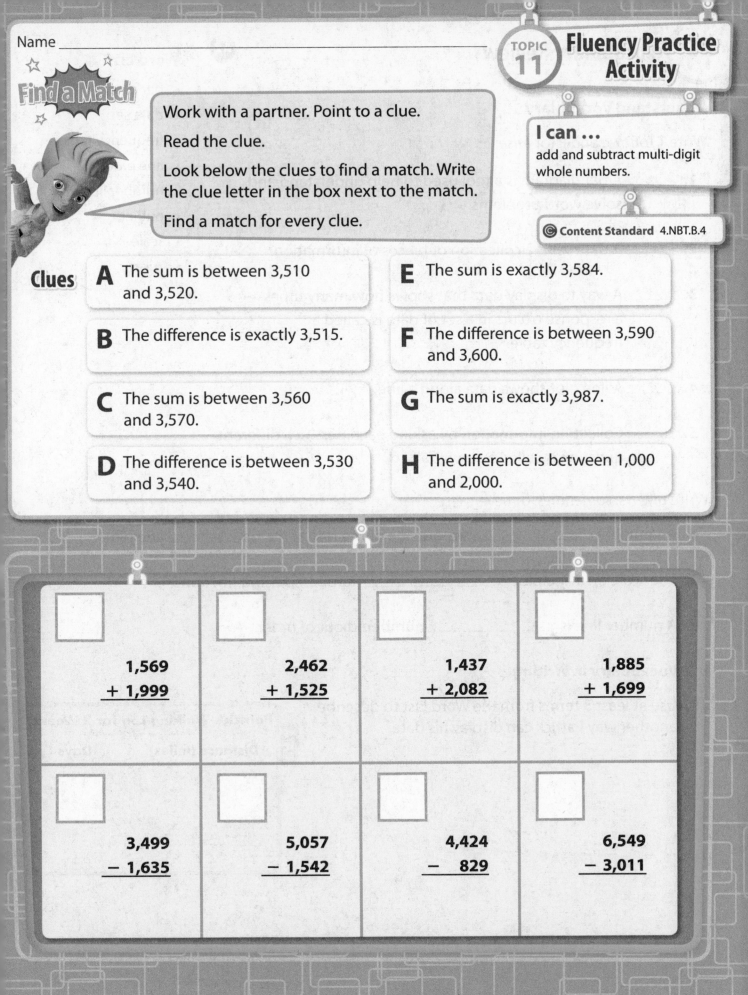

1,569 + 1,999	2,462 + 1,525	1,437 + 2,082	1,885 + 1,699
3,499 − 1,635	5,057 − 1,542	4,424 − 829	6,549 − 3,011

Vocabulary Review

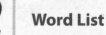
A-Z
Glossary

Word List

- bar diagram
- data set
- frequency table
- line plot
- number line
- outlier
- scale
- survey

Understand Vocabulary

Write T for *true* and F for *false*.

1. _____ A bar diagram is a tool used to help understand and solve word problems.

2. _____ A data set is a collection of pieces of information.

3. _____ A way to display data that shows how many times a response occurs in a set of data is called a frequency table.

4. _____ A line plot shows data along a line.

5. _____ Collecting information by asking each person a different question is called a survey.

Write *always, sometimes,* or *never*.

6. An outlier _____ sits outside of the rest of the data set on a line plot.

7. The scale on a line plot is _____ numbered using fractions.

8. A number line is _____ numbered out of order.

Use Vocabulary in Writing

9. Use at least 3 terms from the Word List to describe another way Patrick can display his data.

Patrick's Walking Log for 2 Weeks

DATA	Distance (miles)	Days
	1	3
	2	2
	3	4
	4	5

© Pearson Education, Inc. 4

Reteaching

Set A pages 591–596

The line plot shows the average hang times of kickers in a football league.

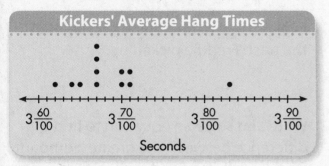

Kickers' Average Hang Times

$3\frac{60}{100}$ $3\frac{70}{100}$ $3\frac{80}{100}$ $3\frac{90}{100}$

Seconds

Each dot above the line plot represents one value in the data set.

Remember an outlier is a number that is very different from the rest of the numbers in a data set.

1. How many hang times are shown on the line plot?

2. What hang time appears most often on the line plot?

3. Is there an outlier in the set?

Set B pages 597–602

Lilly measured the lengths of the ribbons in her craft kit.

Lengths of Lilly's Ribbons	
Ribbon Colors	**Length**
Red	$5\frac{1}{2}$ in.
Blue	4 in.
White	$5\frac{1}{2}$ in.
Yellow	$4\frac{1}{4}$ in.
Pink	$4\frac{3}{4}$ in.

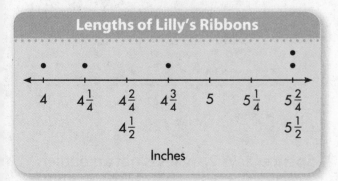

Lengths of Lilly's Ribbons

4   $4\frac{1}{4}$ $4\frac{2}{4}$ $4\frac{3}{4}$ 5 $5\frac{1}{4}$ $5\frac{2}{4}$

$4\frac{1}{2}$ $5\frac{1}{2}$

Inches

The number line shows the lengths from least to greatest. The labels show what the dots represent.

Remember to choose a reasonable scale for your number line.

A zoo in Australia studied platypuses. Their weights are recorded below.

Platypus Weights (kg)				
$1\frac{3}{4}$	2	$2\frac{1}{8}$	$2\frac{1}{2}$	$1\frac{3}{4}$
$2\frac{3}{4}$	2	2	2	$1\frac{3}{4}$
$1\frac{7}{8}$	$1\frac{5}{8}$	$2\frac{1}{4}$	$1\frac{7}{8}$	$2\frac{1}{2}$

1. Draw a line plot for the data set.

2. What scale did you use to create your line plot? Explain.

Carly and Freddie pick up trash. The line plots show how much they picked up each day for 14 days. What is the difference between the greatest and least amounts Carly picked up?

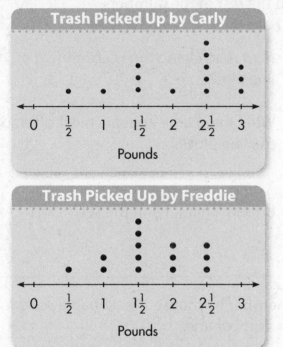

The greatest amount of trash Carly picked up was 3 pounds. The least amount was $\frac{1}{2}$ pound.

Subtract. $3 - \frac{1}{2} = 2\frac{1}{2}$ pounds

Remember to use equivalent fractions when necessary to help solve problems on line plots.

For **1–3**, use the line plots at the left.

1. Explain how to find the total weight of the trash Freddie picked up.

2. Write and solve an equation to find the difference between the greatest amount Freddie collected and the least amount Carly collected.

3. What is the sum of Carly's most frequent weight and Freddie's most frequent weight? Explain.

Think about these questions to help you **critique the reasoning** of others.

Thinking Habits

• What questions can I ask to understand other people's thinking?

• Are there mistakes in other people's thinking?

• Can I improve other people's thinking?

Remember you can use math to identify mistakes in people's thinking.

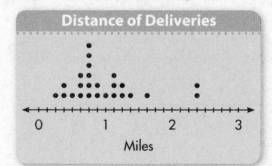

1. Spencer says $2\frac{3}{8}$ miles is not an outlier because there are two dots above it. Do you agree? Explain.

Name _____

1. Which weights are least common?

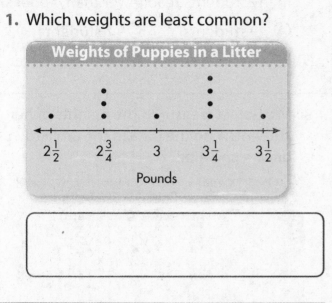

Weights of Puppies in a Litter

Pounds

2. How many dots would be placed above $1\frac{3}{4}$ in a line plot of this data?

DATA

Glasses of Water

$1\frac{1}{2}$	$2\frac{1}{2}$	$1\frac{3}{4}$	2	$1\frac{3}{4}$
$2\frac{1}{4}$	3	$1\frac{1}{2}$	$2\frac{1}{2}$	$3\frac{1}{2}$
$1\frac{3}{4}$	2	$3\frac{1}{2}$	$1\frac{1}{4}$	$2\frac{1}{4}$

Ⓐ 3 dots   Ⓒ 1 dot

Ⓑ 2 dots   Ⓓ 0 dots

3. Which is the most common length of snail Fred has in his backyard?

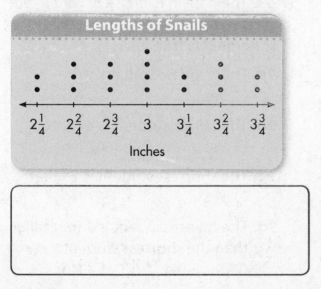

Lengths of Snails

Inches

4. During a sleep study, the number of hours 15 people slept was recorded in the table below.

DATA

Hours of Sleep in One Night				
9	6	7	$6\frac{1}{2}$	$5\frac{1}{2}$
8	$7\frac{1}{2}$	8	$7\frac{1}{2}$	7
6	$5\frac{1}{2}$	$7\frac{1}{2}$	$8\frac{1}{2}$	$6\frac{1}{2}$

Part A

Use the data in the table to draw a line plot.

Part B

How many more hours did the person who slept the greatest number of hours sleep than the person who slept the least number of hours? Explain.

5. Use the line plot below. Select all the true statements.

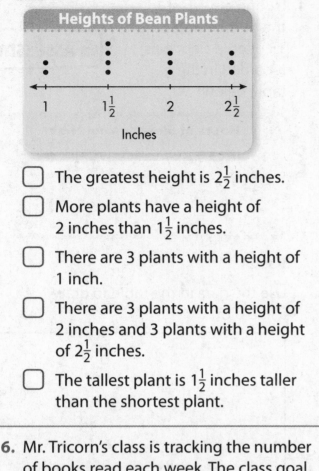

- The greatest height is $2\frac{1}{2}$ inches.
- More plants have a height of 2 inches than $1\frac{1}{2}$ inches.
- There are 3 plants with a height of 1 inch.
- There are 3 plants with a height of 2 inches and 3 plants with a height of $2\frac{1}{2}$ inches.
- The tallest plant is $1\frac{1}{2}$ inches taller than the shortest plant.

6. Mr. Tricorn's class is tracking the number of books read each week. The class goal is to read 50 books. How many more books does the class need to read to meet their goal? Explain.

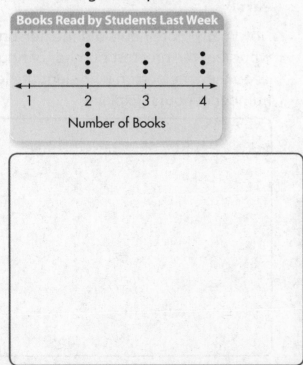

7. Use the line plot from Exercise 6. How many students read fewer than 4 books?

(A) 9 students   (C) 7 students

(B) 8 students   (D) 6 students

8. Ms. Garcia measured the heights of her students. Use the data in the table to draw a line plot.

DATA	Heights of Students in Ms. Garcia's Class (feet)				
	4	$3\frac{3}{4}$	$4\frac{1}{4}$	$4\frac{1}{2}$	4
	$3\frac{3}{4}$	$3\frac{1}{2}$	$4\frac{1}{2}$	4	$3\frac{3}{4}$
	4	$4\frac{1}{4}$	$4\frac{1}{4}$	4	$4\frac{1}{2}$

9. Use the data in Exercise 8. For 9a–9d, choose *Yes* or *No* to tell if each statement is true.

9a. There are no outliers.
○ Yes   ○ No

9b. The tallest student is $4\frac{1}{2}$ feet.
○ Yes   ○ No

9c. The shortest student is $3\frac{3}{4}$ feet.
○ Yes   ○ No

9d. The tallest student is 1 foot taller than the shortest student.
○ Yes   ○ No

Name _____

Measuring Pumpkins

Mr. Chan's class picked small pumpkins from the pumpkin patch and then weighed their pumpkins.

1. The class weighed their pumpkins and made the **Pumpkin Weights** line plot of the data.

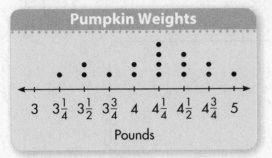

Part A

What is the most common weight of the pumpkins?

Part B

Write and solve an equation to find how much more the heaviest pumpkin weighs than the pumpkin that weighs the least.

Part C

Ayana said 3 pumpkins weigh $4\frac{1}{2}$ pounds. Critique Ayana's reasoning. Is she correct?

2. The class also measures the length around their pumpkins to the nearest half-inch. They recorded their data in the **Pumpkin Size** list.

Pumpkin Size: $19\frac{1}{2}$, $20\frac{1}{2}$, $19\frac{1}{2}$, 20, $20\frac{1}{2}$, $21\frac{1}{2}$, 20, 21, 22, $19\frac{1}{2}$, $20\frac{1}{2}$, $21\frac{1}{2}$, 21, 21, $21\frac{1}{2}$, $20\frac{1}{2}$

Part A

Draw a line plot of **Pumpkin Size** data.

Part B

Drew says 1 more pumpkin was $20\frac{1}{2}$ inches around than was $19\frac{1}{2}$ inches around because $20\frac{1}{2} - 19\frac{1}{2} = 1$. Critique Drew's reasoning. Is Drew correct?

Part C

What is the difference between the longest length and the shortest length? Write and solve an equation.

Understand and Compare Decimals

Essential Questions: How can you write a fraction as a decimal? How can you locate points on a number line? How do you compare decimals?

Digital Resources

Solve   Learn   Glossary   Practice Buddy

Tools   Assessment   Help   Games

Curling is an Olympic sport that uses special stones and a target.

Players can make their stones move the other team's stones by transferring energy when they collide.

Curling must take a lot of energy! Here is a project about energy and decimals.

Math and Science Project: Energy and Decimals

Do Research Use the Internet or other sources to research other sports or games where players transfer energy to cause collisions in order to score points and win.

Journal: Write a Report Include what you found. Also in your report:

- Explain how the transfer of energy helps the player or team score.

- A game of curling is broken into ten rounds called *ends*. Suppose a team wins 6 of the 10 ends. Write a fraction with a denominator of 10 and an equivalent fraction with a denominator of 100. Then, write an equivalent decimal that represents the same value.

Name _____

Review What You Know

Choose the best term from the box.
Write it on the blank.

• hundredth	• tens
• place value	• tenth

1. A _____ is one of 10 equal parts of a whole, written as $\frac{1}{10}$.

2. _____ is the position of a digit in a number that is used to determine the value of the digit.

3. A _____ is one of 100 equal parts of a whole, written as $\frac{1}{100}$.

Comparing Fractions

Write $>$, $<$, or $=$ in the $\bigcirc$.

4. $\frac{5}{100}$ $\bigcirc$ $\frac{5}{10}$

5. $\frac{1}{10}$ $\bigcirc$ $\frac{1}{100}$

6. $\frac{2}{10}$ $\bigcirc$ $\frac{20}{100}$

Parts of a Whole

Complete each fraction to represent the shaded part of the whole.

7. $\frac{\square}{10}$

8. $\frac{\square}{10}$

9. $\frac{\square}{10}$

Shade the part of the whole that represents the fraction.

10. $\frac{22}{100}$

11. $\frac{79}{100}$

12. $\frac{37}{100}$

Problem Solving

13. **© MP.2 Reasoning** Rob walked $\frac{2}{10}$ block. Drew walked $\frac{5}{10}$ block. Write a comparison for the distance Rob and Drew each walked.

My Word Cards

Use the examples for each word on the front of the card to help complete the definitions on the back.

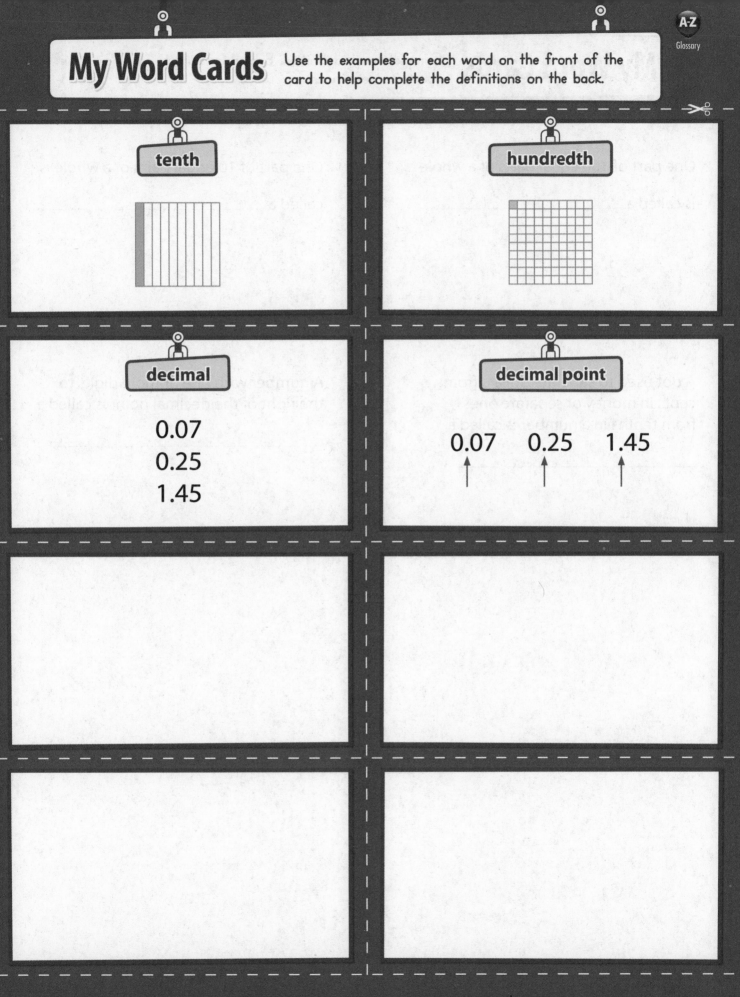

tenth

hundredth

decimal

0.07
0.25
1.45

decimal point

0.07   0.25   1.45

My Word Cards

One part of 100 equal parts of a whole is called a _____.

One part of 10 equal parts of a whole is called a _____.

A dot used to separate dollars from cents in money or separate ones from tenths in a number is called a _____.

A number with one or more digits to the right of the decimal point is called a _____.

Name _____

☆ ☆
Solve & Share

According to a survey, 7 out of 10 pet owners have a dog. Use a drawing to show this relationship. **Solve this problem any way you choose.**

I can ...
relate fractions and decimals.

Ⓒ Content Standard 4.NF.C.6
Mathematical Practices MP.2, MP.3, MP.4

You can model with math. There is more than one way to represent this relationship. *Show your work in the space below!*

Look Back! Ⓒ **MP.2 Reasoning** How many pet owners do **NOT** have a dog? Write a fraction showing this relationship.

Essential Question # How Can You Write a Fraction as a Decimal?

A

On Kelsey Street, 6 out of 10 houses have swing sets in their backyards. Write $\frac{6}{10}$ as a decimal.

Fractions and decimals can be used to show relationships between numbers.

6 out of 10 houses have swing sets.

B

Write $\frac{6}{10}$ as a decimal. Use a grid to help.

There are 10 houses, so each house is one tenth, or $\frac{1}{10}$.

$\frac{1}{10} = 0.1$

$\frac{6}{10}$ is six tenths, or 0.6.

$\frac{6}{10} = 0.6$
 ↑
 └─ decimal point

So, 0.6 of the houses have swing sets.

C

In the Kelsey Street neighborhood, 75 out of 100 houses are two-story homes. Write $\frac{75}{100}$ as a decimal. Use a grid to help.

There are 100 houses, so each house is one hundredth, or $\frac{1}{100}$.

$\frac{1}{100} = 0.01$

$\frac{75}{100}$ is seventy-five hundredths, or 0.75.

$\frac{75}{100} = 0.75$

So, 0.75 of the houses are two-story homes.

Convince Me! © MP.4 Model with Math Would the decimal models for 0.6 and 0.60 be the same or different? Use the grids to explain.

© Pearson Education, Inc. 4

Practice Buddy | Tools | Assessment

Another Example!

Show two dollars and thirty-one cents using fractions and decimals. You can use diagrams to show how money relates to fractions and decimals.

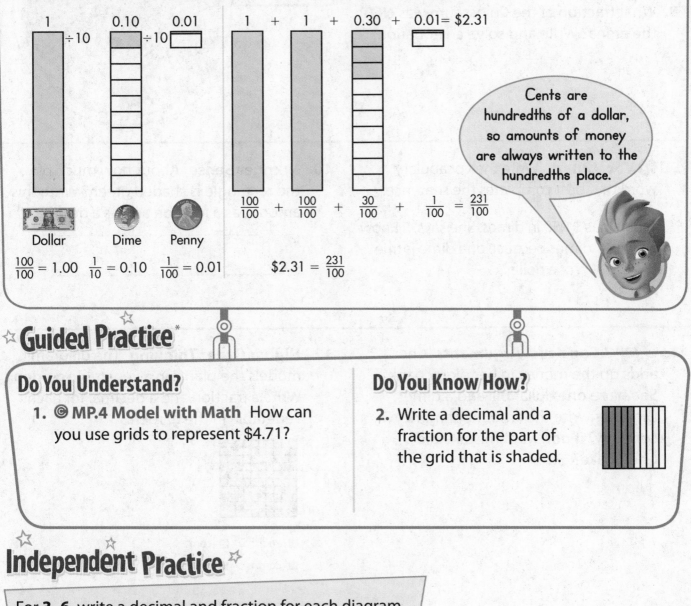

1   ÷10   0.10   ÷10   0.01

Dollar   Dime   Penny

$\frac{100}{100} = 1.00$ $\frac{1}{10} = 0.10$ $\frac{1}{100} = 0.01$

1 + 1 + 0.30 + 0.01 = $2.31

$\frac{100}{100} + \frac{100}{100} + \frac{30}{100} + \frac{1}{100} = \frac{231}{100}$

$2.31 = $\frac{231}{100}$

Cents are hundredths of a dollar, so amounts of money are always written to the hundredths place.

☆ Guided Practice *

Do You Understand?

1. © MP.4 Model with Math How can you use grids to represent $4.71?

Do You Know How?

2. Write a decimal and a fraction for the part of the grid that is shaded.

☆ Independent Practice ☆

For **3–6**, write a decimal and fraction for each diagram.

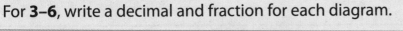

3.   4.   5.   6.

Math Practices and Problem Solving

7. The arena of the Colosseum in Rome was about $\frac{15}{100}$ of the entire Colosseum. Write this amount as a decimal.

8. What fraction of the Colosseum was **NOT** the arena? Write and solve an equation.

> The arena is $\frac{15}{100}$ of the Colosseum.

---

9. **🅐🅩 Vocabulary** Write the vocabulary word that best completes the sentence:

   Jelena has $1.50 in dimes. She says, "I know I have 15 dimes because one dime is one _____ of a dollar."

10. **Number Sense** About how much of the rectangle is shaded green? Write this amount as a fraction and as a decimal.

---

11. **© MP.3 Construct Arguments** Cher adds up the money in her piggy bank. She has a one dollar bill and 3 dimes. Did Cher write the amount of money correctly? If not, what mistake did Cher make?

    $1.3

12. **Higher Order Thinking** The diagram models the plants in a vegetable garden. Write a fraction and a decimal for each vegetable in the garden.

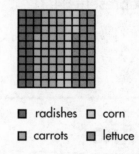

   ■ radishes ☐ corn
   ☐ carrots   ■ lettuce

© Common Core Assessment

13. A school has 100 windows. On a cool day, 95 of the windows were closed. Which decimal represents how many of the windows were open?

    Ⓐ 0.05   Ⓒ 0.50

    Ⓑ 0.5   Ⓓ 0.95

14. A singer wrote 100 songs in her career. She played guitar for 29 of the songs. Which fraction and decimal represent how many songs for which she played guitar?

    Ⓐ 0.29 and $\frac{29}{10}$ Ⓒ 2.9 and $\frac{29}{100}$

    Ⓑ 0.29 and $\frac{100}{29}$ Ⓓ 0.29 and $\frac{29}{100}$

Homework & Practice 12-1
Fractions and Decimals

Another Look!

How can you represent a number as a fraction or a decimal?

30 parts out of 100 is 0.30.

$\frac{30}{100} = 0.30$

3 parts out of 10 is 0.3.

$\frac{3}{10} = 0.3$

You can use grids to help write fractions and decimals.

So, $\frac{30}{100} = \frac{3}{10}$ and $0.30 = 0.3$. These decimals and fractions are equivalent.

For **1–3**, write a decimal and fraction for each grid.

1.

2.

3.

For **4–7**, shade the grid for each fraction and write the decimal.

4. $\frac{1}{10}$

5. $\frac{8}{10}$

6. $\frac{29}{100}$

7. $\frac{4}{100}$

8. On Tuesday, Pierce ran $\frac{3}{4}$ mile and walked $\frac{3}{4}$ mile. On Wednesday, he ran $\frac{2}{4}$ mile and walked $1\frac{1}{4}$ miles. How much farther did Pierce run and walk on Wednesday than on Tuesday? Explain.

9. © MP.3 Critique Reasoning Monique said, "0.70 is greater than 0.7 because 70 is greater than 7." Do you agree with Monique? Why or why not?

10. Jaclynn had 84 cents. Her brother gave her another 61 cents. Write the amount of money Jaclynn now has as a decimal. Explain.

11. Higher Order Thinking Hugh uses 0.63 of a piece of canvas to paint a picture. Draw a model to represent this decimal. How much of the canvas is left?

© Common Core Assessment _____

12. Look at the floor plan below. Which fraction and decimal describe the part of the grocery store that is used for food?

☐ Food ■ Kitchenware
☐ Toiletries ■ Pharmacy

Ⓐ $\frac{7}{100}$; 0.07

Ⓑ $\frac{1}{10}$; 0.1

Ⓒ $\frac{73}{100}$; 0.73

Ⓓ $\frac{73}{10}$; 7.3

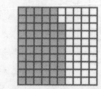

Use the key for the floor plan to find the part of the store that is used for food.

13. Which grid represents 0.85?

Ⓐ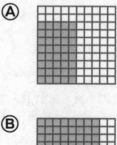

Ⓑ

Ⓒ

Ⓓ

Name _____

Solve & Share

What decimal names the location of each lettered point on the number lines? Tell how you decided. *Solve this problem any way you choose.*

I can ...
locate and describe fractions and decimals on number lines.

© Content Standard 4.NF.C.6
Mathematical Practices MP.1, MP.2, MP.4, MP.6, MP.7

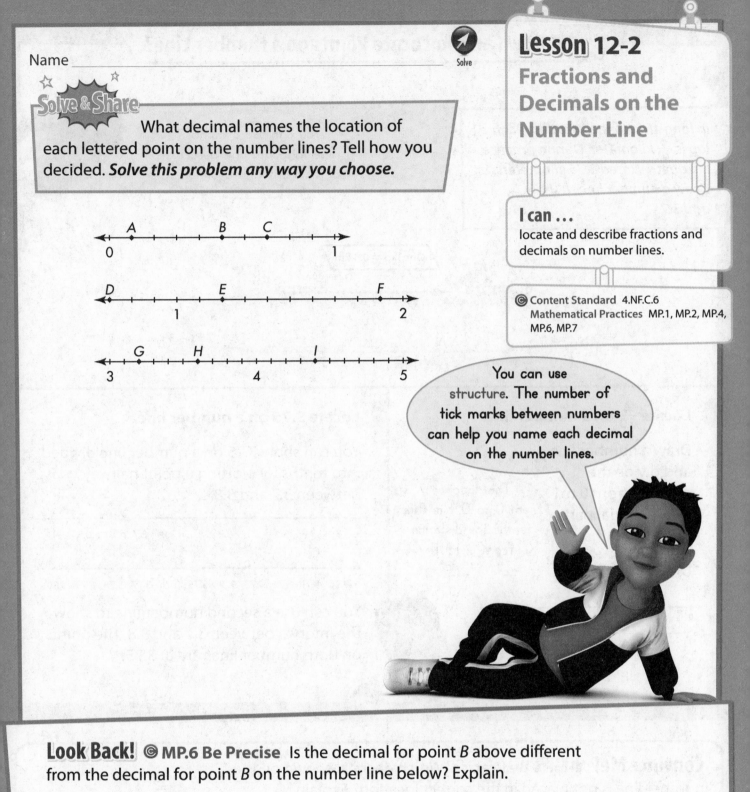

You can use structure. The number of tick marks between numbers can help you name each decimal on the number lines.

Look Back! © **MP.6 Be Precise** Is the decimal for point *B* above different from the decimal for point *B* on the number line below? Explain.

Essential Question How Can You Locate Points on a Number Line?

A

In long-track speed skating, each lap is $\frac{4}{10}$ kilometer. During practice, Elizabeth skated 3.75 kilometers. Draw a number line to show $\frac{4}{10}$ and 3.75.

You can use a number line to locate and describe fractions and decimals.

One lap = 0.4 km

B

Locate $\frac{4}{10}$ on a number line.

Draw a number line and divide the distance from 0 to 1 into 10 equal parts to show tenths.

Draw a point at $\frac{4}{10}$.

The distance from 0 to 0.4 is four tenths the distance from 0 to 1.

0   1

$\frac{4}{10}$ or 0.4

C

Locate 3.75 on a number line.

You can show 3.75 on a number line divided into tenths by plotting a point halfway between 3.7 and 3.8.

3   3.1   3.2   3.3   3.4   3.5   3.6   3.7   3.8   3.9   4

3.70 3.71 3.72 3.73 3.74 3.75 3.76 3.77 3.78 3.79 3.80

You can use a second number line to show the interval between 3.7 and 3.8. The points on both number lines are at 3.75.

Convince Me! © MP.6 Be Precise Which decimal shown on the number line is not placed in the correct location? Explain.

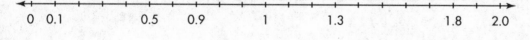

0   0.1   0.5   0.9   1   1.3   1.8   2.0

Name _____

☆ Guided Practice ☆

Do You Understand?

1. Locate $\frac{45}{100}$ on the number line.

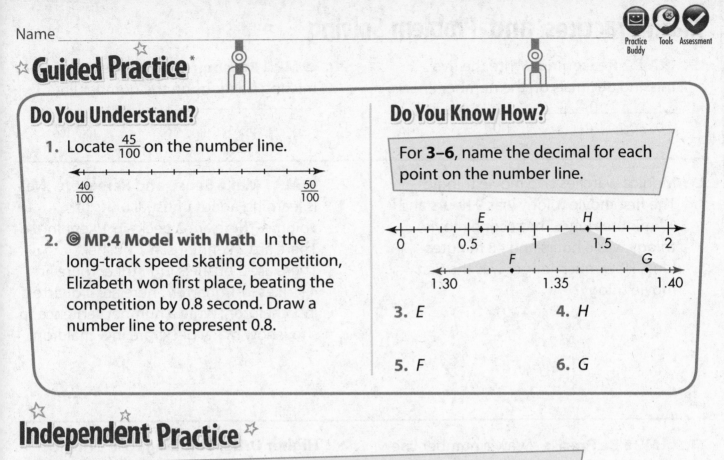

2. ⓒ **MP.4 Model with Math** In the long-track speed skating competition, Elizabeth won first place, beating the competition by 0.8 second. Draw a number line to represent 0.8.

Do You Know How?

For **3–6**, name the decimal for each point on the number line.

3. *E*   4. *H*

5. *F*   6. *G*

Independent Practice ☆

For **7–12**, name the point on the number line for each fraction or decimal.

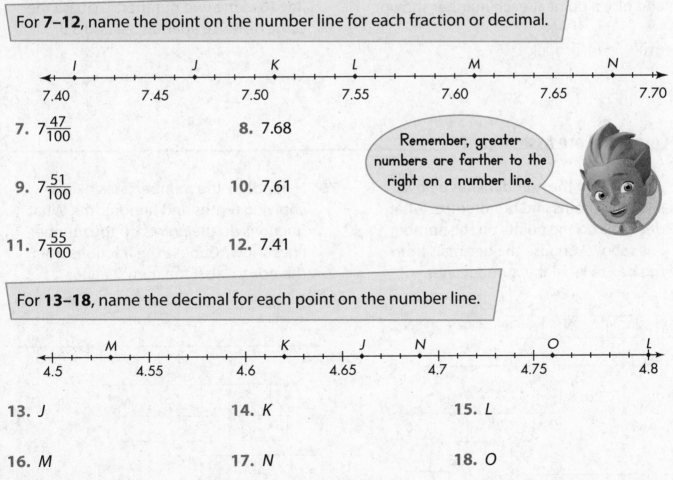

7. $7\frac{47}{100}$ 8. 7.68

9. $7\frac{51}{100}$ 10. 7.61

11. $7\frac{55}{100}$ 12. 7.41

> Remember, greater numbers are farther to the right on a number line.

For **13–18**, name the decimal for each point on the number line.

13. *J*   14. *K*   15. *L*

16. *M*   17. *N*   18. *O*

Math Practices and Problem Solving

19. ⓒ **MP.2 Reasoning** Write the five missing decimals on the number line.

```
◄─┼──┼────────┼────┼─►
  0  0.2      1.0  1.6
```

20. ⓒ **MP.2 Reasoning** Write the five missing fractions on the number line.

```
◄─┼────┼────┼─┼────────┼─┼─►
 40/100 42/100 44/100 45/100  48/100 49/100
```

21. Monica watches two movie trilogies. The first movie trilogy was 9 hours and 17 minutes long. The second movie trilogy was 6 hours and 48 minutes long. How much longer was the first movie trilogy?

22. ⓒ **MP.1 Make Sense and Persevere** Neil is learning about unusual units of volume. There are 2 pecks in 1 kenning. There are 2 kennings in 1 bushel. There are 2 bushels in 1 strike. There are 4 strikes in 1 quarter. There are 4 quarters in 1 chaldron. Write a number sentence to show how many pecks are in a chaldron.

23. ⓒ **MP.6 Be Precise** Draw a number line and plot a point at each number shown.

$$2\frac{71}{100} \quad 2\frac{6}{10} \quad 2\frac{82}{100}$$

24. **Higher Order Thinking** Use a number line to name two numbers that are the same distance apart as 3.2 and 3.8.

ⓒ Common Core Assessment

25. Jimmy drew the number lines below showing tenths and hundredths. What decimals do the points on the number lines show? Choose the decimals from the box to label the number lines.

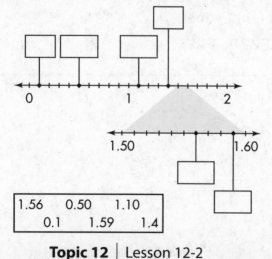

1.56	0.50	1.10
0.1	1.59	1.4

26. Harry drew the number lines below showing tenths and hundredths. What fractions do the points on the number lines show? Choose the fractions from the box to label the number lines.

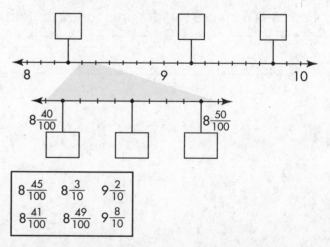

$8\frac{45}{100}$	$8\frac{3}{10}$	$9\frac{2}{10}$
$8\frac{41}{100}$	$8\frac{49}{100}$	$9\frac{8}{10}$

Name _____

Homework & Practice 12-2

Fractions and Decimals on the Number Line

Another Look!

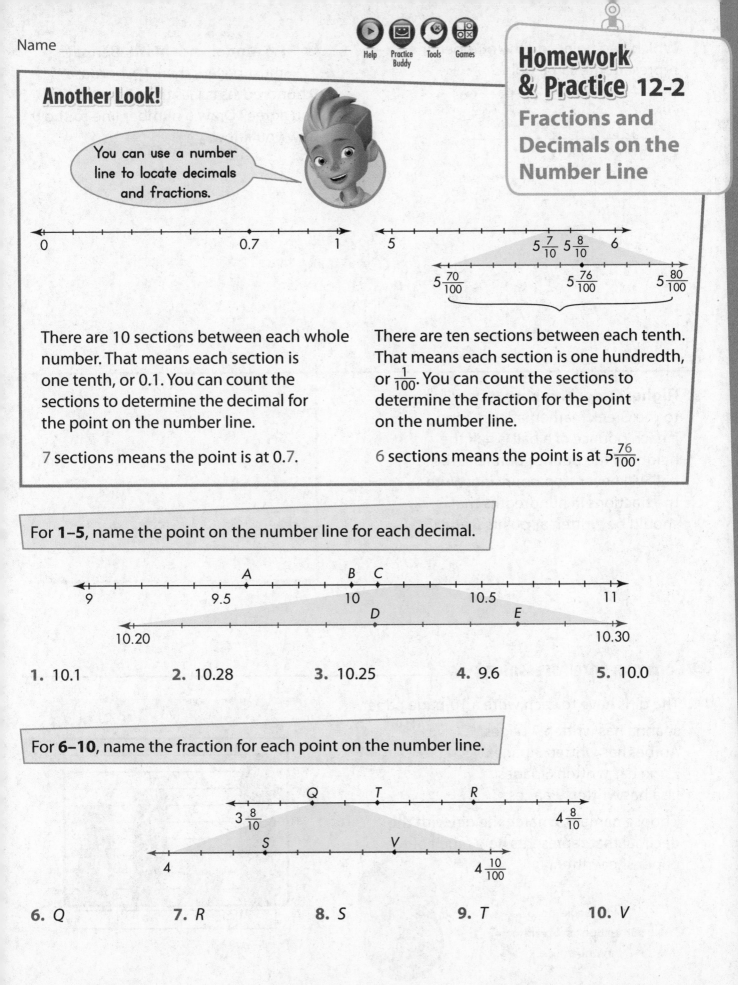

You can use a number line to locate decimals and fractions.

There are 10 sections between each whole number. That means each section is one tenth, or 0.1. You can count the sections to determine the decimal for the point on the number line.

7 sections means the point is at 0.7.

There are ten sections between each tenth. That means each section is one hundredth, or $\frac{1}{100}$. You can count the sections to determine the fraction for the point on the number line.

6 sections means the point is at $5\frac{76}{100}$.

For **1–5**, name the point on the number line for each decimal.

1. 10.1   **2.** 10.28   **3.** 10.25   **4.** 9.6   **5.** 10.0

For **6–10**, name the fraction for each point on the number line.

6. Q   **7.** R   **8.** S   **9.** T   **10.** V

11. Which two points on the number line represent the same point?

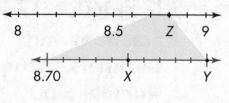

12. ⓒ **MP.4 Model with Math** Ben says $7\frac{9}{100}$ must be less than $7\frac{2}{10}$ because 9 hundredths is less than 2 tenths. Do you agree? Draw a number line to show how you know.

13. Higher Order Thinking According to the Greek mathematician Zeno, if each bounce of a ball is half the height of the bounce before it, the ball will never stop bouncing. Write the fractions in hundredths that should be written at points *B* and *C*.

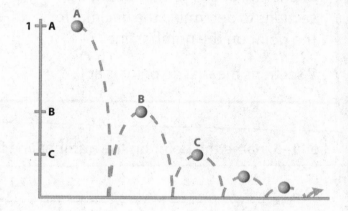

ⓒ **Common Core Assessment**

14. The girls have to each write a 10-page paper.

Joanna has written 7 pages.
Amber has written 3 pages.
Esme has written 6 pages.
Lisa has written 9 pages.

Choose names to match the girl with the decimal that represents how much of the paper she written.

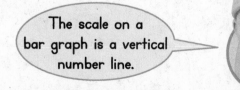

The scale on a bar graph is a vertical number line.

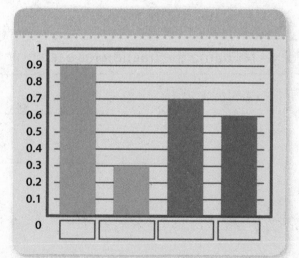

© Pearson Education, Inc. 4

Name _____

Solve & Share

A penny made in 1982 weighs about 0.11 ounce. A penny made in 2013 weighs about 0.09 ounce. Which penny weighs more? *Solve this problem any way you choose.*

I can ...
compare decimals by reasoning about their size.

Content Standards 4.NF.C.7, 4.MD.A.2
Mathematical Practices MP.2, MP.3, MP.5

You can construct arguments. Thinking about what you know about place value can help justify your reasoning.

Look Back! MP.3 Construct Arguments Simon and Danielle are eating oranges. Danielle says, "Because we each have 0.75 of an orange left, we have the same amount left to eat." Do you agree with Danielle? Explain.

Essential Question: How Do You Compare Decimals?

A

Donovan ran the 100-meter race in 10.11 seconds. Sal ran the same race in 10.09 seconds. Who had the faster time?

10.11s

Donovan

10.09 s

Sal

There is more than one way to compare decimals when they refer to the same whole.

B ## One Way

Use hundredths grids.

The digits in the tens and ones places are the same. Compare the digits in the tenths place.

10.11   10.09

10.11 > 10.09

Sal had the faster time.

C ## Another Way

Use place value.

The whole number parts are the same.

The decimal parts are both to the hundredths.

11 hundredths is greater than 9 hundredths.

10.11 > 10.09

Sal had the faster time.

D ## Another Way

Start at the left.

Compare each place value. Look for the first place where the digits are different.

10.11   10.09

1 tenth > 0 tenths

10.11 > 10.09

Sal had the faster time.

Convince Me! © MP.2 Reasoning Write four different digits in the blank spaces to make each comparison true. Explain your reasoning.

0. ____ 8 < 0. ____ 7   0. 5 ____ > 0. ____ 9

Name _____

Another Example!

Compare 0.23 and 0.32.

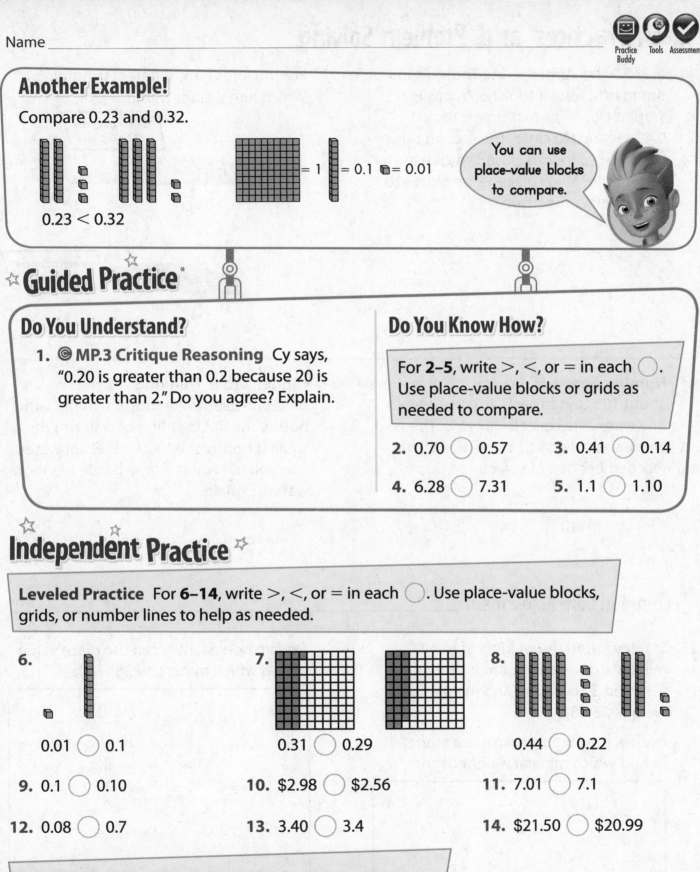

= 1   = 0.1   = 0.01

0.23 < 0.32

You can use place-value blocks to compare.

Guided Practice*

Do You Understand?

1. **MP.3 Critique Reasoning** Cy says, "0.20 is greater than 0.2 because 20 is greater than 2." Do you agree? Explain.

Do You Know How?

For **2–5**, write >, <, or = in each ◯. Use place-value blocks or grids as needed to compare.

2. 0.70 ◯ 0.57   3. 0.41 ◯ 0.14

4. 6.28 ◯ 7.31   5. 1.1 ◯ 1.10

Independent Practice

Leveled Practice For **6–14**, write >, <, or = in each ◯. Use place-value blocks, grids, or number lines to help as needed.

6.

0.01 ◯ 0.1

7.

0.31 ◯ 0.29

8.

0.44 ◯ 0.22

9. 0.1 ◯ 0.10

10. $2.98 ◯ $2.56

11. 7.01 ◯ 7.1

12. 0.08 ◯ 0.7

13. 3.40 ◯ 3.4

14. $21.50 ◯ $20.99

For **15–20**, write a decimal to make the comparison true.

15. _____ < 0.23

16. 8.60 = _____

17. _____ > 4.42

18. 13.2 > _____

19. 5.2 < _____

20. 6.21 = _____

Math Practices and Problem Solving

21. **MP.5 Use Appropriate Tools** Maria timed how long it took her Venus Fly Trap to close. The first time it took 0.43 seconds to close. The second time took 0.6 seconds to close. Which was the faster time? Draw place-value blocks to show your comparison.

22. Fishing lures have different weights. Which lure weighs more?

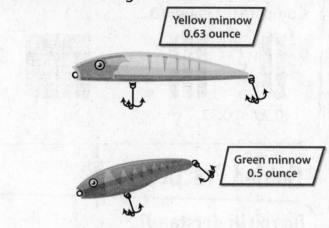

Yellow minnow 0.63 ounce

Green minnow 0.5 ounce

23. **Number Sense** Ellen wants to give about 125 toys to each of 7 charities. In one week, she collects 387 toys. The next week, she collects 515 toys. Has Ellen reached her goal? Explain.

24. **Higher Order Thinking** Tori has two different-sized water bottles. In the larger bottle, she has 0.81 liter of water. In the smaller bottle, she has 1.1 liters of water. Can you tell whether one bottle has more water? Explain.

Common Core Assessment

25. Stanley found the weights of two minerals, quartz and garnet. The quartz weighed 3.76 ounces and the garnet weighed 3.68 ounces.

Explain how Stanley can use a model to find which mineral weighed more.

Explain how Stanley can use place value to find which mineral weighed less.

© Pearson Education, Inc. 4

Another Look!

Patrick collected change for charity. On Friday, he collected $7.28. On Saturday, he collected $7.15. On which day did Patrick collect more money? Use a number line to compare the amounts.

$7.15 $7.28

$7.00 $7.10 $7.20 $7.30 $7.40 $7.50

Because $7.28 is farther to the right on the number line, it is the greater number.

So, $7.28 > $7.15.

Patrick collected more money on Friday.

There are different ways to compare decimals.

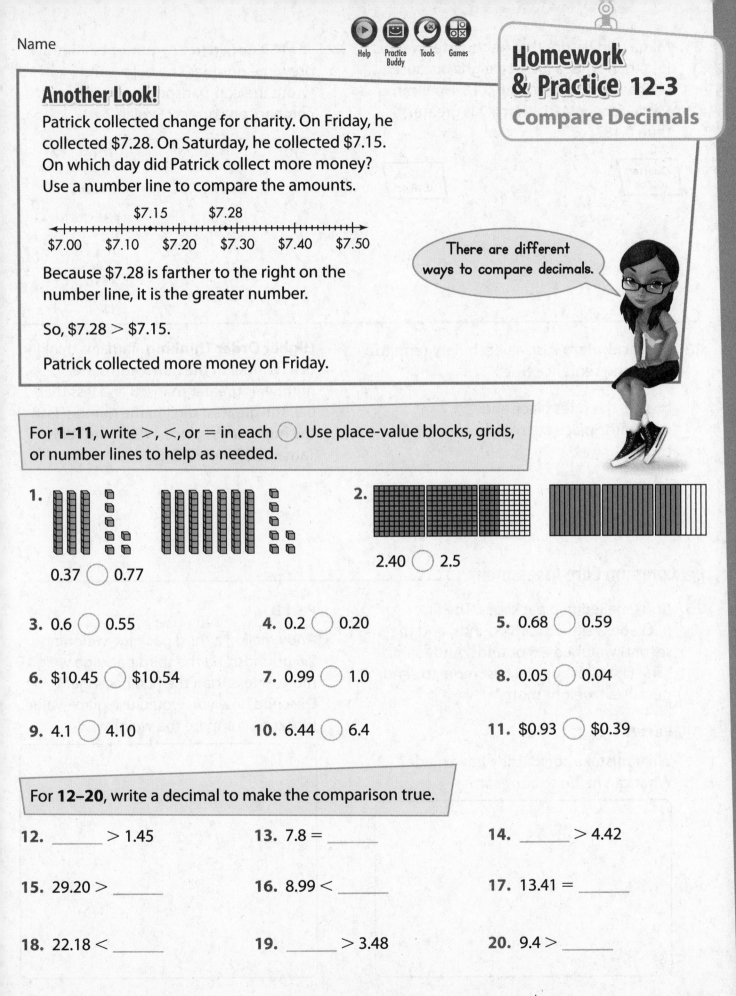

For **1–11**, write >, <, or = in each ◯. Use place-value blocks, grids, or number lines to help as needed.

1.

0.37 ◯ 0.77

2.

2.40 ◯ 2.5

3. 0.6 ◯ 0.55   **4.** 0.2 ◯ 0.20   **5.** 0.68 ◯ 0.59

6. $10.45 ◯ $10.54   **7.** 0.99 ◯ 1.0   **8.** 0.05 ◯ 0.04

9. 4.1 ◯ 4.10   **10.** 6.44 ◯ 6.4   **11.** $0.93 ◯ $0.39

For **12–20**, write a decimal to make the comparison true.

12. _____ > 1.45   **13.** 7.8 = _____   **14.** _____ > 4.42

15. 29.20 > _____   **16.** 8.99 < _____   **17.** 13.41 = _____

18. 22.18 < _____   **19.** _____ > 3.48   **20.** 9.4 > _____

21. Maria told Patrick that her quarter weighs less than what a nickel weighs because 0.2 has fewer digits than 0.18. How can Patrick show Maria that 0.2 is greater than 0.18?

Quarter 0.2 oz

Nickel 0.18 oz

22. © **MP.3 Construct Arguments** Kimmy drew the number line below and wrote the comparison shown. Is her comparison correct? Explain?

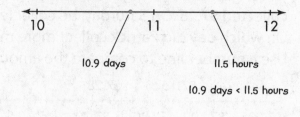

10.9 days < 11.5 hours

23. (A-Z) **Vocabulary** Use a vocabulary term to make the sentence true.

In 37.2, the ones place and the tenths place are separated by a _____.

24. **Higher Order Thinking** Tamar is thinking of a number in the hundredths. Her number is greater than 0.8 and less than 0.9. The greatest digit in the number is in the hundredths place. What number is Tamar thinking of? Explain.

© **Common Core Assessment**

25. Andy mailed two packages. The first package weighed 2.48 pounds, and the second weighed 2.6 pounds. Andy said, "The first package will cost more to send because it weighs more."

Part A

What mistake could Andy have made? What can he do to correct it?

Part B

Andy mailed a third package weighing 2.5 pounds. Did the third package weigh more or less than the first package? Describe how you would use place-value blocks to compare the weights.

Solve

☆ ☆
Solve & Share

The mural is divided into 100 equal parts. Marilyn's class painted $\frac{3}{10}$ of the mural, and Cal's class painted $\frac{27}{100}$ of the mural. How much of the mural have the two classes painted? *Solve this problem any way you choose.*

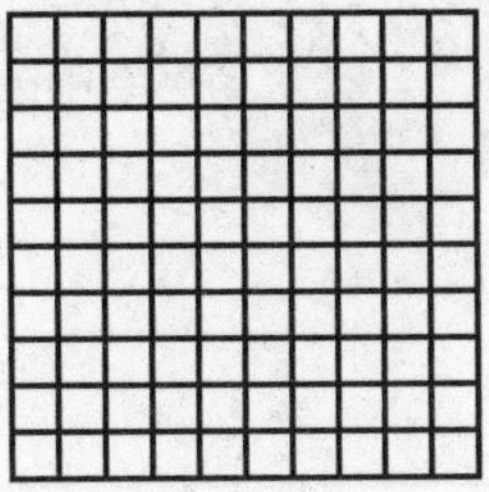

I can ...
use equivalence to add fractions with denominators of 10 and 100.

© Content Standard 4.NF.C.5
Mathematical Practices MP.1, MP.2, MP.3, MP.4, MP.5

You can use appropriate tools. Think about how you can use the grid to find how much of the mural the two classes painted. *Show your work in the space above!*

Look Back! © MP.2 Reasoning How much of the mural remains to be painted? Write the amount as a decimal.

Essential Question # How Can You Add Fractions with Denominators of 10 and 100?

A

Jana and Steve collected money for an animal shelter. Jana collected $\frac{5}{100}$ of their goal while Steve collected $\frac{4}{10}$. How much of their goal did Jana and Steve collect?

Use like denominators to add fractions.

Paws and Tails Animal Shelter

0    $\frac{10}{10}$

B The red shows $\frac{4}{10}$ of the goal and the blue shows $\frac{5}{100}$ of the goal.

The amount they collected can be written as $\frac{4}{10} + \frac{5}{100}$.

You can use equivalent fractions to write tenths as hundredths.

C Rewrite $\frac{4}{10}$ as an equivalent fraction with a denominator of 100.

Multiply the numerator and denominator by 10.

$$\frac{4}{10} \times \frac{10}{10} = \frac{40}{100}$$

D Add the numerators and write the sum over the like denominator.

$$\frac{40}{100} + \frac{5}{100} = \frac{45}{100}$$

Jana and Steve collected $\frac{45}{100}$ of their goal.

Convince Me! © **MP.3 Construct Arguments** In the problem above, why is the denominator 100 and not 200?

☆Guided Practice*

Practice Buddy   Tools   Assessment

Do You Understand?

1. Suppose Jana collected another $\frac{25}{100}$ of their goal. What fraction of the goal have they now collected?

2. ©MP.4 Model with Math Write a problem that represents the addition shown below, then solve.

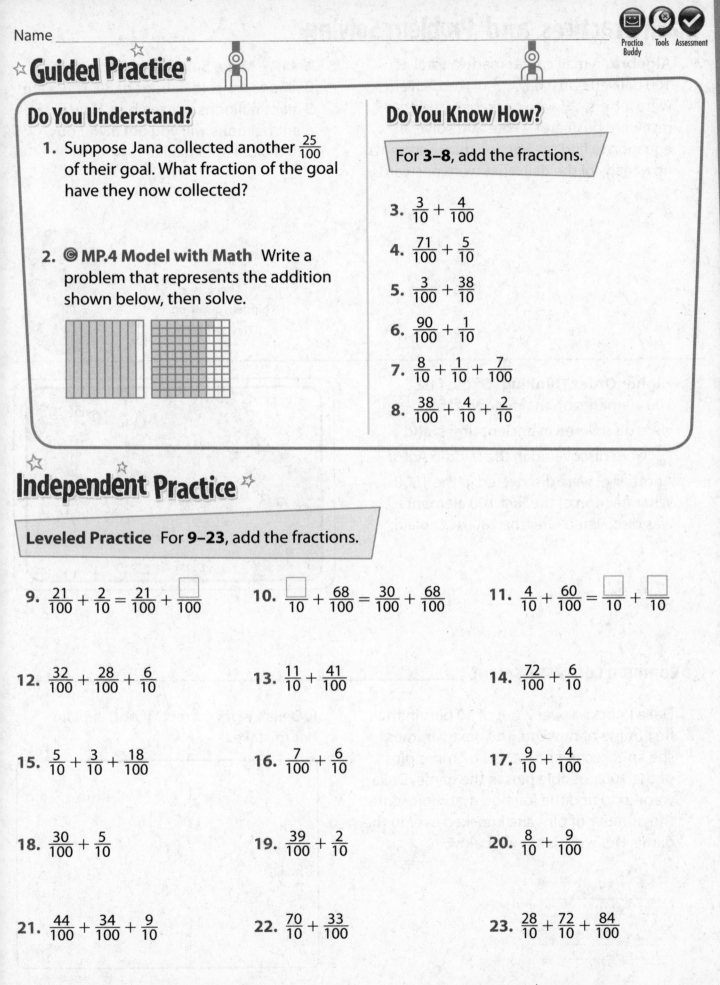

Do You Know How?

For **3–8**, add the fractions.

3. $\frac{3}{10} + \frac{4}{100}$

4. $\frac{71}{100} + \frac{5}{10}$

5. $\frac{3}{100} + \frac{38}{10}$

6. $\frac{90}{100} + \frac{1}{10}$

7. $\frac{8}{10} + \frac{1}{10} + \frac{7}{100}$

8. $\frac{38}{100} + \frac{4}{10} + \frac{2}{10}$

☆Independent Practice ☆

Leveled Practice For **9–23**, add the fractions.

9. $\frac{21}{100} + \frac{2}{10} = \frac{21}{100} + \frac{\square}{100}$

10. $\frac{\square}{10} + \frac{68}{100} = \frac{30}{100} + \frac{68}{100}$

11. $\frac{4}{10} + \frac{60}{100} = \frac{\square}{10} + \frac{\square}{10}$

12. $\frac{32}{100} + \frac{28}{100} + \frac{6}{10}$

13. $\frac{11}{10} + \frac{41}{100}$

14. $\frac{72}{100} + \frac{6}{10}$

15. $\frac{5}{10} + \frac{3}{10} + \frac{18}{100}$

16. $\frac{7}{100} + \frac{6}{10}$

17. $\frac{9}{10} + \frac{4}{100}$

18. $\frac{30}{100} + \frac{5}{10}$

19. $\frac{39}{100} + \frac{2}{10}$

20. $\frac{8}{10} + \frac{9}{100}$

21. $\frac{44}{100} + \frac{34}{100} + \frac{9}{10}$

22. $\frac{70}{10} + \frac{33}{100}$

23. $\frac{28}{10} + \frac{72}{10} + \frac{84}{100}$

*For another example, see Set D on page 666.

Math Practices and Problem Solving

24. Algebra A mail carrier made a total of 100 deliveries in a day. $\frac{76}{100}$ of the deliveries were letters, $\frac{2}{10}$ were packages, and the rest were postcards. Write and solve an equation to find the fraction that represents how many of the deliveries were postcards.

25. © **MP.1 Make Sense and Persevere**
Balloons are sold in bags of 30. There are 5 giant balloons in each bag. How many giant balloons will you get if you buy 120 balloons? Explain.

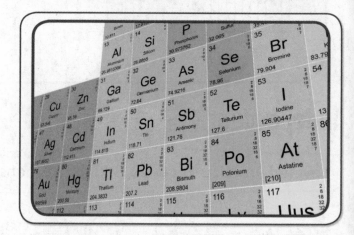

There is a hidden question in this problem.

26. Higher Order Thinking Of the first 100 elements on the periodic table, $\frac{13}{100}$ were discovered in ancient times, and $\frac{21}{100}$ were discovered in the Middle Ages. Another $\frac{5}{10}$ were discovered in the 1800s. What fraction of the first 100 elements was discovered *after* the 1800s? Explain.

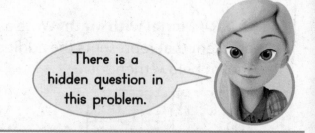

© Common Core Assessment

27. Delia knocked over 7 out of 10 pins in the first frame of bowling. The next 9 frames, she knocked over a total of 67 more pins of the 100 possible pins in the game. Delia wanted to find the fraction that represented the number of pins she knocked over in the game. Her work is shown below.

$$\frac{7}{10} + \frac{67}{100}$$

$$\frac{70}{100} + \frac{67}{100} = \frac{137}{100} \text{ pins}$$

Is Delia's work correct? If not, explain her mistake.

Help Practice Tools Games
     Buddy

Another Look!

In the morning, Duncan sold $\frac{27}{100}$ of the items in his yard sale. In the afternoon, he sold another $\frac{6}{10}$ of the items.

What fraction of the items did Duncan sell?

Find $\frac{27}{100} + \frac{6}{10}$.

> Use equivalent fractions to find how many of the items Duncan sold.

Rename one of the fractions using a common denominator.

$$\frac{6}{10} \times \frac{10}{10} = \frac{60}{100}$$

Add

$$\frac{27}{100} + \frac{60}{100} = \frac{87}{100}$$

Duncan sold $\frac{87}{100}$ of the items.

For **1–15**, add the fractions.

1. $\frac{31}{100} + \frac{4}{10} = \frac{31}{100} + \frac{\square}{100} = \frac{\square}{100}$

2. $\frac{17}{100} + \frac{9}{10} = \frac{17}{100} + \frac{\square}{\square} = 1\frac{7}{100}$

3. $\frac{\square}{100} + \frac{3}{\square} = \frac{2}{\square} + \frac{\square}{10} = \frac{5}{10}$

4. $\frac{6}{10} + \frac{39}{100}$

5. $\frac{7}{10} + \frac{22}{100}$

6. $\frac{9}{100} + \frac{3}{10} + \frac{5}{10}$

7. $2\frac{4}{10} + \frac{33}{100}$

8. $\frac{19}{100} + \frac{21}{100} + \frac{3}{10}$

9. $\frac{9}{10} + \frac{30}{100}$

10. $\frac{1}{100} + \frac{25}{10}$

11. $1\frac{3}{10} + 2\frac{8}{100}$

12. $\frac{27}{100} + \frac{2}{10}$

13. $\frac{3}{10} + \frac{4}{10} + \frac{53}{100}$

14. $\frac{64}{100} + \frac{33}{100}$

15. $3\frac{3}{10} + \frac{42}{100} + \frac{33}{100}$

16. **MP.4 Model with Math** Cecily purchases a box of 100 paper clips. She puts $\frac{37}{100}$ of the paper clips in a jar on her desk and puts another $\frac{6}{10}$ in her drawer at home. Shade a grid that shows how many of the paper clips are in Cecily's jar and drawer, then write the fraction the grid represents.

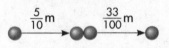

17. Robyn sells 100 tickets to the fourth-grade play. The table shows how many of each ticket she sold. What fraction of the tickets were adult and student tickets?

DATA	Ticket	Number
	Adult	$\frac{38}{100}$
	Child	$\frac{22}{100}$
	Student	$\frac{4}{10}$

18. **Math and Science** Balls colliding on a pool table are an example of how energy changes when objects collide. When two balls collide, the first ball loses speed and the second ball moves. What is the combined distance the two balls traveled?

19. **Higher Order Thinking** Alecia walked $\frac{3}{10}$ of a mile from school, stopped at the grocery store on the way, then walked another $\frac{4}{10}$ of a mile home. Georgia walked $\frac{67}{100}$ of a mile from school to her home. Which of the girls lives farther from school? Explain.

20. Regina kept a reading log of how much of her 100-page book she read each day. She read $\frac{33}{100}$ of the book on Monday, $\frac{4}{10}$ of the book on Tuesday, and another 35 pages on Wednesday. Did Regina fill out her reading log correctly? Explain.

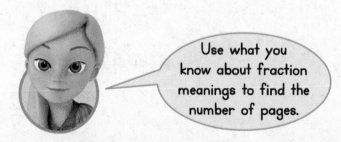

Use what you know about fraction meanings to find the number of pages.

Name _____

☆ ☆
Solve & Share

A flash drive costs $24, including tax. A customer purchases 3 flash drives and pays the cashier $80. How much change should the cashier give back to the customer? **Solve this problem any way you choose.**

Lesson 12-5
Solve Word Problems Involving Money

I can ...
use fractions or decimals to solve word problems involving money.

© **Content Standards** 4.MD.A.2, 4.NF.C.6
Mathematical Practices MP.1, MP.2, MP.4, MP.7, MP.8

You can make sense and persevere. What do you need to find first to answer the question?

$24.00

Look Back! © **MP.8 Generalize** How can you estimate and check if your solution is reasonable?

Essential Question

How Can You Solve Word Problems Involving Money?

A

Marcus buys a toy airplane and a toy car. How much does Marcus spend? How much more does the toy airplane cost than the toy car?

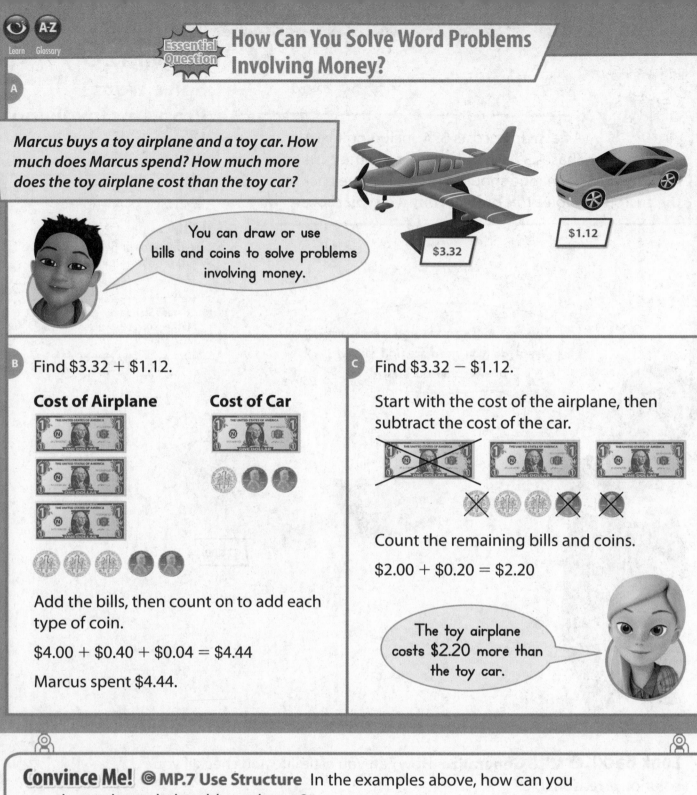

You can draw or use bills and coins to solve problems involving money.

$3.32

$1.12

B Find $3.32 + $1.12.

Cost of Airplane   **Cost of Car**

Add the bills, then count on to add each type of coin.

$4.00 + $0.40 + $0.04 = $4.44

Marcus spent $4.44.

C Find $3.32 − $1.12.

Start with the cost of the airplane, then subtract the cost of the car.

Count the remaining bills and coins.

$2.00 + $0.20 = $2.20

The toy airplane costs $2.20 more than the toy car.

Convince Me! © MP.7 Use Structure In the examples above, how can you use place value to help add or subtract?

Another Example!

Find $6.33 ÷ 3. Draw or use bills and coins to model $6.33.

Divide the bills and coins into 3 equal groups.

> You can use division to solve problems involving money.

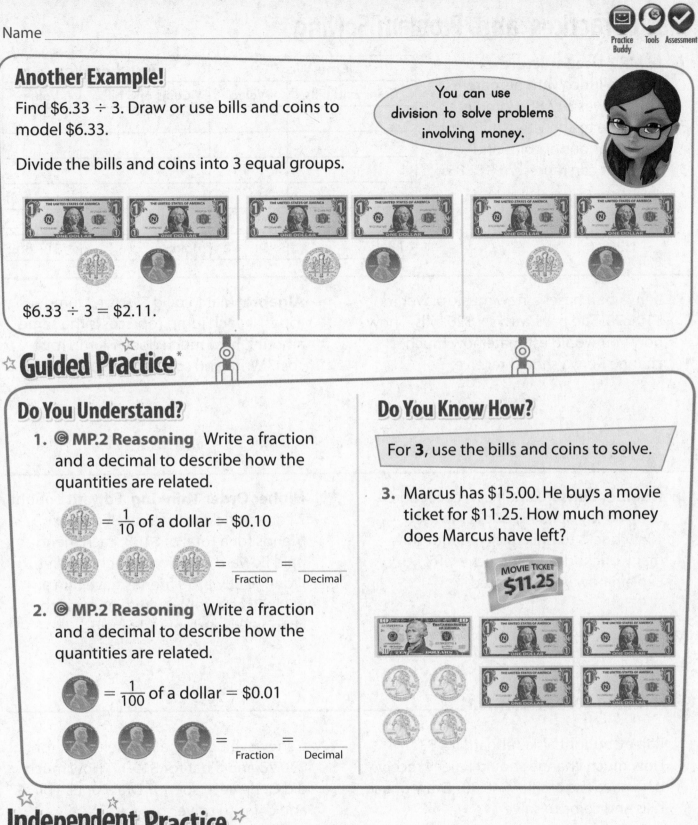

$6.33 ÷ 3 = $2.11.

☆ Guided Practice*

Do You Understand?

1. © **MP.2 Reasoning** Write a fraction and a decimal to describe how the quantities are related.

   = $\frac{1}{10}$ of a dollar = $0.10

   = _____ = _____
         Fraction   Decimal

2. © **MP.2 Reasoning** Write a fraction and a decimal to describe how the quantities are related.

   = $\frac{1}{100}$ of a dollar = $0.01

   = _____ = _____
         Fraction   Decimal

Do You Know How?

For **3**, use the bills and coins to solve.

3. Marcus has $15.00. He buys a movie ticket for $11.25. How much money does Marcus have left?

MOVIE TICKET $11.25

☆ Independent Practice ☆

For **4–5**, draw or use bills and coins to solve.

4. A new jacket costs $65.56 and a new scarf costs $23.21. If Sarah buys both, how much does she spend?

5. Carlos spends $14.38 on equipment. How much change should Carlos receive if he gives the clerk $20.00?

Math Practices and Problem Solving

6. **MP.7 Use Structure** Leo went to lunch with his parents. The bill was $17.85. Complete the table to show two different combinations of coins and bills that can represent $17.85.

One Way		Another Way	
Coins and bills	Value	Coins and bills	Value
Total	$17.85	Total	$17.85

7. Kenya purchases a new music player for $109.78. She pays with six $20 bills. Show how you would estimate how much change Kenya should receive.

8. **Algebra** Marco paid $12 for 3 jump ropes. If each jump rope costs the same amount, how much does 1 jump rope cost? Write and solve an equation.

9. **Number Sense** Jiang has a collection of 3,788 toy building bricks. He used 1,229 bricks to build a city. About how many bricks does Jiang have left? Explain how you estimated.

10. **Higher Order Thinking** Edward bought 7 concert tickets for himself and six friends for a total of $168. Each friend paid Edward back for his or her ticket. If one of Edward's friends gave him a $50 bill, how can you find how much change Edward should return?

Common Core Assessment

11. Rajeev bought a skateboard for $37.74. How much change should Rajeev receive if he gave the cashier $40.00? Draw or use bills and coins to solve.

   Ⓐ $2.26
   Ⓑ $2.74
   Ⓒ $3.26
   Ⓓ $3.74

12. Genevieve bought a catcher's mitt for $30.73 and a bat for $19.17. How much did Genevieve spend? Draw or use bills and coins to solve.

   Ⓐ $11.56
   Ⓑ $49.17
   Ⓒ $49.90
   Ⓓ $50.73

Name _____

Another Look!

Add

$1.25 + $2.01

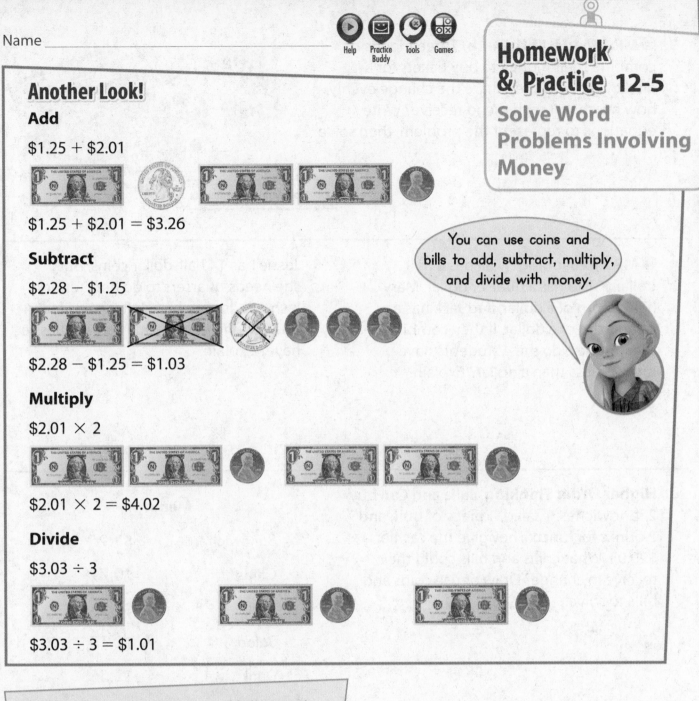

$1.25 + $2.01 = $3.26

Subtract

$2.28 − $1.25

$2.28 − $1.25 = $1.03

You can use coins and bills to add, subtract, multiply, and divide with money.

Multiply

$2.01 × 2

$2.01 × 2 = $4.02

Divide

$3.03 ÷ 3

$3.03 ÷ 3 = $1.01

For **1–2**, draw or use coins and bills to solve.

1. Mrs. Hargrove owes the doctor $34.56. She gives the clerk $50.00.

   a. List Mrs. Hargrove's change using the least number of coins and bills.

   b. What is the total amount of change Mrs. Hargrove should receive?

2. Emma buys a game for $26.84. She gives the clerk $30.00.

   a. List Emma's change using the least number of coins and bills.

   b. What is the total amount of change Emma should receive?

3. **MP.4 Model With Math** Three friends combine their money to buy tickets for a hockey game. If they share the change evenly, how much will each friend receive? Write equations to represent the problem, then solve.

$12
$12
$12

| Money given for tickets |

---

4. **MP.2 Reasoning** Niall has a half dollar, Krista has a quarter dollar, Mary has a tenth of a dollar, and Jack has a hundredth of a dollar. If they combine their money, do the 4 students have more or less than a dollar? Explain.

5. Jessie has 14 half-dollar coins, but she needs quarters to do her laundry. If she trades her half-dollar coins for quarters, how many quarters will Jessie have? Explain.

---

6. **Higher Order Thinking** Julia and Carl buy 2 sandwiches, 1 salad, 1 piece of fruit, and 2 drinks for lunch. They give the cashier $20.03. What coins and bills could they receive in change? Draw or use coins and bills to solve.

Menu	
Sandwich	$3.96
Chips	$0.79
Fruit	$1.24
Salad	$2.17
Drink	$1.55

Common Core Assessment

7. Claire has a $60 gift card. She uses the whole value of the card to buy 4 copies of the same book to give as gifts. How much does each book cost?

　Ⓐ $15

　Ⓑ $20

　Ⓒ $40

　Ⓓ $60

8. Larisa buys 3 purses. Each purse costs $126.32. How much did Larisa spend? Draw or use bills and coins to solve.

　Ⓐ $126.32

　Ⓑ $256.64

　Ⓒ $378.96

　Ⓓ $505.28

Name _____

Solve & Share

Three people hiked the same 1-mile trail. The distance for each hiker is represented in the drawings. Show about where the 1-mile mark should be on each drawing. Explain.

Start   0.5 mi

Start   0.25 mi

Start   0.75 mi

I can ...
use the structure of the place-value system to solve problems.

© Mathematical Practices MP.7 Also MP.1, MP.2, MP.3, MP.4, MP.6
Content Standards 4.NF.C.7, 4.MD.A.2

Thinking Habits

Be a good thinker!
These questions can help you.

- What patterns can I see and describe?

- How can I use the patterns to solve the problem?

- Can I see expressions and objects in different ways?

Look Back! © **MP.7 Look For Relationships** The three drawings represent 0.5, 0.25, and 0.75 mile with equivalent lengths. How does this affect where 1-mile is located on each drawing?

How Can You Look for and Make Use of Structure to Solve Problems?

A

Maps from two different ski resorts show a 1-mile cross-country ski trail for beginners. Show about where to mark 0.25, 0.5, and 0.75 mile on each trail.

Start   1 mile

Start   1 mile

How can you determine where to mark the points on each drawing?

I need to analyze each drawing and decide about where the given decimals should be located on each.

Here's my thinking.

B **How can I make use of structure to solve this problem?**

I can

- break the problem into simpler parts.

- use what I know about decimal meanings to locate the points.

- use equivalent forms of numbers.

C The size of a decimal depends on the size of the whole. The size of the whole is not the same for each drawing. Divide each whole in half to show **0.5** on each whole.

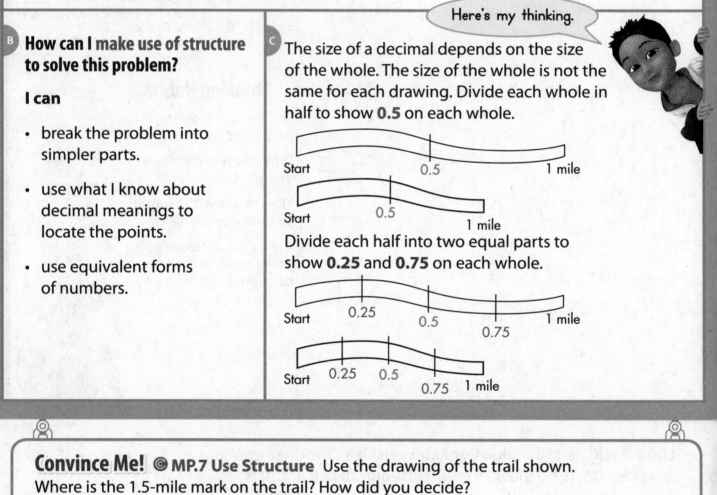

Start   0.5   1 mile

Start   0.5
                      1 mile

Divide each half into two equal parts to show **0.25** and **0.75** on each whole.

Start   0.25   0.5   0.75   1 mile

Start   0.25   0.5   0.75   1 mile

Convince Me! © **MP.7 Use Structure** Use the drawing of the trail shown. Where is the 1.5-mile mark on the trail? How did you decide?

Start   0.5

Name _____

☆ Guided Practice *

© **MP.7 Use Structure**

Margie painted 0.4 of her banner blue.
Helena painted 0.5 of her banner blue.

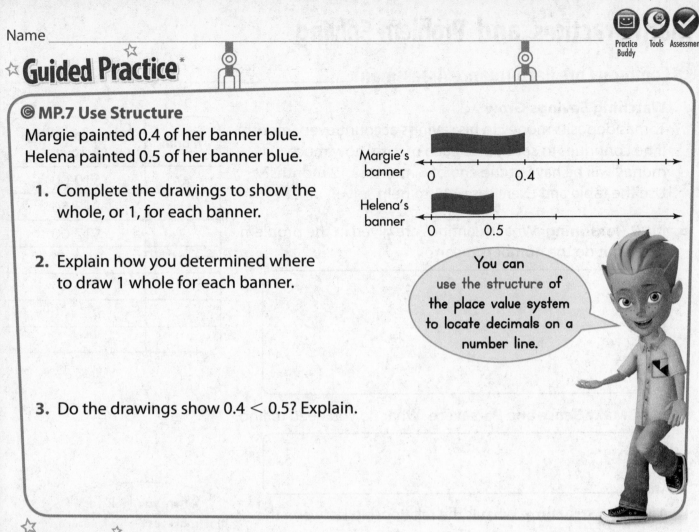

1. Complete the drawings to show the whole, or 1, for each banner.

2. Explain how you determined where to draw 1 whole for each banner.

3. Do the drawings show 0.4 < 0.5? Explain.

> You can use the structure of the place value system to locate decimals on a number line.

☆ Independent Practice ☆

© **MP.7 Use Structure**

Kaitlin is making a map for a 1-mile scavenger hunt. She wants the stops to be 0.5 mile, 0.3 mile, and 0.85 mile from the start.

Start ————————————————— End

4. Label 0.25, 0.5, 0.75 on the number line as a scale reference. Explain how you decided where to mark the number line.

5. Estimate where 0.3 and 0.85 are located compared to the other points. Mark the points 0.3 and 0.85. Explain how you estimated.

*For another example, see Set F on page 666.

Math Practices and Problem Solving

© **Common Core Performance Assessment**

Watching Savings Grow

Tomas deposits money in his savings account every month. If he continues to save $3.50 each month, how much money will he have at the end of 6 months? 12 months? Use the table and Exercises 6–11 to help solve.

Month	Money in Savings Account
0	$10.00
1	$13.50
2	$17.00
3	$20.50

6. **MP.2 Reasoning** What quantities are given in the problem and what do the numbers mean?

7. **MP.1 Make Sense and Persevere** What do you need to find?

8. **MP.7 Use Structure** What is the relationship between the amount of money Tomas will have in his savings account in the fourth month and the amount in the third month?

When you look for and make use of structure, you break a problem into simpler parts.

9. **MP.4 Model with Math** Write an expression that can be used to find the amount saved at the end of 6 months.

10. **MP.4 Model with Math** Complete the table to find how much Tomas will have saved in 6 months.

11. **MP.6 Be Precise** Use the answers from the table to find how much money Tomas will have at the end of 12 months. Show your work.

Help Practice Tools Games
        Buddy

Another Look!

Do the number lines show 0.2 = 0.5?

Tell how you can use the structure of a number line to analyze the relationships between decimals.

- I can break the problem into simpler parts.

- I can use what I know about decimal meanings.

Use the number line to help you find if the decimals represent parts of the same whole.

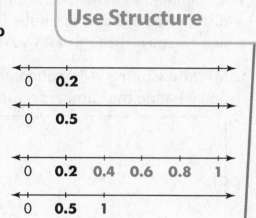

On the third number line, you can use the distance between 0 and 0.2 as a guide to mark **0.4**, **0.6**, **0.8**, and **1**.

On the fourth number line, you can use the distance between 0 and 0.5 as a guide to mark **1**.

To find **1**, you can make a mark that is the same distance to the right of 0.5 as 0.5 is from 0.

When the size of the whole is not the same on the two number lines, the number lines cannot be used to show equivalent decimals.

© **MP.7 Use Structure**

Anton knows it is $\frac{1}{2}$ mile from his home to the store along Main Street. He wants to find how far it is from his home to school.

Home   Store   School

When you look for relationships, you use equivalent forms of numbers.

1. Label 1, 1.5, and 2 on the drawing. Explain how you determined where to label each number.

2. How far does Anton live from school? Explain.

Training

Liz trains for rock climbing 4 days a week. Her first 4 days of training are shown in the table. She plans to increase the distance each time she climbs. Did Liz climb farther on the first two days than the last two days?

Day	Distance Liz Climbed
1	0.09 km
2	0.1 km
3	0.11 km
4	0.07 km

DATA

3. **MP.2 Reasoning** What quantities are given in the problem and what do the numbers mean?

4. **MP.1 Make Sense and Persevere** What do you need to find?

5. **MP.2 Reasoning** What hidden questions need to be answered before answering the main question?

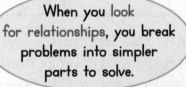

When you look for relationships, you break problems into simpler parts to solve.

6. **MP.4 Model with Math** Use equivalent fractions to write equations to find the distances Liz climbed the first two days and the last two days.

7. **MP.3 Construct Arguments** Did Liz climb farther the first two days or the last two days? Use a number line to justify your answer.

Name _____

Follow the Path

Shade a path from **Start** to **Finish**. Follow the sums or differences that round to 2,000 when rounded to the nearest thousand. You can only move up, down, right, or left.

I can ...
add and subtract multi-digit whole numbers.

© Content Standard 4.NBT.B.4

Start

954 + 871	2,000 − 1,876	3,887 + 369	2,195 − 737	2,698 + 400
8,998 − 7,399	1,810 + 789	8,917 − 5,252	6,295 − 3,290	8,506 − 3,282
1,789 + 210	1,340 − 771	2,615 + 347	9,000 − 6,233	5,896 + 5,601
6,726 − 4,309	1,199 + 468	3,300 − 298	9,444 + 9,444	3,922 − 923
3,856 + 1,144	4,239 − 2,239	5,999 − 4,370	5,607 − 3,605	2,203 + 122

Finish

A-Z
Glossary

Word List

- decimal
- decimal point
- equivalent
- fraction
- greater than symbol (>)
- hundredth
- less than symbol (<)
- tenth

Understand Vocabulary

Choose the best term from the box. Write it on the blank.

1. A dot used to separate dollars from cents or ones from tenths in a number is called a _____.

2. One part of 100 equal parts of a whole is called a _____.

3. Numbers that name the same amount are _____.

4. A symbol, such as $\frac{2}{3}$, $\frac{5}{1}$, or $\frac{8}{5}$, used to name part of a whole, part of a set, or a location on a number line is called a _____.

5. One out of ten equal parts of a whole is called a _____.

For each of these terms, give an example and a non-example.

	Example	Non-example
6. greater than symbol (>)	_____	_____
7. less than symbol (<)	_____	_____
8. decimal	_____	_____

Use Vocabulary in Writing

9. Krista wrote $\frac{75}{100}$ and 0.75. Use at least 3 terms from the Word List to describe Krista's work.

Set A pages 627–632

The essay question on a 100-point test was worth 40 points. Write this amount as a fraction and a decimal.

There are 100 points, so each point is $\frac{1}{100}$. $\frac{40}{100}$ is 0.40.

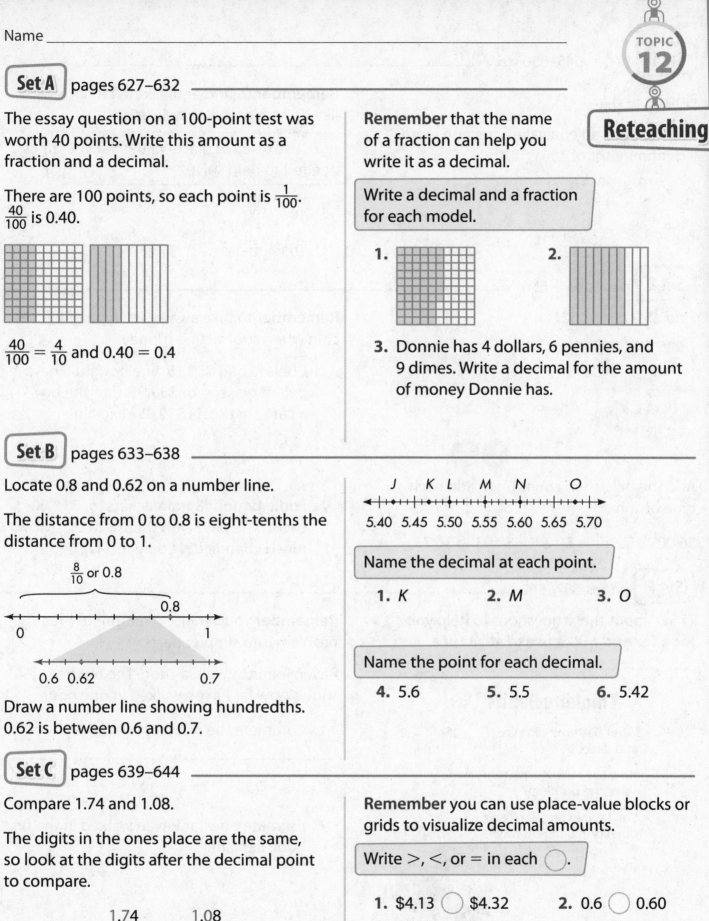

$\frac{40}{100} = \frac{4}{10}$ and 0.40 = 0.4

Remember that the name of a fraction can help you write it as a decimal.

Write a decimal and a fraction for each model.

1. 2.

3. Donnie has 4 dollars, 6 pennies, and 9 dimes. Write a decimal for the amount of money Donnie has.

Set B pages 633–638

Locate 0.8 and 0.62 on a number line.

The distance from 0 to 0.8 is eight-tenths the distance from 0 to 1.

$\frac{8}{10}$ or 0.8

0.8

0   1

0.6 0.62   0.7

Draw a number line showing hundredths. 0.62 is between 0.6 and 0.7.

J   K   L   M   N   O

5.40 5.45 5.50 5.55 5.60 5.65 5.70

Name the decimal at each point.

1. *K*   2. *M*   3. *O*

Name the point for each decimal.

4. 5.6   5. 5.5   6. 5.42

Set C pages 639–644

Compare 1.74 and 1.08.

The digits in the ones place are the same, so look at the digits after the decimal point to compare.

1.74   1.08
7 tenths > 0 tenths
1.74 > 1.08

Remember you can use place-value blocks or grids to visualize decimal amounts.

Write >, <, or = in each ◯.

1. $4.13 ◯ $4.32   2. 0.6 ◯ 0.60

3. 5.29 ◯ 52.9   4. 12.91 ◯ 12.19

Find $\frac{9}{10} + \frac{49}{100}$.

Rewrite $\frac{9}{10}$ as an equivalent fraction with a denominator of 100.

$$\frac{9}{10} \times \frac{10}{10} = \frac{90}{100}$$

$$\frac{90}{100} + \frac{49}{100} = \frac{139}{100} \text{ or } 1\frac{39}{100}$$

Remember to find equivalent fractions with like denominators to help add.

Add. Use grids or place-value blocks as needed to help solve.

1. $\frac{8}{10} + \frac{40}{100}$

2. $\frac{24}{100} + \frac{6}{100}$

Find $\$5.21 + \$1.52$.

Add the bills, then count on to add each type of coin.

$\$6.00 + \$0.50 + \$0.20 + \$0.03 = \$6.73$

Remember to take away each type of bill and coin when subtracting money.

1. Chelsea had $71.18. She bought a new pair of glasses for $59.95. Can she buy a case that costs $12.95? Explain.

2. Eddie bought 3 train tickets for $17.00 each. If he paid with three $20 bills, how much change did Eddie receive?

Think about these questions to help you **look for and make use of structure**.

Thinking Habits

- What patterns can I see and describe?

- How can I use the patterns to solve the problem?

- Can I see expressions and objects in different ways?

Remember you can use structure to break problem into simpler parts.

Raven joined a walk-a-thon. The red dot shows how far Raven walked in one hour.

1. Complete the number line below.

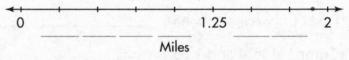

Miles

2. Estimate how far Raven walked in the first hour. Explain.

1. Marvin writes a number that shows 70 parts out of 100. Select all that could be Marvin's number.

☐ 0.07

☐ $\frac{7}{10}$

☐ $\frac{70}{100}$

☐ 0.70

☐ $\frac{70}{10}$

2. Which symbol makes the comparison true? Write the correct symbol from the box.

29.48 ◯ 29.69

| < | > | = |

3. Lucy buys a puzzle for $3.89 and a model airplane for $12.75. How much more did the model airplane cost than the puzzle?

Ⓐ $8.86   Ⓒ $15.64

Ⓑ $9.06   Ⓓ $16.64

4. Which point is incorrectly labeled? Explain.

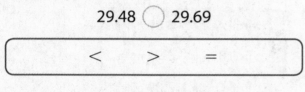

A (3.75)   B (4.5) C (4.9)

3   4   5

5. Catalina takes the money shown to the bookstore.

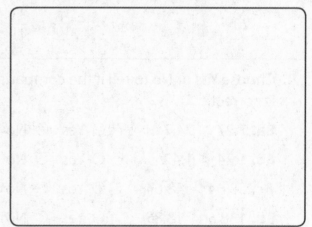

© Assessment

New Releases	
A Story of Two Towns	$14.95
Good Morning, Sun	$16.55
The History of Italy	$16.00

Part A

Does Catalina have enough for all three books? If not, how much more money does Catalina need? Explain.

Part B

Catalina chooses to buy only 2 of the books. Choose two books for Catalina to buy, then find how much money she will have left.

6. Write a fraction and a decimal that represent the part of the grid that is green.

7. Draw a line from the decimal to its equivalent fraction.

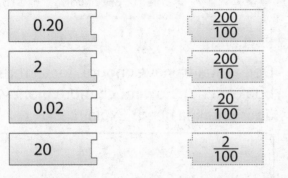

8. Choose Yes or No to tell if the comparison is correct.

8a. 7.27 > 74.7   ○ Yes ○ No

8b. 1.24 < 1.42   ○ Yes ○ No

8c. 58.64 > 48.64   ○ Yes ○ No

8d. 138.5 < 13.85   ○ Yes ○ No

9. Write the fraction that best describes point R on the number line.

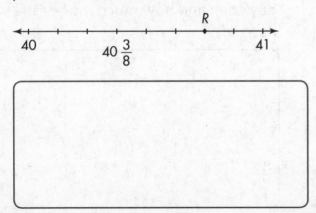

10. Explain how to find the sum of $\frac{3}{10} + \frac{4}{100}$.

11. Use the table below.

DATA		
Trail A	6.89 miles
Trail B	6.95 miles
Trail C	7.09 miles
Trail D	6.98 miles

Create a number line and plot the length of each trail.

12. Phil collected 60 eggs and sold 44 of them to the local grocer. Phil wrote down that he sold 0.44 of the eggs he collected. Did Phil write the decimal correctly? Explain.

Name _____

Nature Club

The nature club at the school devoted a month to learning about different local birds. The **Bird Traits** photos show information about several birds they observed.

Bird Traits

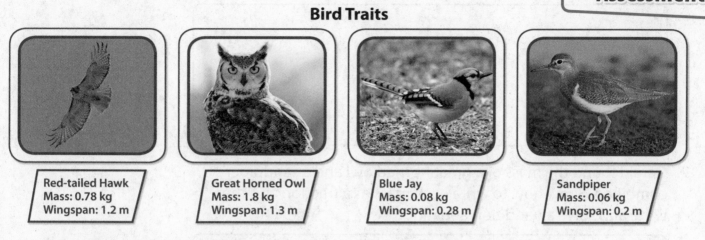

Red-tailed Hawk
Mass: 0.78 kg
Wingspan: 1.2 m

Great Horned Owl
Mass: 1.8 kg
Wingspan: 1.3 m

Blue Jay
Mass: 0.08 kg
Wingspan: 0.28 m

Sandpiper
Mass: 0.06 kg
Wingspan: 0.2 m

1. The club leader asked students to analyze and compare the measures from the **Bird Traits** photos.

Part A

Randall was asked to write the mass of a red-tailed hawk as a fraction. Label the mass on the number line and write the equivalent fraction.

0.70   0.80

Part B

Melanie was assigned to compare the wingspans of the blue jay and the sandpiper. Which bird had longer wings? Show the comparison on the grids, and write the comparison using symbols.

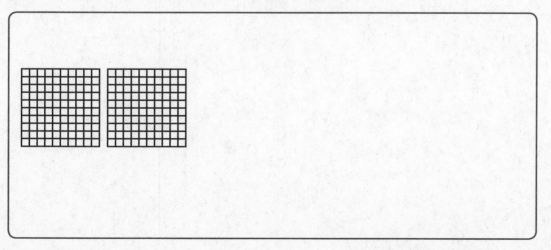

Part C

Mila compared the wingspans of the red-tailed hawk and the great horned owl. Explain how to use place value to find the longer wingspan. Show the comparison using symbols.

2. Gerald found the mass of a great horned owl and a sandpiper combined. Show how to write each mass as a fraction and then write and solve an addition equation.

3. The **Blue Jay** photo shows the wingspan of a blue jay Susannah observed.

   Susannah said the wingspan of the blue jay was greater than the wingspan of the great horned owl since 1.4 > 1.3. Do you agree? Explain.

Blue Jay

Wingspan: 1.4 ft

Measurement: Find Equivalence in Units of Measure

Essential Questions: How can you convert from one unit to another? How can you be precise when solving math problems?

Digital Resources

Solve   Learn   Glossary   Practice Buddy

Tools   Assessment   Help   Games

The Grand Canyon in Arizona was formed by erosion.

The Colorado River cut through the layers of rock. In some places, the canyon is more than a mile deep!

Imagine how it will look in the future! Here is a project on erosion and measurement.

Math and Science Project: Erosion and Measurement

Do Research The Colorado River has played a large part in shaping North America. Use the Internet and other resources to research the states through which the river travels.

Journal: Write a Report Include what you found. Also in your report:

- Look up *geology* and *geometry* in the dictionary. Write the definitions and explain how these words are related. What does the prefix "geo" mean in both words?

- A.J. takes a 4-mile tour of the Grand Canyon. Explain how to convert the length of A.J.'s tour from miles to feet.

Review What You Know

A-Z Vocabulary

Choose the best term from the box. Write it on the blank.

- capacity
- gram
- liter
- mass

1. The amount of liquid a container can hold is called its _____.

2. _____ is the amount of matter that something contains.

3. One metric unit of capacity is a _____.

Perimeter

Find the perimeter of each shape.

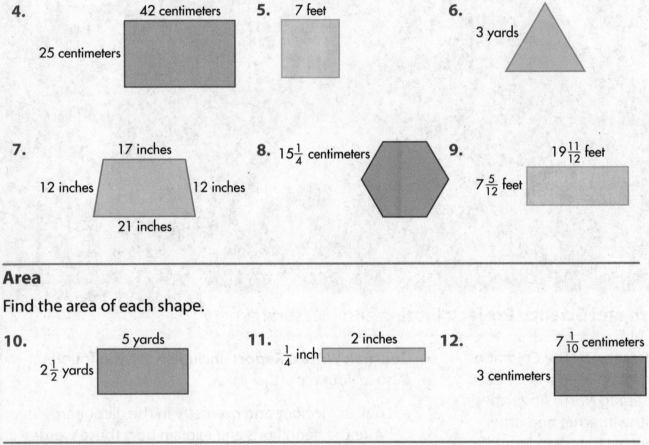

4. 42 centimeters / 25 centimeters

5. 7 feet

6. 3 yards

7. 17 inches / 12 inches / 12 inches / 21 inches

8. $15\frac{1}{4}$ centimeters

9. $19\frac{11}{12}$ feet / $7\frac{5}{12}$ feet

Area

Find the area of each shape.

10. 5 yards / $2\frac{1}{2}$ yards

11. 2 inches / $\frac{1}{4}$ inch

12. $7\frac{1}{10}$ centimeters / 3 centimeters

Problem Solving

13. **◎ MP.1 Make Sense and Persevere** A league is a nautical measurement equal to about 3 miles. If a ship travels 2,000 leagues, about how many miles did the ship travel?

My Word Cards

Use the examples for each word on the front of the card to help complete the definitions on the back.

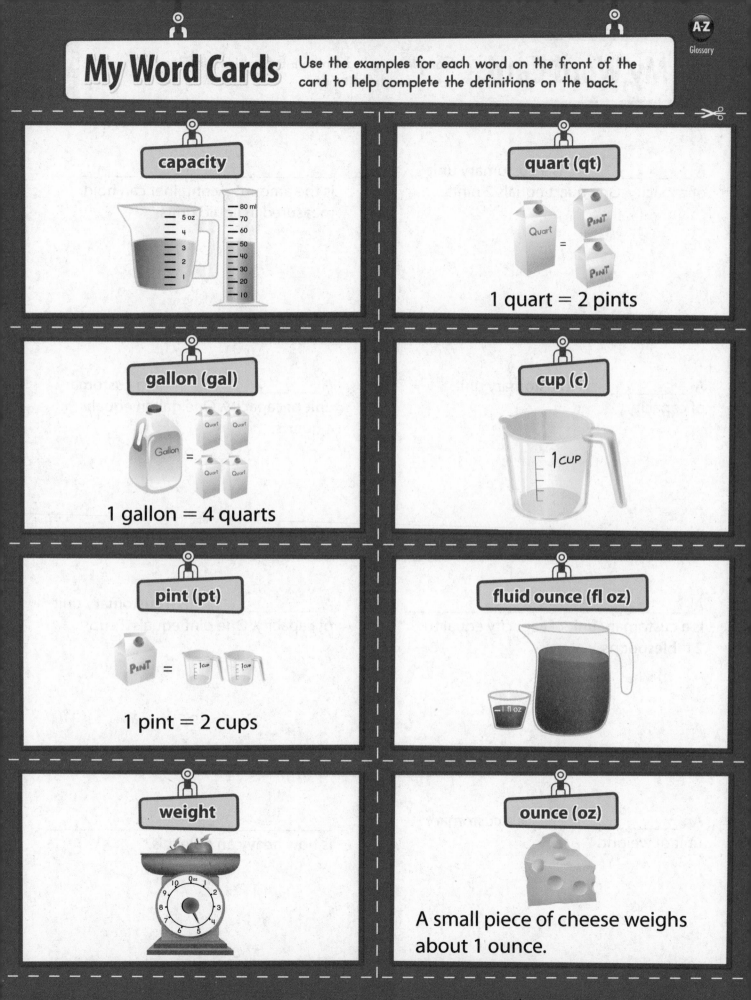

capacity

5 oz
4
3
2
1

80 ml
70
60
50
40
30
20
10

quart (qt)

Quart = PINT PINT

1 quart = 2 pints

gallon (gal)

Gallon = Quart Quart Quart Quart

1 gallon = 4 quarts

cup (c)

1 CUP

pint (pt)

PINT = 1 CUP 1 CUP

1 pint = 2 cups

fluid ounce (fl oz)

1 fl oz

weight

ounce (oz)

A small piece of cheese weighs about 1 ounce.

My Word Cards

Complete each definition. Extend learning by writing your own definitions.

A _____ is a customary unit of capacity. One quart equals 2 pints.

_____ is the amount a container can hold, measured in liquid units.

A _____ is a customary unit of capacity.

A _____ is a customary unit of capacity. One gallon equals 4 quarts.

A _____ is a customary unit of capacity equal to 2 tablespoons.

A _____ is a customary unit of capacity. One pint equals 2 cups.

An _____ is a customary unit of weight.

_____ is how heavy an object is.

My Word Cards

Use the examples for each word on the front of the card to help complete the definitions on the back.

pound (lb)

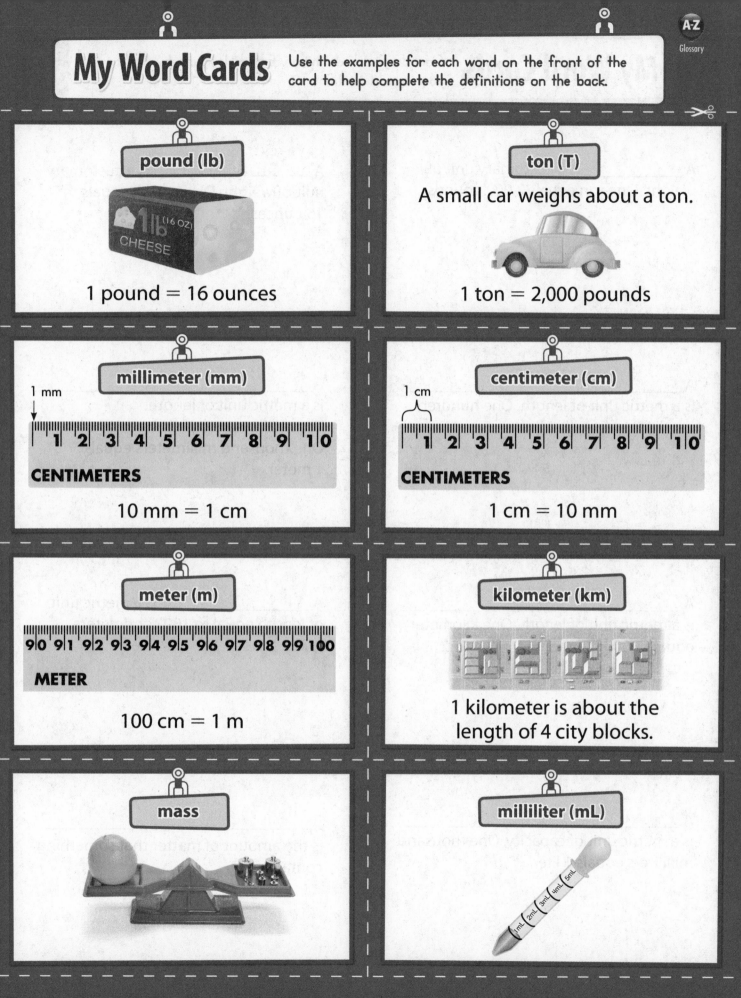

1lb (16 OZ)
CHEESE

1 pound = 16 ounces

ton (T)

A small car weighs about a ton.

1 ton = 2,000 pounds

millimeter (mm)

1 mm

1 2 3 4 5 6 7 8 9 10
CENTIMETERS

10 mm = 1 cm

centimeter (cm)

1 cm

1 2 3 4 5 6 7 8 9 10
CENTIMETERS

1 cm = 10 mm

meter (m)

90 91 92 93 94 95 96 97 98 99 100
METER

100 cm = 1 m

kilometer (km)

1 kilometer is about the length of 4 city blocks.

mass

milliliter (mL)

1mL 2mL 3mL 4mL 5mL

My Word Cards

A _____ is a customary unit of weight. One ton equals 2,000 pounds.

A _____ is a customary unit of weight. One pound equals 16 ounces.

A_____ is a metric unit of length. One hundred centimeters equals 1 meter.

A_____ is a metric unit of length. Ten millimeters equals 1 centimeter. One thousand millimeters equals 1 meter.

A _____ is a metric unit of length. One kilometer equals 1,000 meters.

A _____ is a metric unit of length equal to 100 centimeters.

A _____ is a metric unit of capacity. One thousand milliliters equals 1 liter.

_____ is the amount of matter that something contains.

My Word Cards

Use the examples for each word on the front of the card to help complete the definitions on the back.

A-Z Glossary

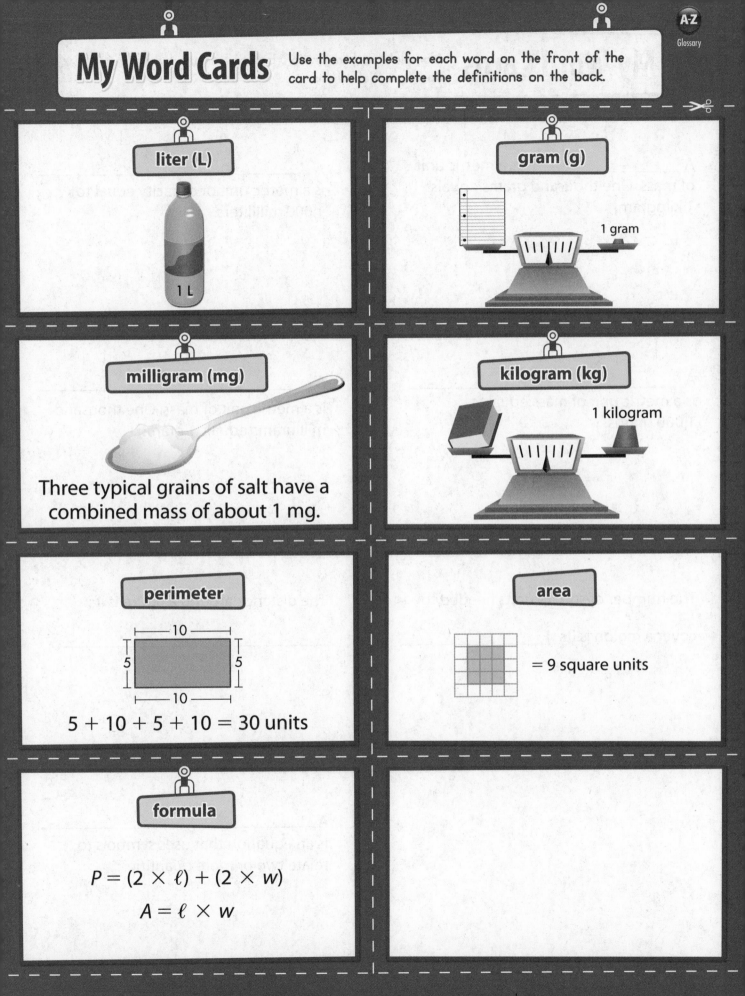

liter (L)

1 L

gram (g)

1 gram

milligram (mg)

Three typical grains of salt have a combined mass of about 1 mg.

kilogram (kg)

1 kilogram

perimeter

10

5   5

10

$5 + 10 + 5 + 10 = 30$ units

area

= 9 square units

formula

$P = (2 \times \ell) + (2 \times w)$

$A = \ell \times w$

My Word Cards

Complete each definition. Extend learning by writing your own definitions.

A _____ is a metric unit of mass. One thousand grams equals 1 kilogram.

A_____ is a metric unit of capacity equal to 1,000 milliliters.

A_____ is a metric unit of mass equal to 1,000 grams.

A_____ is a metric unit of mass. One thousand milligrams equals 1 gram.

The number of square units needed to cover a region is its _____.

The distance around a figure is its _____.

A_____ is an equation that uses symbols to relate two or more quantities.

Name _____

Solve & Share

Jeremy jogged 75 yards from his house to school. How many feet did Jeremy jog? *Solve this problem any way you choose.*

Be precise. Be sure to calculate correctly and use the right units. *Show your work in the space below!*

50 yd   60 yd   70 yd   80 yd

I can ...
convert customary units of length from one unit to another and recognize the relative size of different units.

Ⓒ **Content Standards** 4.MD.A.1, 4.MD.A.2, 4.NF.B.3d, 4.NF.B.4c
Mathematical Practices MP.1, MP.6, MP.7, MP.8

Look Back! Ⓒ **MP.7 Look for Relationships** What do you notice about the relationship between the number of yards and the number of feet Jeremy jogged?

How Can You Convert from One Unit of Length to Another?

Essential Question

A

Maggie has a tree swing. How many inches long is each rope from the bottom of the branch to the swing?

Branch: 10 ft from ground

You can convert feet to inches using multiplication.

DATA

Customary Units of Length

1 foot (ft) = 12 inches (in.)

1 yard (yd) = 3 ft = 36 in.

1 mile (mi) = 1,760 yd = 5,280 ft

Swing: $2\frac{1}{4}$ ft from ground

B

Step 1

Find the length of the rope in feet.

$r = 10 - 2\frac{1}{4}$

10 ft	
r	$2\frac{1}{4}$ ft

$$10 = 9\frac{4}{4}$$
$$- 2\frac{1}{4} = -2\frac{1}{4}$$
$$7\frac{3}{4}$$

Each rope is $7\frac{3}{4}$ feet long.

C

Step 2

Convert the length of the rope to inches.

DATA

Feet	Inches
1	12
2	24
3	36
4	48
5	60
6	72
7	84
$7\frac{3}{4}$	93

There are 12 inches in a foot.

Find 7×12.

$7 \times 12 = 84$ inches

Find $\frac{3}{4} \times 12$.

$$\frac{3}{4} \times 12 = \frac{3 \times 12}{4}$$
$$= \frac{36}{4} \text{ or 9 inches}$$

$84 + 9 = 93$

Each rope is 93 inches long.

Convince Me! © **MP.8 Generalize** How do you know the answer is reasonable when converting a larger unit to a smaller unit?

Another Example!

Convert 6 yards to inches. There are 12 inches in 1 foot, and there are 3 feet in 1 yard.

$12 \times 3 = 36$

There are 36 inches in 1 yard.

$6 \times 36 = 216$ inches

Number   Inches per
of yards   yard

There are 216 inches in 6 yards.

> You need to find how many smaller units are in a number of larger units. Then, multiply the number of larger units by the number of smaller units in each larger unit.

☆ Guided Practice*

Do You Understand?

1. **© MP.8 Generalize** Does it take more inches or feet to equal a given length? Explain.

2. Which is a greater distance, 9 yards or 9 miles?

Do You Know How?

For **3–5**, convert each unit.

3. 2 miles = _____ yards

4. $4\frac{2}{3}$ yards = _____ feet

5. 6 feet = _____ inches

☆ Independent Practice ☆

For **6–13**, convert each unit.

6. 8 yards = _____ inches

7. 28 yards = _____ feet

8. 18 feet = _____ inches

9. 7 miles = _____ yards

10. $\frac{1}{3}$ yard = _____ inches

11. $2\frac{1}{2}$ feet = _____ inches

12. 5 miles = _____ feet

13. $6\frac{1}{3}$ yards = _____ feet

Math Practices and Problem Solving

14. **MP.6 Be Precise** Lou cuts 3 yards from a 9-yard roll of fabric. Then he cuts 4 feet from the roll. How many feet of fabric is left on the roll?

15. **MP.1 Make Sense and Persevere** Tonya bought a sweater that costs $29.99 plus $1.60 tax. She used a coupon for $10 off. She paid the cashier $25. How much change should Tonya receive? Use coins and bills to solve.

16. **Algebra** On the field trip, Toni collected 4 times as many bugs as Kaylie. Kaylie collected 14 bugs. How many bugs did Toni collect? Draw a bar diagram. Write and solve an equation to represent the problem.

17. Which is greater 3 miles or 5,000 yards? How much greater? Explain.

18. **Higher Order Thinking** Jenna uses 18 inches of ribbon for each box she wraps. How many yards of ribbon does she need to wrap 4 boxes? Use the diagram to help solve.

0	1 yd	2 yd	3 yd
0	36 in.	72 in.	108 in.

Common Core Assessment

19. Draw lines to match each measure on the left with its equivalent measure on the right.

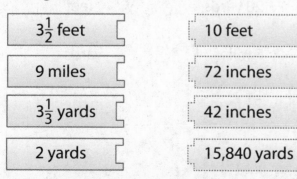

$3\frac{1}{2}$ feet

9 miles

$3\frac{1}{3}$ yards

2 yards

10 feet

72 inches

42 inches

15,840 yards

20. Three students measured the width of the classroom. Lisa got 9, Shanna got 324, and Emma got 27. The teacher said they were all correct. Draw lines to match each student with the unit she was using.

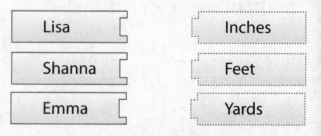

Lisa

Shanna

Emma

Inches

Feet

Yards

Name _____

Another Look!

The longest squid recorded by scientists was $14\frac{1}{3}$ yards long. In 2006, a 24-foot squid was captured. How many feet longer was the longest squid than the captured squid?

Be precise and use the correct units.

Step 1

Convert the length of the longest squid to feet. There are 3 feet in 1 yard.

$$14\frac{1}{3} \times 3 = (14 \times 3) + \left(\frac{1}{3} \times 3\right)$$

$$= 42 + \frac{3}{3}$$

$$= 42 + 1$$

$$= 43$$

$14\frac{1}{3}$ yards = 43 feet

Step 2

Find the difference to compare.

$$\begin{array}{r} \overset{3\ 13}{\cancel{4}\cancel{3}} \\ -\ 2\ 4 \\ \hline 1\ 9 \end{array}$$

The longest squid was 19 feet longer than the captured squid.

For **1–6**, convert each unit.

1. 25 feet = _____ inches

2. 3 miles = _____ feet

3. 4 miles = _____ yards

4. 57 yards = _____ inches

5. $\frac{1}{2}$ yard = _____ inches

6. $2\frac{2}{3}$ yards = _____ feet

For **7–8**, complete each table.

7.

Miles	Feet
$1\frac{1}{2}$	
$2\frac{1}{2}$	
$3\frac{1}{2}$	
$4\frac{1}{2}$	
$5\frac{1}{2}$	
$6\frac{1}{2}$	

8.

Yards	Inches
$1\frac{1}{3}$	
$2\frac{1}{3}$	
$3\frac{1}{3}$	
$4\frac{1}{3}$	
$5\frac{1}{3}$	
$6\frac{1}{3}$	

9. @ **MP.6 Be Precise** How many times wider are the handlebars of the bike than the width of the tire?

10. What is the length of the bike in inches?

11. @ **MP.6 Be Precise** How many more inches is the length of the bike than the height of the bike?

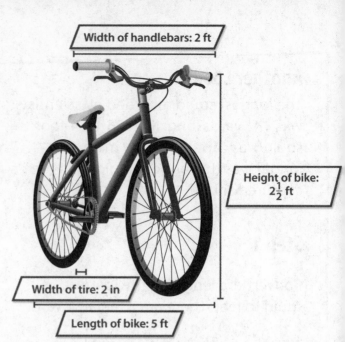

Width of handlebars: 2 ft

Height of bike: $2\frac{1}{2}$ ft

Width of tire: 2 in

Length of bike: 5 ft

---

12. @ **MP.1 Make Sense and Persevere** Harriet rode her bike $2\frac{1}{4}$ miles to the mall. She then rode $\frac{3}{4}$ mile to the grocery store. She came back the way she went. How many miles did Harriet ride in all? Explain.

13. **Higher Order Thinking** Use the number line. What fraction of 1 foot is 3 inches? What fraction of 1 yard is 3 inches? Explain.

```
0   3   6   9 12 in.                    1 yd
              1 ft           2 ft        3 ft
```

@ **Common Core Assessment**

14. Draw lines to match each measure on the left with its equivalent measure on the right.

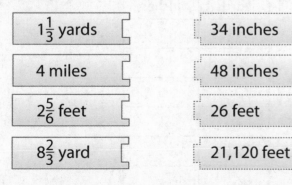

$1\frac{1}{3}$ yards	34 inches
4 miles	48 inches
$2\frac{5}{6}$ feet	26 feet
$8\frac{2}{3}$ yard	21,120 feet

15. Three students measured the width of the whiteboard. Reggie got 2, Jackson got 72, and Pete got 6. The teacher said they were all correct. Draw lines to match each student with the unit he was using.

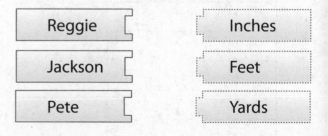

Reggie	Inches
Jackson	Feet
Pete	Yards

Name _____

Solve & Share

Casey has $2\frac{1}{2}$ gallons of juice. How many 1-pint containers can he fill? *Solve this problem any way you choose.*

You can use reasoning. Use what you know about converting a larger unit to a smaller unit. *Show your work in the space below!*

DATA

Customary Units of Capacity

1 cup (c) = 8 fluid ounces (fl oz)

1 pint (pt) = 2 c = 16 fl oz

1 quart (qt) = 2 pt = 4 c

1 gallon (gal) = 4 qt = 8 pt

I can ...
convert customary units of capacity from one unit to another and recognize the relative size of different units.

© Content Standards 4.MD.A.1, 4.MD.A.2, 4.NF.B.3d, 4.NF.B.4c
Mathematical Practices MP.1, MP.2, MP.8

Look Back! © **MP.8 Generalize** How did you change from a larger unit of capacity to a smaller unit of capacity? Did you use the same process you used to change from a larger unit of length to a smaller unit of length? Explain.

How Can You Convert from One Unit of Capacity to Another?

A

Ms. Nealy's class needs 5 gallons of punch for family math night. How much of each ingredient is needed to make enough punch with the recipe shown?

Units of capacity include gallons, quarts, pints, cups, and fluid ounces.

RECIPE #116

Punch Recipe

5 pints of apple juice
4 pints lemon/lime soda
1 pint frozen orange juice

1 gal							
1 qt		1 qt		1 qt		1 qt	
1 pt	1 pt	1 pt	1 pt	1 pt	1 pt	1 pt	1 pt
1 c 1 c	1 c 1 c	1 c 1 c	1 c 1 c	1 c 1 c	1 c 1 c	1 c 1 c	1 c 1 c

B Step 1

Convert 5 gallons to pints.

DATA

Gallons	Quarts	Pints
1	4	8
2	8	16
3	12	24
4	16	32
5	20	40

5 gallons = 40 pints

C Step 2

Add the number of pints in the recipe to find how many batches the class needs to make.

$5 + 4 + 1 = 10$

$10 \times n = 40$

$n = 4$

The class needs to make 4 batches of the recipe.

D Step 3

Find how much of each ingredient is in 4 batches.

$4 \times 5 = 20$ pints
$4 \times 4 = 16$ pints
$4 \times 1 = 4$ pints

20 pints of apple juice, 16 pints of lemon/lime soda, and 4 pints of frozen orange juice are needed.

Convince Me! © **MP.2 Reasoning** Complete the sentence below.

One gallon equals _____ quarts, _____ pints, or _____ cups.

Name _____

☆ Guided Practice ☆

Do You Understand?

1. ⓒ MP.1 Make Sense and Persevere
How many cups of punch does one batch of the recipe on the previous page make? Explain.

Do You Know How?

For **2–4**, convert each unit.

2. 2 cups = _____ fluid ounces

3. $3\frac{1}{2}$ quarts = _____ pints

4. 1 pint = _____ fluid ounces

☆ Independent Practice ☆

For **5–12**, convert each unit.

5. 7 quarts = _____ cups

6. 12 gallons = _____ quarts

7. 3 gallons = _____ cups

8. $1\frac{1}{2}$ quarts = _____ cups

9. $3\frac{3}{4}$ gallons = _____ pints

10. $2\frac{3}{4}$ pints = _____ fluid ounces

11. 9 cups = _____ fluid ounces

12. $3\frac{1}{2}$ pints = _____ fluid ounces

For **13–14**, complete each table.

13.

Pints	Fluid Ounces
$1\frac{1}{2}$	
$2\frac{1}{2}$	
$3\frac{1}{2}$	
$4\frac{1}{2}$	
$5\frac{1}{2}$	
$6\frac{1}{2}$	

14.

Quarts	Cups
$1\frac{1}{2}$	
$2\frac{1}{2}$	
$3\frac{1}{2}$	
$4\frac{1}{2}$	
$5\frac{1}{2}$	
$6\frac{1}{2}$	

*For another example, see Set A on page 723.

Topic 13 | Lesson 13-2

Math Practices and Problem Solving

15. Math and Science Scientists measure how much water and debris flow past a river station at different times of the year. The water and debris are called discharge. The table shows the average discharge at the Camp Verde station on the Verde River in two months. How many more quarts of discharge per second are there in December than November?

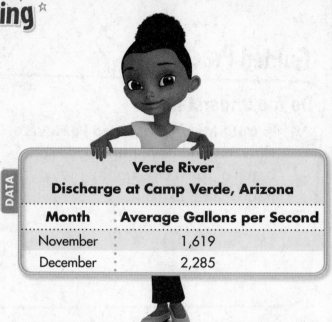

Verde River
Discharge at Camp Verde, Arizona

Month	Average Gallons per Second
November	1,619
December	2,285

16. Vocabulary Use *capacity*, *length*, and *meters* to complete the definitions.

_____ is the amount of liquid a container can hold.

_____ are one unit that can be used to measure _____.

17. Higher Order Thinking A caterer combines 3 quarts of orange juice, 5 pints of milk, and 5 cups of pineapple juice to make smoothies. How many cups can be filled with smoothies? Explain.

© Common Core Assessment

18. Annabelle had the following containers of paint leftover: $\frac{1}{2}$ gallon, $\frac{3}{4}$ quart, and $\frac{1}{4}$ gallon.

Part A
How many quarts of paint does Annabelle have left over? Explain.

Part B
Annabelle put the leftover paint in pint containers. How many pint containers did Annabelle fill? Explain.

Another Look!

Lance has an 8-gallon aquarium. How many 2-quart containers will it take to fill the aquarium?

DATA

Customary Units of Capacity

1 cup (c) = 8 fluid ounces (fl oz)

1 pint (pt) = 2 c = 16 fl oz

1 quart (qt) = 2 pt = 4 c

1 gallon (gal) = 4 qt = 8 pt

Step 1

Convert 8 gallons to quarts.

Gallons	Quarts
2	8
4	16
6	24
8	32

8 gallons = 32 quarts

Use the correct units as you solve measurement problems.

Step 2

Divide 32 quarts by 2.

$$
\begin{array}{r}
16 \\
2{\overline{)32}} \\
-2 \\
\hline
12 \\
-12 \\
\hline
0
\end{array}
$$

It takes 16 of the 2-quart containers to fill the tank.

For **1–6**, convert each unit.

1. 9 pints = _____ fluid ounces

2. 16 quarts = _____ cups

3. 2 gallons = _____ pints

4. $1\frac{1}{2}$ quarts = _____ cups

5. $1\frac{1}{4}$ gallons = _____ pints

6. $5\frac{1}{2}$ pints = _____ fluid ounces

For **7–8**, complete each table.

7.

Quarts	Fluid Ounces
$1\frac{1}{2}$	
$2\frac{1}{2}$	
$3\frac{1}{2}$	
$4\frac{1}{2}$	
$5\frac{1}{2}$	
$6\frac{1}{2}$	

8.

Gallons	Pints
$1\frac{1}{2}$	
$2\frac{1}{2}$	
$3\frac{1}{2}$	
$4\frac{1}{2}$	
$5\frac{1}{2}$	
$6\frac{1}{2}$	

9. **Number Sense** Lauren hiked 16,900 feet in the morning and 14,850 feet in the afternoon. Estimate the total number of miles Lauren hiked that day. Explain.

10. How many minutes are in 3 hours? There are 60 minutes in one hour. Complete the table.

Hours	Minutes
1	
2	
3	

11. **Math and Science** How many pounds of eroded material does the Verde River carry past a given point each hour?

12. How many pounds of eroded material does the Verde River carry past a given point in $\frac{1}{4}$ of a day?

The Verde River in Arizona carries an average of $14\frac{1}{3}$ pounds of eroded material past a given point each minute.

13. A car with a 20-gallon gas tank can go 25 miles on 1 gallon of gas. If the tank is full at the beginning of a 725-mile trip, how many times does the driver have to refill the gas tank?

14. **Higher Order Thinking** Janice needs 3 gallons of lemonade for a party. She has 4 quarts, 6 pints, and 4 cups of lemonade already made. How many cups of lemonade does Janice need? How many more cups does she need?

© Common Core Assessment

15. Edgar has a birdbath that holds 2 gallons of water. He only wants to fill it $\frac{3}{4}$ full.

Part A

How much water, in gallons, should Edgar put in the birdbath? Explain.

Part B

How many 1-pint containers does it take to fill the birdbath? Explain.

Name _____

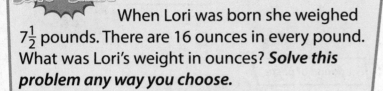

Solve & Share

When Lori was born she weighed $7\frac{1}{2}$ pounds. There are 16 ounces in every pound. What was Lori's weight in ounces? *Solve this problem any way you choose.*

You can generalize and use what you know about converting from a larger unit of measurement to a smaller unit to convert from pounds to ounces.

Lesson 13-3
Equivalence with Customary Units of Weight

I can ...
convert customary units of weight from one unit to another and recognize the relative size of different units.

© **Content Standards** 4.MD.A.1, 4.MD.A.2, 4.NF.B.3d, 4.NF.B.4c
Mathematical Practices MP.1, MP.2, MP.6, MP.8

Look Back! © **MP.6 Be Precise** How did you know you needed to convert units to solve the problem above?

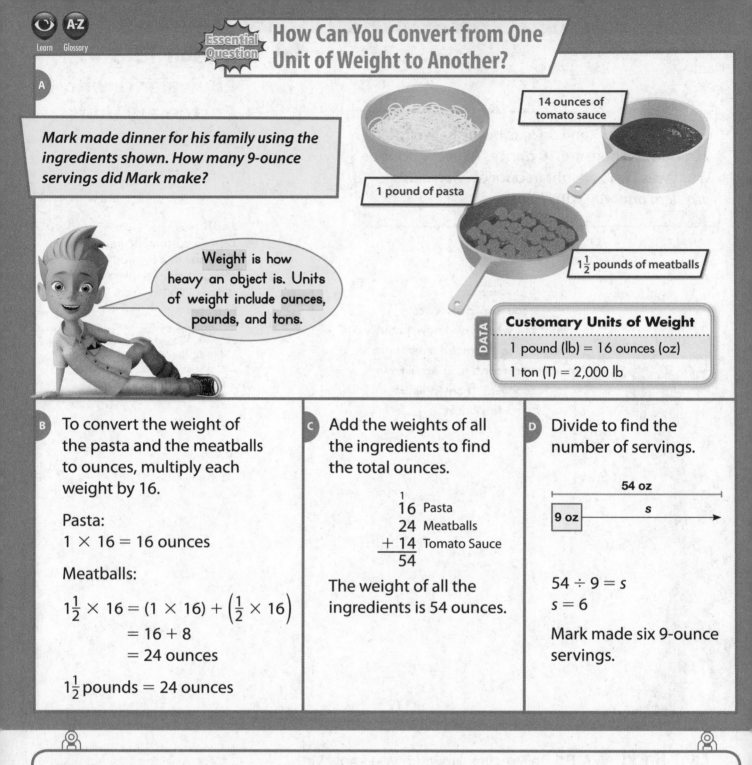

Essential Question **How Can You Convert from One Unit of Weight to Another?**

A

Mark made dinner for his family using the ingredients shown. How many 9-ounce servings did Mark make?

14 ounces of tomato sauce

1 pound of pasta

1½ pounds of meatballs

Weight is how heavy an object is. Units of weight include ounces, pounds, and tons.

DATA

Customary Units of Weight

1 pound (lb) = 16 ounces (oz)

1 ton (T) = 2,000 lb

B To convert the weight of the pasta and the meatballs to ounces, multiply each weight by 16.

Pasta:
1 × 16 = 16 ounces

Meatballs:

$1\frac{1}{2} × 16 = (1 × 16) + \left(\frac{1}{2} × 16\right)$
$= 16 + 8$
$= 24$ ounces

$1\frac{1}{2}$ pounds = 24 ounces

C Add the weights of all the ingredients to find the total ounces.

$$\begin{array}{r} \overset{1}{16} \text{ Pasta} \\ 24 \text{ Meatballs} \\ + 14 \text{ Tomato Sauce} \\ \hline 54 \end{array}$$

The weight of all the ingredients is 54 ounces.

D Divide to find the number of servings.

54 oz

9 oz   s

$54 ÷ 9 = s$
$s = 6$

Mark made six 9-ounce servings.

Convince Me! © **MP.8 Generalize** How do you convert a larger unit of weight to a smaller unit of weight?

Name ______

Practice Buddy | Tools | Assessment

Guided Practice*

Do You Understand?

1. MP.2 Reasoning Would it make sense to describe the total weight of Mark's dinner in tons? Why or why not?

Do You Know How?

For **2–4**, convert each unit.

2. 9 tons = ______ pounds

3. $3\frac{1}{2}$ pounds = ______ ounces

4. 17 pounds = ______ ounces

Independent Practice

For **5–12**, convert each unit.

5. 15 pounds = ______ ounces

6. 7 tons = ______ pounds

7. 46 pounds = ______ ounces

8. $9\frac{1}{2}$ pounds = ______ ounces

9. $5\frac{1}{4}$ pounds = ______ ounces

10. $8\frac{1}{4}$ tons = ______ pounds

11. 6 tons = ______ pounds

12. 3 pounds = ______ ounces

For **13–14**, complete each table.

13.

Tons	Pounds
1	
$1\frac{1}{2}$	
2	
$2\frac{1}{2}$	
3	

14.

Pounds	Ounces
1	
$1\frac{1}{4}$	
$1\frac{2}{4}$	
$1\frac{3}{4}$	
2	

*For another example, see Set A on page 723.

Math Practices and Problem Solving

For **15–19**, use the line plot at the right.

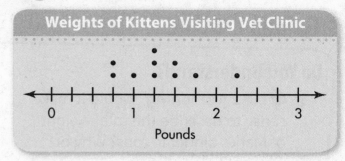

Pounds

15. © **MP.6 Be Precise** What is the total weight in ounces of the three kittens that weigh the least?

16. **Higher Order Thinking** Two kittens had a total weight of $3\frac{1}{4}$ pounds. What could their individual weights have been?

17. **Number Sense** The greatest number of kittens weighed how many pounds?

18. **Algebra** How many more pounds did the heaviest kitten weigh than the lightest kitten?

19. How many ounces did all the kittens weigh?

20. About how many pounds do African elephants weigh? Complete the table to solve.

Tons	$\frac{1}{2}$	$1\frac{1}{2}$	$2\frac{1}{2}$	$3\frac{1}{2}$	$4\frac{1}{2}$	$5\frac{1}{2}$
Pounds						

Male African elephants weigh about $5\frac{1}{2}$ tons.

© Common Core Assessment

21. Which is most likely to weigh 3 ounces?

   Ⓐ A shoe

   Ⓑ A large spider

   Ⓒ A box of cereal

   Ⓓ A math book

22. Lloyd made $3\frac{1}{2}$ pounds of potatoes. He added 4 ounces of butter. How many 6-ounce servings did Lloyd make?

   Ⓐ 6 servings

   Ⓑ 8 servings

   Ⓒ 10 servings

   Ⓓ 12 servings

Another Look!

The world's largest horse weighed almost $1\frac{1}{2}$ tons. An average mature male horse weighs about 1,200 pounds. How much more did the largest horse weigh than an average horse?

Step 1

Convert the weight of the world's largest horse to pounds.

Tons	Pounds
$\frac{1}{2}$	1,000
1	2,000
$1\frac{1}{2}$	3,000

$1\frac{1}{2}$ tons = 3,000 pounds

Step 2

Find the difference.

3,000 lb

1,200 lb	d

$3,000 - 1,200 = d$
$d = 1,800$

The world's largest horse weighed 1,800 pounds more than an average male horse.

> There are 2,000 pounds in a ton.

For **1–6**, convert each unit.

1. 21 pounds = _____ ounces

2. 8 tons = _____ pounds

3. $8\frac{3}{4}$ pounds = _____ ounces

4. $4\frac{3}{8}$ pounds = _____ ounces

5. 6 tons = _____ pounds

6. $6\frac{1}{2}$ pounds = _____ ounces

For **7–8**, complete each table.

7.

Tons	Pounds
1	
2	
3	
4	
5	

8.

Pounds	Ounces
1	
2	
3	
4	
5	

For **9–11**, use the table and art shown at the right.

9. © MP.6 **Be Precise** What is the total weight in ounces of Heidi's 2 guinea pigs?

10. © MP.6 **Be Precise** What is the total weight in ounces of the food for Heidi's guinea pigs?

Heidi's 2 guinea pigs each weigh $2\frac{1}{2}$ pounds.

11. **Higher Order Thinking** A pound of guinea pig pellets is about 3 cups of food. Each guinea pig eats $\frac{1}{4}$ cup of pellets a day. How many days will the pellets last? Explain.

DATA

Food for Heidi's Guinea Pigs	
Food	**Weight**
Grass or hay	$2\frac{1}{2}$ pounds
Vegetables	15 ounces
Pellets	5 pounds

12. © MP.2 **Reasoning** Which product is greater, 9×15 or 9×17? Explain how you can tell without finding the products.

13. © MP.1 **Make Sense and Persevere** What two 1-digit factors could you multiply to get a product between and including 40 and 50?

© **Common Core Assessment**

14. Which is most likely to weigh 4 tons?

   Ⓐ A watermelon

   Ⓑ A man

   Ⓒ A clothes dryer

   Ⓓ A helicopter

15. Each stone in Ally's collection weighs about 4 ounces. Her collection weighs about 24 pounds in all. About how many stones are in Ally's collection?

   Ⓐ 3 stones

   Ⓑ 4 stones

   Ⓒ 36 stones

   Ⓓ 96 stones

Name _____

Solve & Share

Find the length of the marker shown in both centimeters and millimeters. Describe the relationship between the two units.

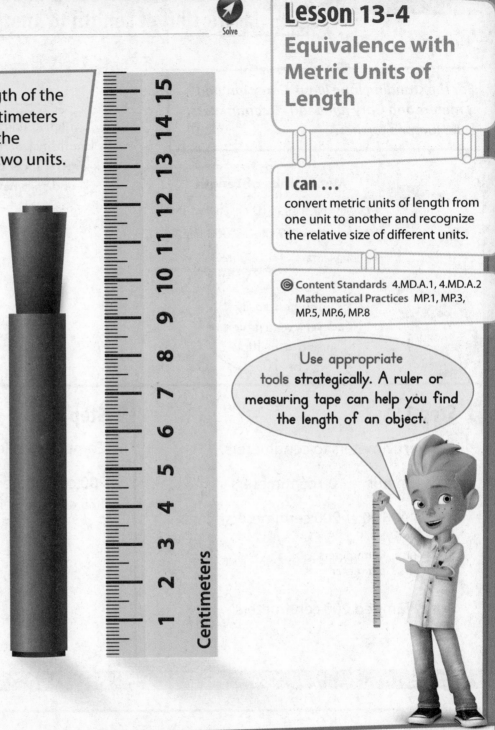

Centimeters

I can ...
convert metric units of length from one unit to another and recognize the relative size of different units.

© Content Standards 4.MD.A.1, 4.MD.A.2
Mathematical Practices MP.1, MP.3, MP.5, MP.6, MP.8

Use appropriate tools strategically. A ruler or measuring tape can help you find the length of an object.

Look Back! © MP.8 Generalize The length of Toby's giant pencil is 25 centimeters. How could you find the length of his pencil in millimeters?

Essential Question **How Can You Convert from One Metric Unit of Length to Another?**

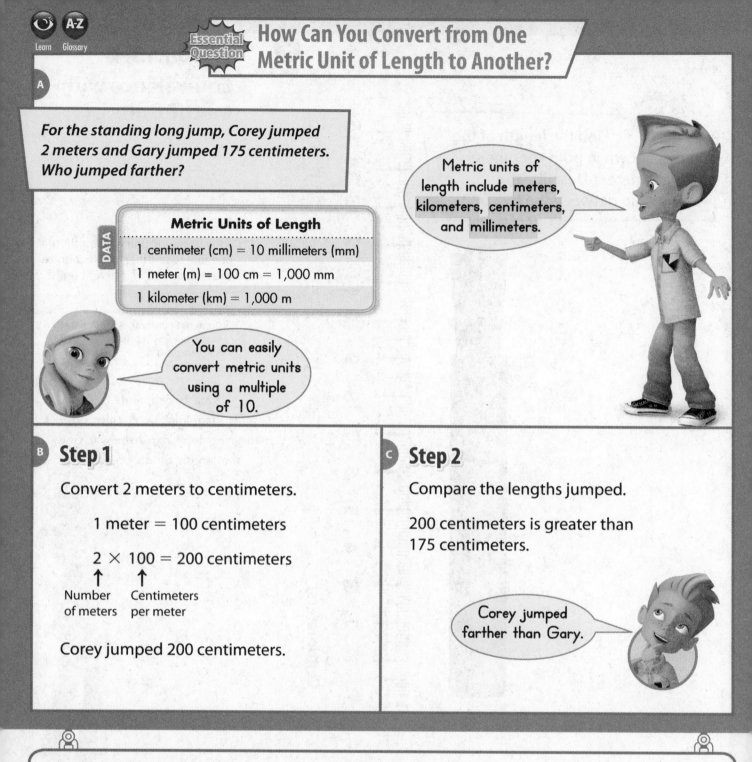

For the standing long jump, Corey jumped 2 meters and Gary jumped 175 centimeters. Who jumped farther?

DATA

Metric Units of Length

1 centimeter (cm) = 10 millimeters (mm)

1 meter (m) = 100 cm = 1,000 mm

1 kilometer (km) = 1,000 m

Metric units of length include meters, kilometers, centimeters, and millimeters.

You can easily convert metric units using a multiple of 10.

B Step 1

Convert 2 meters to centimeters.

1 meter = 100 centimeters

2 × 100 = 200 centimeters
　↑　　　↑
Number　Centimeters
of meters　per meter

Corey jumped 200 centimeters.

C Step 2

Compare the lengths jumped.

200 centimeters is greater than 175 centimeters.

Corey jumped farther than Gary.

Convince Me! © **MP.3 Critique Reasoning** Shayla says 5 kilometers are equal to 500 meters. Do you agree? Explain.

© Pearson Education, Inc. 4

Another Example!

Convert 5 meters to millimeters.

Multiply the larger number of units by the number of smaller units in each larger unit.

$5 \times 1{,}000 = 5{,}000$ millimeters

↑   ↑

Number   Millimeters
of meters   per meter

There are 5,000 millimeters in 5 meters.

> There are 1,000 millimeters in 1 meter.

☆ Guided Practice*

Do You Understand?

1. **© MP.6 Be Precise** In the problem on the previous page, suppose Matthew jumped $\frac{3}{4}$ meter. Who jumped farther, Matthew or Gary? Explain.

Do You Know How?

For **2–3**, convert each unit.

2. 5 kilometers = _____ meters

3. 75 centimeters = _____ millimeters

Independent Practice ☆

For **4–9**, convert each unit.

4. 2 meters = _____ centimeters

5. 5 kilometers = _____ meters

6. 8 centimeters = _____ millimeters

7. 6 meters = _____ millimeters

8. 9 kilometers = _____ meters

9. 6 meters = _____ centimeters

For **10–11**, complete each table.

10.

Meters	Millimeters
1	
2	
3	
4	
5	

11.

Centimeters	Millimeters
1	
2	
3	
4	
5	

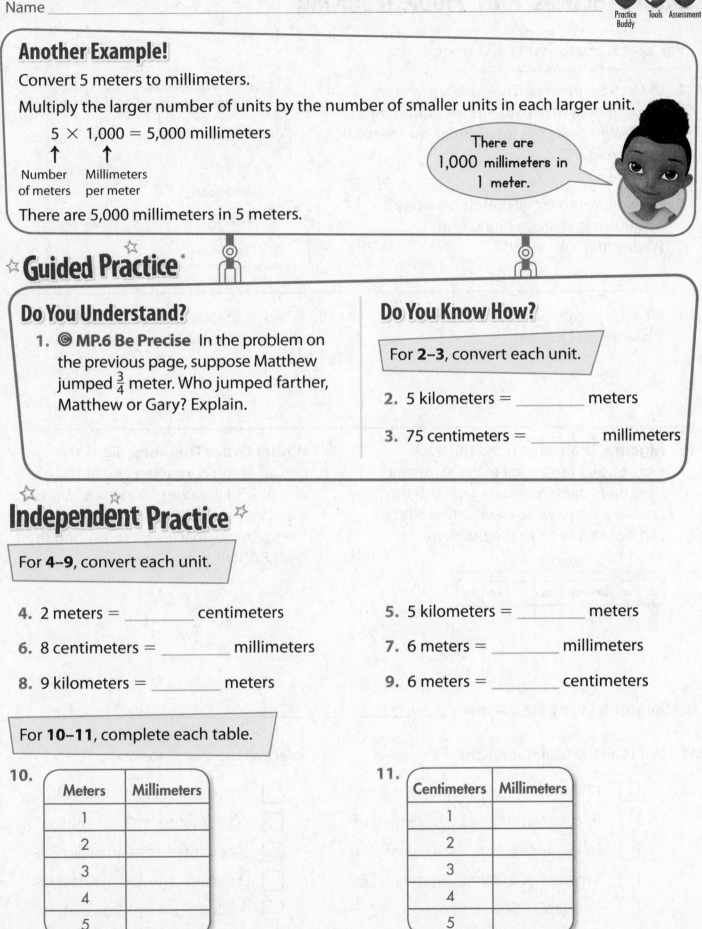

*For another example, see Set B on page 723.

Topic 13 | Lesson 13-4   **699**

Math Practices and Problem Solving

For **12–13**, use the table at the right.

12. **© MP.6 Be Precise** The table shows the amount of rainfall students measured for a week. What was the total rainfall for the week, in millimeters?

13. How many more millimeters of rain fell on Thursday than on Monday and Wednesday combined?

Rainfall Students Measured	
Monday	3 cm
Tuesday	0 cm
Wednesday	1 cm
Thursday	5 cm
Friday	2 cm

---

14. Which is greater, 2,670 meters or 2 kilometers? Explain.

15. Which is greater, 8 hours or 520 minutes? One hour is equal to 60 minutes.

---

16. **Algebra** Leah ran around the track 8 times. She ran a total of 2,000 meters. How many meters equal 1 lap? Use the bar diagram to write an equation which can be used to solve the problem.

2,000 m							
m	m	m	m	m	m	m	m

17. **Higher Order Thinking** Signs are placed at the beginning and at the end of a 3-kilometer hiking trail. Signs are also placed every 500 meters along the trail. How many signs are along the trail? Explain.

© Common Core Assessment

18. Select all the true statements.

☐ 14 meters = 1,400 centimeters
☐ 10 centimeters = 1,000 millimeters
☐ 55 kilometers = 5,500 meters
☐ 3 meters = 3,000 millimeters
☐ 5 meters = 500 centimeters

19. Select all the true statements.

☐ 3 meters = 3,000 centimeters
☐ 2 kilometers = 2,000 meters
☐ 4 centimeters = 40 millimeters
☐ 3 meters = 3,000 millimeters
☐ 5 kilometers = 5,000 meters

Name _____

Help   Practice   Tools   Games
       Buddy

Homework
& Practice 13-4
Equivalence with
Metric Units of
Length

Another Look!

Jasmine finished 9 centimeters of the scarf she is knitting. Manuella finished 108 millimeters of her scarf. How much longer is Manuella's scarf than Jasmine's?

To change from a larger unit like centimeters to a smaller unit like millimeters, multiply.

Step 1

Convert 9 centimeters to millimeters.

1 centimeter = 10 millimeters

$9 \times 10 = 90$ millimeters
↑   ↑
Number of   Millimeters
centimeters per centimeter

9 centimeters = 90 millimeters

Step 2

Find the difference.

108 mm

| 90 mm | d |

$108 - 90 = d$

$d = 18$

Manuella's scarf is 18 millimeters longer than Jasmine's scarf.

For **1–6**, convert each unit.

1. 7 meters = _____ centimeters

2. 8 kilometers = _____ meters

3. 65 centimeters = _____ millimeters

4. 2 meters = _____ centimeters

5. 7 kilometers = _____ meters

6. 8 meters = _____ centimeters

For **7–8**, complete each table.

7.

Kilometers	Meters
1	
2	
3	
4	
5	

8.

Meters	Centimeters
1	
2	
3	
4	
5	

For **9–11**, use the pictures at the right.

9. **© MP.1 Make Sense and Persevere**
José bought the items shown and paid $0.53 tax. He gave the cashier a $10 bill. How much change should José get? Use coins and bills to solve.

$2.88

10. Brittney bought two bottles of shampoo like the one shown and paid $0.52 tax. How much did she spend? Use coins and bills to solve.

11. **Number Sense** How can you tell, without adding, that two bottles of shampoo cost less than a bottle of shampoo and a 2-pack of toothpaste?

$2.98

12. Martha had 2.35 centimeters of her hair cut off. Neil had 2.53 centimeters cut. Who had more hair cut off? Explain.

13. A spider traveled 3 meters in one minute. How many centimeters did it travel?

14. **© MP.6 Be Precise** The ceiling of Mr. Vega's classroom is 3 meters high. The ceiling in the hall is 315 centimeters high. How much taller is the ceiling in the hall than in the classroom?

15. **Higher Order Thinking** A yellow ribbon is 56 centimeters long. It is twice as long as a green ribbon. A brown ribbon is 4 times as long as the green ribbon. What is the length of the brown ribbon?

© Common Core Assessment

16. Select all the true statements.

☐ 1,000 kilometers = 100 meters

☐ 11 meters = 110 centimeters

☐ 17 centimeters = 170 millimeters

☐ 5 meters = 500 millimeters

☐ 5 kilometers = 5,000 meters

17. Select all the true statements.

☐ 5 meters = 5,000 millimeters

☐ 18 kilometers = 1,800 meters

☐ 20 centimeters = 200 millimeters

☐ 7 meters = 70 centimeters

☐ 6 meters = 60,000 millimeters

Name _____

Solve & Share

Jenny has 3 liters of water. How many milliliters of water does she have, and what is the mass of the water in grams? *Solve this problem any way you choose.*

You can generalize about how you change larger units to smaller units when working with customary units or metric units of capacity or mass.

I can ...
convert metric units of capacity and mass from one unit to another and recognize the relative size of different units.

© Content Standards 4.MD.A.1, 4.MD.A.2
Mathematical Practices MP.1, MP.2, MP.6, MP.8

Some water bottles hold 1 liter or 1,000 milliliters of water. 1 liter of water has a mass of 1 kilogram or 1,000 grams.

DRINKING WATER
1 liter

Look Back! © MP.2 Reasoning Why did you need to convert units to solve the problem above?

Essential Question: How Can You Convert from One Metric Unit of Capacity or Mass to Another?

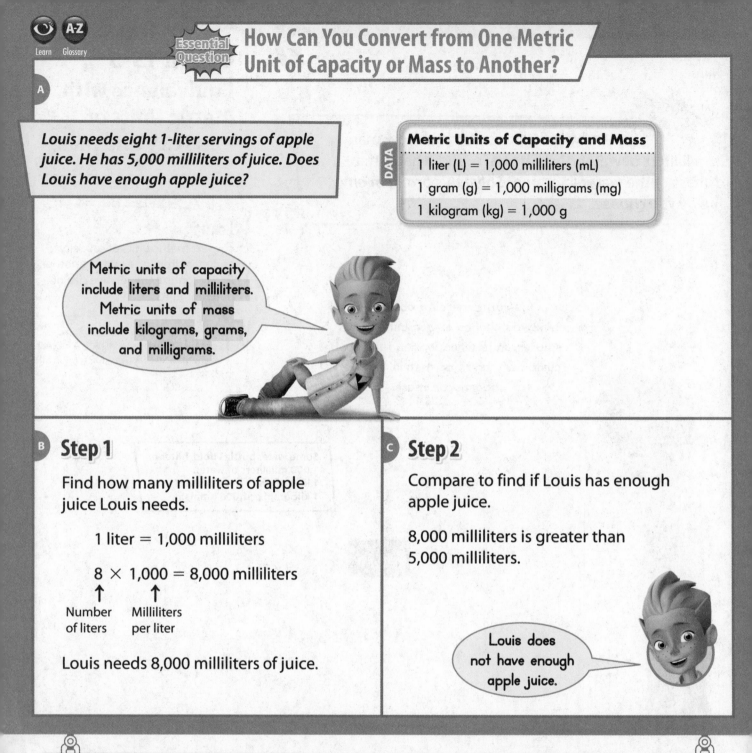

A

Louis needs eight 1-liter servings of apple juice. He has 5,000 milliliters of juice. Does Louis have enough apple juice?

Metric Units of Capacity and Mass

DATA

1 liter (L) = 1,000 milliliters (mL)

1 gram (g) = 1,000 milligrams (mg)

1 kilogram (kg) = 1,000 g

Metric units of capacity include liters and milliliters. Metric units of mass include kilograms, grams, and milligrams.

B Step 1

Find how many milliliters of apple juice Louis needs.

1 liter = 1,000 milliliters

8 × 1,000 = 8,000 milliliters
↑   ↑
Number   Milliliters
of liters   per liter

Louis needs 8,000 milliliters of juice.

C Step 2

Compare to find if Louis has enough apple juice.

8,000 milliliters is greater than 5,000 milliliters.

Louis does not have enough apple juice.

Convince Me! © MP.6 Be Precise Why did you need to convert liters to milliliters?

Name _____

Another Example!

How many grams of apples are needed to make 1 liter of apple juice?

1 kilogram = 1,000 grams

2 kilograms = 2 × 1,000 grams
            = 2,000 grams

2,000 grams of apples make 1 liter of apple juice.

> Mass is the amount of matter that something contains.

2 kilograms of apples makes 1 liter of apple juice.

☆ Guided Practice*

Do You Understand?

1. © MP.1 Make Sense and Persevere
   Margot has 8 kilograms of apples. How many liters of apple juice can Margot make? Explain.

Do You Know How?

For **2–3**, convert each unit.

2. 6 grams = _____ milligrams

3. 9 liters = _____ milliliters

☆ Independent Practice ☆

For **4–11**, convert each unit.

4. 5 kilograms = _____ grams

5. 2 liters = _____ milliliters

6. 4 grams = _____ milligrams

7. 9 kilograms = _____ grams

8. 7 liters = _____ milliliters

9. 1 gram = _____ milligrams

10. 3 liters = _____ milliliters

11. 4 kilograms = _____ grams

*For another example, see Set B on page 723.

Math Practices and Problem Solving

12. **© MP.2 Reasoning** A cardboard box has a mass of 800 grams. When 4 books of equal mass are put into the box, the filled box has a mass of 8 kilograms. What is the mass of each book in grams? Explain.

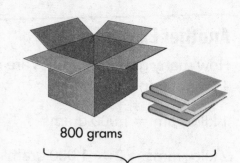

800 grams

8 kilograms

13. **Math and Science** The Cape Hatteras Lighthouse was a kilometer from the shore in 1870. How far was the lighthouse from the shore in 1970? Explain.

The beach near Cape Hatteras Lighthouse in North Carolina has eroded about 8 meters each year.

14. The mass of 4 large zucchini is about 2 kilograms. About how many grams will 1 large zucchini have?

15. **Higher Order Thinking** A small sofa has a mass of 30 kilograms. A pillow on the sofa has a mass of 300 grams. How many pillows would it take to equal the mass of the sofa?

© Common Core Assessment

16. Which shows a correct comparison?

   Ⓐ 5 milliliters > 50 liters

   Ⓑ 2 liters < 200 milliliters

   Ⓒ 100 liters = 1,000 milliliters

   Ⓓ 3,000 milliliters = 3 liters

17. Which shows a correct comparison?

   Ⓐ 1 kilogram > 2,000 grams

   Ⓑ 9,000 milligrams = 9 grams

   Ⓒ 900 grams > 1 kilogram

   Ⓓ 9 milligrams = 9 grams

© Pearson Education, Inc. 4

Name ____________________

Help | Practice Buddy | Tools | Games

Homework & Practice 13-5
Equivalence with Metric Units of Capacity and Mass

Another Look!

Convert each unit.

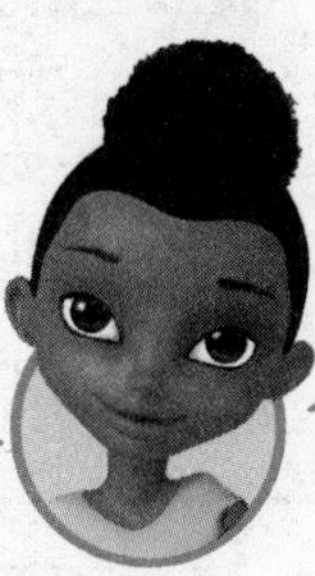

To convert from kilograms to grams, multiply by 1,000.
To convert from liters to milliliters, multiply by 1,000.

Convert 8 liters to milliliters.

1 liter = 1,000 milliliters

$8 \times 1{,}000 = 8{,}000$

8 liters = 8,000 milliliters

Convert 9 grams to milligrams.

1 gram = 1,000 milligrams

$9 \times 1{,}000 = 9{,}000$

9 grams = 9,000 milligrams

For **1–6**, convert each unit.

1. 2 liters = ________ milliliters

2. 8 grams = ________ milligrams

3. 3 kilograms = ________ grams

4. 7 liters = ________ milliliters

5. 4 grams = ________ milligrams

6. 8 kilograms = ________ grams

For **7–8**, complete each table.

7.

Liters	Milliliters
5	
6	
7	
8	
9	

8.

Kilograms	Grams
4	
5	
6	
7	
8	

9. **A-Z Vocabulary** Fill in the blank:
_____ is the amount of matter something contains.
_____ is a measure of how heavy an object is.

10. Jake walks dogs and delivers papers to earn money. This month, he earned $52 delivering papers and $44 walking dogs. Each month, he puts half of his money into his savings account. How much money did Jake save this month?

11. **Math and Science** A glacier moved a boulder with a mass of 9 kilograms. What was the mass of the boulder in grams?

12. Another glacier moved a boulder that weighed 2 tons. How many pounds did the boulder weigh?

Glaciers move boulders, and boulders erode the soil.

13. **© MP.2 Reasoning** Hannah has 3 boxes of rice. One box contains 3 kilograms, the second box contains 150 grams, and the third box contains 500 grams. She wants to divide the rice equally into 5 bags. How much rice should she put into each bag? Explain.

14. **Higher Order Thinking** Rob has a 2-liter bottle of iced tea. He poured an equal amount of the iced tea into 8 containers. How many milliliters did Rob pour into each container?

© Common Core Assessment

15. Which shows a correct comparison?

Ⓐ   1,000 liters < 1,000 milliliters

Ⓑ   40 liters = 400 milliliters

Ⓒ   5,000 milliliters = 5 liters

Ⓓ   900 milliliters > 900 liters

16. Which shows a correct comparison?

Ⓐ   5 grams = 500 milligrams

Ⓑ   1 gram < 10 milligrams

Ⓒ   910 kilograms < 910 grams

Ⓓ   2 kilograms > 2 grams

Name _____

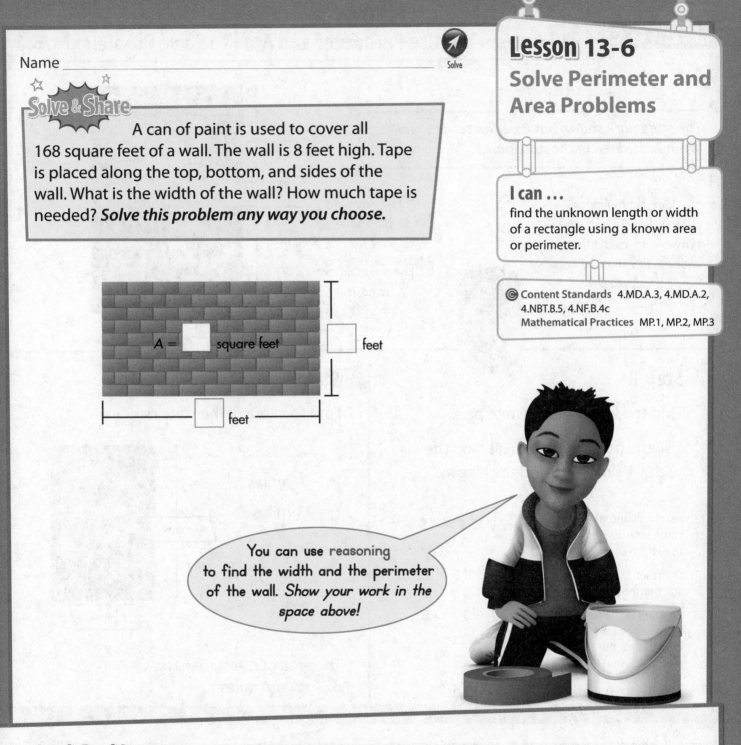

☆ Solve & Share

A can of paint is used to cover all 168 square feet of a wall. The wall is 8 feet high. Tape is placed along the top, bottom, and sides of the wall. What is the width of the wall? How much tape is needed? *Solve this problem any way you choose.*

I can ...
find the unknown length or width of a rectangle using a known area or perimeter.

© **Content Standards** 4.MD.A.3, 4.MD.A.2, 4.NBT.B.5, 4.NF.B.4c
Mathematical Practices MP.1, MP.2, MP.3

A = ☐ square feet

☐ feet

☐ feet

You can use reasoning to find the width and the perimeter of the wall. *Show your work in the space above!*

Look Back! © **MP.1 Make Sense and Persevere** Describe the steps you would use to solve the problem.

Learn Glossary

Essential Question
How Can You Use Perimeter and Area to Solve Problems?

A

The state park shown has a perimeter of 37 miles. What is the area of the state park?

Use formulas or equations, that use symbols to relate two or more quantities to solve this problem.

The formula for perimeter is:
$P = (2 \times \ell) + (2 \times w)$

The formula for area is:
$A = \ell \times w$

length (ℓ)

width (w) = $7\frac{1}{2}$ miles

B ## Step 1

Find the length of the state park.

Use the perimeter, 37 miles, and the width, $7\frac{1}{2}$ miles, to find the length.

Opposite sides of a rectangle are the same length, so multiply the width by 2.

$7\frac{1}{2} \times 2 = 15$

Subtract 15 from the perimeter.

$37 - 15 = 22$

22 miles is the length of two sides of the park. Divide 22 by 2 to find the length of one side.

$22 \div 2 = 11$

The length of the park is 11 miles.

C ## Step 2

Find the area of the state park.

$w = 7\frac{1}{2}$ miles

$\ell = 11$ miles

11 miles

$A = \ell \times w$
$= 11 \times 7\frac{1}{2}$
$= 82\frac{1}{2}$

$7\frac{1}{2}$ miles

The area of the state park is $82\frac{1}{2}$ square miles.

Convince Me! © **MP.1 Make Sense and Persevere** If the area of another state park is 216 square miles, and the park has a width of 8 miles, what is the park's length? What is the perimeter of this state park?

Name _____

☆Guided Practice*

Do You Understand?

1. © MP.3 **Construct Arguments** A sandbox is shaped like a rectangle. The area is 16 square feet. The side lengths are whole numbers. What are the possible dimensions of the sandbox? Do all possible dimensions make sense?

2. Write and solve an equation to find the width of a room if the length of the floor is 8 feet and the area of the room is 96 square feet.

Do You Know How?

For **3–5**, complete each calculation.

3. Find n. Perimeter = 46 in.

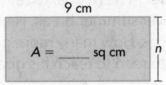
8 in.

n

4. Find n. Perimeter = 26 cm

9 cm

$A = $ _____ sq cm

n

5. Find the perimeter.

$5\frac{1}{2}$ yd

☆Independent Practice☆

For **6–9**, find the missing dimension.

6. Find n.

Area = 60 sq ft   6 ft

n

7. Find n. Perimeter = 65 in.

n

$11\frac{2}{4}$ in.

8. Find n. Perimeter = 84 yd

22 yd

n

9. A rectangle has a length of 9 millimeters and an area of 270 square millimeters. What is the width? What is the perimeter?

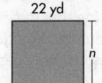
9 mm

w

Math Practices and Problem Solving

10. Greg built the picture frame shown to the right. It has a perimeter of $50\frac{2}{4}$ inches. How wide is the picture frame?

11. Greg covered the back of the picture with a piece of felt. The felt covers both the picture and the frame. What is the area of the felt?

$\ell = 15\frac{1}{4}$ in.

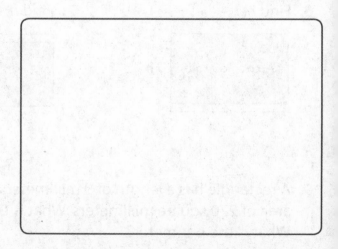

12. **Number Sense** Al has a goal to read 2,000 pages over summer break. He has read 1,248 pages. How many more pages does Al need to read to reach his goal?

13. The area of a tabletop is 18 square feet. The perimeter of the same table is 18 feet. What are the dimensions of the tabletop?

14. Amy and Zach each have 24 feet of fencing for their rectangular gardens. Amy makes her fence 6 feet long. Zach makes his fence 8 feet long. Whose garden has the greater area? How much greater?

15. **Higher Order Thinking** Nancy made a table runner that has an area of 80 square inches. The length and width of the table runner are whole numbers. The length is 5 times greater than the width. What are the dimensions of the table runner?

© Common Core Assessment

16. Which has the greater area: a square with a side that measures 7 meters or a $6\frac{1}{2}$-meter by 8-meter rectangle? How much more area does that figure have?

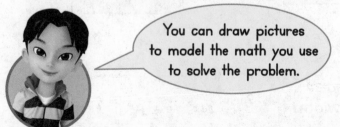

You can draw pictures to model the math you use to solve the problem.

712   **Topic 13** | Lesson 13-6

Help Practice Tools Games
        Buddy

Another Look!

Find the perimeter of the rectangle.

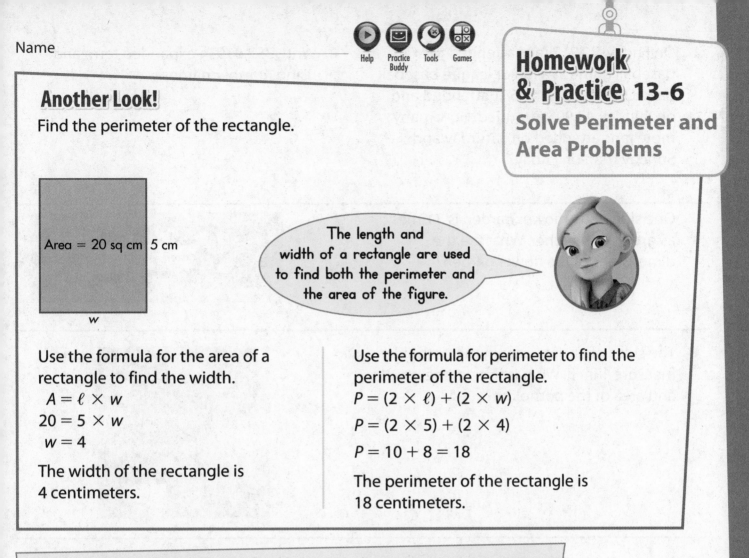

Area = 20 sq cm | 5 cm

w

The length and width of a rectangle are used to find both the perimeter and the area of the figure.

Use the formula for the area of a rectangle to find the width.

$A = \ell \times w$

$20 = 5 \times w$

$w = 4$

The width of the rectangle is 4 centimeters.

Use the formula for perimeter to find the perimeter of the rectangle.

$P = (2 \times \ell) + (2 \times w)$

$P = (2 \times 5) + (2 \times 4)$

$P = 10 + 8 = 18$

The perimeter of the rectangle is 18 centimeters.

For **1–4**, use the formulas for perimeter and area to solve each problem.

1. Find *n*.

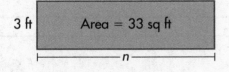

2 ft | Area = 28 sq ft | ← n →

2. Find *n*. Perimeter = 86 in.

25 in.

n

3. Find *n*. Then find the perimeter.

3 ft | Area = 33 sq ft
← n →

4. Find *n*. Then find the area.
Perimeter = $60\frac{2}{4}$ in.

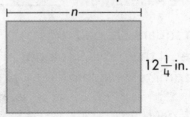

← n →

$12\frac{1}{4}$ in.

5. On Friday, 39,212 fans attended the baseball game at a major league baseball park. On Saturday, 41,681 attended and on Sunday 42,905 attended. How many more fans attended on Saturday and Sunday than on Friday?

6. Write 352,619 in expanded form and using number names.

7. One side of the flower garden is 3 times as great as the other. What are the dimensions of the flower garden?

Area = 48 sq m

8. The sides of each square in the potholder measure 1 inch. What is the perimeter and area of the potholder?

9. How many seconds are in 3 minutes? There are 60 seconds in one minute. Complete the table.

Minutes	Seconds
1	
2	
3	

10. Higher Order Thinking An art class is planning to paint a rectangular mural with an area of 60 square feet. It has to be at least 4 feet high but no more than 6 feet high. The length and width have to be whole numbers. List all possible widths for the mural.

© Common Core Assessment

11. The area of a square-shaped rug is 81 square feet. If the rug is 9 ft long, what is its perimeter? Explain.

Use what you know about squares to help solve the problem.

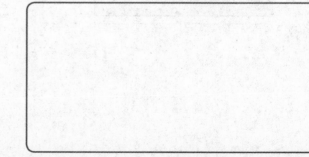

Name _____

Math Practices and Problem Solving

Lesson 13-7
Precision

Solve & Share

Mr. Beasley's science class wants to decorate one wall in the classroom like an underwater scene. They use sheets of blue poster board that are 2 feet long and 2 feet wide. How many sheets of blue poster board are used to cover the entire area of the wall? Use math words and symbols to explain how you solve.

I can ...
be precise when solving math problems.

© **Mathematical Practices** MP.6 Also MP.1, MP.2, MP.4
Content Standards 4.MD.A.2, 4.MD.A.3, 4.NBT.B.5, 4.NBT.B.4

8 feet high

14 feet wide

Thinking Habits
Be a good thinker!
These questions can help you.

- Am I using numbers, units, and symbols appropriately?

- Am I using the correct definitions?

- Am I calculating accurately?

- Is my answer clear?

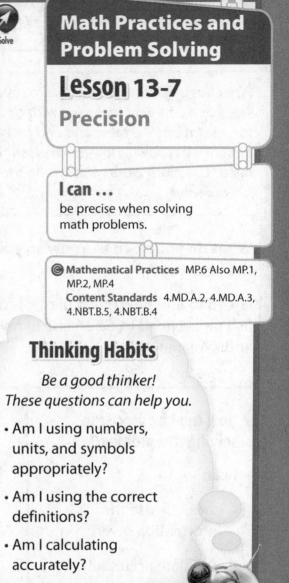

Look Back! © **MP.6 Be Precise** How can calculating the area of the whole wall and the area of one sheet of poster board help you determine the total number of sheets of poster board needed to cover the entire area of the wall?

How Can You Be Precise When Solving Math Problems?

A

length = 12 inches

height = 15 inches

width = 24 inches

Piper has a fish tank and wants to cover all four sides $\frac{6}{10}$ of the way to the top with clear plastic for insulation. She measures and finds the dimensions shown. How much plastic does Piper need? Use math words and symbols to explain how to solve.

What do you need to know so you can solve the problem?

I need to find how much plastic is needed for the fish tank. I need to be precise in my calculations and explanation.

Here's my thinking.

B **How can I be precise in solving this problem?**

I can

- correctly use the information given.

- calculate accurately.

- decide if my answer is clear and appropriate.

- use the correct units.

C The height of the plastic is $\frac{6}{10}$ times 15 inches.

$\frac{6}{10} \times 15 = \frac{90}{10}$ or 9   The plastic is 9 inches high.

Front and back: $A = 9 \times 24$
$A = 216$ square inches

Each side: $A = 9 \times 12$
$A = 108$ square inches

Add: $216 + 216 + 108 + 108 = 648$ square inches

Piper needs 648 square inches of plastic.

Convince Me! © MP.6 Be Precise How did you use math words and numbers to make your explanation clear?

Name _____

☆ Guided Practice *

© **MP.6 Be Precise**

Jeremy uses $1\frac{1}{2}$ feet of tape for each box he packs for shipping. How many inches of tape does Jeremy need to pack 3 boxes?

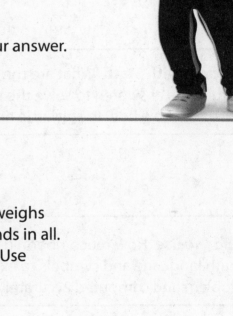

When you are precise, you calculate accurately.

1. How can you use the information given to solve the problem?

2. How many inches of tape does Jeremy need to pack 3 boxes? Explain.

3. Explain why you used the units you did in your answer.

Independent Practice ☆

© **MP.6 Be Precise**

Mrs. Reed collects shells. Each shell in her collection weighs about 4 ounces. Her collection weighs about 12 pounds in all. About how many shells are in Mrs. Reed's collection? Use Exercises 4–6 to solve.

4. How can you use the information given to solve the problem?

5. What is the total weight of Mrs. Reed's shell collection, in ounces?

6. How many shells are in Mrs. Reed's shell collection?

For another example, see Set D on page 724.   **Topic 13** | Lesson 13-7   **717**

Math Practices and Problem Solving

Ⓒ Common Core Performance Assessment

Making Thank You Cards

Tanesha is making cards by gluing 1 ounce of glitter on the front of the card and then making a border out of ribbon. She makes each card the dimensions shown. How much ribbon does Tanesha need?

9 cm

85 mm

7. **MP.2 Reasoning** What quantities are given in the problem and what do the numbers mean?

8. **MP.1 Make Sense and Persevere** What do you need to find?

9. **MP.4 Model with Math** What are the hidden questions which must be answered to solve the problem? Write equations to show how to solve the hidden questions.

When you are precise, you specify and use units of measure appropriately.

10. **MP.6 Be Precise** How much ribbon does Tanesha need? Use math language and symbols to explain how you solved the problem and computed accurately.

11. **MP.2 Reasoning** What information was not needed in the problem?

Homework & Practice 13-7
Precision

Another Look!

Mia has a length of string that is 2 meters long. She cuts it into 4 equal pieces. Is one of the pieces of string long enough to tie around the perimeter of a square box with a side length of 16 centimeters? Explain.

Tell how you can solve the problem with accuracy.

- I can correctly use the information given.

- I can calculate accurately.

- I can decide if my answer is clear and appropriate.

- I can use the correct units.

> When you are precise, you use math symbols and language appropriately.

Attend to precision as you solve.

First, convert 2 meters to centimeters. $2 \times 100 = 200$ centimeters

Next, find the length of each piece Mia has after $200 \div 4 = 50$ centimeters
she cuts the string into 4 equal pieces.

Then, find the perimeter of the square box. $P = 4 \times 16 = 64$ centimeters

The 50-centimeter piece is not long enough to go around the 64-centimeter perimeter of the box.

© MP.6 Be Precise

Susan bought a 1 kilogram bag of grapes. On the way home, she ate 125 grams of the grapes. How many grams of grapes does Susan have left? Use Exercises 1–3 to solve.

1. How can you use the information given to solve the problem?

2. How many grams of grapes does Susan have left? Show that you compute accurately.

3. Use math language and symbols to explain how you solved the problem.

Cell Phone Pouches

Lex wants to make phone bags like the one shown. The pattern shows the material he needs for each side of the bag. He needs to know how much material he will need to make each bag.

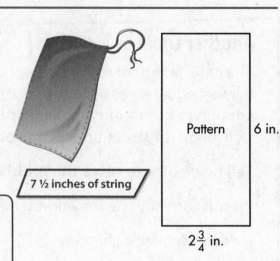

7 ½ inches of string

Pattern   6 in.

$2\frac{3}{4}$ in.

4. **MP.1 Make Sense and Persevere** What do you know and what do you need to find?

5. **MP.4 Model with Math** What is the hidden question? Write an equation to show how to solve it.

6. **MP.1 Make Sense and Persevere** How much material does Lex need to make each bag?

When you are precise, you give carefully formulated explanations that are clear and appropriate.

7. **MP.6 Be Precise** Explain how you know what units to use for your answer.

8. **MP.2 Reasoning** What information was not needed to solve the problem?

★ ☆
Find a Match
☆
☆

Work with a partner. Point to a clue.

Read the clue.

Look below the clues to find a match. Write the clue letter in the box next to the match.

Find a match for every clue.

I can ...
add and subtract multi-digit whole numbers.

© **Content Standard** 4.NBT.B.4

Clues

A The sum is between 2,000 and 2,500.

E The sum is exactly 16,477.

B The difference is exactly 10,000.

F The sum is between 5,500 and 5,600.

C The sum is exactly 6,000.

G The difference is between 1,000 and 2,000.

D The difference is exactly 4,500.

H The difference is between 8,000 and 9,000.

□	□	□	□
10,005 + 6,472	7,513 − 5,676	35,000 − 25,000	1,234 + 4,321
□	□	□	□
1,050 + 1,200	3,778 + 2,222	10,650 − 2,150	9,000 − 4,500

Vocabulary Review

A-Z
Glossary

Word List

- area
- capacity
- centimeter (cm)
- cup (c)
- fluid ounce (fl oz)
- formula
- gallon (gal)
- gram (g)
- kilogram (kg)
- kilometer (km)
- liter (L)
- mass
- meter (m)
- milligram (mg)
- milliliter (mL)
- millimeter (mm)
- ounce (oz)
- perimeter
- pint (pt)
- pound (lb)
- quart (qt)
- ton (T)
- weight

Understand Vocabulary

1. Cross out the units that are **NOT** used to measure length.

centimeter (cm)   pint (pt)

pound (lb)   kilogram (kg)

2. Cross out the units that are **NOT** used to measure capacity.

millimeter (mm)   ounce (oz)

gallon (gal)   milliliter (mL)

3. Cross out the units that are **NOT** used to measure weight.

cup (c)   liter (L)

meter (m)   ton (T)

4. Cross out the units that are **NOT** used to measure mass.

fluid ounce (fl oz)   kilometer (km)

milligram (mg)   quart (qt)

Label each example with a term from the Word List.

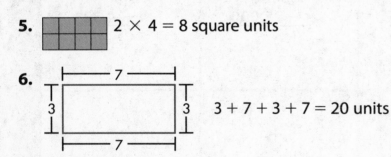

5. $2 \times 4 = 8$ square units   _____

6.   _____

$3 + 7 + 3 + 7 = 20$ units

7. Area $= \ell \times w$ _____

Use Vocabulary in Writing

8. Mike uses 24 meters of fence to enclose a rectangular garden. The length of the garden is 10 meters, what is the width? Use at least 3 terms from the Word List to explain.

Name _____

Set A pages 679–696 _____

Customary units can be used when measuring length, capacity, and weight.

Reteaching

	Length	1 foot (ft) = 12 inches (in.)
DATA		1 yard (yd) = 3 ft = 36 in.
		1 mile (mi) = 1,760 yd = 5,280 ft

	Capacity	1 cup (c) = 8 fluid ounces (fl oz)
DATA		1 pint (pt) = 2 c = 16 fl oz
		1 quart (qt) = 2 pt = 4 c
		1 gallon (gal) = 4 qt = 8 pt

	Weight	1 pound (lb) = 16 ounces (oz)
DATA		1 ton (T) = 2,000 lb

Convert 26 quarts to cups.

Larger Unit		Smaller Unit		Converted to Smaller Unit
26	×	4 cups	=	104 cups

Remember when converting from a larger unit to a smaller unit, you multiply. Use the conversion charts to help solve.

1. 9 yards = _____ inches

2. 5 miles = _____ yards

3. 215 yards = _____ feet

4. 9 pints = _____ fluid ounces

5. 372 quarts = _____ cups

6. 1,620 gallons = _____ pints

7. 9 pounds = _____ ounces

8. 5 tons = _____ pounds

9. 12 feet = _____ inches

Set B pages 697–708 _____

Metric units are commonly used by scientists to measure length, capacity, and mass.

	Length	1 centimeter (cm) = 10 millimeters (mm)
DATA		1 meter (m) = 100 cm = 1,000 mm
		1 kilometer (km) = 1,000 m

	Capacity and Mass	1 liter (L) = 1,000 milliliters (mL)
DATA		1 gram (g) = 1,000 milligrams (mg)
		1 kilogram (kg) = 1,000 g

Convert 30 centimeters to millimeters.

Larger Unit		Smaller Unit		Converted to Smaller Unit
30	×	10 mm	=	300 mm

Remember metric units can be converted using multiples of 10. Use the conversion charts to help.

1. 9 kilometers = _____ meters

2. 55 centimeters = _____ millimeters

3. 2 meters = _____ centimeters

4. 9 liters = _____ milliliters

5. 4 grams = _____ milligrams

6. 5 kilograms = _____ grams

7. 8 kilograms = _____ grams

8. 5 grams = _____ milligrams

The perimeter of Ted's pool is 16 yards. The pool is 3 yards wide. He has a 150-square foot plastic cover. Is Ted's plastic cover large enough to cover his pool?

Use the formula for perimeter to find the length. Substitute the numbers you know.

$$\text{Perimeter} = (2 \times \ell) + (2 \times w)$$
$$16 = (2 \times \ell) + (2 \times 3)$$
$$\ell = 5$$

The length of the pool is 5 yards.

Convert yards to feet.

3 yards wide × 3 feet = 9 feet wide

5 yards long × 3 feet = 15 feet long

$$A = 15 \times 9$$
$$A = 135$$

The area of the pool is 135 square feet. $135 < 150$, so Ted's plastic cover is large enough to cover his pool.

Remember to label your answer with the appropriate unit.

1. Find n.
   $P = 108$ inches

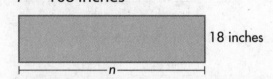
18 inches
n

2. Find the area.

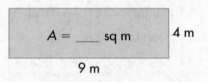
$A = \underline{\quad}$ sq m
4 m
9 m

3. Find the perimeter of the square.

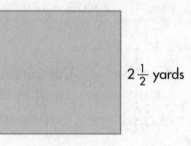
$2\frac{1}{2}$ yards

Think about these questions to help you **be precise.**

Thinking Habits

• Am I using numbers, units, and symbols appropriately?

• Am I using the correct definitions?

• Am I calculating accurately?

• Is my answer clear?

Remember to give an explanation that is clear and appropriate.

A puppy pen is 4 feet wide and 5 feet long.

1. Is 21 square feet of fabric large enough to make a mat for the pen? Explain.

2. Puppy fencing comes in sizes that are 12 feet, 24 feet, and 30 feet in length. Which length would be the best for the pen? How much, if any, will have to be cut off to fit the pen?

1. A window is 5 feet long. What is the length of the window in inches?

2. Mrs. Warren bought 6 liters of lemonade for a party. How many milliliters of lemonade did she buy?

   Ⓐ 9,000 milliliters

   Ⓑ 6,000 milliliters

   Ⓒ 3,000 milliliters

   Ⓓ 1,200 milliliters

3. Draw lines to match the measure on the left to the equivalent measure on the right.

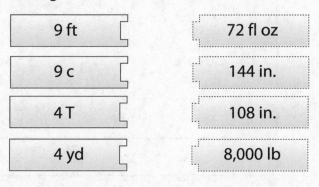

9 ft	72 fl oz
9 c	144 in.
4 T	108 in.
4 yd	8,000 lb

4. A picnic table is 9 feet long and 3 feet wide. Write and solve an equation to find the area of the rectangular surface of the table.

5. The Girl's Club is making muffins. Mindy's recipe calls for 3 cups of buttermilk. Josie's recipe calls for 20 fluid ounces of buttermilk. Georgia's recipe calls for 1 pint of buttermilk. Whose recipe calls for the most buttermilk? Explain.

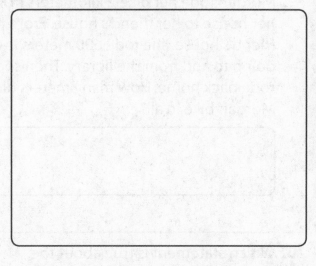

6. Andrea ran 4 kilometers over the weekend. How many meters did Andrea run?

7. Choose numbers from the box to complete the table. Some numbers will not be used.

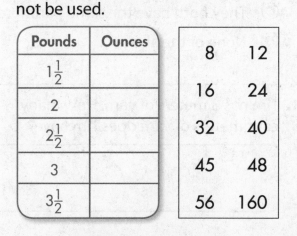

Pounds	Ounces
$1\frac{1}{2}$	
2	
$2\frac{1}{2}$	
3	
$3\frac{1}{2}$	

8	12
16	24
32	40
45	48
56	160

8. Choose Yes or No to tell if the equation is correct.

8a. 1 L = 100 mL   ○ Yes   ○ No

8b. 1 kg = 1,000 g   ○ Yes   ○ No

8c. 4 yd = 14 ft   ○ Yes   ○ No

8d. 15 cm = 150 mm   ○ Yes   ○ No

---

9. Morgan rode her bike 2 kilometers from her house to her friend's house. From her friend's house, she rode 600 meters in all going to and from the library. Then she rode back home. How many meters did Morgan bike in all?

---

10. Which statement is true about the bedrooms in the drawings below?

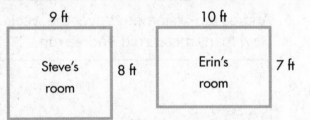

  Ⓐ Erin's room has a greater area than Steve's room.

  Ⓑ Steve's room has a greater perimeter than Erin's room.

  Ⓒ They both have the same perimeter.

  Ⓓ None of the above

---

11. Tim has 3 meters of yarn. How many centimeters of yarn does Tim have?

---

12. Mrs. Li's classroom is 34 feet wide and 42 feet long.

Objects in Classroom	Area of Objects (square feet)
Mrs. Li's Desk	8
Fish Tank	6
Math Center	100
Reading Center	120

Part A

What is the area of the classroom?

Part B

How much area is taken up by the objects in the classroom? How much area is left for the students' desks? Write and solve equations to find the area.

---

13. Draw lines to match the measure on the left to the equivalent measure on the right.

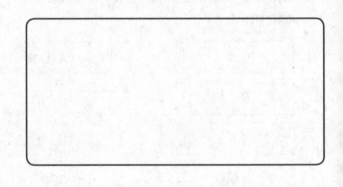

3 g		3,000 mL
3 m		3,000 g
3 L		3,000 mm
3 kg		3,000 mg

Name _____

Watermelons

Kasia grows watermelons.

1. Kasia plants her watermelons in rows. Kasia's watermelon field has a perimeter of $71\frac{1}{3}$ yards and is 44 feet wide. The rows will be planted $2\frac{2}{3}$ yards apart.

Part A

How many rows of watermelons can Kasia plant? Explain.

Watermelon Field

width = 44 feet

First and last row are 6 feet from the edge.

Part B

What is the area of Kasia's field? Complete the table to convert the perimeter to feet. Explain.

Yards	Feet
$1\frac{1}{3}$	4
$11\frac{1}{3}$	
$21\frac{1}{3}$	
$31\frac{1}{3}$	
$41\frac{1}{3}$	
$51\frac{1}{3}$	
$61\frac{1}{3}$	
$71\frac{1}{3}$	

Part C

Explain why you used the units you did in your answer to Part B.

2. Use the information in the 20-Pound **Watermelon** table.

Watermelon

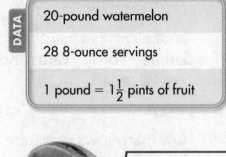

DATA	
20-pound watermelon	
28 8-ounce servings	
1 pound = $1\frac{1}{2}$ pints of fruit	

Part A

If there are twenty-eight 8-ounce servings in a 20-pound watermelon, how many pounds does the rind weigh? Explain.

The part of the watermelon that you do not eat is the rind.

Part B

How many cups of fruit does Kasia get from a 20-pound watermelon? Explain. Show your computations. Do not include the weight of the rind.

3. Use the information from the **Watermelon and Nutrition** picture to answer the question.

Watermelon and Nutrition

How many more milligrams of fiber than potassium are in a serving of watermelon? Explain.

Each serving has 1 gram of fiber and 270 mg of potassium.

Algebra: Generate and Analyze Patterns

Essential Questions: How can you use a rule to continue a pattern? How can you use a table to extend a pattern? How can you use a repeating pattern to predict a shape?

Digital Resources

Solve Learn Glossary Practice Buddy

Tools Assessment Help Games

Scientists can use an instrument called an oscilloscope to see sounds as waves.

Higher sounds have shorter wavelengths.

I can see what you are saying on the oscilloscope. Here is a project about patterns and waves.

Math and Science Project: Patterns and Waves

Do Research Use the Internet or other sources to learn about 2 industries where oscilloscopes can be used. Name the industry and what can be observed using the oscilloscope.

Journal: Write a Report Include what you found. Also in your report:

- Oscilloscopes are also used to observe patterns in waves. Suppose a scientist created a pattern with three levels of sounds: *quiet, loud, medium*. If the scientist repeats the pattern of sounds, what would be the 41st sound in the pattern? Explain.

Name _____

Review What You Know

Addition and Subtraction Patterns

Add or subtract to find the missing number in each pattern.

4. 3, 6, 9, 12, _____, 18

5. 4, 8, 12, _____, 20, 24

6. 8, 7, 6, _____, 4, 3

7. 30, 25, 20, 15, _____, 5

8. 1, 5, 9, _____, 17, 21

9. 12, 10, 8, 6, _____, 2

Multiplication and Division Patterns

Multiply or divide to find the missing number in each pattern.

10. 1, 3, 9, 27, _____, 243

11. 64, 32, 16, _____, 4, 2

12. 1, 5, 25, _____, 625

13. 1, 2, 4, 8, _____, 32

14. 1, 4, 16, _____, 256

15. 729, 243, 81, 27, 9, _____

Problem Solving

16. © MP.7 Look for Relationships James places 1 counter in the first box. He places 2 counters in the second box, 4 counters in the third box, 8 counters in the fourth box, and continues the pattern until he gets to the tenth box. How many counters did James place in the tenth box?

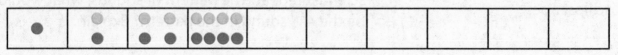

My Word Cards

Use the examples for each word on the front of the card to help complete the definitions on the back.

rule

Rule: Multiply by 3

Input	1	2	3	4
Output	3	6	9	12

repeating pattern

Rule: Triangle, Square

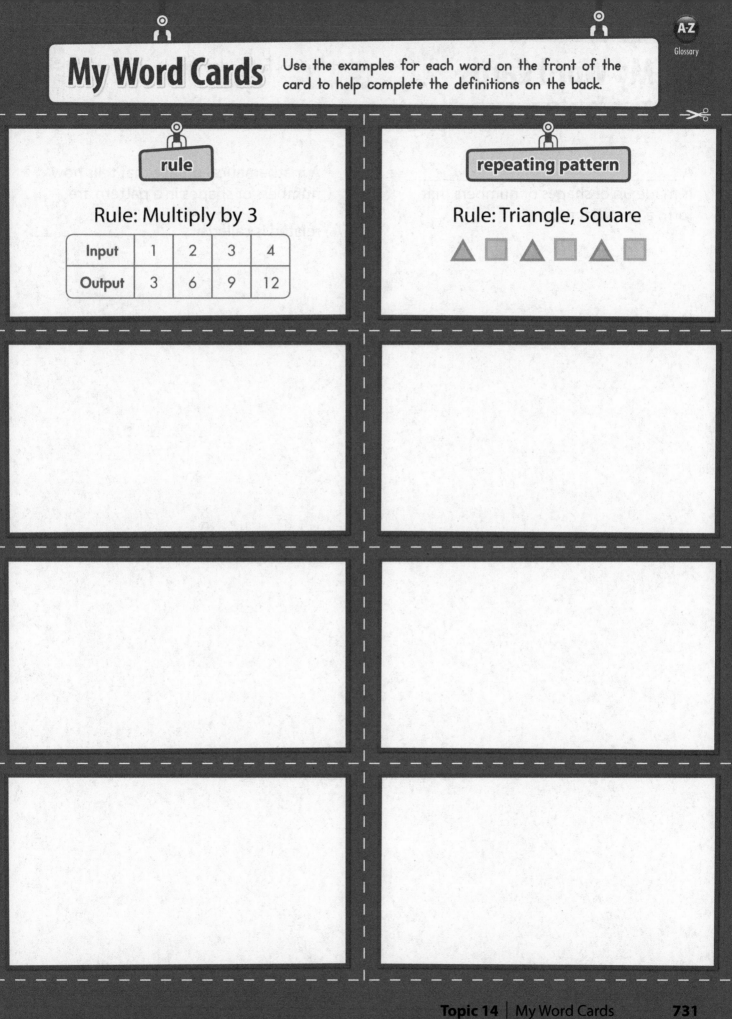

Complete each definition. Extend learning by writing your own definitions.

A _____ is made up of shapes or numbers that form a part that repeats.

A mathematical phrase that tells how numbers or shapes in a pattern are related is called a _____.

Name _____

Solve

Solve & Share

Look at the rules and starting numbers below. What are the next 6 numbers in each pattern? Tell how you decided. Describe features of the patterns. *Solve these problems any way you choose.*

I can ...
use a rule to create and extend a number pattern and identify features of the number pattern not described by the rule.

Content Standard 4.OA.C.5
Mathematical Practices MP.1, MP.2, MP.4, MP.5, MP.7, MP.8

When you use a table to organize your work, you are modeling with math.

Starting Number	Rule	Next 6 Numbers
18	Add 3	
17	Add 2	
40	Subtract 4	

Look Back! MP.7 Look for Relationships Create two patterns that use the same rule but start with different numbers. Identify a feature of each pattern. For example, identify whether the numbers are all even, all odd, or alternate between even and odd.

A

The house numbers on a street follow the rule "Add 4." If the pattern continues, what are the next three house numbers? Describe a feature of the pattern.

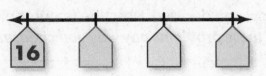

16

You can use a number line to help make sense of the problem and find the next three house numbers.

B **Use a number line to continue the pattern.**

A rule is a mathematical phrase that tells how numbers or shapes in a pattern are related. The rule for the house numbers is "Add 4."

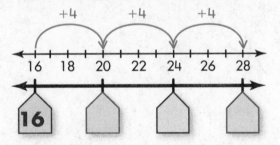

+4   +4   +4

16 18 20 22 24 26 28

16

The next three house numbers are 20, 24, and 28.

C **Describe features of the pattern.**

Some patterns have features that are not given in the rule.

16, 20, 24, 28

One of the features of this pattern is all of the house numbers are even numbers.

Another feature is all of the house numbers are multiples of 4.

Convince Me! © MP.8 Generalize Can you use the rule "Add 4" to create a different pattern with all odd numbers? Explain.

Name _____

Another Example!

On another street, the house numbers follow the rule "Subtract 5." What are the next three house numbers? Describe a feature of the pattern.

$$-5 \quad -5 \quad -5$$
$$25 \quad 20 \quad 15 \quad 10$$

The next three house numbers are 20, 15, and 10. All of the house numbers are multiples of 5.

> Some patterns have rules using addition, while others have rules using subtraction.

☆ Guided Practice *

Do You Understand?

1. **ⓒ MP.2 Reasoning** Rudy's rule is "Add 2." He started with 4 and wrote the numbers below. Which number does **NOT** belong to Rudy's pattern? Explain.

   4, 6, 8, 9, 10, 12

Do You Know How?

Continue the pattern. Describe a feature of the pattern.

2. Subtract 6

   48, 42, 36, 30, 24, _____, _____, _____

Independent Practice ☆

For **3–6**, continue each pattern. Describe a feature of each pattern.

3. Subtract 3: 21, 18, 15, _____, _____

4. Add 7: 4, 11, 18, _____, _____

5. Add 5: 5, 10, 15, _____, _____

6. Add 2: 5, 7, 9, _____, _____

For **7–12**, use the rule to generate each pattern.

7. Rule: Subtract 10

   90, _____, _____

8. Rule: Add 11

   16, _____, _____

9. Rule: Add 5

   96, _____, _____

10. Rule: Add 4

    43, _____, _____

11. Rule: Subtract 15

    120, _____, _____

12. Rule: Subtract 9

    99, _____, _____

*For another example, see Set A on page 759.

Topic 14 | Lesson 14-1   **735**

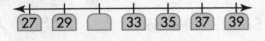
13. © **MP.2 Reasoning** Orlando delivers mail. He sees one mailbox that does not have a number. If the numbers are in a pattern, what is the missing number?

27 29 ☐ 33 35 37 39

14. A bus tour runs 9 times a day, 6 days a week. The bus can carry 30 passengers. Find the greatest number of passengers who can ride the tour bus each week.

15. The year 2005 was the year of the Rooster on the Chinese calendar. The next year of the Rooster will be 2017. The rule is "Add 12." What are the next five years of the Rooster?

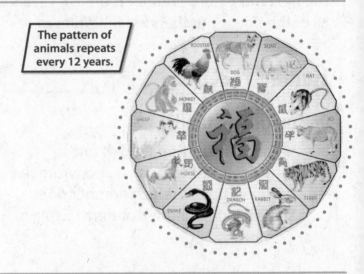

The pattern of animals repeats every 12 years.

16. Suppose you were born in the year of the Snake. How old will you be the next time the year of the Snake is celebrated?

17. 🄰🅉 **Vocabulary** Define *rule*. Create a number pattern using the rule "Subtract 7."

18. **Higher Order Thinking** Some patterns use both addition and subtraction in their rules. The rule is "Add 3, Subtract 2." Find the next three numbers in the pattern.

1, 4, 2, 5, 3, 6, 4, 7, _____, _____, _____

© **Common Core Assessment**

19. Rima used "Subtract 3" as the rule to make a pattern. She started with 60, and wrote the next 6 numbers in her pattern. Which number does **NOT** belong in Rima's pattern?

Which number is NOT a multiple of 3?

  Ⓐ 57
  Ⓑ 54
  Ⓒ 45
  Ⓓ 26

20. Ivan counted all the beans in a jar. If he counted the beans in groups of 7, which list shows the numbers Ivan could have named?

  Ⓐ 7, 14, 21, 24
  Ⓑ 7, 14, 28, 54
  Ⓒ 7, 14, 21, 28
  Ⓓ 14, 24, 34, 44

Help Practice Tools Games
      Buddy

Another Look!

Melanie has to create a pattern using the rule "Add 11." Her starting number is 11. What are the next 5 numbers in Melanie's pattern? Describe a feature of the pattern.

You can use a rule to describe a number pattern.

Use the rule to continue the pattern.

+11 +11 +11 +11 +11
11   22   33   44   55   66

The next 5 numbers in Melanie's pattern are 22, 33, 44, 55, and 66.

Describe features of the pattern.

• The numbers in the pattern are multiples of 11.

• The digits in the ones place increase by one as the pattern continues.

For **1–6**, continue each pattern. Describe a feature of each pattern.

1. Subtract 2: 30, 28, 26, _____, _____

2. Add 8: 14, 22, 30, _____, _____

3. Add 9: 9, 18, 27, _____, _____

4. Subtract 7: 49, 42, 35, _____, _____

5. Add 10: 213; 223; 233; _____; _____

6. Subtract 8: 92, 84, 76, _____, _____

For **7–12**, use the rule to fill in the missing number in each pattern.

7. Add 3

41, 44, _____, 50

8. Subtract 10

429, 419, 409, _____

9. Add 6

11, _____, 23, 29

10. Add 7

1, _____, 15, 22

11. Subtract 2, Add 3

6, 4, 7, _____, _____

12. Add 2, Subtract 4

10, 12, 8, _____, _____

13. **MP.5 Use Appropriate Tools** Emily buys a sandwich, a salad, and a drink. If she gives the cashier $20, how much change will she receive? Use bills and coins to solve.

14. Mimi started a pattern with 5 and used the rule "Add 10." What are the first five numbers in Mimi's pattern? Describe the numbers in the sequence.

15. © **MP.2 Reasoning** Jack arranged the pencils in groups of 6 to make a pattern. His rule is "Add 6." His starting number is 6. What are the next 4 numbers in Jack's pattern?

16. Presidential elections are held every 4 years. There were Presidential elections in 1840, 1844, 1848, and 1852. When were the next three Presidential elections? Describe a feature of the pattern.

17. **Higher Order Thinking** Sarah created a pattern. Her rule was "Add 4." All the numbers in Sarah's pattern were odd. Three of the numbers in Sarah's pattern were less than 10. What was the starting number for Sarah's pattern?

© **Common Core Assessment**

18. The house numbers on Carr Memorial Avenue follow a pattern. The first four houses on the left side of the street are numbered 8, 14, 20, and 26. The rule is "Add 6." How many more houses are on the left side of the street with numbers less than 50?

   Ⓐ 1 house

   Ⓑ 2 houses

   Ⓒ 3 houses

   Ⓓ 4 houses

19. Noreen is training for a race. The first week she runs the route in 54 minutes. The second week, she runs the route in 52 minutes. The third week, she runs the route in 50 minutes. Noreen runs 2 minutes faster each week. If the pattern continues, how many minutes will it take Noreen to run the route the fifth week?

   Ⓐ 44 minutes

   Ⓑ 46 minutes

   Ⓒ 48 minutes

   Ⓓ 50 minutes

Name _____

Solve & Share

There are 6 juice boxes in 1 pack, 12 in 2 packs, and 18 in 3 packs. How many juice boxes are in 4 packs? in 5 packs? in 6 packs? Use the rule to complete the table. Describe features of the pattern. Then find how many juice boxes are in 10 packs and 100 packs.

I can ...
use a rule to extend a number pattern, identify features of the number pattern, and use the number pattern to solve a problem.

Content Standard 4.OA.C.5
Mathematical Practices MP.2, MP.7

Rule: Multiply by 6

Number of Packs	Number of Juice Boxes
1	6
2	12
3	18
4	
5	
6	

You can use reasoning to extend and describe features of the pattern.

Look Back! MP.2 Reasoning Create a table showing the relationship between the number of bicycles and the number of wheels on bicycles. Start with 1 bicycle. Complete 5 rows of the table using the rule "Multiply by 2." Describe features of the pattern.

A

There are 3 leaflets on 1 cloverleaf.
There are 6 leaflets on 2 cloverleaves.
There are 9 leaflets on 3 cloverleaves.
How many leaflets are on 4 cloverleaves?
How many cloverleaves will have 12 leaflets?

A cloverleaf has 3 leaflets.

You can use a table to create, extend, and identify features of a pattern.

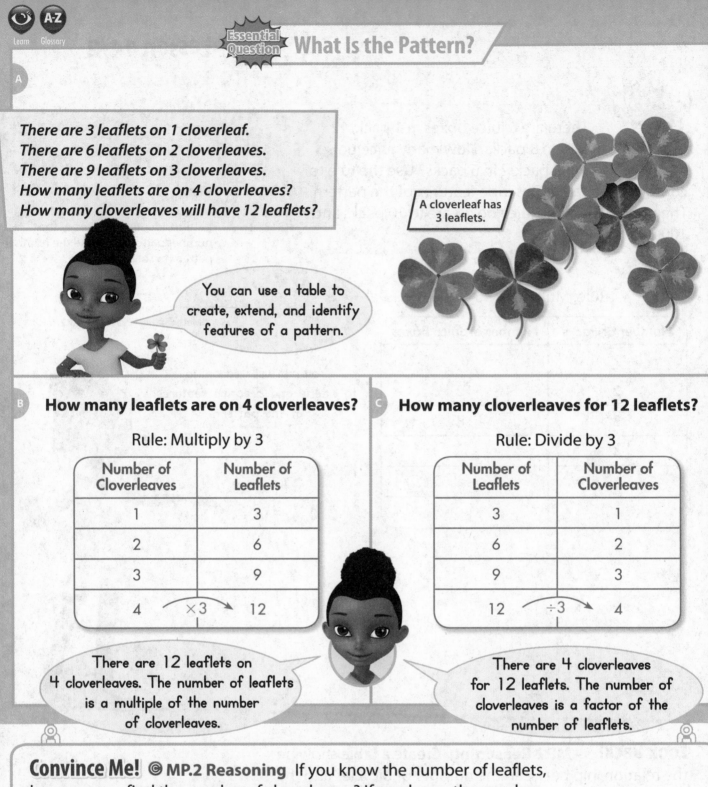

B **How many leaflets are on 4 cloverleaves?**

Rule: Multiply by 3

Number of Cloverleaves	Number of Leaflets
1	3
2	6
3	9
4 ×3→	12

There are 12 leaflets on 4 cloverleaves. The number of leaflets is a multiple of the number of cloverleaves.

C **How many cloverleaves for 12 leaflets?**

Rule: Divide by 3

Number of Leaflets	Number of Cloverleaves
3	1
6	2
9	3
12 ÷3→	4

There are 4 cloverleaves for 12 leaflets. The number of cloverleaves is a factor of the number of leaflets.

Convince Me! © MP.2 Reasoning If you know the number of leaflets, how can you find the number of cloverleaves? If you know the number of cloverleaves, how can you find the number of leaflets?

Guided Practice *

Do You Understand?

1. © **MP.2 Reasoning** The rule for this table is "Multiply by 4." What number does not belong?

My Marbles	John's Marbles
1	4
2	8
3	12
4	15

Do You Know How?

Complete the table. Describe a feature of the pattern.

2. Rule: Divide by 4

Total Number of Wheels	8	12	16	20
Number of Cars	2	3	4	

Independent Practice *

For **3–6**, use the rule to complete each table. Describe a feature of each pattern.

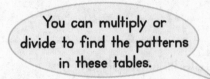

You can multiply or divide to find the patterns in these tables.

3. Rule: Multiply by 8

Number of Spiders	1	2	3	4	5
Number of Legs	8		24	32	

4. Rule: Divide by 5

Number of Fingers	Number of Hands
5	1
10	2
15	
20	

5. Rule: Multiply by 16

Number of Books	1	2	3	4
Weight of Books in Ounces	16	32		

6. Rule: Divide by 2

Number of Shoes	12	14	16	18
Number of Pairs	6	7		

Math Practices and Problem Solving

7. The table shows how much money Joe makes babysitting. How much money will Joe make when he babysits for 6 hours?

Rule: Multiply by 7

Hours of Babysitting	Amount Earned
3	$21
4	$28
5	$35
6	

8. The table shows the total number of pounds of potatoes for different numbers of bags. How many bags does it take to hold 96 pounds of potatoes?

Rule: Divide by 8

Number of Pounds	Number of Bags
72	9
80	10
88	11
96	

9. Number Sense What is the greatest number you can make using each of the digits 1, 7, 0 and 6 once?

10. Algebra A penguin can swim 11 miles per hour. At this speed, how far can it swim in 13 hours? Use *s* as a variable. Write and solve an equation.

For **11–12**, the rule is "Multiply by 3."

11. © MP.2 Reasoning Using the rule, how many batteries do 8 flashlights need? 10 flashlights?

12. Higher Order Thinking How many more batteries do 6 flashlights need than 4 flashlights? Explain.

DATA

Batteries for Flashlights

Number of Flashlights	Number of Batteries
1	3
2	6
3	9

© Common Core Assessment

13. There are 6 rolls in each package. Use the rule "Divide by 6" to show the relationship between the number of rolls and the number of packages. Use each digit from the box once to complete the table.

Number of Rolls	522	528	534	540	546	552
Number of Packages	☐☐	88	89	☐☐	9☐	9☐

0	1
2	7
8	9

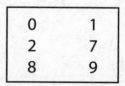

`Name _____`

Help Practice Tools Games
      Buddy

**Homework
& Practice 14-2**

Patterns:
Number Rules

Another Look!

Stephanie wants to know how many players are participating in a competition. There are 6 teams. Each team has 11 players. The rule is "Multiply by 11."

Use the rule to complete the table.

Number of Teams	Number of Players
1	11
2	22
3	33
4	44
5	55
6	66

Describe features of the pattern.

- The number of players are multiples of 11.

- The digits in the ones place increase by 1 for each team added.

- The number of teams is a factor of the number of players for each number pair.

There are 66 players participating.

For **1–4**, use the rule to complete each table. Describe a feature of each pattern.

1. Rule: Multiply by 12

Number of Dozens	4	5	6	7
Number of Eggs	48		72	

2. Rule: Divide by 9

Number of Baseball Players	54	63	72	81
Number of Teams	6	7		

3. Rule: Divide by 6

Number of Legs	162	168	174	180
Number of Insects		28	29	

4. Rule: Multiply by 10

Number of Phone Numbers	33	34	35	36
Number of Digits in Phone Numbers	330	340		

Digital Resources at PearsonRealize.com   **Topic 14** | Lesson 14-2   **743**

5. **© MP.7 Look for Relationships** The table shows the amounts of money Emma earns for different numbers of chores. How much money does Emma earn when she does 6 chores?

Rule: Multiply by 9

Number of Chores	Amount Earned
3	$27
4	$36
5	$45
6	

6. **Math and Science** A *wavelength* is the distance between 1 peak of a wave of light, heat, or other energy to the next peak. Greta measured the distance for 3 wavelengths. What is distance for 1 wavelength?

├─── 168 feet ───┤

7. Write 894,217 in expanded form and using number names.

8. There are 21,611 more students enrolled in elementary school than in middle school in a city district. If there are 16,247 students enrolled in middle school, how many are enrolled in elementary school?

For **9–10**, the rule is "Divide by 7."

9. Using the rule from the table, how many T-shirts would sell for $168?

Do you need to find the price of 30 T-shirts and 9 T-shirts to solve Exercise 10?

10. **Higher Order Thinking** How much more do 30 T-shirts cost than 9 T-shirts? Explain.

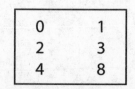

	Price	Number of T-Shirts
DATA	$147	21
	$154	22
	$161	23

© Common Core Assessment

11. There are 24 hours in a day. Use the rule "Multiply by 24" to show the relationship between the number of days and the number of hours. Use each digit from the box once to complete the table.

Number of Days	13	14	15	16	17
Number of Hours	☐☐☐	336	360	384	☐☐☐

0	1
2	3
4	8

Name _____

Solve & Share

The rule for the repeating pattern below is "Square, Triangle." What will be the 37th shape in the pattern? Explain. *Solve this problem any way you choose.*

I can ...
use a rule to predict a number or shape in a pattern.

© Content Standard 4.OA.C.5
Mathematical Practices MP.2, MP.3, MP.6, MP.7

1st   2nd   3rd   4th   5th   6th   ...   37th

You can construct arguments to convince a classmate your answer is correct.

Look Back! © MP.2 Reasoning After the 37th shape is placed, how many triangles are in the pattern?

How Can You Use a Repeating Pattern to Predict a Shape?

A

Rashad is making a repeating pattern for the rule "Triangle, Square, Trapezoid."
What will be the 49th shape in the pattern?

A repeating pattern is made up of shapes or numbers that form a part that repeats.

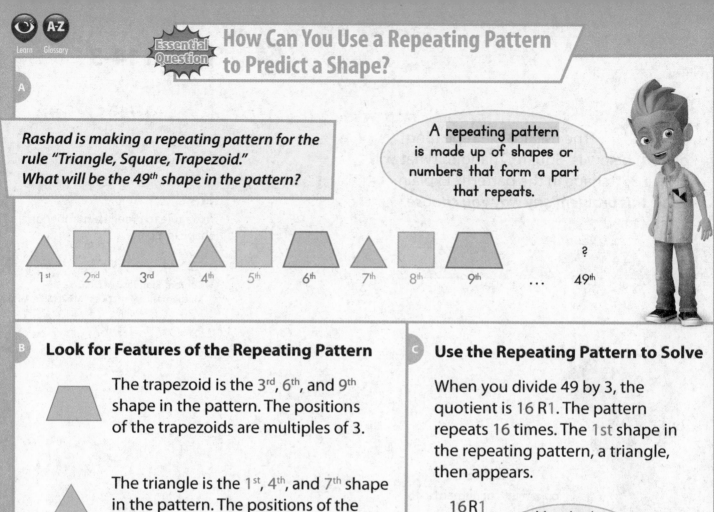

1st 2nd 3rd 4th 5th 6th 7th 8th 9th ... 49th

B

Look for Features of the Repeating Pattern

The trapezoid is the 3rd, 6th, and 9th shape in the pattern. The positions of the trapezoids are multiples of 3.

The triangle is the 1st, 4th, and 7th shape in the pattern. The positions of the triangles are 1 more than a multiple of 3.

The square is the 2nd, 5th, and 8th shape in the pattern. The positions of the squares are 1 less than a multiple of 3.

C

Use the Repeating Pattern to Solve

When you divide 49 by 3, the quotient is 16 R1. The pattern repeats 16 times. The 1st shape in the repeating pattern, a triangle, then appears.

$$3\overline{)49} \quad 16\,R1$$

You divide by 3 because there are 3 items in the repeating pattern.

49 is one more than a multiple of 3.

The 49th shape is a triangle.

Convince Me! © **MP.6 Be Precise** Suppose the rule is "Square, Triangle, Square, Trapezoid" in a repeating pattern. What is the 26th shape in the pattern? Describe features of the repeating pattern. Be precise in your description.

Another Example!

Write the next three numbers in the repeating pattern. Then name the 100th number in the pattern.

Rule: 1, 3, 5, 7

1, 3, 5, 7, 1, 3, 5, 7, 1, 3, 5, 7, __1__ , __3__ , __5__ …

There are 4 items in the repeating pattern. To find the 100th number, divide by 4. The pattern repeats 25 times. The 100th number is 7.

$$\begin{array}{r} 25 \\ 4\overline{)100} \\ -100 \\ \hline 0 \end{array}$$

> A repeating pattern can be made up of shapes or numbers.

☆ Guided Practice *

Do You Understand?

1. **© MP.7 Look for Relationships** In the "Triangle, Square, Trapezoid" example on the previous page, what will be the 48th shape? the 50th shape? Explain.

Do You Know How?

2. What is the 20th shape? The rule is "Triangle, Circle, Circle."

3. Write the next three numbers. The rule is "9, 2, 7, 6."

   9, 2, 7, 6, 9, 2, 7, 6, ____ , ____ , ____

Independent Practice ☆

For **4–7**, draw or write the next three items to continue each repeating pattern.

4. The rule is "Square, Triangle, Square."

   ■ ▲ ■ ■ ▲ ___ ___ ___ …

5. The rule is "Up, Down, Left, Right."

   ⬆⬇⬅➡⬆ ___ ___ ___ …

6. The rule is "1, 1, 2."

   1, 1, 2, 1, 1, 2, ____ , ____ , ____ …

7. The rule is "5, 7, 4, 8."

   5, 7, 4, 8, 5, 7, 4, 8, 5, 7, ____ , 8, 5 …

For **8–9**, determine the given shape or number in each repeating pattern.

8. The rule is "Tree, Apple, Apple." What is the 19th shape?

9. The rule is "1, 2." What is the 42nd number?

   1, 2, 1, 2, 1, 2, …

For another example, see Set C on page 760.

Math Practices and Problem Solving

10. Create a repeating pattern using the rule "Triangle, Square, Square."

11. Math and Science Margot measured the distance for 6 wavelengths of visible light as 2,400 nanometers. What is the distance for 1 wavelength?

12. © MP.7 Look for Relationships Hilda is making a repeating pattern with the shapes below. The rule is "Heart, Square, Triangle." If Hilda continues the pattern, what will be the 11th shape?

 …

13. © MP.7 Look for Relationships Josie puts beads on a string in a repeating pattern. The rule is "Blue, Green, Yellow, Orange." There are 88 beads on her string. How many times did Josie repeat her pattern?

14. How many more years passed between the first steam locomotive and the gasoline-powered automobile than between the gasoline-powered automobile and the first diesel train in the U.S.?

Year	Invention
1804	Steam Locomotive
1885	Gasoline-powered Automobile
1912	Diesel Train in U.S.

15. © MP.2 Reasoning Louisa used the rule "Blue, Green, Green, Green" to make a bracelet with a repeating pattern. She used 18 green beads. How many beads did Louisa use to make the bracelet? How many beads were **NOT** green?

16. Higher Order Thinking Marcus is using shapes to make a repeating pattern. He has twice as many circles as squares. Make a repeating pattern that follows this rule.

© Common Core Assessment

17. Which rules give a repeating pattern that has a square as the 15th shape? Select all that apply.

- ☐ Square, Circle
- ☐ Circle, Square, Triangle
- ☐ Square, Circle, Triangle
- ☐ Circle, Triangle, Square
- ☐ Trapezoid, Circle, Square

18. Which rules give a repeating pattern that has a 7 as the 15th number? Select all that apply.

- ☐ 1, 7
- ☐ 1, 7, 9
- ☐ 1, 9, 7
- ☐ 1, 7, 7
- ☐ 7, 1, 9

Help Practice Tools Games
       Buddy

Another Look!

Alan is using the rule below to make a repeating pattern. What is the 31st shape in Alan's pattern?

Rule: Rectangle, Circle, Square, Triangle

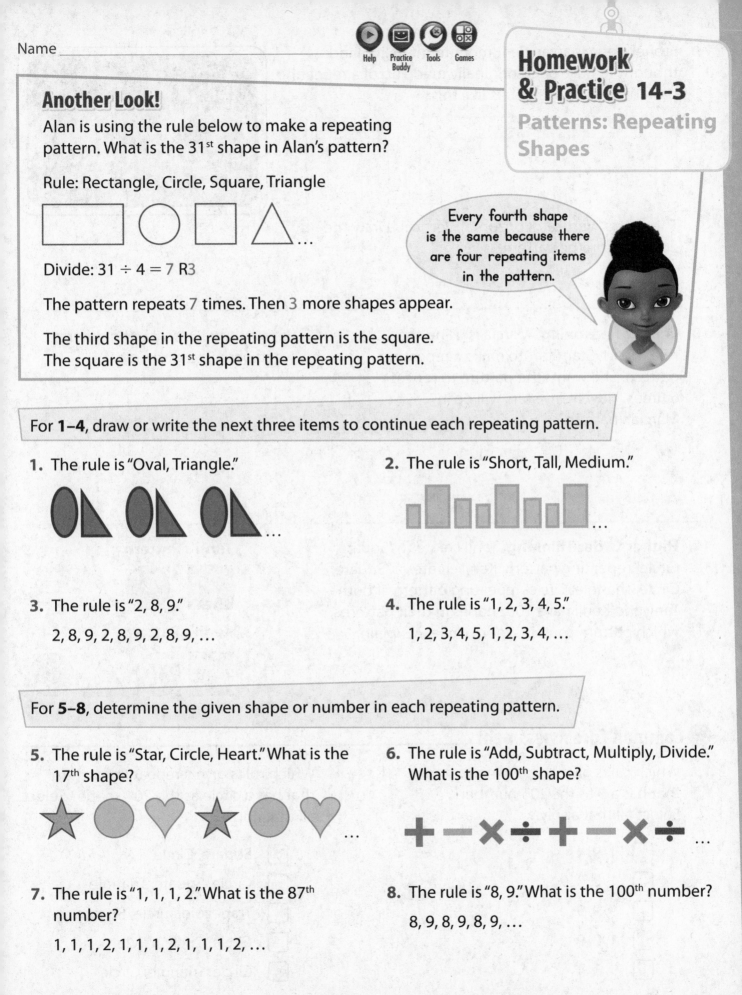

Divide: $31 \div 4 = 7 \text{ R}3$

The pattern repeats 7 times. Then 3 more shapes appear.

The third shape in the repeating pattern is the square.
The square is the 31st shape in the repeating pattern.

> Every fourth shape is the same because there are four repeating items in the pattern.

For **1–4**, draw or write the next three items to continue each repeating pattern.

1. The rule is "Oval, Triangle."

2. The rule is "Short, Tall, Medium."

3. The rule is "2, 8, 9."

2, 8, 9, 2, 8, 9, 2, 8, 9, …

4. The rule is "1, 2, 3, 4, 5."

1, 2, 3, 4, 5, 1, 2, 3, 4, …

For **5–8**, determine the given shape or number in each repeating pattern.

5. The rule is "Star, Circle, Heart." What is the 17th shape?

6. The rule is "Add, Subtract, Multiply, Divide." What is the 100th shape?

7. The rule is "1, 1, 1, 2." What is the 87th number?

1, 1, 1, 2, 1, 1, 1, 2, 1, 1, 1, 2, …

8. The rule is "8, 9." What is the 100th number?

8, 9, 8, 9, 8, 9, …

9. Stonehenge is an ancient monument in England thought to have been originally made up of a repeating pattern of rocks that looks like this:

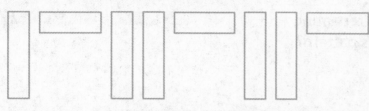

The rule is "Vertical, Horizontal, Vertical." Draw the 26th shape in the pattern.

---

10. © **MP.2 Reasoning** Marcia is using the rule "Heart, Star, Star" to make a repeating pattern. She wants the pattern to repeat 6 times. How many stars will be in Marcia's pattern?

11. A-Z **Vocabulary** Describe the difference between *perimeter* and *area*.

---

12. Higher Order Thinking Tanji creates a "Square, Circle" repeating pattern. Kenji creates a "Square, Circle, Triangle, Circle" repeating pattern. If both Tanji and Kenji have 100 shapes in their patterns, which pattern contains more circles? Explain.

Tanji's Pattern

Kenji's Pattern

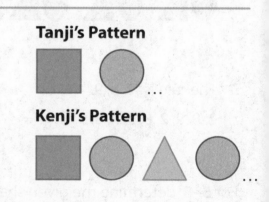

© Common Core Assessment

13. Which rules give a repeating pattern that has a 9 as the 20th number? Select all that apply.

- ☐ 1, 9, 4
- ☐ 1, 2, 3, 9
- ☐ 9, 9, 9
- ☐ 1, 2, 9
- ☐ 9, 1, 4

14. Which rules give a repeating pattern that has a circle as the 20th shape? Select all that apply.

- ☐ Square, Circle
- ☐ Circle, Square, Triangle
- ☐ Trapezoid, Circle, Square
- ☐ Circle, Circle, Circle
- ☐ Circle, Triangle, Circle

Name _____

Solve

Math Practices and
Problem Solving

Lesson 14-4
Look for and
Use Structure

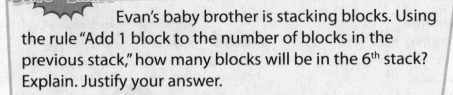

Solve & Share   Evan's baby brother is stacking blocks. Using the rule "Add 1 block to the number of blocks in the previous stack," how many blocks will be in the 6ᵗʰ stack? Explain. Justify your answer.

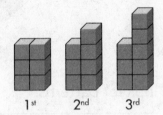

1ˢᵗ   2ⁿᵈ   3ʳᵈ

I can ...
use patterns to help solve problems.

© Mathematical Practices MP.7 Also MP.1, MP.2
Content Standard 4.OA.C.5

Thinking Habits

- What patterns can I see and describe?

- How can I use the patterns to solve the problem?

- Can I see expressions and objects in different ways?

Look Back! © MP.7 Look For Relationships How many blocks are in the 10ᵗʰ stack? Explain.

Essential Question: How Can I Look for and Make Use of Structure?

Rule: Each layer has 4 cubes.

Alisa made three walls with cubes. She recorded her pattern. If she continues the pattern, how many cubes will be in a 10-layer wall? a 100-layer wall?

1 layer
4 cubes

2 layers
8 cubes

3 layers
12 cubes

What do you need to do to find the number of cubes in a 10-layer and 100-layer wall?

I need to continue the pattern using the rule and analyze the pattern to find features not stated in the rule itself.

Here's my thinking.

How can I make use of structure to solve this problem?

I can

- look for and describe patterns in three-dimensional shapes.

- use the rule that describes how objects or values in a pattern are related.

- use features of the pattern not stated in the rule to generate or extend the pattern.

Make a table and look for patterns.

Number of Layers	1	2	3	4	5
Number of Cubes	4	8	12	16	20

1 layer
4 cubes

2 layers
8 cubes

3 layers
12 cubes

4 layers
16 cubes

5 layers
20 cubes

There are 4 cubes in each layer. Multiply the number of layers by 4 to calculate the number of cubes.

A 10-layer wall contains $10 \times 4 = 40$ cubes.

A 100-layer wall contains $100 \times 4 = 400$ cubes.

Convince Me! © **MP.7 Look For Relationships** How could you use multiples to describe Alisa's pattern?

☆ Guided Practice *

© MP.7 Use Structure

Leah arranged triangular tiles in a pattern like the one shown. She used the rule "Multiply the number of rows by itself to get the number of small triangles." How many small triangles would be in the pattern if there were 10 rows?

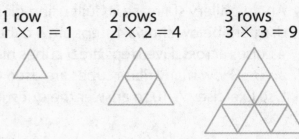

1 row
$1 \times 1 = 1$

2 rows
$2 \times 2 = 4$

3 rows
$3 \times 3 = 9$

1. Complete the table to help describe the pattern.

Number of Rows	1	2	3	4	5
Number of Small Triangles	1	4	9		

> When you look for relationships, you use features of the pattern not stated in the rule to extend the pattern.

2. Describe the pattern another way.

3. How many triangles would be in 10 rows?

Independent Practice ☆

© MP.7 Look for Relationships

Alan built the towers shown using the rule "Each story has 2 blocks." How many blocks will a 10-story tower have? Use Exercises 4–6 to answer the question.

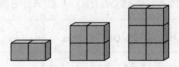

4. Complete the table to help describe the pattern.

Number of Stories	1	2	3	4	5
Number of Blocks	2	4	6		

5. What is another way to describe the pattern that is not described by the rule?

6. How many blocks are in a 10-story tower? Explain.

For another example, see Set D on page 760.   **Topic 14** | Lesson 14-4   **753**

Math Practices and Problem Solving

© Common Core Performance Assessment

Glass Stairs

An art gallery staircase is built using glass cubes. The diagram below shows 4 steps are 4 cubes high and 4 cubes across. Five steps are 5 cubes high and 5 cubes across. How many glass cubes are used to make 7 steps? Use Exercises 7–10 to answer the question.

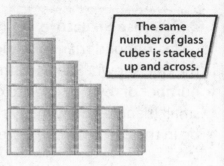

The same number of glass cubes is stacked up and across.

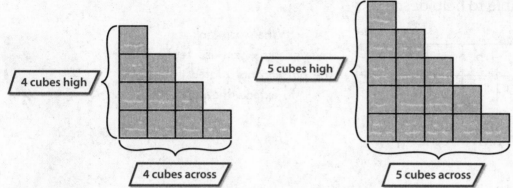

4 cubes high

4 cubes across

5 cubes high

5 cubes across

7. **MP.1 Make Sense and Persevere** What do you know, and what do you need to find?

When you look for relationships, you use the rule that describes how objects or values in a pattern are related.

8. **MP.2 Reasoning** Complete the table.

Cubes Up or Across	2	3	4	5	6
Total Cubes Needed	3	6			

9. **MP.7 Look For Relationships** What pattern can you determine from the table?

10. **MP.2 Reasoning** How many cubes are needed for 7 steps? Write and solve an equation.

Name _____

Homework & Practice 14-4
Look for and
Use Structure

Another Look!

Dwayne built the towers shown. He used the rule that each tower has 1 more block than the tower before it. How many blocks are needed for the 10th tower?

Tell how you can solve the problem.

- I can use the rule that describes how objects or values in a pattern are related.

- I can use features of the pattern not stated in the rule to extend the pattern.

Extend the pattern and find features not stated in the rule.

Tower Number	1	2	3	4	5
Number of Blocks	2	3	4	5	6

The number of blocks in a tower is 1 more than the tower number. The 10th tower contains $10 + 1 = 11$ blocks.

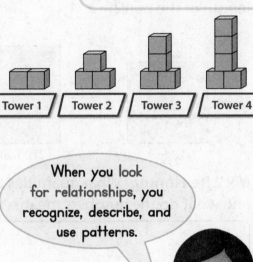
Tower 1 Tower 2 Tower 3 Tower 4

When you look for relationships, you recognize, describe, and use patterns.

© MP.7 Use Structure

Sarah is making diamond shapes with yarn like the ones shown. She adds the length of the sides to determine how much yarn she needs. What is the greatest side length Sarah could make with 48 inches of yarn? Use Exercises 1–3 to answer the question.

2 in. 2 in. 3 in. 3 in. 4 in. 4 in.

1. Complete the table to help describe the pattern.

Inches on One Side	2	3	4	5	6
Inches of Yarn Needed	8	12	16		

2. What is another feature of the pattern that is not described in the rule?

3. What is the side length of the diamond Sarah can make with 48 inches of yarn? Explain.

Swimming Pools

Pete's Pools installs rectangular pools that are all 10 feet wide. The length can vary from 10 feet to 30 feet. The company installed a pool with a perimeter of 76 feet. What was the length of the pool?

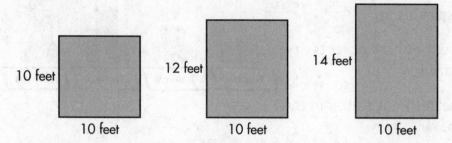

4. **MP.2 Reasoning** What quantities are given in the problem and what do the numbers mean?

5. **MP.1 Make Sense and Persevere** What do you need to find?

When you use structure, you break the problem into simpler parts.

6. **MP.2 Reasoning** Complete the table.

Feet in Length	10	12	14	16	18	20	22	24
Perimeter	40	44	48					

7. **MP.7 Use Structure** What is the length of a pool with a perimeter of 76 feet? Explain how you found the answer. Then describe how you can use a feature of the pattern to find the length.

Find a partner. Get paper and a pencil. Each partner chooses a different color: light blue or dark blue.

Partner 1 and Partner 2 each point to a black number at the same time. Each partner adds the two numbers.

If the answer is on your color, you get a tally mark. Work until one partner has twelve tally marks.

I can ...
add multi-digit whole numbers.

 **Content Standard** 4.NBT.B.4

Partner 1					**Partner 2**
5,150	49,495	14,245	47,250	30,081	**500**
10,101	32,326	17,850	40,900	12,000	**1,999**
11,000	8,650	11,500	16,951	42,399	**3,500**
23,231	26,731	12,100	23,731	7,149	**6,850**
40,400	13,601	10,601	19,196	43,900	**9,095**
	14,500	20,095	5,650	12,999	

Tally Marks for Partner 1

Tally Marks for Partner 2

TOPIC 14 Vocabulary Review

A-Z Glossary

Word List

- equation
- even number
- factor
- multiple
- odd number
- repeating pattern
- rule
- unknown

Understand Vocabulary

1. Circle the term that best describes 28.

even odd equation unknown

2. Circle the term that best completes this sentence:
4 is a ________ of 16.

even odd factor multiple

3. Circle the term that best describes 17.

even odd equation unknown

4. Circle the term that best completes this sentence:
9 is a ________ of 3.

even odd factor multiple

5. Draw a line from each term to its example.

equation	Multiply by 3
repeating pattern	$14 \div 2 = n$
rule	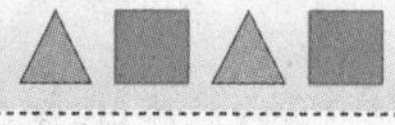
unknown	$4 + 7 = 11$

Use Vocabulary in Writing

6. Use at least 3 terms from the Word List to describe the pattern.

50, 48, 46, 44, 42 …

Set A pages 733–738

You can use the rule "Subtract 3" to continue the pattern.

24 → 21 → 18 → 15 → 12 → 9 → 6 → 3
  −3 −3 −3 −3 −3 −3 −3

The next three numbers in the pattern are 9, 6, and 3.

A feature of the pattern is all the numbers are multiples of 3.

Another feature is all the numbers in the pattern alternate even, odd.

Reteaching

Remember to check that the numbers in your pattern follow the rule.

Use the rule to continue each pattern. Describe a feature of the pattern.

1. Rule: Add 2

   1, 3, 5, _____, _____, _____

2. Rule: Subtract 4

   22, 18, 14, _____, _____, _____

Set B pages 739–744

The regular price is twice the sale price. You can use the rule "Divide by 2" to continue the pattern.

Regular Price	Sale Price
$44	$22
$42	$21
$40	$20
$38	$19
$36	$18
$34	$17

The regular price is a multiple of the sale price, and the sale price is a factor of the regular price.

Remember to look for features of the pattern not described by the rule.

Use the rule to continue each pattern. Describe a feature of the pattern.

1. Rule: Multiply by 18

Trucks	3	5	7	9
Wheels	54	90	126	

2. Rule: Divide by 3

Earned	$12	$18	$24	$30
Saved	$4	$6	$8	

3. Rule: Multiply by 4

Chairs	5	10	15	20
Legs	20	40	60	

You can use the rule "Circle, Triangle, Square" to continue the repeating pattern.

You can use the rule to find the 25th shape in the pattern.

$25 \div 3 = 8$ R1.

The pattern will repeat 8 times, then the 1st shape will appear.

The circle is the 25th shape in the pattern.

Remember to use the rule to continue the pattern.

1. **a.** Draw the next three shapes in the repeating pattern. The rule is "Right, Up, Up."

   b. Draw the 50th shape in the pattern.

2. **a.** Write the next three numbers in the repeating pattern. The rule is "3, 5, 7, 9."

   3, 5, 7, 9, 3, 5, 7, _____, _____, _____

   b. What will be the 100th number in the pattern?

Think about these questions to help you **look for relationships**.

Thinking Habits

- What patterns can I see and describe?

- How can I use the patterns to solve the problem?

- Can I see expressions and objects in different ways?

Remember to use the rule that describes how objects or values in a pattern are related.

Sam creates a pattern using the rule "Each layer has 3 cubes."

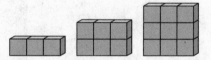

1. Draw the next shape in Sam's pattern.

2. Use the rule to continue Sam's pattern.

Stories	1	2	3	4
Blocks	3	6	9	

3. How many blocks are in the 10th shape in Sam's pattern?

1. Football players come out of the tunnel, and their jerseys have the number pattern shown below. They follow the rule "Add 4."

Part A

What number belongs on the front of the blank jersey? Explain.

Part B

Describe two features of the pattern.

2. One dozen eggs is 12 eggs. Two dozen eggs is 24 eggs. The rule for this pattern is "Multiply by 12." Draw lines to connect the number of dozens with the number of eggs.

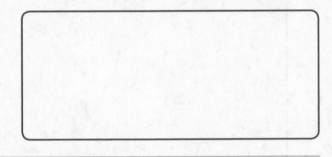

8 dozen	168 eggs
10 dozen	60 eggs
14 dozen	96 eggs
5 dozen	120 eggs

3. Use the rule "Multiply by 6" to continue the pattern.

Number of Grasshoppers	3	5	7	9
Number of Legs	18	30	42	

4. Which statement is true? Use the table and rule in Exercise 3.

Ⓐ The number of legs in the table will always be an even number.

Ⓑ The number of grasshoppers will always be an even number.

Ⓒ The number of grasshoppers must be odd to follow the rule.

Ⓓ The number of legs on grasshoppers will always be less than the number of grasshoppers.

5. Choose the correct word from the box to complete each statement that describes the table in Exercise 3.

Multiple	Factor

The number of legs on a grasshopper is a _____ of the number of grasshoppers.

The number of grasshoppers is a _____ of the number of legs on grasshoppers.

6. Choose numbers from the box to continue the pattern for the rule "Divide by 3." Use each number from the box once.

729, 243, ⬜⬜ , ⬜⬜ , ⬜ , ⬜

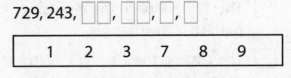

| 1 | 2 | 3 | 7 | 8 | 9 |

7. The rule for the repeating pattern is "5, 7, 2, 8." Write the next three numbers in the pattern. Then tell what will be the 25th number in the pattern. Explain.

5, 7, 2, 8, 5, 7, 2, 8, 5, ____, ____, ____

8. Claire wrote different patterns for the rule "Subtract 5". Which patterns could Claire have written?

8a. 27, 22, 17, 12, 7   ○ Yes ○ No

8b. 5, 10, 15, 20, 25   ○ Yes ○ No

8c. 55, 50, 35, 30, 25   ○ Yes ○ No

8d. 100, 95, 90, 85, 80   ○ Yes ○ No

9. Select all the true statements. The rule is "Circle, Heart, Triangle."

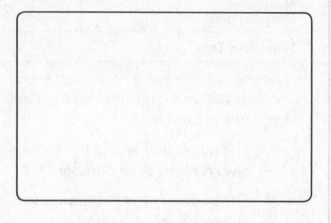

☐ The next shape in the repeating pattern is the circle.

☐ The circle only repeats twice in the repeating pattern.

☐ The 10th shape in the repeating pattern is the heart.

☐ The 12th shape in the repeating pattern is the triangle.

☐ The circle is the 1st, 4th, 7th, etc. shape in the repeating pattern.

10. The table shows the different number of teams formed by different numbers of players. The rule is "Divide by 8."

Players	24	32	40	72
Teams	3	4	t	9

How many teams can be formed with 40 players?

Ⓐ   5 teams

Ⓑ   32 teams

Ⓒ   48 teams

Ⓓ   320 teams

11. Marcus lives on a street where all the house numbers are multiples of 9. If the first number on the street is 9, what are the next 3 possible house numbers? Explain.

12. The rule is "Subtract 7." What are the next 3 numbers in the pattern? Describe two features of the pattern.

70, 63, 56, 49, 42, 35

© Pearson Education, Inc. 4

Name _____

Wall Hangings

Michael uses knots to make wall hangings to sell.

© Performance Assessment

1. The **Michael's Basic Wall Hanging** figure shows a simple wall hanging Michael makes by repeating the shapes shown. What is the 16th shape in the repeating pattern? The rule is "Circle, Triangle, Square." Explain.

Michael's Basic Wall Hanging

2. The **Snowflake Design** figure shows a knot Michael likes to use.

Part A

List the number of knots that Michael uses to form 1 to 6 snowflake designs. The rule is "Add 11."

Snowflake Design

Uses 11 knots

Part B

Describe a feature of the pattern you listed in Part A that is not part of the rule. Explain why it works.

3. The **Michael's Wall Hanging** figure shows the design of a wall hanging Michael makes using the **Snowflake Design**. Answer the following to find how many knots Michael ties to make a wall hanging with 28 snowflakes.

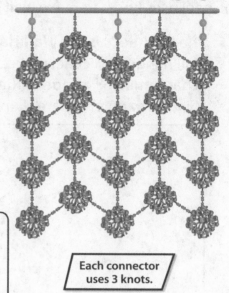

Michael's Wall Hanging

Each connector uses 3 knots.

Part A

Each up-and-down row of 4 snowflakes has 4 connectors. There are also 4 connectors between rows. Complete the **Connectors** table using the rule "Add 8 connectors for each row." Describe a feature of the pattern.

Connectors

Rows	1	2	3	4	5
Connectors	4	12			

Part B

Complete the **Total Knots** table using the following rules.

Snowflake Knots rule: Multiply the number of snowflakes by 11.

Connector Knots rule: Multiply the number of connectors from the **Connectors** table by 3.

Total Knots rule: Add the number of snowflake knots and the number of connector knots.

Total Knots

Columns	Snowflakes	Snowflake Knots	Connector Knots	Total Knots
1	4	44	12	56
2	8			
3	12			
4	16			
5	20			

Geometric Measurement: Understand Concepts of Angles and Angle Measurement

Essential Questions: What are some common geometric terms? How can you measure angles?

Digital Resources

Solve   Learn   Glossary   Practice Buddy

Tools   Assessment   Help   Games

Fasten your seatbelts! Here is a project about lines and angles.

The collisions cause cars to change direction, stop, or start moving.

When bumper cars collide, they transfer energy.

Math and Science Project: Lines and Angles

Do Research Use the Internet or other sources to research the area of the world's largest bumper car floor. Find where it is located and when it was built.

Journal: Write a Report Include what you found. Also in your report:

- Draw a diagram of a bumper car collision. Use an angle to show how a car might change direction after it collides with something. Measure and label the angle you drew.

- Describe your angle using some of the vocabulary terms on the My Word Cards.

Name _____

Review What You Know

A-Z Vocabulary

Choose the best term from the box.
Write it on the blank.

- angle
- right angle
- line
- sixth

1. A(n) _____ is one of 6 equal parts of a whole, written as $\frac{1}{6}$.

2. A(n) _____ is a figure formed by two rays that share the same endpoint.

3. A(n) _____ is an angle that forms a square corner.

Adding and Subtracting

Find the sum or difference.

4. $45 + 90$ **5.** $120 - 45$ **6.** $30 + 150$

7. $180 - 135$ **8.** $60 + 120$ **9.** $90 - 45$

Parts of a Whole

Tell the fraction that represents the shaded part of the whole.

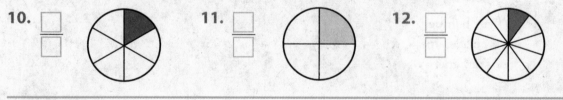

10. ▢/▢   **11.** ▢/▢   **12.** ▢/▢

Dividing

Find the quotient.

13. $360 \div 6$ **14.** $180 \div 9$ **15.** $360 \div 4$

Problem Solving

16. © **MP.1 Make Sense and Persevere** Gary has $4. Mary has twice as many dollars as Gary. Larry has 4 fewer dollars than Mary. How much money do Gary, Mary, and Larry have in all?

My Word Cards

Use the examples for each word on the front of the card to help complete the definitions on the back.

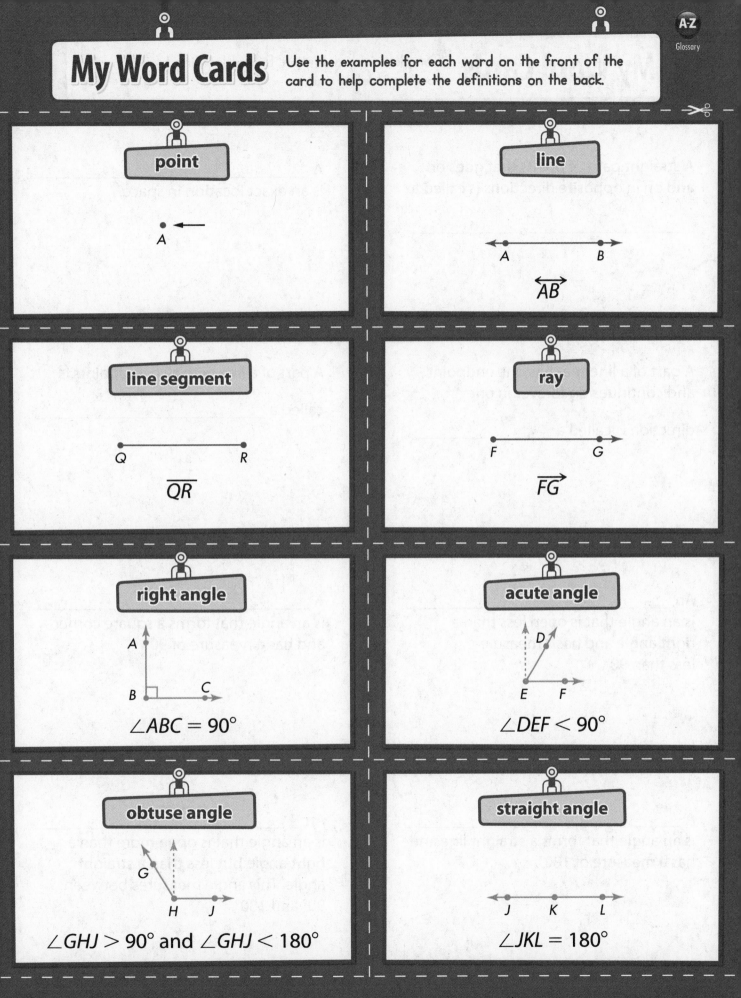

point

A

line

A   B

$\overleftrightarrow{AB}$

line segment

Q   R

$\overline{QR}$

ray

F   G

$\overrightarrow{FG}$

right angle

A

B   C

$\angle ABC = 90°$

acute angle

D

E   F

$\angle DEF < 90°$

obtuse angle

G

H   J

$\angle GHJ > 90°$ and $\angle GHJ < 180°$

straight angle

J   K   L

$\angle JKL = 180°$

Complete each definition. Extend learning by writing your own definitions.

A straight path of points that goes on and on in opposite directions is called a _____.

A _____ is an exact location in space.

A part of a line that has one endpoint and continues on forever in one direction is called a _____.

A part of a line with two endpoints is called a _____.

An _____ is an angle that is open less than a right angle and has a measure less than 90°.

A _____ is an angle that forms a square corner and has a measure of 90°.

A _____ is an angle that forms a straight line and has a measure of 180°.

An _____ is an angle that is open more than a right angle but less than a straight angle. This angle measures between 90° and 180°.

My Word Cards

Use the examples for each word on the front of the card to help complete the definitions on the back.

degree (°)

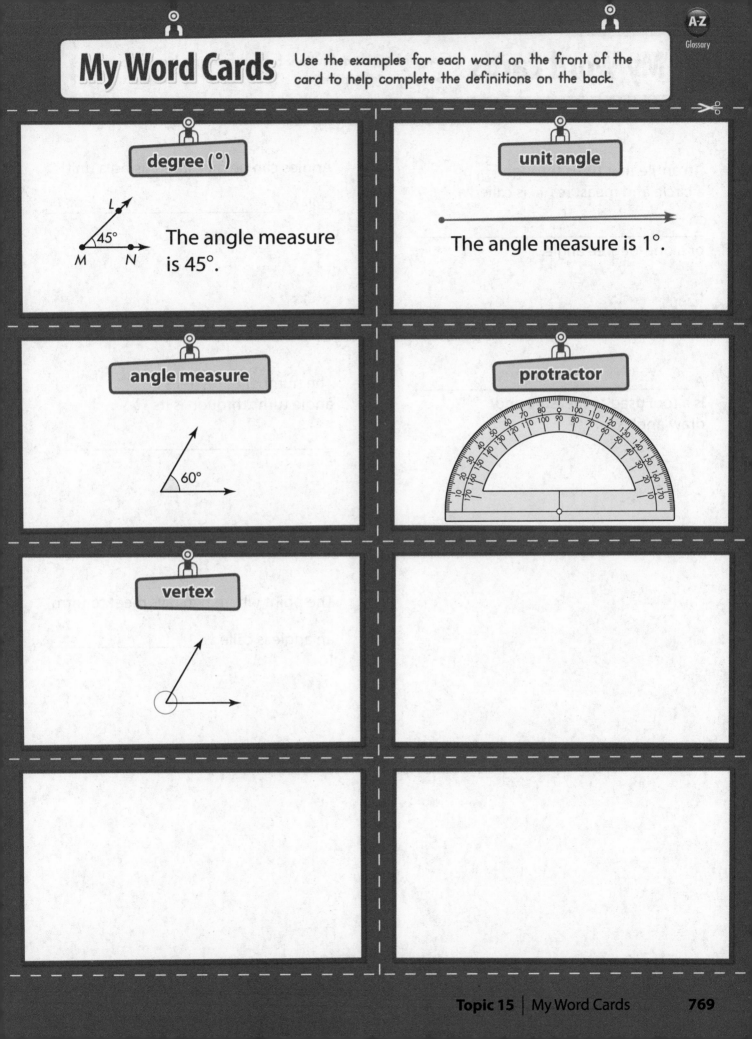

The angle measure is 45°.

unit angle

The angle measure is 1°.

angle measure

60°

protractor

vertex

Complete each definition. Extend learning by writing your own definitions.

An angle that turns through $\frac{1}{360}$ of a circle and measures 1° is called a

_____,

or a one-degree angle.

Angles can be measured using a unit

called a _____.

A _____
is a tool used to measure and
draw angles.

The number of degrees an
angle turns through is its

_____.

The point where two rays meet to form

an angle is called a _____.

Name _____

A right angle forms a square corner, like the one shown below. Draw two angles that are open less than the right angle. *Solve this problem any way you choose.*

I can ...
recognize and draw lines, rays, and angles with different measures.

© **Content Standards** 4.MD.C.5, 4.G.A.1
Mathematical Practices MP.2, MP.4, MP.6, MP.7

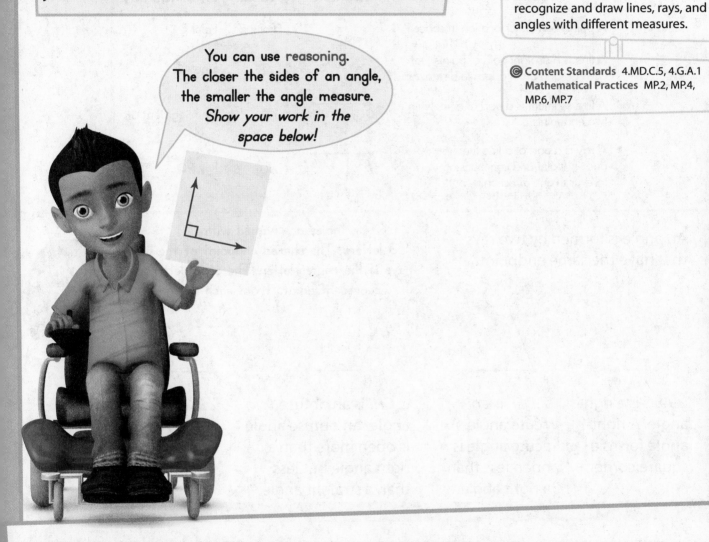

You can use reasoning. The closer the sides of an angle, the smaller the angle measure. *Show your work in the space below!*

Look Back! © **MP.2 Reasoning** Draw an angle that is open more than a right angle.

Essential Question: What Are Some Common Geometric Terms?

A

Point, line, line segment, ray, right angle, acute angle, obtuse angle, and straight angle are common geometric terms.

> Lines and parts of lines are named for their points. A ray is named with its endpoint first.

Geometric Term	Example	Label	What You Say
A point is an exact location in space.	• Z	Point Z	Point Z
A line is a straight path of points that goes on and on in opposite directions.	←•——•→ A B	$\overleftrightarrow{AB}$	Line AB
A line segment is a part of a line with two endpoints.	•——• G R	$\overline{GR}$	Line Segment GR
A ray is a part of a line that has one endpoint and continues on forever in one direction.	•——→ N O	$\overrightarrow{NO}$	Ray NO

B

An angle is formed by two rays that have the same endpoint.

> Angles are named with 3 letters. The shared endpoint of the rays is the center letter. The other letters represent points from each ray.

∠ABC is a right angle. A right angle forms a square corner.

∠DEF is an acute angle. An acute angle is open less than a right angle.

∠GHI is an obtuse angle. An obtuse angle is open more than a right angle but less than a straight angle.

∠JKL is a straight angle. A straight angle forms a straight line.

Convince Me! © **MP.7 Look for Relationships** Complete each figure to show the given angle.

←——— Obtuse angle

←——— Straight angle

•———→ Acute angle

↑ Right angle

☆Guided Practice*

Do You Understand?

1. © **MP.6 Be Precise** What geometric term describes a part of a line that has one endpoint? Draw an example.

2. What geometric term describes a part of a line that has two endpoints? Draw an example.

3. Which geometric term describes an angle that forms a square corner? Draw an example.

Do You Know How?

For **4–7**, use geometric terms to describe what is shown.

4. P •————————• X

5. P •↑ Q⌐ R →

6. B •————————→ Y

7. L ↗ M •— N →

Independent Practice ☆

For **8–11**, use geometric terms to describe what is shown.

8. H↖ O• S→

9. B •————————• D

10. X •————————→ Y

11. P• S •—⌐ T

For **12–14**, use the diagram at the right.

12. Name four line segments.

13. Name four rays.

14. Name 2 right angles.

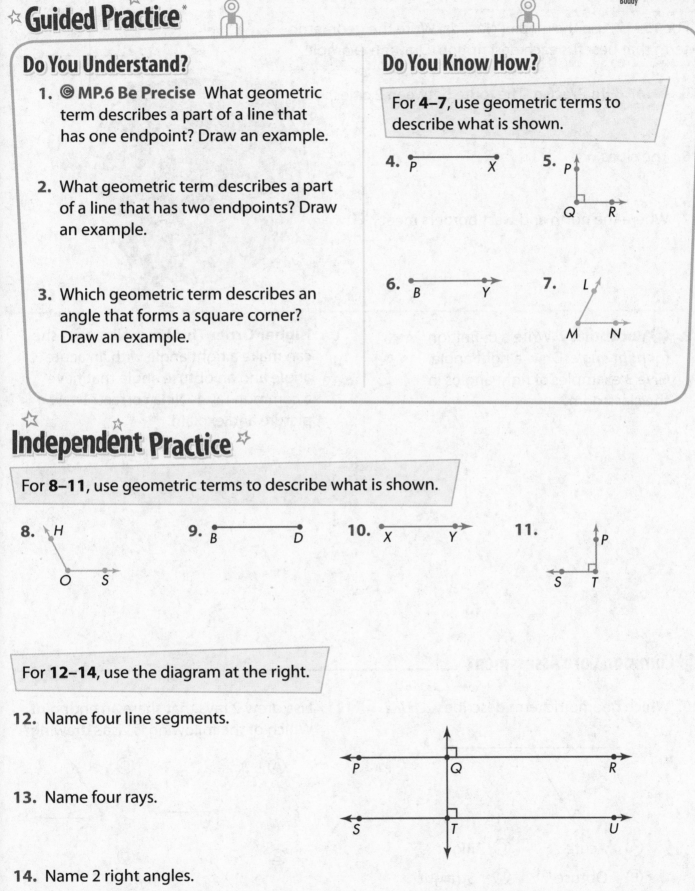

Math Practices and Problem Solving

For **15–17**, use the map of Nevada. Write the geometric term that best fits each description. Draw an example.

15. © **MP.6 Be Precise** The route between 2 cities.

16. The cities

17. Where the north and west borders meet

18. A-Z **Vocabulary** Write a definition for *right angle*. Draw a right angle. Give 3 examples of right angles in the classroom.

19. **Higher Order Thinking** Nina says she can make a right angle with an acute angle and an obtuse angle that have a common ray. Is Nina correct? Draw a picture and explain.

© **Common Core Assessment**

20. Which geometric term describes ∠HJK?

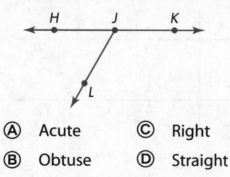

  Ⓐ Acute   Ⓒ Right
  Ⓑ Obtuse   Ⓓ Straight

21. Lisa drew 2 rays that share an endpoint. Which of the following is Lisa's drawing?

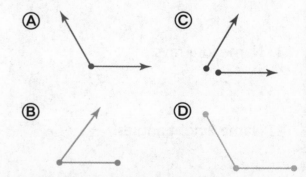

Help Practice Tools Games
      Buddy

Another Look!

Here are some important geometric terms.

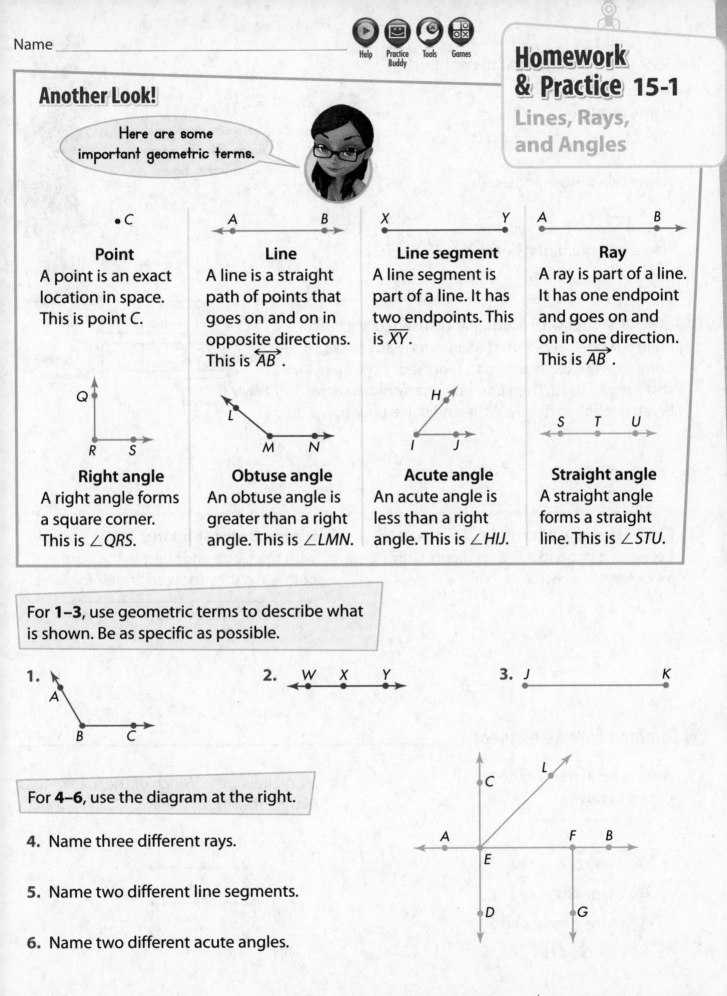

Point
A point is an exact location in space. This is point C.

Line
A line is a straight path of points that goes on and on in opposite directions. This is $\overleftrightarrow{AB}$.

Line segment
A line segment is part of a line. It has two endpoints. This is $\overline{XY}$.

Ray
A ray is part of a line. It has one endpoint and goes on and on in one direction. This is $\overrightarrow{AB}$.

Right angle
A right angle forms a square corner. This is $\angle QRS$.

Obtuse angle
An obtuse angle is greater than a right angle. This is $\angle LMN$.

Acute angle
An acute angle is less than a right angle. This is $\angle HIJ$.

Straight angle
A straight angle forms a straight line. This is $\angle STU$.

For **1–3**, use geometric terms to describe what is shown. Be as specific as possible.

1.

2.   W   X   Y

3.   J   K

For **4–6**, use the diagram at the right.

4. Name three different rays.

5. Name two different line segments.

6. Name two different acute angles.

For **7–9**, use the diagram at the right.

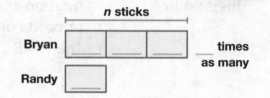

7. Name two lines.

8. Name two obtuse angles.

There may be more than one name for the same geometric figure.

9. Name one point that lies on two lines.

10. © **MP.4 Model with Math** Randy used 92 sticks to build a model. Bryan used 3 times as many sticks. Complete the bar diagram to represent how many sticks Bryan used. Then find how many more sticks Bryan used than Randy. Write and solve equations.

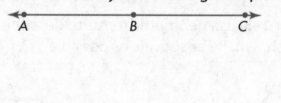

11. **Vocabulary** What is the difference between a *line* and a *line segment*? Draw an example of each.

12. **Higher Order Thinking** Name two rays with the same endpoint in the figure below. Do they form an angle? Explain.

A   B   C

© **Common Core Assessment** _____

13. What is the name for the figure shown below?

G   H

   Ⓐ   Ray *GH*

   Ⓑ   Line *GH*

   Ⓒ   Line Segment *HG*

   Ⓓ   Angle *GH*

14. Mary drew $\overleftrightarrow{XY}$. Which of the following is Mary's drawing?

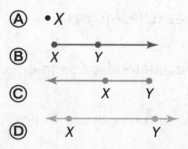

Ⓐ   •*X*

Ⓑ   *X*   *Y*

Ⓒ   *X*   *Y*

Ⓓ   *X*   *Y*

© Pearson Education, Inc. 4

Name _____

 Solve

Solve & Share

If a clock shows it is 3 o'clock, how could you describe the smaller angle made by the two hands of the clock? *Solve this problem any way you choose.*

I can ...
use what I know about fractions to measure angles.

Content Standard 4.MD.C.5a
Mathematical Practices MP.1, MP.2, MP.3, MP.4

You can make sense of the problem by using what you know about acute, right, and obtuse angles. *Show your work in the space below!*

Look Back! © MP.2 Reasoning What two fractions do the hands divide the clock into?

What is the Unit Used to Measure Angles?

A

An angle is measured with units called **degrees.** An angle that turns through $\frac{1}{360}$ of a circle is called a **unit angle.** How can you determine the angle measure of a right angle and the angles that turn through $\frac{1}{6}$ and $\frac{2}{6}$ of a circle?

> An angle that measures 1° is a unit angle or one-degree angle.

$1° = \frac{1}{360}$ of a circle

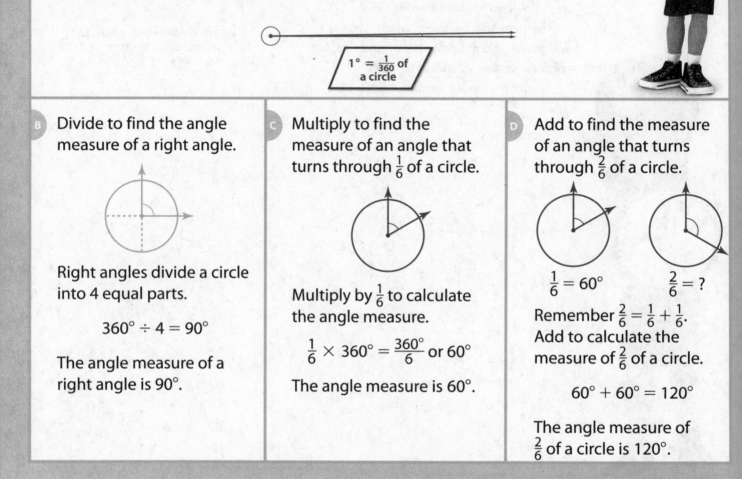

B Divide to find the angle measure of a right angle.

Right angles divide a circle into 4 equal parts.

$$360° \div 4 = 90°$$

The angle measure of a right angle is 90°.

C Multiply to find the measure of an angle that turns through $\frac{1}{6}$ of a circle.

Multiply by $\frac{1}{6}$ to calculate the angle measure.

$$\frac{1}{6} \times 360° = \frac{360°}{6} \text{ or } 60°$$

The angle measure is 60°.

D Add to find the measure of an angle that turns through $\frac{2}{6}$ of a circle.

$\frac{1}{6} = 60°$ $\frac{2}{6} = ?$

Remember $\frac{2}{6} = \frac{1}{6} + \frac{1}{6}$. Add to calculate the measure of $\frac{2}{6}$ of a circle.

$$60° + 60° = 120°$$

The angle measure of $\frac{2}{6}$ of a circle is 120°.

Convince Me! ◎ **MP.3 Critique Reasoning** Susan thinks the measure of angle *B* is greater than the measure of angle *A*. Do you agree? Explain.

A

B

Another Example!

Find the fraction of a circle that an angle with a measure of 45° turns through.

A 45° angle turns through $\frac{45}{360}$ of a circle.

$45° \times 8 = 360°$, so 45° is $\frac{1}{8}$ of 360°.

One 45° angle is $\frac{1}{8}$ of a circle.

$45° = \frac{1}{8}$ of a 360° circle

☆ Guided Practice *

Do You Understand?

1. What fraction of the circle does a 120° angle turn through?

2. ⓒ **MP.4 Model with Math** Mike cuts a pie into 4 equal pieces. What is the angle measure of each piece? Write and solve an equation.

Do You Know How?

3. A circle is divided into 9 equal parts. What is the angle measure of one of those parts?

4. An angle turns through $\frac{2}{8}$ of the circle. What is the measure of this angle?

Independent Practice ☆

For **5–8**, find the measure of each angle.

5. The angle turns through $\frac{1}{5}$ of the circle.

6. The angle turns through $\frac{3}{8}$ of the circle.

7. The angle turns through $\frac{2}{5}$ of the circle.

8. The angle turns through $\frac{2}{6}$ of the circle.

Math Practices and Problem Solving

9. **MP.2 Reasoning** Use the clock to find the measure of the smaller angle formed by the hands at each time.

    a. 3:00

    b. 11:00

    c. 2:00

    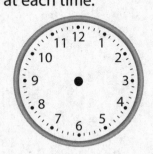

10. **Algebra** Jacey wrote an equation to find an angle measure. What do the variables a and b represent in Jacey's equation?
    $$360° \div a = b$$

11. **Math and Science** A mirror can be used to reflect a beam of light at an angle. What fraction of a circle would the angle shown turn through?

    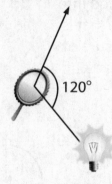

    120°

12. Malik paid $32.37 for three books. One book cost $16.59. The second book cost $4.27. How much did the third book cost? Use bills and coins to solve.

    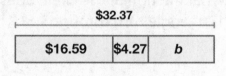

$32.37		
$16.59	$4.27	b

13. **MP.1 Make Sense and Persevere** A pie was cut into equal parts. Four pieces of the pie were eaten. The 5 pieces that remained created an angle that measured 200°. What was the angle measure of one piece of pie?

14. **Higher Order Thinking** Jake cut a round gelatin dessert into 8 equal pieces. Five of the pieces were eaten. What is the angle measure of the dessert that was left?

Common Core Assessment

15. Draw a line from the time to the smaller angle the time would show on a clock. Use the clock to help.

    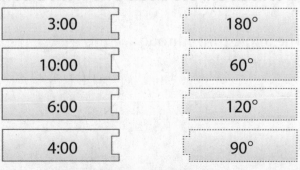

3:00		180°
10:00		60°
6:00		120°
4:00		90°

Another Look!

You can find the measure of an angle using fractions of a circle.

The angle shown is $\frac{2}{5}$ of a circle.

What is the measure of this angle?

Remember that $\frac{2}{5} = \frac{1}{5} + \frac{1}{5}$.
Divide to find the angle measure of $\frac{1}{5}$ of a circle.

$360° \div 5 = 72°$

An angle that turns through $\frac{1}{5}$ of a circle measures 72°.

$72° + 72° = 144°$

The measure of this angle is 144°.

Fractions of a circle can help with the understanding of angle measures.

For **1–4**, find the measure of each angle.

1. The angle turns through $\frac{1}{9}$ of the circle.

2. A circle is divided into 6 equal parts. What is the total angle measure of 1 part?

$\frac{1}{6} \times$ _____ = _____

3. A circle is divided into 5 equal parts. What is the total angle measure of 4 parts?

4. A circle is divided into 8 equal parts. What is the total angle measure of 4 parts?

5. **◎ MP.2 Reasoning** Noah used a bar diagram to find the measure of an angle that turns through $\frac{1}{5}$ of a circle. Write an equation to find the measure of the angle.

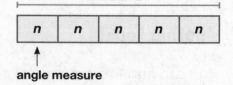

angle measure

6. **Number Sense** Miguel cut $\frac{1}{4}$ from a round pie. Mariah cut a piece from the same pie with an angle measure of 60°. Who cut the larger piece? Explain.

7. **◎ MP.3 Construct Arguments** Janie served 4 same-size pizzas at the class party. Explain how to find how many slices of pizza Janie served if the angle for each slice turns through a right angle.

8. Wendy's older brother is buying a car. He can make 24 payments of $95 or 30 payments of $80 each. Which costs less? How much less?

9. **Higher Order Thinking** A circle is divided into 18 equal parts. How many degrees is the angle measure for each part? How many degrees is the angle measure for 5 of those parts? Break apart 18 to solve. Explain.

◎ Common Core Assessment

10. Draw a line to match the angle in the circle with its angle measure.

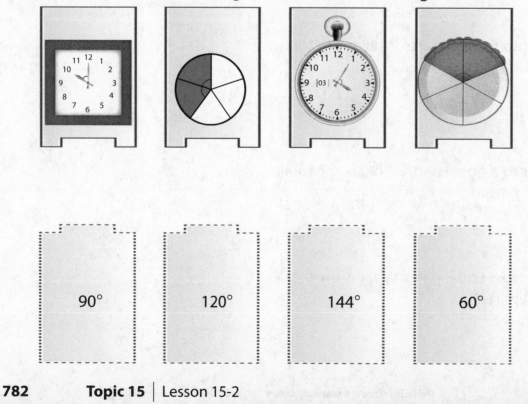

| 90° | 120° | 144° | 60° |

© Pearson Education, Inc. 4

Name _____

Solve & Share

The smaller angles on the tan pattern block shown each measure 30°. How can you use the angles on the pattern block to determine the measure of the angle below? **Solve this problem any way you choose.**

I can ...
use angles I know to measure
angles I do not know.

© Content Standards 4.MD.C.5a, 4.MD.C.5b
Mathematical Practices MP.1, MP.3, MP.4,
MP.5, MP.8

You can make sense and persevere in solving the problem. *Show your work in the space below!*

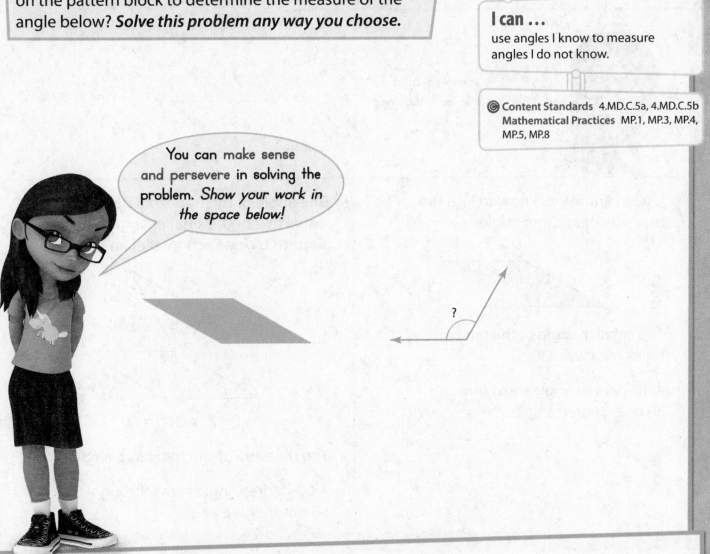

Look Back! © MP.1 Make Sense and Persevere Two right angles make a straight angle. How many 45° angles form a straight angle? Explain.

A

Holly traced around a trapezoid pattern block. She wants to find the measure of the angle formed shown to the right. What can Holly use to measure the angle?

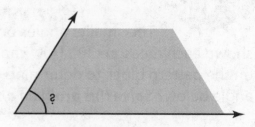

> The measure of a unit angle is 1 degree.

B

Use an angle you know to find the measure of another angle.

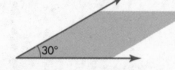

The smaller angle of the tan pattern block measures 30°.

A 30-degree angle turns through 30 one-degree angles.

C

The angle of the trapezoid pattern block is equal to 2 of the smaller angles of the tan pattern block. Each smaller angle is 30°.

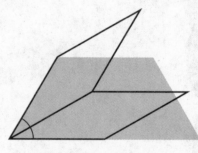

$$2 \times 30° = 60°$$

The measure of the trapezoid angle is 60°.

A 60-degree angle turns through 60 one-degree angles.

Convince Me! © **MP.8 Generalize** What do you notice about the number of one-degree angles in an angle measure?

Name _____

☆ Guided Practice ☆

Do You Understand?

1. How many 30° degree angles are in a 180° angle? Explain.

2. © **MP.1 Make Sense and Persevere**
How many 15° angles are in a 180° angle? Use your answer to Exercise 1 to explain.

Do You Know How?

For **3–4**, use angles you know to find the measure of each angle. Explain how the angles in the square can help.

3.

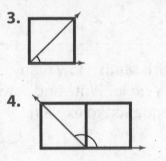

4.

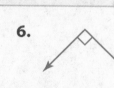 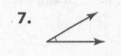

☆ Independent Practice ☆

For **5–13**, find the measure of each angle. Use pattern blocks to help.

5. **6.** **7.**

8. **9.** **10.**

11. **12.** **13.**

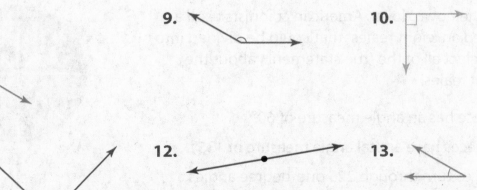

For another example, see Set C on page 809.

Topic 15 │ Lesson 15-3   **785**

Math Practices and Problem Solving

14. **MP.5 Use Appropriate Tools** What is the measure of the angle of the yellow hexagon pattern block?

15. What is the measure of the smaller angle formed by the clock hands when it is 5:00?

16. **MP.4 Model with Math** How many 30° angles are in a circle? Write and solve a multiplication equation to explain.

17. **MP.1 Make Sense and Persevere** How many unit angles make up the smaller angle formed by the hands of a clock when it is 3:00? Explain.

18. Veronica purchases a rug with a length of 16 feet and a width of 4 feet. One fourth of the rug is purple and the rest is blue. What is the area of the blue part of the rug?

19. **Higher Order Thinking** The hands of a clock form a 120° angle. Name two different times it could be.

Common Core Assessment

20. Before creating their own dollar, American colonists used a circular coin called an "eight reales" that could be divided into 8 equal pieces. Select all of the true statements about the pieces of an eight reales.

- ☐ Each piece has an angle measure of 60°.
- ☐ Three pieces have a total angle measure of 135°.
- ☐ Five pieces turn through 225 one-degree angles.
- ☐ Three 30° angles can fit into 2 pieces of an eight reales.
- ☐ Half of an eight reales has an angle measure of 90°.

Help Practice Tools Games
Buddy

Another Look!

The smaller angle of the tan pattern block measures 30°.

Use the tan pattern block to find the measure of the angle below.

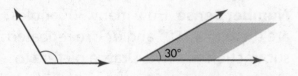

Four of the 30° angles will fit into the angle.

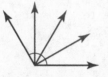

You can use an angle you know to find the measure of an angle you do not know.

$30° + 30° + 30° + 30° = 120°$
The measure of this angle is 120°.
It turns through 120 one-degree angles.

For **1–6**, find the measure of each angle. Use pattern blocks to help.

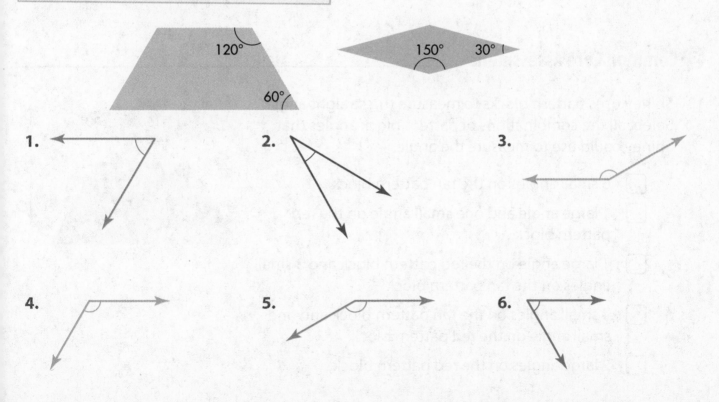

120°

150°   30°

60°

1.

2.

3.

4.

5.

6.

7. **© MP.3 Construct Arguments** A round classroom table is made from 5 identical wedges. What is the measure of each angle formed at the center of the classroom table? Explain.

8. **© MP.8 Generalize** How many unit angles does the smaller angle of a tan pattern block turn through? Explain.

9. Mario cut a circular pizza into 9 equal slices. He put a slice of pizza on each of 5 plates. What is the measure for the angle of the slices that are left?

10. **Number Sense** How many 30° angles are there in a 150° angle? Use repeated subtraction to solve. Draw a picture to justify your solution.

11. Matt's parents pay him $5.50 for each half hour he babysits his sister, plus a two dollar tip. If Matt made $18.50, for how long did he babysit?

12. **Higher Order Thinking** If a clock face reads 1:00, how many hours must pass for the hands to form a straight angle?

Common Core Assessment

13. Shirley uses pattern blocks to measure the straight angle. Select all the combinations of pattern block angles that Shirley could use to measure the angle.

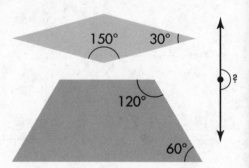

- [ ] 6 small angles on the tan pattern block
- [ ] 1 large angle and one small angle on the red pattern block
- [ ] 1 large angle on the red pattern block and 3 small angles on the tan pattern block
- [ ] 4 small angles on the tan pattern block and one small angle on the red pattern block
- [ ] 2 large angles on the red pattern block

Name _____

☆ Solve & Share ☆

Find the measure of ∠ABC. **Solve this
problem any way you choose.**

I can ...
use a protractor to measure and
draw angles.

© Content Standard 4.MD.C.6
Mathematical Practices MP.1, MP.2, MP.3,
MP.5, MP.6

You can use appropriate
tools. A protractor can help you
measure and draw angles.

Look Back! © **MP.5 Use Appropriate Tools** Use the
protractor to draw an angle that measures 110°.

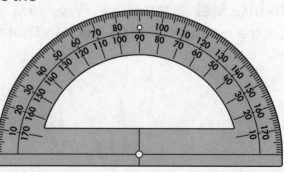

A

A protractor is a tool that is used to measure and draw angles. A partially folded crane is shown at the right. Measure ∠PQR.

The angle, ∠PQR, can also be written as ∠RQP.

B **Measure Angles**

Measure ∠PQR.

Place the protractor's center on the angle's vertex, Q. Place one side of the bottom edge on one side of the angle. Read the measure where the other side of the angle crosses the protractor. If the angle is acute, use the lesser number. If the angle is obtuse, use the greater number.

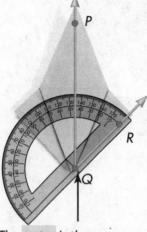

The vertex is the common endpoint of the rays that form the angle.

The measure of ∠PQR is 45°.

C **Draw Angles**

Draw an angle that measures 130°.

Draw a ray. Label the endpoint T. Place the protractor so the middle of the bottom edge is over the endpoint of the ray. Place a point at 130°. Label it W. Draw $\overrightarrow{TW}$.

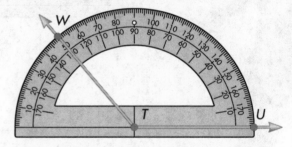

The measure of ∠WTU is 130°.

Convince Me! © **MP.6 Be Precise** How do you know the measure of ∠UTS is 60° and not 120°?

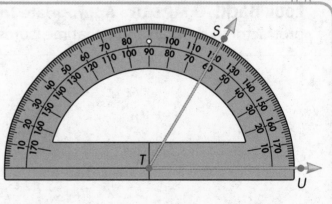

☆ Guided Practice *

Do You Understand?

1. What is the angle measure of a straight line?

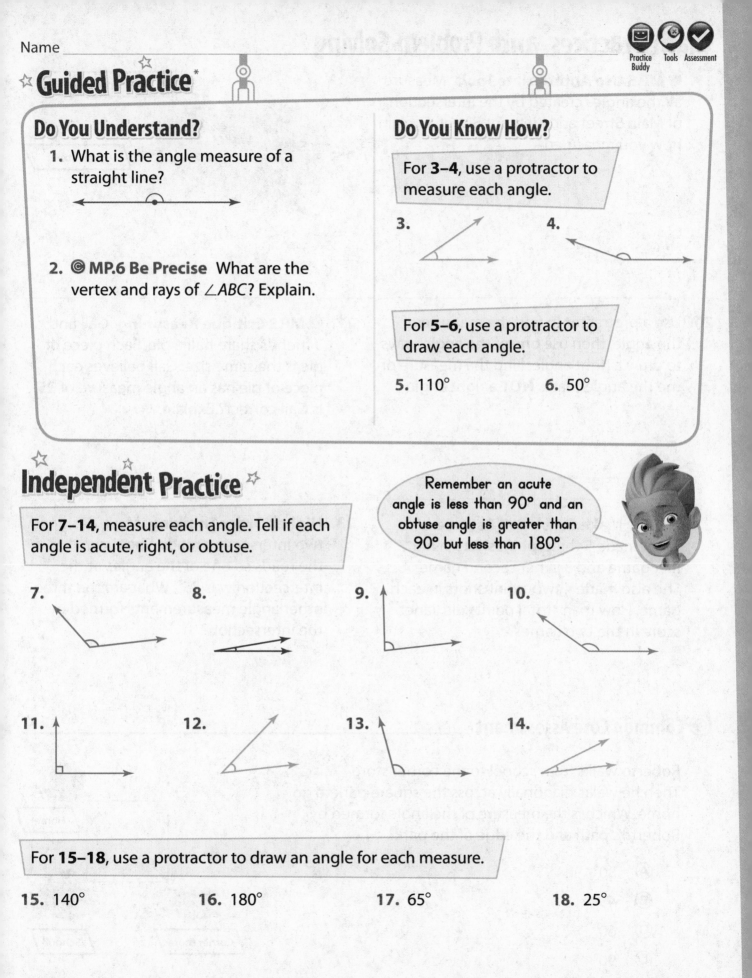

2. © MP.6 Be Precise What are the vertex and rays of ∠*ABC*? Explain.

Do You Know How?

For **3–4**, use a protractor to measure each angle.

3.

4.

For **5–6**, use a protractor to draw each angle.

5. 110°   6. 50°

☆ Independent Practice ☆

For **7–14**, measure each angle. Tell if each angle is acute, right, or obtuse.

> Remember an acute angle is less than 90° and an obtuse angle is greater than 90° but less than 180°.

7.   8.   9.   10.

11.   12.   13.   14.

For **15–18**, use a protractor to draw an angle for each measure.

15. 140°   16. 180°   17. 65°   18. 25°

Math Practices and Problem Solving

19. ☺ **MP.5 Use Appropriate Tools** Measure all the angles created by the intersection of Main Street and Pleasant Street. Explain how you measured.

20. Use a protractor to find the measure of the angle, then use one of the angle's rays to draw a right angle. Find the measure of the the angle that is **NOT** a right angle.

21. ☺ **MP.3 Critique Reasoning** Gail and 3 friends share half a pie. Each piece of pie is the same size. Gail believes each piece of pie has an angle measure of 25°. Is Gail correct? Explain.

22. ☺ **MP.1 Make Sense and Persevere** Janet made 5 three-point shots in her first game and 3 in her second game. She also made 4 two-point shots in each game. How many total points did Janet score in the two games?

23. **Higher Order Thinking** Maya designed two intersecting roads. She drew the roads so one of the angles at the intersection was 35°. What are the three other angle measurements formed by the intersection?

☺ Common Core Assessment

24. Roberto walks from school to the corner store. Then he walks diagonally across the square park to go home. Which is the measure of the angle formed by Roberto's path and the edge of the park?

  Ⓐ 30°

  Ⓑ 45°

  Ⓒ 60°

  Ⓓ 90°

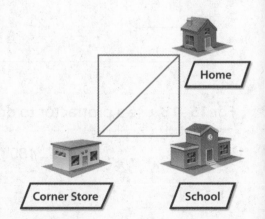

© Pearson Education, Inc. 4

Name _____

Another Look!

To measure an angle:

Place the protractor's center on the vertex of the angle and the 0° mark on one of the angle's rays. Read the number in degrees where the other ray of the angle crosses the protractor. If the angle is acute, use the lesser number. If the angle is obtuse, use the greater number.

To draw an angle:

Draw a dot to show the vertex of the angle. Place the center of the protractor on the vertex point. Draw another point at the 0° mark and another point at the angle degree mark. Draw rays from the vertex through the other points.

> You can use a protractor to measure or draw angles.

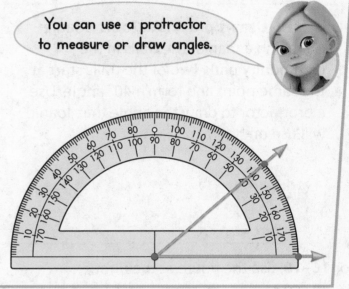

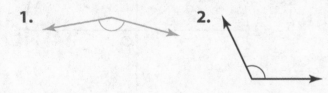

For **1–4**, measure each angle. Tell if each angle is acute, right, or obtuse.

1.

2.

3.

4.

For **5–12**, use a protractor to draw an angle for each measure.

5. 75°

6. 80°

7. 155°

8. 45°

9. 135°

10. 180°

11. 5°

12. 90°

13. **© MP.2 Reasoning** The angle turns through $\frac{1}{5}$ of the circle. What is the measure of the angle?

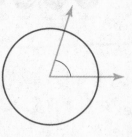

There are multiple ways to determine an angle's measure.

14. **© MP.5 Use Appropriate Tools** Joanie is making a map of the trails in the community park. Two of the trails start at the same point and form a 40° angle. Use a protractor to draw the angle that Joanie will use on her map.

15. **Math and Science** Watts, volts, and amps are used to measure electricity. There is a formula that shows the relationship between watts, volts, and amps. Volts × Amps = Watts. If the volts are 120 and the amps are 5, how many watts are there?

For **16–18**, use the figure at the right.

16. **© MP.2 Reasoning** Does the measure of ∠COA equal the measure of ∠EOD? What are their measures?

17. Name an acute, an obtuse, and a right angle.

18. **Higher Order Thinking** The measure of ∠EOF is 35°. The measure of ∠FOB is 120°. What is the measure of ∠BOC?

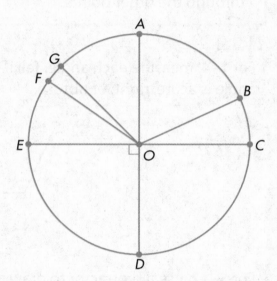

© **Common Core Assessment**

19. Stuart drew 4 angles. Which of Stuart's angles measures 25°?

Ⓐ Ⓑ Ⓒ Ⓓ

© Pearson Education, Inc. 4

Name _____

Solve

Solve & Share

Draw $\overrightarrow{BC}$ that divides $\angle ABD$ into two smaller angles. Measure each angle. **Solve this problem any way you choose.**

I can ...
use addition and subtraction to solve problems with unknown angle measures.

Ⓒ **Content Standard** 4.MD.C.7
Mathematical Practices MP.1, MP.2, MP.3, MP.4, MP.7

You can look for relationships with the three angles you measure. How is the sum of the measures of the two smaller angles related to the measure of the larger angle?

A
B
D

Look Back! Ⓒ **MP.2 Reasoning** How can you relate the measures of the two smaller angles to the measure of the larger angle above using an equation?

Essential Question ## How Can You Add and Subtract to Find Unknown Angle Measures?

A

Elinor designs wings for biplanes. First she draws a right angle, ∠ABC. Then she draws BE. She finds ∠EBC measures 30°. How can Elinor find the measure of ∠ABE without using a protractor?

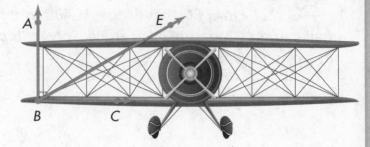

∠ABC is decomposed into two non-overlapping parts.

B ∠EBC and ∠ABE do not overlap, so the measure of right ∠ABC is equal to the sum of the measures of its parts.

The measure of ∠ABC equals the measure of ∠ABE plus the measure of ∠EBC.

C Write an equation to determine the missing angle measure.

$$n + 30° = 90°$$

Solve the equation.

$$n = 90° - 30°$$
$$n = 60°$$

All right angles measure 90°.

The measure of ∠ABE is 60°.

Convince Me! © MP.1 Make Sense and Persevere ∠ABD is a straight angle. What is the measure of ∠ABE if the measure of ∠DBC is 115° and the measure of ∠CBE is 20°? How did you decide? Write and solve an equation.

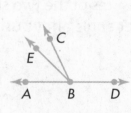

© Pearson Education, Inc. 4

Name _____

☆ Guided Practice ☆

Do You Understand?

1. **© MP.4 Model with Math** Use the information below to draw and label a diagram.
   ∠PQR measures 45°.
   ∠RQS measures 40°.
   ∠PQR and ∠RQS do not overlap.
   Write and solve an equation to find the measure of ∠PQS.

Do You Know How?

For **2–3**, use the diagram to the right of each exercise. Write and solve an equation to find the missing angle measure.

2. What is the measure of ∠EBC if ∠ABE measures 20°?

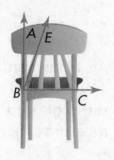

3. What is the measure of ∠AEB if ∠CEB measures 68°?

Independent Practice ☆

For **4–7**, use the diagrams to the right. Write and solve an addition or subtraction equation to find the missing angle measure.

4. What is the measure of ∠FGJ if ∠JGH measures 22°?

5. What is the measure of ∠KGF if ∠EGK measures 59°?

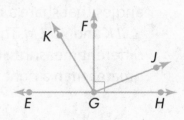

6. Use the angle measures you know to write an equation to find the angle measure of ∠EGH. What kind of angle is ∠EGH?

7. Which two non-overlapping angles that share a ray make an obtuse angle? Use addition to explain.

Math Practices and Problem Solving

8. Shane says a straight angle always has 180° degrees. Is Shane correct? Explain.

9. © **MP.4 Model with Math** Talla earns 85¢ for cans she recycles. If she gets a nickel for each can, how many cans does Talla recycle? Draw a bar diagram to represent how to solve the problem.

10. Alex draws an angle that measures 110°. He then draws a ray that divides the angle into 2 equal parts. What is the measure of each smaller angle?

11. Six angles share a vertex. Each of the angles has the same measure. The sum of the measures of the angles is 330°. What is the measure of one angle?

12. Higher Order Thinking Li uses pattern blocks to make a design. He puts 5 pattern blocks together, as shown in the diagram. The measure of ∠LJK is 30°. Name all the 60° angles shown that have point J as a vertex.

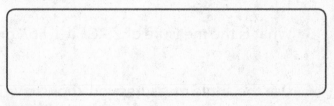

© Common Core Assessment

13. Carla drew two acute nonoverlapping angles that share a ray and labeled them ∠JLK and ∠KLM. The two angles have different measures. Carla says ∠JLM is greater than a right angle.

An acute angle is open less than a right angle.

Part A

Is it possible for Carla to be correct? Write to explain.

Part B

Write an equation showing one possible sum for Carla's angles.

Help Practice Tools Games
      Buddy

Another Look!

Addition

∠ADC is decomposed into 2 non-overlapping angles, ∠BDC and ∠ADB.

If the measure of ∠ADB is 90° and the measure of ∠BDC is 75°, what is the measure of ∠ADC?

$90° + 75° = 165°$

$∠ADC = 165°$

Subtraction

∠ADC is decomposed into 2 non-overlapping angles, ∠ADB and ∠BDC.

If the measure of ∠ADC is 165° and the measure of ∠ADB is 90°, what is the measure of ∠BDC?

$165° - 90° = 75°$

$∠BDC = 75°$

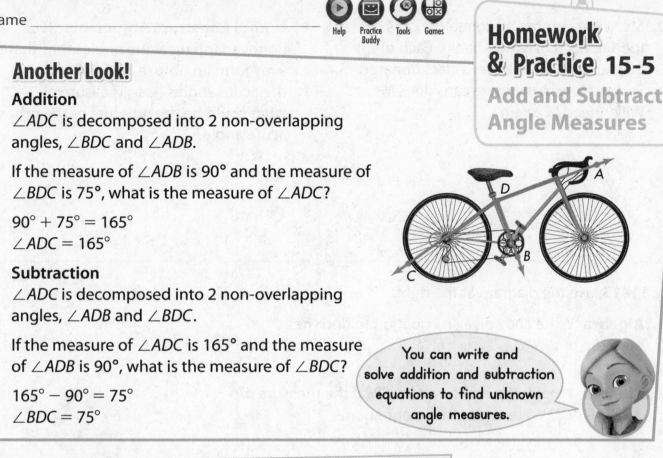

You can write and solve addition and subtraction equations to find unknown angle measures.

For **1–5**, add or subtract to find the missing angle measures.

∠TUW and ∠WUV share a ray. Together, they form ∠TUV.

A table can help you see the relationships between angles.

	Angle Measure		
	∠TUW	∠WUV	∠TUV
1.	120°	45°	
2.	105°		155°
3.	100°		170°
4.		25°	150°
5.	112°	36°	

For **6–8**, write and solve an addition or subtraction equation to find the missing angle measure.

6.
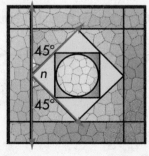
45°
n
45°

7.
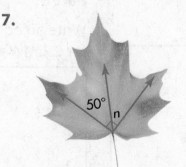
50°
n

8.
60° n 60°

---

9. Ms. Willer wanted to donate 27 cans of food to each of 8 food banks. Each of the 23 students in Ms. Willer's class donated 9 cans. How many more cans does Ms. Willer need? Explain.

10. © **MP.3 Construct Arguments** Two nonoverlapping acute angles that share a ray form an obtuse angle. If one of the acute angles has a measure of 50°, what could be the measure of the other acute angle?

For **11–13**, use the diagram at the right.

11. **Algebra** Write and solve an equation to find the measure of ∠NPO.

12. **Algebra** What is the measure of ∠SPR if the measure of ∠RPQ is 40°? Write and solve an equation.

13. **Higher Order Thinking** ∠NPO and ∠RPQ both share rays with ∠QPO. Do ∠NPO and ∠RPQ have the same measure? How do you know?

© **Common Core Assessment**

14. ∠CMW and ∠WML together form ∠CML. ∠CMW is a right angle.

Part A

Describe ∠CML.

Part B

Write an equation showing one possible sum for ∠CMW and ∠WML.

Name _____

Solve & Share

Caleb is standing next to the tallest building in a city. Determine the measure of the 3 angles with the vertex at the tallest building and rays on the music hall, the live theater, and the art museum. Tell what tool you used and explain why the measures make sense relative to each other.

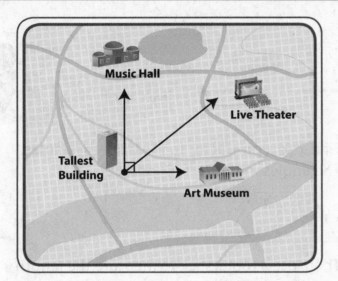

I can ...
use appropriate tools strategically to solve problems.

© Mathematical Practices MP.5 Also MP.1, MP.2, MP.4
Content Standards 4.MD.C.6, 4.MD.C.7

Thinking Habits
Be a good thinker!
These questions can help you.

- Which tools can I use?
- Why should I use this tool to help me solve the problem?
- Is there a different tool I could use?
- Am I using the tool appropriately?

Look Back! © **MP.5 Use Appropriate Tools** Could you use a ruler to find the angle measures? Explain.

Essential Question

How Can You Select and Use Appropriate Tools to Solve Problems?

Trevor and Holly are tracing large trapezoids to make a wall mural. They need to find the measures of the angles formed by the sides of the trapezoid and the length of each side of the trapezoid. What tools are needed to find the measures of the angles and the lengths of the sides?

What do you need to do to copy the trapezoid?

I need to measure the angles, then measure the sides.

Here's my thinking.

Which tool can I use to help me solve this problem?

I can

- decide which tool is appropriate.

- explain why it is the best tool to use.

- use the tool correctly.

First, use a protractor to measure the angles. The angles measure 120° and 60°.

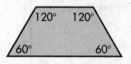

Then, use a meterstick to measure the length of each side. The lengths are 1 meter, 1 meter, 1 meter, and 2 meters.

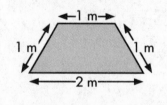

Convince Me! © **MP.5 Use Appropriate Tools** What other tools could be used to solve this problem? Why are a protractor and a meterstick more appropriate than other tools?

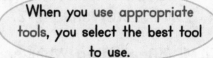

☆ Guided Practice ☆

ⓒ MP.5 Use Appropriate Tools

Lee brought $1\frac{3}{5}$ pounds of apples to the picnic. Hannah brought $\frac{4}{5}$ pounds of oranges. Lee said they brought $2\frac{2}{5}$ pounds of fruit in all. Lee needs to justify that $1\frac{3}{5} + \frac{4}{5} = 2\frac{2}{5}$.

1. What tool could Lee use to justify the sum?

2. How can Lee use a tool to justify the sum? Draw pictures of the tool you used to explain.

> When you use appropriate tools, you select the best tool to use.

Available Tools
Place-value blocks
Fraction strips
Rulers to $\frac{1}{8}$ inch
Grid paper
Counters

Independent Practice ☆

ⓒ MP.5 Use Appropriate Tools

What are the measures of the sides and angles of the parallelogram shown? Use Exercises 3–5 to help solve.

3. What tools can you use to solve this problem?

4. Explain how to use the tool you chose to find the measures of the angles. Label the figure with the measures you find.

5. Explain how to use the tool you chose to find the lengths of the sides. Label the figure with the measures you find.

For another example, see Set F on page 810.

Math Practices and Problem Solving

© Common Core Performance Assessment

Mural

Before Nadia paints a mural, she plans what she is going to paint. She sketches the diagram shown and wants to know the measures of ∠WVX, ∠WVY, ∠XVY, and ∠YVZ.

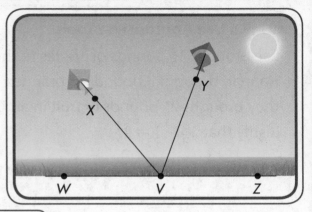

6. **MP.2 Reasoning** What quantities are given in the problem and what do the numbers mean? What do you know from the diagram?

7. **MP.1 Make Sense and Persevere** What do you need to find?

8. **MP.5 Use Appropriate Tools** Measure ∠WVX, ∠WVY, and ∠YVZ. What is the best tool to use?

When you use appropriate tools, you decide if the results you get with the tool make sense.

9. **MP.4 Model with Math** Write and solve an equation which could be used to find the measure of ∠XVY. What is the measure of the angle?

Help   Practice   Tools   Games
Buddy

Another Look!

When light hits a mirror, it reflects at the same angle as it hits. In the diagram shown, $\angle ABC$ has the same measure as $\angle CBD$, where $\overline{BC}$ makes a right angle with the mirror.

Measure $\angle ABC$. Then, write and solve an equation to find the measure of $\angle DBE$.

Tell how you can strategically choose a tool to solve the problem.

- I can decide which tool is appropriate.

- I can explain why it is the best tool to use.

- I can use the tool correctly.

The measure of $\angle ABC$ is 25°. The measure of $\angle CBD$ is also 25° and the sum of $\angle CBD$ and $\angle DBE$ is 90°. So, $25° + d = 90°$, $d = 90° - 25° = 65°$. The measure of $\angle DBE$ is 65°.

Mirror

© **MP.5 Use Appropriate Tools**

Jason wants to set up blocks for a game. He wants to set up the blocks in an array, so there are the same number of rows as columns. He wants to use between 20 and 90 blocks. How can Jason set up the blocks? Use Exercises 1–2 to help solve.

1. What tool could Jason use? Explain how Jason could use the tool to find at least one way to set up the blocks.

When you use appropriate tools, you consider options before selecting a tool.

Available Tools
Place-value blocks
Fraction strips
Rulers
Grid paper
Counters

2. What are all the ways Jason can set up the blocks?

Common Core Performance Assessment

Tiling

Marcus created the tile pattern shown. All the angles of each hexagon have the same measure and all the angles of each equilateral triangle have the same measure. Find the measure of each angle.

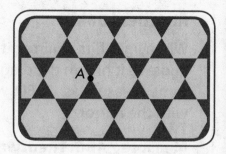

3. MP.1 Make Sense and Persevere What do you know and what do you need to find?

4. MP.5 Use Appropriate Tools What tool could you use to measure the angle of a hexagon? Explain how to use the tool you chose. What is the measure?

When you use appropriate tools, you use the tool you chose correctly.

5. MP.4 Model with Math Write and solve an equation which could be used to find the measure of one angle of a triangle. What is the measure of the angle? Explain.

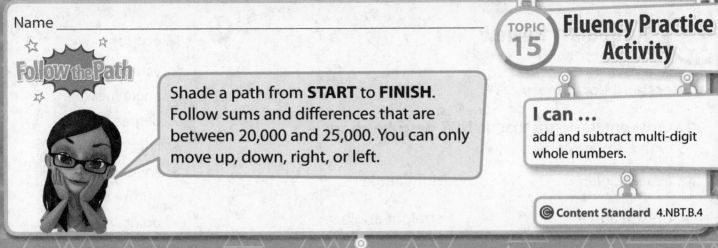

Follow the Path

Shade a path from **START** to **FINISH**. Follow sums and differences that are between 20,000 and 25,000. You can only move up, down, right, or left.

I can ...

add and subtract multi-digit whole numbers.

© **Content Standard** 4.NBT.B.4

Start				
66,149 − 44,297	13,000 + 13,000	11,407 + 13,493	35,900 − 12,605	30,000 − 9,825
40,350 − 20,149	18,890 + 190	13,050 + 11,150	60,000 − 33,900	41,776 − 18,950
89,000 − 68,900	12,175 + 18,125	12,910 + 12,089	67,010 − 42,009	42,082 − 19,582
56,111 − 32,523	22,009 + 991	11,725 + 11,450	75,000 − 45,350	65,508 − 42,158
99,000 − 81,750	9,125 + 9,725	18,517 + 8,588	38,000 − 19,001	37,520 − 16,215
				Finish

Understand Vocabulary

Word List

- acute angle
- angle measure
- degree (°)
- line
- line segment
- obtuse angle
- point
- protractor
- ray
- right angle
- straight angle
- unit angle
- vertex

1. Cross out the terms that do **NOT** describe an angle with a square corner.

   acute angle   right angle

   obtuse angle   straight angle

2. Cross out the terms that do **NOT** describe an angle open less than a right angle.

   acute angle   right angle

   obtuse angle   straight angle

3. Cross out the terms that do **NOT** describe an angle that forms a straight line.

   acute angle   right angle   obtuse angle   straight angle

4. Cross out the terms that do **NOT** describe an angle open more than a right angle, but less than a straight angle.

   acute angle   right angle   obtuse angle   straight angle

Label each example with a term from the Word List.

5. ←————→ _____   6. •————• _____

7. •————→ _____   8. _____

Use Vocabulary in Writing

9. Describe how to measure an angle. Use at least 3 terms from the Word List in your explanation.

Reteaching

Set A pages 771–776

A ray has one endpoint and continues on forever in one direction.

A **line segment** is a part of a line with two endpoints.

An **angle** is formed by two rays with a common endpoint.

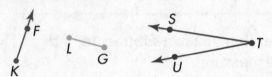

Remember that a line segment is a part of a line.

Use geometric terms to describe what is shown.

1.

2.

3.

4.

Set B pages 777–782

The angle below is $\frac{1}{3}$ of the circle.

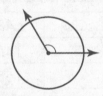

$\frac{1}{3}$ means 1 of 3 equal parts.

$360° \div 3 = 120°$

$\frac{1}{3} \times 360° = \frac{360°}{3}$ or $120°$

The measure of this angle is 120°.

Remember there are 360° in a circle.

A circle is cut into eighths. What is the angle measure of each piece?

1. Use division to solve.

2. Use multiplication to solve.

Set C pages 783–788

You can use an angle you know to find the measure of other angles. The smaller angle of the tan pattern block has a measure of 30°.

Three of the 30° angles will fit into the angle.
Add: $30° + 30° + 30° = 90°$

The measure of this angle is 90°.

Remember you can use any angle that you know the measure of to find the measure of other angles.

Find the measure of each angle. Use pattern blocks.

1.

2.

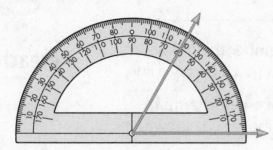

The measure of this angle is 60°.

Remember that a straight angle has a measure of 180°.

| Measure the angles. |

1. 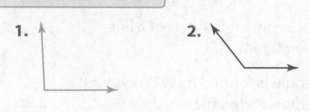 2.

When an angle is decomposed into non-overlapping parts, the angle measure of the whole is the sum of the angle measures of the parts.

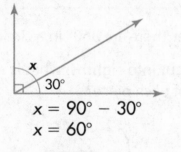

$$x = 90° - 30°$$
$$x = 60°$$

Remember you can subtract to find angle measures.

$\angle ABD$ is decomposed into two non-overlapping angles, $\angle ABC$ and $\angle CBD$. Complete the table.

Angle Measure (degrees)		
$\angle ABC$	$\angle CBD$	$\angle ABD$
100°	45°	145°
95°		155°
105°		170°
	25°	140°
122°	36°	

Think about these questions to help you **use appropriate tools** strategically.

Thinking Habits

- Which tools can I use?

- Why should I use this tool to help me solve the problem?

- Is there a different tool I could use?

- Am I using the tool appropriately?

Remember there may be more than one appropriate tool to use to solve a problem.

One-eighth of the pie is missing from the tin.

1. What tools can Delia use to measure the angle of the missing piece?

2. How can you calculate the measure?

Name _____

© **Assessment**

1. What is the measure of the angle shown below?

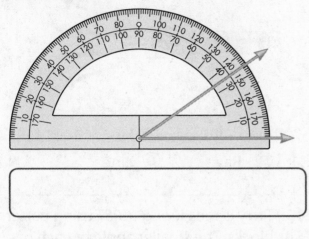

_____

2. Megan needs to find the measures of the angles on a bridge.

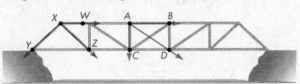

Part A

Find the measure of ∠YXW if ∠YXZ is 85° and ∠ZXW is 40°. Write and solve an addition equation.

_____

Part B

Find the measure of ∠CAD if ∠CAB is a right angle and ∠DAB is 45°. Write and solve a subtraction equation.

3. If you divide a circle into 360 equal angles, what is the angle measure of each angle? What term describes this measure?

_____

4. Choose the correct term from the box to complete each statement.

Line Segment	Ray

A _____ has one endpoint.

A _____ has two endpoints.

5. Draw an example of a point A, a line segment BC, a line DE, and a ray FG.

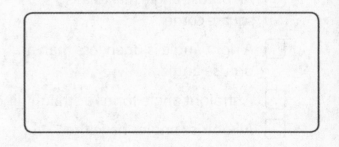

6. ∠JKL is decomposed into 2 non-overlapping right angles, ∠JKM and ∠MKL. What kind of angle is ∠JKL?

Ⓐ Acute

Ⓑ Right

Ⓒ Obtuse

Ⓓ Straight

7. ∠ABC has a measure of 40°. ∠CBD has a measure of 23°. The angles share a ray and form ∠ABD. Which is the measure of ∠ABD?

Ⓐ 17°　　　Ⓒ 63°

Ⓑ 27°　　　Ⓓ 73°

---

8. Emma cut slices from pies. Draw lines to match the fractions with the angle measures.

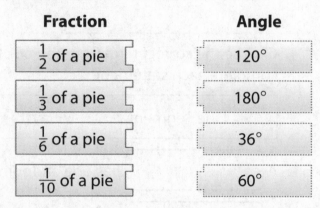

Fraction	Angle
$\frac{1}{2}$ of a pie	120°
$\frac{1}{3}$ of a pie	180°
$\frac{1}{6}$ of a pie	36°
$\frac{1}{10}$ of a pie	60°

---

9. Select all the true statements.

☐ An acute angle is open less than a right angle.

☐ An obtuse angle makes a square corner.

☐ A right angle is open less than an obtuse angle.

☐ A straight angle forms a straight line.

☐ All obtuse angles have the same measure.

---

10. Two wooden roof beams meet at a 60° angle. Draw an angle to represent how the beams meet.

---

11. Which geometric term best describes the light that shines from a flashlight?

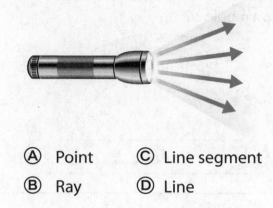

Ⓐ Point　　　Ⓒ Line segment

Ⓑ Ray　　　Ⓓ Line

---

12. Terry is measuring ∠RST using pattern blocks. The smaller angle of each of the tan pattern blocks shown below measures 30°. What is the measure of ∠RST? Explain.

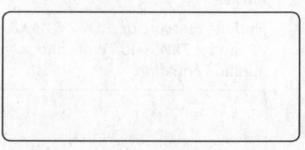

---

13. Identify an acute angle, a right angle, and an obtuse angle in the figure below.

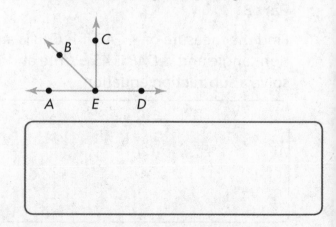

Name _____

Ancient Roads

The ancient Romans built roads throughout their empire.
Many roads were paved with stones that fit together.
The spaces between the stones were filled with sand
and gravel. Many of these roads still exist today,
over 2,000 years after they were built.

1. As seen in the **Roman Road** figure, the stones formed
   angles and other geometric figures.

Roman Road

 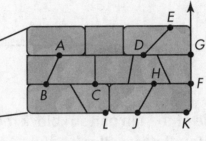

Part A

What geometric figure has one endpoint at *F* and goes on
forever through point *G*?

Part B

Is ∠*EDA* right, acute, or obtuse? Explain.

Part C

∠*EDG* turns through $\frac{1}{8}$ of a circle. What is its angle
measure? Explain.

2. Answer the following to find the measure of ∠*HJK* and ∠*HJL* in the **Measuring a Roman Road** figure.

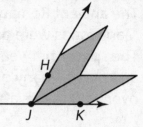

Part A

Name two tools you could use to measure the angles.

Part B

The smaller angle of the tan pattern block measures 30°, as shown in the **Tan Pattern Block** figure. A 30-degree angle is 30 one-degree angles. What is the measure of ∠*HJK* in the **Measuring a Roman Road** figure? Explain.

Tan Pattern Block

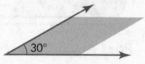

30°

You can write and solve equations to find unknown angle measures.

Part C

What is the measure of ∠*HJL* in the **Measuring a Roman Road** figure? Write and solve an equation to find the measure of the angle.

TOPIC 16

Lines, Angles, and Shapes

Essential Questions: How can you classify triangles and quadrilaterals? What is line symmetry?

Digital Resources

Solve Learn Glossary Practice Buddy

Tools Assessment Help Games

> They can see the math that is all around them! Here is a project about senses and symmetry!

> Chameleons can move their eyes one at a time!

> When they do, they are able to see in two directions at once, helping them find food and stay safe.

Math and Science Project: Senses and Symmetry

Do Research The location of an animal's eyes helps it to survive in the wild. Use the Internet or other sources to find why some animals have eyes on the sides of their head and others have eyes on the front.

Journal: Write a Report Include what you found. Also in your report:

- Most animals are the same on both sides of their body. Use a line of symmetry to help make a simple drawing of your favorite animal's face. Draw both sides of the animal's face the same. Explain how you know that both sides of your drawing are the same.

Name _____

Review What You Know

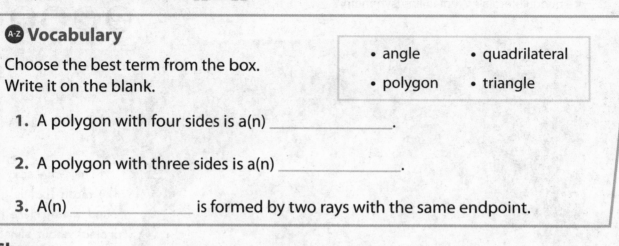

A-Z Vocabulary

Choose the best term from the box.
Write it on the blank.

- angle
- polygon
- quadrilateral
- triangle

1. A polygon with four sides is a(n) _____.

2. A polygon with three sides is a(n) _____.

3. A(n) _____ is formed by two rays with the same endpoint.

Shapes

Choose the best term to describe each shape. Use each term once.

Rectangle   Rhombus   Trapezoid

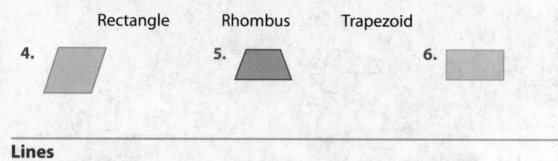

4.   5.   6.

Lines

Use geometric terms to describe what is shown.

7.   8.   9.

Problem Solving

10. **© MP.8 Generalize** Which generalization about these figures is **NOT** true?

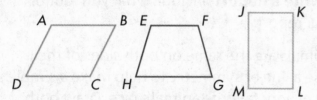

Ⓐ Each figure is a quadrilateral.

Ⓑ Each figure has two pairs of parallel sides.

Ⓒ Each figure has at least two sides of equal length.

Ⓓ Each figure has 4 angles.

My Word Cards

Use the examples for each word on the front of the card to help complete the definitions on the back.

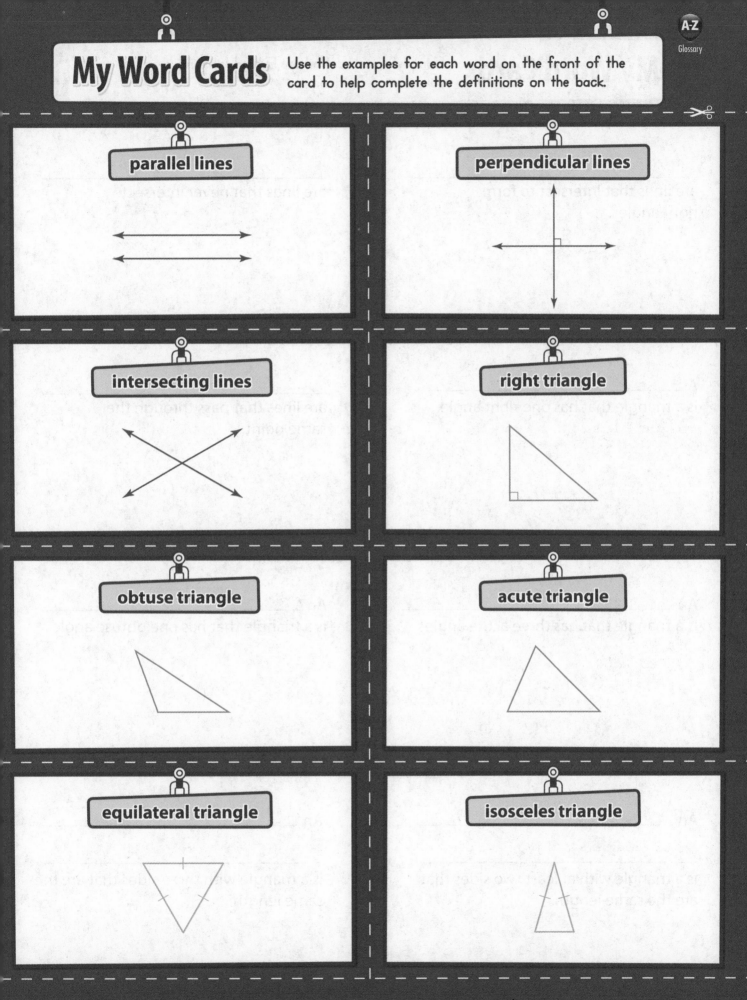

parallel lines

perpendicular lines

intersecting lines

right triangle

obtuse triangle

acute triangle

equilateral triangle

isosceles triangle

My Word Cards

Complete each definition. Extend learning by writing your own definitions.

______________ are lines that intersect to form right angles.

______________ are lines that never intersect.

A ______________ is a triangle that has one right angle.

______________ are lines that pass through the same point.

An ______________ is a triangle that has three acute angles.

An ______________ is a triangle that has one obtuse angle.

An ______________ ______________ is a triangle with at least two sides that are the same length.

An ______________ ______________ is a triangle with three sides that are the same length.

My Word Cards

Use the examples for each word on the front of the card to help complete the definitions on the back.

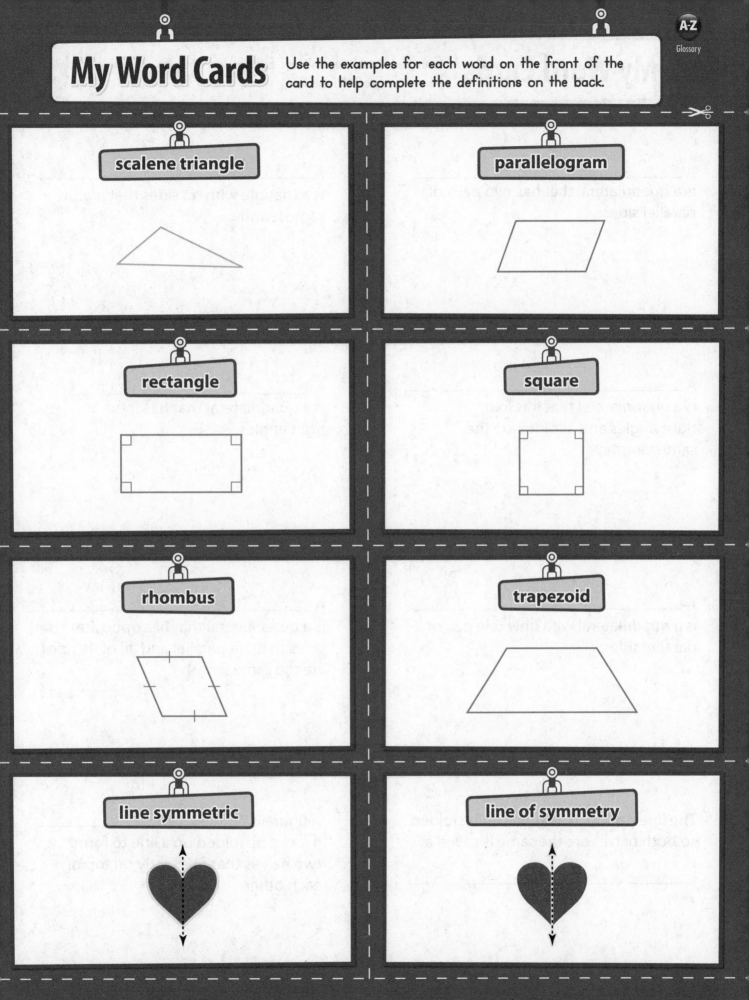

scalene triangle

parallelogram

rectangle

square

rhombus

trapezoid

line symmetric

line of symmetry

My Word Cards

Complete each definition. Extend learning by writing your own definitions.

A _____
is a quadrilateral that has two pairs of parallel sides.

A _____
is a triangle with no sides that are the same length.

A _____
is a quadrilateral that has four right angles and all sides are the same length.

A _____
is a quadrilateral that has four right angles.

A _____
is a quadrilateral with only one pair of parallel sides.

A _____
is a quadrilateral that has opposite sides that are parallel and all of its sides are the same length.

The line on which a figure can be folded so both halves are the same is called a
_____.

A figure is _____
if it can be folded on a line to form two halves that fit exactly on top of each other.

Name _____

I can ...
draw and identify perpendicular, parallel, and intersecting lines.

© Content Standard 4.G.A.1
Mathematical Practices MP.3, MP.4, MP.6

Solve & Share

The number line below is an example of a line. A line goes on forever in a straight path in two directions. Draw the following pairs of lines: two lines that will never cross, two lines that cross at one point, two lines that cross at two points. If you cannot draw the lines, tell why.

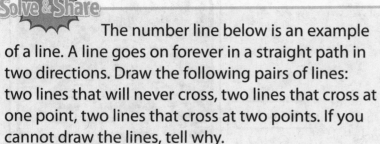

0 1 2 3 4 5 6 7 8 9

Be precise. Think of and use math language you already know. *Show your work in the space below!*

Look Back! © MP.6 Be Precise Terry said, "The lines shown intersect at three points." Is Terry correct? Explain.

Essential Question: How Can You Describe Pairs of Lines?

A

A line is a straight path of points that goes on and on in opposite directions. A pair of lines can be described as parallel, perpendicular, or intersecting.

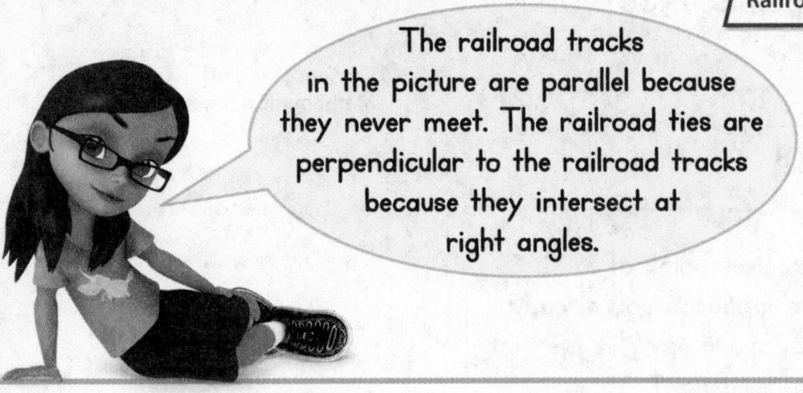

The railroad tracks in the picture are parallel because they never meet. The railroad ties are perpendicular to the railroad tracks because they intersect at right angles.

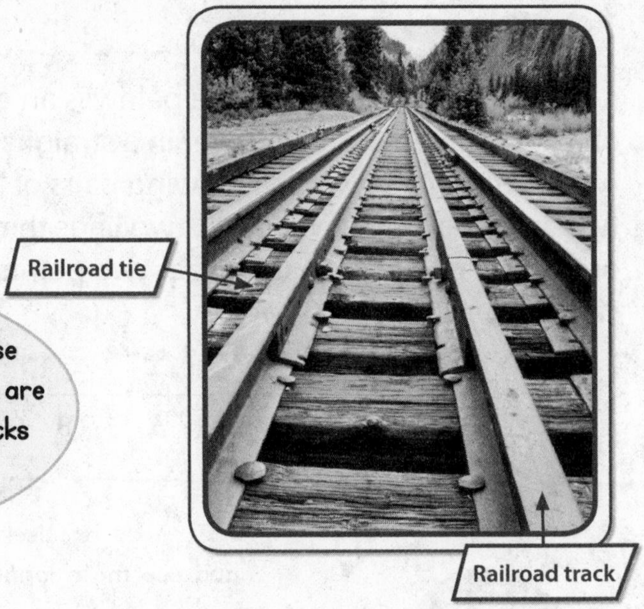

Railroad tie

Railroad track

B Pairs of lines are given special names depending on their relationship.

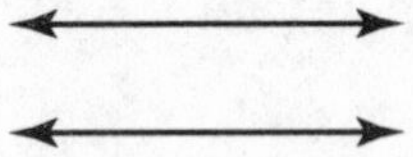

Parallel lines
never intersect.

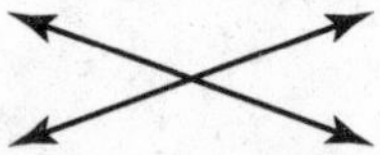

Intersecting lines
pass through the
same point.

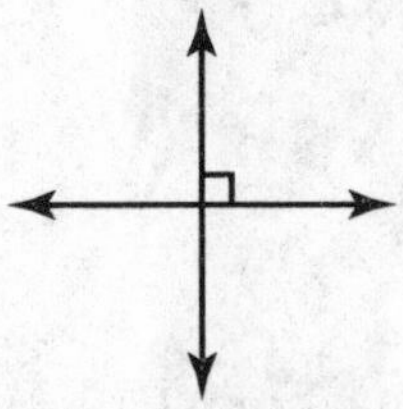

Perpendicular lines
are lines that intersect
to form right angles.

Convince Me! © MP.6 Be Precise Find examples in your classroom
where you can identify parallel lines, intersecting lines, and
perpendicular lines. Explain.

Name _____

☆Guided Practice*

Do You Understand?

1. Ⓒ **MP.6 Be Precise** What geometric term could you use to describe the top and bottom edges of a book? Why?

2. What pair of lines looks like the blades of an open pair of scissors? Why?

Do You Know How?

For **3–6**, use the diagram.

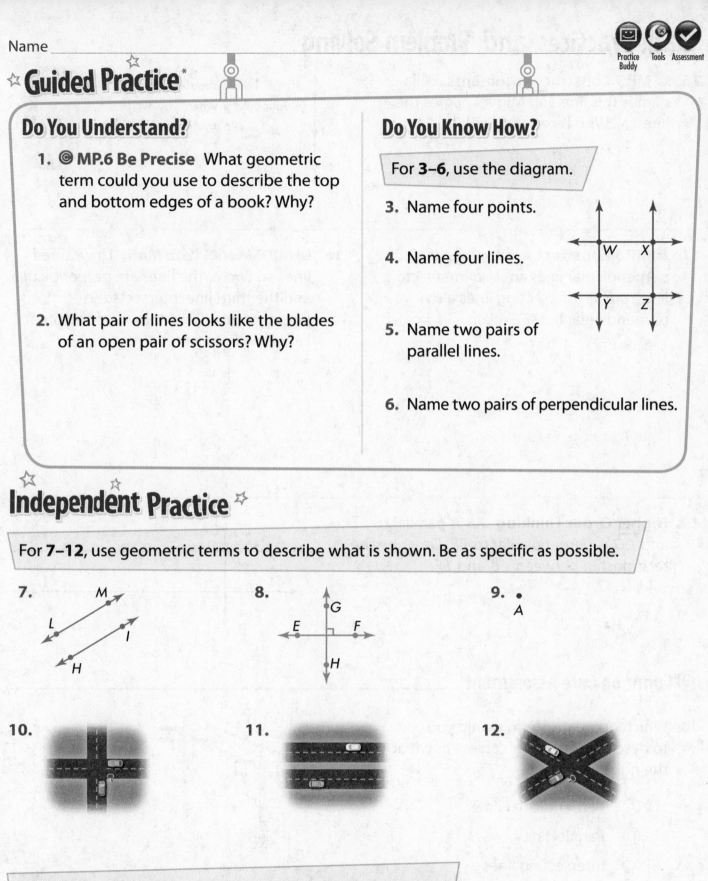

3. Name four points.

4. Name four lines.

5. Name two pairs of parallel lines.

6. Name two pairs of perpendicular lines.

Independent Practice ☆

For **7–12**, use geometric terms to describe what is shown. Be as specific as possible.

7. M L I H

8. G E F H

9. • A

10.

11.

12.

For **13–15**, draw what is described by the geometic terms.

13. Perpendicular lines

14. Intersecting lines

15. Parallel lines

Math Practices and Problem Solving

16. **MP.3 Construct Arguments** Bella names this line $\overleftrightarrow{LM}$. Miguel names the line $\overleftrightarrow{LN}$. Who is correct? Explain.

> Think about math vocabulary when you write explanations.

L •
M •
N •

17. **MP.3 Construct Arguments** If all perpendicular lines are also intersecting lines, are all intersecting lines also perpendicular lines? Explain.

18. **MP.4 Model with Math** Draw three lines so two of the lines are perpendicular and the third line intersects the perpendicular lines at exactly one point. Label the lines with points.

19. **Higher Order Thinking** $\overleftrightarrow{AB}$ is parallel to $\overleftrightarrow{CD}$, and $\overleftrightarrow{CD}$ is perpendicular to $\overleftrightarrow{EF}$. Describe the relationship between $\overleftrightarrow{AB}$ and $\overleftrightarrow{EF}$.

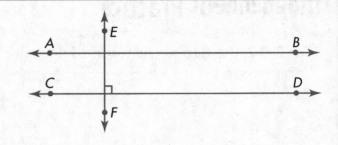

Common Core Assessment

20. Which geometric term would you use to describe the power cables shown at the right?

    (A)   Perpendicular lines

    (B)   Parallel lines

    (C)   Intersecting lines

    (D)   Points

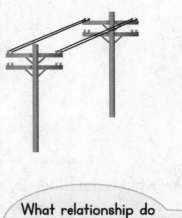

> What relationship do the power cables have to each other?

© Pearson Education, Inc. 4

Help Practice Buddy Tools Games

Another Look!

You can use geometric terms to describe what you draw.

Parallel lines

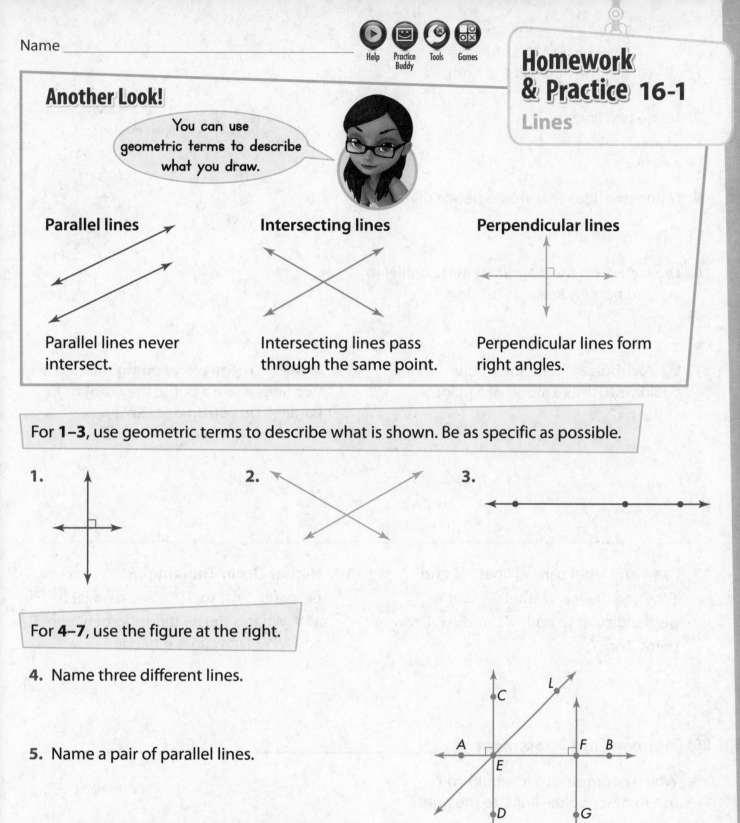

Parallel lines never intersect.

Intersecting lines

Intersecting lines pass through the same point.

Perpendicular lines

Perpendicular lines form right angles.

For **1–3**, use geometric terms to describe what is shown. Be as specific as possible.

1.

2.

3.

For **4–7**, use the figure at the right.

4. Name three different lines.

5. Name a pair of parallel lines.

6. Name two lines that are perpendicular.

7. Name two intersecting lines.

For **8–10**, use the figure at the right.

8. Name two lines.

9. Name two lines that are perpendicular.

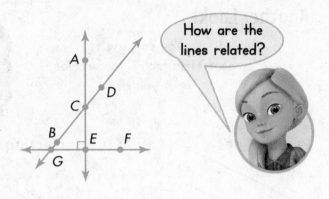

How are the lines related?

10. Draw a $\overleftrightarrow{HF}$ on the diagram that is parallel to $\overleftrightarrow{AE}$ and perpendicular to $\overleftrightarrow{GF}$.

---

11. **A-Z Vocabulary** Describe a point. What could you use as a model of a point?

12. **© MP.3 Critique Reasoning** Ali says if two lines share a point, they cannot be parallel. Do you agree? Explain.

---

13. Draw and label parallel lines $\overleftrightarrow{XY}$ and $\overleftrightarrow{RS}$. Then draw and label $\overleftrightarrow{TS}$ so it is perpendicular to both $\overleftrightarrow{XY}$ and $\overleftrightarrow{RS}$. Draw point Z on $\overleftrightarrow{TS}$.

14. **Higher Order Thinking** $\overleftrightarrow{RS}$ is perpendicular to $\overleftrightarrow{TU}$. $\overleftrightarrow{RS}$ is parallel to $\overleftrightarrow{VW}$. What is the relationship between $\overleftrightarrow{TU}$ and $\overleftrightarrow{VW}$? Draw lines if needed.

© Common Core Assessment

15. Which geometric term would you use to describe the lines to the right?

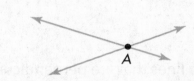

    Ⓐ   Perpendicular lines

    Ⓑ   Point A

    Ⓒ   Parallel lines

    Ⓓ   Intersecting lines

Think about the relationship between the two lines.

Name _____

Solve & Share

Sort the triangles shown below into two or more groups. Explain how you sorted them. **Solve this problem any way you choose.**

I can ...
reason about line segments and angles to classify triangles.

© Content Standard 4.G.A.2
Mathematical Practices MP.3, MP.6, MP.8

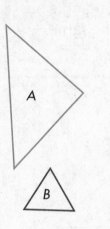
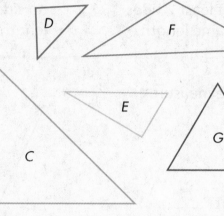

You can construct arguments and use different ways of describing and classifying triangles. *Show your work in the space above!*

Look Back! © MP.8 Generalize What is true about all 7 triangles you sorted?

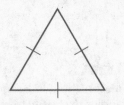
A Triangles can be classified by the line segments that make their sides.

An **equilateral triangle** has 3 sides the same length.

An **isosceles triangle** has at least 2 sides the same length.

A **scalene triangle** has no sides the same length.

B Triangles can be classified by their angle measures.

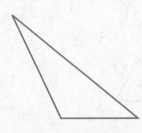

A **right triangle** has one right angle.

An **acute triangle** has three acute angles. All of its angles measure less than a right angle.

An **obtuse triangle** has one obtuse angle. One angle has a measure greater than a right angle.

Triangles can also be classified by both their angle measures and their sides. The red triangle is an obtuse scalene triangle.

Convince Me! © **MP.6 Be Precise** Can a triangle have more than one obtuse angle? Explain.

Name _____

☆ Guided Practice *

Do You Understand?

1. ⓒ **MP.3 Critique Reasoning** Sally classified a triangle as an obtuse acute triangle. Is this a possible classification? Explain.

2. Can a triangle have more than one right angle? If so, draw an example.

Do You Know How?

For **3–6**, classify each triangle by its sides, and then by its angles.

3.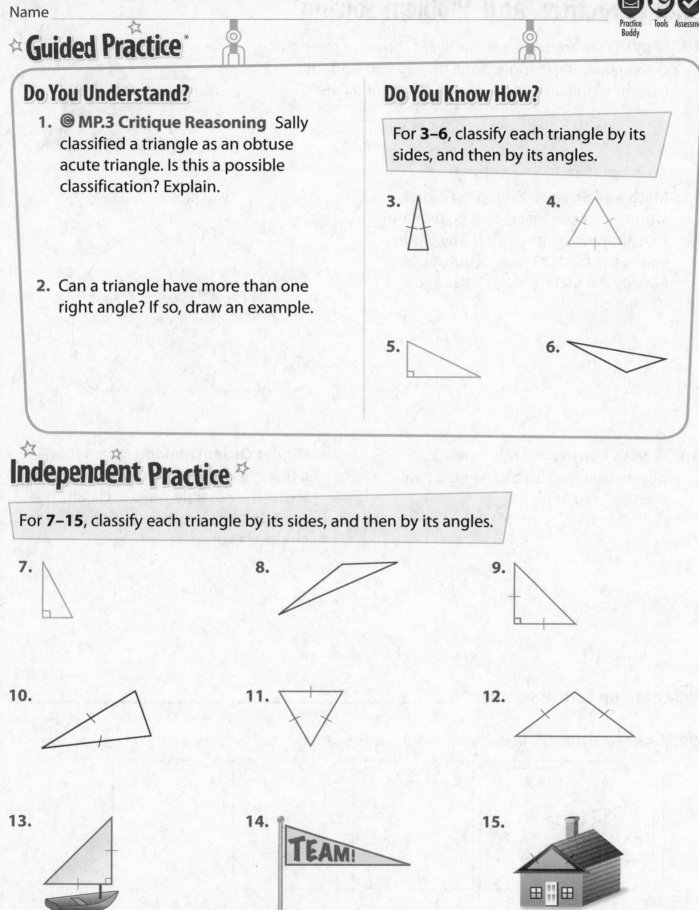

4.

5.

6.

Independent Practice ☆

For **7–15**, classify each triangle by its sides, and then by its angles.

7.

8.

9.

10.

11.

12.

13.

14. TEAM!

15.

Math Practices and Problem Solving

16. **© MP.8 Generalize** If the backyard shown at the right is an equilateral triangle. What do you know about the lengths of the other two sides that are not labeled?

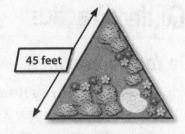

45 feet

17. **Math and Science** A rabbit's field of vision is so wide that it can see predators that approach from behind. The diagram shows the field of vision of one rabbit. Classify the triangle by its sides and its angles.

Seen by both eyes

Seen by left eye

Seen by right eye

18. **© MP.3 Construct Arguments** Can an obtuse triangle also be an equilateral triangle? Explain.

19. **Higher Order Thinking** Mitch draws a triangle with one obtuse angle. What are all the possible ways to classify the triangle by its angle measures and side lengths? Explain.

© Common Core Assessment

20. Draw each triangle in its correct angle classification.

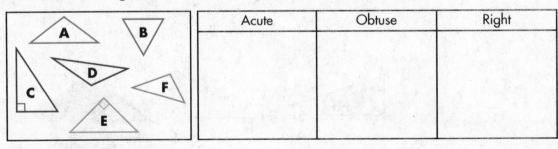

Acute	Obtuse	Right

Help | Practice Buddy | Tools | Games

Another Look!

Triangles can be classified by their angle measures, side lengths, or both.

Equilateral triangle
All sides are the same length.

Isosceles triangle
At least two sides are the same length.

Scalene triangle
No sides are the same length.

Right triangle
One angle is a right angle.

Acute triangle
All three angles are acute angles.

Obtuse triangle
One angle is an obtuse angle.

For **1–6**, classify each triangle by its sides and then by its angles.

1.

2.

3.

4.

5.

6.

For **7–8**, use the figure at the right.

7. Hilary flew from Denver to Atlanta for business. From Atlanta, she flew to Chicago to visit her aunt. From Chicago, she flew back home to Denver. Classify the triangle made by her complete flight path.

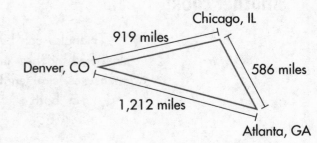

8. How many miles complete the triangle made by Hilary's flight path?

9. **Algebra** The triangle shown is an equilateral triangle. Write an addition equation and a multiplication equation to show how to find the perimeter, *p*, of the triangle when *s* is the measure of one side.

10. **A-Z Vocabulary** Fill in the blanks to correctly complete the sentences:

A _____ triangle has no sides the same length.

A triangle with one 90° angle is called a _____ triangle.

An isosceles triangle has _____ sides the same length.

11. **MP.3 Critique Reasoning** Sylvia says a right triangle can have only one right angle. Joel says a right triangle can have more than one right angle. Who is correct? Explain.

12. **Higher Order Thinking** Dani measured the angles of a triangle as 120°, 36°, and 24°. Then, she measured the side lengths as 25.3 cm, 17.2 cm, and 11.8 cm. She said her triangle is an isosceles obtuse triangle. Do you agree? Explain.

© Common Core Assessment

13. Draw each triangle in its correct side classification.

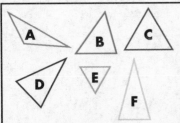

Isosceles	Equilateral	Scalene

Name _____

Draw three different four-sided shapes that have opposite sides parallel. *Solve this problem any way you choose.*

I can ...
reason about line segments and angles to classify quadrilaterals.

ⓒ **Content Standard** 4.G.A.2
Mathematical Practices MP.2, MP.3, MP.6, MP.7, MP.8

You can generalize and use what you know about parallel lines and angles to draw quadrilaterals. *Show your work in the space below!*

Look Back! ⓒ **MP.7 Use Structure** What attributes do your shapes have in common?

Essential Question **How Can You Classify Quadrilaterals?**

A

Quadrilaterals can be classified by their angles or the line segments that make their sides. Which of the quadrilaterals shown have only one pair of parallel sides? Which have two pairs of parallel sides?

A parallelogram has 2 pairs of parallel sides.

A rectangle has 4 right angles. It is also a parallelogram.

A square has 4 right angles and all sides are the same length. It is a parallelogram, a rectangle, and a rhombus.

Any four-sided shape can be called a quadrilateral.

B

A rhombus is a quadrilateral that has opposite sides that are parallel and all of its sides are the same length. It is also a parallelogram.

A trapezoid is a quadrilateral with only one pair of parallel sides.

Trapezoids have only one pair of parallel sides. Parallelograms, rectangles, squares, and rhombuses all have two pairs of parallel sides.

Convince Me! © **MP.6 Be Precise** How are a parallelogram and a rectangle the same? How are they different?

Another Example!

Perpendicular sides form right angles. Can a trapezoid have perpendicular sides?

A trapezoid can have two right angles that form perpendicular sides. A trapezoid with two right angles is called a right trapezoid.

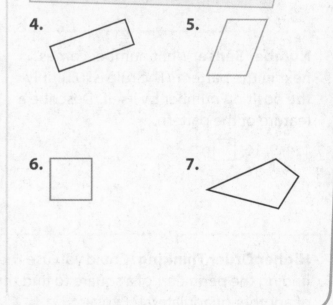

☆ Guided Practice *

Do You Understand?

1. **ⓒ MP.7 Use Structure** What is true about all quadrilaterals?

2. What is the difference between a square and a rhombus?

3. Shane drew a quadrilateral with at least 2 right angles and at least 1 pair of parallel sides. Name three quadrilaterals Shane could have drawn.

Do You Know How?

For **4–7**, write all the names possible for each quadrilateral.

4.   5.

6.   7.

Independent Practice ☆

For **8–11**, write all the names possible for each quadrilateral.

8. 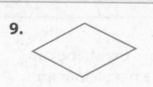   9.    10.    11.

Math Practices and Problem Solving

12. **Algebra** Jamie swims at a swimming pool. The length of the pool is 25 yards. She swam a total of 150 yards. How many times did she swim the length of the pool? Use the bar diagram to write and solve an equation to find the answer.

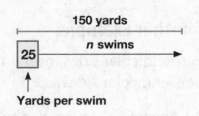

150 yards

n swims

25

Yards per swim

---

13. ⊚ **MP.3 Critique Reasoning** Tia says every square is a rectangle, and every square is a rhombus, so every rectangle must be a rhombus. Do you agree? Explain.

14. ⊚ **MP.3 Construct Arguments** Is it possible for a quadrilateral to be both a rhombus and parallelogram? Explain.

---

15. **Number Sense** What number comes next in the pattern? The rule is "Multiply the position number by itself." Describe a feature of the pattern.

1, 4, 9, 16, ☐

16. ⊚ **MP.2 Reasoning** All the sides of an equilateral triangle are the same length. Is an equilateral triangle also a rhombus? Explain.

---

17. **Higher Order Thinking** Could you use the formula for finding the perimeter of a square to find the perimeter of another quadrilateral? Explain.

> The formula for perimeter of a square is $P = 4 \times s$.

⊚ **Common Core Assessment**

18. Ben draws the shape shown at the right. He says the shape can be classified as a quadrilateral, trapezoid, and a parallelogram. Is Ben correct? Explain.

Name _____

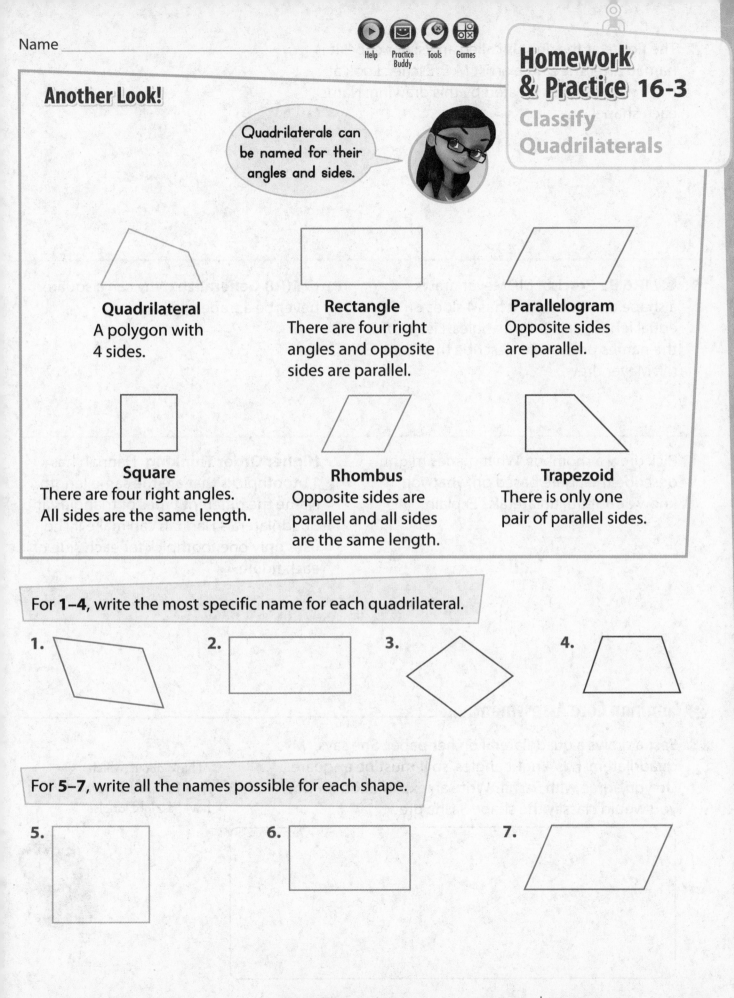

Help Practice Tools Games
      Buddy

Another Look!

Quadrilaterals can be named for their angles and sides.

Quadrilateral
A polygon with 4 sides.

Rectangle
There are four right angles and opposite sides are parallel.

Parallelogram
Opposite sides are parallel.

Square
There are four right angles. All sides are the same length.

Rhombus
Opposite sides are parallel and all sides are the same length.

Trapezoid
There is only one pair of parallel sides.

For **1–4**, write the most specific name for each quadrilateral.

1.

2.

3.

4.

For **5–7**, write all the names possible for each shape.

5.

6.

7.

8. The figure at the right is called an Escher cube. It is named after the Dutch artist M.C. Escher. Look at the 7 white shapes created by this drawing. Name each shape.

9. © **MP.6 Be Precise** Mr. Meyer draws a shape on the board. It has 4 sides of equal length and 4 right angles. List all of the names possible to describe the shape Mr. Meyer drew.

10. © **MP.8 Generalize** Why can a square never be a trapezoid?

11. Rick drew a rhombus. What names might describe the figure based on what you know about quadrilaterals? Explain.

12. **Higher Order Thinking** Hannah has 11 toothpicks that are the same length. Name the different types of triangles and quadrilaterals Hannah can make if she uses only one toothpick for each side of each figure.

© **Common Core Assessment**

13. Sasha draws a quadrilateral on her paper. She says, "My quadrilateral has 4 right angles, so it must be a square." Do you agree with Sasha? Write an explanation for how you would classify the shape Sasha drew.

Think about which types of quadrilaterals have 4 right angles.

Name _____

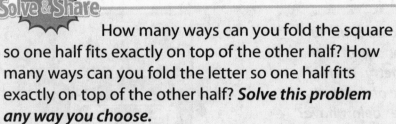

Solve & Share

How many ways can you fold the square so one half fits exactly on top of the other half? How many ways can you fold the letter so one half fits exactly on top of the other half? *Solve this problem any way you choose.*

Solve

I can ...
recognize and draw lines of symmetry and identify line-symmetric figures.

© **Content Standard** 4.G.A.3
Mathematical Practices MP.2, MP.3, MP.5, MP.7

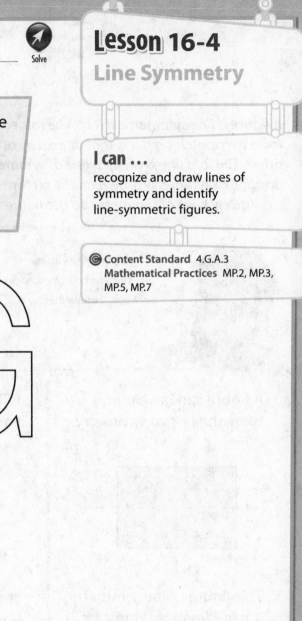

You can use appropriate tools. How can the edge of a ruler help you solve this problem?

Look Back! © **MP.2 Reasoning** What figures can you form when you fold a square in half?

Essential Question **What Is Line Symmetry?**

A

A figure is **line symmetric** if it can be folded on a line to form two matching parts that fit exactly on top of each other. The fold line is called a **line of symmetry**. There is one line of symmetry drawn on the picture of the truck. How many lines of symmetry do the figures below have?

Count the lines of symmetry drawn on each figure below.

B

A figure can have more than one line of symmetry.

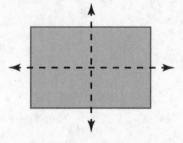

This figure is line symmetric. It has 2 lines of symmetry. It can be folded on each line of symmetry into matching parts.

C

A figure can have many lines of symmetry.

This figure is line symmetric. It has 6 lines of symmetry. It can be folded on each line of symmetry into matching parts.

D

A figure can have no lines of symmetry.

This figure is **NOT** line symmetric. It has 0 lines of symmetry. It cannot be folded to have matching parts.

Convince Me! © **MP.7 Look for Relationships** Find two capital letters that have exactly one line of symmetry. Find two capital letters that have exactly two lines of symmetry.

☆ Guided Practice ☆

Do You Understand?

1. How many lines of symmetry does the letter R have?

2. How many lines of symmetry does the figure below have?

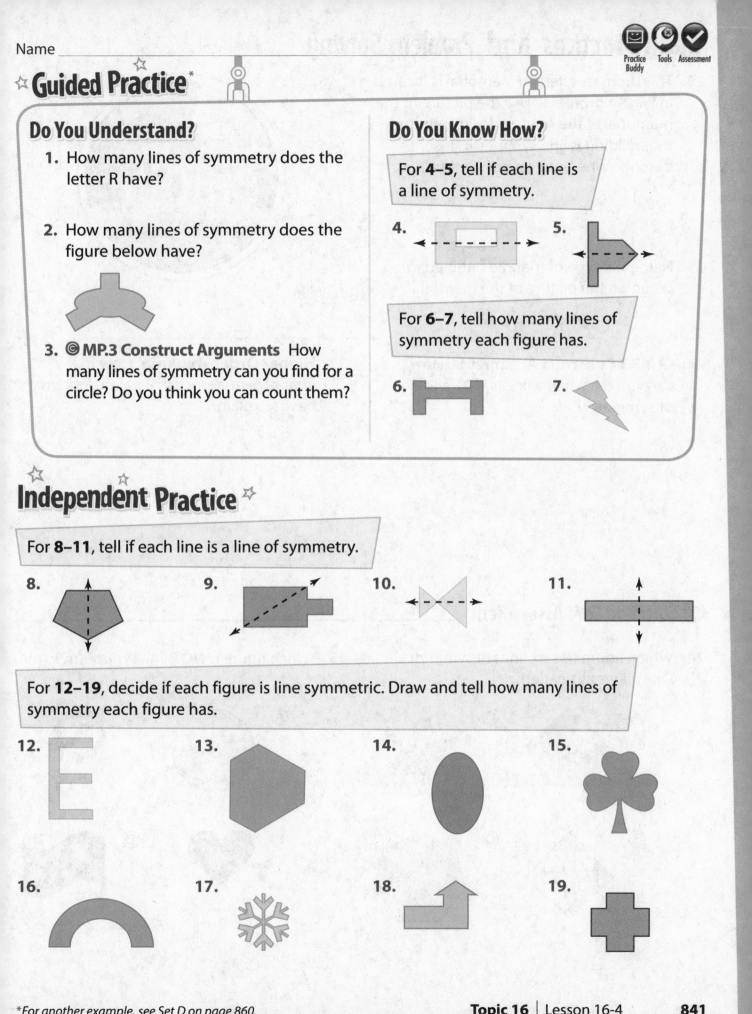

3. ©MP.3 **Construct Arguments** How many lines of symmetry can you find for a circle? Do you think you can count them?

Do You Know How?

For **4–5**, tell if each line is a line of symmetry.

4.

5.

For **6–7**, tell how many lines of symmetry each figure has.

6.

7.

Independent Practice ☆

For **8–11**, tell if each line is a line of symmetry.

8.

9.

10.

11.

For **12–19**, decide if each figure is line symmetric. Draw and tell how many lines of symmetry each figure has.

12. E

13.

14.

15.

16.

17.

18.

19.

Math Practices and Problem Solving

20. The Thomas Jefferson Memorial is located in Washington, D.C. Use the picture of the memorial at the right to decide whether the building is line symmetric. If so, describe where the line of symmetry is.

21. Name the type of triangle outlined in green on the picture of the memorial.

22. © **MP.3 Construct Arguments** How can you tell when a line is **NOT** a line of symmetry?

23. **Higher Order Thinking** How many lines of symmetry can a parallelogram have? Explain.

© **Common Core Assessment**

24. Which figure has six lines of symmetry? Draw lines as needed.

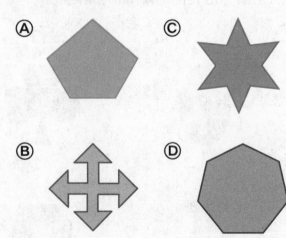

25. Which figure is **NOT** line symmetric?

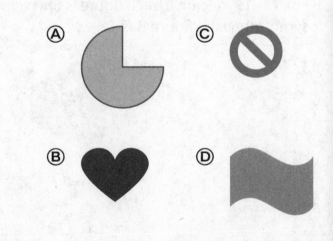

Name _____

Another Look!

Line-symmetric figures are figures that can be folded to make matching parts.

How many lines of symmetry does a square have?

If you fold the square along any of the 4 dashed lines, the two matching parts will lie on top of each other.

A square has 4 lines of symmetry. It is a line-symmetric figure.

For **1–4**, tell if each line is a line of symmetry.

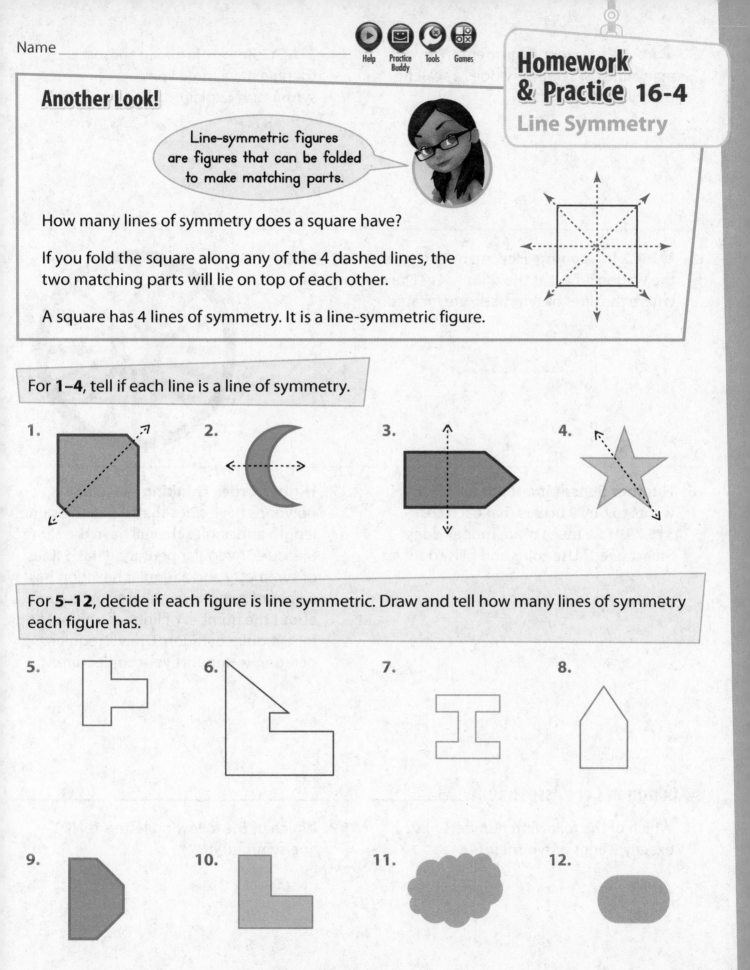

1.

2.

3.

4.

For **5–12**, decide if each figure is line symmetric. Draw and tell how many lines of symmetry each figure has.

5.

6.

7.

8.

9.

10.

11.

12.

13. **© MP.3 Construct Arguments** How many lines of symmetry does a scalene triangle have? Explain.

14. **© MP.2 Reasoning** Can an isosceles triangle have three lines of symmetry? Explain.

15. **© MP.2 Reasoning** How many lines of symmetry does the wagon wheel at the right have? Draw or explain where the lines of symmetry are located.

16. **Number Sense** Stuart has $23.75. He wants to buy 2 tickets that each cost $15.75. How much more money does Stuart need? Use coins and bills to solve.

17. **Higher Order Thinking** Regular polygons have sides that are all the same length and angles that all have the same measure. A regular pentagon has 5 lines of symmetry and a regular hexagon has 6 lines of symmetry. Make a conjecture about the number of lines of symmetry for a regular octagon. Draw a regular octagon to support your conjecture.

© Common Core Assessment

18. Which of the following numbers has exactly 2 lines of symmetry?

　Ⓐ 1
　Ⓑ 3
　Ⓒ 7
　Ⓓ 8

19. Which of the following letters is **NOT** line symmetric?

　Ⓐ W
　Ⓑ T
　Ⓒ S
　Ⓓ A

Name _____

Solve & Share

Craig and Julia are designing kites. A kite will fly well if the kite has line symmetry. Does Craig's or Julia's kite have line symmetry? Explain. Then, design your own kites. Design one kite with 2 lines of symmetry and another kite with 3 lines of symmetry. **Solve this problem any way you choose.**

I can ...
draw a figure that has line symmetry.

© **Content Standard** 4.G.A.3
Mathematical Practices MP.1, MP.2, MP.3, MP.4

Craig's Design

Julia's Design

You can construct arguments. What math vocabulary can you use to explain why Craig's or Julia's kite designs will fly well?

Look Back! © **MP.1 Make Sense and Persevere** Can both Craig's and Julia's kites can be folded into matching parts? If one of the kites is not line symmetric, can it be changed so that it is? Explain.

Essential Question **How Can You Draw Figures with Line Symmetry?**

A

Sarah wants to design a line-symmetric tabletop. She sketched half of the tabletop. What are two ways Sarah can complete her design?

The tabletop is line symmetric if the design can be folded along a line of symmetry into matching parts.

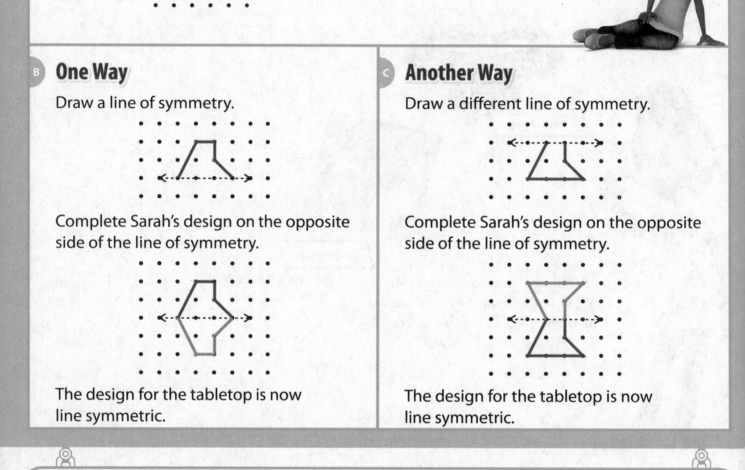

B **One Way**

Draw a line of symmetry.

Complete Sarah's design on the opposite side of the line of symmetry.

The design for the tabletop is now line symmetric.

C **Another Way**

Draw a different line of symmetry.

Complete Sarah's design on the opposite side of the line of symmetry.

The design for the tabletop is now line symmetric.

Convince Me! **© MP.4 Model with Math** Sarah sketched a different design for a smaller tabletop. Use the lines of symmetry to draw two ways Sarah can complete her design.

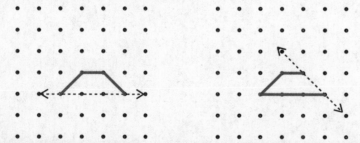

☆ Guided Practice *

Practice Buddy · Tools · Assessment

Do You Understand?

1. ⓒ **MP.3 Critique Reasoning** Chandler tried to complete Sarah's design from the previous page. Describe the error Chandler made.

2. How can folding a piece of paper help to determine if a line in a figure is a line of symmetry?

Do You Know How?

For **3–4**, draw a line of symmetry and complete the designs.

3.

4.

☆ Independent Practice ☆

For **5–10**, use the line of symmetry to draw a line-symmetric figure.

5.

6.

7.

8.

9.

10.

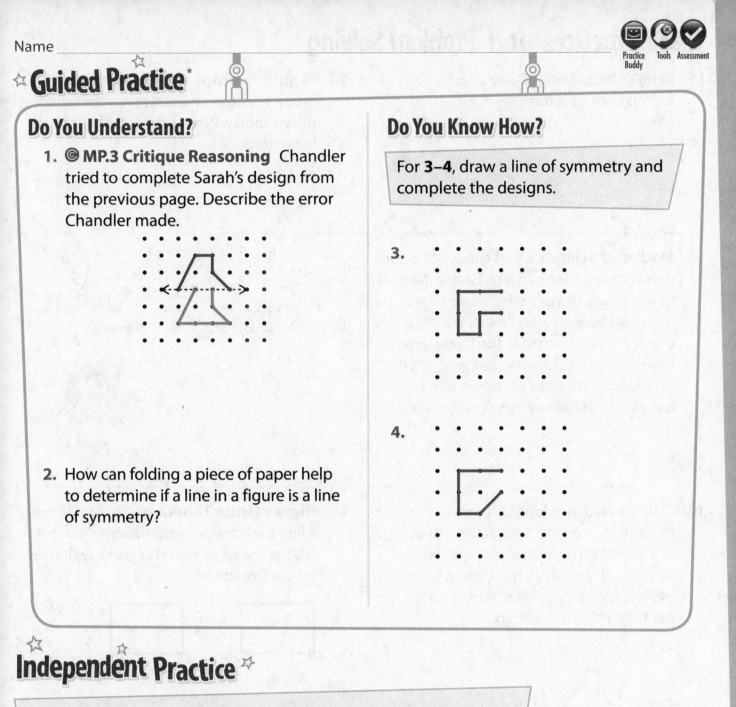

Math Practices and Problem Solving

11. **© MP.2 Reasoning** Draw a figure that has no lines of symmetry.

12. **© MP.2 Reasoning** Vanessa drew a figure that has an infinite number of lines of symmetry. What figure could Vanessa have drawn?

13. **Math and Science** Dogs can smell odors that humans cannot. Dogs can be trained to alert their owners when they smell odors associated with illness. If a dog trains 2 hours every day for 1 year, how many hours has the dog trained? What do the total number of training hours equal in days? About how many weeks?

> Remember, there are 365 days in a year, 24 hours in a day, and 7 days in a week.

14. Clare trained for a long distance marathon. She ran a total of 225 miles in 3 months. The first month she ran 50 miles. If she ran 25 more miles each month, how many miles did she run in her third month of training?

15. **Higher Order Thinking** Can you draw a line that divides a figure in half, but is **NOT** a line of symmetry? Use the figures below to explain.

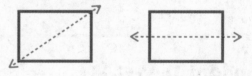

© Common Core Assessment

16. Which of the following figures is symmetric about the dashed line?

Ⓐ   Ⓑ   Ⓒ   Ⓓ

© Pearson Education, Inc. 4

Homework & Practice 16-5

Draw Shapes with Line Symmetry

Another Look!

You can use dot paper to draw line-symmetric figures.

How to draw a line-symmetric figure:

Step 1

Draw a figure on dot paper.

Step 2

Draw a line of symmetry.

Step 3

Complete the figure on the opposite side of the line of symmetry.

For **1–6**, use the line of symmetry to draw a line-symmetric figure.

1.

2.

3.

4.

5.

6.

7. **MP.2 Reasoning** Draw a quadrilateral that has no lines of symmetry.

8. **MP.4 Model with Math** Draw a figure with exactly 2 lines of symmetry.

9. A storage compartment for a gym locker room can hold up to 7 folded towels. There are 22 compartments for towels. Katie has 150 towels to fold and put away. How many of the compartments will be filled? How many towels will be in a compartment that is not completely filled?

10. **MP.4 Model with Math** James bought $175 in accessories for his video game console. He spent $15 on a new power cord and the rest of his money on 5 new video games. Each video game cost the same amount. Write two equations you could use to find the cost of each video game.

11. Create a line symmetric figure. Draw half of a figure. Then draw a line of symmetry. Complete your figure on the opposite side of the line of symmetry.

12. **A-Z Vocabulary** Describe the difference between *parallel* and *intersecting lines*.

13. **Higher Order Thinking** Draw a figure that has both horizontal and vertical symmetry.

Common Core Assessment

14. Which of the following figures has 4 lines of symmetry? Draw lines as needed.

Ⓐ   Ⓑ   Ⓒ   Ⓓ

© Pearson Education, Inc. 4

Name _____

☆ ☆
Solve & Share

Nathan gave the answer shown to the following question. True or False? All right triangles have two sides the same length. How do you respond to Nathan's reasoning?

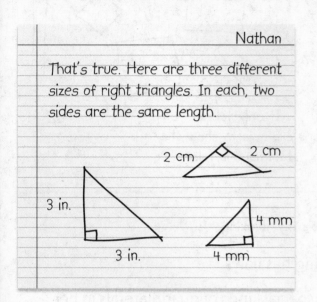

Nathan

That's true. Here are three different sizes of right triangles. In each, two sides are the same length.

2 cm — 2 cm

3 in.

3 in.

4 mm

4 mm

I can ...
critique the reasoning of others by using what I know about two-dimensional shapes.

© **Mathematical Practices** MP.3 Also MP.1, MP.2, MP.6, MP.7
Content Standard 4.G.A.2

Thinking Habits
Be a good thinker!
These questions can help you.

- What questions can I ask to understand other people's thinking?

- Are there mistakes in other people's thinking?

- Can I improve other people's thinking?

Look Back! © **MP.3 Critique Reasoning** If Nathan had drawn even more triangles, would it show that the statement is true? Explain.

A

Abby gave the answer shown to the following question.

True or False? Every quadrilateral has at least one right angle.

What is Abby's reasoning to support her statement?

Abby drew quadrilaterals that have right angles.

Abby

True. Here are different quadrilaterals. They all have four sides and four right angles.

It only takes one example to show the statement is false.

B

How can I critique the reasoning of others?

I can

- ask questions about Abby's reasoning.

- look for flaws in her reasoning.

- decide whether all cases have been considered.

C

Here's my thinking.

Abby's reasoning has flaws.

She used only special kinds of quadrilaterals in her argument. For these special cases, the statement is true.

Here is a quadrilateral that has no right angles. It shows the statement is not true about **every** quadrilateral.

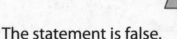

The statement is false.

Convince Me! © **MP.6 Be Precise** Would Abby's reasoning be correct if the question was changed to: True or False? Some quadrilaterals have at least one right angle. Explain.

☆ Guided Practice *

© **MP.3 Critique Reasoning**

Anthony said all multiples of 4 end in 2, 4 or 8. He gave 4, 8, 12, 24, and 28 as examples.

1. What is Anthony's argument? How does he support it?

2. Describe at least one thing you could do to critique Anthony's reasoning.

3. Does Anthony's reasoning make sense? Explain.

Independent Practice ☆

© **MP.3 Critique Reasoning**

Marista said the polygons shown all have the same number of angles as they have sides.

4. Describe at least one thing you could do to critique Marista's reasoning.

5. Does Marista's reasoning make sense? Explain.

> When you critique reasoning, you decide whether or not another student's conclusion is logical.

6. Can you think of any examples that prove Marista wrong? Explain.

Math Practices and Problem Solving

Common Core Performance Assessment

Dog Pen
Caleb is designing a dog pen for the animal shelter. He has 16 feet of fence, including the gate. His designs and explanation are shown. Critique Caleb's reasoning.

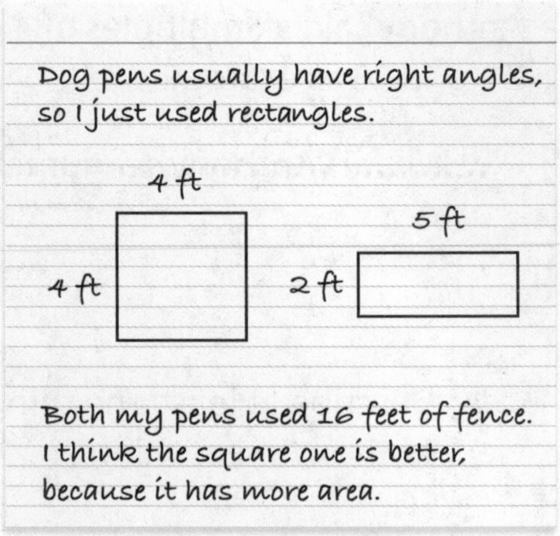

7. **MP.2 Reasoning** What quantities are given in the problem and what do the numbers mean?

8. **MP.3 Critique Reasoning** What can you do to critique Caleb's thinking?

9. **MP.6 Be Precise** Did Caleb correctly calculate the perimeter of each fence? Explain.

10. **MP.3 Critique Reasoning** Does Caleb's reasoning make sense? Explain.

11. **MP.2 Reasoning** Explain how you know what units to use in your explanation.

Dog pens usually have right angles, so I just used rectangles.

4 ft

4 ft

5 ft

2 ft

Both my pens used 16 feet of fence. I think the square one is better, because it has more area.

When you critique reasoning, you ask questions to help understand someone's thinking.

Another Look!

Alisa said all obtuse triangles have acute angles because you cannot draw an obtuse triangle with all obtuse angles. Critique Alisa's reasoning.

Tell how you can critique the reasoning of others.

- I can look for flaws in her reasoning.

- I can decide whether all cases have been considered.

When you critique reasoning, you need to carefully consider all parts of an argument.

Decide whether or not you think Alisa's statement is true. Then, explain why.

Alisa is correct. All obtuse triangles have one obtuse angle that is greater than 90°. The remaining angles are acute. An obtuse triangle cannot have a right angle.

© **MP.3 Critique Reasoning**

Ronnie said that if all of the sides of a polygon have equal length, then all of the angles will have the same measure. He drew the figures shown.

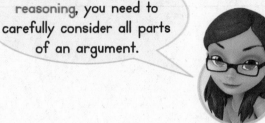

1. Describe at least one thing you could do to critique Ronnie's reasoning.

2. Does Ronnie's reasoning make sense? Explain.

Rachel said the sum of three odd numbers is always odd. She gave the examples shown.

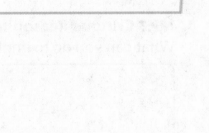

Rachel

$5 + 3 + 7 = 15$

$21 + 33 + 45 = 99$

$127 + 901 + 65 = 1,093$

3. Describe at least one thing you could do to critique Rachel's reasoning

4. Does Rachel's reasoning make sense? Explain.

Common Core Performance Assessment

Designing a Logo

Tamara was asked to design a logo for the Writing Club. The logo needs to be a scalene triangle. Tamara reasons about how to draw the logo. Critique Tamara's reasoning.

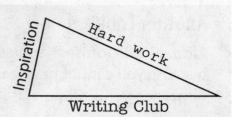

5. MP.1 Make Sense and Persevere What do you know and what do you need to do?

Tamara's Reasoning

A scalene triangle has 3 sides of differing lengths. Each of the angles is acute because I cannot draw a triangle with 3 different right angles or 3 different obtuse angles.

6. MP.3 Critique Reasoning Critique Tamara's reasoning. What can you do to improve her reasoning?

When you critique reasoning you carefully read someone else's argument.

7. MP.7 Use Structure Describe three possible logo designs Tamara could make using a scalene triangle and acute, right, or obtuse angles.

Name _____

Find a Match

Work with a partner. Point to a clue. Read the clue.

Look below the clues to find a match. Write the clue letter in the box next to the match.

Find a match for every clue.

I can ...
add multi-digit whole numbers

© **Content Standard** 4.NBT.B.4

Clues

A The sum is between 650 and 750.

B The sum is between 1,470 and 1,480.

C The sum is exactly 1,550.

D The sum is between 1,350 and 1,450.

E The sum is exactly 790.

F The sum is exactly 1,068.

G The sum is between 1,100 and 1,225.

H The sum is exactly 1,300.

510 240 + 550	225 350 + 125	400 850 + 150	50 390 + 1,110
125 125 225 + 315	475 475 + 175	500 425 325 + 225	500 250 250 + 68

Vocabulary Review

A-Z
Glossary

Understand Vocabulary

Write T for *true* and F for *false*.

1. _____ An acute triangle is a triangle with one acute angle.

2. _____ An isosceles triangle has at least two equal sides.

3. _____ A figure is line symmetric if it has at least one line of symmetry.

4. _____ Perpendicular lines form obtuse angles where they intersect.

5. _____ A trapezoid has two pairs of parallel sides.

Write *always, sometimes,* or *never*.

6. An equilateral triangle _____ has three equal sides.

7. Parallel lines _____ intersect.

8. A scalene triangle _____ has equal sides.

9. A rectangle is _____ a square.

10. A rhombus _____ has opposite sides that are parallel.

Word List

- acute triangle
- equilateral triangle
- intersecting lines
- isosceles triangle
- line of symmetry
- line symmetric
- obtuse triangle
- parallel lines
- parallelogram
- perpendicular lines
- rectangle
- rhombus
- right triangle
- scalene triangle
- square
- trapezoid

Use Vocabulary in Writing

11. Rebecca drew a figure. Describe Rebecca's figure. Use at least 3 terms from the Word List in your description.

Name _____

Set A   pages 821–826

Pairs of lines are given special names: parallel, intersecting, or perpendicular.

$\overleftrightarrow{DE}$ and $\overleftrightarrow{FG}$ are parallel lines.

Reteaching

Remember to use geometric terms when describing what is shown.

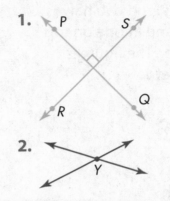

1.

2.

Set B   pages 827–832

Triangles can be classified by their sides and angles.

Two sides are the same length, and each angle measures less than a right angle. It is an isosceles, acute triangle.

Remember to classify each triangle by its sides and then by its angles.

1.

2.

Set C   pages 833–838

Name the quadrilateral.

Opposite sides are parallel. There are no right angles. All sides are not the same length. It is a parallelogram.

Remember that a quadrilateral can be a rectangle, square, trapezoid, parallelogram, or rhombus.

Write all the names possible for each quadrilateral.

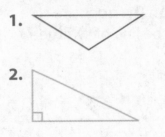

1.

2.

Set D pages 839–844

How many lines of symmetry does the figure have?

Fold the figure along the dashed line. The two halves are equal and fit one on top of the other. The figure is line symmetric.

It has 1 line of symmetry.

Remember that figures can have many lines of symmetry.

Draw and tell how many lines of symmetry for each figure.

1.

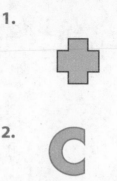

2.

Set E pages 845–850

Complete a design with line symmetry.

Draw a line of symmetry for the shape.

Complete the design on the opposite side of the line of symmetry.

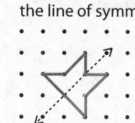

Remember, for a figure to be line symmetric, it must have a line of symmetry.

Draw a line of symmetry and complete the designs.

1.   2.

Set F pages 851–856

Think about these questions to help you **critique the reasoning** of others.

Thinking Habits

Be a good thinker! These questions can help you.

- What questions can I ask to understand other people's thinking?

- Are there mistakes in other people's thinking?

- Can I improve other people's thinking?

Remember that it only takes one example to show the statement is false.

Derek says, "All triangles have 1 right angle."

1. Use the figures above to critique Derek's statement.

2. What kinds of triangles do **NOT** have right angles?

Name _____

1. Danica incorrectly thinks a square is an example of a parallelogram, rectangle, rhombus, and trapezoid. Identify the shape that cannot be classified as a square. Explain.

2. Which type of triangle has no equal side lengths?

Ⓐ Isosceles

Ⓑ Equilateral

Ⓒ Scalene

Ⓓ None of the above

3. Gavin drew different-colored lines. Draw a line that is parallel to $\overleftrightarrow{SR}$.

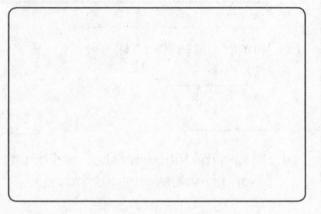

4. Marci described the light from the sun as a line that starts at the sun and continues on forever. Which geometric term best describes Marci's description of the sun's light?

5. Four of Mrs. Cromwell's students decorated a bulletin board with the shapes shown below. Who made a shape with 8 lines of symmetry?

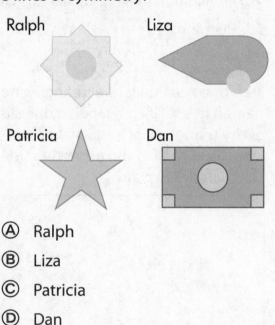

Ⓐ Ralph

Ⓑ Liza

Ⓒ Patricia

Ⓓ Dan

6. Are all intersecting lines perpendicular? Draw a picture to help explain your answer.

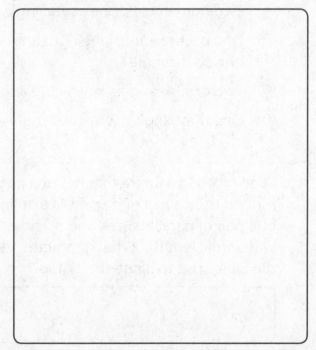

7. For questions 7a–7d, choose Yes or No to tell if each quadrilateral always has opposite sides that are parallel and right angles.

7a. Square   ○ Yes   ○ No

7b. Rhombus   ○ Yes   ○ No

7c. Parallelogram   ○ Yes   ○ No

7d. Rectangle   ○ Yes   ○ No

8. Fran drew an equilateral triangle and named it ABC. If Fran labeled one side of the triangle 4 inches, what are the lengths of each of the other two sides of the triangle? Explain.

9. Which set of angles could form a triangle?

   Ⓐ   Two right angles, one acute angle

   Ⓑ   One obtuse angle, one right angle, one acute angle

   Ⓒ   Two obtuse angles, one acute angle

   Ⓓ   One right angle, two acute angles

10. Lance named a figure that has one angle formed from a pair of perpendicular lines, one pair of parallel sides, and no sides with equal lengths. What geometric term did Lance use to name this figure?

11. Dina's teacher asks her to describe the top and bottom edges of her ruler using a geometric term. What term could Dina use?

12. Tanner chose these shapes.

He said the following shapes did not belong with the ones he chose.

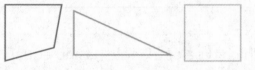

What generalization can be made about the shapes Tanner chose?

13. Complete the drawing so the figure is line symmetric.

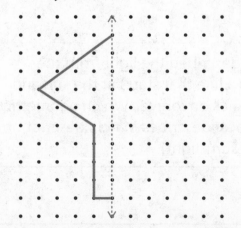

Ottoman Art

The Ottoman Empire lasted from 1299 until 1922.
Much of the art from this period contained geometric shapes.

© **Performance Assessment**

1. Use the **Ottoman Empire** figure to answer the following.

Part A

Name a pair of parallel lines and explain why the lines
are parallel.

Ottoman Empire

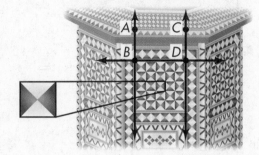

Part B

The enlarged part of the figure shows 4 triangles that
are all the same type. Classify these triangles by their
sides and by their angles. Explain.

Part C

Olivia said the 4 triangles were inside a square. When
asked other possible names for the square, she said it was
a quadrilateral, a parallelogram, and a rectangle. Critique
Olivia's reasoning.

2. The basic shape used in the **Ottoman Scarf** is a quadrilateral. Answer the following about this shape.

Part A

What are all the names you can use for this quadrilateral? Explain.

Part B

Corbin said the triangle named WXY is acute because it has acute angles. Critique Corbin's reasoning.

Part C

Draw all lines of symmetry on the **Decorative Plate**. How many lines of symmetry does the plate have? Explain why the plate is line symmetric.

Decorative Plate

© Pearson Education, Inc. 4

Step Up to Grade 5

Here's a preview of next year. These lessons help you step up to Grade 5.

Lessons

1 Understand Decimal Place Value 5.NBT.A.3a 867

2 Compare Decimals 5.NBT.A.3b 871

3 Use Models to Add and
Subtract Decimals 5.NBT.B.7 875

4 Estimate the Product of a Decimal
and a Whole Number 5.NBT.B.7 879

5 Find Common Denominators 5.NF.A.1, 5.NF.A.2 ... 883

6 Add Fractions with
Unlike Denominators 5.NF.A.1, 5.NF.A.2 887

7 Subtract Fractions with
Unlike Denominators 5.NF.A.1, 5.NF.A.2 891

8 Multiply Fractions and
Whole Numbers 5.NF.B.4a 895

9 Divide Whole Numbers by Unit Fractions
5.NF.B.7b, 5.NF.B.7c 899

10 Model Volume 5.MD.C.3a, 5.MD.C.3b,
5.MD.C.4 903

Name _____

Step Up to Grade 5

Lesson 1
Understand Decimal Place Value

I can ...
read and write decimals in
different ways.

© Content Standard 5.NBT.A.3a
Mathematical Practices MP.1, MP.2, MP.4,
MP.7, MP.8

Solve & Share

A runner won a 100-meter race with a
time of 9.85 seconds. How can you use place value
to explain this time? Complete a place-value chart to
show this time.

Generalize
You can use what you know
about whole-number place value
to help you understand decimal
place value.

Look Back! © **MP.7 Use Structure** In the decimal 9.85,
what is the value of the 8? the value of the 5?

Essential Question **How Can You Represent Decimals?**

A

Jo picked a seed from her flower. The seed has a mass of 0.245 gram. What are some different ways you can represent 0.245?

You can write the standard form, expanded form, and number name for a decimal just like you can for a whole number.

B

ones		tenths	hundredths	thousandths
0	.	2	4	5

A place-value chart can help you identify the tenths, hundredths, and thousandths place in a decimal.

Standard Form: 0.245

└─ The 5 is in the thousandths place. Its value is 0.005.

Expanded Form:

$$\left(2 \times \frac{1}{10}\right) + \left(4 \times \frac{1}{100}\right) + \left(5 \times \frac{1}{1,000}\right)$$

Number Name: two hundred forty-five thousandths

Convince Me! © **MP.2 Reasoning** How many hundredths are in one tenth? How many thousandths are in one hundredth? Tell how you know.

Tools Assessment

Another Example

Equivalent decimals name the same amount.

What are two other decimals equivalent to 1.4?

One and four tenths is the same as one and forty hundredths.

$$1.4 = 1.40$$

One and four tenths is the same as one and four hundred thousandths.

$$1.4 = 1.400$$

So, 1.4 = 1.40 = 1.400.

1 hundredth is equal to 10 thousandths.

1 whole

4 columns = 4 tenths
40 small squares = 40 hundredths
40 hundredths = 400 thousandths

☆ Guided Practice

Do You Understand?

1. © MP.2 Reasoning The number 2.452 has two 2s. Why does each 2 have a different value?

Do You Know How?

For **2–3**, write each number in standard form.

2. 5 + 0.5 + 0.03 + 0.006

3. two and sixty-nine thousandths

Independent Practice

For **4–6**, write each number in standard form.

4. $(3 \times 1) + \left(6 \times \frac{1}{100}\right)$

5. $(7 \times 1) + \left(3 \times \frac{1}{10}\right) + \left(4 \times \frac{1}{1,000}\right)$

6. five and twenty hundredths

For **7–10**, write two decimals that are equivalent to the given decimal.

7. 3.300

8. 9.1

9. 9.60

10. 4.400

Math Practices and Problem Solving

11. **MP.4 Model with Math** The annual fundraising goal of a college is $100,000. So far $58,743 has been raised. How much more money is needed to reach the goal?

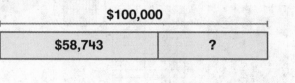

12. Trisha has a ribbon that measures $\left(5 \times \frac{1}{10}\right) + \left(3 \times \frac{1}{100}\right) + \left(5 \times \frac{1}{1,000}\right)$ meter. How can this measurement be written as a decimal?

13. **MP.2 Reasoning** How can you tell that 4.620 and 4.62 are equivalent decimals?

14. **MP.1 Make Sense and Persevere** During a sports assembly, 0.555 students wore something blue. The rest of the students wore something red. If there were 1,000 students at the assembly, how many were wearing blue? How many red?

15. Collette incorrectly placed the decimal point when she wrote 0.065 inch for the width of her tablet. What is the correct decimal number for the width?

16. **Higher Order Thinking** Meg shades 1 whole and $\frac{1}{10}$, Corky shades $\frac{1}{2}$, and Derek does not shade a grid. Shade the grids to show the fractions. What decimal represents the amount each student shades?

Common Core Assessment

17. Find two decimals that are equivalent to $(6 \times 10) + \left(5 \times \frac{1}{100}\right)$. Write the decimals in the box.

| 60.5 | 60.05 | 6.5 | 60.050 | 6.50 | 60.50 |

Name _____

☆ Solve & Share ☆

The lengths of three ants were measured in a laboratory. The lengths were 0.521 centimeter, 0.498 centimeter, and 0.550 centimeter. Which ant was the longest? Which ant was the shortest?

Step Up to Grade 5

Lesson 2
Compare Decimals

I can ...
compare decimals to the thousandths.

© Content Standard 5.NBT.A.3b
Mathematical Practices MP.3, MP.6, MP.7

How can you use structure to compare and order the decimals? Tell how you decided.

ones   tenths   hundredths   thousandths

Look Back! © MP.6 Be Precise What are the lengths of the ants in order from least to greatest?

Essential Question: How Can You Compare Decimals?

A

Scientists collected and measured the lengths of different cockroach species. Which cockroach had the greater length, the American or the Oriental cockroach?

Comparing decimals is like comparing whole numbers!

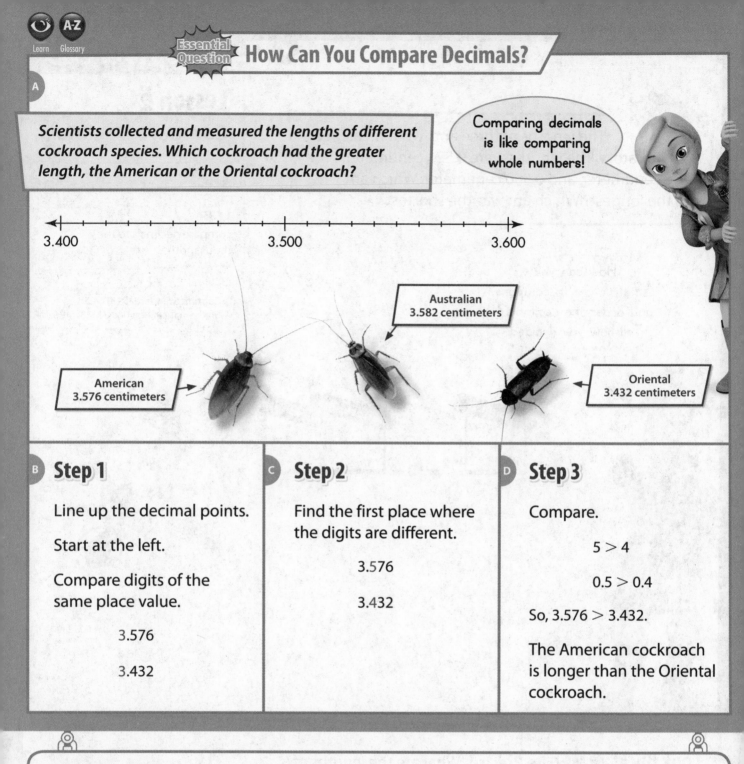

3.400   3.500   3.600

Australian
3.582 centimeters

American
3.576 centimeters

Oriental
3.432 centimeters

B **Step 1**

Line up the decimal points.

Start at the left.

Compare digits of the same place value.

   3.576

   3.432

C **Step 2**

Find the first place where the digits are different.

   3.576

   3.432

D **Step 3**

Compare.

   5 > 4

   0.5 > 0.4

So, 3.576 > 3.432.

The American cockroach is longer than the Oriental cockroach.

Convince Me! © **MP.3 Critique Reasoning** Valerie said, "12.68 is greater than 12.8 because 68 is greater than 8." Is she correct? Explain.

Another Example

Order the cockroaches from least to greatest length.

Step 1

Write the numbers, lining up the decimal points. Start at the left. Compare digits of the same place value.

3.576
3.432
3.582

3.432 is the least.

Step 2

Write the remaining numbers, lining up the decimal points. Start at the left. Compare.

3.576
3.582

3.582 is greater than 3.576.

Step 3

Write the numbers from least to greatest.

3.432   3.576   3.582

From least to greatest lengths are the Oriental, the American, and the Australian.

☆ Guided Practice

Do You Understand?

1. © MP.3 Critique Reasoning Scientists measured a Madeira cockroach and found it to be 3.44 centimeters long. Toby says that the Madeira is shorter than the Oriental because 3.44 has fewer digits than 3.438. Is he correct? Explain.

Do You Know How?

For **2–3**, write >, <, or = for each ◯.

2. 2.345 ◯ 3.509   3. 7.317 ◯ 7.203

For **4–5**, order the decimals from least to greatest.

4. 4.540, 4.631, 4.625

5. 0.575, 1.429, 1.35, 0.593

Independent Practice ☆

For **6–8**, compare the two numbers. Write >, <, or = for each ◯.

6. 0.790 ◯ 0.79   7. 5.783 ◯ 4.692   8. 6.717 ◯ 6.718

For **9–10**, order the decimals from greatest to least.

9. 606.314, 606.219, 616.208   10. 234.639, 219.646, 234.630

Math Practices and Problem Solving

11. © **MP.3 Critique Reasoning** Explain why it is not reasonable to say that 6.24 is less than 6.231 because 6.24 has fewer digits after the decimal point than 6.231.

12. **Number Sense** Krystal wrote three numbers between 0.63 and 0.64. What numbers could Krystal have written?

13. **A-Z** **Vocabulary** Write an *equivalent decimal* for each given decimal.

0.85 _____

1.6 _____

2.07 _____

1.02 _____

14. Is 0.6 greater than or less than $\frac{7}{10}$? Draw a number line to show your answer.

15. **Higher Order Thinking** Team Spirit's cheerleading scores were posted on the scoreboard in order from highest to lowest score. One digit in the team's dance score is not visible. List all the possible digits for the missing number.

16. Team Extreme's jumps score is 95.050. How does it compare to Team Spirit's jumps score?

Team Spirit's Scores	
Jumps	95.500
Dance	95._66
Stunts	95.133
Pyramid	94.200

DATA

© **Common Core Assessment**

17. A grain of fine sand can have a diameter of 0.120 millimeter. Which numbers are less than 0.120?

☐ 0.1

☐ 0.10

☐ 0.121

☐ 0.122

☐ 0.126

18. Kara weighed some oranges at the grocery store. The oranges weighed 4.16 pounds. Which numbers are greater than 4.16?

☐ 4.15

☐ 4.19

☐ 4.2

☐ 4.24

☐ 4.26

Name _____

★ ☆ ★
Solve & Share

Gloria rode her bicycle 0.75 mile in the morning and 1.10 miles in the afternoon. How many miles did Gloria ride in all? *Solve this problem any way you choose.*

You can use appropriate tools, such as decimal grids, to help determine how many miles Gloria rode.

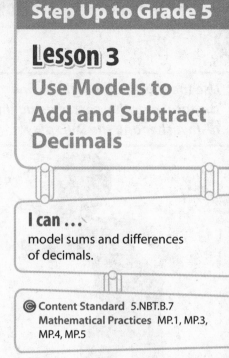

Lesson 3
Use Models to Add and Subtract Decimals

I can ...
model sums and differences of decimals.

© **Content Standard** 5.NBT.B.7
Mathematical Practices MP.1, MP.3, MP.4, MP.5

Look Back! © **MP.1 Make Sense and Persevere** How can you check that your answer is correct?

Essential Question **How Can You Use Grids to Add Decimals?**

A

Use the table at the right to find the total monthly cost of using the dishwasher and the DVD player.

A model can be used to add decimals.

DATA	Device	Monthly Cost
	DVD player	$0.40
	Microwave oven	$3.57
	Ceiling light	$0.89
	Dishwasher	$0.85

B

Use hundredths grids to add $0.85 + $0.40.

It costs $0.85 to use the dishwasher per month.

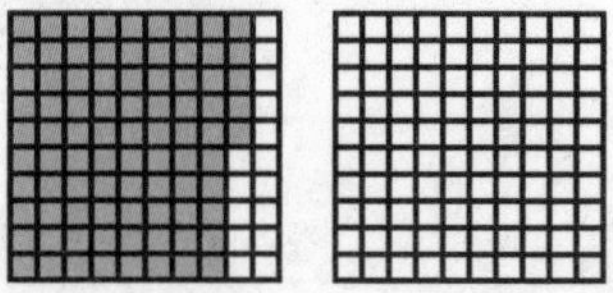

Shade 85 squares to show $0.85.

C

It costs $0.40 to use the DVD player per month.

Use a different color and shade 40 more squares to show $0.40. Count all of the shaded squares to find the sum.

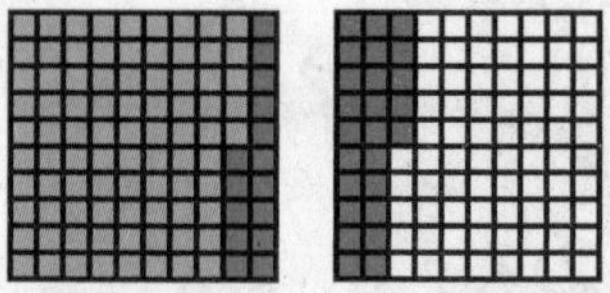

$0.85 + $0.40 = $1.25

The monthly cost of using the dishwasher and DVD player is $1.25.

Convince Me! © **MP.3 Critique Reasoning** For the example above, Jesse said, "The total monthly cost of using the ceiling light and the dishwasher was $0.74." Is Jesse correct? Explain.

Another Example

You can subtract decimals with grids.

Use hundredths grids to find 1.57 − 0.89.

Step 1

Shade 1 grid and 57 squares to show 1.57.

Step 2

Cross out 8 columns and 9 squares of the shaded grid. The difference is the squares that are shaded but not crossed out.

1.57 − 0.89 = 0.68

☆ Guided Practice

Do You Understand?

1. © **MP.4 Model with Math** Explain how to use grids to find the difference between the monthly cost of using the DVD player and the dishwasher. Then find the difference.

Do You Know How?

For **2–7**, use hundredths grids to add or subtract.

2. 1.45 + 0.37   3. 0.89 + 0.41

4. 4.89 − 0.94   5. $1.45 − $0.76

6. 0.41 − 0.37   7. 2.28 + 0.6

Independent Practice ☆

For **8–11**, add or subtract. Use hundredths grids to help.

8. 0.2 + 0.73   9. $1.33 − $0.25   10. $0.37 + $0.57   11. 1.01 + 0.99

Math Practices and Problem Solving

12. © **MP.3 Construct Arguments** How is adding 5.51 + 2.31 similar to adding $2.31 + $5.51?

13. © **MP.4 Model with Math** Write an expression that is represented by the model below.

14. Is the sum of 0.57 + 0.31 less than or greater than one? Explain.

15. **Number Sense** Estimate to decide if the sum of 321 + 267 is more or less than 600.

16. **Higher Order Thinking** Do you think the difference of 1.45 − 0.97 is less than one or greater than one? Explain.

17. ⒶⓏ **Vocabulary** Estimate 53.7 − 27.5. Circle the *compatible numbers* to substitute.

54 − 28   53 − 28   55 − 27   55 − 25

18. **Algebra** Write an expression that can be used to find the perimeter of the pool shown to the right. Remember, perimeter is the distance around a figure.

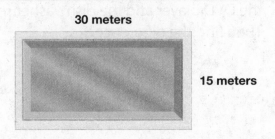

30 meters

15 meters

© **Common Core Assessment**

19. Each shaded area in the grids below represents a decimal.

Part A

What is the sum of the decimals?

Part B

Explain how you found your answer.

Name _____

Solve

Solve & Share

Renee needs 32 strands of twine for an art project. Each strand must be 1.25 centimeters long. About how many centimeters of twine does she need? *Solve this problem any way you choose!*

Generalize
How can you relate what you know about estimating with whole numbers to estimating with decimals? *Show your work!*

I can ...
use rounding and compatible numbers to estimate the product of a decimal and a whole number.

Ⓒ Content Standard 5.NBT.B.7
Mathematical Practices MP.2, MP.6, MP. 8

Look Back! Ⓒ **MP.2 Reasoning** Is your estimate an overestimate or an underestimate? How can you tell?

What Are Some Ways to Estimate Products with Decimals?

Essential Question

A

A wedding planner needs to buy 16 pounds of sliced cheddar cheese. About how much will the cheese cost?

You can use different strategies to estimate a product.

The words *about how much* mean you only need an estimate.

$2.15 per pound

B ## One Way

Round each number to the nearest dollar and nearest ten.

$$\$2.15 \times 16$$
$$\downarrow \qquad \downarrow$$
$$\$2 \quad \times \quad 20$$

$\$2 \times 20 = \$40$

The cheese will cost about $40.

C ## Another Way

Use compatible numbers that you can multiply mentally.

$$\$2.15 \times 16$$
$$\downarrow \qquad \downarrow$$
$$\$2 \quad \times \quad 15$$

$\$2 \times 15 = \$30$

The cheese will cost about $30.

Convince Me! © **MP.2 Reasoning** About how much money would 18 pounds of cheese cost if the price is $3.95 per pound? Use two different ways to estimate the product. Are your estimates overestimates or underestimates? Explain.

Another Example

Manuel walks a total of 0.75 mile to and from school each day. If there have been 105 school days so far this year, about how many miles has he walked in all?

Round to the nearest whole number.

105×0.75

$\downarrow \qquad \downarrow$

$105 \times 1 = 105$

Use compatible numbers.

105×0.75

$\downarrow \qquad \downarrow$

$100 \times 0.8 = 80$

Be sure to place the decimal point correctly.

Both methods provide reasonable estimates of how far Manuel has walked.

☆ Guided Practice

Do You Understand?

1. **Number Sense** There are about 20 school days in a month. About how many miles does Manuel walk each month? Write an equation to show your work.

2. **© MP.2 Reasoning** Without multiplying, which estimate in the Another Example do you think is closer to the exact answer? Explain your reasoning.

Do You Know How?

For **3–8**, estimate each product using rounding or compatible numbers.

3. 2.87×412

4. 943×1.98

5. 107×5.15

6. 4.06×73

7. 41.05×300

8. 8.95×21

Independent Practice ☆

For **9–16**, estimate each product.

9. 119×2.8

10. 4.7×69

11. 107×2.3

12. 35×3.5

13. 1.6×7

14. 9.1×53

15. 39×1.22

16. 4×7.8

Math Practices and Problem Solving

17. About how much money does Isaac need to buy 3 bags of balloons and 4 packs of gift bags?

DATA	Party Supply	Cost
	Balloons	$3.95 per bag
	Gift Bags	$7.95 per pack

18. Charlie buys a cake for $23.99 and 6 bags of balloons. About how much money does he spend?

19. Isabel walks 0.83 mile total to and from the library 3 days a week. About how many miles does she walk in 4 weeks?

20. © **MP.6 Be Precise** One basketball weighs 20.2 ounces. The basketball team has a total of 15 basketballs. If each basketball weighs the same, how much do the basketballs weigh in all? Explain.

21. The side lengths of a square measure 25.3 cm. Estimate the area of the square.

22. **Higher Order Thinking** Carol drives 23.5 miles to work and 21.7 miles round trip to school each day, Monday to Friday. How many miles does Carol drive in one week?

© Common Core Assessment

23. Rounding to the nearest tenth, which of the following give an **underestimate**?

- ☐ 38.45 × 1.7
- ☐ 28.54 × 0.74
- ☐ 9.91 × 8.73
- ☐ 78.95 × 1.25
- ☐ 18.19 × 2.28

24. Rounding to the nearest whole number, which of the following give an **overestimate**?

- ☐ 11.7 × 9.4
- ☐ 4.48 × 8.3
- ☐ 13.9 × 0.9
- ☐ 0.63 × 1.5
- ☐ 8.46 × 7.39

Name _____

Solve & Share

Sue wants $\frac{1}{2}$ of a rectangular pan of cornbread. Dena wants $\frac{1}{3}$ of the same pan of cornbread. How should you cut the cornbread so that each girl gets the size portion she wants? *Solve this problem any way you choose.*

I can ...
find common denominators for fractions with unlike denominators.

© **Content Standards** 5.NF.A.1, 5.NF.A.2
Mathematical Practices MP.3, MP.4

Model with Math
You can draw a picture to represent the pan as 1 whole. Then solve. *Show your work!*

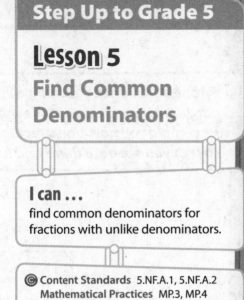

Look Back! © **MP.3 Construct Arguments** Is there more than one way to divide the pan of cornbread into equal-sized parts? Explain how you know.

Essential Question **How Can You Find Common Denominators?**

A

Tyrone partitioned a rectangle into thirds. Sally partitioned a rectangle of the same size into fourths. How could you partition a rectangle of the same size so that you see both thirds and fourths?

You can partition a rectangle to show thirds or fourths.

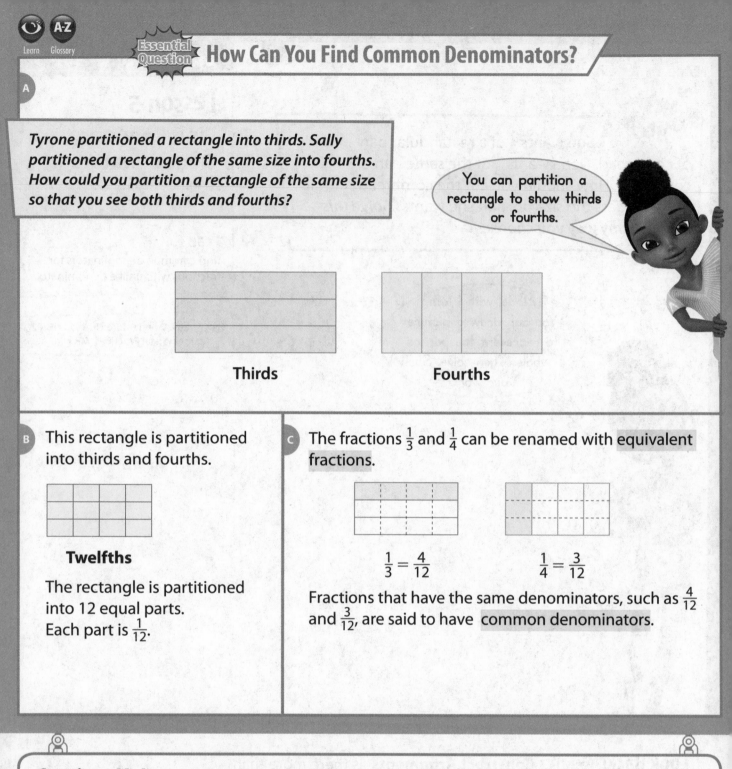

Thirds   **Fourths**

B This rectangle is partitioned into thirds and fourths.

Twelfths

The rectangle is partitioned into 12 equal parts. Each part is $\frac{1}{12}$.

C The fractions $\frac{1}{3}$ and $\frac{1}{4}$ can be renamed with equivalent fractions.

$$\frac{1}{3} = \frac{4}{12}$$ $$\frac{1}{4} = \frac{3}{12}$$

Fractions that have the same denominators, such as $\frac{4}{12}$ and $\frac{3}{12}$, are said to have common denominators.

Convince Me! © MP.4 Model with Math Draw rectangles such as the ones above to find fractions equivalent to $\frac{2}{5}$ and $\frac{1}{3}$ that have the same denominator.

Another Example

Find a common denominator for $\frac{7}{12}$ and $\frac{5}{6}$. Then rename each fraction with an equivalent fraction.

One Way

Multiply the denominators to find a common denominator: $12 \times 6 = 72$.

Write equivalent fractions with denominators of 72.

$\frac{7}{12} = \frac{7 \times 6}{12 \times 6} = \frac{42}{72}$ $\frac{5}{6} = \frac{5 \times 12}{6 \times 12} = \frac{60}{72}$

So, $\frac{42}{72}$ and $\frac{60}{72}$ is one way to name $\frac{7}{12}$ and $\frac{5}{6}$ with a common denominator.

Another Way

Think of a number that is a multiple of the other.

You know that 12 is a multiple of 6.

$\frac{5}{6} = \frac{5 \times 2}{6 \times 2} = \frac{10}{12}$

So, $\frac{7}{12}$ and $\frac{10}{12}$ is another way to name $\frac{7}{12}$ and $\frac{5}{6}$ with a common denominator.

☆ Guided Practice

Do You Understand?

1. In the example on the previous page, how many twelfths are in each $\frac{1}{3}$ section of Tyrone's rectangle? How many twelfths are in each $\frac{1}{4}$ section of Sally's rectangle?

Do You Know How?

For **2–3**, find a common denominator for each pair of fractions.

2. $\frac{1}{6}$ and $\frac{1}{2}$ 3. $\frac{2}{3}$ and $\frac{3}{4}$

Independent Practice ☆

For **4–11**, find a common denominator for each pair of fractions. Then write equivalent fractions with the common denominator.

4. $\frac{3}{5}$ and $\frac{3}{8}$ 5. $\frac{5}{8}$ and $\frac{3}{4}$ 6. $\frac{1}{3}$ and $\frac{4}{5}$ 7. $\frac{3}{12}$ and $\frac{9}{8}$

8. $\frac{4}{7}$ and $\frac{1}{2}$ 9. $\frac{4}{5}$ and $\frac{3}{4}$ 10. $\frac{2}{8}$ and $\frac{7}{20}$ 11. $\frac{1}{9}$ and $\frac{2}{3}$

Math Practices and Problem Solving

12. ⓒ **MP.3 Critique Reasoning** Clara says the only common denominator of $\frac{3}{4}$ and $\frac{3}{5}$ is 20. Do you agree? Explain.

13. Higher Order Thinking The least common denominator is the least common multiple of the two denominators. What is the least common denominator of $\frac{3}{4}$ and $\frac{5}{6}$? Explain.

14. ⓒ **MP.4 Model with Math** Gemma bought two cakes that are the same size. The first one was divided into 3 equal sections. The second one was divided into 2 equal sections. Gemma wants to cut the cakes so that there are 6 pieces in each cake. Draw on the pictures to show how Gemma should cut each cake.

15. Number Sense The table shows the price for three different sandwiches sold at a local deli. What are the prices of the sandwiches rounded to the nearest dollar? nearest dime?

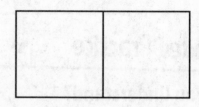

Lunch Menu	
Sandwich	**Price**
Ham	$3.89
Turkey	$4.09
Chicken	$3.79

ⓒ Common Core Assessment

16. Choose all the common denominators for $\frac{1}{3}$ and $\frac{2}{4}$.

- ☐ 8
- ☐ 12
- ☐ 16
- ☐ 36
- ☐ 48

17. Choose all the common denominators for $\frac{2}{3}$ and $\frac{4}{5}$.

- ☐ 12
- ☐ 15
- ☐ 30
- ☐ 60
- ☐ 72

Name _____

☆ ☆
Solve & Share

Over the weekend, Eleni ate $\frac{1}{4}$ box of cereal, and Freddie ate $\frac{3}{8}$ of the same box. What portion of the box of cereal did they eat in all?

I can ...
add fractions with unlike denominators.

© Content Standards 5.NF.A.1, 5.NF.A.2
Mathematical Practices MP.1, MP.3, MP.4, MP.5

$\frac{3}{8}$

$\frac{1}{4}$

Use Appropriate Tools
You can use fraction strips to represent adding fractions. *Show your work!*

Look Back! © **MP.1 Make Sense and Persevere**
What steps did you take to solve this problem?

A

Alex rode his scooter from his house to the park. Later, he rode from the park to baseball practice. How far did Alex ride?

You can add to find the total distance that Alex rode his scooter.

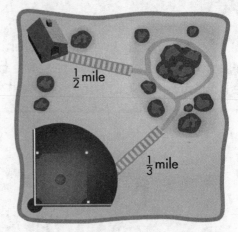

$\frac{1}{2}$ mile

$\frac{1}{3}$ mile

B **Step 1**

Change the fractions to equivalent fractions with a common, or like, denominator.

1

$\frac{1}{2}$	$\frac{1}{3}$

Multiples of 2: 2, 4, 6, 8, 10, 12, . . .

Multiples of 3: 3, 6, 9, 12, . . .

The number 6 is a common multiple of 2 and 3, so $\frac{1}{2}$ and $\frac{1}{3}$ can both be rewritten with a common denominator of 6.

C **Step 2**

Write equivalent fractions with a common denominator.

1

$\frac{1}{2}$	$\frac{1}{3}$

$\frac{1}{6}$	$\frac{1}{6}$	$\frac{1}{6}$	$\frac{1}{6}$	$\frac{1}{6}$

$\frac{1}{2} \times \frac{3}{3} = \frac{3}{6}$

$\frac{1}{3} \times \frac{2}{2} = \frac{2}{6}$

D **Step 3**

Add the fractions to find the total number of sixths.

$$\begin{array}{r} \frac{1}{2} = \frac{3}{6} \\ + \frac{1}{3} = \frac{2}{6} \\ \hline \frac{5}{6} \end{array}$$

Alex rode his scooter $\frac{5}{6}$ mile.

Convince Me! © MP.3 Construct Arguments In the example above, would you get the same sum if you used 12 as the common denominator? Explain.

Another Example

Find $\frac{5}{12} + \frac{1}{4}$.

$$\frac{5}{12} + \frac{1}{4} = \frac{5}{12} + \frac{3}{12}$$ Write equivalent fractions with common denominators.

$$= \frac{5 + 3}{12} = \frac{8}{12} \text{ or } \frac{2}{3}$$ Find the total number of twelfths by adding the numerators.

☆ Guided Practice

Do You Understand?

1. In the example at the top of page 888, if the park was $\frac{1}{8}$ mile from baseball practice instead of $\frac{1}{3}$ mile, how far would Alex ride his scooter in all?

2. **A-Z Vocabulary** Rico and Nita solved the same problem. Rico got $\frac{6}{8}$ for an answer, and Nita got $\frac{3}{4}$. Which answer is correct? Use the term *equivalent fraction* in your explanation.

Do You Know How?

For **3**, find the sum. Use fraction strips to help.

3. $\frac{1}{2} + \frac{2}{4} = \frac{\square}{\square} + \frac{\square}{\square} = \frac{\square}{\square}$

1		
$\frac{1}{2}$	$\frac{1}{4}$	$\frac{1}{4}$
$\frac{1}{4}$	$\frac{1}{4}$	$\frac{1}{4}$	$\frac{1}{4}$

Independent Practice ☆

For **4–5**, find each sum. Use fraction strips to help.

> Remember that you can use multiples to find a common denominator.

4. $\frac{1}{3} + \frac{1}{4} = \frac{\square}{\square} + \frac{\square}{\square} = \frac{\square}{\square}$

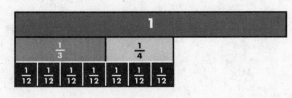

5. $\frac{1}{8} + \frac{1}{4} + \frac{1}{8} =$

$\frac{\square}{\square} + \frac{\square}{\square} + \frac{\square}{\square} = \frac{\square}{\square}$

1		
$\frac{1}{8}$	$\frac{1}{4}$	$\frac{1}{8}$
$\frac{1}{8}$	$\frac{1}{8}$	$\frac{1}{8}$	$\frac{1}{8}$

Math Practices and Problem Solving

6. **MP.3 Construct Arguments** Explain why the denominator 12 in $\frac{5}{12}$ is not changed when adding the fractions.

$$\begin{aligned} \frac{5}{12} &= \frac{5}{12} \\ + \frac{1}{3} &= \frac{4}{12} \\ \hline & \frac{9}{12} \end{aligned}$$

7. **MP.4 Model with Math** To make juice, Cindy added $\frac{5}{8}$ cup of water to $\frac{1}{4}$ cup of juice concentrate. How much juice did Cindy make? Write and solve an equation.

8. **Math and Science** Of 36 chemical elements, 2 are named for women scientists and 25 are named for places. What fraction are named for women? Write two equivalent fractions.

9. **Higher Order Thinking** Alicia is making tropical punch for a picnic. What is the total amount of lemon juice and orange juice Alicia will need? Is this amount more than the amount of sugar she will need? Explain.

Tropical Punch Recipe	
Ingredient	**Amount**
Lemon Juice	$\frac{1}{3}$ cup
Water	4 cups
Sugar	$\frac{2}{3}$ cup
Orange Juice	$\frac{1}{2}$ cup

DATA

Common Core Assessment

10. Choose Yes or No to tell if the fraction $\frac{1}{2}$ will make each equation true.

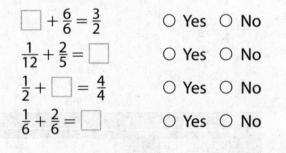

$\square + \frac{6}{6} = \frac{3}{2}$ ○ Yes   ○ No

$\frac{1}{12} + \frac{2}{5} = \square$ ○ Yes   ○ No

$\frac{1}{2} + \square = \frac{4}{4}$ ○ Yes   ○ No

$\frac{1}{6} + \frac{2}{6} = \square$ ○ Yes   ○ No

11. Choose Yes or No to tell if the fraction $\frac{4}{8}$ will make each equation true.

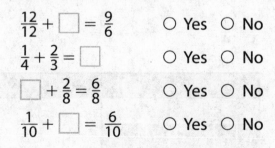

$\frac{12}{12} + \square = \frac{9}{6}$ ○ Yes   ○ No

$\frac{1}{4} + \frac{2}{3} = \square$ ○ Yes   ○ No

$\square + \frac{2}{8} = \frac{6}{8}$ ○ Yes   ○ No

$\frac{1}{10} + \square = \frac{6}{10}$ ○ Yes   ○ No

Name _____

Solve & Share

Rose bought the length of copper pipe shown below. She used $\frac{1}{2}$ yard to repair a water line in her house. How much pipe does she have left? **Solve this problem any way you choose.**

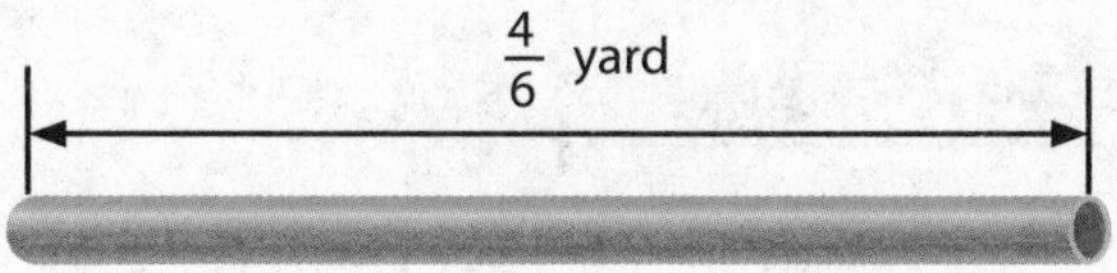

$\frac{4}{6}$ yard

Lesson 7
Subtract Fractions with Unlike Denominators

I can ...
subtract fractions with unlike denominators.

© **Content Standards** 5.NF.A.1, 5.NF.A.2
Mathematical Practices MP.2, MP.3, MP.4, MP.7, MP.8

Use Structure You can use mental math to find equivalent fractions so that $\frac{1}{2}$ and $\frac{4}{6}$ will have like denominators. *Show your work!*

Look Back! © **MP.8 Generalize** How is subtracting fractions with unlike denominators similar to adding fractions with unlike denominators?

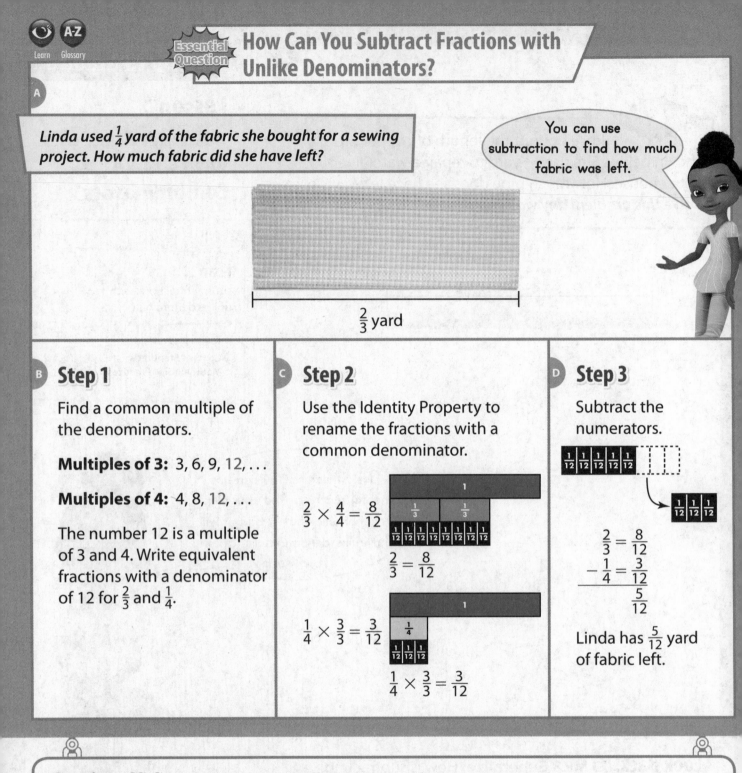

How Can You Subtract Fractions with Unlike Denominators?

A

Linda used $\frac{1}{4}$ yard of the fabric she bought for a sewing project. How much fabric did she have left?

You can use subtraction to find how much fabric was left.

$\frac{2}{3}$ yard

B Step 1

Find a common multiple of the denominators.

Multiples of 3: 3, 6, 9, 12, ...

Multiples of 4: 4, 8, 12, ...

The number 12 is a multiple of 3 and 4. Write equivalent fractions with a denominator of 12 for $\frac{2}{3}$ and $\frac{1}{4}$.

C Step 2

Use the Identity Property to rename the fractions with a common denominator.

$\frac{2}{3} \times \frac{4}{4} = \frac{8}{12}$

$\frac{2}{3} = \frac{8}{12}$

$\frac{1}{4} \times \frac{3}{3} = \frac{3}{12}$

$\frac{1}{4} \times \frac{3}{3} = \frac{3}{12}$

D Step 3

Subtract the numerators.

$\frac{2}{3} = \frac{8}{12}$
$-\frac{1}{4} = \frac{3}{12}$
$\overline{\frac{5}{12}}$

Linda has $\frac{5}{12}$ yard of fabric left.

Convince Me! © **MP.3 Critique Reasoning** Suppose Linda had $\frac{2}{3}$ of a yard of fabric and told Sandra that she used $\frac{3}{4}$ of a yard. Sandra says this is not possible. Do you agree? Explain your answer.

Name _____

☆ Guided Practice

Do You Understand?

1. **© MP.2 Reasoning** In the example on page 892, is it possible to use a common denominator greater than 12 and get the correct answer? Why or why not?

2. In the example on page 892, if Linda had started with 1 yard of fabric and used $\frac{5}{8}$ yard, how much fabric would be left?

Do You Know How?

For **3–6**, find each difference.

3.
$$\frac{3}{4} = \frac{9}{12}$$
$$-\frac{1}{3} = \frac{4}{12}$$

4.
$$\frac{5}{12} = \frac{10}{24}$$
$$-\frac{1}{8} = \frac{3}{24}$$

5.
$$\frac{2}{3}$$
$$-\frac{1}{6}$$

6.
$$\frac{7}{10}$$
$$-\frac{3}{8}$$

☆ Independent Practice ☆

Leveled Practice For **7–16**, find each difference.

7.
$$\frac{3}{5} = \frac{\boxed{}}{10}$$
$$-\frac{3}{10} = \frac{\boxed{}}{10}$$
$$\frac{\boxed{}}{\boxed{}}$$

8.
$$\frac{1}{2} = \frac{\boxed{}}{6}$$
$$-\frac{2}{6} = \frac{\boxed{}}{6}$$
$$\frac{\boxed{}}{\boxed{}}$$

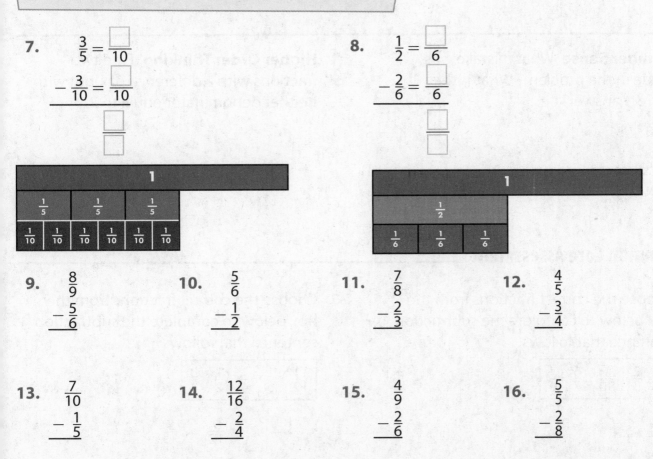

9.
$$\frac{8}{9}$$
$$-\frac{5}{6}$$

10.
$$\frac{5}{6}$$
$$-\frac{1}{2}$$

11.
$$\frac{7}{8}$$
$$-\frac{2}{3}$$

12.
$$\frac{4}{5}$$
$$-\frac{3}{4}$$

13.
$$\frac{7}{10}$$
$$-\frac{1}{5}$$

14.
$$\frac{12}{16}$$
$$-\frac{2}{4}$$

15.
$$\frac{4}{9}$$
$$-\frac{2}{6}$$

16.
$$\frac{5}{5}$$
$$-\frac{2}{8}$$

Math Practices and Problem Solving

17. **© MP.4 Model with Math** Write and solve an equation to find the difference between the location of Point *A* and Point *B* on the ruler.

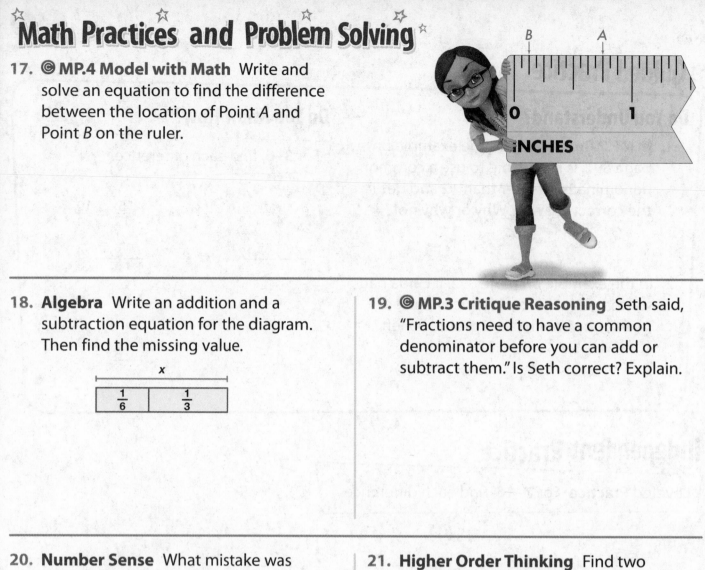

18. **Algebra** Write an addition and a subtraction equation for the diagram. Then find the missing value.

$$x$$

$\frac{1}{6}$	$\frac{1}{3}$

19. **© MP.3 Critique Reasoning** Seth said, "Fractions need to have a common denominator before you can add or subtract them." Is Seth correct? Explain.

20. **Number Sense** What mistake was made in the problem? What is the correct answer?

$$\frac{7}{8} = \frac{7}{8}$$
$$-\frac{1}{4} = \frac{1}{8}$$
$$\overline{\quad \frac{6}{8}}$$

21. **Higher Order Thinking** Find two fractions with a difference of $\frac{1}{2}$ but with neither denominator equal to 2.

© Common Core Assessment

22. Choose the correct fractions from the box below to complete the subtraction sentence that follows.

$\frac{5}{6}$	$\frac{2}{3}$	$\frac{1}{30}$	$\frac{6}{7}$	$\frac{3}{6}$

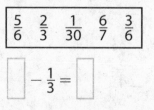

$$\square - \frac{1}{3} = \square$$

23. Choose the correct fractions from the box below to complete the subtraction sentence that follows.

$\frac{11}{12}$	$\frac{1}{6}$	$\frac{1}{4}$	$\frac{1}{2}$	$\frac{3}{4}$

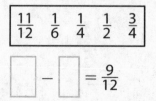

$$\square - \square = \frac{9}{12}$$

Name _____

Solve & Share

Julie has 10 yards of ribbon. She divides the ribbon into 3 equal pieces and uses 2 of the pieces on gifts. How much ribbon does she use? *Solve this problem any way you choose.*

10 yd

I can ...
multiply fractions and whole numbers.

© **Content Standard** 5.NF.B.4a
Mathematical Practices MP.2, MP.3, MP.4, MP.6

Model with Math You can use words, pictures, and equations to solve the problem. *Show your work in the space above!*

Look Back! © **MP.2 Reasoning** Should the answer be less than or greater than 5? How do you know?

Essential Question

How Can You Multiply Fractions and Whole Numbers?

A

Hal spent $\frac{3}{4}$ hour reading each day for 7 days. How much total time did he spend reading?

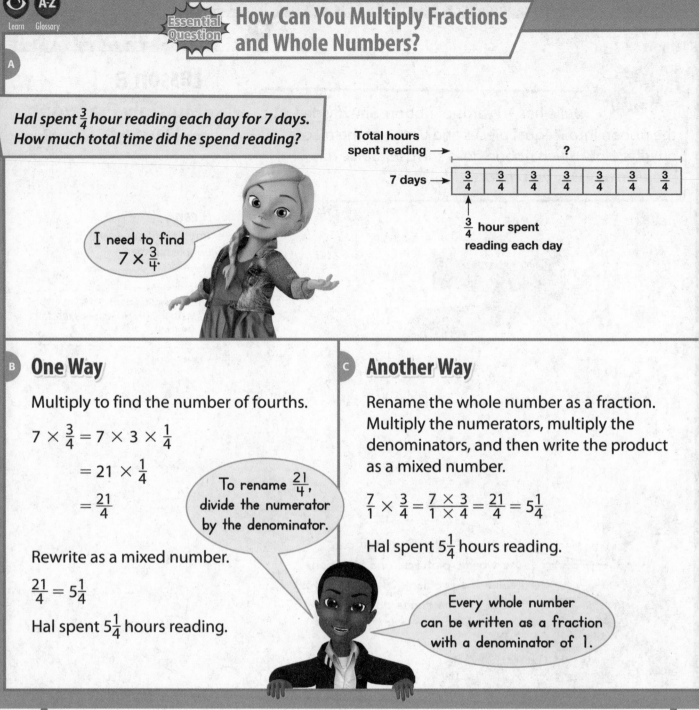

I need to find $7 \times \frac{3}{4}$.

Total hours spent reading → ?

7 days →

| $\frac{3}{4}$ | $\frac{3}{4}$ | $\frac{3}{4}$ | $\frac{3}{4}$ | $\frac{3}{4}$ | $\frac{3}{4}$ | $\frac{3}{4}$ |

$\frac{3}{4}$ hour spent reading each day

B ## One Way

Multiply to find the number of fourths.

$7 \times \frac{3}{4} = 7 \times 3 \times \frac{1}{4}$

$= 21 \times \frac{1}{4}$

$= \frac{21}{4}$

To rename $\frac{21}{4}$, divide the numerator by the denominator.

Rewrite as a mixed number.

$\frac{21}{4} = 5\frac{1}{4}$

Hal spent $5\frac{1}{4}$ hours reading.

C ## Another Way

Rename the whole number as a fraction. Multiply the numerators, multiply the denominators, and then write the product as a mixed number.

$\frac{7}{1} \times \frac{3}{4} = \frac{7 \times 3}{1 \times 4} = \frac{21}{4} = 5\frac{1}{4}$

Hal spent $5\frac{1}{4}$ hours reading.

Every whole number can be written as a fraction with a denominator of 1.

Convince Me! © **MP.6 Be Precise** Find $6 \times \frac{4}{9}$. Then use repeated addition to justify your answer.

Name _____

☆ Guided Practice

Do You Understand?

1. ⓒ **MP.2 Reasoning** In the example at the top of the previous page, how can finding $\frac{1}{4}$ of 7 help you find $\frac{3}{4}$ of 7?

2. If Hal spent $\frac{2}{3}$ of an hour reading each day for 7 days, how much time, in all, did he spend reading? Show how you found your answer.

Do You Know How?

For **3–5**, find each product. Write the product as a mixed number.

3. $\frac{1}{3} \times 18 = \dfrac{\square \times \square}{\square} = \dfrac{\square}{\square} = \square$

4. $\frac{5}{6} \times 35 = \dfrac{\square \times \square}{\square} = \dfrac{\square}{\square} = \square\dfrac{\square}{\square}$

5. $\frac{2}{3} \times 26 = \dfrac{\square \times \square}{\square} = \dfrac{\square}{\square} = \square\dfrac{\square}{\square}$

Independent Practice ☆

Leveled Practice For **6–16**, find each product. Write the product as a mixed number.

Remember: You can use division to rename a fraction as a mixed number.

6. $\frac{3}{5} \times 40 = \dfrac{\square \times \square}{\square}$
$= \dfrac{\square}{\square} = \square$

7. $\frac{7}{8} \times 56 = \dfrac{\square \times \square}{\square}$
$= \dfrac{\square}{\square} = \square$

8. $\frac{2}{3} \times 80 = \dfrac{\square \times \square}{\square}$
$= \dfrac{\square}{\square} = \square\dfrac{\square}{\square}$

9. $\frac{2}{5}$ of 35

10. $\frac{4}{7}$ of 45

11. $\frac{1}{4}$ of 28

12. $\frac{3}{7}$ of 63

13. $\frac{1}{6}$ of 205

14. $\frac{3}{4}$ of 100

15. $\frac{4}{5}$ of 231

16. $\frac{2}{3}$ of 204

Math Practices and Problem Solving

17. On Mars, your weight is about $\frac{1}{3}$ of your weight on Earth. If a fourth grader weighs 96 pounds on Earth, about how much would he or she weigh on Mars?

18. **Number Sense** How can you use mental math to find $25 \times \frac{2}{10}$?

19. During a nature walk, Mary identified 24 species of animals and plants.

   a **© MP.3 Construct Arguments** Mary said $\frac{1}{5}$ of the species she identified were animals. Can this be correct? Explain.

   b If $\frac{1}{3}$ of the species Mary identified were animals, how many plants did Mary identify?

20. A rectangular painting is 3 feet long and $\frac{5}{6}$ foot wide. What is the area of the painting?

21. **Higher Order Thinking** One recipe calls for $\frac{1}{3}$ cup flour per batch and the other calls for $\frac{1}{2}$ cup flour per batch. How much flour will Marcy use if she makes 12 batches of each type of cookie?

22. **Math and Science** A water molecule is made up of 3 atoms. One third of the atoms are oxygen and the remaining atoms are hydrogen. If there are 125 water molecules, how many hydrogen atoms are there? Show your work.

© **Common Core Assessment**

23. Which is the product of 21 and $\frac{3}{7}$?

   Ⓐ $2\frac{3}{7}$

   Ⓑ 5

   Ⓒ 9

   Ⓓ $32\frac{2}{3}$

24. Which is the product of $\frac{11}{12}$ and 3?

   Ⓐ $1\frac{1}{4}$

   Ⓑ $2\frac{3}{4}$

   Ⓒ $4\frac{1}{3}$

   Ⓓ 33

Name _____

Solve & Share

One ball of dough can be stretched into a circle to make a pizza. After the pizza is cooked, it is cut into 8 equal slices. How many slices of pizza can you make with 3 balls of dough? **Solve this problem any way you choose.**

I can ...
divide a whole number by a unit fraction.

© **Content Standards** 5.NF.B.7b, 5.NF.B.7c
Mathematical Practices MP.1, MP.2, MP.4, MP.5

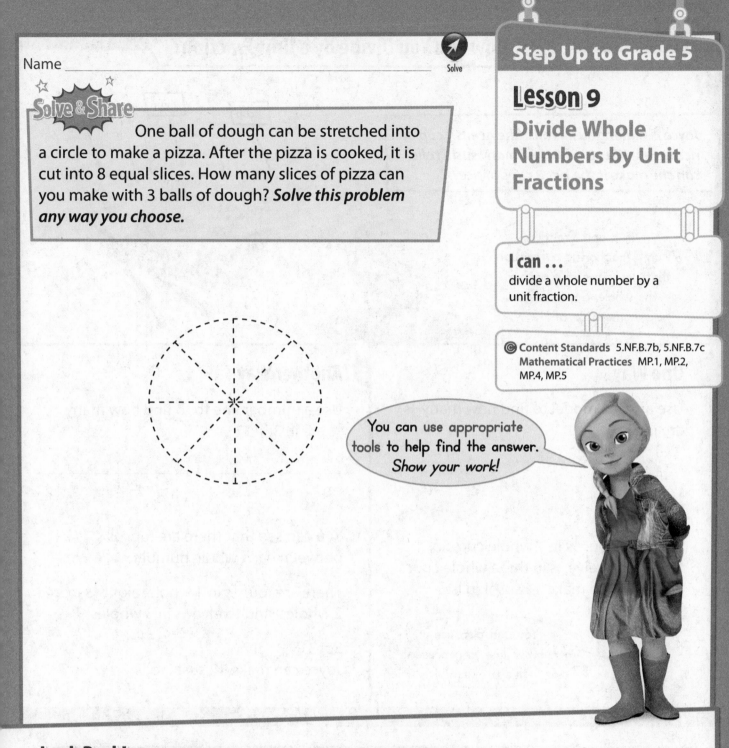

You can use appropriate tools to help find the answer. Show your work!

Look Back! © **MP.2 Reasoning** Into how many slices of pizza will each ball of dough be divided? What fraction of a whole pizza does 1 slice represent?

Essential Question: How Can You Divide by a Unit Fraction?

A

Joyce is making sushi rolls. She needs $\frac{1}{4}$ cup of rice for each sushi roll. How many sushi rolls can she make if she has 3 cups of rice?

1 cup 1 cup 1 cup

$\frac{1}{4}$ is a unit fraction. A unit fraction is a fraction that describes one part of the whole. So, it has a numerator of 1.

B One Way

Use an area model to find how many $\frac{1}{4}$s are in 3.

There are four $\frac{1}{4}$s in 1 whole cup. So, there are twelve $\frac{1}{4}$s in three whole cups. So, Joyce can make 12 sushi rolls.

You can also use a number line to represent this problem.

C Another Way

Use a number line to to find how many $\frac{1}{4}$s are in 3.

$$0 \quad \frac{1}{4} \quad \frac{2}{4} \quad \frac{3}{4} \quad 1 \quad \frac{1}{4} \quad \frac{2}{4} \quad \frac{3}{4} \quad 2 \quad \frac{1}{4} \quad \frac{2}{4} \quad \frac{3}{4} \quad 3$$

You can see that there are four $\frac{1}{4}$s between each whole number.

There are four $\frac{1}{4}$s in 1 whole, eight $\frac{1}{4}$s in 2 wholes, and twelve $\frac{1}{4}$s in 3 wholes.

So, $3 \div \frac{1}{4} = 12$.
Joyce can make 12 sushi rolls.

Convince Me! © MP.4 Model with Math Use the diagram below to find $4 \div \frac{1}{3}$.

$4 \div \frac{1}{3} =$ _____

Name _____

☆Guided Practice

Do You Understand?

1. In the example at the top of page 900, if Joyce had 4 cups of rice, how many rolls could she make?

2. In the example at the top of page 900, how does the number line help to show that $3 \div \frac{1}{4}$ is equal to 3×4?

Do You Know How?

For **3–4**, use the picture below to find each quotient.

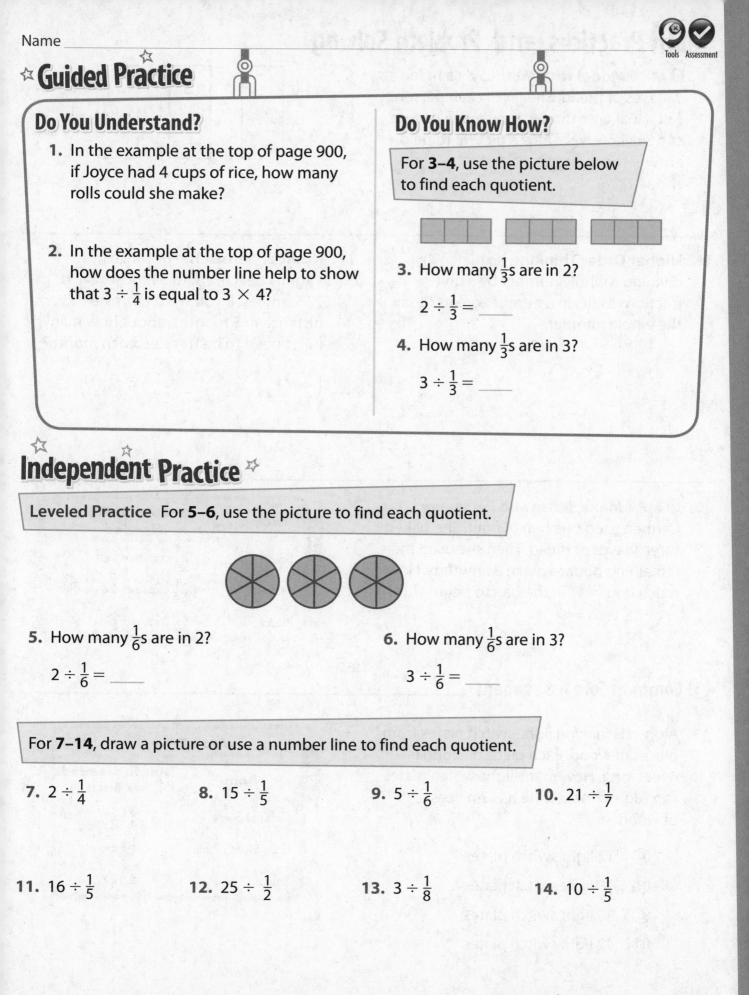

3. How many $\frac{1}{3}$s are in 2?

$2 \div \frac{1}{3} =$ _____

4. How many $\frac{1}{3}$s are in 3?

$3 \div \frac{1}{3} =$ _____

Independent Practice

Leveled Practice For **5–6**, use the picture to find each quotient.

5. How many $\frac{1}{6}$s are in 2?

$2 \div \frac{1}{6} =$ _____

6. How many $\frac{1}{6}$s are in 3?

$3 \div \frac{1}{6} =$ _____

For **7–14**, draw a picture or use a number line to find each quotient.

7. $2 \div \frac{1}{4}$

8. $15 \div \frac{1}{5}$

9. $5 \div \frac{1}{6}$

10. $21 \div \frac{1}{7}$

11. $16 \div \frac{1}{5}$

12. $25 \div \frac{1}{2}$

13. $3 \div \frac{1}{8}$

14. $10 \div \frac{1}{5}$

Math Practices and Problem Solving

15. **MP.4 Model with Math** Sylvia made 3 loaves of bread. She gives each person $\frac{1}{6}$ of a loaf with dinner. How many people can Sylvia serve? Draw a picture to help answer the question.

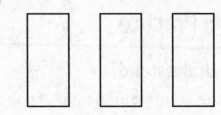

16. **Higher Order Thinking** Explain why dividing a whole number by a unit fraction results in a number greater than the whole number.

17. **Number Sense** The distance from Virginia Beach, VA, to San Jose, CA, is 2,990 miles. If you want to travel this distance in 3 months, about how many miles need to be traveled each month?

18. **MP.1 Make Sense and Persevere** Carmen used one bag of flour. She baked three loaves of bread. Then she used the remaining flour to make 24 muffins. How much flour was in the bag to begin with?

DATA	Recipe	Amount of Flour Needed
	Bread	$2\frac{1}{4}$ cups per loaf
	Muffins	$3\frac{1}{4}$ cups per 24 muffins
	Pizza	$1\frac{1}{2}$ cups per pie

Common Core Assessment

19. Alonso is making light-switch plates from pieces of wood. Each piece of wood is 6 feet long. How many light switch plates can Alonso make if he has 2 pieces of wood?

Ⓐ 12 light switch plates

Ⓑ 18 light switch plates

Ⓒ 36 light switch plates

Ⓓ 42 light switch plates

DATA	Wood Projects	
	Item	Length Needed for Each
	Cabinet Shelf	$\frac{3}{4}$ foot
	Light Switch Plate	$\frac{1}{3}$ foot
	Shingle	$\frac{2}{3}$ foot

Name _____

Solve & Share

Gina is building a rectangular prism out of sugar cubes for her art class project. She started by drawing a diagram of the rectangular prism that is 4 cubes high and 4 cubes long. How many cubes does she use to make the prism? *Solve this problem any way you choose.*

I can ...
find the volume of solid figures.

© Content Standards 5.MD.C.3a, 5.MD.C.3b, 5.MD.C.4
Mathematical Practices MP.2, MP.5

Use Appropriate Tools
You can draw a picture to find the number of cubes in a rectangular prism. *Show your work!*

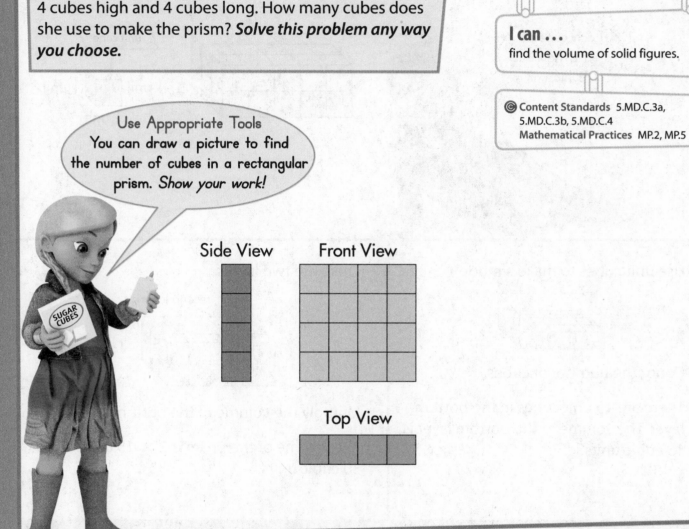

Side View   Front View

Top View

Look Back! © **MP.2 Reasoning** Gina decided to change her art project and build a rectangular prism that is 3 cubes long, 4 cubes wide, and 2 cubes high. Use the picture to determine the number of cubes she used.

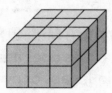

Essential Question **How Can You Measure Space Inside a Solid Figure?**

A

Volume is the number of cubic units needed to pack a solid figure without gaps or overlaps. A cubic unit is the volume of a cube measuring 1 unit on each edge. What is the volume of this rectangular prism?

Each cube of a solid figure is 1 cubic unit.

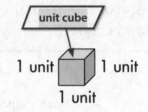

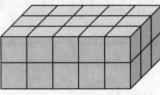

unit cube

1 unit   1 unit

1 unit

B Use unit cubes to make a model.

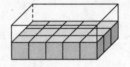

Count the number of cubes.

There are 15 unit cubes in the bottom layer. The volume of the bottom layer is 15 cubic units.

C There are two layers.

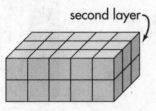

second layer

Multiply the volume of the bottom layer by 2.

The volume of the prism is 2 × 15 or 30 cubic units.

Convince Me! Ⓒ **MP.2 Reasoning** In the picture below, how many unit cubes does it take to make the rectangular prism on the left without gaps or overlaps? How many 2-unit cubes does it take to make the rectangular prism?

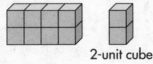

2-unit cube

904   **Step Up** | Lesson 10

Tools Assessment

☆ Guided Practice

Do You Understand?

1. Make a model of a rectangular prism with a bottom layer that is 4 cubes long by 3 cubes wide. Make a top layer that is the same as the bottom layer. Then draw a picture of your model. What is the volume?

2. **A-Z Vocabulary** Describe how to find the *volume* of a *rectangular prism*.

Do You Know How?

For **3–4**, use unit cubes to make a model of each rectangular prism. Find the volume.

3.

4.

☆ Independent Practice ☆

For **5–13**, find the volume of each solid. Use unit cubes to help.

5.

6.

7.

8.

9.

10.

11.

12.

13.

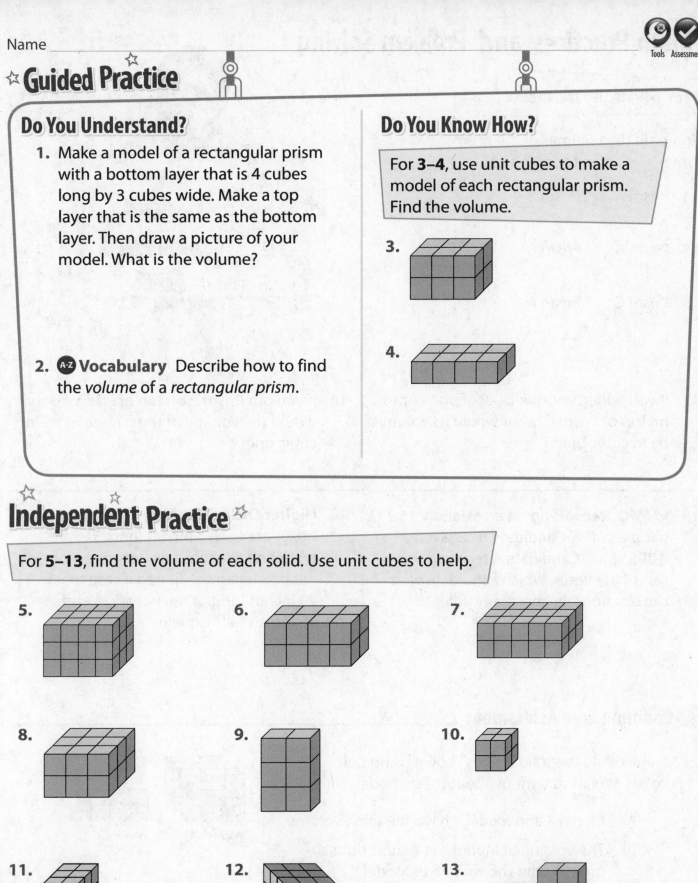

Math Practices and Problem Solving

For **14–18**, use the table.

Compare the volumes of the prisms.
Write >, <, or = for each ◯.

14. Prism A ◯ Prism B

15. Prism B ◯ Prism C

16. Prism C ◯ Prism A

Prism	Model
A	
B	
C	

17. If you added another layer of unit cubes on top of Prism C, what would its volume be in cubic units?

18. If you put Prism C on top of Prism A, what would the volume of the new solid be in cubic units?

19. © **MP.2 Reasoning** In an election, 15,392 people voted. Candidate B received 8,205 votes. Candidate A received the rest of the votes. Which candidate won the election? By how many votes?

20. **Higher Order Thinking** Ms. Smith's boxes are each 5 inches long, 5 inches wide, and 5 inches tall. How many of her boxes can she fit into a case that is 20 inches long, 20 inches wide, and 20 inches tall? Explain.

© Common Core Assessment

21. Frank made the solid figures shown using unit cubes. Which statement about these models is true?

Model X   Model Y

Ⓐ Model X and Model Y have the same volume.

Ⓑ The volume of Model X is 7 cubic units greater than the volume of Model Y.

Ⓒ The volume of Model X is 15 cubic units greater than the volume of Model Y.

Ⓓ The volume of Model X and Model Y combined is 55 cubic units.

Glossary

A

acute angle An angle that is open less than a right angle.

acute triangle A triangle that has three acute angles.

addends The numbers that are added together to find a sum.
Example: $2 + 7 = 9$
↖ ↗
Addends

algorithm A set of steps used to solve a math problem.

angle A figure formed by two rays that have the same endpoint.

angle measure The number of degrees in an angle.

area The number of square units needed to cover a region.

array A way of displaying objects in rows and columns.

Associative Property of Addition Addends can be regrouped and the sum remains the same.

Associative Property of Multiplication Factors can be regrouped and the product stays the same.

B

bar diagram A tool used to help understand and solve word problems.

bar graph A graph using bars to show data.

benchmark fraction A known fraction that is commonly used for estimating.
Examples: $\frac{1}{4}$, $\frac{1}{3}$, $\frac{1}{2}$, $\frac{2}{3}$, and $\frac{3}{4}$.

billions A period of three places to the left of the millions period.

breaking apart Mental math method used to rewrite a number as the sum of numbers to form an easier problem.

C

capacity The amount a container can hold, measured in liquid units.

center A point within a circle that is the same distance from all points on a circle.

centimeter (cm) A metric unit used to measure length. 100 centimeters = 1 meter

century A unit of time equal to 100 years.

circle A closed plane figure in which all the points are the same distance from a point called the center.

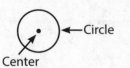
Circle
Center

common denominator A number that is the denominator of two or more fractions.

common factor A number that is a factor of two or more given numbers.

Commutative Property of Addition Numbers can be added in any order and the sum remains the same.

Commutative Property of Multiplication Factors can be multiplied in any order and the product stays the same.

compare Decide if one number is greater than, less than, or equal to another number.

compatible numbers Numbers that are easy to compute mentally.

compensation Choosing numbers close to the numbers in a problem to make the computation easier, and then adjusting the answer for the numbers chosen.

compose To combine parts.

composite number A whole number greater than 1 with more than two factors.

conjecture Statement that is believed to be true but has not been proven.

coordinate grid A grid used to show ordered pairs.

counting on Counting up from the lesser number to the greater number to find the difference of two numbers.

cube A solid figure with six identical squares as its faces.

cubic unit The volume of a cube that measures 1 unit on each edge.

cup (c) A customary unit of capacity. 1 cup = 8 fluid ounces

customary units of measure Units of measure that are used in the United States.

D

data Pieces of collected information.

day A unit of time equal to 24 hours.

decade A unit of time equal to 10 years.

decimal A number with one or more digits to the right of the decimal point.

decimal point A dot used to separate dollars from cents in money or to separate ones from tenths in a number.

decimeter (dm) A metric unit of length equal to 10 centimeters.

decompose To break into parts.

degree (°) A unit of measure for angles. $1° = \frac{1}{360}$ of a circle. Also a unit of measure for temperature.

denominator The number below the fraction bar in a fraction that represents the total number of equal parts in one whole.

difference The answer when subtracting two numbers.

digits The symbols used to write a number: 0, 1, 2, 3, 4, 5, 6, 7, 8, and 9.

Distributive Property Multiplying a sum (or difference) by a number is the same as multiplying each number in the sum (or difference) by that number and adding (or subtracting) the products. *Example:* $(3 \times 21) = (3 \times 20) + (3 \times 1)$

divide An operation to find the number in each group or the number of equal groups.

dividend The number to be divided.

divisibility rules The rules that state when a number is divisible by another number.

divisible Can be divided by another number without leaving a remainder. *Example:* 10 is divisible by 2

divisor The number by which another number is divided. *Example:* $32 \div 4 = 8$
Divisor

dot plot A type of line plot that uses dots to indicate the number of times a response occurred.

elapsed time The amount of time between the beginning of an event and the end of the event.

equation A number sentence that uses the equal sign (=) to show that two expressions have the same value. *Example:* $9 + 3 = 12$

equilateral triangle A triangle with three sides that are the same length.

equivalent Numbers that name the same amount.

equivalent fractions Fractions that name the same region, part of a set, or part of a segment.

estimate To give an approximate value rather than an exact answer.

expanded form A number written as the sum of the values of its digits. *Example:* $2,476 = 2,000 + 400 + 70 + 6$

expression A mathematical phrase. *Examples:* $x - 3$ or $2 + 7$

F

fact family A group of related facts using the same set of numbers.

factor pairs Numbers that when multiplied together give a certain product.

factors The numbers that are multiplied together to give a product.
Example: 3 × 6 = 18
Factors

fluid ounce (fl oz) A customary unit of capacity. 1 fluid ounce = 2 tablespoons; 8 fluid ounces = 1 cup

foot (ft) A customary unit of length. 1 foot = 12 inches

formula An equation that uses symbols to relate two or more quantities.
Example: $A = \ell \times w$

fraction A symbol, such as $\frac{2}{3}$, $\frac{5}{1}$, or $\frac{8}{5}$, used to name a part of a whole, a part of a set, or a location on a number line.

frequency The number of times that a response occurs in a set of data.

frequency table A way to display data that shows how many times a response occurs in a set of data.

G

gallon (gal) A customary unit of capacity. 1 gallon = 4 quarts

generalize To make a general statement.

gram (g) A metric unit of mass. 1,000 grams = 1 kilogram

greater than symbol (>) A symbol that points away from a greater number or expression. *Example:* 450 > 449

H

hexagon A polygon with 6 sides.

hour A unit of time equal to 60 minutes.

hundredth One part of 100 equal parts of a whole.

I

Identity Property of Addition The sum of any number and zero is that number.

Identity Property of Multiplication The product of any number and one is that number.

inch (in.) A customary unit of length.
12 inches = 1 foot

inequality A number sentence that uses the greater than sign (>) or the less than sign (<) to show that two expressions do not have the same value. *Example:* 5 > 3

intersecting lines Lines that pass through the same point.

interval A number which is the difference between two consecutive numbers on the scale of a graph.

inverse operations Operations that undo each other.
Examples: Adding 6 and subtracting 6;
          Multiplying by 4 and dividing by 4.

isosceles triangle A triangle with at least two equal sides.

key Part of a graph that tells what each symbol stands for.

kilogram (kg) A metric unit of mass equal to 1,000 grams. 1 kilogram = 1,000 grams

kilometer (km) A metric unit of length equal to 1,000 meters.
1 kilometer = 1,000 meters

leap year A calendar occurrence that happens every four years when an extra day is added to February. Leap years have 366 days.

less than symbol (<) A symbol that points towards a lesser number or expression. *Example:* 305 < 320

line A straight path of points that goes on and on in opposite directions.

line of symmetry
A line on which a figure can be folded so both halves are the same.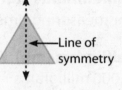

line plot A way to display data along a number line, where each dot represents one number in a set of data.

line segment A part of a line that has two endpoints.

line symmetric A figure that can be folded on a line to form two halves that fit exactly on top of each other.

liter (L) A metric unit of capacity.
1 liter = 1,000 milliliters

mass The amount of matter that something contains.

meter (m) A metric unit of length. 1 meter = 100 centimeters

metric units of measure Units of measure commonly used by scientists.

mile (mi) A customary unit of length. 1 mile = 5,280 feet

millennium (plural: millennia) A unit for measuring time equal to 1,000 years.

milligram (mg) A metric unit of mass. 1,000 milligrams = 1 gram

milliliter (mL) A metric unit of capacity. 1,000 milliliters = 1 liter

millimeter (mm) A metric unit of length. 1,000 millimeters = 1 meter

millions In a number, a period of three places to the left of the thousands period.

minute A unit of time equal to 60 seconds.

mixed number A number that has a whole number part and a fraction part.

month One of the 12 parts into which a year is divided.

multiple The product of a given whole number and any non-zero whole number.

number name A way to write a number in words. *Example:* Four thousand, six hundred thirty-two.

numerator In a fraction, the number above the fraction bar that represents the part of the whole.

numerical expression An expression that contains numbers and at least one operation. *Example:* 35 + 12

obtuse angle An angle that is open more than a right angle but less than a straight angle.

obtuse triangle A triangle that has one obtuse angle.

octagon A polygon with 8 sides.

ounce (oz) A customary unit of weight. 16 ounces = 1 pound

outlier Any number in a data set that is very different from the rest of the numbers.

overestimate An estimate that is greater than the exact answer.

P

parallel lines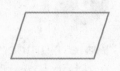
Lines that never intersect.

parallelogram
A quadrilateral that has
two pairs of parallel sides.

partial products Products found by
breaking one factor in a multiplication
problem into ones, tens, hundreds, and so
on and then multiplying each of these by
the other factor.

partial quotients A way to divide
that finds quotients in parts until only
a remainder, if any, is left.

pentagon A plane figure with 5 sides.

perimeter The distance around a figure.

period In a number, a group of three
digits, separated by commas, starting
from the right.

perpendicular lines Intersecting
lines that form right angles.

pint (pt) A customary unit of capacity.
1 pint = 2 cups

place value The value given to a place a
digit has in a number.
Example: In 3,946, the 9 is in the hundreds
place. So, the 9 has a value of 900.

point An exact location in space.

polygon A closed plane figure made up
of line segments.

pound (lb) A customary unit of weight.
1 pound = 16 ounces

prime number A whole number greater
than 1 that has exactly two factors, itself
and 1.

product The answer to a
multiplication problem.

protractor A tool used to measure and
draw angles.

Q

quadrilateral A polygon with 4 sides.

quart (qt) A customary unit of capacity.
1 quart = 2 pints

quotient The answer to a
division problem.

ray A part of a line that has one endpoint and continues on forever in one direction.

rectangle A quadrilateral that has four right angles.

rectangular prism A solid figure with 6 rectangular faces.

regroup To name a whole number in a different way. *Example:* 32 = 2 tens 12 ones

remainder The number that remains after the division is complete.

repeated addition A way to write a multiplication expression as an addition expression. *Example:* 3 × 5 = 5 + 5 + 5

repeating pattern Made up of shapes or numbers that form a part that repeats.

rhombus A quadrilateral that has opposite sides that are parallel and all of its sides are the same length.

right angle An angle that forms a square corner.

right triangle A triangle that has one right angle.

rounding A process that determines which multiple of 10, 100, 1,000, and so on a number is closest to.

rule A mathematical phrase that tells how numbers in a table are related.

scale Numbers that show the units used on a graph.

scalene triangle A triangle with no sides that are the same length.

second A unit of time. 60 seconds = 1 minute

sequence A set of numbers that follows a pattern.

side Each of the line segments of a polygon.

solid figure A figure with three dimensions that has length, width, and height.

solution The value of the variable that makes an equation true.

solve an equation Find a solution to an equation.

square A quadrilateral that has four right angles and all sides are the same length.

square unit A square with sides one unit long used to measure area.

standard form A way to write a number showing only its digits. Commas separate groups of three digits starting from the right. *Example:* 613,095

straight angle An angle that forms a straight line.

sum The result of adding numbers together.

survey Collecting information by asking a number of people the same question and recording their answers.

T

tablespoon (tbsp) A customary unit of capacity. 1 tablespoon = 3 teaspoons

teaspoon (tsp) A customary unit of capacity. 3 teaspoons = 1 tablespoon

tenth One part of 10 equal parts of a whole.

terms Numbers in a sequence or variables, such as *x* and *y*, in an expression.

ton (T) A customary unit of weight. 1 ton = 2,000 pounds

trapezoid A quadrilateral with only one pair of parallel sides.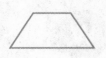

triangle A polygon with 3 sides.

U

underestimate An estimate that is less than the exact answer.

unit angle An angle that cuts off $\frac{1}{360}$ of a circle and measures 1°.

unit fraction A fraction with a numerator of 1. *Example:* $\frac{1}{2}$

unknown A symbol or letter, such as *x*, that represents a number in an expression or equation.

V

variable A symbol or letter that stands for a number.

vertex (plural: vertices) The point where two rays meet to form an angle.

volume The number of cubic units needed to fill a solid figure.

week A unit of time equal to 7 days.

weight A measure of how heavy an object is.

whole numbers The numbers 0, 1, 2, 3, 4, and so on.

Zero Property of Multiplication The product of any number and zero is zero. *Examples:* $3 \times 0 = 0$; $5 \times 0 = 0$

yard (yd) A customary unit of length. 1 yard = 3 feet

year A unit of time equal to 365 days or 52 weeks or 12 months.

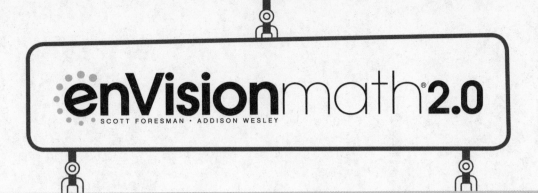

Photographs

Every effort has been made to secure permission and provide appropriate credit for photographic material. The publisher deeply regrets any omission and pledges to correct errors called to its attention in subsequent editions.

Unless otherwise acknowledged, all photographs are the property of Pearson Education, Inc.

Photo locators denoted as follows: Top (T), Center (C), Bottom (B), Left (L), Right (R), Background (Bkgd)

001 MarclSchauer/Shutterstock; **032** petr84/Fotolia; **043** forkArt Photography/Fotolia; **060** Alexey Usachev/Fotolia; **068** Digital Vision/Thinkstock; **091** John Hoffman/Shutterstock; **108** Stevanzz/Fotolia; **118** Pearson Education; **134CL** Andreanita/Fotolia; **134CR** Algre/Fotolia; **134L** EcoView/Fotolia; **134R** Eduardo Rivero/Fotolia; **138** Bork/Shutterstock; **152** Andrew Breeden/Fotolia; **167** Majeczka/Shutterstock; **184** Pearson Education; **204** Steve Byland/Shutterstock; **210** 2011/Photos To Go; **214** Pearson Education; **222** Rikke/Fotolia; **224** Fotolia; **236L** Neelsky/Shutterstock; **236R** Serg64/Shutterstock; **249** Mark McClare/Shutterstock; **254** Pearson Education; **260** Pearson Education; **274** Pearson Education; **325** ShutterStock; **340** Flashon Studio/Shutterstock; **344** Cbpix/Shutterstock; **348L** JackF/Fotolia; **348R** Smileus/Shutterstock; **365** ShutterStock; **378** Comstock Images/Jupiter Images; **382** Womue/Fotolia; **407** Kletr/Shutterstock; **414** Hamik/Fotolia; **461** Adrio/Fotolia; **468** Oleksii Sagitov/Shutterstock; **470** Africa Studio/Fotolia; **514** Pearson Education; **516** Werner Dreblow/Fotolia; **520** Image Source/Jupiter Images; **524C** Melinda Fawver/Shutterstock; **524L** Yaping/Shutterstock; **524R** Undy/Fotolia; **539** pk7comcastnet/Fotolia; **556** JLV Image Works/Fotolia; **587** NASA; **623** Bork/Shutterstock; **630** Hemera Technologies/ThinkStock; **648** Concept w/Fotolia;

651 StockPhotosArt/Fotolia; **669CL** Donfink/Fotolia; **669CR** Tim elliott/Fotolia; **669L** Proedding/Fotolia; **669R** Petergyure/Fotolia; **670** Redwood/Fotolia; **671** Katrina Brown/Fotolia; **675** Pearson Education; **690** CristinaMuraca/Shutterstock; **694** Duncan Noakes/Fotolia; **696** Viorel Sima/Shutterstock; **706** Sergio Martínez/Fotolia; **708** Pascal Rateau/Fotolia; **728B** LittleMiss/Shutterstock; **728T** Margouillat photo/Shutterstock; **729** luchschen/Shutterstock; **750** Justin Black/Shutterstock; **765** James Kingman/Shutterstock; **786** Tom Grundy/Shutterstock; **813** WitR/Shutterstock; **815** Dja65/Shutterstock; **822** Arina P Habich/Shutterstock; **842** Gary Blakeley/Fotolia; **863** EvrenKalinbacak/Shutterstock; **864B** Orhan Cam/Shutterstock; **864T** Thampapon/Shutterstock; **900** Pearson Education.